Industry and ideology

Industry and ideology
IG Farben in the Nazi era

Peter Hayes
Northwestern University

The right of the
University of Cambridge
to print and sell
all manner of books
was granted by
Henry VIII in 1534.
The University has printed
and published continuously
since 1584.

Cambridge University Press

Cambridge
New York   New Rochelle
Melbourne   Sydney

Published by the Press Syndicate of the University of Cambridge
The Pitt Building, Trumpington Street, Cambridge CB2 1RP
32 East 57th Street, New York, NY 10022, USA
10 Stamford Road, Oakleigh, Melbourne, 3166, Australia

First published 1987
First paperback edition 1989

Printed in the United States of America

Library of Congress Cataloging-in-Publication Data
Hayes, Peter, 1946–
Industry and ideology.
Bibliography: p.
Includes index.
1. Interessengemeinschaft Farbenindustrie
Aktiengesellschaft – Political activity – History –
20th century.   2. Nationalsozialistische Deutsche
Arbeiter-Partei – History.   3. Chemical industry –
Political aspects – History – 20th century.   4. Mineral
industries – Political aspects – Germany – History –
20th century.   5. Germany – Politics and government –
1933–1945.   6. World War, 1939–1945.   I. Title.
HD9654.9.15H39   1987   338.7′66′00943   86–28388
ISBN 0 521 32948 5 hard covers
ISBN 0 521 36823 5 paperback

British Library Cataloguing-in-Publication Data applied for.

For my son, Kenneth

If, however, economic ambitions are good servants, they are bad masters. Harnessed to a social purpose, they will turn the mill and grind the corn. But the question, to what end the wheels revolve, still remains. . . . Mankind may wring her secrets from nature, and use their knowledge to destroy themselves.

R. H. Tawney
Religion and the Rise of Capitalism

If I understand what was going on, it was the negative character of the young man's fighting position which was his undoing. . . . *Not* to want to do something may be in the long run a mental content impossible to subsist on. Between not willing a certain thing and not willing at all — in other words, yielding to another person's will — there may lie too small a space for the idea of freedom to squeeze into.

Thomas Mann
"Mario and the Magician"

But so long as virtue is not rewarded here on earth, ethics will, I fancy, preach in vain.

Sigmund Freud
Civilization and Its Discontents

Contents

Illustrations

Preface

The problem in history, someone once said, is to explain, not why bad men do evil, but why good men do. The leaders of IG Farben, Europe's largest private corporation between 1925 and 1945, were conventionally good men. Serious, talented, and well educated, they brought the world a succession of beneficial inventions, such as sulfa drugs, magnetic tape, and a host of artificial fibers. Though steeped in the nationalism and class consciousness of the Wilhelmian Reich, they helped during the 1920s to attenuate the antagonisms between labor and management within Germany and between the country and its former enemies. Nearly all of them sensed the dangers Nazism posed and shunned the movement before 1933. While Hitler ruled, most of them futilely dissented from his worst excesses: Aryanization, autarky, aggression, and forced labor. These were not small men, failed vacuum cleaner salesmen like Adolf Eichmann, whose pathetic desire for advancement and approval from his Nazi superiors made him the eager executor of their most vicious orders and thus the personification to Hannah Arendt of "the banality of evil."[1] Nor were they greedy, union-bashing, revanchist wire pullers who, according to vulgar Marxist caricatures, hired Hitler's party to serve their rapacious interests.

Yet within the Third Reich, these executives presided over the firm most widely credited, then and since, with carving out a lucrative and murderous place for itself. Farben's products became ubiquitous and essential. It made not only the synthetic rubber on which most Nazi war vehicles rode and the fuel-from-coal that powered many of them, but also the gas that murdered more than a million people at Auschwitz and even several of the drugs that Dr. Theo Morell, Hitler's physician, pumped into the führer's bloodstream.[2] By 1943, the concern's 334 plants and mines across Germany and occupied Europe

[1] See Hannah Arendt, *Eichmann in Jerusalem* (New York, 1965).
[2] David Irving (ed.), *The Secret Diaries of Hitler's Doctor* (New York, 1983), pp. 62–3.

were turning out more than 3 billion marks' worth of goods and earning net profits of more than 0.5 billion.[3] Nearly 50% of IG's 330,000-person work force had come to consist of conscript or slave laborers, among whom were some of the perhaps 30,000 inmates of Auschwitz who eventually died in the company's new factory and mines near the camp.[4]

Even before the full extent of this record became clear, Franklin Roosevelt declared that "the history of the use of the IG Farben trust by the Nazi reads like a detective story. Defeat of the Nazi armies will have to be followed by the eradication of those weapons of economic warfare."[5] Hence, one of the first acts of the American occupation authorities in 1945 was to seize the enterprise as punishment for "knowingly and prominently . . . building up and maintaining German war potential."[6] Two years later, twenty-three of the firm's principal officers went on trial at Nürnberg for crimes against peace, humanity, and property rights. Though the tribunal of three American judges acquitted all the defendants of having conspired to prepare and launch a war, thirteen of the businessmen were sentenced to prison on one charge or another. By the time John McCloy, the American high commissioner, pardoned the last of them in 1951, IG Farben scarcely existed. Its holdings in the German Democratic Republic had been nationalized; those in the Federal Republic had been divided into six, later chiefly three, separate corporations: BASF, Bayer, and Hoechst.

How and why IG traveled this path are the subjects of this book. I am, of course, not the first person to take them up. The relationship between private capitalism and the Nazi regime has intrigued authors almost since its inception.[7] In nearly all treatments of that topic,

---

[3] For the number of plants, see NI-8325/68, Affidavit by E. Struss, 29.V.47; for the financial data, see NI-10002-03/82, Affidavits by H. Deichfischer, 11.VI.47. Throughout this volume, the term "billion" denotes a thousand million (American usage).

[4] On total employment, see Hermann Gross, *Further Facts and Figures Relating to the Deconcentration of the IG Farbenindustrie Aktiengesellschaft* (Kiel, 1950), p. 35, Table VIa. On the death toll at Auschwitz, see Chapter 8.

[5] Quoted in Howard Ambruster, *Treason's Peace* (New York, 1947), p. 383.

[6] Josiah DuBois, *The Devil's Chemists* (Boston, 1952), p. 199; Joseph Borkin, *The Crime and Punishment of I. G. Farben* (New York, 1978), p. 158.

[7] For convenient guides to this vast literature, see Pierre Ayçoberry, *The Nazi Question* (New York, 1981), pp. 47–68, 92–7, 150–61; Renzo DeFelice, *Interpretations of Fascism* (Cambridge, Mass., 1977), pp. 30–54, 187–90; A. James Gregor, *Fascism: The Classic Interpretations of the Interwar Period* and *Fascism: The Contemporary Interpretations* (both Morristown, N.J., 1983), pp. 32–9 and 16–26, respectively;

Farben has figured prominently – as the guiding hand, opportunistic partner, or pliant tool of Nazi policy. But the existing literature has notable defects. Much of the critical writing on Farben adopts the dramatic tone of President Roosevelt's letter in 1944. Whether produced by trust-busting Americans in the aftermath of the war or by Marxist commentators of various shades since, these works echo the two best-known early exposés, Victor Lefebure's *The Riddle of the Rhine* (New York, 1923), which called the emergent German dye trust "a monster camouflaged floating mine in the troubled sea of world peace," and Helmut Wickel's *I.-G. Deutschland* (Berlin, 1932), wherein the concern became "the secret government of the German Republic." As recently as 1978, Joseph Borkin, a former prosecutor at Nürnberg, revived these charges, minus a few of their least convincing features, in *The Crime and Punishment of I.G. Farben*.[8] From vet-

Anson Rabinbach, "Toward a Marxist Theory of Fascism and National Socialism," *New German Critique*, 1 (1974), pp. 127–53; and Wolfgang Wippermann, "The Postwar German Left and Fascism," *JCH*, 11 (1976), pp. 185–219. The most important recent contributions to the discussion are Avraham Barkai, *Das Wirtschaftssystem des Nationalsozialismus* (Köln, 1977); R. Beckenbach, *Der Staat im Faschismus* (East Berlin, 1974); Fritz Blaich, "Wirtschaftspolitik und Wirtschaftsverfassung im Dritten Reich," *Aus Politik und Zeitgeschichte*, Beilage 8 (1971), pp. 3–18; John Gillingham, "Die Rolle der Privatwirtschaft im Dritten Reich," *Zeitgeschichte*, 2 (1974) pp. 20–7; Dieter Grosser, "Die nationalsozialistische Wirtschaft," *Das Argument*, 7 (1965), pp. 1–11; Dieter Halfmann, *Der Anteil der Industrie und Banken an der faschistischen Innenpolitik* (Köln, 1974); Eike Hennig, *Thesen zur deutschen Sozial- und Wirtschaftsgeschichte 1933 bis 1938* (Frankfurt, 1973); Tim Mason, "The Primacy of Politics," in Henry A. Turner, Jr. (ed.), *Nazism and the Third Reich* (New York, 1972), pp. 175–200; Alan S. Milward, "Fascism and the Economy," in Walter Laqueur (ed.), *Fascism: A Reader's Guide* (Berkeley, Calif., 1976), pp. 379–412; Hans-Heinrich Rubbert, "Die 'gelenkte Marktwirtschaft' des Nationalsozialismus: Ein Literaturbericht," *Hamburger Jahrbuch für Wirtschafts- und Gesellschaftspolitik*, 8 (1963), pp. 215–34; Arthur Schweitzer, *Big Business in the Third Reich* (Bloomington, Ind., 1964); Alfred Sohn-Rethel, *Oekonomie und Klassenstruktur des deutschen Faschismus* (Frankfurt, 1973); George W. F. Hallgarten and Joachim Radkau, *Deutsche Industrie und Politik* (Frankfurt, 1974); Henry A. Turner, *Big Business and the Rise of Hitler* (New York, 1985); and John R. Gillingham, *Industry and Politics in the Third Reich: Ruhr Coal, Hitler and Europe* (New York, 1985).
8 The other main American accounts are Ambruster, *Treason's Peace*; DuBois, *Devil's Chemists*; and Richard Sasuly, *IG Farben* (New York, 1947). See also the report of the Finance Division of the Office of Military Government for Germany, United States, September 1945, recently republished with commentary as Dokumentationsstelle zur NS-Sozialpolitik Hamburg (ed.), *O.M.G.U.S. Ermittlungen gegen die I.G. Farbenindustrie AG* (Nördlingen, 1986).The chief Marxist critiques are D. Eichholtz, "Zum Anteil des IG Farben Konzerns an der Vorbereitung des Zweiten Weltkrieges," *JfW*, 10 (1969), pp. 83–105; Ferdinand Grocek, "Ein Staat im Staate – Der IG-Farben Konzern," *Marxistische Blätter*, 4 (1966), pp. 41–8; Giesela Kahl, "Zu den Kriegsvorbereitungen und Kriegsdurchführung des IG-Farben-Konzerns in

erans or admirers of the firm have come equally unbalanced accounts, which ask their readers to believe that any connection between Farben's actions and those of the Nazi state was purely coincidental or coerced.[9]

On the basis of extensive records that earlier authors have underexploited or not seen, I have tried here to improve on these overdrawn versions of the past. Some of my sources, notably the testimony and documents assembled for the Nürnberg tribunal, have long been in the public domain and accessible to American scholars in the form of microfilm reels obtainable from the National Archives. But their daunting scope, amounting to 6,384 exhibits placed in evidence, thousands of documents not presented to the court, and more than 16,000 pages of trial transcript, has contributed to their highly selective use by previous students of IG Farben. Moreover, the stakes and the highly charged nature of the proceedings in 1947–8, along with the considerable opportunities provided for collusion among the witnesses, make the testimony and affidavits submitted subject to even more than the usual reservations about the trustworthiness of oral history. That these pieces of evidence were often self-serving does not mean that all parts of them were false, however. Fortunately, the extent of the records that survived the Third Reich permits checking the contentions in most affidavits against contemporary documentation – not only that collected for the trial, but also that preserved in the archives of the German Federal Republic and many private German firms. These

zwei Weltkriegen," *Wissenschaftliche Zeitschrift der Fr.-Schiller Universität, Jena,* 8 (1958–9), pp. 605–24; Willi Kling, *Kleine Geschichte der IG Farben – Der Grossfabrikanten des Todes* (East Berlin, 1957); Hans Radandt (ed.), *Fall 6: Ausgewählte Dokumente und Urteil des IG-Farben-Prozesses* (East Berlin, 1970); André Leisewitz, "Die Auswirkungen der Verwissenschaftlichung der Produktion auf die Monopolbildung und auf das Verhältnis von Oekonomie und Politik dargestellt am Beispiel der chemischen Industrie," *Das Argument,* 14 (1972), pp. 444–508; Hartmut Raupert, *Rolle und Bedeutung der I.G.-Farben im Rahmen der nationalsozialistischen Wirtschaftspolitik* (Diplom-Arbeit, Bochum, 1976); and Hellmuth Tammen, *Die I. G. Farbenindustrie Aktiengesellschaft (1925–1933)* (Dissertation, Freie Universität, Berlin, 1978).

[9] The principal defenses of the concern are those of Hans-Joachim Flechtner, *Carl Duisberg – vom Chemiker zum Wirtschaftsführer* (Düsseldorf, 1959); Hermann Gross, *Material zur Aufteilung der I. G. Farbenindustrie Aktiengesellschaft* (Kiel, 1950) and two *Nachträge* to this brochure (Kiel, 1950); Karl Holdermann, *Im Banne der Chemie. Carl Bosch, Leben und Werke* (Düsseldorf, 1953); Fritz terMeer, *Die I. G. Farben Industrie Aktiengesellschaft* (Düsseldorf, 1953); Werner Reichelt, *Das Erbe der I.G. Farben* (Düsseldorf, 1956); and the memoirs of Curt Duisberg, *Nur ein Sohn* (Stuttgart, 1981) and Heinrich Gattineau, *Durch die Klippen des 20. Jahrhunderts* (Stuttgart, 1983).

corporate holdings constitute the second principal, and often new, group of sources for this book. With the aid of these materials, I have cross-examined the evidence, both written and oral, more thoroughly than could the hard-pressed lawyers for each side at Nürnberg, who worked under constraints of time, resources, and the state of communications and transportation in postwar Germany. Where I have had nonetheless to rely on uncorroborated accounts provided on the stand or in affidavits, I have done so when (1) merely conveying what Farben's leaders claimed after the Third Reich to have thought, heard, and felt during it, or (2) the information cited seems believable by virtue of having satisfied at least one of three tests: (a) Several other specific facts or assertions in the same source have proved accurate when checked against more reliable sources (the test of general veracity); (b) the information cited is incidental to the main thrust of the document in question, hence not likely to have been bent to serve a purpose (the test of probability); and (c) the data derived from the account in question, though not confirmed elsewhere, fit the pattern of evidence on the subject at hand established by other documents (the test of compatibility). As a result of this method, applied in a spirit of skepticism toward the testimony, I have left out much that both friends and foes of IG Farben have long maintained but have also clarified many matters that had stood in darkness or dispute.

My work differs from its predecessors in its tone as well as in the strength and breadth of its underpinnings. Every historian must both enter into the subject at hand and stand back from it, attempting, in a sense, the impossible task of being in two places at one time. For this book, that attempt has entailed efforts both to reimagine the situation and reasoning of Farben's leaders from 1925 to 1945 and to analyze at some remove what their deeds really signified. In so doing, I have been guided, as on many specific points, by an observation of Tim Mason, namely, that "if historians do have a public responsibility, if hating is part of their method and warning part of their task, it is necessary that they should hate precisely."[10] At the same time, I have also borne in mind Franklin Ford's admonition that "standing aghast is an unrewarding posture for anyone trying to pay close attention to the thread

10 Tim Mason, "Intention and Explanation: A Current Controversy about the Interpretation of National Socialism," in G. Hirschfeld and L. Kettenacker (eds.), *Der Führerstaat: Mythos und Realität* (Stuttgart, 1981), p. 40.

of history."[11] The studied neutrality of my account reflects my desire not to reindict or to exonerate the leaders of IG Farben, but to highlight the mainsprings of their actions. Those mainsprings are with us still. The amoral pragmatism and professionalism that propelled Farben's executives dwell within all large-scale organizations, whether they be corporate or political, whether they seek to maximize power or profits, whether they claim to serve the individual, a class, or a race. These drives make Farben an instructive case study in the plasticity of private interests and the consequences of permitting any single-minded doctrine to grasp the levers of a state. Lest that point be lost and readers distance themselves too far and easily from Farben's behavior, I have emphasized here the specious rationality of the concern's deeds and largely let the self-evident wickedness of some of them speak for itself.

Timeless or timely as IG's experience may be, however, this is a work of history. I hope here to better our understanding of the political economy of Nazism, and to do so precisely by moving discussion of this topic out of the realm of abstractions. One of the most curious lacunae in the vast body of modern writing about Hitler's Reich is the absence to date of any full-dress, scholarly studies of the interaction between a single major corporation and that regime. Instead, readers have encountered a stream of popular and frequently unreliable surveys of particular firms, sanitized or commissioned business histories, exculpatory memoirs and testimonial biographies of individual executives, and orthodox Marxist or neo-Marxist studies dedicated to unmasking the responsibility, either direct or "objective," of German industry for the crimes of the Nazi state. Not until 1981 did a German academician publish a disinterested and well-researched examination of even a leading armaments firm, and that turned out to be an attempt, however valuable, to write "social history from below."[12] In consequence, a penchant for schematic formulations of business's rela-

---

[11] Quoted in Eberhard Jäckel, *Hitler's World View*, Foreword to the second American edition (Cambridge, Mass., 1982), p. 3.

[12] Gustav-Hermann Seebold, *Ein Stahlkonzern im Dritten Reich* (Wuppertal, 1981). Three earlier corporate studies are "official" histories, sanctioned by the postwar management of the enterprises concerned: Wolfram Fischer, *WASAG: Die Geschichte eines Unternehmens* (Berlin, 1966); Erich Maschke, *Es entsteht ein Konzern. Paul Reusch und die GHH* (Tübingen, 1969); and Hans Radandt, *Kriegsverbrecher-Konzern Mansfeld* (East Berlin, 1958). William Manchester, *The Arms of Krupp* (New York, 1968), is an example of how this sort of work ought not to be conceived or written.

tions with the Third Reich has long since outrun our empirical knowledge. It has proved tempting for people to write of "bilateral power structures," "industrial factionalism," "monopoly groups," "corporatism," "organized capitalism," the "dual state," "partial fascism," "state monopoly capitalism," and the like because such constructs seem to order the mess of the past without requiring one to navigate the morass of the archives. But conceptualization of this sort distorts and disembodies what occurred in Germany, and it is premature. The need for historians to get down to cases has become inescapable.

Of course, my account seeks to contribute more than just greater specificity to our knowledge of the Third Reich. A close examination of IG Farben yields, I believe, results that undermine much of the previous writing on business in Nazi Germany catalogued in the footnotes to this preface. The enterprise's fate indicates that the survival of private property under Nazism did not equal the survival of private political power. Of the concern's leaders, one may fairly say what a fellow historian has of their counterparts in another time and place: "As shrewdly as some of them pursued the main chance, they were also trapped by the present, scurrying where they appeared to stalk."[13] What made them behave so were the two facets of Nazism that always seemed most menacing to them: not only its obvious "promiscuity of aggressive intentions," but also its equally characteristic libertinism as to means.[14] Hitler threatened the fundamental assumptions of the strategy of capitalist reproduction that Farben's leaders had derived from decades of experience in a highly changeable industry: that economic success required political peace, both foreign and domestic, and predominance at the cutting edge of technological development. To preserve both, the concern first opposed the Nazi führer, then let itself be drawn into uneasy and uneven cooperation with him between 1933 and 1939, then began to share in his crimes once his victories and defeats undid the world in which their assumptions had taken shape. The story presented here is thus one of the manipulation and partial remaking of an industrial mentality by an ideological one. The argument suggests that German businessmen *were* "coordinated" like other social groups in the Third Reich, but also that they were defeated by their own desires.

---

13 Robert Wiebe, *The Search for Order 1877–1920* (New York, 1967), p. 18.
14 The phrase is from Mason in Hirschfeld and Kettenacker (eds.), *Der Führerstaat*, pp. 33–4.

Such an analysis stresses interests as the basis of corporate action. Noting this, one advance reader of this book complained that it deals too much with businessmen's interests and not enough with their ideology (as distinct from that of the Nazi Party, to which my title refers and on which I say a good deal). I should state at the outset that my emphasis is intentional. In the early stages of Nazi rule, some executives were disposed to cooperate with the regime because it shared a number of their assumptions about the value of individual initiative, the inevitability of inequality, the proper place of the working class, and the inefficiency of democratic decision making. As my analysis makes clear, however, accumulating evidence indicates that these perceived affinities rapidly moved from disarming big businessmen to consoling them, since the differences between corporate and Party world views, always great with regard to entrepreneurial freedom of action and the sovereignty of the market, grew steadily wider. In short, the ideological bonds between most corporate managers and Nazism were never strong enough to close the ideological gap between them, and the bonds became weaker with time.[15] Interests, given this context, counted for more in business–state relations than partial philosophical compatibilities; hence, interests predominate in my narrative.[16]

Finally, let me summarize the limitations and assumptions of this book, insofar as I am conscious of them. This is an examination of IG Farben's role in and relations with the Nazi regime, not a comprehensive study of the concern analogous to W. J. Reader's admirable volumes on the Imperial Chemical Industries.[17] Labor relations, managerial styles, and the internal operations of IG's many factories, for example, are among several subjects not treated in depth here, and much work remains to be done on them. Nor have I undertaken to compare more than intermittently Farben's behavior with that of other large German firms. An integrated history of industry in the

[15] See in this connection the findings of Gillingham, *Industry and Politics*, chaps. 2–3.
[16] I do not mean here to denigrate the importance of examining businessmen's general world view or ideology. But I believe that historians' knowledge of it during this and later eras is less sure and extensive than we often think, which is why its development in the twentieth century is the subject of my current research. For now, see Volker Berghahn's excellent *The Americanization of West German Industry, 1945–1973* (New York, 1986), pp. 13–39.
[17] W. J. Reader, *Imperial Chemical Industries: A History*, 2 vols. (London, 1970, 1975).

Third Reich also remains to be written, and other books like this one will have to appear before it can be.

As for my a priori judgments, from which no historian, however dedicated an empiricist, is entirely free, they rest on the conviction that the organizing framework for good and evil in the modern age is not capitalism or socialism, but industrialization and its corollaries of bureaucratism and professionalism.[18] These phenomena have placed similar demands on and posed similar moral challenges to people in very different systems of accumulating and applying knowledge and wealth. None of these systems has refrained from making inroads on human rights in the name of productivity and self-perpetuation.[19] As Aristotle's *Politics* demonstrated long ago, every political, economic, and social pattern can degenerate into its own form of perversion. Human ambition, avarice, apprehension, and alienation regularly see to that. They did so in the Germany of the 1930s. There and then, acute pressures permitted a pathological leader to alter the nature and forms of the economic and social system within which he ostensibly operated. That system and its national context provided the devices and idioms of the dictator's domination and the populace's acquiescence. This is the dialectic of history that I have seen at work in the events depicted in this book. It structures my attempt to show how the interaction of Hitler's will, the pressures of competition, the heritage of a single industry, the logic of professionalism, and the frailties of ordinary people produced the behavior of a particular enterprise in Nazi Germany.

"If there is any lesson to be learned," Willy Brandt has written of the Nazi years, "it is that decent men and women learn to make choices in favor of the good, and to do this before criminal power is established and gets stabilized."[20] Of course, Brandt is right, though choosing is not enough; action is also necessary and success not guaranteed. But heeding even Brandt's call has proved difficult in our age of highly professionalized industrial structures. This book documents how and why this is so and to what it can lead.

18 On the implications of this distinction, see John P. Scott, *Corporations, Classes and Capitalism* (New York, 1980), pp. 15–29, 134.
19 For a succinct and elegant statement in this vein, see W. N. Parker, "European Development in Millennial Perspective," in C. Kindleberger and G. DiTella (eds.). *The Economics of the Long View*, vol. 2 (New York, 1982), p. 17.
20 Foreword to Frances Henry, *Victims and Neighbors* (South Hadley, Mass., 1984), p. viii.

Acknowledgments

Books get finished, I am told, when authors tire of their subjects. Perhaps I have been slow to weary of IG Farben because so many people have made studying it an enriching experience. Henry Turner, who advised the dissertation from which this book emerged, shared with me his vast knowledge of modern German history and provided a model of scrupulous scholarship. Among his colleagues at Yale, Hans Gatzke, William Parker, and David Large read and remarked most helpfully on all or part of the manuscript, and Peter Gay and Donald Kagan heard me out and stimulated my thinking on countless occasions. Both in graduate school and since, my friend Robert Luchs sharpened my ideas, often by freely offering his own. Since moving to Northwestern, I have had the benefit of incisive commentaries on my work by T. H. Breen, Karen Halttunen, T. W. Heyck, David Joravsky, Robert Lerner, Sarah Maza, Michael Sherry, Lacey Baldwin Smith, and Robert Wiebe. Several expert readers went over my manuscript before publication. One of them, Gerald Feldman, I may thank by name; to the others, I am no less grateful. In addition, specific passages have benefited from the assistance of Larry Jones, William Patch, and Neal Pease. All of these people deserve a share of the credit for such merits as this book may contain but no blame for any errors of fact or interpretation that remain.

I am also grateful to several organizations that funded or lent ancillary support to my research and writing: the Social Science Research Council, the Deutscher Akademischer Austauschdienst, the Giles Whiting Foundation, and the Department of History and the University Research Grants Committee at Northwestern. The archivists and staffs of the Sterling Memorial Library at Yale, the Bayer-Archiv in Leverkusen, the Firmenarchiv der Hoechst AG in Frankfurt, the Unternehmensarchiv der BASF in Ludwigshafen, the Bundesarchiv in Koblenz, the Historisches Archiv of the Gutehoffnungshütte Aktienverein in Oberhausen, the Historisches Archiv of the Metallgesellschaft AG and the IG Farbenindustrie AG in Abwicklung in Frankfurt, the Historisches Archiv of the Fried. Krupp GmbH in Essen, the Werner von Siemens Institut in Munich, and the Center for Research Libraries in Chicago were all extremely helpful, as were the personnel of the Interlibrary Loan Office of the University Library at North-western. Among these people, I must single out Herr Peter Göb and his colleagues at Bayer, Ms. Pat Finney of the Center for Research Librar-ies, Herr Bodo Herzog of the Gutehoffnungshütte, and Dr. Manfred Simon of Hoechst. They gave me the run of their treasures and a warm reception besides. Dr. Curt Duisberg, Dr. Hanns Gierlichs, Herr Hans Kehrl, and Generalkonsul a. D. Wilhelm R. Mann kindly agreed to share their recollections of some of the people and events I have de-scribed. In addition, Herr Michael Wiest opened several personal con-tacts, and Herr Armin Danco gave me access to family papers. None of these institutions or individuals sought or exercised any control over my findings or bears responsibility for them.

There are, of course, more personal debts to acknowledge. Mr. and Mrs. John E. Drick extended material support at several stages; I wish he had lived to see the result. Through much of the research and writing, Holly Hayes also lent both aid and comfort. At a critical juncture, my sister Pamela Ewing made the completion of the work possible. So, in a different way, did Steven Kaplan and Harry and Judy Warren, who sustained me during dark days. Two German families also deserve an expression of my affection and appreciation. The Kleemanns of Düsseldorf kindled my interest in their country and language years ago and have fueled it regularly since; the Broils of Cologne offered friendship and practical help in 1977–8, as this pro-ject was beginning.

Finally, I note with pleasure the contributions of Joan Stahl, who typed both the dissertation and the final manuscript; of Frank Smith, Janis Bolster, and Mary Nevader of Cambridge University Press; and of Kazlinn J. Sugiyama, who drew the Appendixes.

Abbreviations

AA	Working Committee (Arbeitsausschuss)
AfS	*Archiv für Sozialgeschichte*
AHR	*American Historical Review*
AO	Auslandsorganisation (Foreign Organization of the Nazi Party)
BA	Bundesarchiv
BASF	Badische Anilin- und Soda-Fabrik
BDC	Berlin Document Center
BHR	*Business History Review*
CEH	*Central European History*
DAF	German Labor Front
EHR	*Economic History Review*
G&G	*Geschichte und Gesellschaft*
GHH	Gutehoffnungshütte
GWU	*Geschichte in Wissenschaft und Unterricht*
HGW	Hermann Göring Werke
IG in Abw.	IG Farbenindustrie AG in Abwicklung (in Dissolution)
IMT	International Military Tribunal (Nürnberg)
JCH	*Journal of Contemporary History*
JEH	*Journal of Economic History*
JfG	*Jahrbuch für Geschichte*
JfW	*Jahrbuch für Wirtschaftsgeschichte*
JMH	*Journal of Modern History*
JNS	*Jahrbücher für Nationalokonomie und Statistik*
KA	Commercial Committee (Kaufmännischer Ausschuss)
MM	*Militärgeschichtliche Mitteilungen*
MWT	Mitteleuropäischer Wirtschaftstag
NI	Nürnberg Industrialists Document
NL	Nachlass
NMT	Nürnberg Military Tribunal

NSBO	Nazi Factory Cells Organization
P&P	Past & Present
PSQ	Political Science Quarterly
QJE	Quarterly Journal of Economics
RDI	Reichsverband der deutschen Industrie
RGBl.	Reichsgesetzblatt
RGI	Reichsgruppe Industrie
RLM	Reich Air Ministry (Luftfahrtministerium)
RVB	Rheinische Vierteljahrsblätter
RWM	German Economics Ministry (Wirtschaftsministerium)
SAA	Siemens Archiv
SOA	Southeast Europe Committee (Südost-Ausschuss)
TEA	Technical Committee (Technischer Ausschuss)
VfZ	Vierteljahrshefte für Zeitgeschichte
Vowi	Volkswirtschaftliche Abteilung
Wigru Chemie	Economic Group for Chemicals
Wipo	Wirtschaftspolitische Abteilung
ZA	Central Committee (Zentralausschuss)
Zefi	Central Finance Section
ZfG	Zeitschrift für Geschichte
ZfN	Zeitschrift für Nationalökonomie

Sources and citations

My debts to the hundreds of books, articles, and other published sources employed in the preparation of this book are largely indicated in the footnotes. Readers interested in pursuing particular subjects or checking my account or interpretation will find a complete reference to the source at its initial citation in the Preface, each of the five parts, and the Epilogue. Thereafter, I have given the author's last name, an abbreviated title of the appropriate book or journal, and the pertinent page number(s).

Many of the footnotes refer to documents collected for the trial of twenty-three Farben officers at Nürnberg in 1947–8. Those sources prefixed with the letters NI were assembled by the prosecution for this and other judicial proceedings against German industrialists and eventually copied on the 163 reels of microfilm of National Archives Record Group 238, T301, Records of the Office of the United States Chief Counsel for War Crimes, Nürnberg. The footnotes cite individual documents by NI number, followed by that of the reel containing the document, a brief description, and a date of origin, for example, NI-7330/58, Affidavit by A. Reithinger, 19.VI.47, the roman numerals referring to the month.

The trial transcript and the exhibits produced by the defense staffs were not included in the T301 collection, but can be found in a separate subset of 113 reels labeled Record Group 238, M892, Records of the United States of America vs. Carl Krauch et al. (Case VI), August 14, 1947–July 30, 1948. I have cited testimony in the following form: M892/reel number, name of the witness, and page of the transcript. References to the defense exhibits consist of the appropriate defendant's name, a roman numeral to indicate the document book number, an arabic numeral for the document number, a brief description, and in most cases the date of origin, for example, Schmitz I/4, Affidavit by W. F. Kalle, 8.IX.47.

For assiduous students, there is a useful, though inexhaustive published index to the trial transcript and the documents introduced:

Hans-Günther Seraphim, *Indices zu den zwölf Nürnberger US.-Militärgerichtsprozessen,* vol. V, A: *Personenindex zum Verfahren gegen Carl Krauch u. a.,* and vol. V, B u. C: *Sach- und Dokumentenindex zum Verfahren gegen Carl Krauch u. a.* ([Göttingen], 1964).

A portion of the testimony and documents used at the trial was published in vols. 7 and 8 of *Trials of the War Criminals Before the Nürnberg Military Tribunals under Control Council Law No. 10,* Case VI, "The Farben Case" (Washington, D.C., 1953), and related material appeared in vols. 12–14, Case XI, "The Ministries Case" (Washington, D.C., 1952). I have cited documents included in these publications by their prosecution or defense number, a short description, their date of origin, the letters *NMT,* the pertinent volume number, and the pages on which the material appears.

I have also had recourse to several additional collections of microfilmed material from the U. S. National Archives:

RG242/T83   Records of private Dutch, Austrian, and German firms, including the *Vorstand* minutes for the Degussa Corporation and the diary of IG's Eduard Weber-Andreä

RG242/T253   Records of private industrialists

RG1004/T71   Records of the Reich Ministry of Economics

RG1035/T81   Records of the NSDAP

Citations to these documents give the appropriate record group prefix, the reel number on which the document is to be found, a description or heading for the document, its date of origin, and the frames of microfilm bearing the source.

References to materials preserved in Germany include an abbreviation of the name of the appropriate repository, numbers indicating the pertinent collection and file, the heading of the document being cited or a description of it, and its date of origin. The principal archives and holdings consulted are as follows:

Berlin Document Center, Berlin

Nazi Party records (*Personalakten*) of numerous Farben officers

Bundesarchiv, Koblenz

Nachlass (NL) 2   Eduard Dingeldey

Nachlass 19   Paul Moldenhauer

Nachlass 158	Wichard von Moellendorf
Nachlass 231	Alfred Hugenberg
NS 20	Kleine Erwerbungen NSDAP, vol. 122
NS 43	Aussenpolitisches Amt der NSDAP
R2/	Reichsfinanzministerium, files 13150, 13154–5, 13424–24a, 13720–1, 15302, 15306–11, 15458, 15460, 15467, 16304, 16347, 16708, 16986, 17780, 17837, 19491, 19536, 19452, 19547, 19562, 21047, 21370, 21469, 21602
R8/VIII	Reichsstelle Chemie, vols. 1, 3, 8, 11, 26, 51, 53–67, 70–5, 80–2, 86, 98–9, 133, 314, 320, 341–3, 348, 350
R10/X	Stickstoffsyndikat GmbH
R12/I	Reichsgruppe Industrie
R13/XII	Wirtschaftsgruppe Chemie, vols. 10–11, 14–16, 30–1, 102, 106–9, 113–22, 125, 138, 146, 156, 158–66, 173, 176, 185, 191–2, 201–11, 228–35, 433–41, 471–95, 550, 552, 562–3, 570, 582–82c, 588–9
R25/	Reichsamt für Wirtschaftsausbau, vols. 6, 9, 14, 18–21, 22, 25, 36–9, 47–9, 83–4, 86, 89–95, 98, 100–13, 133, 148–52b, 159–62, 171–4, 176, 190–1
R26/I	Beauftragten für den Vierjahresplan (Zentrale), vols. 1a, 5, 15–18, 36
R43/II	Reichskanzlei, vols. 320–1, 362
R125/	Wirtschaftliche Forschungsgesellschaft (Wifo), vols. 131, 271–74, and Mappe X
ZSg 127	Presseausschnitt Sammlung des Chemie Vereins, vols. 40–2, 823–38

Deutsches Museum, München
  Jahresversammlung, 1939
Firmenarchiv der Degussa AG, Frankfurt
  Biographische Unterlagen Dr. Fritz Roessler

Firmenarchiv der Hoechst AG, Frankfurt-Hoechst
Büro des Technischen Ausschusses (TEA), vols. 70, 80–1, 85–
6, 108a–15, 191, 207, 235, 253, 255, 262–5, 290–5, 351–83,
391, 393–9, 400–1, 404, 483, 527, 757–61, 775, 901, 921,
943–4, 957, 1028–33, 1071, 1077–82, 1086–90, 1196–7,
1250, 1256, 1261, 1264, 1296, 1306, 1308, 1324–8, 1331,
1334–40, 1343–6, 1348–51, 1390, 1488, 2199, 2788, 2911,
2915–23
Historisches Archiv der Friedrich Krupp GmbH, Essen
FAH IV C 203, 205, 3694
FAH IV E 152, 178, 180, 202, 203 498–99, 776, 885, 1186
Historisches Archiv der Gutehoffnungshütte AG, Oberhausen
400 101 24 15,16a–b; 400 101 220 14a–b; 400 101 290 3, 5a,
10; 400 101 293 4a–b; 400 101 2007 16
Historisches Archiv der Metallgesellschaft AG, Frankfurt
Korrespondenz von Richard Merton
I. G. Farbenindustrie in Abwicklung, Frankfurt
Assorted *Personalakten* and files of the Zentralfinanz and Ju-
ristische Abteilungen
Klöckner-Archiv, Duisburg
Bestand Peter Klöckner
Politisches Archiv des Auswärtigen Amtes, Bonn
Gesandtschaft Prag, Pakete: 6, 174, 176, 178, 181, 186, 191,
258, 316, 318
Unternehmensarchiv der BASF AG, Ludwigshafen
Bde. 32, 36, 39, 83; C6321/01–04; M02/1; M04/3;
M3205/1; T51/1–2; T52/4, 7–9, 13, 15a–e; W1; "Unveröf-
fentlichte BASF-Chronik von Dr. Voigtländer-Tetzner," Bd. II
Werksarchiv der Bayer AG, Leverkusen
Autographensammlung Duisberg (AS)
Direktions-Abteilung, Leverkusen (DA), vols. 21, 67, 116,
180–1, 183, 311, 330, 377, 429, 461, 464, 481, 497, 551, 566,
909, 913, 935, 950, 1010, 1056, 1110–1, 1136, 1164–5a,
1288, 1320, 1390, 1425, 1427, 1431, 1436, 1476, 1538, 1556,
1629, 1645, 1670, 1731, 1743, 1748, 1759, 2067, 2077, 2084,
2106, 2112, 2162, 2200, 2230–1, 2236, 2439, 5283, 5375,
5384, 5388, 8080, 8133

Hauptsignaturen

4B/36, 4C3, 4C6, 4C9, 4C14–17, 4C25, 4D/W, 6/1, 6/14, 10/3, 11/A.1.a, 11/3, 12/2–3, 12/19, 13/2, 13/6, 13/9, 13/11, 13/12, 13/13, 13/15, 13/16, 13/25–6, 14, 15/B47–68, 15/D–Da, 15/F6, 15/G, 62/10.1–11, 62/40, 64/3, 64/6, 64/9, 64/12, 66/A2, 66/20, 76–7, 81A, 84, 91, 91/1, 96, 110, 134/12, 151–4, 156/7, 158/5, 186/D2, 214/1, 214/10, 221/6, 271

Unnumbered folder: Akten aus dem IG Zentralarchiv, Frankfurt

Werner von Siemens Institut zur Geschichte des Hauses Siemens, München

Nachlass Carl-Friedrich von Siemens

4/Lf 670, 675, 676, 688, 761, 779

11/Lo 806

PART I
The nascent concern, 1860–1933

If the dimensions and products of the German chemical industry changed strikingly from 1860 to 1945, its governing principle did not. From their inception, the nation's major manufacturers strove to make the most of Germany's naturally limited resources. Instead of specializing in acids, alkalies, and explosives like their European and American counterparts, these firms transmuted virtually their only abundant domestic raw materials – coal, water, wood, earth, and air – into one synthetic compound after another. At first, their efforts centered on organic chemicals, like dyes, drugs, and photographic aids; later, they turned to nitrogen, rubber, fuel, fibers, and light metals. In each instance, the impetus was the same: the desire to find substitutes for expensive and uncertain imports.

Concentrating on synthetics bred both high profits and chronic insecurity. By virtue of lower prices, better quality, and more aggressive salesmanship, German dyes and pharmaceuticals rapidly crowded competing natural substances out of international markets. Between 1880 and 1912, dye exports became the nation's ranking source of earnings from foreign trade, and profits and dividends in the organic chemical field widely exceeded the averages for all other German industries.[1] Such returns invited vigorous competition, expressed in constant innovation and price warfare. Old processes or products became vulnerable or obsolete overnight; proceeds frequently tumbled as fast. In so capital-intensive an industry, such fluctuations were

---

[1] For detailed statistics, see Otto Lindemann, *Die Arbeiterverhältnisse und die Arbeiterpolitik in der chemischen Industrie* (Dissertation, Hamburg, 1928), p. 16; Curt Paschke, *Der Aufbau der deutschen Teerfarbenindustrie und ihre Stellung in der Zollpolitik des Auslandes* (Dissertation, Giessen, 1927), pp. 22, 29; Franz Thissen, *Die Stellung der deutschen Teerfarbenindustrie in der Weltwirtschaft (Vor, in und nach dem Kriege)* (Dissertation, Giessen, 1922), pp. 7, 18–19; Friedrich M. Vogel, *Die Entwicklung des Exportes und Importes der chemischen Industrie in Deutschland* (Dissertation, Erlangen, 1914), pp. 74, 99; and Walter Fraund, *Betriebswirtschaftliche Studie über die Entwicklung und Finanzierung der IG Farbenindustrie Aktiengesellschaft* (Dissertation, Giessen, 1929), pp. 25–7. For a somewhat biased description of the German dye industry's sharp marketing practices overseas, see Howard W. Ambruster, *Treason's Peace* (New York, 1947), pp. 1–14.

particularly unnerving. Output depended on expensive laboratories and miles of apparatus, which translated into high fixed costs. Without steady flows of new inventions and investment and unusually large liquid and hidden reserves, no producer could rest easy.[2]

Well before 1900, a standard set of responses to the relentless pressure of costs and risks began to take shape. One expedient was government assistance, in the guise of the Reich patent laws, which the industry helped draft in the 1870s. By safeguarding domestic discoveries for fifteen years and denying protection to those foreign applicants unable to assume the great expense of employing their secrets within Germany, this legislation went far toward protecting the home markets of the German manufacturers.[3] Other defensive steps gradually altered the structure of the industry. Numerous small individual partnerships blended into a handful of large stock corporations in which leadership passed from the founding families and great investors to a corps of technically expert managers with relatively small personal shareholdings. These enterprises tentatively branched out into new product lines, experimented with scattered and ephemeral cartel agreements, and took over the preparation of their own working chemicals, thus beginning the practice of vertical integration.[4]

During the early decades of the twentieth century, however, accelerating commercial and technical changes made the synthetics industry's appetite for capital and inventions progressively more difficult to satisfy. As one of the business's modern shapers explained:

A great research accomplishment requires ten years to reach the production stage; for ten more years it brings returns; in the next ten years, it sags. Then another problem already must have been solved. What we earn on a successful discovery has to be poured into the preparation of a new product.[5]

[2] Thissen, *Die Stellung*, pp. 6–7; Paschke, *Der Aufbau*, pp. 29–30; L. F. Haber, *The Chemical Industry during the Nineteenth Century* (Oxford, 1958), p. 174; and L. F. Haber, *The Chemical Industry, 1900–1930* (Oxford, 1971), p. 123.
[3] Thissen, *Die Stellung*, pp. 3–4, 12; Paschke, *Der Aufbau*, p. 20; W. Greiling, *75 Jahre Chemieverband* (Frankfurt, 1952), pp. 21–2; J. J. Beer, *The Emergence of the German Dye Industry* (Urbana, Ill., 1959), p. 56; and Thomas Kuczynski, "Die Stellung der deutschen Teerfarbenindustrie zum Stoff- und Verfahrenspatent in der Zeit bis . . . 1891," *JfW*, 11 (1970), pp. 115–40. The industry preferred patents to tariffs as a protectionist device out of fear that the latter would provoke foreign nations to reply in kind.
[4] See the relevant chapters in the works of Thissen and Haber, cited in footnotes 1 and 2, respectively, and in the centennial volumes of BASF, *Im Reiche der Chemie* (Düsseldorf, 1965), and of Hoechst, Ernst Bäumler, *A Century of Chemistry* (Düsseldorf, 1968), which was also published in German as *Ein Jahrhundert Chemie*.
[5] Carl Bosch quoted in Josef Winschuh, *Männer, Traditionen, Signale* (Berlin, 1940), pp. 102–3.

This was the pattern of "senescence and rejuvenation" set by the dyes trade and its successor, synthetic nitrogen, in the years surrounding the First World War.[6] During the 1920s, the same underlying dynamic gave rise to a third generation of laboratory creations, liquid fuels made from coal, and inspired work on a fourth, synthetic rubber. The industry thus came to define the essence of its business as the exploitation of overlapping, but short-lived monopolies, each nurtured with government help in its embryonic stage, each dominating international markets during its mature period, when it provided the wherewithal for a new line of growth, and each retiring in the face of imitators into service of specialized demands during its declining phase.[7] With each turn of the wheel, mounting financial demands pushed the producers into greater consolidation, cartelization, and diversification.

Chapter 1 relates how this sequence of product cycles engendered the giant IG Farben corporation in 1925, as well as three aspects of the mentality that guided it over the ensuing twenty years. The first of these was a disposition to weigh long-range and technical considerations more heavily in decision making than immediate, commercial calculations. Purposely dominated by trained chemists, the firm tended to select priorities on the basis of their inventive promise. As Carl Bosch, Farben's first chairman, informed the occasionally disgruntled recipients of the company's modest dividends, "IG is not here to give big profits to its stockholders. Our pride and our duty is to work for those who come after us to establish the processes on which they will work."[8] This emphasis on creativity reinforced a second attribute of the new corporation: its inclination toward decentralization and the encouragement of initiative and teamwork at the lower levels of the enterprise. Though hardly egalitarian, Farben's internal ethos reflected Bosch's mistrust in both business and public life of "the call for a strongman." He insisted, on the contrary, that the organization of states and firms "concede to individual citizens . . . the freest possible activity" and recognize that "today, considering the enormous tasks

[6] The quoted phrase is from Raymond Vernon, *Sovereignty at Bay* (New York, 1971), which offers a somewhat different formulation of the product cycles of American industry, especially pp. 65–77, 81–6. An interesting, but highly derivative application of Vernon's model to German circumstances, among others, is James R. Kurth's "The Political Consequences of the Product Cycle: Industrial History and Political Outcomes," *International Organization*, 33 (1979), pp. 1–34.

[7] Walter Silbermann, *Chemie-Industrie und Aussenhandel* (Hamburg, 1938), pp. 11–12, 191, and chap. 4.

[8] Quoted by Carl Krauch in M892/15, p. 5122.

to be mastered, a single man will never be in a position to fulfill all that is expected of him."[9] IG Farben thus emerged as a notably inner-directed and loosely articulated enterprise, one that designed itself around the imperatives of research. An automatous view of those imperatives constituted the third salient element of the firm's mentality. Again, it was Bosch who stated the prevailing faith. Reflecting on the destructive uses to which nations could put the products of his industry, he dismissed second thoughts on such grounds by remarking that

progress in science and technology cannot be stopped. They are in many respects akin to art. One can persuade the one to halt as little as the others. They drive the people who are born for them to activity.[10]

In IG Farben, the task of the researcher was to invent, that of the executive to foster invention.

Yet because neither science nor commerce exists in a vacuum, Farben's mentality had a political side. Dependence on product cycles imparted a fourth trait to the huge corporation: a need for economic and political stability. This is the subject of Chapter 2. Given the natural fluctuations of the firm's business, IG's leaders saw their major extramural task as securing an orderly, predictable context in which to operate. Given the importance of exports to the corporation's health, that context embraced Farben's interaction with foreign competitors and Germany's relations with other nations, as well as the political arena of the Weimar Republic. In other words, smoothing the ups and downs of successive product cycles into a composite line of growth required the enterprise's managers to promote calm and cooperation among chemical producers around the world, the governments that presided over them, and the factions that contended within Germany.

The result during the 1920s was not a heartfelt acceptance of the consequences of World War l, but a recognition that their amelioration demanded realism and patience at home and abroad. Hence, Carl Duisberg, one of IG's founding fathers, admonished German executives in 1929–30 to find their places within the Reich's new republic, not against or alongside it, and urged them to expose the "un-

[9] Bosch's address to the Verein Deutscher Chemiker, May 1921, quoted in Karl Holdermann, *Im Banne der Chemie. Carl Bosch, Leben und Werke* (Düsseldorf, 1953), pp. 260–1.
[10] BASF Wı, Copy of Bosch's remarks in Vienna upon receipt of the Exner Medal, 16.XII.32.

workability" of the Versailles treaty, not to defy it.[11] The diversity, delicacy, and extent of Farben's business placed it in a constant brokering role – between native and foreign markets, agricultural and industrial interests, and the claims of capital and labor. The concern tried, therefore, to find a "state supporting middle line" in all these spheres, one that preserved the domestic prerequisites of profitability without harming the overseas ones.[12] But the Great Depression complicated this effort in two respects: It upset international economic arrangements and helped make the firm's own resources inadequate for the requirements of the product cycles; and it swelled the ranks of extremist political movements that threatened the preconditions of Farben's prosperity.

In 1933, these leitmotifs in the history of IG Farben – its subordination to the rhythm of product cycles, its responsiveness to "technological momentum," its internal looseness, its illusorily apolitical professionalism, and its quest for stability – added up to a complex of potential affinities and differences with the new masters of Germany.[13]

---

[11] Duisberg to the Reichsverband der deutschen Industrie, as quoted in the *Frankfurter Zeitung*, 23.IX.29, and reprinted in Jens Flemming, Claus-Dieter Krohn, Dirk Stegmann, and Peter-Christian Witt (eds.), *Die Republik von Weimar*, vol. 1 (Königstein/Ts., 1979), p. 210, and to the same group on 26.XI.30, as quoted in Heinrich Gattineau, *Durch die Klippen des 20. Jahrhunderts* (Stuttgart, 1983), p. 35.

[12] The phrase quoted appears in Bayer 4C9.25, unpublished manuscript by R. W. Mueller and Dr. von Knieriem, "Die I. G. Farbenindustrie Aktiengesellschaft. Das Schicksal eines deutschen Unternehmens," March 1951, p. 85. On the company's determination to appear *immer regierungstreu*, that is, always ostentatiously loyal to the prevailing political order in Germany, see Hartmut Raupert, *Rolle und Bedeutung der I. G.-Farben im Rahmen der nationalsozialistischen Wirtschaftspolitik* (Diplom Arbeit, Ruhr-Universität, Bochum, 1976), p. 140, and NI-5196/38, Affidavit by Georg von Schnitzler, 18.III.47.

[13] The phrase quoted is from Thomas Parke Hughes's path-breaking essay, "Technological Momentum in History: Hydrogenation in Germany 1898–1933," *P&P*, no. 44 (August 1969), pp. 106–32.

1. Origins and organization

At the beginning of the twentieth century, satisfaction with the profitability of the organic chemical industry began to give way to concern
over its future. To be sure, German corporations and their foreign
branches still controlled just less than 90% of world dye production
and paid annual dividends averaging around 20% of their stock capital. However, they appeared to have nearly depleted nature's store of
dyeing compounds. Small improvements required great outlays for
research and marketing. Large breakthroughs, as demonstrated by the
40 million marks spent on synthesizing indigo, almost exhausted the
finances of single firms.[1] The saturation of the rather inelastic dye
market foretold more than customarily vicious and expensive infighting; so did the steady expiration of patents and the rise of tariff walls.
In the related and even more volatile pharmaceuticals field, American
sellers made "dangerous" inroads on European markets.[2] Nor was the
overall situation reassuring. Despite substantial increases in total German output and workers employed in the industry, the Reich's share
of world chemical production dropped between 1897 and 1905 from
nearly one-third to one-quarter.[3]

In January 1904, Carl Duisberg took note of such signs of decline in
a memorandum he circulated among the principal German dye and
drug companies.[4] A chemist by training with modest research finds to
his credit, Duisberg had risen to the top of the Bayer corporation on
more than technical ability. He had married into the family of the
company's namesake and demonstrated a rare organizational talent,

[1] Herman Pinnow, *Zur Erinnerung an die 75. Wiederkehr des Gründungstages der
Farbwerke vorm. Meister Lucius & Brüning* (München, 1938), p. 91; Bäumler, *Century of Chemistry*, p. 192.
[2] Vogel, *Die Entwicklung des Exportes und Importes*, pp. 74, 81.
[3] Claus Ungewitter (ed.), *Chemie in Deutschland* (Berlin, 1938), p. 38; K. Barkin,
"Germany's Path to Industrial Maturity," *Laurentian University Review*, 5 (1973),
p. 25.
[4] Reprinted in Carl Duisberg, *Abhandlungen, Vorträge und Reden aus den Jahren
1882–1921* (Berlin, 1923), pp. 343–69.

Carl Duisberg (1861–1935), chairman of the *Aufsichtsrat*, 1925–35. (*Source:* Bayer-Archiv, Leverkusen)

in which he took justifiable, though sometimes rather pompous pride. During a recent visit to the United States, he thought he had discovered a means of channeling competition among the German producers to serve their common advantage. He urged the manufacturers to federate into a single giant trust that would merge the capital but preserve the energizing individual identities of the participating firms. Under a "republican constitution" and a collegial leadership composed only of experienced businessmen, the producers would reap savings from common administration and planning, cooperation on research, and clear divisions of market spheres, while their plants would continue to vie at producing most efficiently.

Duisberg's ambitious program proved premature, but between 1904 and 1907, two blocs crystallized among the largest dye makers: the Dreibund, consisting of the Badische Anilin- und Soda-Fabrik (BASF) of Ludwigshafen, the Farbenfabriken vorm. Friedrich Bayer & Co. (Bayer) of Leverkusen, and the Aktiengesellschaft für Anilin-Fabrikation (Agfa) of Berlin; and the Dreiverband, comprising the Farbwerke vorm. Meister Lucius & Brüning of Hoechst am Main (Hoechst), Leopold Cassella & Co. GmbH of Frankfurt am Main, and Kalle & Co. Aktiengesellschaft of Biebrich am Main. Members of the former group pooled their profits; interlocking shareholdings and directorships ensured a similar arrangement in the latter. Although these industrial alliances did not end wrangling over patents, competition abroad, or duplication of plants, they took some of the uncertainty out of costs, markets, and prices.[5]

The three largest participants now felt free to pursue new ventures. Bayer promptly turned out hard artificial rubber tires, a promising accomplishment, even though technical problems and underselling by rubber planters rendered it impracticable for the moment. Hoechst moved into the electrothermic manufacture of carbide, which led to the fabrication of limited quantities of nitric acid and, more importantly, to acetylene chemistry. From BASF came the revolutionary

[5] On the emergence and functioning of the two blocs, see, above all, Beer, *German Dye Industry*, pp. 94–101; Haber, *Chemical Industry, 1900–1930*, pp. 124–8; Peter Waller, *Probleme der deutschen chemischen Industrie* (Halberstadt, 1928), pp. 57, 81. Also relevant are Haber, *Chemical Industry during the Nineteenth Century*, pp. 170–1; Werner Reichelt, *Das Erbe der IG Farben* (Düsseldorf, 1956), pp. 18–24; Hans-Joachim Flechtner, *Carl Duisberg – vom Chemiker zum Wirtschaftsführer* (Düsseldorf, 1959), pp. 187–214; Bäumler, *Century of Chemistry*, pp. 74–88; Paschke, *Der Aufbau*, pp. 43–9; and Fraund, *Betriebswirtschaftliche Studie*, pp. 9–13.

Haber–Bosch process for obtaining nitrogen from the air by combining it with hydrogen. Not only did the result, synthetic ammonia, free Germany of dependence on foreign sources for basic components of fertilizers and explosives, but the procedure, called hydrogenation, opened the way to further applications of catalysts under extremely high pressures.[6]

World War I forced the pace of these incipient shifts in production and organization. While the dye plants profiteered off military orders for munitions and poison gases, the Allied blockade of Germany created a hothouse environment for the fledgling prewar inventions. The Reich provided not only lucrative contracts, but also, at the urging of some producers, the labor of prisoners of war and conscripted Belgians, as well as loans for half the cost of erecting and operating an enormous nitrogen fixation plant at Leuna near Merseburg.[7] Concurrently, however, the interruption of normal commerce and production undermined the traditional commercial foundations of the chemical companies. They exported 75 to 85% of their dyes output on the eve of the war; the returns amounted to 63% of the earnings from sales of the eight leading producers.[8] Given the hectic enlargement of this industry in the Allied nations during the fighting, these firms could expect an intense postwar struggle resulting in, at best, partial recovery of their former position. Alone among the new products, nitrogen promised substantial, sustained peacetime demand and thus a means of alleviating the looming crisis of overcapacity and price warfare.

[6] Beer, *German Dye Industry*, p. 101; Bäumler, *Century of Chemistry*, pp. 60–5; Hughes, *P&P*, no. 44 (August 1969), pp. 107–9; Haber, *Chemical Industry, 1900–1930*, pp. 129–30; and Gottfried Plumpe, "Industrie, technischer Fortschritt und Staat: Die Kautschuksynthese in Deutschland 1906–1944/45," *G&G*, 9 (1983), pp. 565–7.

[7] Holdermann, *Im Banne der Chemie*, pp. 136–46; Heinz Beike, "Zur Rolle von Fritz Haber und Carl Bosch in Politik und Gesellschaft," *Wissenschaftliche Zeitschrift der Technischen Hochschule für Chemie Leuna-Merseburg*, 3 (1960–1), pp. 64–5; Joseph Borkin, *The Crime and Punishment of I.G. Farben* (New York, 1978), pp. 21–3; and André Leisewitz, "Die Auswirkungen der Verwissenschaftlichung der Produktion auf die Monopolbildung und auf das Verhältnis von Ökonomie und Politik. . . ," *Das Argument*, 14 (1972), which notes that net profits of the principal dye firms rose from 25.8 million reichsmarks in 1914 to 52.2 million in 1917 (pp. 483–4).

[8] Bayer 15 D1.1, Dr. W. Thiele, Statistische Abteilung, Leverkusen, "Die Umsätze der IG im Jahre 1924. (Ein Vergleich mit 1923 und dem letzten Vorkriegsjahr 1913)," 22.IV.25, pp. 10–11; Bayer 4C9.32, Office of the Military Government for Germany (U.S.), I. G. Farben Control Office [Hans Kugler], *The Activities of I.G. Farbenindustrie in the Dyestuffs Industry* (1946), p. 28; Lindemann, *Die Arbeiterverhältnisse*, p. 12.

BASF, however, could not exploit this advantage single-handedly, lest it collapse under the weight of the borrowing necessary to expand the nitrogen installations. Again Duisberg stated the case for cooperation. Alarmed by their prospects and by the increasingly assertive trade unions, prodded by the government, and eager to insure themselves by jointly developing the nitrogen operation, the main dye companies decided once more to pull together.[9]

A new Interessengemeinschaft der deutschen Teerfarbenfabriken (Community of Interests of the German Tar Dye Factories) united the Dreibund and Dreiverband in August 1916.[10] Within a year, it all but perfected its monopoly of the German dye industry by signing on the Chemische Fabrik vorm. Weiler-terMeer of Uerdingen and the Chemische Fabrik Griesheim Elektron of Frankfurt am Main and buying up several smaller factories. This so-called Little IG aligned and expanded the common spheres of action laid down in the two earlier agreements. Serious competition among the members ceased within Germany. Having cautiously retained the legal right to withdraw from the new pact and, therefore, outward independence and control over their production programs, the firms nonetheless abridged their sovereignties in important respects. One of the numerous joint commissions took up the sensitive matter of voluntary reductions in overlapping domestic and foreign plants. A council of leaders from each firm, the *Gemeinschaftsrat,* acted on acquisitions, exchanges of know-how, and capital issues and settled disputed questions. A table of fixed percentages apportioned votes in the council, as well as the pooled profits, which excluded receipts from certain products reserved to Griesheim, Hoechst, and BASF. Almost immediately, BASF surrendered its right to withhold the proceeds from nitrogen production at Leuna in return for capital commitments by the other firms to this

---

[9] Rudolf K. Michels, *Cartels, Combines and Trusts in Post-War Germany* (New York, 1928), pp. 152–4; Beer, *German Dye Industry,* pp. 140–1; Hellmuth Tammen, *Die I. G. Farbenindustrie Aktiengesellschaft (1925–1933)* (Dissertation, Freie Universität, Berlin, 1978), pp. 13–14. Duisberg's second memorandum appears in W. Treue, "Carl Duisbergs Denkschrift von 1915 zur Gründung der 'Kleinen IG,'" *Tradition,* 8 (1963), pp. 193–227; cf. Rolf Sonnemann, "Ueber die Duisberg-Denkschrift aus dem Jahre 1915," *JfW,* 7 (1966), pp. 119–45.

[10] The original contract is NI-5179/38, 18.VIII.16. Useful summaries appear in Fritz terMeer's *Die I. G. Farben Industrie Aktiengesellschaft* (Düsseldorf, 1953), pp. 17–21; Beer, *German Dye Industry,* pp. 134–41; and Hermann Schreyer, "Der IG-Farben Konzern, Seine Vorgänger und Nachfolger," *Archivmitteilungen,* 16 (1966), pp. 103–4. Several careless errors and questionable interpretations weaken Haber's comments in *Chemical Industry, 1900–1930,* pp. 279–84.

operation. So profitable was the new confederation that the participants easily bought up extensive coal mines during 1916–17 and
reconverted to peacetime production in 1918–19.

The postwar sales crisis surpassed the worst expectations of the dye
firms without seriously damaging them. Partly as a result of the confiscation of foreign patents and subsidiaries under the Versailles treaty, German dye output in 1924 languished at 45% of capacity, having
fallen from 88% of world production in 1913 to 46%. By the following year, dye exports came to less than one-third of their prewar
volume, leaving the companies with inventories equal to demand for
the next one and a half years. But continuing technical superiority and
shrewd advertising preserved German dominance in the most specialized lines, for which prices rose rapidly. If the deterioration in
exports of pharmaceuticals and photographic chemicals was even
more pronounced, new products, like film, took up the slack. In 1925,
the pattern of the Little IG's trade mirrored that of German chemicals
as a whole: diminished quantities but nearly constant or increased
values in comparison with 1913. Exclusive of nitrogen and light metals, the sales proceeds of the member firms, adjusted for inflation,
actually rose from 1913 to 1924 by 12.9%; a fair estimate of the gain
including these areas is probably about 50%. The principal impact of
the postwar crisis was not on the volume of revenue but on its source:
The share from dyes, sold mostly abroad, shrank to about 45%,
whereas that from nitrogen, purchased predominantly within Germany, swelled to about one-third. By 1924, synthetic nitrogen, not
dyes, was bringing in the greater part of the Little IG's profits.[11]

Meanwhile, vertical integration armed the Little IG against such
problems as the national coal shortage, and enormous accumulated
reserves enabled the companies to ride out the bitter labor troubles of
1919–21. As for the gathering inflation, which went out of control in
1923, it simply piled on windfall profits in stable foreign exchange by
lowering the cost of German goods abroad. The Little IG availed itself
unashamedly of the opportunity to pay off the wartime government

[11] Bayer 15 D1.1, Thiele memo, pp. 5–11, and 4C9.32, Control Office, *Dyestuffs*, p.
30; Tammen, *I. G. Farbenindustrie*, pp. 14–15; Waller, *Probleme*, pp. 125–6, 128;
Bäumler, *Century of Chemistry*, p. 95; Schwarz, Goldschmidt & Co., *Die I. G.
Farbenindustrie und ihre Bedeutung* (Berlin, 1926), pp. 56, 59; Lindemann, *Arbeiterverhältnisse*, p. 15; Robert A. Brady, *The Rationalization Movement in German Industry* (Berkeley, Calif., 1933), p. 236; and D. Warriner, *Combines and
Rationalization in Germany, 1924–1928* (London, 1931), pp. 83, 171.

loans for the Leuna plant in worthless paper marks. Turning the other cheek, the Republic then made good most of the losses attendant on the French intervention in the Rhineland and Ruhr.[12] Even the compulsory sales of dyes and fertilizers as war reparations benefited the German producers by providing a secure minimum market and undercutting the efforts of manufacturers in the Allied countries to establish themselves.[13] When the member firms revalued their stock capital in 1924, their aggregate worth in gold was three and a half times higher than in 1913.[14] In sum, the Little IG participants remained highly profitable, largely by virtue of diversification, temporary export advantages, and a measured reorientation around the nitrogen sector.

So long as earnings held up, the companies clung to their independence. They agreed to exchanges of stock in order to block the influence of potential foreign investors, and they formed a commonly owned nitrogen company, the Ammoniak-Werke Merseburg-Oppau GmbH, when the new Republic refused to guarantee BASF against the risks of operating Leuna in peacetime unless the government got a majority of the plant's stock. However, the pleas of Carl Bosch of BASF, who now outstripped Duisberg as the most insistent proponent of closer union, achieved little else.[15] Although joint administration of purchasing, finance, legal affairs, and reparations payments accustomed the partners to centralization, they kept up their guards against withdrawal by any member. With each firm fighting to protect its employees from layoffs and its relative position in the industry against plant closings, rationalization (i.e., the reduction of superfluous works) made but modest headway.[16]

Beginning in the final months of 1923, a series of circumstances reconciled the producers to complete consolidation. Changes in Ger-

12 Bayer 15 D1.1, Thiele memo, pp. 4–5.
13 Haber, *Chemical Industry 1900–1930*, p. 250. Neither this observation, nor the later German complaints about the burden of reparations should be overemphasized. Though Versailles entitled the Allies to take 25% of German dye production as reparations, they in fact took only about 7% between 1920 and 1923 (NI-5193/38, Affidavit by G. von Schnitzler, 7.III.47, p. 2). As of 1926, IG estimated the value of its goods paid over as reparations at 70 million reichsmarks (NI-11252/93, IG's New Order Plan, 3.VIII.40, p. 10).
14 Michels, *Cartels, Combines and Trusts*, p. 142; Fraund, *Betriebswirtschaftliche Studie*, p. 42.
15 Thissen, *Die Stellung*, pp. 74–75; Beer, *German Dye Industry*, p. 144; Fraund, *Betriebswirtschaftliche Studie*, p. 39; Holdermann, *Im Banne der Chemie*, pp. 170–2.
16 Bayer 4C9.32, Control Office, *Dyestuffs*, p. 26; Reichelt, *Das Erbe*, pp. 29–33; Bäumler, *Century of Chemistry*, p. 95.

Carl Bosch (1874–1940), chairman of the *Vorstand*, 1925–35, and of the *Aufsichtsrat*, 1935–40. (*Source*: Bayer-Archiv, Leverkusen)

man corporate and tax laws made an amalgamation more attractive, while the stabilization of the mark spelled the end of Germany's fortuitous sales advantage abroad, and the spread of nitrogen fixation to other lands presaged a leveling off of income from that source.[17] Ruthless pruning of overhead in the dyes sector became urgent. To forestall a similar overcapacity problem in nitrogen, millions of marks were needed to finance BASF's project for the hydrogenation of coal into liquid fuels. Just as in 1915–16, the keys to escape from a threatening situation seemed at hand, and their possessor, in this case the Little IG, lacked the financial strength to turn them in the lock. Bosch now pressed home BASF's advantages as the partner with the greatest facilities and reserves, the most promising new technology, and the largest output of basic chemicals on which the others depended.

Despite the apparent urgency of the situation, disputes between Duisberg and Bosch held up a merger agreement. These two godfathers of IG Farben, though both self-made men, could not have differed more sharply in temperament or experience. Bosch, the younger by some thirteen years, assumed managerial responsibility only during World War I, following a brilliant scientific and engineering career that eventuated in his receipt of the Nobel Prize for Chemistry in 1931. Contemplative, somewhat melancholy, and lacking his buoyant colleague's vanity and taste for hierarchy, Bosch took an unprejudiced attitude toward relations with his work force, developed an uncommonly talented cadre of subordinates, and shunned the limelight in which Duisberg obviously bathed. Whereas Duisberg saw the advantages of merger primarily in traditional commercial terms, Bosch was concerned chiefly with funding new and pressing technical tasks. While Duisberg placed his faith in elaborate and precise organizational schemes, Bosch preferred to match problems to able individuals on an ad hoc basis. Though Duisberg thought the formation of a holding company would meet the producers' needs, Bosch would settle for nothing short of fusion into a single corporation under his leadership. At the price of concessions regarding the structure and name of the new enterprise, Bosch finally obtained his main objective.[18]

17 See Fraund, *Betriebswirtschaftliche Studie,* pp. 43–4.
18 See, for this and the following paragraph, terMeer, *I. G. Farben,* pp. 22–4, 56; Reichelt, *Das Erbe,* pp. 29–33; Borkin, *Crime and Punishment,* pp. 42–5; Michels, *Cartels, Combines and Trusts,* pp. 142–4; Tammen, *I. G. Farbenindustrie,* pp. 15–

On December 2, 1925, representatives of BASF, Bayer, Hoechst, Agfa, Griesheim, and Weiler-terMeer signed the merger contract. The other two members of the Little IG, Cassella and Kalle, remained almost wholly owned subsidiaries, legally distinct but administered as part of the new corporation. To execute the agreement, BASF raised its capitalization to equal that of all six signatories, exchanged its stock for theirs, elected new governing boards, moved its headquarters to Frankfurt, and retitled itself the IG Farbenindustrie Aktiengesellschaft (Interest Community of the Dye Industry, Inc.). The mechanics of the merger attested to the existing and future distribution of weight within the new enterprise. In a sense, BASF had swallowed the others: Its style and personnel exerted a fateful influence on the twenty-year history of IG Farben.

The new colossus bestrode the German chemical industry. Indeed, it was the largest corporation, not just in Germany, but in all of Europe and, by most indices, the fourth largest in the world behind General Motors, United States Steel, and Standard Oil of New Jersey.[19] Its name hardly did justice to its extent, for IG Farben was neither a federation of formally independent companies, as the vestigial initials implied, nor confined to the dye industry; nor was it merely a single corporation. Instead, it fit the description of a vertically and horizontally integrated concern or combine, encompassing one core firm and more than fifty semiautonomous dependents.[20] Within a few years, these holdings included not only the properties of the eight forerunner companies, but also the film and fiber factories grouped in the Köln-Rottweil AG, the explosives plants operated independently by the Dynamit AG (DAG) and the Westfälische-Anhaltische Sprengstoff AG

18; Flechtner, *Carl Duisberg*, pp. 333–49; Holdermann, *Im Banne der Chemie*, pp. 195–208; Louis Lochner, *Tycoons and Tyrant* (Chicago, 1954), pp. 38–47; and Wolfram Fischer, "Dezentralisation oder Zentralisation – kollegiale oder autoritäre Führung?" in Norbert Horn and Jürgen Kocka (eds.), *Recht und Entwicklung der Grossunternehmen im 19. und frühen 20. Jahrhundert* (Göttingen, 1979), pp. 476–88.

19 Comparisons appear in Hermann Gross, *Further Facts and Figures Relating to the Deconcentration of the I. G. Farbenindustrie Aktiengesellschaft* (Kiel, 1950), pp. 35–40, which was also published in German. The statistics for IG refer only to the core corporation, however, not the wider concern, and are thus understatements.

20 For definitions of these designations, see Michels, *Cartels, Combines and Trusts*, pp. 17, 25–6, 28–30. Tammen, *I. G. Farbenindustrie*, contains a useful graphic depiction of Farben's far-flung solar system, between pp. 20 and 21.

(WASAG), the fuel sales organization of the Deutsche Gasolin AG, and 47% of the stock in the Rheinische Stahlwerke.[21] From birth, IG Farben defied classification into any one of the categories by which historians sometimes group German industries: heavy or light, basic or finishing, export- or domestic-oriented, traditional or dynamic.

More than one hundred IG plants and mines belonged to the core firm alone by 1929 (see Appendix A), employing close to 120,000 people and grossing more than 1.4 billion reichsmarks from sales.[22] Shortly after the merger, the book value of the corporation's stock climbed from 646 million to 1.1 billion reichsmarks; market value on the exchanges crested at three times that amount in 1928.[23] No independent chemical firm in Germany wielded even 10% of this capital; the next fifteen companies in order of size accounted for less than one-third of IG's total at book, and the concern owned a majority of two of them plus substantial fractions of several of the others.[24] Under the Republic, the combine consistently held about 48% of the invested capital of the German chemical industry, about 4% of that in industry as a whole.[25] More to the point, from 1925 to 1929, IG generated two-thirds of the chemical industry's profits, exports, and new capital outlays.[26] According to two American analysts, by 1930 the concern turned out 100% of German dyes, 65–85% of the country's nitrogen, nearly all its explosives, 90% of its mineral acids, 40% of its pharmaceuticals, 30% of its rayon – altogether more than 40% of German chemical products.[27] A contemporary German critic calculated that IG also controlled 8% of lignite or brown coal production in the Rhineland and 39% in central Germany, where it also had 16% of

21 On the process by which Farben "rounded off" its holdings in the late 1920s, see Peter Hayes, The Gleichschaltung of IG Farben (Dissertation, Yale Univ., New Haven, Conn., 1982), pp. 40–1.
22 Tammen, I. G. Farbenindustrie, pp. 67–8.
23 Das Spezial-Archiv der deutschen Wirtschaft, Der I. G. Farben-Konzern 1932 (Berlin, 1932), pp. 28–9; Michels, Cartels, Combines and Trusts, p. 145; Tammen, I.G. Farbenindustrie, pp. 17–19, 66.
24 Tammen, I. G. Farbenindustrie, p. 19 and note 46, p. 347; NI-9052/75, Affidavit of Werner Hagert, 26.VII.47; Brady, Rationalization, p. 235.
25 Gross, Facts and Figures, p. 27.
26 Claus Ungewitter's estimate in Spezial-Archiv, Der I. G. Farben-Konzern 1932, p. 12. Compare the figures on dividends as a proportion of invested capital in Wilhelm Hagemann, Das Verhältnis der deutschen Grossbanken zur Industrie (Dissertation, Handels-Hochschule Berlin, 1931), p. 106.
27 George Stocking and Myron Watkins, Cartels in Action (New York, 1947), pp. 413–14. Insofar as their figures can be checked against documentation, they are slightly high across the board.

briquette output.[28] The combine's lignite holdings were the second largest in the nation, amounting, by IG's own reckoning, to 12% of the brown coal surface mines; its bituminous coal possessions, covering 2.5% of the entire Ruhr region, were allotted 4.5% of the production under the Rhenish-Westphalian Coal Syndicate.[29] None of these indications of economic power takes into consideration the concern's modest ownerships in banking, its interests in oil research and sales, its 20% share in the German light-metal business, and its rapidly growing output of other nonferrous metals.[30]

Vast as Farben was, it developed within conscious limits. By design, IG slighted older or middlingly profitable chemical fields, such as paints, soaps, and retail inorganic products, in order to concentrate on the perceived growth sectors of the industry.[31] And the concern was no conglomerate. Its operations remained linked by common raw materials or interlocking manufacturing processes, largely because any more inclusive pattern of acquisitions would threaten the enterprise's collegial style of leadership.[32] Finally, the combine stopped short of becoming a truly multinational corporation. By 1932, IG had recovered the prewar American properties of the predecessor firms, established a handful of productive facilities in Spain, Italy, Norway, Poland, and Switzerland, and founded the IG Chemie of Basel as its international holding and financing agency. Nonetheless, Farben continued to prefer active exporting to projects that would scatter capital.[33]

That this empire evolved a complicated, rather diffuse organization was both inevitable and intentional. Sheer size and diversity, coupled

---

[28] Helmut Wickel, *IG-Deutschland* (Berlin, 1932), p. 148; nearly identical figures appear in Waller, *Probleme*, p. 37.

[29] Tammen, *I. G. Farbenindustrie*, pp. 59–60 and notes 211, p. 357, and 215, p. 358; RG 242/T83, Reel 88, Item 5, document concerning the extent of IG, undated, probably 1934.

[30] Statistiches Reichsamt, *Konzerne, Interessengemeinschaften und ähnliche Zusammenschlüsse im Deutschen Reiche Ende 1926* (Berlin, 1927), pp. 119–24; NI-8034/66, Bürgin and Moschel to Schmitz, terMeer, and Weber-Andreä, 23.X.40.

[31] Haber, *Chemical Industry, 1900–1930*, p. 287.

[32] Spezial-Archiv, *Der I. G. Farben-Konzern 1932*, p. 24; NI-5191/38, Affidavit by G. von Schnitzler, 4.III.47; Warriner, *Combines and Rationalization*, p. 46; and Hayes, *Gleichschaltung*, pp. 43–4.

[33] For a more detailed description of IG's foreign operations and the motives behind them, see Hayes, *Gleichschaltung*, pp. 44–5, and Verena Schröter, *Die deutsche Industrie auf dem Weltmarkt 1929 bis 1933* (Frankfurt, 1984), pp. 163–4, 401–14, 431–2.

with the disparate arrangements that bound the ancillary companies
to the whole, ruled out a simple, hierarchical system. Moreover, the
founders set out to extract the economic rewards of unified planning
and administration without fostering an overarching bureaucracy that
would stifle the inventiveness, individual responsibility, and initiative
to which the predecessor firms owed their success. The upshot was a
costly, but flexible system of widely dispersed authority. A clear chain
of command from the top down never existed. Instead, decisions were
made at the lowest level possible, and only the broadest, most expensive, and most precedential matters percolated upward.[34] To the outside world, IG apotheosized the scheme under the ungainly title "decentralized centralism." Within the firm, it was known rather more
aptly, with a nod to another composite of pyramided dynastic unions,
proud local magnates, and heterogeneous dominions, as "the Habs-
burg Model."[35] True to that metaphor IG's structure unfolded gradually and never seamlessly wove the firm together.[36]

For about five years the design of IG followed the blueprint of Carl
Duisberg, who became the first chairman of the supervisory board, or
Aufsichtsrat.[37] Still determined to harness, not destroy, creative competition among the merged companies and to restrict the influence of
lawyers and financiers, Duisberg merely remodeled the Little IG to fit
under one rather thin corporate roof. Centralization of sales took just
a small step forward: In dyes and chemicals, specific markets were
parceled out among the various works. Scattered main offices for
purchasing, bookkeeping, taxes, advertising, transport, social questions, and patents and other legal matters performed service and recording functions for corresponding units within the plants. The details of production and research remained the province of these
relatively autonomous, self-contained factories. They dealt with common problems informally and through countless commissions, committees, and study groups, as well as through the four, later five, plant

34 NI-5186/38, Affidavit by F. terMeer, 23.IV.47, p. 11; NI-9487/78, Affidavit by
Ernst Struss, 5.VIII.47, p. 50.
35 Interview with W. R. Mann, Jr., 13.VII.78.
36 See Karl Winnacker's memoir, *Nie den Mut verlieren* (Düsseldorf, 1971), pp. 74–6.
37 Unless otherwise acknowledged below, my summary of the concern's organization
rests on the two documents cited in footnote 34, as well as NI-5184/38, Affidavit by
Fritz terMeer, 29.IV.47; Tammen, *I. G. Farbenindustrie*, pp. 22–28; terMeer, *I. G.
Farben*, pp. 48–57; Schreyer, *Archivmitteilungen*, 16 (1966), pp. 148–52; and
Rudolf Schröder, "Die Ausschussprotokolle der IG Farben," *JfW*, 8 (1967), pp.
250–69.

associations, or *Betriebsgemeinschaften*. Intended to cluster small and medium-sized works around one plant on a regional basis, the factory groupings in reality roughly perpetuated the outlines of the principal forerunner firms.

Between 1929 and 1932, however, Carl Bosch, the first chairman of the managing board, or *Vorstand*, acted on his belief "that the Depression period must be used to simplify the organization of the firm and make it more effective."[38] Convinced that the complexity of Duisberg's edifice wasted the scientific staff's time and impeded action, Bosch began building the structure depicted in Appendix B. It compressed the marketing agencies and more or less subsumed all of the technical and commercial groupings under three Product Divisions, or Sparten.[39] Each division had its own leader and central office to supervise planning, expansion, pricing, finances, and the advancement of personnel within its field. Sparte I, chaired by Karl Krekeler briefly, then by Carl Krauch until 1938, and thereafter by Christian Schneider, centered on the practice of high-pressure chemistry. It consisted of IG's coal mines and nitrogen and synthetic fuel installations with their sales units, the Mining Administration in Halle, the Nitrogen Syndicate of Berlin, and the German Gasoline Corporation or the IG-Department for Oil, both in Berlin. Sparte II, under Fritz terMeer, bracketed the mainstream chemical products, often related by common intermediate materials or similar production processes: inorganic and organic chemicals, light metals, and solvents; dyes, rubber, plastics, bleaches, detergents, and tanning substances; and insecticides and pharmaceuticals. Marketing agents were the sales combines for chemicals and dyes, both in Frankfurt, and the Bayer sales combine for pharmaceuticals in Leverkusen. Sparte III was Fritz Gajewski's domain. Built around the use of cellulose or applications of vulcanization, it comprised photographic supplies, sold by the Sales Combine Agfa in Berlin; artificial fibers, which reached the public via several syndicates; explosives, manufactured and sold by the formally independent munition firms controlled by IG; and cellophane and special papers for blueprints and photocopying (Ozalid), made and disposed

[38] NI-1941/18, Minutes of the ZA meeting, 9.I.31.
[39] On the commercial organization, see Bayer 4C9.24, Büro Anderhub, pp. 4–7; NI-9267/77, Affidavit by H. Bässler, 1.VIII.47; NI-7318/58, Affidavit by K. von Heider, 28.VI.47; and Waller, *Probleme*, pp. 18–19.

of by Kalle & Co. of Biebrich. Unavoidably, some of the larger plants of the combine housed operations that reported to different Sparten.

The Sparten varied in their cohesiveness, hence also in the complexity of their internal organization and in their modes of making policy. In Sparten I and III, the plant and sales chiefs worked out at regular meetings the divisional plans and budgets and coordinated commercial and technical considerations. Gajewski held his Sparte, with the exception of the explosives sector, on a tight leash, but the three segments of Sparte I tolerated little interference from their leader. Matters were ambiguous within Sparte II. Its heterogeneity dictated the survival of the plant associations, albeit along somewhat modified lines, and of the welter of special committees, whereas Sparten I and III could dispense with these groupings. Moreover, Sparte II embraced the spheres of several individuals whose prominence in the forerunner firms' marketing organizations forbade subordinating them to ter-Meer. Sales leaders, therefore, seldom attended the regular Sparte sessions; instead, commercial and technical personnel cooperated and arrived at production targets in three independent-minded main committees: the Chemicals Committee under Eduard Weber-Andreä, the Dyes Committee under Georg von Schnitzler, and the Pharmaceuticals Main Conference directed by Wilhelm Mann, Jr. and Heinrich Hoerlein.

The Sparten, the sales combines, and the main committees all reported in principle directly to the managing board, or *Vorstand,* but in practice their recommendations filtered through either of two advisory committees, which met on the morning before the board's session. However, one of these, the Commercial Committee (KA) under Schnitzler, failed to carve out a convincing role for itself in the early years, partly because the Sparten leaders snubbed it. It lapsed into dormancy between 1932 and 1937, reviving only when Nazi policy complicated IG's foreign activities. Far more significant initially was the Technical Committee (TEA), which Bosch conducted until 1933, when terMeer took over. Consisting of the technical members of the *Vorstand* and several engineers and lower-ranking leaders of important plants, the TEA also invited financial and legal advisers, the chairman of the KA, and the chairmen of the two boards to its meetings. In broad outline, it reviewed production plans, requests for construction funds, patent or license agreements, and research developments, all of which had been worked out in detail by its forty-one subcommittees and commissions. Both committees possessed small supporting offices to handle correspondence and prepare their discussions.[40]

As prescribed by German law, three bodies capped this structure. Legal responsibility for the management of the corporation resided in a board of active executives called the *Vorstand*. It was appointed and supervised by an *Aufsichtsrat,* composed of retired IG executives and representatives of companies and banks that worked closely with the concern. The latter group, in turn, was responsible to and chosen by the general meeting of the stockholders. None of these organizations exercised the degree of control theoretically assigned to it, a fact that reinforced as much as it reflected the scattering of authority ordained by "decentralized centralism."

The *Aufsichtsrat* at first combined the supervisory boards of the forerunner firms, minus some retirees, plus a few men who had been "kicked upstairs" from the several managing boards. This resulted in an initial membership of fifty-five. Though a government decree of September 1931 slashed the number to twenty-eight as an economy measure, an administrative council, or *Verwaltungsrat*, of about eleven members continued to meet three or four times annually until 1938 and to function in place of the larger, purely honorary group.[41] The board's duties were mainly formalities: the approval of nominees to the *Vorstand,* authorization of share and bond issues, consideration of alterations in the charter (*Satzung*) or bylaws of the firm, and presentation of the annual business report and balance sheets to the shareholders. Members of the administrative council made their influence felt individually in private conversations and at meetings of subordinate committees. After 1938, retirements and replacements balanced

---

[40] NI-5169/38 lists the members of the KA, 1926–45; NI-10043/82 those of the TEA for the same period. The minutes of the KA sessions are in Bayer 13/9, and those of the TEA meetings in Bayer 13/13-17 and among the vast collection of the TEA's files housed at the Hoechst Archiv. The bylaws of the TEA are NI-7603/62.

[41] NI-5186/38, Affidavit by F. terMeer, 23.IV.47; NI-6120/46, Affidavit by Carl Krauch, 28.VII.47; *RGBl.* no. 1 (1931) p. 493; BA, ZSg 127, Bd. 838. Members of the *Aufsichtsrat* and of the *Verwaltungsrat* are listed in NI-7957/66, Affidavit by H. Bässler, 17.VII.47. The records of the *Verwaltungsrat* have not survived, since each member returned his copies upon retirement at age 75, and the firm systematically destroyed them: Bayer AS, Duisberg to Walther vom Rath, 6.I.33, and Schmitz I/5, Deposition by W. F. Kalle, 4.X.47. NI-5178/38 includes the group's bylaws. The minutes of the *Aufsichtsrat* are at Bayer 11/3; its bylaws are NI-8933/74.

out at a manageable complement of about twenty for the *Aufsichtsrat*, which henceforth met as a whole, but the members lost the right to attend committee sessions, and changes in the laws governing corporations reduced the board to a cipher. Duisberg served as chairman until 1935, Bosch until 1940, and Carl Krauch thereafter.

The evolution of the *Vorstand* paralleled that of the supervisory board. Initially composed of eighty-three full and deputy members drawn from the previous managing boards, it delegated its powers to two more compact groups. The Working Committee (Arbeitsausschuss), or AA, consisted of twenty-five to thirty active managers of the main plants and plant associations, the sales combines, and the main committees, as well as a few legal and financial officers, all of whom were charged with training and nominating their own successors. With final say over such questions as major purchases, construction projects at home and abroad, involvement in cartels, charitable and political contributions, plant closings, and patent policies, this body, "in effect, constituted the responsible management of IG Farben from 1925 to 1937."[42] However, swollen by the attendance of the members of the administrative council, the Working Committee was too cumbersome for Carl Bosch's taste. In 1930–1, he formed an inner circle, called the Central Committee (Zentralausschuss), or ZA, of seven other members under his direction, with Duisberg as an adviser. This committee met on the afternoon before the Working Committee sessions to settle the outstanding issues, and for five years "may be considered to have been the supreme directing group of IG Farben."[43] After Bosch retired from the *Vorstand* in 1935, the Central Committee handled only special financial and personnel questions. Two years later, the whole managing board, now reduced to twenty-seven men, began meeting as a group an average of seven times per year, and the Working Committee disappeared along with the increasingly empty

---

42 NI-5184/38, Affidavit by F. terMeer, 29.IV.47. NI-10044/82, Affidavit by H. Bässler, 4.VIII.47, lists the members of the Working Committee, 1926-37; Bayer 13/12, 1-3, contains the minutes of the 107 meetings of the AA from 14.X.25 to 7.IV.38.

43 NI-5184/38, Affidavit by Fritz terMeer, 29.IV.47. NI-7956/66, Affidavit by H. Bässler, 17.VII.47, lists the members of the *Vorstand* and the ZA. On the operations of the latter, see NI-7366/59, Affidavit by H. Bässler, 28.VI.47; its minutes for the period from 1930 to 1939 are in NI-1941/18. For the background to its formation, see Bayer AS, Selck to Duisberg and Bosch, 20.II.30, and Duisberg's reply of the following day; Curt Duisberg, *Nur ein Sohn* (Stuttgart, 1981), pp. 139-40; and NI-1941/18, ZA meetings of 9.I and 9.II.31.

distinction between full and deputy members. During the war years, the full strength of the *Vorstand* stabilized at about twenty-one. As in the case of the *Aufsichtsrat*, it so happened that effectiveness and size declined simultaneously.

Though implicitly ranked by salary differentials, the members of the managing board stood on formally equal footing.[44] They regarded their chairman as primus inter pares, no more. Whether in committee or as a whole, they assembled less to deliberate on common policy than to inform one another, to the degree that each saw fit, about their highly specialized fields and to answer questions. Still less did they familiarize their colleagues with the operations and finances of the subsidiaries to whose boards they were assigned. The members lacked the time or inclination to meddle in one another's bailiwicks; where their concerns overlapped, they reached agreement privately or through some lower-level committee. Consequently, *Vorstand* meetings seldom lasted longer than four hours, formal votes were almost never taken, and the participants nearly always ratified the course of action that had worked its way onto the agenda.[45] After 1938, each member saw only that portion of the minutes and IG's balance sheets related to his sphere of operations.[46] From time to time, conscientious members protested against this excess of "republican" procedure, claiming that it prevented them from discharging their legal obligations.[47] But the spiraling growth of IG only strengthened centrifugal forces within the firm. By the time the reduced size of the managing board made collective decision possible, most members were quite unwilling to add real oversight to their already inordinate workloads.

---

[44] According to the scattered but representative compensation records in eight *Person-alakten* at IG in Abw., each *Vorständler* received a relatively modest basic salary plus a variable fraction of 1% of the concern's net profits. In 1927, the basic wage ranged from 30,000 to 63,000 marks, the fraction between 0.08 and 0.33%, and the resulting compensation between 83,463 and 275,427 reichsmarks per year.

[45] See terMeer, *I. G. Farben*, pp. 53–5; Knieriem V/34, Affidavit by Knieriem, 31.III.48; Oster I/16, Affidavit by G. Pistor, 9.II.48; and Haefliger IV/56, Affidavit by Karl von Heider, 17.II.48, concerning Eduard Weber-Andreä's reports to the *Vorstand*. Copies of the *Vorstand* minutes for 1938–45 are in Bayer 12/19 and in RG242/T83, Reel 82. Its bylaws are in NI-5178/38.

[46] Bayer 12/19, Hoyer of the ZA Büro to Hermann, 12.VIII.38, and Hoyer to Fritz Gajewski, 17.VIII.38. Similarly, *Vorstand* members could gain only partial access to the minutes and statistics of important Farben subsidiaries; see, e.g., IG in Abw., Jur. Abt., v.H. 5/I, Dynamit Nobel Pressburg I, Gattineau to Weber-Andreä, 3.IX.42.

[47] terMeer, *I. G. Farben*, pp. 56–7; Bayer 13/25, Kühne to Ilgner, 15.I.41.

Hermann Schmitz (1881–1960), head of the Central Finance Office, 1925–
35, and chairman of the *Vorstand*, 1935–45. (*Source:* Bayer-Archiv,
Leverkusen)

Strong-willed and well-placed personalities could go their own ways, as long as they did not offend the interests of powerful colleagues.

This was all the more evident after April 1935, when Hermann Schmitz succeeded Bosch as chairman of the *Vorstand*.[48] Bosch could generally use his imposing prestige to good effect in that group – indeed, he continued to attend meetings for the next five years, and his word remained, according to one participant, "more or less law."[49] Schmitz's authority therefore developed slowly, and it never equaled that of his predecessor. Lacking scientific training and experience in managing a factory or sales organization, the new chairman was precisely the sort of figure Duisberg dreaded seeing at the head of the enterprise. Without benefit of a university degree, Schmitz had risen rapidly within the Metallgesellschaft and several wartime economic regulatory offices on the strength of his genius as a financier. Bosch recruited him to the *Vorstand* of BASF in 1919 and after the fusion gave him exclusive control over IG's foreign activities and labyrinthine financial affairs. These subjects continued to preoccupy Schmitz as chairman, and he brought a penchant for caution and secrecy to his work. A nephew once remarked that his working motto might as well have been Wait, Reconsider, Then Wait Again; a knowledgeable contemporary observed that the official balance sheets Schmitz issued "carried reticence beyond the limits of decency acknowledged even by trusts."[50] By the early 1930s, his financial skills were in such demand that he served on some twenty supervisory boards and had accumulated a small fortune in director's fees, much of which he began donating to several charitable foundations that he established.[51] Although he kept informed in detail on all aspects of the combine's operations, an unofficial division of labor evolved: Schmitz's mastery of the concern's

[48] On Schmitz, see NI-6539/50, Affidavit by H. Schmitz, 2.V.47; NI-5092/37, Affidavit by E. Struss, 11.I.47; and NI-5135/38, Affidavit by P. Ester, 15.V.47.
[49] NI-9761/81, Affidavit by F. Jähne, 13.VIII.47. See also Gattineau, *Klippen*, p. 84.
[50] BA Koblenz, NL 158, R. Ilgner to W. von Moellendorf, 5.I.29; Warriner, *Combines and Rationalization*, p. 117. See also Duisberg, *Nur ein Sohn*, pp. 143–4.
[51] See IG in Abw., Personalakten Schmitz, records of his personal accounts, 23.VI.31. For the subsequent growth of his fortune, see NI-308/4, an undated chart from Griesheim File no. 103. On his philanthropic activities, I am relying on photocopies of the following documents furnished me by the Schmitz family: Schmitz to the Kuratorium of the Liebig Oberrealschule, Darmstadt, 26.IV.28 and 1.X.37; Paula Ester to H. Gierlichs, 26.X.47; Schmitz to the liquidators of IG Farben, 21.XI.53; Müller to F. Silcher, 28.X.54; and the Westdeutsche Handelsbank AG to Schmitz, 15.IV.55. The last-named letter lists gifts of stock bearing face values of 811,800 reichsmarks and an additional 61,700 deutschmarks.

financial side and corporate relations and his nominal subordinates' expertise in their respective spheres went equally unchallenged.

Largely unaccountable to one another or to the *Aufsichtsrat*, IG's managers also enjoyed considerable freedom from outside influence. This enabled them to plow returns back into the most promising fields and pay less heed to dividends, which fell steadily as a percentage of earnings from sales.[52] The concern controlled its own general meeting, since a subsidiary held all of the multivote preferred shares and no single bank or shareholder disposed of an appreciable block of stock before the war years.[53] Only once or twice in twenty years did a participant criticize the management of the firm from the floor of the sparsely attended sessions.[54] For the most part, IG financed its needs out of stock and debenture issues, receipts, and reserves and entrusted its banking transactions to the Deutsche Länderbank, whose stock, management, and business it dominated. The latter arrangement guaranteed the concern savings on taxes and privileged interest rates on its deposits while providing convenient financial leverage over subsidiaries and independent companies.[55] Similarly, a wholly owned insurance firm, the Pallas GmbH, shielded IG from another sort of external interference and reduced both premiums and taxes.[56]

The backgrounds of the men who guarded their own and Farben's independence during the 1930s varied within relatively predictable parameters. Selection to the *Aufsichtsrat* still reflected a noticeable bias toward inherited wealth or status. The Kalle, Meister, Brüning, vom Rath, von Böttinger, and Bayer who belonged to that group represented the founding families of the predecessor firms, and the von Weinberg brothers, who had owned Casella, were literally business

52 See Spezial-Archiv, *Der I.G. Farben-Konzern 1932*, pp. 12, 47; Gross, *Facts and Figures*, pp. 13–14, 17; terMeer, *I. G. Farben*, pp. 108–9.
53 Das Spezial-Archiv der deutschen Wirtschaft, *Der Farben-Konzern 1927* (Berlin, 1927), pp. 18–19; Spezial-Archiv, *Der I.G. Farben-Konzern 1932*, p. 43; NI-5196/38, Affidavit by F. terMeer, 23.IV.47; NI-8113/67, Affidavit by P. Dencker, 7.II.47; R. Levassort, "Quelques aperçus sur l'I. G. Farbenindustrie A. G.," in Edmond Vermeil (ed.), *Etudes Economiques Allemandes* (Paris, 1951), p. 74; Warriner, *Combines and Rationalization*, p. 117. For indications of the rising role of the Deutsche Bank during the war, see Dokumentationsstelle zur NS-Politik Hamburg, *O.M.G.U.S. Ermittlungen gegen die Deutsche Bank* (Nördlingen, 1985), pp. 116–19.
54 NI-5184/38, Affidavit by F. terMeer, 29.IV.47, p. 21; for one example, see Holderman, *Im Banne der Chemie*, p. 255.
55 Tammen, *I. G. Farbenindustrie*, p. 26; NI-4441/32, Affidavit by M. Ilgner, 28.VI.45; NI-4440/32, Affidavit by G. Frank-Fahle, 28.VI.45; Hagemann, *Verhältnis*, pp. 104, 179–80.
56 terMeer, *I. G. Farben*, p. 49.

aristocrats, having been ennobled by Wilhelm II.[57] But the *Vor-ständler* generally had conventional middle-class origins, with a few deviations in either direction on the social scale. Only Fritz terMeer, the head of Sparte II, and Wilhelm R. Mann, the leader of the Bayer sales combine, carried on family traditions in top management roles. Probably only Georg von Schnitzler, the concern's commercial chief, could claim social eminence both within and beyond the corporate world, the former by virtue of blood ties to the vom Raths and the original owners of the J. H. Stein Banking House of Cologne, the latter partly in consequence of having married Lily von Mallinckrodt.[58] Both Gajewski of Sparte III and Hermann Schmitz, in contrast, had risen from straitened circumstances by pluck and intelligence. Sketchy data suggest that Protestants predominated on both boards; in 1933, however, seven Jews sat on the *Aufsichtsrat,* most of them former associates of the two putatively "Jewish" forerunner companies, Agfa and Casella.[59] Of the thirty-five men who served on the Working Committee between 1933 and 1938 or the *Vorstand* thereafter, at least sixteen hailed from the Rhenish-Westphalian or Main-Neckar regions of western and southwestern Germany, at least twenty-four held earned doctorates, more than two-thirds of them in chemistry, and at least sixteen were veterans of the First World War, including seven recipients of Iron Crosses. In both 1933 and 1938, the median age of the members of the two bodies was 53; nearly all were married and fathers. Eleven of the managing board members had cut their professional teeth in BASF, six in Griesheim, and four each in Bayer and Hoechst; sixteen became affiliated with Sparte II, six with Sparte I, and three with Sparte III; the remainder in both cases sprang from or served in the combine's various central offices or joined IG after the fusion.[60]

Of course, the personalities of some of these individuals acquired distinct reputations within the enterprise. A few, such as Erwin Selck, who supervised IG's central staffs, were known as stereotypically Prussian in their manners and militarism; others, notably those associ-

---

[57] Duisberg, *Nur ein Sohn,* pp. 92–102, 109.

[58] See Gert Eynern, *Die Unternehmungen der Familie vom Rath* (Bonn, 1958), pp. 159–60; on Frau Schnitzler, see Hans-Georg von Studnitz, *Menschen aus meiner Welt* (Frankfurt, 1985), pp. 55–69.

[59] For the characterization, see Duisberg, *Nur ein Sohn,* p. 83.

[60] Compiled from numerous personal affidavits submitted at the postwar trial and the records of the BDC.

ated with IG's sales operations and cartel connections, like Eduard
Weber-Andreä and Paul Haefliger, appeared to be flexible and inter-
nationalist. Schnitzler's cosmopolitan charm and Schmitz's smooth
reserve contrasted sharply with Carl Krauch's intensity, Heinrich
Hoerlein's bullishness, and terMeer's icy belligerence.[61] Similarly, the
lifestyles of Farben's leaders ran the gamut from the unassuming,
academic demeanor of Carl Bosch to the "childish" personal display
of Duisberg, who filled his villa next to the Leverkusen factory
grounds with plaques and honorary awards and with busts and portraits of himself and even designed his own "royal standard" to be
hoisted when he was in residence.[62] These were extremes, however. So
far as one can gather from the surviving records, Farben's managers
were generally typical of their profession and day: accomplished, responsible, hard working, demanding, church going, patriotic, and generous to their communities, universities, and preferred charities. Proud
to have climbed the greasy pole in the nation's most visible and competitive corporate structure, they jealously defended their stature outside their enterprise, as well as their prerogatives within it.

Financially self-sufficient and held together by several commanding,
experienced figures in its early years, Farben could afford initially to
integrate its precursors, subsidiaries, and subdivisions haltingly and
imperfectly. So long as the concern encompassed a manageable
number of related plants and contended only with market forces,
"decentralized centralism" seemed vindicated. Its defects protruded
only in the form of excessive paper work and a certain slowness in
making decisions.[63] But in the early 1930s, external pressures began
to undermine the fragile coherence of the firm. The harbinger of this
process was the formation "more or less against the resistance of the
Vorstand" of a complex of offices known collectively as Berlin NW7,
after their postal address.[64]

---

61 Interview with Curt Duisberg, 20.I.78. Also, on terMeer, see Winnacker, *Nie den
Mut verlieren*, pp. 118–19; on Hoerlein, see Duisberg, *Nur ein Sohn*, pp. 87, 164;
and on Krauch, interview with Hans Kehrl, 11.VII.78.
62 Friedrich Glum, *Zwischen Wissenschaft, Wirtschaft und Politik* (Bonn, 1964), pp.
268–70, 311; Duisberg, *Nur ein Sohn*, p. 151.
63 Haber, *Chemical Industry, 1900–1930*, pp. 340, 342. On IG's *Schwerfälligkeit*, see
Degussa, Biographische Unterlagen, "Zur Geschichte der Scheideanstalt 1927 bis
1932" by Dr. Fritz Roessler, Abschrift, p. 71. For a critical assessment of the effects
of Farben's structure on its research work, see Peter J. T. Morris, *The Development
of Acetylene Chemistry and Synthetic Rubber by I.G. Farbenindustrie Aktiengesellschaft: 1926–1945* (Dissertation, University of Oxford, 1982).
64 For the quotation, NI-4928, Affidavit by K. Krüger, 18.III.47, *NMT*, vol. 7, p. 440.

Erwin Selck, IG's principal legal specialist, nominally presided over NW7, but its real driving spirit came from a young, anomalous presence within Farben's top ranks, Max Ilgner. The product of a long line of officers, Ilgner had attended a cadet school at Berlin-Lichterfelde, seen active duty on the western front in 1918, and then helped suppress the German Communists as a member of various *Freikorps* units until early 1920. Because the Versailles treaty's limitations on the size of the German army barred a military career, he had cast around for another profession and opted for that of his uncle, Hermann Schmitz. After obtaining a doctorate in political science for his dissertation on the supply of raw materials to the German sulfuric acid industry and acquiring commercial experience in several companies, he joined Casella in October 1924, at the age of 25. By then, he had already arrived at the idea that animated his work thereafter: the conviction that in eastern Europe "great sales possibilities for German goods will be opened in the future."[65] In 1926, IG posted him to Berlin to act as liaison with Schmitz, who was directing the concern's Central Finance Section (Zefi) from an office in the Deutsche Länderbank. On the strength of Schmitz's patronage and his own indefatigable enthusiasm, Ilgner gradually parlayed this new position into growing jurisdiction and prominence. Though he never realized his project for attaching IG's bookkeeping, purchasing, and tax offices to his command, he became by 1934 a deputy member of the *Vorstand* with responsibility for the consolidated departments of finance, press relations, market research, and contacts with the government, all of which he used to promote himself as much as IG Farben. Most of his colleagues atop the concern regarded him as a loud and loose cannon, and he never gained their confidence. But most of them also bore his ties to Schmitz in mind and treated him gingerly.[66] He was thus able in the period between 1930 and 1945 to attract attention in Berlin out of all proportion to his influence within the corporation.

The chief vehicles of Ilgner's ambition turned out to be two subsections of NW7. The Volkswirtschaftliche Abteilung (Vowi), like to a degree the existence and the decentralization of IG, owed its inspira-

---

[65] BA, NL 158, Bd. 40, Ilgner to Moellendorf, 26.I.24.
[66] NI-6544/50, Affidavit by M. Ilgner, 30.IV.47; NI-012/2, excerpt from *Das Deutsche Führerlexikon 1934/35*, pp. 208–9; Tammen, *I. G. Farbenindustrie*, pp. 155–61; IG in Abw., Personal-Kartei Ilgner; and my conversations with W. R. Mann, Jr., 13.VII.78, and with Curt Duisberg, 20.I.78.

tion to American models.[67] It studied currency questions, IG's markets and competitors, and the development of important branches of industry in major foreign nations. Much of its personnel, including its chief Anton Reithinger, came from the Reich Statistical Office, and from 1929 its reports circulated among interested ministries and private organizations, where their timeliness and quality made them indispensable.[68] The Wirtschaftspolitische Abteilung (Wipo), formed from several separate staffs in 1932 as an arm of the Central Committee of the *Vorstand,* concentrated on foreign trade, economic negotiations with foreign states, tax and legal measures that affected IG, and such other matters that bore on dealings with government agencies. Its leader until 1939 was Heinrich Gattineau, an athletic and engaging young veteran of the nationalist, paramilitary Bund Oberland who had studied under Professor Karl Haushofer at Munich and published a doctoral dissertation analyzing the adverse effects of urbanization and "worker egoism" on the prospects for the white race in Australia. When he moved up to his new post after two years of work as Duisberg's personal secretary and two more as his and Bosch's representative in Berlin, Gattineau was only 27. From 1931 until 1934 he also handled IG's press contacts.[69]

The emergence of Berlin NW7 and of Ilgner, Gattineau, and the views they espoused represented in microcosm the economic and political challenges to IG Farben in the turbulent closing years of the Weimar Republic. Driven by the needs for more detailed knowledge of foreign economic and political developments and greater influence over government policy during the Depression, the concern established a satellite organization that in the context of "decentralized centralism" constantly threatened to spin out of control.

---

[67] See Bosch's comments in Ilgner II/49, 19th meeting of the Working Committee, 13.I.27.

[68] NI-4975/36, Affidavit by A. Reithinger, 3.II.47; NI-8149/67, Affidavit by H. Bannert, 19.V.47; NI-8514/70, Affidavit by Ritter, 4.VI.47. For a complete list of the Vowi documents recovered after the war, see Ilgner III/44-45; many of these are preserved at the Bayer Archiv under the headings 4B/36, 66/A.2, 84, and 91/1.

[69] NI-9569/79, 71st meeting of the Working Committee, 7.IX.32; NI-8788/72, Affidavit by H. Gattineau, 12.VI.47; Gattineau II/6, Affidavit by Adolf Weber; NI-4833/35, Affidavit by Gattineau, 13.III.47; Gattineau, *Klippen,* pp. 18–22, 84. The dissertation was published as *Verstädterung und Arbeiter-Herrschaft* (Berlin, 1929); see especially pp. 9–10, 51, 66, 103–5, 147–9, and 220–22.

2. The search for stability

The formation of IG Farben reflected a general crisis in the international chemical industry after the First World War. As some old and many newly independent nations put up factories and tariffs, supply rapidly outstripped demand. Everywhere in the industrialized world, manufacturers pulled together to rationalize output, achieve economies of scale, diversify production, corner their home markets, and undersell their rivals abroad.[1] Between 1918 and 1928, this process stimulated the emergence of Allied Chemical and Dye and the ascent of DuPont in America, the preeminence of Montecatini in Italy, the founding of a Swiss IG by that nation's three principal dye firms, and the establishment of Imperial Chemical Industries (ICI) in Britain, a loose alliance of the twelve leading organics companies in France, and a Belgian trust dominated by Solvay's Compagnie Belge pour les Industries Chimiques.[2] But these intranational efforts scarcely sufficed to master the problem of excess capacity. By 1926, 21% of the French, 31% of the Swiss, 33% of the American, 38% of the British, and 61% of the German dye plants lay idle; by the early 1930s, unused facilities came to 40% of the nitrogen sector in Italy, 45% in Britain, 48% in Belgium, 51% in Switzerland, 54% in France, and 70% in Germany.[3] As the most resourceful and versatile of the major producers, as well as the one most burdened by paralyzed plant, IG Farben took the lead in seeking escapes from the crisis. In doing so, the concern adapted its traditional strategy to a transnational setting. IG tried to coordinate

---

[1] Brady, *Rationalization;* and Charles S. Maier, "Between Taylorism and Technocracy: European Ideologies and the Vision of Industrial Productivity in the 1920s," *JCH,* 5 (1970), pp. 27–62. On the market trends, see Enquête Ausschuss zur Untersuchung der Erzeugungs- und Absatzbedingungen der deutschen Wirtschaft, III. Unterausschuss *Gesamtbericht* (Berlin, 1931), pp. 10, 84; W. J. Reader, *Imperial Chemical Industries: A History,* vol. 2: *The First Quarter Century, 1926–1952* (London, 1975), p. 187; Stocking and Watkins, *Cartels,* Table 10, p. 126. On Farben's cost-cutting efforts, see Hayes, *Gleichschaltung,* p. 39 and the sources cited there.
[2] See Haber, *Chemical Industry, 1900–1930,* pp. 302–18, on all of these firms.
[3] Bayer 4C9.32, Control Office, *Dyestuffs,* pp. 26, 29; Reader, *Imperial Chemical Industries,* vol. 2, pp. 147, 153, and Table 7, between pp. 108–9.

the activities of the various manufacturers while it conquered a new monopoly, this time over synthetic fuel, the product whose prospects had propelled the merger of 1925.

The first prong of Farben's offensive called for rationalization on an international scale, no doubt in the expectation that the combine's greater capacity and technical superiority would entitle it to the lion's share of world output. To guarantee that outcome, IG offered its stock to Allied Chemical and each of the foremost European producers in return for majorities in their enterprises. When the French, British, Belgian, and Swiss firms refused to martyr themselves in this manner, the German concern fell back with qualified success on a second solution: cartelization.[4] By the late 1920s, financial stability was becoming the cardinal value for all the major manufacturers, Live and Let Live the motto of the day. All, therefore, increasingly shared IG's desire to channel competition into research, to distribute discoveries though production licenses and patent exchanges, and to substitute negotiation for the erratic market as the arbiter of output, prices, and sales.[5]

The upshot for IG consisted of three major and a host of lesser international corporate treaties. A European dyes cartel developed between 1927 and 1932 as first the French, then most of the Swiss, and finally the English makers fell into line.[6] IG's quota came to 65.5% of world export sales, but the French and British retained special privileges within their empires, as did the Swiss in southern Europe. The lucrative China market was subject to separate agreement among the four parties plus the American, Italian, and Japanese manufacturers. Subsequent conventions with the Greek, Italian, Polish, Swiss, and Czech outsiders cut into the export shares reserved to the original parties. The small producers adeptly exploited the threat of increased tariffs in their homelands and unsettling price warfare to extract export quotas larger than those to which their previous sales

[4] Haber, *Chemical Industry, 1900–1930*, pp. 275, 296; Reader, *Imperial Chemical Industries*, vol. 2, pp. 41–3, 151; A. Bürgin, *Geschichte des Geigy-Unternehmens von 1758 bis 1939* (Basel, 1958), pp. 254–5. Since IG courted the British and American producers, it is inaccurate to argue that the concern initially sought to form a purely Continental bloc, as do Wickel, *IG-Deutschland*, pp. 167–70; Tammen, *I.G. Farbenindustrie*, p. 31; and Kurt Gossweiler, *Grossbanken–Industriemonopole–Staat* (East Berlin, 1975), p. 335.

[5] On this mentality, see the superb discussion in Stocking and Watkins, *Cartels*, chap. 9, especially pp. 377–80, 418–28.

[6] See the cartel contracts of 1927, 1929, and 1932, Schnitzler X/180-81, and the detailed discussion in Schröter, *Deutsche Industrie auf dem Weltmarkt*, pp. 295–313.

IG's factory at Leverkusen, ca. 1930. (*Source:* Bayer-Archiv, Leverkusen)

entitled them.[7] As a result, although it is true that the other nations exchanged immunity from German competition at home for quite small allotments of international trade, the dyes cartel only slowed the descent of IG's share of world production by volume from 46% in 1924 to 34.6% in 1928 to 24.5% in 1936.[8]

Nor did the international nitrogen cartel serve as much more than a branch for IG to cling to. Despite repeated efforts, the concern made no progress toward international cooperation in this field until the expansion bubble burst in 1929.[9] In that year, ICI and Norsk-Hydro S/A of Oslo joined with the German Nitrogen Syndicate, dominated by IG, in the DEN Agreement.[10] A year later, nearly all the non-

[7] Haber, *Chemical Industry, 1900–1930*, pp. 275–6; Bayer 4C9.32, Control Office, *Dyestuffs*, pp. 31–6; and Reader, *Imperial Chemical Industries*, vol. 2, pp. 187–95.
[8] Stocking and Watkins, *Cartels*, p. 510; Tammen, *I. G. Farbenindustrie*, p. 35; Bayer 4C9.32, Control Office, *Dyestuffs*, Annex VIII.
[9] Stocking and Watkins, *Cartels*, p. 469; Reader, *Imperial Chemical Industries*, vol. 2, p. 45.
[10] For the details of the DEN Agreement, see Haber, *Chemical Industry, 1900–1930*, pp. 276–7; and Reader, *Imperial Chemical Industries*, vol. 2, pp. 113–14, 151. For

American manufacturers associated in the Convention Internationale de l'Industrie d l'Azote (CIA), chaired by Hermann Schmitz of IG. Each member of the cartel retained exclusive rights to its home market at whatever prices it would bear, and all synthetic nitrogen exports were pooled and sold at uniform prices through a single organization belonging to ICI and IG. Proceeds were then apportioned according to quotas established periodically on the basis of productive capacities by a trustee, the International Nitrogen Association. From a central fund the cartel bought up surplus stocks, offset domestic competition to the partners from outsiders, and compensated those participants whose production fell below 70% of capacity. Although the CIA continued almost uninterruptedly until World War II, its attempts to sustain prices and discourage new production worked at cross-purposes.[11] International sales of nitrogen slid by 31% between 1929 and 1934.[12] Moreover, as in the case of dyes, the largest producers sacrificed part of their sales for peace with the smaller companies; the DEN group's proportion of total exports fell from 85 to 70% in the first half of the 1930s. IG took the bulk of the losses.[13] Within the German Nitrogen Syndicate the same motives for concessions to the lesser manufacturers between 1929–30 and 1933–4 combined with the effects of the Depression to reduce IG's share of total business from 65 to 45%, its share of the export trade from 88 to 51%, the volume of its exports by more than half, their value by 80%.[14] By mid-1932, IG anticipated losses of about 33 million reichsmarks in the nitrogen business for that year alone, a considerable comedown from the profit of between 257 and 300 million reichsmarks for 1928.[15]

Not all of IG's cartel commitments had such onerous outcomes: Satisfactory conventions governing synthetic fibers, light metals, explosives, and specific chemical products sheltered these businesses rea-

IG's controlling position in the German syndicate, see Tammen, *I. G. Farbenindustrie*, pp. 40–1, 122. In general, see the thorough treatment by Schröter, *Deutsche Industrie auf dem Weltmarkt*, pp. 313–31.

[11] NI-7745/63, Affidavit by W. Jacobi, manager of the cartel, 1935–9, 7.VII.47; Stocking and Watkins, *Cartels*, pp. 145–7, 163; Reader, *Imperial Chemical Industries*, vol. 2, pp. 146–50.

[12] Tammen, *I. G. Farbenindustrie*, p. 130.

[13] Reader, *Imperial Chemical Industries*, vol. 2, p. 155; Tammen, *I. G. Farbenindustrie*, pp. 133–5.

[14] Tammen, *I. G. Farbenindustrie*, pp. 115, 118–24.

[15] Ibid., p. 42 (for 1928) and p. 118 (for 1932). Waller, *Probleme*, p. 158, estimates a profit of 330 million marks for 1928.

sonably well from the economic crisis.[16] But these arrangements could not recompense the combine for the vulnerability of the dye and nitrogen lines that brought in 18 and 65% of its profits, respectively, in 1926. That fact, recognized before the fusion, helps explain the renewal of work on synthetic rubber in 1927, as well as the urgency of IG's synthetic fuel project.[17] Here is where the second prong of Farben's strategy intersected with the first, for the concern's attempt to stake out a new monopoly with fuel-from-coal brought on IG's third major liaison.

In 1913, Friedrich Bergius, a professor at Heidelberg, discovered a process for liquefying coal and increasing its hydrogen content under pressure so that its properties would resemble those of oil. In the next thirteen years, however, his backers grew weary of the long struggle to apply the process on an industrial scale, and the oil and coal industries shifted their attention toward alternative processes. IG was therefore able in 1925–6 to gain control of Bergius's company, the Erdölverwertungs GmbH (EVAG), its foreign licensing organization, the International Bergin Company, and the inventor's patents and services in return for stock in the concern worth perhaps 10 million reichsmarks.[18] The allure of Bergius's process dated from Carl Bosch's decision in 1923 to order research into alternative uses for the huge synthetic nitrogen factories and their gifted scientific staffs. These works

[16] On the fibers agreements and their consequences, see Wickel, *IG-Deutschland*, p. 188, and Bayer 4C9.19, Pinnow manuscript, pp. 70–1; on explosives, see Joseph Borkin and Charles A. Welsh, *Germany's Master Plan* (New York, 1943), pp. 89–90; on metals, see NI-10968/90, Agreement of 23.X.31 between IG and Alcoa, Borkin and Welsh, pp. 212–21, 226–33, and Stocking and Watkins, *Cartels*, pp. 260–4, 284–302. On Farben's commercial conventions with DuPont, see the useful summary in BASF T52/4, Verhältnis I.G./DuPont, 10.VI.31. Bosch stated that IG participated in fifty treaties concerning chemical and pharmaceutical products, Enquête Ausschuss, pp. 132–3.
[17] For the profit shares, see Bayer 4C9.32, Control Office, *Dyestuffs*, p. 27. Of course, work on rubber would not have resumed but for several momentarily favorable circumstances: prodding by Kontinentale Gummiwerke, rising natural rubber prices and the resulting potential shortages, and the declining cost of acetylene, the basic feedstock; see Morris, *Synthetic Rubber*, pp. 151–5.
[18] Wolfgang Birkenfeld, *Der synthetische Treibstoff, 1933–1945* (Göttingen, 1964), pp. 14–15; Tammen, *I. G. Farbenindustrie*, note 159, p. 354; Anthony N. Stranges, "Friedrich Bergius and the Rise of the German Synthetic Fuel Industry," *Isis*, 75 (1984), pp. 643–67; and Deutsches Bergbau-Museum (ed.), *Friedrich Bergius und die Kohleverflüssigung* (Bochum, 1985). BA, ZSg 127, Bd. 827, "I.G. Farbenindustrie und Berginverfahren," *Berliner Börsen-Zeitung*, 29.IX.26, provides the most complete history of the successive ownerships of Bergius's patents and processes but should be supplemented by Bd. 828, "Die Beziehungen zwischen Stahltrust und Chemietrust," *Wirtschaftsdienst*, no. 52, 30.XII.27.

also employed hydrogen under high pressures, but in the presence of a catalyst. Fresh from their success in hydrogenating carbon monoxide to obtain methanol, IG's scientists had reason to anticipate rapid progress in synthesizing fuel.

The concern pinned its long-range commercial hopes for the new product on two forecasts: that world petroleum sources were approaching depletion and that Germany could not stand the inevitable hemorrhage of foreign exchange to pay for fuel once motorization picked up momentum. Fuel production also promised unmistakable short-range benefits to kindred operations. By activating idle capacity at IG's brown coal mines and the costly hydrogen-making facilities, the fuel program would generate valuable economies of scale, thereby reducing, above all, the unit costs of synthetic nitrogen. At the outset certainly, the concern had no reason or need to posit large-scale military demand for its creation.[19]

Scarcely had the ink dried on the contract with Bergius when IG set to building a plant at Leuna to convert brown coal to 100,000 tons of fuel yearly at a competitive wholesale price of 20 pfennigs per liter.[20] It was an ill-fated action. Ample new oil fields drove down the price of refined gasoline by more than a third between 1925 and 1929; within two more years, the Depression more than halved the price again.[21] Until 1932, technical difficulties bedeviled the manufacturing process and required the successive substitutions of tar, oil, and hard coal for the concern's own, cheaper brown coal. Full production was attained only in 1931, the now-dated cost target during the following year.[22] By then, IG had sunk some 426 million reichsmarks into the fuel project and incurred a net loss of 152 million reichsmarks.[23] Had the work not attracted in the interim the interest of Standard Oil of New Jersey, the deficit would have been twice as large.

The American giant wanted to hydrogenate crude oil in order to increase the yield of gasoline. Having gained nothing by dangling the hydrogenation process as bait for an exchange of shares with the British chemical companies, Allied Chemical, and Solvay of Brussels,

[19] Hughes, *P&P*, no. 44 (August 1969), pp. 116–18.
[20] Birkenfeld, *Treibstoff*, pp. 15, 17–18.
[21] Hughes, *P&P*, no. 44 (August 1969), p. 122.
[22] Tammen, *I. G. Farbenindustrie*, p. 95; Birkenfeld, *Treibstoff*, pp. 16, 19.
[23] Tammen, *I. G. Farbenindustrie*, pp. 50–52. Hughes considerably understates IG's synthetic fuel expenses, *P&P*, no. 44 (August 1969), p. 118.

IG in 1927 granted the right to conduct oil research under its patents to Standard.[24] This arrangement aroused mutual misgivings almost immediately, and both sides soon found reasons for seeking a broader deal: Standard wished to corner a potentially competing technology, whereas IG's accumulating expenses made it eager to head off a conscious price offensive by the oil companies that would surely force the combine to jettison its vast investment in fuel. Thus, the concern cut its losses in 1929 by selling all but its German rights to the hydrogenation of fuel for stock in Standard worth $35 million, or more than 149 million reichsmarks. Title to the patents was vested in a new Standard-IG Corporation, in which IG's 20% holding proved to be worth another 2.5 million reichsmarks annually. To administer hydrocarbon processes that could not be classified as relating solely to the chemical or the petroleum industry, notably synthetic rubber, the two parties formed the Joint American Study Company (JASCO) in 1930. Each donor reserved control of the inventions it contributed to the new company and five-eighths of any proceeds derived from them, and IG's German market for these products was declared inviolate.[25] A year later, Standard-IG, Royal Dutch Shell, and ICI signed an interlocking set of four contracts, known collectively as the International Hydrogenation Patents Agreement. This, along with the radically altered economics of synthetic fuel production, completed the oil industry's containment of the new technology.[26] In short, in return for cash, exclusive rights to all purely chemical applications of hydrogenation, guaranteed predominance in synthetic rubber production, and a somewhat protected internal market, IG restricted its synthetic fuel business to Germany. Given the state of the fuel undertaking, this did not seem a bad bargain.[27]

However advantageous, the understanding with Standard only briefly delayed a serious dispute within the concern over the Leuna

24 Haber, *Chemical Industry 1900–1930*, p. 296; W. J. Reader, "The Chemical Industry," in N. Buxton and D. Aldcroft (eds.), *British Industry between the Wars* (London, 1979), p. 168.
25 See Tammen, *I. G. Farbenindustrie*, pp. 50, 55–7; Henrietta M. Larson, Evelyn H. Knowlton, and Charles S. Popple, *History of the Standard Oil Company (New Jersey)*, vol. 3: *New Horizons 1927–1950* (New York, 1971), pp. 153–7; Bennett H. Wall and George S. Gibb, *Teagle of Jersey Standard* (New Orleans, La., 1974), pp. 299–302.
26 Reader, *Imperial Chemical Industries*, vol. 2, pp. 169–70; Schröter, *Deutsche Industrie auf dem Weltmarkt*, pp. 247–53.
27 See Bosch's testimony, Enquête Ausschuss, pp. 133–5.

plant. Always dubious about the fuel program, the leaders of IG's dye and pharmaceutical lines held their peace while Leuna's earnings on nitrogen paid the project's way. But as nitrogen sales plunged during 1929–30 and the continuing losses on fuel started to siphon off their profits, these men ran out of patience. With Duisberg in the vanguard, they began clamoring for their confreres to close the Leuna plant, abandon synthetic fuel, and produce nitrogen only at Oppau, BASF's original installation for that purpose.[28] At the direction of the *Verwaltungsrat*, chaired by Duisberg, a special commission composed of Friedrich Jaehne, Wilhelm Gaus, and a Dr. Moeg examined the prospects for synthetic fuel in early 1931 and concluded that only government subsidies could put Leuna in the black. Rejecting these for fear of state influence over the concern, the commission recommended that the lamed hydrogenation plant be shut down.[29] This proposal, which clashed with the findings of another review evidently conducted simultaneously by terMeer and Gajewski for the Working Committee, struck Bosch, Schmitz, and Krauch as the counsel of callousness and stagnation.[30] Closing Leuna, they contended, would throw around 10,000 people out of work, discard the concern's main hope of generating new jobs, slash IG's assets by 161 million marks, increase the unit costs of manufacturing nitrogen, and nip in the bud extremely promising discoveries in hydrocarbon substitutes for imported raw materials – all in order to calm the nerves of representatives of two largely static lines of production.[31] Experience also fortified the three men, all veterans of BASF, against the storm: They recalled parallel faintheartedness within that company's boards over indigo synthesis and nitrogen fixation, as well as the ease with which they had rebuffed the government's financial claims on the Leuna nitrogen plant once it reached maturity.[32]

Sure that synthetic fuel would eventually justify itself but unable simply to overrule Leuna's critics, Bosch outflanked them. In May

[28] NI-6524/49, Affidavit by Carl Krauch, 29.IV.47.
[29] NI-6765/52, Affidavit by F. Jaehne, 2.V.47.
[30] NI-5184/18, Affidavit by F. terMeer, 29.IV.47.
[31] Tammen, *I. G. Farbenindustrie*, pp. 105–7, 112. The employment figure is an estimate based on data for proximate dates in ibid., p. 67; H. R. Knickerbocker, *The German Crisis* (New York, 1932), p. 91; and R. Pfretzschner, "Zum Kampf um die Herstellung der Einheitsfront . . . ," *Wissenschaftliche Zeitschrift der Karl-Marx-Universität*, 2 (1963), p. 242.
[32] Hughes, *P&P*, no. 44 (August 1969), p. 120; Borkin, *Crime and Punishment*, pp. 7, 9.

1931, he met with Finance Minister Dietrich to discuss increases in the German tariff on mineral oils, hoping to add greater customs protection to the support that the government already had provided Leuna through tax abatements and reduced transport rates on the national railroads.[33] Buttressed by the demands of the Ruhr producers of benzol and nitrogen and perhaps by further lobbying on the part of Hermann Schmitz, Bosch's timely intervention helped shape two provisions of the impending emergency decree by which the Brüning cabinet sought to slake the economic crisis and close a growing budget deficit.[34] That edict, released on June 5, not only raised German imposts on most oil products by 70% to the highest level in Europe, but also authorized subsequent changes in the market regulations and tariffs governing nitrogen in order to secure Germany's supply of fertilizers.[35] Though stiff charges on previously duty-free nitrogenous goods were not announced until July 14, Bosch probably used knowledge of what was in store when he persuaded Duisberg in mid-June that changed conditions warranted another look at the hydrogenation program. The two men agreed to assign Wilhelm Gaus of Sparte I sole responsibility for merging the two earlier studies of Leuna into an updated set of recommendations for IG's Central Committee.[36] As Gaus took up this ticklish task, the government came to Leuna's aid once more. On August 17, after negotiations for the renewal of the international nitrogen cartel broke down, the cabinet blocked imports of nitrogenous fertilizers.[37]

Coupled with rigorous cost cutting at the Leuna plant, including the practice of working parts of the cavernous and underutilized factory to exhaustion and then shifting manufacturing to another quarter, these forms of official assistance had the effect Bosch desired.[38] They saved Leuna, though just barely. During the ensuing fall and winter, Gaus put off a conclusive report, while the oil tariffs lifted IG's fuel

[33] NI-1941/18, ZA meeting of 18.V.31; Birkenfeld, *Treibstoff*, pp. 18–19.

[34] Tammen, *I. G. Farbenindustrie*, p. 254; Wickel, *IG-Deutschland*, p. 144.

[35] Cuno Horkenbach, *Das Deutsche Reich von 1918 bis Heute, Jahrgang 1931* (Berlin, 1932), pp. 195, 197, 244; Hughes, *P&P*, no. 44 (August 1969), p. 123.

[36] NI-1941/18, ZA meeting of 20.VI.31; Holdermann, *Im Banne der Chemie*, p. 256, whose misdating of this assignment to 1930 accounts, in part, for Hughes's error in conflating it with Jaehne's review and ascribing that to 1929; see *P&P*, no. 44 (August 1969), p. 120.

[37] Horkenbach, *Das Deutsche Reich, 1931*, p. 280.

[38] Tammen, *I. G. Farbenindustrie*, pp. 52, 117.

proceeds toward the break-even point for the first time in the project's history, and the import prohibition kept nitrogen prices in Germany about 60% higher than elsewhere.[39] Still, as late as March 1932, "the largest chemical plant in the world" was functioning at only 20% of capacity, and Gaus projected its losses for the year at about 15 million marks on fuel operations and 25 million marks on nitrogen.[40] Reluctantly, he sanctioned a final attempt to turn brown coal into gasoline, doubting that even success would achieve profitability unless the major oil companies reversed themselves and agreed to raise prices or lower retail costs or mix IG's output with their refined product.[41] Moreover, if the protectionist measures seemed inadequate to keep Leuna afloat, relying on them was uncomfortable even to the factory's defenders. Trade barriers invited reprisals abroad and thus further antagonized IG's dye and pharmaceutical divisions. In Germany, such restrictions angered consumers and held down sales. To buy time, the concern told foreigners that German self-sufficiency in fuel would free about $100 million in former import purchases for the repayment of reparations and overseas debts and offered officials of the nation's political parties expense-paid opportunities to visit and be awed by the Leuna works.[42] However, by the spring of 1932, it was clear that Jaehne's committee had been on the right track. Only a state subvention in the form of a promise to purchase IG's output at a remunerative price would serve the interests of both Leuna and the rest of the combine. Gaus remained opposed to accepting such support, but his scruples ceased to count in July, when a report by IG's Profitability Examination Section demonstrated that shutting down the plant would actually cost 3.3 million reichsmarks more during 1932–33 than would operating it at the expected rate of loss.[43] In view of the

39 See NI-1941/18, Gaus's comments to the ZA meetings on 11.IX.31, 10.X.31, 3.XII.31, 21-22.XII.31, and 15.II.32; Tammen, *I. G. Farbenindustrie*, pp. 52, 96–97; and NI-7745/63, Affidavit by Walter Jacobi, 7.VII.47.
40 Knickerbocker, *German Crisis*, pp. 83, 91; NI-1941/18, Gaus to ZA meeting of 15.II.32; BASF, Bd. 39, "Der Stand der Hydrierung, . . ." 23.III.32.
41 NI-1941/18, Gaus to ZA meeting of 15.II.32; BASF, Bd. 39, "Der Stand der Hydrierung, . . ." 23.III.32. On IG's discussions with the oil companies and the reasons for their recalcitrance, see Tammen, *I. G. Farbenindustrie*, pp. 100–5.
42 Knickerbocker, *German Crisis*, pp. 86–90; NI-15257/123, Bericht über den Besuch der Leuna-Werk durch Presse und Politik, 12.X.31; and for the invitation to the Nazis, see RG1035/T81, Reel 116, Wagener and Hierl to Sauckel, 30.IX.31, Frame 136985.
43 Bayer 13/12, vol. 2, Abteilung für Wirtschaftlichkeitsprüfung, 1.VII.32; Tammen, *I. G. Farbenindustrie*, pp. 109–11, reproduces this document.

choices now available to the concern, Duisberg probably approved as the reprieved advocates of hydrogenation opened negotiations with the German government for a state guarantee against further red ink, and the internal struggle over Leuna came to an end.[44]

The fuel catastrophe combined with the inexorable displacement of IG's profit leaders from foreign markets and the spreading impact of the Depression to wipe out by 1932 most of the economic gains that followed the fusion. Sales peaked in 1929, then dropped by 38.4% over the next three years, bottoming out at 85% of their level in 1926. Net profits deteriorated by 55% between 1929 and 1932, and the volume of dividends as well as their ratio to sales was halved. Payments to shareholders came to rest at 70% of their 1926 level.[45] Employment fell by a quarter between the merger and the low point on October 1, 1932. Furthermore, the decline in workers by 46% since 1929 considerably exceeded the drop in the entire German chemical sector (29%) and in German industry as a whole (33%). Neither reductions in the number and fees of managing board members nor curtailments in the wages and hours of nearly all the concern's employees could arrest the trend.[46] Research, the lifeblood of the combine, came almost to a standstill.[47] Admittedly, few German firms withstood the economic debacle as well as IG Farben. At its nadir in 1932, the concern distributed a profit of more than 47 million marks, largely because IG's exports had tumbled by only 39% since 1929, compared with 58% for Germany as a whole. Total assets shown on the balance sheets actually rose by between 1 and 6% during 1926–32 (the available statistics vary), and these financial statements underrepresented the value of the plant, into which the combine managed to pour more than 380 million marks in capital

---

[44] Birkenfeld, *Treibstoff,* p. 19; Bütefisch IV/31, Affidavit by B. Mulert, leader of the chemicals section in the Economics Ministry, 1922–33, 14.VII.47, which dates the onset of these negotiations to late 1931 or early 1932. Since Gaus's summary of March 23 referred to various contemplated forms of government help but said nothing of this sort of subsidy, the talks probably began between early April and late July of 1932.

[45] Defense Basic Information II/4, Distribution of Total Proceeds, 1926–1944; Tammen, *I. G. Farbenindustrie,* p. 140.

[46] NI-1941/18, ZA meetings of 19.XI.31, 7.I.32 and 3.X.32; IG in Abw., Personalakten Wolff, Duisberg to members of the *Vorstand,* 20.X.32; Bayer 221/6, E. Schwarz to Duisberg and the ZA, 9.III.33; Tammen, *I. G. Farbenindustrie,* pp. 80–6.

[47] terMeer, *I. G. Farben,* pp. 78, 110, 119; Tammen, *I. G. Farbenindustrie,* p. 36. See also the figures for Sparte I in Bütefisch II/282, Affidavit by G. Kunze, 18.II.48, and for rubber in terMeer IV/186, Affidavit by E. Struss, 30.XI.47. On the suspension of the rubber project, see Plumpe, *G&G,* 9 (1983), pp. 574–9.

investments and repairs during the worst years of the economic crisis.[48] Gone forever, however, were the initiative and dominant bargaining position the concern possessed in international corporate negotiations during the mid-1920s, not to mention IG's chances of recovering the ground lost since 1913. Declining demand had converted the firm's great size into its chief weakness. By 1932, IG had failed to stake out an international monopoly over a single major chemical field or to free itself of market constraints.[49]

Moreover, the period from 1926 to 1932 fundamentally altered IG Farben's commercial orientation. Although the concern continued to make about 55% of its total sales abroad and the exported proportion of each major product line also held nearly constant, the home market, especially the agricultural sector, loomed ever larger in IG's calculations.[50] Clearly, the most export-oriented sections of the firm – dyes and pharmaceuticals – carried the concern through the Depression.[51] Equally clearly, the global trends toward industrialization, tariffs, and market divisions through cartels ran against significant increases in the returns from these products. IG managed to boost its percentage of world chemical trade during the period, but not enough to compensate for the decline in total value of that commerce.[52] The direction of IG's trade, moreover, was shifting toward underdeveloped lands, whose already limited purchasing power suffered from falling raw material prices and where the political influence of other powers told against German business.[53] Little relief could come from that quarter, as Carl Duisberg pointed out in an effort to dampen NW7's growing interest

[48] NI-10003/82, Net profit of I. G. Farbenindustrie A. G., Affidavit by H. Deichfischer, 11.VI.47; Defense Basic Information II/4, Distribution of Total Proceeds, 1926–1944; Spezial-Archiv, *Der I. G. Farben-Konzern 1932*, p. 33; Defense Basic Information I/Bilanzen, pp. 70–1; Gustav Stolper, *The German Economy 1870 to the Present* (New York, 1967), p. 145; Tammen, *I. G. Farbenindustrie*, p. 74. For a good summary of the effects of the Depression on Farben, see Schröter, *Deutsche Industrie auf dem Weltmarkt*, pp. 159–61.
[49] Tammen, *I. G. Farbenindustrie*, p. 69, comes to a similar conclusion.
[50] For the figures on dyes, chemicals, photographic products, pharmaceuticals, and insecticides, see Defense Basic Information II/6, pp. 33–6; for the totals for the concern, II/8, p. 38; for the nitrogen figures, Tammen, *I. G. Farbenindustrie*, p. 113.
[51] Tammen, *I. G. Farbenindustrie*, pp. 30, 89–90, 130, 143–4; Bayer 4C9.32, Control Office, *Dyestuffs*, p. 27.
[52] Defense Basic Information II/14, p. 51, and II/16, between pp. 52–3. The variations in the percentages given in the two documents do not affect my summary of the situation.
[53] Bosch to the Enquête Ausschuss, pp. 86–7; Bayer 4C6, Volkswirtschaftliches Archiv, "Neue Ziele und Aufgaben für die Forschungs- und Produktionspolitik der

in the Balkans. "The value of grain export surpluses from the Southeast European states," he wrote in December 1931, "is so limited that a considerable expansion of German exports from these sums is not to be expected."[54]

Considering these circumstances and the concern's massive financial commitment to the nitrogen sector, even Duisberg, the foremost spokesman for IG's dyes and pharmaceutical branches, concluded that "our attention must return primarily to the internal market, which will always remain the backbone of our economy."[55] More specifically, Carl Bosch and the chemical industry's trade association, the Verein zur Wahrung der Interessen der chemischen Industrie Deutschlands, came out vigorously for rationalization in German agriculture and price supports for the farmers who consumed IG's nitrogenous fertilizers.[56] But no leader of the firm went so far as to share the judgments of the Verein's business manager, Claus Ungewitter. He asserted that only a "great German Ten Year Plan" could propel the indispensable domestic revival, one that would be based on "substitution for foreign raw materials and the best possible application of domestic raw material supplies."[57]

Aside from advocating tariffs on nitrogen and gasoline imports and subsidies for the agricultural sector, IG Farben clung, on the whole, to the twin pillars of its traditional economic liberalism: free trade abroad and free enterprise at home. Notwithstanding IG's difficulties with fuel and nitrogen, Bosch and Duisberg consistently defended the most-favored-nation principle and unfettered private initiative as essential to their industry and to the welfare of the Reich. Despite their common call for a firm hand to direct national economic policy, neither man wavered in his opposition to autarky, which each considered a recipe for unemployment, to preferential bilateral trade treaties and

IG," 30.VI.34. By the end of the period, 50% of IG's dyes exports went to Asia, exclusive of the Soviet Union; Tammen, *I. G. Farbenindustrie*, p. 367, note 47. See also Schröter, *Deutsche Industrie auf dem Weltmarkt*, pp. 84–5.

54 BASF W1, Duisberg to Gattineau, 12.XII.31. Farben also kept its distance from attempts to increase trade with Russia; see Kurt Laser, "Der Russlandausschuss der deutschen Wirtschaft," *ZfG*, 20 (1972), p. 1387.

55 Carl Duisberg, *Abhandlungen, Vorträge und Reden aus den Jahren 1922–1933* (Berlin, 1933), p. 356.

56 Tammen, *I. G. Farbenindustrie*, pp. 229–36.

57 See Ungewitter's speech of 25.II.32, quoted in ibid., p. 206, and note 236, p. 405; and C. Ungewitter, "Ist chemiewirtschaftliche Aktivität gerechtfertigt?" in Spezial-Archiv, *Der I. G. Farben-Konzern 1932*, p. 12.

clearing agreements, to all "experiments in economic planning," such as "childish" schemes for a "five-year plan on the Russian model," and to "all attempts to steer the clear course of private business into the impenetrable fog spread by Marxism, state capitalism, and similar notions." Sporadic deviations from these positions, they insisted, could be countenanced only as transitory defensive measures.[58] Thus, whatever the eventual value of increasing German commerce with southeastern Europe, IG's leaders made an understanding with France the essential precondition for this development and envisioned an "economic block from Bordeaux to Sofia" only in the form of a customs union that would practice the most-favored-nation principle.[59] Hence, too, Bosch's solution to the crisis of German agriculture

[58] See Duisberg's speeches of 12.XI.30, 24.III.31, 3.VI.32, and 17.I.33 in *Abhandlungen* . . . *1922–1933*, pp. 123–30, 142–6, 147–51, 165–73; Greiling, *75 Jahre Chemieverband*, p. 56; Knieriem's remarks in Gattineau Nachtrag I/101, 68th meeting of the AA, 15.IV.32, pp. 1–2; the reports of speeches by Bosch in BASF W1, "Wirtschaftsblock und Meistbegünstigung," *Berliner Börsen-Courier*, no. 88, 21.II.31, and "Gegen den selbstmörderischen Wirtschaftsprotektionismus," *Mannheimer Volksstimme*, no. 128, 12.V.32, and in BA, ZSg 127, Bd. 40, "Die Autarkiebestrebungen und die deutsche chemische Industrie," *Chemiker-Zeitung*, 22.VI.32, p. 497; HA Krupp, FAH IV C 205, "Handelspolitische Notwendigkeiten," by Carl Bosch, November 1932, especially pp. 3–4, 15–16; BASF W1, Draft of Bosch's Exner-Medal speech in Vienna, 16.XII.32; and Tammen, *I. G. Farbenindustrie*, pp. 236–53. For similar views held by individuals close to the concern, see Clemens Lammers, *Autarkie, Planwirtschaft und berufständischer Staat?* (Berlin, 1932), pp. 7–16, 24–6, 31, 34–5, and 44; and Edmund Pietrkowski of the Chemie Verein to the *Vorstand* of the RDI, 25.XI.32, in Fleming et al. (eds.), *Die Republik von Weimar*, vol. 2, pp. 294–5.
[59] Duisberg's speech of 24.III.31 in *Abhandlungen* . . . *1922–1933*, pp. 172–3. See also Bosch's newspaper articles of 17–18.II.31 and 13.IV.32 and the study by IG's Zefi section of July 1931, all discussed in Tammen, *I. G. Farbenindustrie*, pp. 241–6, and the findings of Schröter, *Deutsche Industrie auf dem Weltmarkt*, pp. 507–8. IG Farben's involvement in the Mitteleuropäischer Wirtschaftstag and that organization's importance in the early 1930s have been vastly overrated. Despite the claims of Alfred Sohn-Rethel, *Economy and Class Structure of German Fascism* (London, 1978), especially pp. 63–6, and David Abraham, *The Collapse of the Weimar Republic* (Princeton, N.J., 1981), note 111, p. 224, IG's demonstrable role in the group during the early 1930s was slight, amounting to occupying two seats on its twenty-five member board and contributing some 10,000 marks annually to the MWT's budget of 55,000 marks; see Dirk Stegmann, "'Mitteleuropa' 1925–1934," in D. Stegmann, Bernd-Jürgen Wendt, and Peter-Christian Witt (eds.), *Industrielle Gesellschaft und politisches System* (Bonn, 1978), p. 218; Tammen, *I. G. Farbenindustrie*, pp. 248–53; and, in general, Bayer 62/40, "Entstehung, Entwicklung und Arbeit des Mitteleuropäischen Wirtschaftstages," by Thilo von Wilmowsky, 22.XI.38, excerpted in D. Eichholtz and W. Schumann (eds.), *Anatomie des Krieges* (East Berlin, 1969), pp. 86–7. Nor was the MWT "the forum" through which heavy-industry and chemicals producers sought to arrive at a common agricultural policy, as Abraham, relying on Sohn-Rethel, asserts (*Collapse*, pp. 224, 226–8). If any organizations played that part, they were probably the as yet largely uninvesti-

rejected protectionism except in the case of grain. Otherwise, he favored constructing an international agricultural cartel capable of setting prices and production quotas for each state without governmental interference. Such an organization would reestablish market stability as the basis for a "renaissance of international trade."[60]

Convinced that "foreign trade and domestic business stand in a mutual relationship," IG refused to choose between the two sources of its wealth and insisted that Germany could not afford to do so.[61] Though the domestic market seemed more urgent and manipulable for the moment, neither the concern nor the Reich could forgo potential earnings, however long delayed, when international commerce revived. That is one reason IG continued selling at a loss in some countries and tolerated the sacrifices imposed by the international cartels, which were the firm's chief bulwark against a recurrence of chaotic overbuilding and a renewed collapse of international trade.[62] That is also why the combine never split into two factions, one domestic-oriented and sympathetic to the Nazis and one export-oriented and hostile to Hitler's party.[63]

For thirty years the German organic chemical industry labored to insure itself: with nitrogen against the collapse of dyes sales, with synthetic fuel against the downfall of nitrogen, with concentration and cartels at home and abroad against fluctuations in either market. But the nitrogen program tottered before the backup for it matured. Moreover, the Depression sapped IG of the financial strength to develop

gated German Nitrogen Syndicate and certainly the Agricultural Policy Committee of the RDI, formed in 1930. The latter's proposals of May 1930 (Veröffentlichungen des RDI, no. 52, which does not appear in Abraham's bibliography) long anticipated the program suggested by associates of the MWT in mid-1932. Compare Abraham's discussion, Duisberg's remarks at the turn of 1930–1 in Abhandlungen . . . 1922–1933, p. 347, and Tammen, pp. 229–35, which also includes important corrections to Sohn-Rethel's account.

60 HA Krupp, FAH IV C 205, Carl Bosch, "Handelspolitische Notwendigkeiten," November 1932. On this pamphlet, compare the misleading account in Abraham, Collapse, p. 225, which relies solely on a newspaper report, and Tammen's discussion in I. G. Farbenindustrie, pp. 235–7.

61 Duisberg on 3.VI.32 in Abhandlungen . . . 1922–1933, p. 144. For other comments in the same vein, see the sources cited in footnote 58 and E. Pietrkowski, "Industrie und Landwirtschaft," Veröffentlichungen des RDI, no. 60 (Berlin, 1932), p. 5.

62 See Schnitzler's paper for the AA meeting of 26.I.33; Hoechst, TEA 110.

63 Cf. Tammen's overschematic interpretation in I. G. Farbenindustrie, passim, which is contradicted by the evidence he presents (especially pp. 236–53) and by the case of W. R. Mann, Jr., the only senior IG official to join the NSDAP before 1933. Mann spent his entire career in the export-oriented dyes and pharmaceuticals sectors. See footnote 121 and the discussion to which it refers.

synthetic rubber as an alternative profit source, turned the concern's size into a liability, and undercut the effectiveness of the combine's international conventions. If the life-giving product cycles were to flow normally again, Farben badly needed a stable German government pursuing policies congenial to the firm. After 1929, however, it found its political props just as shaky as its economic ones.

IG's leaders believed that the purpose of micro- and macroeconomic policy was to generate the profits that powered the product cycles; the goal of corporate political activity was to retain an optimal share of those profits. Exercising political influence thus boiled down to fending off claimants to undue portions of the concern's income. In the Germany created at Versailles and Weimar during 1919, these aspirants included the Allies with their reparations bills, labor unions demanding wage gains, landholders who clamored for subsidies, and the elected officials whose competition for votes bid up taxes. All had to be persuaded that their desires exceeded the concern's and Germany's resources, hence threatened to extinguish them. But defeat and democracy had made "persuade" the operative word. A business could not simply assert its needs and defy all who disputed them, lest it mobilize anti-German passions abroad and anticapitalist feeling at home.

Thus, Bosch and Duisberg arrived at a common view of Germany's requirements after the currency stabilization and reparations settlement of 1924. Toward former enemies, the nation had to show sufficient reasonableness and good faith to maintain the flow of foreign loans on which economic recovery rested, to facilitate the international cartel agreements vital to IG, and to obtain gradual revision of the most offensive parts of the Versailles treaty. To workers, German business had to extend the same appearance of good will, bonuses in return for increased productivity, and an array of company-organized social and athletic activities that would "keep them on the beer bench and in assemblies and away from the dangerous field of politics."[64]

---

[64] Bayer AS, Duisberg to Moldenhauer, "Auf der Fahrt von Shanghai," ?.?.26; Gattineau, *Klippen*, p. 111. See Duisberg's response to the antilabor Silverberg program of 1923 and his endorsement of the conciliatory Silverberg program of 1926; Bayer 62/10/6, Duisberg to Silverberg, 12.I.23, and Reinhard Neebe, *Grossindustrie, Staat und NSDAP 1930–1933* (Göttingen, 1981), pp. 31–2, 45, 48; as well as Clemens Lammers' postwar testimony, M892/7, p. 5622.

With agriculture and the politicians, the corporate world had to seek mutually tolerable compromises but also to stand up for the greater good of the economy over the long term. To be sure, Bosch's and Duisberg's shared convictions left room for disagreements of tone or detail. The latter man's nationalism and paternalism had a decidedly Wilhelmian cast that Bosch disliked. On fundamentals, however, the two executives thought virtually as one. IG's fortunes depended on the restoration of German unity and power; that, in turn, demanded patience and conciliation.[65]

Under the Weimar Republic, the concern chose political sides on the basis of these conclusions. They made Farben the foremost corporate supporter of the man and group that came to embody them best, Gustav Stresemann and the German People's Party (DVP). Conversely, the firm's policy preferences aligned it unflaggingly against the person and organization most identified with hostility to organized labor, renunciation of Versailles, and protectionism for agriculture, Alfred Hugenberg and the Nationalists (DNVP). Given the splintering of representation in the German Reichstag, however, and the consequent inescapability of coalition government, IG could not rely on association with a single party. Carl Duisberg therefore deduced, partly from his observations of corporate practice in America, that the surest protection for IG's and other firms' interests lay in the active engagement of businessmen and their companies' resources in several parties simultaneously. Neither cogent arguments nor vigorous lobbying organizations, he maintained, could substitute for generous rations of money and immediate and broad influence in Parliament.[66]

As a first step toward implementing this "System Duisberg," the Little IG formed a "political commission" in late 1922 or early 1923.[67] Soon called the Kalle circle after its chairman, Wilhelm Ferdinand Kalle, the group consisted after 1925 of Carl Bosch and four supervisory board members who also sat in the Reichstag with Ger-

65 On Bosch's and Duisberg's political philosophies, see Reichelt, *Das Erbe*, pp. 26–8; Tammen, *I. G. Farbenindustrie*, pp. 149–51; Flechtner, *Carl Duisberg*, especially pp. 295–331, 355–80; Gattineau, *Klippen*, pp. 27–9; and Holdermann, *Im Banne der Chemie*, pp. 187–9, 229–79.

66 [Richard Lewinsohn] Morus, *Das Geld in der Politik* (Berlin, 1930), pp. 82–4; Tammen, *I. G. Farbenindustrie*, p. 147; Michael Schneider, *Unternehmer und Demokratie* (Bonn, 1975), p. 170; Duisberg's remarks on 23.V.30, excerpted in J. Herle, *C. Duisberg. Ein deutscher Industrieller* (Berlin [1931]), pp. 102–3.

67 See Bayer AS, Duisberg to Otto Wolff, 29.I.23. I am indebted to Larry Jones for bringing this document to my attention.

many's three pivotal, prorepublican, and procapitalist parties. Kalle, a firm adherent of Stresemann, belonged to the DVP, as did Paul Moldenhauer, though his outspokenly antisocialist and quietly anti-Semitic views placed him closer to the right wing of their party.[68] Slightly farther to the left on the political spectrum stood Hermann Hummel, the former state president of Baden, who served from 1924 to 1930 as a Democratic Party (DDP) deputy for the electoral district that included Farben's central German works at Wolfen, Bitterfeld, and Leuna.[69] Finally, there was Clemens Lammers, a lawyer and participant in the predominantly Catholic Center Party. He resigned his parliamentary seat, however, in early 1929.[70] Together these men worked out IG's positions on important public questions and argued for those stances to their respective delegations. On occasion, they solicited the advice of other politically prominent men associated with Farben, such as Hermann Warmbold of the *Vorstand,* Wichard von Moellendorf and Ernst von Simson from the *Aufsichtsrat,* Professor Julius Flechtheim, the concern's legal adviser, and Hermann Bücher, who counseled the firm until he became chairman of the managing board of the Allgemeine Elektricitäts Gesellschaft (AEG) in 1928.[71] But for the most part, Kalle's circle reached decisions informally and in private conversations, so much so, in fact, that its meetings appear to have grown fewer and farther between from 1925 to 1932.[72]

Until the middle of 1932, IG spread its political contributions almost without exception among the moderate, predominantly middle-class parties represented in the Kalle circle. Duisberg, Bosch, and Kalle

[68] On the group and its composition, see Schmitz I/4-5, Affidavits by W. F. Kalle, 8.IX.47 and 4.X.47; and Bayer 4C9.25, Mueller/Knieriem manuscript, March 1951, p. 85. Contemporary records of the circle's meetings have not survived. Kalle's political convictions are conveyed in his "Es war einmal . . . Erinnerungen an die Zeit von 1870 bis 1932," a forty-two-page manuscript dated 26.VI.33, with an afterword dated 20.II.47. I extend my thanks to Larry Jones for allowing me to read the copy in his possession. For Moldenhauer's political views, see the "Political Memories" that he compiled in 1940 from diaries written during 1930–3; BA Koblenz, NL 19, vols. 1–4, especially vol. 1, Bl. 63–4, 123–4.
[69] On Hummel, see "Die leitenden Köpfe der I.G.-Farben," *Berliner Börsen-Zeitung,* no. 303, 6.XI.26, and the two essays by Benno Reifenberg in Werner Wirthle, *Frankfurter Zeitung und Frankfurter Societäts-Druckerei GmbH. Die wirtschaftlichen Verhältnisse 1927–1939* (Frankfurt, 1977), pp. 59–63.
[70] On Lammers, see M892/7, pp. 5618–23.
[71] Bayer 4C9.25, Mueller/Knieriem manuscript, p. 85; Schmitz I/5, Kalle's affidavit, 4.X.47; NI-6544/50, Affidavit by M. Ilgner, 30.IV.47.
[72] See Bayer AS, Moldenhauer to Duisberg, 15.VIII.31; BA Koblenz, NL 19, Bd. 1, Bl. 141.

Wilhelm Ferdinand Kalle (1870–1954), chairman of the "political commission" and the Kalle circle, 1923–33, and member of the *Aufsichtsrat*, 1925–45. (*Source:* Firmenarchiv der Hoechst AG, Frankfurt-Hoechst)

determined the amounts and recipients, and Hermann Schmitz distributed the funds.[73] After the war, Kalle's personal secretary stated from memory that the disbursements included annual payments of 200,000 reichsmarks to the DVP, 30,000 marks to the DDP and its successor, the Deutsche Staatspartei, and 50,000 marks to the Center, as well as special gifts for each national and state legislative election of 200,000 marks to the DVP, 50,000 marks to the DDP or Staatspartei, and 70,000 marks to the Center.[74] Additional donations went to the DVP and collateral organizations on the recommendation of Gustav Stresemann and to the DDP/Staatspartei via Hummel on Bosch's authority.[75] Historians have no more exhaustive or reliable information on the Kalle circle's political grants or those by other IG offices. Fragmentary evidence indicates, however, that the latter were inconsequential, comprising small purses handed out by Duisberg or Berlin NW7.[76] In the main, such funds went to opponents of Alfred Hugenberg within the Nationalist Party, not least because his charges of treason leveled against anyone connected to the "Versailles System" infuriated both Bosch, a member of the German delegation to the Paris Peace Conference, and Duisberg, who had endorsed the Dawes and Young Plans governing reparations payments. Thus, in 1929 Duisberg routed 20,000 marks to dissidents in the DNVP. A year later, both Heinrich Gattineau, one of the officers in Berlin authorized to dispense minor sums, and Jakob Hasslacher, the general director of the Rheinische Stahlwerke recently elected to the IG's supervisory board, aligned themselves with the seceding Nationalists who formed the Konservative Volkspartei.[77] If the larger subsidiaries made separate offerings to local political affiliates, none have come to light, and the minutes of the Central Committee, which acted on appeals from ostensibly charitable and service organizations, disclose no overtly polit-

73 Schmitz II/25, Affidavit by W. F. Kalle, 8.IX.47.
74 Schmitz II/24, Affidavit by E. Pfeiffer, 8.IX.47.
75 Schmitz II/25, Kalle's affidavit, 8.IX.47.
76 See NI-7082/55, Affidavit by M. Ilgner, 1.V.47; NI-4833/35, Affidavit by H. Gattineau, 13.III.47.
77 On the 20,000 marks, see Bayer AS, Werner von Alvensleben to Duisberg, 28.XI.29, and reply of 29.XI.29. It is not clear, however, that the money was IG's. On Gattineau's actions, see Gattineau I/30, Affidavit by W. Steinberg, 16.III.48, and I/31, Affidavit by E. Kritzler, 1.X.47; and Gattineau, Klippen, pp. 29–30. On Hasslacher, see Tammen, I. G. Farbenindustrie, p. 146; John A. Leopold, Alfred Hugenberg: The Radical Nationalist Campaign against the Weimar Republic (New Haven, Conn., 1977), pp. 44, 80–1; and NI-7957/66, Affidavit by H. Bässler, 17.VII.47.

ical donations, unless one counts IG's gifts to endow President von Hindenburg's estate at Neudeck. So respectful of the Kalle circle's prerogatives was the committee, in fact, that it turned down a petition for funds in 1931 from the Bund zur Erneuerung des Reiches. Its reputation as a vehicle for Chancellor Brüning's rival Hans Luther probably tainted the nominally nonpartisan group.[78]

After Stresemann's death and the onset of the Depression in October 1929, the thrust of Farben's political efforts naturally shifted somewhat. Like many German businessmen, IG's chiefs embraced the notion of merging the divided bourgeois parties into a single force attractive enough to check the alarming swing of voters toward the extremes of Communism and Nazism.[79] But unlike many of their colleagues atop other corporations, IG's managers continued to regard Hugenberg's DNVP as an unacceptable partner in this "*Bürgerblock*" and to maintain that efforts to keep the state on a sensible economic course had to proceed "within the bounds of our present constitutional order."[80] Kalle took an increasingly prominent role within the DVP, weighing in decisively in favor of electing Eduard Dingeldey to succeed Stresemann as the party's leader and then pressuring him hard to resist the pulls of "the Hitler psychosis and the bandwagon effect" of Nazism.[81] In Kalle's view, the DVP could save the political situation only by allying with the Catholic Center, not Hugenberg, and by holding out against the trends toward "the repression of all individualism and the corpselike obedience to leaders" that increasingly characterized the other parties.[82]

[78] NI-1941/18, ZA meetings of 28.IV.31, 20.VII.31, and 5.IX.32. See also Bayer 15/G.1, the records of IG's Zentralstelle für Spenden. On the *Bund* and its relations with business, see the entry by Kurt Gossweiler in D. Fricke, M. Weissbecker, H. Schwab, S. Schmidt, G. Fesser, and H. Gottwald (eds.), *Die bürgerlichen Parteien in Deutschland* (East Berlin, 1968), pp. 195–200; Neebe, *Grossindustrie*, pp. 58–9, 74–5, 89, 109, 113, 123, and 147.
[79] For evidence that Bosch, Hummel, Kalle, and Schmitz worked in 1931–2 to gather the bourgeois parties together, see Glum, *Zwischen*, pp. 405–7. There is a suggestive, though overdrawn, left-wing analysis of the reasons IG preferred this course to cultivating relations with the Nazis and of the pressures the concern allegedly used on the parties in Johann Kunkel, "Synthetische Politik," *Die Weltbühne*, no. 41 (13.X.31), pp. 545–7.
[80] Duisberg to the RDI, 23.V.30, quoted by Neebe, *Grossindustrie*, pp. 61–2.
[81] Hans Booms, "Die deutsche Volkspartei," in E. Matthias and R. Morsey (eds.), *Das Ende der Parteien 1933* (Königstein/Ts., 1979), p. 527; BA Koblenz, NL 2, Bd. 75, Kalle to Dingeldey, 7.XII.31. See also Dingeldey to Kalle, 17.I.31, and the reply of 8.III.31.
[82] BA Koblenz, NL 2, Bd. 75, Kalle to Dingeldey, 1.II.32.

By mid-1932, however, IG had little to show for its political largesse. Within the combine's own labor force, the radicalization of public opinion had begun to erode the strength of the relatively moderate Socialist unions. Thus, the factory council elections of 1931 produced a combined Nazi–Communist vote of 46.8% at Leuna, 45.7% at Leverkusen, 42% at Hoechst, and 31.1% at Ludwigshafen, compared with only 3.9% at all the nation's plants.[83] In the balloting for the Reichstag, the concern's chosen parties, with the exception of the Catholic Center, had continued their uninterrupted decline since December 1924. Not only had the Volkskonservativen also failed and Hugenberg survived as the head of the DNVP, but also the remnants of the Democratic and People's Parties had been unable to pull together against the Nazi onslaught. Instead, while the DDP explored electoral alliances with the Center and the Social Democrats, the DVP gravitated toward the Nationalists.[84]

The DVP's drift constituted a major defeat for IG. Whereas Kalle had helped hold the party in line behind Brüning in June 1931 by threatening the termination of IG's support and his own resignation, these possibilities had ceased to restrain the DVP by October. Then, and again in February and May 1932, Kalle found himself in the minority as the party endorsed no confidence motions against the chancellor.[85] Although Kalle agreed to run on the DVP ticket for his

83 For the results at Leuna, see BA Koblenz, ZSg. 127, Bd. 25, "Betriebsrätewahlen in Leuna-Werk," *Frankfurter Zeitung*, no. 434–6, 14.VI.31; at Leverkusen, Bayer 214/10; at Hoechst (first round of balloting), Bayer 214/10, Schwamborn and Häuser to Sozialkommission, 30.V.31; at Ludwigshafen, BASF, "Das Mensch in der BASF," by Dr. Voigtländer-Tetzner, Bd. II, Bl. 390; and for the nation as a whole, John Moses, *German Trade Unionism from Bismarck to Hitler, 1869–1933*, vol. 2 (Totowa, N.J., 1982), p. 518.
84 Matthias and Morsey (eds.), *Das Ende der Parteien*, pp. 55, 58–66, 530–3. The minutes of the meeting of the DDP *Gesamtvorstand* on 7.VI.32, where the advisability of a deal with the SPD was debated, give no sign that Hummel participated; see Konstanze Wegner and Lother Albertin (eds.), *Linksliberalismus in der Weimarer Republik* (Düsseldorf, 1980), pp. 731–8.
85 See Kalle's letter to Dingeldey, the DVP leader, 14.VI.31, reprinted in Lothar Döhn, *Politik und Interesse* (Meisenheim am Glan, 1970), pp. 436–7. Its impact can be traced in Horkenbach, *Deutsche Reich, 1931*, pp. 189, 201, 205, 211, and 225. On the votes of no confidence, see the same book, pp. 332–3; its companion volume for 1932, pp. 61–2; and Abraham, *Collapse*, note 92, p. 310, and note 97, p. 312. Kalle's position earned him the furious hostility of the Nazis; see Ilse Maurer and Udo Wengst (eds.), *Politik und Wirtschaft in der Krise* (Düsseldorf, 1980), Document 350, p. 1077. Within the DVP on the regional level, another IG official, Max Kuhbier, a director of the concern's Duisburger Kupferhütte and the chairman of the party's organization in the electoral district Düsseldorf-West, fought the same hold-

electoral district in the July elections, he refused to be entered on the party's national list of candidates. Worn out by the struggle against "the two false prophets," Hitler and Hugenberg, he drafted his own plans for a loose confederation of liberal parties allied against the socialist menace that he saw in both the Communists and Nazis, and he began curtailing IG's donations to the DVP. The electoral compact that his party sealed with the Nationalists four weeks before the voting and renewed two months later won his grudging acceptance, but only temporarily. In September, he and IG finally gave up. Acting on instructions from Duisberg, Kalle ended IG's direct payments to the DVP and his own career as a candidate under the party's banner.[86] He and Paul Moldenhauer, the combine's last two Reichstag deputies, already had been swept out of office by the Nazi landslide of July 31, their defeats confirming once more that "economic power did not translate readily into political power in the Weimar Republic."[87]

The concern's efforts to shape public opinion were similarly unrewarding. Before the fusion, the Little IG set aside 2 million marks to help found a newspaper called *Die Zeit* as a nationwide outlet for the views of Gustav Stresemann, then contributed another 10 million inflated marks to keep it going during 1923. Nonetheless, chronic financial losses forced Stresemann to sell the journal in June 1925, only three and a half years after its first issue was published.[88] Just as he did so, Farben apparently made a small grant toward the launching of a

ing action; see Horst Romeyk, "Die deutsche Volkspartei in Rheinland und Westfalen 1918–1933," *RVB*, 39 (1975), pp. 195, 209–11.

[86] On Kalle's thoughts and actions, see BA Koblenz, NL 2, Kalle to Dingeldey, 7.III.32, 21.V.32, 2.VII.32, 12.VIII.32, 30.IX.32, and 13.X.32. See also Larry Eugene Jones, "Sammlung oder Zersplittung?" *VfZ*, 25 (1977), p. 284; Döhn, *Politik und Interesse*, pp. 207–8, 373. The latter author mistakenly traces Kalle's capitulation to the DVP's support for Papen, whom Duisberg, in fact, backed strongly.

[87] H. A. Turner, Jr., "Big Business and the Rise of Hitler," in H. A. Turner, Jr. (ed.), *Nazism and the Third Reich* (New York, 1972), p. 91. About the only political success the concern could claim in July was the election of Dr. Respondek, whom IG and the AEG funded, as Center Party deputy for the Oppeln election district; see Kommission für Zeitgeschichte, Bonn, NL Friedrich Dessauer, vol. 12, Respondek to Dessauer, 14.VI.32 and 6.VII.32. I am indebted to William Patch for drawing this source to my attention.

[88] See Bayer 4C9.25, Mueller/Knieriem manuscript, p. 87; Tammen, *I. G. Farbenindustrie*, note 20a, p. 380 (although Tammen states erroneously that nothing came of the idea of founding *Die Zeit*); and Larry Eugene Jones, *The Dying Middle: German Liberalism and the Dissolution of the Weimar Party System, 1918–1933* (Chapel Hill, N.C., forthcoming), chap. 2, sec. 3, and chap. 3, sec. 3. On the paper's brief life, see Henry Ashby Turner, Jr., *Stresemann and the Politics of the Weimar Republic* (Princeton, N.J., 1963), pp. 95–6.

rather highbrow monthly called the *Europäische Revue,* published in
Vienna under the direction of Karl Anton Prinz Rohan. Designed to
promote European cultural integration, the journal contained economic, political, philosophical, and literary essays from figures as
diverse as José Ortega y Gasset, Benedetto Croce, Luigi Pirandello,
Leo Baeck, and Winston Churchill, as well as from assorted businessmen, including Georg von Schnitzler and Erwin Selck. It won a
diverse and serious readership, but no mass appeal. There is no proof
that IG's contributions continued after 1926 or influenced the *Revue*'s
composition, though Frau von Schnitzler remained an enthusiastic
promoter of the Austrian prince, even as he moved steadily toward a
Germanocentric view of Europe's future.[89]

The combine abstained from further ventures into political publishing until February 1929, when Carl Bosch, without consulting the
concern's boards, decided to bail the liberal *Frankfurter Zeitung* (FZ)
out of mounting financial difficulties. Motivated by the desire to bolster the moderate and democratic parties and to fan popular support
for the capitalist system, IG's synthetic fuel program, and higher gasoline tariffs, Bosch used his discretionary funds to acquire a camouflaged holding of 35% of the paper's stock at a price of 1.4 million
marks. He also loaned the paper an additional 1.5 million marks at
5% interest. A year later, the combine took over another 14.5% of the
FZ, as well as three-fourths of the shares in a second newspaper
associated with the DVP, the *Frankfurter Nachrichten,* again concealing its role in both cases. It appears that IG sought and exercised only
marginal influence on the overall editorial policies of the two liberal

---

[89] See the excerpts of Ilgner's statement of 18.VI.45, printed in R. Sasuly, *IG Farben*
(New York, 1947), especially p. 282, and the mistaken assertions of Abraham,
Collapse, p. 224, note 110. On Rohan's evolving views, see Carl N. Pegg, *Evolution
of the European Idea, 1914–1932* (Chapel Hill, N.C., 1983), pp. 128–9. According
to a confidential source who knew Frau von Schnitzler well, her long-running affair
with Prinz Rohan continued until his marriage in June 1933 and was well known
and accepted in Frankfurt society. For portraits of the Prince and Lily by an un-
critical friend, see Hans Georg von Studnitz, *Menschen aus meiner Welt* ([Frankfurt,
1985]), pp. 55–69, 113–21. The only documented big-business funder of the *Europäische Revue* was Richard Merton of the Metallgesellschaft, who later recalled
being "part owner" of the journal, apparently into at least 1934; see Hans Achinger,
Richard Merton (Frankfurt, 1970), p. 88; Metallgesellschaft, R. Merton to F. Eu-
lenstein, 25.IV.56; R.M. to Sir A. McFadyean, 24.V.39; and the exchange of letters
between R.M. and Lily von Schnitzler, 17–18.II.55, enclosing a copy of R.M. to L.S.
of 31.XII.36. In the early years of the Third Reich, the Propaganda and Foreign
Ministries subsidized the *ER;* see Margret Boveri, *Wir lügen alle* (Olten, 1965), p.
600.

organs.[90] Nor did even smaller financial involvement prove any more determinative within the *Deutsche Allgemeine Zeitung;* the Deutsche Provinz-Verlag, a supplier of articles to local papers; the Transocean GmbH, an overseas wire service; and the UFA, Germany's largest film company.[91] Primarily because the value of the newspapers did not measure up to their costs, Bosch participated at the turn of 1931–2 in discussions concerning integrating them with several more conservative dailies into a network of probusiness publications, but nothing came of the scheme.[92]

Of course, notwithstanding Duisberg's tactical views, the parties and the press were not the only avenues to influence in Weimar political life. Extensive contacts with the ministerial bureaucracy assured IG's interests a hearing in Berlin.[93] The combine also carried weight within important industrial groups, chief among them the Verein zur Wahrung der Interessen der chemischen Industrie Deutschlands, chaired by Duisberg in the years 1919–24 and by Bosch from 1927 to 1933. The executives of the Verein did not come from IG's ranks, Duisberg having insisted on representatives of other companies in order to maintain the unity of the organization. However, the concern paid the principal part of their salaries and of the annual levy on the member corporations, which funded the Verein's budget and the wages of Dr. Ungewitter, the business manager from 1920 to 1945.[94] Within the Deutsche Industrie- und Handelstag (DIHT) and the Reichsverband der deutschen Industrie (RDI), however, IG's significance depended more on Duisberg's effectiveness than vice versa.[95]

[90] See Kurt Koszyk, *Deutsche Presse 1914–1945* (Berlin, 1972), pp. 263–4; Modris Eksteins, *The Limits of Reason* (New York, 1975), pp. 166–78; Schmitz II/27, Affidavit by E. Pfeiffer, 18.XII.47. Tammen, *I. G. Farbenindustrie*, pp. 152–4, overlooks Eksteins's thorough research, and Koszyk's account falls victim to IG's efforts to conceal its stake in the *FZ;* see the article in that journal, "Frankfurter Zeitung," 25.I.31, in BA Koblenz, ZSg 127, Bd. 824. On IG's inability to control the paper's editorial policy, see Bayer AS, Hummel to Duisberg, 5.II.30. The slightly different account of Farben's investment in the *FZ*, the source of the funds, and the editorial consequences in Wolfgang Schivelbusch, *Intellektuellendämmerung* (Frankfurt, 1985), pp. 69–72, rests on Wirthle, *Frankfurter Zeitung*, pp. 17–36, which makes less complete use of the surviving sources than does Eksteins's work.
[91] Tammen, *I. G. Farbenindustrie*, pp. 153–5; also on Transocean, Ilgner II/115, Affidavit by M. Passarge, 3.III.47.
[92] Koszyk, *Deutsche Presse*, pp. 217–18, and note 9, p. 478.
[93] See footnote 68 to Chapter 1.
[94] NI-9086/76, Affidavit by F. Ehrmann, 25.VII.47; Tammen, *I. G. Farbenindustrie*, pp. 161–3. For IG's annual contributions to the Verein, see Bayer 15/G.1, Jahresbericht der Zentralstelle für Spenden, Ludwigshafen a.Rh. für das Jahr 1929.
[95] Duisberg was a member of the *Vorstand* of the DIHT and of the *Präsidium* of the

Elected chairman of the RDI in 1925 after two industrialists from the Ruhr declined the post, Duisberg was regarded as uniquely qualified to bridge disagreements between German heavy industry and the leaders of more consumer-oriented firms, and he tried to fulfill this function.[96] That fact, as well as the orthodoxy of his economic views, meant that this tireless, voluble, and flamboyant man did not always speak for the entire leadership of IG Farben.

The concern endorsed Duisberg's opportunistic adaptation to parliamentary government, his pragmatic belief that "the best state is the best administered state," his patient revisionism concerning the Versailles treaty, and his somewhat contradictory practice of seeking a "reconciliation" between business and the labor unions while complaining repetitiously against the tax, wage, and fringe benefit burdens sanctioned by the Republic.[97] IG also rallied around Duisberg's labors for President Hindenburg's reelection drive against Hitler in 1932, providing more than one-third of the funds collected by the committee Duisberg headed and perhaps as much as 1 million reichsmarks in all.[98] During 1930–2, however, he and Bosch diverged not only over

RDI from 1919 to 1931. While he chaired the latter organization from 1925 to 1931, Bosch, who also sat on the *Präsidium*, retreated into the background; see his letter to Krupp of 11.VI.31, cited in Michael Wolffsohn, *Industrie und Handwerk in Konflikt mit staatlicher Wirtschaftspolitik?* (Berlin, 1977), p. 296. Clemens Lammers also belonged to the *Präsidium* of roughly thirty-four members, as did Hermann Bücher and Ernst von Simson of IG, who occupied two of the twenty seats on the RDI's important Advisory Committee on Political Economy, along with Pietrkowski of the Chemie Verein; see Bernd Weisbrod, *Schwerindustrie in der Weimarer Republik* (Wuppertal, 1978), p. 223. From early 1931, Schmitz was one of the approximately 100 members of the RDI *Vorstand*. For the composition of the RDI's directing groups, see Bayer 62/10/1.

96 On Duisberg's election, see Weisbrod, *Schwerindustrie*, pp. 220–6; the distorted account in Abraham, *Collapse*, pp. 132–4; and Jürgen John, "Die Faschismus 'Kritik' in der Zeitschrift 'Der Arbeitgeber,'" *ZfG*, 30 (1982), pp. 1076–7. The chemical industry's position as the linchpin between the two major industrial associations of the Wilhelmian era was illustrated in February 1918, when a German industrial council was formed. It emerged from a conference among thirty representatives of heavy industry's CDI, thirty delegates of the more flexible BdI, and four emissaries from the chemical firms. See the Stresemann Nachlass, 3051/6818/122821-32, a bulletin of the BdI central office.

97 Tammen, *I. G. Farbenindustrie*, pp. 149–51; Reichelt, *Das Erbe*, pp. 24–8; Fricke et al. (eds.), *Die bürgerlichen Parteien*, p. 604.

98 Tammen, *I. G. Farbenindustrie*, pp. 176–81, provides, on the basis of hitherto unnoticed lists of contributors in Bayer 76/9, the most comprehensive estimates of IG's efforts on Hindenburg's behalf. He errs, however, in failing to reckon the gifts of Louis Hagen, a member of IG's supervisory board, into the firm's total contribution, which, when corrected, exceeded 159,000 marks. This is much less than the donation of 1 million marks ascribed to IG by Günther Gereke, who chaired the national Working Committee of the Hindenburg campaign; Schmitz II/26, Affidavit

Leuna's fate, but over the larger question of which that issue was only a part: the proper role of government in combating the Depression. Duisberg's thinking on both matters grew out of his lifelong involvement in the export-oriented dyes and pharmaceutical trades and in Bayer, a company then distinguished more for commercial acumen than for pioneering, large-scale research. With the rationalization and modernization of these branches largely completed, he concentrated on other means of reducing overhead costs and thereby increasing the attraction of German products, especially, but not only, abroad. Thus, he cleaved to the liberal dogma that the mere lifting of government's heavy hand from business life would precipitate a recovery.

Bosch, Schmitz, Ilgner, and Warmbold, all intimately associated with the unusually capital-intensive hydrogenation program, went beyond Duisberg's demands with calls for more positive official action. Alarmed by the increasing radicalization of the electorate, Bosch even briefly floated the heretical proposition that the Reich imitate Austria and create jobs by financing the construction of a national network of toll roads.[99] However, he and his associates preferred a less direct form of government stimulus to the domestic economy: expansion of the money supply and the credit available to private industry.[100] This difference of opinion at the top of the concern followed hard on the heels of another contretemps, for Duisberg's old-fashioned mentality brooked no such sentimental "nonsense" as Bosch's proposals for universal reductions in the normal working day and week in order to dilute the impact of the Depression on labor.[101]

None of this, however, had any outward effect before April 1932 on IG's loyalty to the man whom Bosch admired and Duisberg rated as Germany's "best chancellor" next to Bismarck, Heinrich Brüning.[102] Hoping to bring him around to an expansionist program, the con-

by Gereke, 21.X.47. The same figure appears in Schmitz II/24, Affidavit by E. Pfeiffer, 8.IX.47.

[99] Holdermann, *Im Banne der Chemie*, pp. 258–60.

[100] On IG's preferences and proposals, see Wolffsohn, *Industrie und Handwerk*, pp. 158, 189–91, 286, 288–90; Tammen, *I. G. Farbenindustrie*, pp. 204–5; Neebe, *Grossindustrie*, pp. 111–12; and Heinrich Brüning, *Memoiren 1918–1934* (Stuttgart, 1970), pp. 425–6.

[101] Wolffsohn, *Industrie und Handwerk*, pp. 125, 184, 295–6; Duisberg's remarks of 31.X.30 in *Abhandlungen : . . . 1922–1933*, pp. 119–20; and Michael Grübler, *Die Spitzenverbände der Wirtschaft und das erste Kabinett Brüning* (Düsseldorf, 1982), pp. 341–2, 346–9, and 425–30.

[102] Bayer AS, Duisberg to E. Kirdorf, 26.VI.31.

cern's representatives in Berlin importuned Brüning in October 1931 to appoint Hermann Warmbold, Hermann Schmitz, Karl Bachem, and Wichard von Moellendorf to the cabinet. Invited to present IG's proposals to the chancellor and Finance Minister Schwerin von Krosigk, Ilgner impressed them as a "political innocent." Only Warmbold was taken into the government, as economics minister, whereupon he resigned from the *Vorstand* of IG.[103] Almost immediately, he ran up against Brüning's determination to continue his deflationary course at least until the wretched condition of the German economy induced the Western powers to cancel the Reich's reparation bill. As a matter of principle, Warmbold unavailingly withdrew his signature from the Fourth Emergency Decree of December 1931, which, inter alia, reduced prices, and tendered his resignation. Brüning refused to pass it on to the president. Instead, the chancellor promised to consider more generous monetary policies at a later date and impressed on Warmbold the importance of his remaining in office until Hindenburg had been reelected. The latter argument brought both the minister and the concern back into step with Brüning. While Kalle stressed the primacy of foreign over economic policy to the rebellious DVP in February, Warmbold did the same in the cabinet during the early part of 1932. In particular, he sided with the chancellor in deferring action on a plan for credit creation advanced by Ernst Wagemann, the economics minister's brother-in-law, and devised in cooperation with Bachem, Moellendorf, Ilgner, and Schmitz.[104] Not until the end of April, with the president safely back in office, the Brüning government already

---

103 Wolffsohn, *Industrie und Handwerk*, pp. 287–8. Schmitz appears to have lost out for several reasons: loose talk about his intentions by Ilgner; opposition from other German businessmen, including Paul Reusch, and even within Farben; and rumors of his involvement in potentially scandalous tax evasion by IG; see Brüning, *Memoiren*, pp. 425–6; GHH 400 101 293/4a, Gilsa to Reusch, 9.X.31; and Klaus Sator, *Grosskapital im Faschismus* (Frankfurt, 1978), pp. 28–9.

104 Schmitz II/23, Affidavit by H. Warmbold, 5.X.47; Warmbold's letter to the *Frankfurter Allgemeine Zeitung*, no. 242 (17.X.68), reprinted in G. Zeimer, *Inflation and Deflation zerstören die Demokratie* (Stuttgart, 1971), p. 145; Brüning, *Memoiren*, pp. 478–9, 503–4, 567–8; Wolffsohn, *Industrie und Handwerk* pp. 67, 287–8; 379; Neebe, *Grossindustrie*, pp. 112–13, 115; Tammen, *I. G. Farbenindustrie*, pp. 207–10; Döhn, *Politik und Interesse*, p. 204. Though Warmbold sympathized with Wagemann's monetary ideas, the minister did not become a convert to autarky, as his brother-in-law did in March. Cf. Wagemann's announcement, summarized in Horkenbach, *Deutsche Reich, 1932*, p. 88, and Warmbold's comments, reported in the same source, pp. 383, 418. On Schmitz's guarded enthusiasm for the plan, see HA Krupp, FAH IV C 369, Schmitz to Krupp, 23.I.32, and reply of 26.I.32; and Metallgesellschaft, R. Merton Privatbriefe 1919–38, Schmitz to Merton, 23.I.32.

tottering, and the chancellor's sincerity concerning credit creation open to doubt, did Warmbold formally submit his resignation.[105]

Under Brüning's successors, Franz von Papen and Kurt von Schleicher, Warmbold reassumed his portfolio and began to assert himself enough to still the critics of his ineffectiveness who had surfaced even within the concern.[106] Forearming himself against the proponents of agrarian protection and tight money in the cabinet, he allegedly prevailed on Papen to name a special economic advisory council, consisting of Schmitz, Wagemann, and Johannes Popitz, as a court of last resort in disputes between the economics minister and his colleagues.[107] Whether formed or not, such a group proved unnecessary. The virtual elimination of reparations by the Lausanne Conference in July cleared the way for a more vigorous economic program, while action became imperative after the Nazi electoral triumph at the end of the month and the failure two weeks later of negotiations aimed at bringing Hitler into the government. On September 4, an emergency decree formalized a new and decidedly probusiness anticyclical course. Attacking the Depression largely via the private sector, the government prescribed and permitted further curtailments of wages and enacted Warmbold's brainchild, a system of tax relief and rebates for industry designed to stimulate hiring and provide investment capital.[108] Duisberg, like most German executives, was delighted.[109] Bosch, with whom Papen and Warmbold had discussed their plans on August 25, exhibited less enthusiasm. Seeing little advantage in the fiscal measures for a concern that had tried to avoid layoffs by spreading work, he continued to recommend that as the only sound approach to the unemployment problem. Thus, Pietrkowski of the Chemie Verein ruled out additional wage cuts on September 9, and Bosch directed the Central Committee on October 5 "to support the

[105] See Warmbold's statements of 1947 and 1968, cited in footnote 104; Neebe's speculations in *Grossindustrie*, pp. 155–8; and BA Koblenz, R43 I/1309, Warmbold to Hindenburg, 28.IV.32, the accompanying draft press release by Wolff's Telegraphisches Büro, and a memo by Secretary Meissner, which recorded Warmbold's promise not to discuss the reasons for his actions publicly.

[106] BA Koblenz, NL 158, H. Bachem to Moellendorf, 21.VIII.32.

[107] Wolffsohn, *Industrie und Handwerk*, pp. 82–3.

[108] On the development of the program, ibid., pp. 87–92. Cf. Willi A. Boelcke, *Die deutsche Wirtschaft 1930–1945* (Düsseldorf, 1983), p. 26, which traces the tax changes to two senior officials of the RWM.

[109] See Duisberg's remarks of 17.I.33, *Abhandlungen . . . 1922–1933*, p. 150. On the general corporate reaction, see Volker Hentschel, *Weimars letzte Monate* (Düsseldorf, 1978), p. 129.

government in its stimulus program" by generating projects that would increase take-home pay.[110]

Nonetheless, the Papen–Warmbold program was a step in the right direction, all the more so as Warmbold generally succeeded in blocking the introduction of agricultural tariffs and import quotas, which the agriculture minister had promised. On this issue, Schleicher's short-lived cabinet was even more steadfast until mid-January 1933, thereby enraging the agrarian interests.[111] Along with the revocation of Papen's wage reductions, this stance compensated to some degree for Bosch's and Duisberg's joint distaste for Schleicher's endorsement of Günther Gereke's expanded program of direct work creation by the state.[112] If Warmbold's official position failed to secure the subsidy that IG sought for Leuna or to shape every aspect of national economic policy around Bosch's or Duisberg's occasionally incompatible preferences, these facts paled in comparison to the onset of economic recovery in the final quarter of 1932. Between September and December, IG's sales totals began to rise for every division save benzin and pharmaceuticals, and the gains appeared in both domestic and to a lesser extent foreign markets. The combine added some four thousand new employees to its work force within that three-month period, followed by one thousand more in January 1933.[113] With the upturn, the frustration and uncertainty that had gripped Farben's managers during the summer dissipated and so, therefore, did their brief attempt to establish ties to Hitler's movement.

There was never very much to Farben's overtures to the Nazis. Admittedly, Paul Moldenhauer's conservatism and hatred of the Nationalists began to get the better of him in January 1932. Dubbing them "the eternal men of yesterday," he wrote Dingeldey to confess, "I prefer the National Socialists. . . . At least here there is movement, a search for new ways and new goals."[114] But his lapse was transitory, and in any case IG had quietly demoted him since his ouster from a

110 BA Koblenz, R43 I/1141, Bl. 234-40, Aufzeichnung über das Empfang von Vertretern des Reichsverbandes der deutschen Industrie beim Reichskanzler am 25.VIII.32; Wolffsohn, *Industrie und Handwerk*, pp. 125, 289, 297, 380; NI-1941/18, ZA meeting of 5.X.32.
111 D. Petzina, "Hauptprobleme der deutschen Wirtschaftspolitik 1932–1933," *VfZ*, 15 (1967), pp. 32–8; Horkenbach, *Deutsche Reich, 1932*, pp. 335, 344, 358.
112 Wolffsohn, *Industrie und Handwerk*, pp. 290-2.
113 See BA Koblenz, ZSg 127, Bd. 838, "Belebung bei I.G. Farben," *Vossische Zeitung*, no. 44 (28.I.33).
114 BA Koblenz, NL 2, Bd. 78, Moldenhauer to Dingeldey, 19.I.32.

term as finance minister in 1929–30. After refusing him a seat on the managing board, Kalle and Duisberg treated him as an employee and reduced his annual compensation to about half its level before his government service.[115] Nor did Moldenhauer waver in public. Like most of Farben's chiefs, he kept his distance from the Nazis throughout their rise. Thus, the only figure associated with the combine even to attend Hitler's famous Industrie-Klub speech in Düsseldorf on January 26, 1932, was Jakob Hasslacher, a member of the supervisory board.[116] The Keppler circle, formed in early 1932 to advise the Nazi Party on economic matters and to link it to the business community, counted no representative of IG Farben among its members.[117] Though the banker Otto Fischer of Stuttgart did join an advisory committee to Otto Wagener's Nazi Wirtschaftspolitische Abteilung, this occurred shortly before or just after his departure from IG's *Aufsichtsrat* in early 1932.[118] No one connected to Farben signed the famous "industrialists' petition" of November 1932 urging Hindenburg to appoint Hitler chancellor.[119] Finally, among the members of the managing board, only Wilhelm R. Mann, Jr. belonged to the NSDAP before Hitler's selection as chancellor, a fact he later claimed not to have discussed with his colleagues.[120] In February 1932, Mann applied for membership and was admitted, effective from the preceding December, with Party card 760,728. However, he ceased paying dues in June and apparently informed the Gauleitung Köln-Aachen of his withdrawal from the movement sometime in the latter half of the year.[121] Other members of the *Vorstand* maintained after the war that

[115] See BA Koblenz, NL 19, Bd. 3, Bl. 138–42; Bd. 4, Bl. 1–4.

[116] Henry Ashby Turner, Jr., *German Big Business and the Rise of Hitler* (New York, 1985), pp. 420–1, note 18.

[117] Klaus Drobisch, "Der Freundeskreis Himmler," *ZfG*, 8 (1960), p. 309; Michael H. Kater, "Heinrich Himmler's Circle of Friends 1931–1945," *Marab*, 2 (1965–6), p. 76; Tammen, *I. G. Farbenindustrie*, p. 281.

[118] Avraham Barkai, "Die Wirtschaftsauffassung der NSDAP," *Aus Politik und Zeitgeschichte*, Beilage 9 (March 1975), p. 9; NI-7957/56, Affidavit by H. Bässler, 17.VII.47.

[119] Bayer 4C9.25, Mueller/Knieriem manuscript, p. 89. The petition is reprinted in Eberhard Czichon, *Wer verhalf Hitler*, Document 9, pp. 69–71. It appears from Document 8, pp. 68–9, that no officer of IG was asked to sign either.

[120] See his postwar testimony, M892/55, p. 10438.

[121] NI-5167/38, Affidavit by W. R. Mann, Jr., 2.V.47, mentions his admission in December 1931 but is silent on his brief wandering from the fold. For that information, see BDC, Partei Kanzlei Korrespondenz, exchange of letters between Kassenverwaltung of the Gauleitung Köln-Aachen and Kassenverwaltung of the Reichsleitung, München, 29.III.33–22.IV.33. On Mann's putative reasons for joining, see his testimony, M892/55, pp. 10434–5; Mann II/70, Affidavit by M. Weigandt; and II/168, Affidavit by P. Schramm. All three accounts stress antibolshevism.

they spurned invitations to enroll themselves during 1932.[122] True or not, after the Party imposed a ban on new recruits in May 1933, only Erwin Selck among the directors could obtain dispensation by producing evidence of previous support for the Nazis, namely, financial contributions to an SA unit that may have begun after Hitler's accession.[123]

Though money finally did change hands between the concern and the Nazis during 1932, the contributions were neither large nor exclusive. As the NSDAP became the nation's largest party, IG allotted it, according to Max Ilgner's recollection, some 10 to 15% of the firm's total grants for one of the parliamentary campaigns, that is, somewhere between 20,000 and 45,000 marks.[124] Berlin NW7 also plied Walther Funk, a recent convert to Nazism and former editor of the *Berliner Börsenzeitung*, with about 3,000 marks over six months for office expenses and his press service, perhaps in thanks for his support of the Wagemann Plan. The payments stopped toward the end of 1932, just as Funk was emerging as Hitler's principal economic adviser.[125] Yet during preparatory meetings in July, the organizers of the new Deutscher Nationalverein reckoned with help from IG for their effort to pull the German bourgeoisie together behind "the free individual and private enterprise" and against the "collectivist-bolshevist wave from Right and Left."[126] Similarly, Hermann Bücher, who was close to Bosch, told a group of leading businessmen in Berlin on

122 Carl Krauch's testimony, *NMT,* vol. 7, pp. 607–8; Hans Kühne's testimony *NMT,* vol. 7, p. 634.
123 BDC, Personalakte Erwin Selck.
124 NI-1293/13, Affidavit by M. Ilgner, 21.VI.45; NI-7082/55, Affidavit by M. Ilgner, 1.V.47. Kalle, however, later denied that these payments were made; see Turner, *German Big Business,* pp. 262–3. It is worth noting in this connection that the Nazi *Gauleiter* for the area containing the mammoth Leuna works stoutly denies ever receiving money from the region's industry; see R. Jordan, *Erlebt und Erlitten* (Leoni, 1971), p. 39.
125 NI-7082/55, Ilgner's affidavit, 1.V.47; NI-4933/35, Affidavit by H. Gattineau, 13.III.47; Ilgner I/4, Affidavit by Ilgner. See also Turner, *German Big Business,* pp. 261–2. Another frequently suggested indication of Berlin NW7's support for the Nazis is the story that Gattineau owned about one-quarter of the shares in the biweekly *Deutsche Führerbriefe* and the daily *Veltenbriefe,* both of which took on a pro-Nazi tone from the beginning of 1932; see W. Müller and J. Stockfisch, "Die 'Veltenbriefe,'" *ZfG,* 17 (1969), especially pp. 1565–66. Tammen could find no trace of Gattineau's ownership and doubts he wrote for either journal (*I. G. Farbenindustrie,* pp. 387–8, note 96). Wolffsohn, *Industrie und Handwerk,* p. 235, comes to a similar conclusion. Gattineau's memoirs say nothing of these publications.
126 Jones, *VfZ,* 25 (1977), pp. 292–3; for the quotations, the article by Kurt Rüss in D. Fricke et al. (eds.), *Die bürgerlichen Parteien,* pp. 497–8.

October 19 that he hoped for "a minimum of 100,000 reichsmarks" from IG toward the war chest these men were raising to build support for the Papen government during and after the current election campaign.[127] Edmund Pietrkowski, the chemical industry's representative at this meeting, made no recorded comment; no evidence has yet verified that IG donated to this Papen fund; and the prospect of giving money largely destined for the DNVP and DVP probably galled Bosch.[128] Still, the businessmen's decisions to retain complete control over the funds collected and to release them to the government only in return for good behavior probably overcame his reservations. Without the obvious need to insure IG's investment in the fuel program against a change of government, the concern might not have inaugurated even its highly tentative contacts with Hitler's party.

There were numerous reasons for IG's aloofness from the Nazi Party before January 30, 1933. Aside from the vulgarity of the movement, its foreign policy counteracted the export-sensitive concern's championing of international economic and political cooperation. If the NSDAP's work creation program showed an increasing resemblance to the Wagemann Plan, the Party's attitudes toward private property, large corporations, and autarky still seemed, at best, questionable.[129] Hasty clarification of these subjects during the fall of 1932 hardly neutralized the impression created by Nazi solidarity with the Communists in attempts to bring down the government of Danzig and in the strikes by the Berlin transport workers and the jute spinners of Brandenburg.[130] Nor were the concern's leaders indifferent to Nazi

[127] Dirk Stegmann, "Zum Verhältnis von Grossindustrie und Nationalsozialismus 1930–1933," AfS, 13 (1973), Document 15, p. 475.
[128] A contribution of 100,000 marks to Papen by Farben does show up in documents from March 1933, but it is unclear whether the money was given in response to Bücher's request or to the famous meeting between Hitler and German industrialists on February 20, 1933. See Chapter 3.
[129] There is no indication that IG accomplished this change in Nazi work creation policy, and Tammen's elaborate discussion in I. G. Farbenindustrie, pp. 278–80, establishes only that Wagemann contributed to a plan that, in turn, the Nazis drew on. It is worth noting, however, Richard Merton's suspicion "that Wagemann's suggestions attempt . . . to build a bridge to the National Socialist line of thought" and his rejection of them in part for that reason (Metallgesellschaft, Privatbriefe R. Merton 1919–38, Merton to Hermann Schmitz, 27.I.32).
[130] For a quite undocumented and dubious assertion to the contrary, see Alfred Sohn-Rethel, Oekonomie und Klassenstruktur des deutschen Faschismus (Frankfurt, 1973), p. 94. On the Danzig matter, see GHH, 400 101 293/4b, Gilsa to Reusch, 19.IX.32. On the strikes, see especially Hermann Roth, "Die nationalsozialistische Betriebszellenorganisation (NSBO) von der Gründung bis zur Röhm Affäre (1928

propaganda in agricultural regions against supposed price gouging by fertilizer makers.[131] In addition, unlike some reactionary leaders of heavy industry, IG did not hanker to demolish the unions. Since 1925, the chemical sector had known exceptional peace, and Bosch favored resurrecting the relatively amicable procedures and tone that characterized the labor–management *Arbeitsgemeinschaften* of the early 1920s.[132] Also in contrast to some German industrialists, Bosch did not hold labor costs responsible for the onset of the Depression in Germany; that blame he reserved for the framers of Weimar's reparations burden.[133]

The preeminent stumbling block in the path of good relations between IG and the NSDAP was the Party's propaganda against the concern as an agent of destructive Jewish international finance. The presence of about ten Jews on IG's governing boards, as well as IG's involvement in occasionally disadvantageous global cartels, served as pretexts for the slur.[134] Anti-Semitism set off the first documented altercation between the Party and the concern in late 1927, when Robert Ley, a chemist at Leverkusen who had become the *Gauleiter* of Rhineland-South two years earlier, delivered a speech denouncing the Warburg brothers, one of whom sat on IG's *Aufsichtsrat*. Called to account by his corporate superiors, Ley refused to renounce further political activity, so Farben dismissed him without severance pay but agreed to provide him a monthly allowance if he did not offer his skills to any competing firm. Ley used the money to found a Party news-

bis 1934)," *JfW*, 19 (1978), p. 53. On the Party's disclaimers concerning autarky, see Hans-Erich Volkmann, "Das aussenwirtschaftliche Programm der NSDAP, 1930–1933," *AfS*, 17 (1977), p. 256, and Hughes, *P&P*, no. 44 (August 1969), p. 120.

131 Testimony by F. terMeer, *NMT*, vol. 7, p. 616.
132 For explanations and evidence of the social calm, see Enquête Ausschuss, pp. 53–5, 60–1; Eduard Gartmayr, *Angestellte und Arbeiter der deutschen chemischen Industrie* (Dissertation, München, 1930), p. 46; and Tammen, *I. G. Farbenindustrie*, pp. 192–7. On Bosch's views concerning labor, see Dirk Stegmann's articles, *AfS* (1973), p. 409, and (1977), p. 282, as well as Udo Wengst, "Unternehmerverbände und Gewerkschaften in Deutschland im Jahre 1930," *VfZ*, 25 (1977), p. 100, which follows Holdermann, *Im Banne der Chemie*, p. 251. Cf. Lammer's remarks in *Autarkie, Planwirtschaft und berufstandischer Staat?* p. 31.
133 See BASF T51/1, Vowi 314, "Die Ursachen der Arbeitslosigkeit in Deutschland und Vorschläge zu ihrer Bekämpfung," Anfang Januar 1932, especially p. 32; and Bosch's remarks to IG's general meeting, as reported in BA Koblenz, ZSg 127, Bd. 838, "Wachsende Absatzsorgen," *Berliner Börsen-Courier*, no. 216 (10.V.32).
134 Bayer 4C9.25, Mueller/Knieriem manuscript, p. 87. Gajewski I/4, Affidavit by Dr. G. Ollendorf, 24.IV.47. Ollendorf was a Jew, the leader of Wolfen Film, and a member of the IG *Vorstand* until 1932.

paper for Rhineland-Westphalia, the *Westdeutscher Beobachter*.[135]
By June 1931, further Nazi defamation of the "Moloch IG" as a tool
of international capital and the "Jew Warburg" prompted Heinrich
Gattineau to seek the intercession of his former professor Karl Haushofer with Rudolf Hess.[136] Then, on October 5, 1931, Gattineau gave
thirteen Nazi economic specialists a tour of the Leuna works, finding
among them an "extraordinary interest" in IG's synthetic fuel project
and obtaining from their leader Otto Wagener the statement that "the
further supplying of the German market with German gasoline ac-
cords completely with the goals of his movement."[137] But the fruits of
Gattineau's efforts withered rapidly. During the first half of 1932, the
Völkischer Beobachter attacked IG in articles with titles like "Foreign
Domination over the German Economy and Its Dangers," charging
that the concern's monopoly over synthetic fuel production opened
that vital German resource to un-German influences.[138]

Both at the war-crimes trial of IG's surviving leaders in 1947–8 and
in the academic literature since, the most important fact about the
Nazi criticism has been obscured. The target was not synthetic fuel or
the tariff protection it enjoyed, which Wagener already had endorsed,
but IG's role in its production. And the Party took aim just when the
combine was seeking a subsidy from a government that shortly might
include Nazi ministers. On the eve of the Nazi landslide of July 1932,
which delivered to the Party 230 out of 608 seats in the Reichstag,
Bosch drew the inevitable conclusion. He sent an inconspicuous depu-

[135] Ley's speech was reported in the *Nordhausener Allgemeine Zeitung*, 16.IX.27. The Bayer archive contains this document, as well as the correspondence between Krekeler of IG and Ley concerning his removal. See also Schmitz I/5, Affidavit by Kalle, 4.X.47; Testimony by Hans Kühne, *NMT*, vol. 7, p. 634; Kurt Gossweiler, "Hitler und das Kapital (II)," *Blätter für deutsche und internationale Politik*, 23 (1978), pp. 1005–6; and Duisberg, *Nur ein Sohn*, p. 155.
[136] See Gattineau's letter to Haushofer, 6.VI.31, enclosing a copy of another to August Heinrichsbauer of the same date, as well as the article "Moloch IG" by K. E. Weiss, published in the *Grossdeutscher Pressedienst*, 2.VI.31, RG242/T253, Reel 57, Frames 1513247–53; Hughes, *P&P*, no. 44 (August 1969), p. 124; and Borkin, *Crime and Punishment*, p. 54. Max Warburg sat on the supervisory board from 1926 to 1932.
[137] NI-15237/123, Gattineau's report of 12.X.31.
[138] See Gattineau III/47, Affidavit by H. Rechenberg; III/48, excerpts from the *Völkischer Beobachter* (VB), 10.II.32; III/51, excerpts from the VB, 28.IV.32; III/52, excerpts from the VB, 11.III.32 (the complete article, "I.G. Farben und Oppau," is in BA Koblenz, ZSg 127, Bd. 825); Hughes, *P&P*, no. 44 (August 1969), note 57. See also Gattineau Nachtrag II/108, excerpt from *Der Führer*, 21.I.32; Nachtrag II/109, excerpts from *Rote Erde*, 10.II.32 and 1.IX.32.

tation to Munich in the hope of sounding Hitler's attitude and convincing him of the reasonableness and patriotism of the concern's fuel program. It is tempting to suppose that IG's first contributions to the Party were timed to grease the wheels of this mission. The two rather junior emissaries, Heinrich Gattineau, IG's press chief, who arranged the meeting through Rudolf Hess, and Heinrich Bütefisch, a chemist and the head of the Leuna works, conversed with the führer for more than two hours. As usual, Hitler did most of the talking. That IG's men came away with a ringing endorsement of German self-sufficiency in fuel is hardly surprising, since that had not been at issue in the first place.[139] Otherwise, neither side made any specific commitments. Bosch felt relieved nonetheless. He concluded, after hearing Bütefisch's narration of Hitler's comments, that "the man is more sensible than I thought."[140] Over the next few months, however, the Nazis' electoral advance peaked and then receded. As impatient Party activists returned to their rhetorical onslaught on the capitalist system and Farben in particular, the concern recoiled.[141] There was no follow-up to the mission to Munich.

Concerning IG Farben, even more than German big business in general, the repeated attempt by some historians to draw an ascending curve of support for Nazism from 1930 to 1933 runs afoul of the ample surviving evidence. The pattern of corporate interest in Nazism resembled a "fever chart," which moved in direct relation to the elec-

[139] Our knowledge of the meeting rests almost entirely on postwar recollections, since apparently no contemporary written record was prepared (Birkenfeld, *Treibstoff*, p. 30). The most significant of the many pertinent documents presented at the IG trial were NI-4833/35, Affidavit by H. Gattineau, 13.III.47, and NI-8637/71, Interrogation of H. Bütefisch, 16.IV.47. See also Bütefisch's testimony, *NMT*, vol. 7, pp. 544–50; and Gattineau, *Klippen*, pp. 127–8. The best scholarly discussion of the meeting to date is that of Hughes, *P&P*, no. 44 (August 1969), which discredits the supposition that IG's representatives and Hitler sealed a political alliance with promises of mutual efforts for rearmament. Dating the meeting is problematic, since after World War II the surviving participants gave various times in the autumn of 1932, whereas the earliest written account places the session in June 1932 (NI-14304, an excerpt from "Twenty-five Years at the Leuna Works," a celebratory volume written by W. Greiling in 1941, *NMT*, vol. 7, pp. 536–41). When questioned about Greiling's account at the postwar trial, Bütefisch said that Greiling had made up many details but did not challenge the date directly (*NMT*, vol. 7, pp. 541–3). Henry Turner has argued convincingly for the earlier date, and I am following him here; see *German Big Business*, pp. 248–9.
[140] NI-8637/71, Interrogation of H. Bütefisch, 16.IV.47.
[141] See, for example, the attack on Warmbold and IG in Terboven's Nazi paper in Essen, the *National-Zeitung*, "I. G. Farben vorläufig behauptet," 4.XII.32, and the instances mentioned in NI-6787/52, Affidavit by Heinrich Hoerlein, 2.V.47.

tion returns and inverse relation to the economic indicators. As public support for Hitler ebbed in late 1932 and both the ruling cabinets and the national economy moved in directions satisfactory to industry, willingness to gamble on the Nazis declined. Most big businessmen placed their hopes once more on the consolidation of the moderate and conservative middle-class parties behind presidential rule.[142] Farben's leaders did so rather more emphatically than most, having never really deviated from this course. In the last half of 1932, the minor exceptions to this stance largely disappeared. Not only did Mann let his Party membership drop and Ilgner cease passing money to Funk, but also Josef Klein, the secretary of the social welfare section of IG's Uerdingen plant, had to choose between his newly acquired seat in the Reichstag as a Nazi and his post with the concern. At the end of December 1932, he left Farben "because of his activity in the NSDAP."[143] On the brink of the National Revolution, IG's chief executives had no warm ties to its standard-bearers and disliked the prospect of a Nazi government.[144]

Yet Bosch's remark about Hitler captured the mood of the ensuing three years. It soon appeared that the concern had exaggerated the immediate dangers of Nazi rule and underestimated the degree to which the economic interests of the firm and the Party, if not their respective mentalities and goals, could be harmonized.

[142] See Turner, *German Big Business,* especially pp. 344–5. See also Thomas Trumpp, "Zur Finanzierung der NSDAP durch die deutsche Grossindustrie: Versuch einer Bilanz," *GWU,* 32 (1981), especially pp. 231–3.
[143] On Klein, see Bayer Personalkartei, from which the quotation comes; BDC, Personalakten Klein; and Fritz Thyssen, *I Paid Hitler* (1941), p. 124.
[144] There is nothing to the story, invented by Kurt Gossweiler and taken up by soberer commentators, of links between IG Farben and Gregor Strasser of the NSDAP. These rest entirely on a tortuous set of purported bonds between IG and the firm of Schering-Kahlbaum, which employed Strasser after his break with Hitler in December 1932. See Kurt Gossweiler, *Die Röhm Affäre* (Köln, 1983), pp. 246–8; and Peter Stachura, "Der Fall Strasser,'" in P. Stachura (ed.), *The Shaping of the Nazi State* (New York, 1978), p. 96. Udo Kissenkoetter has established that Albert Pietzsch negotiated Hitler's approval of Strasser's appointment with Schering, which suggests that that small-scale chemical industrialist arranged it; see *Gregor Strasser und die NSDAP* (Stuttgart, 1978), pp. 192–3. Similarly, I have found no confirmation of Gossweiler's contention that Werner Daitz, an associate of the Aussenpolitisches Amt of the NSDAP from 1931, "became a plant leader of IG Farben after its founding;" see *Blätter für deutsche und internationale Politik,* 23 (1978), p. 1008. In his *Kapital, Reichswehr und NSDAP* (Köln, 1982), pp. 82–3, Gossweiler says only that the firm of which Daitz was general director from 1912 to 1922 was later taken over by IG. Of course, some lower-level Farben officials must have been active in Nazi local organizations. One such, according to a confidential source, was Dr. Wittwer, the *Ortsgruppenleiter* of Ludwigshafen.

PART II
The national revival, 1933–1936

In the course of the 1920s, Adolf Hitler constructed a utopian ideology around the concepts of race and space, *Rasse und Raum*. Conceiving of history as an unremitting conflict among peoples for their "daily bread," the Nazi führer believed that victory always belonged to the most fecund, valorous, and racially healthy group – to those who by weight of number, force of arms, and purity of blood could periodically seize and hold sufficient new territory from which to feed their swelling ranks. For a land-poor nation like Germany, the peaceful expansion of industry and trade, in Hitler's view, would provide neither an alternative to this "natural imperialism" nor the physical preconditions for its fulfillment. Exchanging manufactures for foreign foodstuffs on the basis of comparative advantage would leave the Reich's lifelines at the mercy of potentially hostile powers and "international Jewish finance." Export earnings would inevitably decline with the spread of industrialization, the rise of foreign competition, and the likely founding of branch factories and subsidiaries abroad. Instead of fostering the essential "heroic virtues," increasing industrialism would encourage materialism and "commercial egoism," qualities on which Hitler blamed the collapse of the Wilhelmian Empire and the "indolence" of a bourgeoisie that "has already become worthless for every exalted human task."[1] And with industrial growth the Nazi leader linked those twin sores on "the national body," cities and Jews. International "political and economic agreements, such as Papen and Hugenberg dream of," would therefore do Germany no good; on the contrary, "these are liberal games, which end in the

---

[1] All the quoted remarks are Hitler's. They and similar ones appear in his essay "Der Weg zum Wiederaufstieg," reprinted in Henry Turner, "Hitler's Secret Pamphlet for Industrialists, 1927," *JMH*, 40 (1968), pp. 367, 369; in Turner's "Hitlers Einstellung zu Wirtschaft und Gesellschaft vor 1933," *G&G*, 2 (1976), pp. 91–3, 96–7; in Peter Krüger, "Zu Hitlers 'nationalsozialistischen Wirtschaftserkenntnissen,'" *G&G*, 6 (1980), pp. 268–70, 274–5 (note 28); and in Berenice Carroll, *Design for Total War* (The Hague, 1968), pp. 95–7.

bankruptcy of the nation."[2] The *Volk* had, Hitler concluded, only one escape from strangulation and decay: the conquest and colonization of a vast, contiguous, agriculturally self-sufficient empire purged of Jews.[3] Along the way, Germany would experience an idealistic renewal and bring forth a "new master class" whose creation the NSDAP proclaimed as "the task of the twentieth century."[4] Thus fortified, the Aryan race could proceed in later ages toward the world domination to which cultural superiority entitled it.

Though bent on transforming the German state into the executor of this vision, Hitler prided himself on being a politician as well as an ideologue. He therefore shaped the Nazi Party's domestic policies around two preliminary duties: to gain office and "to secure the inner strength of [the] people so that it can assert itself in the sphere of foreign policy."[5] In practice, this meant applying the lessons drawn from two Novembers. That of 1918, when the workers overthrew the monarchy and allegedly stabbed Germany's soldiers in the back, underscored the need for a "complete incorporation of the so-called Fourth Estate into the national community." Accordingly, Party propaganda highlighted the populist aspects of the *Volksgemeinschaft*, insisting on every person's right to a job and "declaring war on gigantic interest groups."[6] On the other hand, while the routing of the Beer

---

2 Hermann Rauschning, *The Voice of Destruction* (New York, 1940), p. 39, where the words are dated to the summer of 1932. Rauschning's reliability as a source has been challenged quite powerfully by Wolfgang Hänel, *Hermann Rauschning's "Gespräche mit Hitler" – Eine Geschichtsfälschung* (Ingolstadt, 1984), which demonstrates that Rauschning conversed with Hitler far too seldom to have gathered the numerous quotations Rauschning purports to be repeating and that he cobbled these together out of his own analyses of Nazism, assorted speeches by the führer and *Mein Kampf*, and the remarks of other contemporaries. This does not mean, however, that the picture of Hitler's views presented by Rauschning's book is false, provided, of course, that one can corroborate it with reference to other accounts. I have employed Rauschning's putative citations rarely, only when they seem to me to capture the realities of the situation, and always on the understanding that they do not necessarily convey Hitler's actual words.
3 See in addition to Carroll, *Design*, p. 97, Hitler's remarks to the military commanders on 3.II.33, summarized in Wolfram Fischer, *Deutsche Wirtschaftspolitik 1918–1945* ([Hannover], 1961), p. 61.
4 See the passages quoted in Joachim Fest, *The Face of the Third Reich* (London, 1970), pp. 292–3.
5 Telford Taylor (ed.), *Hitler's Secret Book* (New York, 1961), p. 34. See also the excerpts from *Mein Kampf* in Fischer, *Deutsche Wirtschaftspolitik*, p. 54.
6 The quotations are from Hitler's pamphlet of 1927, Turner, *JMH*, 40 (1968), p. 373. On the implications of November 1918 for Nazi theory and practice, see Timothy W. Mason, *Sozialpolitik im Dritten Reich* (Opladen, 1977), pp. 15–41, and the same author's essay, "The Legacy of 1918 for National Socialism," in A. J. Nicholls and E.

Hall Putsch in November 1923 confirmed the importance of building
mass support, the Nazi führer also construed the debacle as a warning
against arousing the overt opposition of the nation's established elites.
The NSDAP consequently touted its specious legality policy and gradually vitiated those sections of the Party's Twenty-five Point Program
that appeared threatening to propertied interests. With regard to real
economic restructuring Hitler reminded one of the Party's leading
reformers in 1932, the Nazis would have to "hide the glowing torch
behind closed doors," perhaps into the next generation.[7] Since the
appeal of Nazism to Germany's propertied classes depended not only
on such moderation, but also on the ability to attract a mass following, the NSDAP learned to excel at cultivating ambiguity about its
economic aims. Aided by this practice and by brilliant, largely grass-
roots organizational work, the führer stood by 1932 at the head of a
quite broadly based, though fissiparous popular movement. It embraced Germans from all classes and locales, advocates of both revolution and restoration.[8]

Influenced by a long tradition of statist German economic writing
and by the need to appeal to such diverse audiences, the National
Socialists hammered out a distinct, if rather hybrid economic doctrine.
It honored the appearances of capitalism but denied most of their
liberal corollaries.[9] Hitler was too much of a social Darwinist to
dispense with private property and competition. He nonetheless saw
ample room to better their yield. If the Depression illustrated the
tendency of unfettered acquisitiveness to produce destructive cycles of
boom and bust, a glance at Germany's industrial elite convinced the
führer that the free play of economic forces did not unfailingly elevate

Matthias (eds.), *German Democracy and the Triumph of Hitler* (London, 1971), pp.
215–39.
[7] H. A. Turner, Jr. (ed.), *Hitler aus nächster Nähe* (Frankfurt, 1978), p. 444.
[8] Among the many works on the Party's organization, propaganda, and voting base,
see especially Dietrich Orlow, *The History of the Nazi Party: 1919–1933* (Pittsburgh,
Pa., 1969); Jeremy Noakes, *The Nazi Party in Lower Saxony 1921–1933* (London,
1971), especially pp. 89–200; Thomas Childers, *The Nazi Voter* (Chapel Hill, N.C.,
1983); Michael H. Kater, *The Nazi Party* (Cambridge, Mass., 1983); and Heinrich
August Winkler, "German Society, Hitler and the Illusion of Restoration 1930–
1933," *JCH*, 11 (1976), pp. 1–16.
[9] This is the convincing conclusion of Avraham Barkai's work: "Sozialdarwinismus
und Antiliberalismus in Hitlers Wirtschaftskonzept," *G&G*, 3 (1977), pp. 406–17;
"Die Wirtschaftsauffassung der NSDAP," *Aus Politik und Zeitgeschichte*, Beilage 9
(1975), pp. 3–16; and *Das Wirtschaftssystem des Nationalsozialismus* (Köln, 1977).

the fittest to prominence.[10] Obviously, the Nazi leader and his followers argued, "one can no longer allow things to work themselves out."[11] Until years, perhaps even generations, of education in the Party's *Weltanschauung* broke the hegemony of bourgeois individualism in Germany, the state would have to steer the drive for personal gain "onto paths appropriate to the people." Two Party manifestoes from the "period of struggle" largely foretold how this would be done: the "Fundamental Economic Views and Goals of the NSDAP" of March 1931 and the "Economic Emergency Program" issued in June 1932. That Hitler blocked the publication of the first document and withdrew the second from circulation after a few months attests to his concern about political fallout among businessmen, not necessarily to disagreement with the contents. In fact, the pamphlets recommended economic policies substantially identical to those enacted during the first years of the Third Reich.[12] Their common thrust was to cut the economy off from international influences, to increase government control over the factors of production, and to make the rights of ownership contingent on their exercise as the state sanctioned – to create, in short, an environment in which the institution of private property was never abandoned but the disposition and possession of it were always in question.

Summarized in the slogans Autarky, The Primacy of Politics, and The Common Good before Private Interest, these ideas made up the NSDAP's solution to the widespread European quest between the wars for a "Third Way" between capitalism and socialism. Admittedly, from time to time in private Hitler found it politic or satisfying to contemplate the nationalization of large firms or the redistribution

---

[10] Hitler's attitude toward industrialists is difficult to pinpoint, since his utterances varied with time and his moods. For examples of contempt for most businessmen, from which he exempted only those few persons, like Paul Pleiger, Willy Messerschmitt, and Hermann Röchling, whom he regarded as being in his own adventurous mold, see Fischer, *Deutsche Wirtschaftspolitik*, p. 79; G. Hallgarten and J. Radkau, *Deutsche Industrie und Politik* (Frankfurt, 1974), pp. 292–3; and Rauschning, *Voice*, pp. 21, 29. None of Hitler's reputed favorites worked for IG Farben, and as Radkau points out, most of them had strained relations with the combine.

[11] Quoted in Rauschning, *Voice*, p. 24. See also the speeches of Herbert Backe collected in *Volk und Wirtschaft im nationalsozialistischen Deutschland* (München, 1936), especially pp. 5, 14.

[12] See Barkai, *G&G*, 3 (1977), pp. 411–13; and idem, *Wirtschaftssystem*, pp. 10–11, 38–39, 140.

of stockholdings, but his regime seldom acted along these lines.[13] As Hermann Rauschning later formulated the führer's thoughts:

The needs of a state, varying according to time and circumstances, are the sole determining factor. . . . There will be no license, no free space, in which the individual belongs to himself. This is Socialism – not such trifles as the private possession of the means of production. Of what importance is that if I range men firmly within a discipline they cannot escape? . . . Why need we trouble to socialize banks and factories? We socialize human beings.[14]

Thus, though Hitler imagined the eventual unfolding of "a new order for which all expressions used hitherto will be quite inadequate," his immediate plans did not entail revolutionizing the German economy so much as conscripting it.[15] Once his corporate draftees had made conquest possible, he would retain or cashier them as he deemed fit. Meanwhile, he played on their fear of Marxism and advertised his readiness to reward the most useful among them appropriately.

This eclectic doctrine did not produce thoroughly coherent economic policies any more than the führer's territorial ambitions translated into consistent diplomatic practices. In both spheres, the Nazis knew only in general terms what they wanted and found some of their desires contradictory. Rearmament and economic preference for the Mittelstand proved as hard to combine as militant expansion and an alliance with Britain. Even when forced to choose among desiderata, Hitler was unsure of how to achieve his ends and tended to wait for events to suggest a way. Once he was offered one, however, "his moves followed a logical (though not a predetermined) course."[16] This was as true for economic policy as for foreign affairs. If the former often had consequences apparently at odds with Party ideology, favoring, for instance, increased economic concentration at the expense of the little man, that resulted from the Nazi view of expansion as a precondition for social change.[17] Hitler's emphasis on never

13 For examples of such musings, see Albert Speer, Spandau: The Secret Diaries (New York, 1976), pp. 77–8; and Turner, G&G, 2 (1976), pp. 112–14.
14 Rauschning, Voice, pp. 188, 191, 193; see footnote 2.
15 For the quotation, ibid., p. 192; for the metaphor, Norbert Schausberger, "Oesterreich und die deutsche Wirtschaftsexpansion nach dem Donauraum," Oesterreich in Geschichte und Literatur, 16 (1972), p. 197.
16 Alan Bullock, "Hitler and the Origins of the Second World War," in H. A. Turner (ed.), Nazism and the Third Reich (New York, 1967), p. 223.
17 David Schoenbaum, Hitler's Social Revolution (New York, 1967), especially pp. xxi–xxii.

taking more than one step at a time accounted in the same manner for his decision to let the Russian border move west in 1939 in order to erase it altogether later.

Thus, after 1933 as well as before, Nazi economic doctrine served as both a blueprint and a billboard, a blend of half-revealed ideological goals and political blandishments. By presupposing conquest, the führer knew that he presupposed the combined best efforts of the Reich's deeply divided social and economic classes. Therefore, while propaganda, *Gleichschaltung*, terror, and Hitler's charisma kept the populace in line and the Nazi movement together, the regime also contrived to spread employment and nearly restore the living standards of most citizens to pre-Depression levels. After a slow start in 1933, Germany accomplished within the next three years the most rapid and sustained economic recovery in the industrialized world.[18] Still, the bulk of the new national income went into rearmament, not personal consumption. As compensation for forgone monetary gains and lost political freedom, workers, peasants, and the long discontented lower middle classes got a reborn sense of national might, large doses of official flattery, and assorted and relatively inexpensive social innovations designed to betoken the establishment of a classless society. The Third Reich enticed businessmen, on the whole, with less praise and more wealth than any other social group, but deceived them similarly nonetheless.[19]

In 1933, most executives still professed the self-serving view that what had taken place in Germany since 1929 was primarily a political rather than economic breakdown, a product of reparations burdens

[18] See the figures conveniently tabulated in Mason, *Sozialpolitik*, p. 149. On living standards, see Mason's discussion, pp. 150–3; Arthur Schweitzer, *Big Business in the Third Reich* (Bloomington, Ind., 1964), pp. 317–21, 333–37; and the data on real incomes, food consumption, and the availability of consumer goods provided by Walther G. Hoffmann, *Das Wachstum der deutschen Wirtschaft* (Heidelberg, 1965), pp. 632–3, 636–7, 640–1, 644–5, 648–9, 652–3, 659, and by Schoenbaum, *Social Revolution*, pp. 98–104. For balanced summaries, see D. Petzina, *Die deutsche Wirtschaft in der Zwischenkriegszeit* (Wiesbaden, 1977), pp. 146–7; and R. J. Overy, *The Nazi Economic Recovery 1932–1938* (London, 1982).

[19] Schoenbaum, *Social Revolution*, especially pp. 113–51. On the economic gains of businessmen, see Rene Erbe, *Die nationalsozialistische Wirtschaftspolitik im Lichte der modernen Theorie* (Zurich, 1958), pp. 156–9. On corporate profits, see the varying calculations in Hoffmann, *Wachstum*, p. 503; Alan Milward, "Fascism and the Economy," in Walter Laqueur (ed.), *Fascism: A Reader's Guide* (Berkeley, Calif., 1976), p. 399; Maxine Sweezy, "German Corporate Profits 1926–1938," *QJE*, 54 (1940), p. 391; and Georges Castellan, "Bilan social du IIIe Reich," *Revue d'histoire moderne et contemporaine*, 15 (1968), p. 508.

and partisan pressures that had prevented the capitalist system from stabilizing itself. While the system repaired its damaged mechanisms, most industrialists wanted a government that would provide the necessary political firmness at home and abroad, coupled with either absolute noninterference in economic life or a short-lived activist countercyclical course.[20] These convictions had led the odd big businessman, like Fritz Thyssen, to back the NSDAP before Hitler's takeover and others to flirt with doing so. Yet even they, like the majority of their colleagues, doubted that an efficient economy could be autarkic or indefinitely substitute the decisions of the state for those of the market, as the plebeian elements in the Party seemed to believe. Nor is there any evidence that more than a handful of corporate executives saw the Nazis' ill-defined expansionist designs as a solution to business's commercial problems.[21] Trotsky was right in June 1933, when he observed that "while the Nazis acted as a party and not a state power . . . the big bourgeoisie, even those who supported Hitler with money, did not consider his party theirs."[22]

Knowing this, the new regime labored to disarm business's mistrust. Autarky, chorused leaders of both the Party and the state, would apply to vital materials only and was, in any case, being forced on Germany by the protectionism of other nations.[23] Denounced as a vestige of Marxist thought and redefined virtually out of existence, the concept

[20] Cf. Eberhard Czichon's belabored discussion of such near anachronisms as "German Keynesianism," "Left Keynesianism," and "Right Keynesianism," in *Wer Verhalf Hitler zur Macht?* (Köln, 1967), especially pp. 39, 48–52. A deeply flawed overstatement of the political consequences of industrial factionalism is David Abraham's *The Collapse of the Weimar Republic* (Princeton, N.J., 1981). On the differences between the kind of rearmament program some businessmen hoped for and the kind they got, see the incisive comments of Michael Geyer, "Etudes in Political History," in Peter Stachura (ed.), *The Nazi Machtergreifung* (Winchester, Mass., 1983). p. 114, and "Zum Einfluss der nationalsozialistischen Rüstungspolitik auf das Ruhrgebiet," *RVB*, 45 (1981), pp. 216–19.
[21] Cf. the assertions to this effect in Alfred Sohn-Rethel, *Economy and Class Structure of German Fascism* (London, 1978), and Abraham, *Collapse*, which rest on the rather elastic Marxist definition of imperialism.
[22] Leon Trotsky, "What is National Socialism?" in Ernest Mandel (ed.), *The Struggle Against Fascism in Germany* (New York, 1971), p. 402. Cf. G. Gassert, *Werden und Wesen der Sozialistischen Deutschen Wirtschaft* (Berlin, 1939), p. 273: "The majority of employers remained distant from the Party until the revolution [1933]. It followed the new leadership at the beginning only hesitantly and doubtfully and thus aroused the suspicion of intending sabotage. It remains in many respects even today the refuge of reaction and the remnant of bourgeois politics." For a good summary, see Kater, *Nazi Party*, pp. 62–4.
[23] Kurt Schmitt, *Die Wirtschaft in neuen Reich* (München, 1934), pp. 8–11; H. Zeck, *Die deutsche Wirtschaft und Südosteuropa* (Leipzig, 1938), p. 13; Hellmuth Tam-

of "excess" profits faded from Nazi publications.[24] Sometimes out of craft, sometimes out of conviction, official spokesmen repeatedly stressed the provisional, emergency nature of the regime's steadily growing power over the economy. They excused each new regulation as an improvised means of heading off inflation and facilitating an eventual return to normal commercial practice on the "healthier" basis of Germany's international economic and political equality.[25] Trusting to their understanding of the "laws" of economics, most industrialists accepted this explanation and gladly pocketed the proceeds. The few skeptics bided their time, expecting that "the real test of strength will come when the armaments boom is ended."[26]

Behind this smoke screen of verbal reluctance, the state increasingly intruded on the autonomy of managers and markets. Business's existing vehicles for discussing, assessing, and influencing government policy – namely, the Deutsche Industrie- und Handelstag, the various *Arbeitgeberverbände,* and the Reichsverband der deutschen Industrie – all disappeared into an internally fragmented Reichsgruppe Industrie, which was "intended to preclude any effective organization of interest" and to function merely as a "receiver of orders from the government."[27] Official controls soon policed imports and exports, costs and prices, wages and working conditions, raw material supplies, investments, and the flow of foreign exchange. As the Reich became virtually the sole external source of a company's funds, the rate of interest lost its allocative function, and the banks declined in importance. In conjunction with changes in the tax structure, all these restrictions on entrepreneurial freedom of action began channeling resources into takeovers of Jewish-owned firms and into industrial projects that promoted autarky and rearmament.[28] All in all, while the

men, *Die I. G. Farbenindustrie Aktiengesellschaft (1925–1933)* (Dissertation, Freie Universität Berlin, 1978), pp. 262, 272–4.

24 Bernhard Köhler, *Die Eroberung der Wirtschaft* (Munchen, 1937), p. 18.

25 Otto Christian Fischer, *Nationale Weltwirtschaft?* (Berlin, 1933), pp. 34–45; Leonhard Miksch, "Wo herrscht noch freier Wettbewerb?" *Die Wirtschaftskurve,* 15 (1936), p. 340; C. W. Guillebaud, *The Economic Recovery of Germany* (London, 1939), p. 223; Fischer, *Deutsche Wirtschaftspolitik,* p. 63. Illustrations of business's acceptance of this argument appear in Barkai, *Wirtschaftssystem,* p. 100, and NI-5187/38, Affidavit by F. terMeer, 15.IV.47. Conversely, the Party excused the subordination of ideology to immediate needs as merely temporary; see Barkai, *Wirtschaftssystem,* pp. 91–2.

26 Stephen H. Roberts, *The House That Hitler Built* (London, 1938), p. 168.

27 Schoenbaum, *Social Revolution,* p. 124.

28 On the specific measures discussed in this paragraph, see Barkai, *Wirtschaftssystem,*

regime paid lip service to property rights, removed much of the risk from private enterprise, and invoked the national welfare, the Nazis also prevented business from arriving at common positions, blocked unsanctioned uses of corporate funds, prevented capital flight, and established administrative procedures for punishing uncooperative employers. In this manner, businessmen were tempted, threatened, and trapped into serving an economic system that confined their choices and the rates of return on their sales and capital.[29]

As this system took shape from 1933 to 1936, industry won a few deceptive policy victories. On occasion, large corporations profited from clashes between the needs of the Party's varied constituencies. The apparent defeat of German artisans in 1934, when the regime abandoned attempts to stop the installation of labor- and cost-saving machinery in factories, served not only corporate interests, but also the Party's desire to stem the flight of workers from agriculture.[30] More frequently, business owed brief successes to a self-liquidating advantage: the new government's dependence on demonstrating a prompt economic upturn. Though the Cartel Law of 1933 was based on a draft presented by industrial organizations, the Reich began to turn against cartelization as early as February 1934.[31] In subsequent years, the state reduced the cartels to "mere shells," since in the Party's opinion, they were "far too liberal a form of organization."[32] The

pp. 96, 98, 154–7; Hans-Erich Volkmann, "Aspekte der nationalsozialistischen 'Wehrwirtschaft' 1933–1936," *Francia*, 5 (1977), pp. 513–23; L. Hamburger, *How Nazi Germany Has Controlled Business* (Washington, D.C., 1943), pp. 20–37, 85–93; Dörte Doering, *Deutsche Aussenwirtschaftspolitik 1933–35* (Dissertation, Freie Universität Berlin, 1969), pp. 47–54; Samuel Lurie, *Private Investment in a Controlled Economy* (New York, 1947), pp. 88–9, 146–53, 165; Guillebaud, *Economic Recovery*, p. 200; Schoenbaum, *Social Revolution*, pp. 89–90, 124–25; N. A. Pelcovits, "The Social Honor Courts of Nazi Germany," *PSQ.* 53 (1938), pp. 350–71; and Gerhard Kroll, *Von der Weltwirtschaftskrise zur Staatskonjunktur* (Berlin, 1958), pp. 539–62. On the ways in which economic controls fostered so-called Aryanization, see Degussa, Biographische Unterlagen, Zur Geschichte der Scheideanstalt, 1933 bis 1936 by Fritz Roessler, Abschrift, pp. 121–5.
29 Thomas Balogh, "The National Economy of Germany," *Economic Journal*, 48 (1938), pp. 487–8. Sweezy, *QJE*, 54 (1940), Table 1, pp. 390–1, shows that the average pretax profit rate for all German industry in 1926–30 was 5.1% and in 1933–8, 4.3%; for the chemical industry the averages were 9.7 and 5.8%.
30 Schoenbaum, *Social Revolution*, p. 46; Erich Welter, *Der Weg der deutschen Industrie* (Frankfurt, 1943), pp. 91–3.
31 See Herle to Reusch, 22.VII.33, reproduced in Dirk Stegmann, "Zum Verhältnis von Grossindustrie und Nationalsozialismus 1930–1933," *AfS*, 13 (1973), Document 21, p. 482; Hallgarten and Radkau, *Deutsche Industrie*, pp. 204–41; and Miksch, *Die Wirtschaftskurve*, 5 (1936), pp. 346–8.
32 Fritz Voight, "German Experience with Cartels and Their Control during the Pre-

German Labor Front (DAF) evolved from a promising means of containing workers' demands at the end of 1933 into an insistent advocate of these after 1936.[33] Similarly, the Party-sponsored works councils (*Vertrauensräte*), mandated for each plant by the Labor Law (AOG) of January 1934, began as mere advisory bodies subordinate to management but soon developed into mechanisms "used to terrorize both the workers and the employer."[34]

Transient or not, industry's successes were inconsequential in comparison with the government's major achievement: the simultaneous bridling and spurring of competition.[35] As Franz Neumann wrote, "Each restriction imposed upon the entrepreneur sharpens the sting of the profit motive. Each regimentation strengthens the need of business to have pull with the authorities."[36] But pull was largely a matter of performance, and "submission was the condition for success."[37] Nazi legal theorists put the necessary juridical gloss on this reality by declaring that "property was . . . a kind of state concession," and economic publicists pointed out that public or private ownership was, in the Party's eyes, "merely a question of expediency" and that industry had "become a weapon, a constituent part of the state."[38] Executives who dared doubt this claim had only to look at the example made of the uncooperative Professor Hugo Junkers, from whom the Reich extorted the sale of a majority interest in two aircraft firms at the turn of 1933–4. Upon Junkers's death in April 1935, the regime briefly nationalized both companies.[39] Under these circumstances, business retained only limited control over the details, not the direction, of Nazi policy.[40] Tritely, but without great exaggeration, the economics editor

War and Post-War Periods," in J. P. Miller (ed.), *Competition, Cartels and Their Regulation* (Amsterdam, 1962), pp. 184–7; and Philip C. Newman, "Key German Cartels under the Nazi Regime," *QJE*, 62 (1948), p. 577.

[33] Mason, *Sozialpolitik*, pp. 105–20, 175, 198–9; Kater, *Nazi Party*, pp. 103–4.

[34] Franz Neumann, *Behemoth* (New York, 1944), p. 424.

[35] Tim Mason has also stressed the importance of this point; see his "Primat der Industrie? – Eine Erwiderung," *Das Argument*, 10 (1968), especially pp. 199–200, 207–9.

[36] Neumann, *Behemoth*, p. 315.

[37] Schoenbaum, *Social Revolution*, p. 116.

[38] Ibid., pp. 51, 146–7; Welter, *Weg*, pp. 3, 11.

[39] Edward L. Homze, *Arming the Luftwaffe: The Reich Air Ministry and the German Aircraft Industry, 1919–1939* (Lincoln, Neb., 1976), pp. 192–3.

[40] Tim Mason, "The Primacy of Politics," in Turner (ed.), *Nazism and the Third Reich*, pp. 183, 190, 193; and Barkai, *Wirtschaftssystem*, p. 20, which persuasively refutes the distribution of power posited by Schweitzer in *Big Business in the Third Reich* and his other publications.

of the *Völkischer Beobachter* could boast in 1936 that "where capitalism considers itself still untouched, it is, in fact, already harnessed
to politics. . . . National Socialist economic policy corresponds to the
technical age. It lets capitalism run as the motor, uses its dynamic
energies, but shifts the gears."[41]

Though evocative, analogies with conscription and automobile
transmissions fail to do justice to what the Nazis had wrought by
1936. It is perhaps more accurate to say that, to German industry, the
emergent economic system was still capitalism, but only in the same
sense that for a professional gambler poker remains poker, even when
the house shuffles, deals, determines the ante and the wild cards, and
can change them at will, even when there is a ceiling on winnings,
which may be spent only as the casino permits and for the most part
only on the premises. Historians generally do not believe that these
changes in the rules amounted to a change in the game.[42] As accelerated rearmament and full employment intensified the struggle over
chips, more and more contemporaries thought otherwise.[43]

How and to what extent IG Farben proved a willing mark for this
sort of cardsharping are the main questions behind the following two
chapters. Chapter 3 describes the means by which the developing Nazi
state coaxed and cowed IG into line during 1933–4. Though in many
respects the firm attempted to continue doing business as usual, a
mixture of habit, fear, complacence, and satisfaction among IG's leaders gave rise to a policy of "howling with the wolves."[44] Chapter 4
details the concern's subsequent attempts to redefine and assert its
commercial interests within the new economic and political context.
In this regard, Farben encountered considerable difficulties, less with
the man often treated as both business's guardian and IG's antagonist
in the early Third Reich, Hjalmar Schacht, than with the military
procurement offices and a new coterie of Nazi economic policy
makers. Convinced that the Party men were on the ascent and dan-

41 F. Nonnenbruch, *Die dynamische Wirtschaft* (München, 1936), pp. 42–3.
42 For example, Fritz Blaich, "Wirtschaftspolitik und Wirtschaftsverfassung im Dritten
Reich," *Aus Politik und Zeitgeschichte*, no. 8 (20.II.71), pp. 3–12.
43 See, for example, "V," "The Destruction of Capitalism in Germany," *Foreign Affairs*, 15 (1937), pp. 595–607; Frieda Wunderlich, "Germany's Defense Economy
and the Decay of Capitalism," *QJE*, 52 (1938), pp. 401–30; Graham Hutton,
"German Economic Tension: Causes and Results," *Foreign Affairs*, 52 (1939), pp.
524–38; and Peter Drucker, *The End of Economic Man* (New York, 1939), especially pp. 129–66.
44 Testimony of Kurt Krüger, NMT, vol. 7, p. 445.

gerous, IG tried to tack cautiously between them and Schacht while seeking a reliable means of counteracting their influence. As both chapters make clear, neither the government nor the firm forgot during these years that their interests were, at best, merely compatible. Theirs was a relationship of convenience, held together by each side's wager that over time the terms of cooperation would shift in its favor.[45]

---

[45] For a succinct, contemporaneous description of business–state relations in this period, see the letter of a junior official in the RGI to his sister on 10.VII.35, reprinted in Rolf Lahr, *Zeuge von Fall und Aufstieg. Private Briefe 1934–1974* (Hamburg, 1981), p. 30.

3. Revolution and reflation

During the first eighteen months of his projected Thousand Year Reich, Adolf Hitler executed a "coup d'etat by installments."[1] Its rapidity stunned most Germans and may have surprised the Nazi chieftains themselves.[2] Luck contributed in countless ways to the NSDAP's success, yet it seems in retrospect almost foreordained, aptly summarized by two French clichés: *faute de mieux* and *sauve qui peut*. Most Germans were exhausted by the Depression, confused by the Party's fork-tongued propaganda, intimidated by the thuggery of the SA, and afraid of civil war. Not yet willing to vote for the Nazis, neither was a popular majority disposed to fight them. Somewhat desperately, people deluded themselves according to their partisan persuasions. Communists predicted that openly fascist rule would hasten the proletarian revolution, and Socialists expected, at worst, a period of self-defeating repression à la Bismarck. Catholics, the established elites, and adherents of the various bourgeois factions counted on a variety of influences to domesticate the NSDAP: governing responsibility, the army, President Hindenburg, Vice-Chancellor von Papen, and the preponderance of non-Nazis in the coalition cabinet named on January 30, 1933. Unable any longer to imagine, let alone forge, an alternative political combination that could break the deadlock in the Reichstag, the leaders of all these parties and groups surrendered the political initiative. Under such circumstances, the Nazis had little difficulty crushing or coopting one potential center of opposition after another during 1933. Among the nation's major institutions, only the army emerged intact for the moment and capable of exacting a price for its support. The result was the Röhm Purge of mid-1934 by which Hitler propitiated the generals, ensured his succession to Hindenburg, and capped the Nazi conquest of power.

1 Konrad Heiden, *Der Fuehrer* (New York, 1944), p. 529.
2 See Gordon Craig, *Germany 1866–1945* (New York, 1980), pp. 569–70; and Hans Mommsen, "The Political Effects of the Reichstag Fire," in Turner (ed.), *Nazism and the Third Reich*, pp. 109–50.

Though big business escaped the worst of Nazi "coordination," it did not survive the regime's formative period unscathed. Throughout 1933–4, the new rulers initiated industry in "the carrot-and-stick principle that was the de facto constitutional premise of the Third Reich." They thereby completed what the long economic and political crisis had begun: the "conclusive demoralization" – in both senses of that word – "of the industrialists."[3] Alternately bribed and bullied, businessmen descended into increasing collaboration with the Nazi state.

The prototypical step in this process occurred on February 20, 1933, scarcely three weeks after Hitler took office. The occasion was a meeting at the Reichstag President's Palace in Berlin, to which Hermann Göring attracted some two dozen corporate barons with telegrams promising that "the Reich Chancellor will explain his policies."[4] To the four invited members of IG's *Vorstand*, Göring's invitation cannot have been unwelcome. None of the concern's leaders had played any role in arranging the new government; none knew quite what to expect of it. Probably most of them regarded the political turn of events with mixed feelings. Such comfort as they derived from the prominence of Papen and the NSDAP's minority position in the cabinet was offset by the reappointment of the interventionist Gereke as commissioner of work creation, by the replacement of Warmbold as minister of economics with Alfred Hugenberg, and by the turmoil in the streets, factories, and government offices caused by the jubilant Nazis. Yet if the auguries were disquieting, even more so was the probable effect on economic confidence, which was showing fragile signs of revival, should a fourth cabinet collapse within less than a year.[5]

Always desirous of being on good terms with Berlin and both more

---

[3] For both quotations, see Schoenbaum, *Social Revolution*, p. 277.

[4] D-201, Göring to Krupp von Bohlen und Halbach, 16.II.33, *NMT*, vol. 7, p. 557. The surviving sources give varying figures for the number of people in attendance: EC-439, Affidavit by Georg von Schnitzler, undated, *NMT*, vol. 7, pp. 555–6, refers to "about 20 persons"; D-204, Memorandum by Gustav Krupp, 22.II.33, *NMT*, vol. 7, p. 562, mentions "approximately 25 industrialists present"; Blank to Reusch, 21.II.33, in Dirk Stegmann, *AfS*, 13 (1973), Document 18, pp. 477–80, lists 19 attendees; and Springorum to Reusch, 21.II.33, in the same article, Document 19, pp. 480–1, refers to "all 27 men who were present," but adds only one name to the roster provided by Blank.

[5] K. D. Bracher, *Die Auflösung der Weimarer Republik*, 5th ed. (Villingen, 1971), pp. 203–4; Karl Hardach, *The Political Economy of Germany in the Twentieth Century* (Berkeley, Calif., 1980), p. 59.

curious and more nervous than usual about this latest change in government, IG sent Georg von Schnitzler to hear the new chancellor on February 20. Gustav Stein, the head of the Gewerkschaft Auguste-Victoria, reportedly also represented the concern.[6] Like most of the other executives present, IG's men probably hoped that the gathering would lay the groundwork for a mutually satisfactory relationship between the corporate community and an orderly and stable government. Signaling its terms for such a relationship, the *Präsidium* of the Reichsverband der deutschen Industrie (RDI) had concluded its sessions on February 17 by issuing a communiqué that made business's support for the new coalition contingent on a clarification of its economic program and proof that "disturbances of domestic order and social peace would be avoided."[7] During the following three days, Gustav Krupp, the president of the Reichsverband, elaborated industry's desires in a memorandum he prepared for the meeting at Göring's house. Calling for a clear "demarcation line between the state and the economy," Krupp tactfully summarized his colleague's "misgivings" about the new rulers' initial policies toward the economy and the civil service.[8] But if Krupp and the other guests went to the session of February 20 expecting some give and take, they got a sort quite different from what they had bargained for.

Hitler made a point of shaking hands with each member of the audience and then talked for about ninety minutes.[9] Speaking without pause or notes and apparently at the top of his form, the führer largely

6 EC-439, Schnitzler's affidavit, *NMT*, vol. 7, p. 555. Bosch certainly was not present, contrary to Tammen's assertion in *I. G. Farbenindustrie*, p. 293. William Manchester's claim that four IG Farben directors sat immediately behind Krupp at the meeting is typically careless; see *The Arms of Krupp* (New York, 1970), p. 406. Aside from Schnitzler's affidavit, none of the sources listed in footnote 4 mentions the presence of Stein.

7 *Schulthess' Europäischer Geschichtskalender*, Bd. 74 (1933), p. 48. HA Krupp FAH IV E203, contains the official report of the meetings of the *Präsidium* and the *Vorstand*, dated 18.II.33.

8 *NMT*, Case X, Bülow II/182, Notes of the Business Management of the National Association of German Industry for the Conference at Reich Minister Göring's on 20 February 1933, undated. See the discussion in Gerhard Schulz, *Die Anfänge des totalitären Massnahmestaates*, Part II of K. D. Bracher, G. Schulz, and W. Sauer, *Die nationalsozialistische Machtergreifung*, paperback ed. (Frankfurt, 1974), pp. 315–16.

9 My account of the meeting rests on the sources cited in footnote 4, as well as on D-203, a report of Hitler's remarks found in Krupp's files, *NMT*, vol. 7, pp. 557–62; and NI-406, extract from the interrogation of Hjalmar Schacht, 20.VII.45, *NMT*, vol. 7, p. 563. See also PS-2828, Walter Funk's interrogation, 26.VI.45, *IMT*, vol. 13 pp. 40, 141; and Louis Lochner, *Tycoons and Tyrant* (Chicago, 1954), pp. 143–7.

followed the pattern of his previous statements directed at businessmen.[10] The Jews went unmentioned. Alluding to rearmament but briefly, he contented himself with an emphasis on the need for martial spirit ("*Wehrhaftigkeit*") and with the assertions that "only a martial nation can have a flourishing economy" and that Germany alone would decide "the question of the restoration of the Wehrmacht," an obvious reference to the stalled disarmament negotiations in Geneva.[11] On specific economic matters, according to one contemporary account, "he said relatively little."[12] Hitler merely reiterated his conviction that "economics and politics cannot be separated," his commitment to the rights of private property and inheritance, and his opposition to the social and economic leveling promoted by democracy and Marxism.[13] The bulk of the speech consisted of a depiction of recent German history as a losing battle between "creative and decomposing forces," a struggle that had now reached the point where "salvation from the Communist danger is possible only through the NSDAP."[14]

Most of the assembled industrialists had heard all of this before without falling in behind the Nazi movement. Indeed, had solid connections between German big business and Hitler already existed, the meeting of February 20 would have been unnecessary. Therefore, the führer added one relatively new element to his set speech. The time had come, he apparently decided, to show the businessmen that their wish for stability gave him, not them, the whip hand. Turning to the topic of the parliamentary balloting scheduled for March 5, the Nazi leader set his sights on obtaining an absolute majority for his coalition and warned:

We stand before the last election. Regardless of the outcome, there will be no retreat. . . . One way or another, if the election does not decide, the decision simply will have to be brought about by other means. . . . There are only two possibilities, either to crowd back the opponent on constitutional grounds . . .

[10] See Turner, *JMH*, 40 (1968), pp. 348–74; the report of Hitler's speech to the Nationalklub von 1919 in Hamburg on 1.XII.30, in Werner Jochmann (ed.), *Nationalsozialismus und Revolution* (Frankfurt, 1963), Document 99, pp. 309–14; Adolf Hitler, *Vortrag Adolf Hitlers vor westdeutschen Wirtschaftlern im Industrie-Klub Düsseldorf* (München, 1932), excerpted in Erhard Klöss (ed.), *Reden des Führers* (Köln, 1967), pp. 55–74.
[11] D-203, *NMT*, vol. 7, p. 561; Blank to Reusch, 21.II.33, *AfS*, p. 479.
[12] Blank to Reusch, 21.II.33, *AfS*, p. 478.
[13] Ibid.; D-203, *NMT*, vol. 7, pp. 558–60.
[14] D-203, *NMT*, vol. 7, p. 560; Blank to Reusch, *AfS*, p. 479.

or a struggle will be conducted with other weapons, which may demand greater sacrifices.[15]

Having presented his listeners with the stark choice between his government's victory at the polls and the prospect of civil war, Hitler sat down.

Perhaps this ultimatum or perhaps simply the length of the chancellor's address persuaded Gustav Krupp to revise his hopes for the meeting. In any case, rising to reply to the Party's führer, Krupp abandoned his prepared statement and announced that "it would not be advisable to enter into a detailed discussion." Instead, he thanked Hitler briefly in terms both courtly and ambiguous enough to warrant the steelmaker's pride in his training as a diplomat.[16] His deftness, however, did not bring the evening to an end.

Hermann Göring now took the floor to reassure the businessmen and to unveil the hidden agenda of the meeting. Promising that after the election the "domestic economy would also quiet down" and that in the cabinet "the distribution of forces would remain the same," the Reichstag president brought up the matter of the NSDAP's need for money with which to wage the campaign.[17] Because the government would refrain from employing state funds for this purpose, Göring suggested that "business should carry the burden of this struggle as befits its position." He softened this blow by commenting in conclusion that "the sacrifices asked for surely would be so much easier for industry to bear if it realized that the election of 5 March would certainly be the last one for the next ten years, probably even for the next hundred years."[18] In other words, in return for business's help, Göring offered an indefinite "cabinet of national concentration" in which the Nazis would remain a minority.

After Hitler and Göring departed, Hjalmar Schacht finished the shakedown of the executives. Leaving nothing to chance, he proposed a formula for raising a campaign chest of 3 million reichsmarks. The Ruhr iron and coal industries were assessed 1 million marks, the chemical, potash, and brown coal producers 500,000 each, and the

---

[15] D-203, NMT, vol. 7, p. 561. Cf. Blank's report that "one will not let oneself be pushed from power, if the goal of an absolute majority is not reached" (AfS, p. 479).
[16] D-204, Memo by Krupp, 22.II.33, NMT, vol. 7, p. 562.
[17] D-203, NMT, vol. 7, pp. 561–2.
[18] Springorum to Reusch, 21.II.33, AfS, p. 481; D-203, NMT, vol. 7, p. 562.

electrical, auto, and machinery firms the remaining 500,000.[19] Although the industrialists accepted Schacht's idea readily in principle, Fritz Springorum and other representatives of heavy industry suggested two provisos. These men wanted all other claims for political contributions canceled out by this collection and its proceeds apportioned on the basis of relative parliamentary strength between the NSDAP and the Kampffront Schwarz-Weiss-Rot, a loose electoral alliance of the DNVP, the Stahlhelm, and Vice-Chancellor von Papen. Schacht agreed and apparently also conceded that recent donations to the components of the Kampffront might be deducted from a firm's obligations.[20] Within six weeks, 2.6 million marks were credited to the fund drive, from which the NSDAP received just more than 1.9 million, or 72.9% of the total. The Kampffront split the balance between the DNVP (536,500 marks, or 20.4%) and a special fund controlled by Papen (177,500 marks, or 6.7%).[21] Thus, the NSDAP seems to have netted slightly less than two-thirds of the 3 million marks it set out to obtain.[22]

Lacking the authority to commit the concern's funds, IG's Schnitzler left on February 20 without having pledged a contribution.[23] A day or two later, he recounted the meeting to Carl Bosch, who purportedly "shrugged his shoulders" in reply.[24] Apparently without convening

[19] Blank to Reusch, *AfS*, p. 480.

[20] Ibid.; Springorum to Reusch, *AfS*, p. 481.

[21] This distribution was calculated from the figures provided by NI-391, Entries in the account "National Trusteeship" found in the files of Delbrueck, Schickler Co. Bank, *NMT*, vol. 7, pp. 567–8, and the following documents in BA Koblenz, NL 231, Bd. 38, Bl. 230–42: Schacht to Hugenberg, 3.III.33; Scheibe to Hugenberg, 15.III.33; Hugenberg to Papen, 19.III.33; Schacht to Mann, 15.III.33; and Hugenberg to Schacht, 19.III.33.

[22] Possibly Schacht took in during April an additional 500,000 to 600,000 marks, which he later transmitted to Joachim von Ribbentrop. However, no records have surfaced to confirm Schacht's recollection to this effect, and the rest of his testimony concerning February 20 has proved thoroughly inaccurate. See NI-9550, Affidavit by H. Schacht, 12.VIII.47, *NMT*, vol. 7, p. 564. In 1933, Ribbentrop headed a special *Dienststelle* for foreign affairs as part of Rudolf Hess's staff. The fact that this office was later funded from the Adolf Hitler Spende exacted from business may be the source of Schacht's confusion; see Paul Seabury, *The Wilhelmstrasse* (Berkeley, Calif., 1954), p. 52. In his *Confessions of "The Old Wizard"* (Cambridge, Mass., 1956), p. 276, Schacht also refers to an initially unused "balance of six hundred thousand marks" but says nothing of its eventual destination.

[23] EC-439, Schnitzler's affidavit, *NMT*, vol. 7, p. 556; cf. Blank to Reusch, 21.III.33, *AfS*, p. 480: "For the chemical industry . . . no assent could yet be given." Schnitzler contended that Stein of the Gewerkschaft Auguste-Victoria urged the inclusion of the DVP among the beneficiaries of the campaign fund, but no other source confirms this request, and the financial records indicate that the DVP was not cut in.

[24] EC-439, Schnitzler's affidavit, *NMT*, vol. 7, p. 566.

the Central Committee or the Kalle circle, Bosch subsequently decided
that financing Hitler and Papen was preferable to offending them or to
another government crisis and the possibility of more fighting in the
streets and perhaps even in the plants.[25] On February 27, the morning
before the Reichstag burned, IG deposited 400,000 reichsmarks to the
fund controlled by Schacht, from which the money went to various
Nazi Party accounts.[26] Sometime between then and March 15, the
concern sent another 100,000 marks to Vice-Chancellor von Papen,
thereby cutting Hugenberg and the DNVP entirely out of IG's donation.[27] Germany's largest corporation thus made the largest campaign
gift of any single firm. At half a million reichsmarks, the sum still fell
short of the combine's customary political contributions in election
years and of the amount probably granted to the Hindenburg reelection effort a year earlier.[28] By complying with the Nazi demand for
protection money, providing exactly the amount Schacht designated,
and snubbing the proagrarian Nationalists, Bosch implied his motives.
He was practicing IG's usual politics, trying to insure his firm against
instability, to demonstrate that Farben remained "*immer regierungstreu*," and to move the German government toward policies tolerable
to his enterprise.

For the remainder of 1933, and far beyond, neither IG Farben nor
the Nazis varied their tactics much from those delineated during the
episode surrounding February 20. Certainly Hitler encouraged a tendency in parts of the German upper classes to fix on him as the reliable
pole amidst an unruly and dangerous movement.[29] On March 2, the
führer declared that civil liberties would return once the Communist
danger had disappeared.[30] He told the Reichstag on March 23 that he

25 The ZA did not meet between January 25 and March 2. The minutes of the session
on the latter date make no mention of the donation but note that a thorough political
discussion was held (NI-1941/18). Christian Schneider later stated that he could not
recall the AA discussing the contribution at the time (*NMT*, vol. 7, p. 623). No trace
of a discussion by the Kalle circle or even with its namesake shows up in the
surviving documentation, and after the war, Lammers denied that the group met
during this period.
26 NI-391, Selck and Bangert to Delbrueck, Schickler & Co., 27.II.33, *NMT*, vol. 7, p.
565.
27 BA Koblenz, NL 231, Bd. 38, Scheibe to Hugenberg, 15.III.33, and Schacht to
Mann, 15.III.33.
28 On IG's previous contributions, see Chapter 2.
29 Hans Mommsen, "Zur Verschränkung traditioneller und faschistischer Führungsgruppen in Deutschland beim Übergang von der Bewegungs- zur Systemphase," in
W. Schieder (ed.), *Faschismus als soziale Bewegung* (Hamburg, 1976), p. 165.
30 Craig, *Germany 1866–1945*, p. 575.

favored "increased encouragement of private initiative and the recognition of property" and stressed that "nothing is more foreign to the government than opposition to exports."[31] At the end of May, having rid himself of Gereke, Hitler requested the advice of several top industrialists, Carl Bosch among them, concerning government work creation policy. No doubt the chancellor pleased them with the remark that "the burden of corporate taxation during the next five years will not be allowed to exceed the level of 1932"; hence, public expenditures for social welfare must fall.[32] Six weeks later, the creation of the Generalrat der Wirtschaft seemed to institutionalize regular consultation between the regime and business leaders.[33] Perhaps most important, on March 10, April 22, and July 6, Hitler spoke out against eruptions of economic radicalism among the Party rank and file.[34] However, he either could or would not swiftly enforce his admonitions, and even in the most widely noted of these addresses, that to the Reichsstatthalter in July, he explained his restraint in somewhat ominous terms:

It is not permissible to dismiss a business leader when he is a good business leader but not a National Socialist. . . . In the economy, only efficiency may be decisive. . . . one should not rummage around to see if something more is to be revolutionized; rather we have the task of securing one position after another in order to hold them and gradually to fill them exemplarily. We must therefore adjust our methods over many years and calculate in quite large time periods.[35]

When Alfred Hugenberg brought himself down – much to the pleasure of Carl Bosch and other industrialists – with some ill-considered demands at the London Economic Conference in June, Hitler acted on his own advice.[36] He named Kurt Schmitt, the head of the nation's

---

[31] Quoted in Fritz Meystre (ed.), *Sozialismus, wie ihn der Führer sieht* (München, 1935), p. 43; Barkai, *Wirtschaftssystem*, p. 137.

[32] Quoted in Hallgarten and Radkau, *Deutsche Industrie*, p. 238.

[33] Martin Broszat, *Der Staat Hitlers* (München, 1969), p. 219.

[34] Udo Wengst, "Der Reichsverband der deutschen Industrie in den ersten Monaten des Dritten Reiches," *VfZ*, 28 (1980), p. 97; Orlow, *Nazi Party, 1933–1945*, pp. 51–2.

[35] Quoted in Schoenbaum, *Social Revolution*, p. 49, and Meystre, *Sozialismus*, p. 53. For the same passage, rendered slightly differently, see J. Noakes and G. Pridham, *Documents on Nazism* (New York, 1975), p. 204.

[36] For an indication of the intensified opposition to Hugenberg among German big businessmen, see SAA 4/Lf 676, Robert Bosch to Siemens, 29.V.33, an attempt to organize an industrialists' petition to President Hindenburg for the removal of the economics minister. Carl Bosch's name appeared on the list of prospective signers, since his distaste for Hugenberg was well known and unabated.

largest insurance firm, as the new economics minister but also used the opportunity to insert the NSDAP's chief economic theorist, Gottfried Feder, as one of Schmitt's two state secretaries. Veteran Nazis now held the second-ranking positions in the Economics and Finance Ministries. The führer's comments and choices reflected his desire to calm the surging revolution from below, not to halt that from above.

The distinction was good enough for most German executives. Harassed during the spring by continuous demands for money from Nazi organizations and confronted with an invasion of the headquarters of the RDI by Party activists demanding a purge of that body, businessmen were only too eager to make such high-pressure tactics seem superfluous. "In order . . . to avoid worse," as Hugenberg advised, Gustav Krupp presided over a restructuring of the Reichsverband and a cleansing of its staff so as, in his words, "to bring the organization into agreement with the political goals of the Reich." On June 16, the RDI merged with the Verein deutscher Arbeitgeberverbände and formally disappeared into the Reichsstand der deutschen Industrie (RSI) with Krupp as president.[37] Other industrialists took the lead in establishing a central and predictable Party fund-raising mechanism, also inaugurated in June, the Adolf Hitler Spende der deutschen Wirtschaft.[38] Under the new system, intended to last for one year only, corporations were to make quarterly payments totaling one-half of 1% of their annual wage and salary bills and to receive in return a certificate exempting them from further political contributions.[39] Though this enormous exaction came to 30 million reichsmarks in 1933–4, it did not, in fact, deter appeals from fervid local Party functionaries, whom most firms prudently continued to oblige.[40]

Involved only peripherally in these attempts to buy off the NSDAP,

37 Wengst, VfZ, 28 (1980), pp. 101–10; Reinhard Neebe, Grossindustrie, Staat and NSDAP 1930–1933 (Göttingen, 1981), pp. 181–8. For an overview of the resulting structure, see Cuno Horkenbach, Das Deutsche Reich von 1918 bis Heute, Jahrgang 1932 (Berlin, 1933), pp. 579–80. HA Krupp FAH IV C205, Krupp to Bosch, 12.IV.33, reply of the following day, and Krupp to Bosch, 19.V.33, establish that the two men were in constant contact concerning the reorganization, but Bosch's advice is not recorded. When Jacob Herle was forced out as the business manager of the Reichsverband, he became a member of the managing board of the IG-controlled WASAG; Curt Duisberg, Nur ein Sohn (Stuttgart, 1981), p. 178.
38 M892/16, D-151, Assorted Documents on the Adolf Hitler Spende, early 1933; Tammen, I. G. Farbenindustrie, pp. 302–3.
39 Bayer 13/11, v. 2, Beratungspunkte ZA-Sitzung vom 12.VI.33, Anlage 3, 8.VI.33.
40 Orlow, Nazi Party, 1933–1945, pp. 65, 76; Lochner, Tycoons, p. 123; Bayer 13/11, v. 2, ZA Büro to Duisberg and ZA members, 25.VI.34.

IG's own initial concessions to Party pressure resulted from the Nazis' prompt assault on the Jews. During March, as foreign newspapers reported the increasing frequency and violence of anti-Semitic incidents across the Reich, indignation mounted abroad, along with calls for boycotts of German exports, salesmen, and shipping. Typically, the Party excused the viciousness of its faithful as a legitimate, understandable response to unprincipled opponents, in this case mendacious perpetrators of "atrocity propaganda." As a "defense measure," the NSDAP scheduled a preemptive German boycott of Jewish businesses and professional people for April 1. Once more, Hitler contrived to sound both responsible and menacing. He justified the boycott as a necessary method of venting explosive public fury at the Jews but threatened worse measures in the event that the "Jewish war against Germany" continued overseas.[41]

IG could not calmly contemplate the prospect of a cycle of persecutions and foreign reprisals. Many of the firm's principal administrators and researchers were Jewish, most notably four of the eight members of the *Verwaltungsrat,* including Ernst von Simson, one of the principal targets of the Party's move against the Reichsverband.[42] The concern earned 54% of its total sales income abroad in 1932, including 74% of that from dyes and 72% of that from pharmaceuticals.[43] Nor could the hostage German Jewish community afford to take Hitler's warning lightly. Thus, at the end of March, several national and regional Jewish organizations and the Bayer pharmaceutical sales combine of IG were among the numerous German groups that succumbed to government pressure and wrote their foreign affiliates denying that disorder and mistreatment of Jews were widespread in Germany.[44] Wilhelm R. Mann's letter to the Bayer sales agents in seventy-five countries reflected the seriousness with which the concern viewed the situation. In an effort to enlist the sympathies of the recipients, Mann credited the new regime in Germany with "a

[41] Helmut Genschel, *Die Verdrängung der Juden aus der Wirtschaft im Dritten Reich* (Göttingen, 1966), pp. 44–7; Karl A. Schleunes, *The Twisted Road to Auschwitz* (Urbana, Ill., 1970), pp. 62–91.
[42] NI-7957/66, Affidavit by H. Bässler, 17.VII.47; on Simson, see Wengst, *VfZ,* 28 (1980), p. 102, and Lochner, *Tycoons,* p. 157.
[43] Defense Basic Information II/6, pp. 33, 35; II/8, p. 38.
[44] Genschel, *Verdrängung,* pp. 47–8, especially note 18. See also SAA 4/Lf676, Carl Friedrich von Siemens's letter of 8.IV.33; and GHH 400 109/66, the GHH's letters of 1.IV.33 and 3.IV.33, along with similar letters from trade associations.

IG's headquarters on the Grüneburg, Frankfurt a.M., ca. 1931. (*Source:* Firmenarchiv der Hoechst AG, Frankfurt-Hoechst)

victory against bolshevism, the enemy of the entire world." As to the impending boycott, Mann toed the Party line, regretting "that the conduct of certain elements abroad" had provoked what he hoped would be merely a temporary "retaliatory action in Germany against Jewish businesses." He requested his representatives to put an end to the crisis by calming opinion in their respective nations.[45] Thus, in responding publicly to the boycott of April 1, at least one division of IG fell into a common Nazi trap, participating in a lesser evil on pain of promoting a greater one. In private negotiations, however, the concern ventured a slightly stronger stand.

Carl Bosch opposed Nazi anti-Semitism on both personal and professional grounds. Several Jews were among his closest colleagues in 1933, including Edmund Pietrkowski, the vice-chairman and managing director of the Chemie Verein, and Ernst Schwarz, Bosch's secre-

---

[45] Mann II/525, Mann to Hauser, 29.III.33, *NMT*, vol. 7, pp. 649–50. On compliance with Mann's letter, see, e.g., NI-9898/82, Siering to Pharma Leverkusen, 13.IV.33 and 20.IV.33.

tary for the preceding fifteen years and the son of a rabbi.[46] Fearful for their future, Bosch also worried that attacks on the Jews would harm IG's exports and result in a debilitating exodus of Jewish scientists from Germany. During April, two events confirmed his fears: Hermann Schmitz's report on a recent trip to the United States, and the fate of Fritz Haber, a baptized Jew and Bosch's old research partner. Though exempt from a new law excluding most Jews from Prussian government employ, Haber felt honor-bound to resign his chair at the University of Berlin and, two months later, to leave Germany.[47] Bosch reacted by lobbying the Prussian authorities and several Jewish academicians individually in an effort to retain their services for the various scientific institutes organized under the Kaiser-Wilhelm Gesellschaft, which IG had long patronized.[48] He also decided, after accepting an invitation to call at the Chancellery during May, to raise the "Jewish question" with the führer directly. The resulting conversation permanently poisoned relations between the two men. According to Bosch's own, unconfirmed report, as he discreetly outlined the side effects of the Party's racism, Hitler grew furious, then silenced the executive by snapping that he understood nothing of politics and that Germany would, if necessary, "work one hundred years without physics and chemistry." The Nazi leader allegedly concluded his tirade by ringing for his adjutant and announcing brusquely, "The *Geheimrat* wishes to leave."[49]

---

[46] Lochner, *Tycoons*, pp. 44–5; Schmitz I/8, Affidavit by K. Holdermann, 6.III.47.

[47] Haber's resignation letter of 30.IV.33 appears in Rudolf Stern, "Fritz Haber," *Leo Baeck Institute Yearbook*, 8 (1963), p. 99.

[48] BASF W1, transcriptions of von Laue to Bosch, 22.IV.33; Bosch to Fräulein Meitner, 26.IV.33; Bosch to Gerullis of the Prussian Kultusministerium, 26.IV.33.

[49] See Joseph Borkin, *The Crime and Punishment of I. G. Farben* (New York, 1978), pp. 56–8, 115, which slightly expands on the rather worshipful work of a former employee in IG's Patent Section, Karl Holdermann: *Im Banne der Chemie. Carl Bosch, Leben und Werk* (Düsseldorf, 1953), pp. 271–3. His source was one Dr. Willstätter, a Jewish chemistry professor at Munich and Nobel Laureate. Heinrich Gattineau, *Durch die Klippen des 20. Jahrhunderts* (Stuttgart, 1983), pp. 113–14, repeats the story, noting that he never saw Bosch so "aroused" as on the day he met Hitler. A tale remarkably similar to Holdermann's was current in German academic circles by 1937, only the physicist Max Planck, not Bosch, was Hitler's reported interlocutor; see the recounting in Edward Y. Hartshorne, *The German Universities and National Socialism* (London, 1937), pp. 111–12. However, in the *Physikalische Blätter*, 3 (1947), p. 143, Planck recalled discussing Haber and the Jews with Hitler in the spring of 1933 and quoted the Nazi leader's remarks verbatim. These do not tally with either Holdermann's narrative or the rumor of 1937 as restated by Hartshorne. It appears, then, that Hartshorne falsely telescoped two similar and almost simultaneous confrontations into one and ascribed it to Planck, as does Alan

Perhaps Bosch's clash with Hitler had something to do with a simultaneous falling-out between Heinrich Hoerlein of IG's pharmaceutical division and a leader of the SA. Shortly after Hitler's accession, Hoerlein claimed in 1947, he began canvassing various Nazi officials in search of one who could dissuade the führer from crippling IG's drug research by keeping his promise to ban experimentation with animals, which the Party linked to ritual slaughter.[50] Hoerlein's quest led to Ernst Röhm's adjutant, Standartenführer Julius Uhl, who paid an affable visit to IG's laboratories at Elberfeld. But when Hoerlein tried to capitalize on this contact some weeks later, Uhl vehemently turned on the concern. After denouncing IG for inventing and selling tropical medicines that benefited only the usurpers of Germany's former colonies, Uhl proclaimed, according to Hoerlein, "that he wished to have nothing more to do with us, that we were not only an international Jewish undertaking, but simply traitors . . . [and that] in the future, we should be dealt with in quite a different manner." Stunned, the IG executive could ascribe Uhl's striking change of attitude only to the intervention of Hitler.[51]

In any case, having learned that talking to Hitler on the subject of Jews was like talking to a wall, Bosch wrote a sympathetic letter to Haber and regretfully inaugurated what became Farben's fairly standard internal response to Nazi racism. Schwarz and Pietrkowski went into paid exile, the former as head of IG's troubled Agfa-Ansco subsidiary in New York, the latter under contract to aid the concern's export efforts from Switzerland.[52] Simson and most other Jewish members of the governing boards stayed on; Bosch persevered in his efforts to protect Jewish scientists and compensate those driven out of

Beyerchen in *Scientists under Hitler* (New Haven, Conn., 1977), pp. 40–3. Borkin considers the Planck meeting a sequel to Bosch's; so do David Nachmansohn in a passing reference in his *German-Jewish Pioneers in Science 1900–1933* (New York, 1979), p. 175; K. Mendelssohn in *The World of Walther Nernst* (Pittsburgh, Pa., 1973), pp. 146, 148; and I.

50 For an illustration of this connection, see W. S. Allen, *The Nazi Seizure of Power* (Chicago, 1965), p. 51.

51 NI-6787/52, Affidavit by H. Hoerlein, 2.V.47.

52 The letter and Haber's reply appear in Holdermann, *Im Banne der Chemie*, pp. 270–1. On Schwarz, see Schmitz I/8, Affidavit by Holdermann. After World War II, Schwarz wrote a short, spirited defense of IG (RG242/T83, Reel 88, Frames 3460765–81). The Agfa Company's commercial difficulties dated from 1931 and are recorded in NI-1941/18, ZA meetings of 11.IX.31, 24.III.32, and 5.IX.32. On Pietrkowski, see BASF W1, Pietrkowski to Bosch, 9.VI.33, with the enclosed deposition for Bosch's signature.

the country; and the combine's executives did not shrink from paying public homage to Jews like Haber and Arthur von Weinberg, who had served Farben. The concern, however, fearing export losses and trying to offset its "Jewish" reputation among Nazis, continued to echo the Party's excuses for racial incidents to the outside world.[53]

While this crisis unfolded, IG Farben felt pressure to conform to the new Germany on several other fronts. Trivial but symbolic was the experience of Anton Reithinger, the chief of the Vowi section, whose monthly dinner club asked him in June to declare his support for the present trend in state policy as a condition for receiving further invitations from the group. Reithinger replied rather stiffly that he had always been a patriot.[54] More seriously, in April the regime added a new dimension to its political scare tactics by ordering costly and disruptive air raid exercises at IG's westernmost works. Hans Kühne, the manager at Leverkusen, set the general tone for the concern's response when he told the other factory heads that "only such steps are to be taken which can be forced on the plants. Above all, everyone is to remain calm and not to exaggerate the matter."[55] But within a month, IG's most vulnerable production sites were engaged in full-scale planning for defense against air attack.[56] On other matters, IG tried to make a virtue of necessity. After the government preempted May 1 as an official "holiday of industrial labor," Kühne added his own proclamation calling on "all colleagues and associates to join the rally on this day of demonstration and thus prove our will to cooperate."[57] Another bow to the inevitable followed a few weeks later, as the management at Leverkusen said it would "welcome" a "suitable

---

[53] See, e.g., BASF W1, Thum to Bosch, 5.V.33; Wilmanns to Bosch, 4.VII.33; Hochheim's handwritten notes, 19.IV.34; Grimm to Bosch, 22.IV.34; von Laue to Hochheim, 5.XII.34; Bodenstein to Bosch, 21.I.35; and Paschen to Bosch, 31.I.35. See also Lochner, *Tycoons*, p. 45; Friedrich Glum, *Zwischen Wissenschaft, Wirtschaft und Politik* (Bonn, 1964), pp. 487–91; Holdermann, *Im Banne der Chemie*, p. 285; Duisberg, *Nur ein Sohn*, p. 188; Beyerchen, *Scientists*, pp. 66–8; and Hartshorne, *German Universities*, pp. 135, 137. Duisberg apparently made similar efforts; see Gattineau, *Klippen*, p. 63, and Duisberg, *Nur ein Sohn*, p. 183. For a particularly distasteful example of rhetorical collaboration, see the discussion of the Chemie Verein's memo of 29.VI.33 in Neebe, *Grossindustrie*, pp. 195–6.
[54] NI-15145/123, G. Lüttge to Reithinger, 7.VI.33, and reply of the following day.
[55] NI-8461, Conference of Plant Leaders at Leverkusen, 21.VI.33, *NMT*, vol. 7, p. 1226.
[56] See the documents covering 1933–8 compiled in M892/36, Prosecution Book VII, pp. 31–74.
[57] NI-6960, Kühne to Leverkusen employees, 25.IV.33, *NMT*, vol. 7. p. 570.

representation" of the Nazi Factory Cell Organization (NSBO) at the plant.[58] Finally, as early as March 2, IG's Central Committee recognized that managerial hirings and promotions had become politically delicate, and it therefore "decided to postpone the handling of personnel matters for some months."[59] Equivalent delaying tactics at the factory level were, however, no longer possible by June. On the twenty-first, the concern's Social Welfare Committee rejected a demand by Nazi-dominated workers' committees for "a deciding vote when new employees are engaged" but conceded that the committees might submit nominees for new posts and that "it should be a matter of course" to give preference among those qualified to members of paramilitary organizations such as the SA.[60] This announcement antedated by exactly a week a government decree mandating such preference.[61]

Given the momentum and variety of the Nazi political blitzkriegs from January to June 1933, it is hardly surprising that IG Farben adopted the course of least resistance. Most of the practical businessmen atop the concern simply begged the question of cooperating with an increasingly naked dictatorship, regarding any other course as luxuriously shortsighted.[62] Citing their responsibility to the stockholders and employees or the firm's traditional stance of supposedly apolitical patriotism, these executives saw their choice as one between an embrace and a handshake. The widespread argument that "the ability to adapt oneself to a situation is indeed the central quality of a capitalist businessman" had particular force among those of the combine's leaders who thought their situation resembled that of 1918–19.[63] They believed that their duty was, as Duisberg had said then, "to save what is savable" ("zu retten, was zu retten ist"), if necessary by, in Schnitzler's words after the war, "partaking in the socialistic

58 NI-1091/16, Farben Abteilung Leverkusen to Wahl, 19.V.33.
59 NI-1941/18, ZA meeting of 2.III.33. Thus, Carl Krauch was notified that his naming to the *Vorstand* was being put off "in consideration of the political conditions" (IG in Abw., Personalakte Krauch, Duisberg to Krauch, 2.V.33). The same sense of political uncertainty underlay the concern's unwillingness at this time to extend or renew labor contracts at various plants; see Mason, *Sozialpolitik*, p. 122, note 58.
60 NI-4884, Minutes of the Sozialausschuss, 21.VI.33, *NMT*, vol. 7, pp. 570–1.
61 Wolfgang Sauer, *Die Mobilmachung der Gewalt*, Part 3 of *Die nationalsozialistische Machtergreifung*, paperback ed. (Frankfurt, 1974), p. 278. Cf. Conan Fischer, *Stormtroopers* (Boston, 1983), pp. 96, 98.
62 Testimony of Kurt Krüger, *NMT*, vol. 7, p. 445.
63 Quotation from Fischer, *Nationale Weltwirtschaft?* p. 53.

part of the Hitler program and gaining the confidence of the masses back."[64]

During the May Day celebrations at IG's headquarters at Frankfurt, Erwin Selck made the pragmatists' case for active involvement with the new regime. Reminding his co-workers of the delicacy of social and economic structures, of "how easily they can be torn by inexperienced hands," he emphasized that

the success or failure of this beautiful movement depends considerably on whether upright men or petty spirits lead it. . . . We must create institutions which permit morally and mentally mature men to express encouraging criticism. . . . We must hope that in all the vital positions the right men gradually will appear. On that depends everything.[65]

Max Ilgner, especially, endorsed this line of thought, not least because he saw the need for improved contacts with the NSDAP as his ticket to greater prominence both inside and outside IG. At least a half dozen members of the *Vorstand,* including Gajewski, Mann, Otto, and Oster, as well as Selck and Schnitzler, stood with Ilgner. Diverse in ages, backgrounds, and professional specializations, these men agreed that the concern already had "missed the bus" once and would have to pay for IG's earlier reserve unless they curried favor with the Party and acquired influence over its policies.[66]

Several developments during May and June lent weight to this argument. Without bothering to confer with the combine, Party planners decided that the exceptional capital intensity of the chemical industry justified fixing its donation to the Adolf Hitler Spende at 1.0% of each firm's labor costs, rather than the usual 0.5%. Carl Duisberg's protests secured a compromise that lowered the assessments for the largest chemical firms to the normal level, which still resulted in a bill for IG of 934,000 reichsmarks during 1933–4.[67] That Duisberg had to exert himself at all, however, probably stemmed from another alarming consequence of the changes in business organizations and leadership during these months. The chemical industry's representa-

[64] Bayer 62/94b, Duisberg to Merck, 8.XI.18; NI-5191/38, Affidavit by G. von Schnitzler, 4.III.47.
[65] BA Koblenz, ZSg 127, Bd. 832, "Wovon der Erfolg abhängt," *Frankfurter Zeitung,* 3.V.33. On Selck's view of the Nazis, see Duisberg, *Nur ein Sohn,* p. 190.
[66] NI-4928/36, Affidavit by K. Krüger, 18.III.47; Testimony by Krüger, *NMT,* vol. 7, p. 443.
[67] NI-3799/28, Duisberg's file note, 16.VI.33; Bayer 13/11, vol. 2, Beratungspunkte . . . , Anlage 3, 8.VI.33.

tive on the Spende's Kuratorium and recently installed head of the Employers' Association of the German Chemical Industry did not come from the ranks of IG or any major, like-minded corporation. Although the employers had chosen Carl Bosch as their spokesman, the economics minister dictated, instead, the selection of Albert Pietzsch, a founder of the small Munich Electro-Chemical Works of Höllriegelskreuth. Pietzsch, a financial backer of the NSDAP since 1923, joined the Party in 1927.[68] Moreover, at the end of June, the elevation of Feder brought to the number two position in the Economics Ministry a man who had called in print for public sharing in the profits of large concerns, citing IG Farben as a prime candidate.[69]

Pushed toward collaboration by these events but repelled by the Party's attacks on Jews and the churches, the concern's opportunistic captains took refuge in a highly selective assessment of the Nazis' actions and grab-bag program. Hans Kühne admitted after the war that the regime's promises to create political unity, jobs, and "a sound relationship between employers and workers" had attracted him during 1933 and that he had downplayed the NSDAP's darker side:

I considered it to be quite certain that the radical and less educated elements of the Party would be pushed into the background because they would not be capable of the management of responsible governmental agencies, and I hoped that Hitler would make use of better counsel.[70]

Gajewski claimed to have thought similarly, and Ilgner turned a blind eye to Nazi excesses, dismissing them as inevitable accompaniments of revolutionary change.[71] Even Bosch, who continued to worry about the Nazis' inclination to "experiment around" with the economy, diverted himself with Hitler's plan to construct *Autobahnen*, a project IG had recommended for years.[72]

Among the aging members of the now defunct Kalle circle, however, adjustment to the new circumstances came slowly, if at all. Paul Moldenhauer displayed the most flexibility. Defeated on March 5 in a final

68 Holdermann, *Im Banne der Chemie*, p. 274; Tammen, *I. G. Farbenindustrie*, pp. 302–3; NI-017/2, *Das Deutsche Führerlexikon*, p. 355; Lochner, *Tycoons*, p. 18; BDC, Akten des Obersten Parteigerichts, I. Kammer.
69 G. Feder, *Das Programm der NSDAP* (München, 1931), p. 58.
70 Kühne's testimony, *NMT*, vol. 7, pp. 634–6; the passage quoted is on p. 635.
71 M892/9, Gajewski's testimony, pp. 8177–8, 8316; NI-7330/58, Affidavit by A. Reithinger, 19.VI.47.
72 See BASF W1, Bosch's speech at the retirement celebration for Duisberg, 30.IX.33; and Holdermann, *Im Banne der Chemie*, pp. 259–60.

race for the Reichstag as a candidate of the People's Party, he advised that organization to disband and in July accepted membership in the German delegation to the Geneva disarmament conference.[73] Duisberg, clinging to his habitual optimism, slowly came to expect a normalization of conditions in Germany and to believe that a change of government would risk throwing the baby out with the bath.[74] Still, despite his erstwhile cheerleading for a strong state, he fell uncharacteristically silent during 1933. His autobiography, completed in September and published toward the end of the year, mentioned neither Hitler nor Nazism and contained only one reference to the "renewal of 1933."[75] Hermann Hummel, who continued to counsel the firm from retirement and to draw a salary, henceforth concentrated his energies on the *Frankfurter Zeitung*, hoping to restore its financial health and preserve its political independence. In April 1939, having accomplished the first task but having failed in the second, he emigrated, first to Switzerland and then to the United States. Hermann Warmbold also withdrew from political life; his subsequent activities consisted largely of serving on the supervisory board of IG's Deutsche Länderbank and advising Schmitz. And both Wichard von Moellendorf and Kalle himself flatly refused to make their peace with Nazism. Though Moellendorf's proposals for state direction of the economy and national self-sufficiency had anticipated those of the Nazis, he now likened himself to a trained surgeon being forced to watch butchers claim the right to perform operations.[76] In June, he wrote the chairman of the Kaiser-Wilhelm-Gesellschaft to express his satisfaction with the government's decision to remove him from that organization's senate, since he did not feel able to remain associated with the current trend in national affairs.[77] Kalle fought stubbornly to keep the

---

[73] BA Koblenz, NL 19, Bd. 4, pp. 1–4. Thereafter his political career evaporated, and he remained associated with IG only as a consultant on insurance matters, a role that involved him in efforts to prevent the regime from nationalizing the insurance industry; see pp. 21–2 of his manuscript.

[74] Duisberg, *Nur ein Sohn*, p. 183.

[75] Carl Duisberg, *Lebenserinnerungen* (Leipzig, 1933); the quoted phrase is on p. 149.

[76] On Hummel, see Werner Wirthle, *Frankfurter Zeitung und Frankfurter Societäts-Druckerei GmbH. Die wirtschaftlichen Verhältnisse 1927–1939* (Frankfurt, 1977), pp. 36–45, 59–63; and Wolfgang Schivelbusch, *Intellektuellendämmerung* (Frankfurt, 1985), pp. 69–70. On Moellendorf, see Schmitz V/74, Affidavit by Wilhelm von Flügge, 16.III.48, and Moellendorf's own *Konservativer Sozialismus* (Berlin, 1932).

[77] BA Koblenz, NL 158, Bd. 188, Moellendorf to Planck, 19.V.33; Planck to Moellendorf, 30.V.33; and Moellendorf to Planck, 2.VI.33.

DVP alive until the regime dissolved the party in July and then labored to prevent the closing of its last newspaper because he wanted to keep reminding the public of the "catastrophic situation of our foreign policy . . . the hostile atmosphere in almost the entire world."[78] Unsuccessful in these efforts, Kalle nonetheless hung onto both his political convictions and his seat on Farben's supervisory board throughout the Third Reich. As late as 1942, an investigation by the *Gau* leadership in Hessen-Nassau produced the conclusions that he "has no use for the NSDAP" and that "he cannot reconcile himself to National Socialism."[79]

But the guard was changing at IG; hence, the opinions of these elders carried less weight than in earlier years. Twenty-five members of the supervisory board and six members of the managing board had died or been pensioned off in 1932. Since 1930, these bodies had lost twenty-nine and thirty-one members, respectively, including thirteen participants in the *Vorstand's* operative arm, the Working Committee.[80] Four of nine members of the pivotal Central Committee attended their first meetings during 1933.[81] Among the rising generation of executives, the temptation to put the best face on events ran very strong.[82] By July 1933, when Hitler told the Reichsstatthalter that revolution must give way to evolution, wishful thinking predominated in the boardrooms of IG Farben.

The forms this thinking took and some of the problems that induced it emerge clearly from the record of a visit to Germany at midyear by two representatives of the DuPont corporation.[83] Homer Ewing and Jasper Crane came not merely "to renew old friendships," as they told Carl Bosch. Their real purpose, outlined to Hermann Schmitz on July 11, was to explore, in view of "the growth of nationalism in different

78 BA Koblenz, NL 2, Kalle to Dingeldey, 28.IV.33 and 31.V.33, Kalle to Stocksiek, 30.VIII.33.
79 BDC, Personalakte Kalle, DAF Gauwaltung München-Oberbayern to Gauleitung, 14.III.42, and report of the *Kreisleiter* in Starnberg, 16.I.42.
80 NI-7956-57/66, Affidavits by Hermann Bässler on the composition of the *Vorstand, Aufsichtsrat,* and *Verwaltungsrat,* 8.VII.47 and 17.VII.47; NI-10044/83, his affidavit on the AA, 4.VIII.47. NI-9487/78, Affidavit by E. Struss, 5.VIII.47, provides detailed information on the large turnover among plant managers, 1932–4.
81 NI-1941/18, ZA Meeting of 2.III.33.
82 NI-4928/36, Affidavit by K. Krüger, 18.III.47, and his testimony, *NMT,* vol. 7, p. 445.
83 For this and the following paragraph, see NI-9784/81, Homer Ewing to Wendell Swint, 17.VII.33. The dramatized account by Dietrich Eichholtz in H. Bock et al. *Sturz ins Dritte Reich* (Jena, 1983) pp. 250–2, is just that.

countries," DuPont's divestiture of its stock in IG Farben and DAG, Troisdorf. Though willing to exchange these shares for ones in related enterprises outside the Reich, either the IG Chemie holding company in Basel or the American IG Chemical Corporation, DuPont preferred a clear sale for convertible currency. Determined not to lose a valuable international connection, the concern's leaders pulled out all the stops in trying to dissuade the emissaries from DuPont. While Bosch gave them an extremely optimistic account of prospects for synthetic fuel production, Schmitz threw various financial roadblocks in the way of the proposed stock transactions, Müller of DAG appealed to the "sentimental attachment" between the German and American firms, and Krauch and his associates tempted DuPont with technical cooperation on nitrogen production. However, IG claimed it could make no definite agreements on the last-named subject for fear of "the suspicion which would follow an international cooperative movement of this kind."

Unwilling to fulfill DuPont's wishes and unable to offer concrete compensation, the concern's leaders concentrated on sending DuPont's men home with their doubts about the new Germany assuaged. Bosch argued for understanding and forbearance on the part of the American firm, appraising the trend of political events in Germany as follows:

For industry, the last few weeks have been especially difficult. . . . The present revolution consists of the lower and middle classes against the upper classes and industry. Just now it is a question of Fascism and Bolshevism, and industry must support the present government to prevent further chaos. In the beginning, Hitler did not consult industrial leaders, but in recent weeks he has shown his stability by curbing the more extreme element of the Party and bringing the industrial leaders into consultation.

Krauch seconded Bosch's judgment that "in the end sane views will prevail," and Schnitzler, terMeer, and Weber-Andreä explained "the positive position of the government against the Jews." To allay residual doubts on that score, Carl von Weinberg, the aged, Jewish-born deputy chairman of the *Aufsichtsrat,* gave "the movement his full stamp of approval," and as a sign of his confidence in the future, pointed out that he was keeping all of his money invested in Germany.

Despite these expressions of growing confidence, only five members of the Working Committee went so far as to join the NSDAP during

1933, and those who did showed as much prudence as passion.[84] Wilhelm R. Mann, Jr., moved first, hastening in March to correct his now embarrassing resignation from the Party during the previous year.[85] Kühne and Gajewski followed suit readily enough when prodded by Robert Ley and a particularly assertive NSBO chapter at the Wolfen factory, respectively.[86] Moreover, like Wilhelm Otto, the sales leader of Sparte III who also enrolled in 1933, Gajewski was involved in parallel negotiations aimed at aiding the faltering synthetic fibers industry. IG's officials sought a commitment from the Party to buy 90% of its fiber needs from German firms; from the government, they wanted a national requirement that wool clothing henceforth contain a 10% admixture of artificial thread.[87] Both men had reason to seek the bargaining advantage of a Party lapel badge. The same motivation figured in the case of Erwin Selck, the *Vorstand* member in charge of IG's offices in Berlin. Already well connected to the coalition government by virtue of his long-standing participation in the Stahlhelm and more recent financial support for an SA cavalry unit, Selck did not petition for membership in the NSDAP until mid-July 1933, after the dissolution of the Deutschnationale Front and after the Central Committee of IG turned over to him Ernst Schwarz's former responsibility for policy toward the work force.[88] Interestingly, none of the executives associated with the hydrogenation sector, which historians have thought had the most to gain from a Nazi government, requested admission to the NSDAP.[89]

[84] On the subject of Party membership, compare the discussion that follows with the misleading chart compiled by the prosecution at the postwar trial, NI-12042/98. One deputy member of the *Vorstand*, who did not sit on the Working Committee, also enrolled in the NSDAP as of April 1, 1933: Friedrich Wilhelm Mühlen; see BDC, Personalakte Mühlen. When the *Vorstand* was consolidated in 1937, he was dropped from the group; see NI-7956/66, and NI-10044/83, Affidavits by H. Bässler, 8.VII.47 and 4.VIII.47.
[85] BDC, Personalakte Wilhelm Mann, Kassenverwaltung of the Gauleitung Köln-Aachen to Kassenverwaltung of the Reichsleitung, München, 29.III.33.
[86] Kühne's testimony, *NMT*, vol. 7, pp. 634–6; M892/9, Gajewski's testimony, pp. 8177–8, 8316.
[87] Gajewski II/55, Affidavit by E. Hermann, 7.VII.47; NI-14105/115, Gajewski to terMeer, 24.VI.33.
[88] NI-1941/18, ZA meeting of 17.VII.33; BDC, Personalakte Erwin Selck.
[89] The converts of 1933–7 are not distinguishable from their peers on any other basis. Their median age was nearly identical to that of the whole Working Committee in 1933; they came from Sparten II and III and from technical, commercial, and administrative backgrounds in roughly the same proportions as their colleagues. Their

Only three other leading figures in IG subsequently availed themselves of loopholes in the ban on new recruits enforced by the Party treasurer between May 1933 and May 1937. One was Heinrich Hoerlein, the cochairman of the Pharmaceuticals Main Conference, who entered the NSDAP in June 1934, allegedly at the behest of the Nazi organization in Wuppertal and as a condition for retaining his position as local councilor there.[90] The second was Ludwig Hermann of the Hoechst plant, whose case remains unexplained. His admission date of August 1, 1935, suggests that he may have acted tardily in 1933 and been subjected to the Party's statutory two-year proving period.[91] Heinrich Gattineau of the Wipo office probably had the same experience. Hans Hinkel, one of his former comrades in the Bund Oberland and now a Nazi deputy in the Reichstag, claimed in July 1933 to have put Gattineau up for membership immediately after Hitler's accession, but his letter to this effect smacks of an attempt to cover up for the hesitation of an old friend. In any case, neither Hinkel's efforts nor those of an SA adjutant in March 1934 could get Gattineau's application expedited. By the time the logjam broke, he had been dropped from the Working Committee.[92] Since Hermann's enrollment merely offset Kühne's expulsion in late 1934 for being a Freemason, the number of Party initiates on the Working Committee stabilized at six.[93]

In purely statistical terms, IG's managers demonstrated only slightly more caution (or less eagerness) toward affiliating themselves with Nazism than did other German big-business figures. The eight joiners constituted just less than one-third of the twenty-six men who served on the Working Committee between 1933 and 1936. On the Central Committee, which included Gajewski, Hoerlein, and Selck, the proportion reached 33% during 1934.[94] In contrast, one rather prelimi-

particular responsibilities made them representative of the concern's interests in both domestic and foreign markets.

[90] M892–7, Hoerlein's testimony, p. 6340. His Party card was backdated to May 1933; BDC, Personalakte Heinrich Hoerlein.

[91] BDC, Personalakte Ludwig Hermann. On Hermann, see BA Koblenz, ZSg 127, Bd. 837, Von Werk zu Werk, May 1936.

[92] BDC, Personalakte Heinrich Gattineau, Hinkel to Gattineau, 10.VII.33; R. Bergmann to Schwarz, 4.III.34; Gattineau's membership card.

[93] BDC, Personalakte Hans Kühne, corrects his postwar claim that his expulsion occurred "in the fall of 1933," NMT, vol. 7, p. 636.

[94] The percentages are based on NI-7956/66, Bässler's affidavit, 8.VII.47.

nary study of leading Ruhr industrialists estimates that about 37% signed up as Nazis by the end of 1933 alone.[95]

However, the most important of the combine's executives kept their distance. The somewhat Olympian Fritz terMeer, Duisberg's candidate to succeed Bosch, chose not to seek a Party card, in part, as he said after the war, because he had "no intention . . . of attending meetings of the local party members and listening to lectures by people far below me socially and with respect to their education."[96] Even Max Ilgner declined to resign from Rotary International as the price of a proffered exemption from the membership freeze.[97] Duisberg died in 1935 and Bosch in 1940 without having joined the Party. The "coming man" in the firm, Hermann Schmitz, also held out, although he did let the Nazis, who were eager to adorn their rubber-stamp legislature with "prominent personalities . . . from various groups of the population," list him as a Reichstag delegate and guest of the Party *Fraktion*.[98] Among the nine oligarchs on the administrative council between 1933 and 1936, there was not a single Party member.[99]

Short of enlisting in the NSDAP, IG's leaders tried a variety of devices for generating good will within the new ruling circles and speeding the predicted moderating trend in Party policy. Schnitzler opened a "salon" in Berlin, Christian Schneider of the Leuna plant became a "sponsoring member" of the SS, Selck joined its mounted auxiliary, and Gattineau got Bosch's approval to accept a commission in the SA. As the young former *Freikorps* fighter rapidly established ties to Röhm and his staff, he grew convinced that they represented within the NSDAP "a comparatively mild and humane" position toward the unions, churches, Jews, and relations with France. Along

---

95 Mommsen in Schieder (ed.), *Faschismus als soziale Bewegung*, p. 179. On the general pattern of business enlistment, see Kater, *Nazi Party*, pp. 100–1.

96 See terMeer's testimony, *NMT*, vol. 7, pp. 616–17. On Carl Duisberg's plans for terMeer, Interview with Curt Duisberg, 20.I.78.

97 NI-4928/36, Krüger's affidavit, 18.III.47; Krüger's testimony, *NMT*, vol. 7, p. 443; NI-7330/58, Reithinger's affidavit, 19.VI.47; NI-4833/35, Gattineau's affidavit, 13.III.47; Josiah DuBois, *The Devil's Chemists* (Boston, 1952), p. 56; Ilgner I/10, Affidavit by T. von Wilmowsky; and Ilgner I/11, Affidavit by H. Albert. On the Party's view of Rotary Clubs, see Donald M. McKale, *The Nazi Party Courts* (Lawrence, Kan., 1974), p. 148.

98 Schmitz V/92, Affidavit by H. Globke, who supervised the Reichstag elections in Prussia, 1932–4, 26.II.48; V/93, Affidavit by P. Kronmueller, 17.III.48, including Duisberg to Schmitz, 31.IX.33; V/94, *Das Grossdeutsche Reichstag*, pp. 130–4.

99 See NI-7957/66, Bässler's affidavit, 17.VII.47, as compared with the Party membership records in the BDC.

with Mann and one Director Uhl of Agfa, Schnitzler and Gattineau also took seats on the government-sponsored Advertising Council of the German Economy.[100] Ilgner provided his services to both the Propaganda and Economics Ministries, placed some of the Vowi office's files at the disposal of military planners, and may have offered to furnish the Prussian Political Police with information gathered from IG's sources abroad. He also supported the Dirksen-Stiftung, an appendage of the elite Deutscher Herrenklub designed to bring eminent Nazis together with significant figures from all branches of the economy, education, the arts, and public life.[101] And in Frankfurt, the administrative counsel authorized Selck to join the reorganized supervisory board of the Adlerwerke, since the group would include "leading personalities in the present movement" and IG would benefit from this expansion of his already good contacts with the local Party leaders.[102]

Above all, substantial donations flowed into the Party's coffers. In 1933 alone, IG gave roughly 2 million reichsmarks to the NSDAP and its affiliates, over and above the approximately 700,000 marks contributed to the Hitler Spende during the calendar year, the million or so marks that went in September to the Winterhilfswerk relief program, the 400,000 marks for the election campaign, and a host of miscellaneous offerings to the SA, such as flat monthly payments, the use of a house in Munich adjoining Röhm's residence, and about 200,000 marks for uniforms. Altogether, then, the Nazis and activities they sponsored received some 4.5 million reichsmarks from IG Farben in 1933. This was merely the first installment of grants totaling about 40 million marks by 1945 and nearly equaling all of IG's other charitable contributions combined.[103]

100 NI-6702/51, Affidavit by M. Ilgner, 25.IV.47; Schneider's testimony, *NMT*, vol. 7. p. 622; NI-5170/38, Affidavit by H. Gattineau, 31.V.47; Gattineau, *Klippen*, pp. 132–8. Though farfetched to later ears, Gattineau's view of Röhm was widespread at the time.
101 NI-1105/11, Excerpt from dispatch of Wolff's Telegraphisches Büro, 30.X.33; NI-4833/35, Gattineau's affidavit, 13.III.47; M892/57, Gattineau's testimony, p. 12408; Hallgarten and Radkau, *Deutsche Industrie*, pp. 319–20; NI-15132/123, Draft of Ilgner to General Thomas, 23.V.34; and NI-4671/34, Affidavit by R. Diels, 30.I.47.
102 IG in Abw., Personalakte Selck, Selck to Schmitz, 18.IX.33, and Duisberg to Selck, 5.X.33.
103 The principal and inconsistent sources on funds routed to the NSDAP are NI-4056/29, Receipts of IG Farben's contributions to the Adolf Hitler Spende, October 1944; Defense Basic Information II/4, Affidavit by H. Walter, 25.III.48;

Finally, in both the field and the factories, IG moved, albeit inconsistently, toward overt identification with the new regime. Abroad, competing commercial and political demands pulled the concern's conduct in different directions. On the one hand, if left uncombated, the Third Reich's unsavory international reputation seemed bound to harm IG's sales. At least, that was the thinking in Berlin and the justification for a burst of activity by Max Ilgner. Not only did he form a council of advisers to the Propaganda Ministry, organize tours of German industrial districts to impress foreign businessmen, and assign Ivy Lee, a celebrated American public relations expert, the task of improving Hitler's image in the United States, Ilgner also seized the opportunities presented by his periodic trips abroad to trumpet the peaceful intent and the social and political accomplishments of Nazi rule.[104] On the other hand, after spending nearly a decade and a half overcoming the effects of wartime propaganda against "the Huns," Farben's salesmen did not want to be tarred with the Nazi brush. Schnitzler summarized their views in August 1933, when he complained to Selck about Ilgner's journeys:

We now appear as the champion of the German cause in general and as auxiliary government agents without even knowing whether the government considers this desirable. . . . But, however this may be, these trips that are organized on such propaganda lines do not in any case appear of any use whatsoever to our firm. . . . Politics and political economy have nothing to do with this or should have nothing to do with it. The less one mixes business matters with questions of sympathy or antipathy to various forms of government or with the national psychological attitude, the better it will be for business.[105]

NI-9200/76, Affidavit by H. Bässler, 30.VII.47, and NI-7366/59, Affidavit by H. Bässler, 28.VI.47. None of these documents appears to include the election fund, wartime contributions to the Himmler circle, miscellaneous presents to local and national Nazi potentates, and the services to the SA mentioned above. Concerning the SA, see NI-4833/35, Gattineau's affidavit, 13.III.47; and NI-4928/36, Affidavit by K. Krüger, 18.III.47, which is clarified and extended in important respects by M892/57, Gattineau's testimony, pp. 12407, 12410. Conan Fischer reports gifts to the SA by IG of 44,528 marks in 1933, 74,224 marks in 1934, and 29,446 in 1935 (Stormtroopers, p. 113). For illustrations of the numerous smaller extractions by provincial Nazis, see Schneider's testimony, NMT, vol. 7, pp. 624–5; Bayer 13/25, Ilgner to Kühne, 4.XII.41; and Kühne I/36, Affidavit by W. Roettger, 27.II.48, a compilation of gifts made by the Leverkusen, Elberfeld, and Dormagen plants.
104 NI-6702/51, Ilgner's affidavit, 25.IV.47; Bayer AS, Ilgner to Duisberg, 3.VII.33; Ilgner's outline of a lecture to the AA, 3.X.33, reprinted in Hans Radandt, "Die IG-Farbenindustrie AG in Südosteuropa bis 1938," JfW, 7 (1966), pp. 192–5.
105 NI-697/7, Schnitzler to Selck, 28.VII.33.

Ilgner was irrepressible, but Schnitzler stood by his arguments, which he reiterated to the Central Committee, and for a time they prevailed.[106]

During the summer and fall of 1933, IG dodged close public connection overseas with the Nazi government. Thus, when the German embassy in Montevideo prepared a propaganda magazine for local doctors and pharmacists and asked Bayer's field office to provide the appropriate addresses and do the mailing, Leverkusen acceded to the first request but dragged its feet on the second.[107] A few weeks later, several associates of the firm undertook a fact-finding mission to Southeast Europe for the Foreign Office, and IG told its local representatives, in essence, to speak to the visitors only if spoken to.[108] The rule of thumb was laid down in October by a letter in which the pharmaceutical sales combine directed its subdivisions to extend the NSDAP "friendly support without at the same time allowing our business interests to assume a political character."[109]

However, this attempt to separate business and politics abroad rapidly degenerated into a holding action. IG soon thought better of turning over its address lists to official agencies and opted to distribute propaganda itself, when necessary.[110] As early as January 1934, probably as part of the government's response to the ill effects of Germany's withdrawal from the League of Nations, one of the combine's overseas outlets dispatched to Brazilian physicians some 16,000 copies of one of Hitler's more pacific addresses to the Reichstag.[111] Moreover, while contending with recurrent anti-German sentiment, the concern had to fend off attacks by the emigré kingpins of the Party's Foreign Organization (Auslandsorganisation), or AO, whose Foreign Trade Office was led by Alfred Hess, the brother of the führer's deputy. Often composed of small-scale local businessmen who resented the wealthier representatives of large German firms, the branches of the AO continuously berated IG for putting profits before political purity,

[106] NI-1941/18, ZA meeting of 9.XI.33.
[107] NI-9897/82, Montevideo office to Pharma Direktion, 29.VII.33, and reply of 18.VIII.33.
[108] NI-15146/123, Voight and Hoppen to Krüger, 13.IX.33, including letter to field representatives of the previous day.
[109] NI-8418, Meeting of Sales Combine Pharmaceuticals, 25.X.33, NMT, vol. 7, p. 651.
[110] See NI-8139/68, Internal Bayer memo, 14.VIII.40.
[111] NI-8420, Meeting of Bayer directors, 23.I.34, NMT, vol. 7, p. 655.

chiefly by placing advertisements in the often anti-Nazi, sometimes Jewish-owned newspapers read by Latin American doctors and druggists.[112] At the end of 1933, to counter "the boycott propaganda abroad, which is still noticeable," the Bayer pharmaceuticals division sent its foreign agencies a carefully worded defense of the National Socialist government for restoring order, safety, and honesty to the Reich and "belief in itself" to the German people.[113] Three months later, Bayer's capitulation to the AO apparently became complete when the directors ordered their foreign employees to swear "personal political reliability to Germany," "refrain from any political activity against the German Reich," and terminate advertising in periodicals that "publish insulting or abusive articles against the German Reich."[114] Yet IG had not entirely abandoned Schnitzler's position. On March 1, 1934, the concern prepared its first "strictly confidential" memorandum concerning ways of concealing "for tax and other reasons" IG's connections to foreign sales firms.[115]

At home, IG's leaders also tried to balance divergent interests, with the scales tipping steadily toward accommodating the Party. During the latter half of 1933 and early 1934, the NSDAP increasingly appeared to have internalized rather than smashed the menace to Germany's propertied elites formerly represented by the Marxist parties. While the NSBO and the DAF vigorously prosecuted workers' demands and tried to "Nazify" factory life, Ernst Röhm of the SA took the position that "it is in fact high time that the national revolution stopped and became the National Socialist one."[116] In response to the

---

112 On IG's differences with the AO, see NI-1295/13, Statement by G. Frank-Fahle, no date; Ilgner's testimony, *NMT*, vol. 7, pp. 724–30; and Donald M. McKale, *The Swastika Outside Germany* (Kent, Ohio, 1977), pp. 51–3. The most comprehensive discussion of the organization is in Hans-Adolf Jacobsen, *Nationalsozialistische Aussenpolitik, 1933–1938* (München, 1968), pp. 90–160.

113 NI-10267, Mann to Winthrop Chemical Co., New York, 14.XII.33, *NMT*, vol. 7, pp. 652–4.

114 NI-8421-22, Meetings of the Bayer directors, 13.II.34 and 27.II.34, *NMT*, vol. 7, pp. 656–57.

115 NI-1084/11, Einige rechtliche Gesichtspunkte für die Organisation unseres Auslandsverkaufes, 1.III.34, illegibly signed, perhaps by Ilgner.

116 Röhm's newspaper article of June 1933 is quoted in Noakes and Pridham, *Documents on Nazism*, pp. 202–3. On other such statements and the turbulence of the labor groups, see GHH 400 101 220/14b, RSI to Fachgruppen und landschaftlichen Verbände, 26.I.34; Schulz, *Anfänge*, p. 333; Tim W. Mason, "Zur Entstehung des Gesetzes zur Ordnung der nationalen Arbeit, vom 20. Januar 1934," in Hans Mommsen, Dietmar Petzina, and Bernd Weisbrod (eds.), *Industrielles System und politische Entwicklung in der Weimarer Republik*, vol. 1 (Kron-

former problem, IG's leaders walked a fine line between satisfying Party activists and preserving not only managerial control, but also the morale and efficiency of the numerous workers who continued to loathe Nazism. Thus, during the summer of 1933, the directors of the Hoechst plant declined to make the Hitler-Gruss mandatory but then warned "against the contempt shown toward the German salute." They also coupled a ban on collections for the NSDAP in the factory with a contribution to the SS House in Marburg.[117] In October, the same men accepted invitations to attend a public lecture series on *Mein Kampf* by the Party's regional education leader.[118] Although at least some plant leaders were willing to recommend that appropriate employees participate in the highly ideological training courses of the fellow-traveling Deutsches Institut für technische Arbeitsschulung (DINTA), IG's Central Committee decided to evade a bid by Carl Arnhold, the DINTA's chief, for control of the firm's monthly magazine.[119] The Central Committee also opposed a proposal to create a single Nazi-sponsored labor council to speak for the workers at all the combine's plants, but the *Aufsichtsrat* apparently acceded to the NSBO's claim to the two seats in that body occupied under the Republic by union representatives, admitting a pair of Nazi workmen to the sessions in February, March, and April 1934.[120] During the same period, IG's leaders backed away from other possible confrontations. When Party zealots at the Wolfen plant denounced as illegal the contracts being offered to newly hired workers, Fritz Gajewski dismissed the objections, only to be overruled later on this and other disputed points by his superiors.[121] At Hoechst, the managers agreed to release personnel with pay for participation in paramilitary sports training camps.[122]

On matters affecting IG's international corporate connections,

berg/Ts., 1977), pp. 346–9; and Mathilde Jamin, "Zur Rolle der SA im nationalsozialistischen Herrschaftssystem," in G. Hirschfeld and L. Kettenacker (eds.), *Der Führerstaat* (Stuttgart, 1981), pp. 335–41.
[117] NI-5867-68/44, Meetings of Hoechst directors, 14 and 28.VIII.33.
[118] NI-5869/44, Meeting of Hoechst directors, 30.X.33.
[119] NI-4840/35, Hoechst Engineering Committee meeting, 14.XI.34; NI-1941/18, ZA meeting of 2.X.33. On the DINTA, see Robert A. Brady, *The Spirit and Structure of German Fascism* (New York, 1937), pp. 161–72; and John Gillingham, "Ruhr Coal Miners and Hitler's War," *Journal of Social History*, 15 (1981), pp. 638–40.
[120] NI-1941/18, ZA meeting of 2.X.33; Bayer 11/3, vol. 5, 33rd to 35th Aufsichtsrat meetings, 16.II.–28.IV.34.
[121] Gajewski I/1, Hingst to Gestapo, 26.IX.39.
[122] NI-5873/44, Hoechst Technical *Vorstand* meeting, 5.III.34.

research interests, and reputation, the firm put up a greater fight. Alarmed by the vague and sweeping language of the Ministry of Justice's draft legislation on military and economic high treason, IG's legal department protested that "if this bill becomes law, the continuation of business relations abroad would hardly be possible for a world organization such as we are."[123] Bosch engaged in a running, sometimes public dispute with Reich Physicians Leader Gerhard Wagner over his insistence on subjecting scientific inquiry to ideological criteria.[124] What that might mean had been foreshadowed in August, when Göring issued the long-threatened prohibition on experimentation with animals.[125] From then until the turn of the year, IG's past practices and Hoerlein's strenuous opposition to the ban came under fire from antivivisectionist publications.[126] Almost simultaneously, the Nürnberg Party organization began distributing a crude propaganda sheet for doctors and pharmacists under the heading *Deutsche Volksgesundheit aus Blut und Boden*. It featured a cartoon strip titled "Life and Deeds of Isidor G. Faerber" in which grotesquely drawn, price-gouging professors, either Jewish or with Jewish wives, peddled substances poisonous to the German racial stock. Hoerlein was able to get the comic suppressed after several months, and he eventually succeeded in having the freedom to use laboratory animals restored.[127] IG's arguments probably also helped delay until 1936 the enactment of restrictions on exchanges of inventions and technical information with foreign corporations. But these outcomes were in doubt as of 1933, and the firm's struggles reinforced the message of IG's difficulties earlier in the year. Once more, increased influence with Hitler and the more "responsible" Nazi leaders seemed the only possible protection against radicals within the NSDAP.

There was thus no doubt an element of defensiveness and a desire to

123 Knieriem II/12, Knieriem and Brendel to Justice Minister Gürtner, 20.XI.33. Cf. Knieriem Document 11, excerpts from *National Socialist Penal Law* (1933) by Prussian Minister of Justice von Decker, NMT, vol. 7, pp. 1266–9.
124 Holdermann, *Im Banne der Chemie*, pp. 285–6; BASF W1, "National und Weltoffen," *Frankfurter Zeitung*, no. 473 (17.IX.34), an account of Wagner's and Bosch's speeches to a meeting of the Deutsche Naturforscher und Ärzte.
125 NI-6787/52, Affidavit by H. Hoerlein, 2.V.47.
126 Hoerlein I/53, "Tierrecht und Tierschutz," 3.IX.33; I/55, "Der Deutsche Tierfreund," no. 1 (Dec. 1933/Jan. 1934).
127 NI-6787/52, Hoerlein's affidavit, 2.V.47; Hoerlein I/52, photocopies of *Deutsche Volksgesundheit aus Blut und Boden*, nos. 3–6 (Oct.–Dec. 1933), and of a brief reappearance of the comic in the same journal, vol. 3, no. 9 (1.V.35).

ingratiate behind Bosch's decision toward the end of 1933 to abandon his long public silence concerning the new government. His widely reprinted article, "Where There Is a Will, There Is a Way," rejoiced in the "wave of new trust and new confidence" flowing through the German economy, which Bosch traced to the resolution shown by Hitler and the National Socialist government in creating jobs, reducing taxes on industry, rooting out Communism, and restoring pride in labor.[128] But however politic this endorsement, it reflected the beginnings of genuine satisfaction. During the latter half of 1933, the apparent economic advantages of Nazi rule went far toward fitting IG's conduct to Brecht's biting comment on human motives, "Erst kommt das Fressen, dann kommt die Moral."

As early as September 1933, Bosch surveyed the rising curves of IG's sales and employment figures and reported to the *Aufsichtsrat* that the worst of the Depression was over, "thanks to the stabilization of domestic political affairs and to the energetic measures of the government for the relief of unemployment."[129] And by the end of the year, IG's books did record modest, but gratifying improvements over the previous twelve-month period. While total sales rose by only 20 million reichsmarks, or 2.5%, the combine retired about 30% of its bonded indebtedness, increased employment at the factories by 15.5%, and for the first time since 1928 enlarged its expenditures for research and new plant.[130] Despite these added outlays, gross profits expanded by a striking 70%, and net profits, which the firm announced at 49 million marks, or up by only 4.5%, actually reached 65 million marks, an improvement of 32%.[131] Even though a wave of foreign devaluations in 1931–2 had made German products relatively expensive abroad, the annual rate of decline in IG's exports slowed to only 4.4% in 1933,

[128] BASF W1 contains the original text that appeared in a journal of the chemical section of the Deutscher Handlungsgehilfen-Verband on 30.XI.33 and numerous clippings of condensations published elsewhere.

[129] Bayer 11/3, vol. 5, 32nd *Aufsichtsrat* meeting, 29.IX.33.

[130] Bayer 15/Da 1.1, Umsätze; NI-10001/82, Affidavit by H. Deichfischer, 11.VI.47; Defense Basic Information I, pp. 64, 70–1; Defense Basic Information II/4, p. 29; Bütefisch II/282, Affidavit by G. Kunze, 18.II.48; and II/287, Affidavit by F. Schwoerer, 24.II.48.

[131] NI-10002-03/82, Affidavits by H. Deichfischer, 11.VI.47; Defense Basic Information I, p. 71. The actual profits were arrived at by a tax audit now in the BA Koblenz, R 2/21047.

compared with 14% for the Reich as a whole.[132] As a result of these favorable trends the market value of the concern's shares averaged almost 18% more than in the preceding year.[133]

Ironically, the Hitler government's policies made little immediate and direct contribution to this revival of IG's fortunes. The rehiring of workers had begun in October 1932, before the Nazis entered the cabinet, and Carl Bosch remained doubtful that either public works spending or Schacht's schemes to expand the credit supply could shorten or mitigate the normal, necessarily painful process of economic recovery.[134] Contrary to Hitler's promises, the public treasury took back more in corporate income taxes during 1933 than it relinquished with reduced duties on property, even if specific exemptions and liberalized depreciation allowances did enable IG to begin making up for deferred maintenance and modernization.[135] As a whole, the combine benefited slightly from the boom in munitions production at DAG, Troisdorf, where sales rose by almost a quarter and the previous year's loss of 1.7 million marks turned into a profit of 2.4 million.[136] But spending on arms and road construction expanded too slowly to boost IG's own sagging turnover on nitrogen for explosives. The military market, which the concern had been reluctant to pursue under the Republic, made no significant difference to IG's balance sheet for 1933.[137] Meanwhile, Economics Minister Schmitt's determination to

132 Hermann Gross, *Material zur Aufteilung der IG Farbenindustrie Aktiengesellschaft* (Kiel, 1950), pp. 18–19; Gustav Stolper, *The German Economy* (New York, 1967), p. 145. Rudolf Schröder, "Die Ausschussprotokolle der IG Farben," *JfW*, 8 (1967), p. 254, cites a report by the KA showing that IG's exports actually rose by 1% in 1932–3, but none of the records available to me is consistent with this information.

133 Defense Basic Information I, p. 69.

134 On the rehiring, see Bayer 221/6, Schwarz to Duisberg and the ZA, 9.III.33, p. 1; BA Koblenz, ZSg 127, Bd. 838, "Belebung bei IG Farben," *Vossische Zeitung*, 28.I.33. On Bosch's skepticism, see his comments to the Generalrat der Wirtschaft, 20.IX.33, BA Koblenz, R43 II/321, Bl. 43-47, 75-77, and Michael Wolffsohn, *Industrie und Handwerk im Konflikt mit staatlicher Wirtschaftspolitik?* (Berlin, 1977), pp. 139–40.

135 Lurie, *Private Investment*, pp. 138–9; Bayer 13/16, vol. 1, Special Session of Sparte II, 6.VI.33, pp. 3–4; Tammen, *I.G. Farbenindustrie*, p. 74; Hoechst TEA 1296, Erläuterungen zum Gesetz über Steuererleichterungen, 15.VII.33; and BA Koblenz, ZSg 127, Bd. 832, IG press release of 9.X.33, announcing an increase of more than 45 million marks in such expenditures between 1932 and 1933.

136 NI-10008/82, Affidavit by H. Deichfischer, 11.VI.47.

137 On IG's rejection of military work under the Republic, see the testimony of General Rudolf Huenerman, 4–5.V.48, *NMT*, vol. 7, p. 425; and General Thomas's re-

block price increases on most chemical products, despite rising manufacturing costs, inconvenienced producers so much that the Chemie
Verein had to warn them against attempted evasions, lest the ministry
dissolve the organization.[138]

Official anti-Semitism also continued to cost the firm money. A
sharply increased advertising budget, necessitated by resistance to
German goods abroad, was responsible for about 1.1 million reichsmarks of the decline in IG's gross profits on pharmaceuticals and
insecticides between 1932 and 1933.[139] Hence, the concern made a
renewed effort in January 1934 to influence important figures in the
government against its racist course. When Ivy Lee advised IG's leaders that no amount of German propaganda would reconcile Americans to the Reich's treatment of the Jews, Ilgner promptly arranged for
Lee to repeat this information to Goebbels, Papen, Schmitt, and Foreign Minister von Neurath, but without perceptible success.[140]

To be sure, the regime did, as a by-product of its severe limitations
on the repayment and service of German obligations to external creditors, drive down the price of IG's bonds overseas and permit the
combine to use scarce foreign exchange to buy these back at well
below par. By these actions, as well as intervention in the Balkan
capitals, the government facilitated IG's operation of involved "compensation deals." Under the terms of such arrangements, the concern
bought Balkan agricultural goods at their high domestic prices, resold
them abroad at the lower international ones, and made good the loss
by purchasing its bonds cheaply and marking up the exports that the
Balkan nations accepted in return for IG's retailing. The firm as a
result maintained the value of its exports to Southeast Europe at
roughly the level of 1928 and reduced its debts by 72.3 million marks.
Furthermore, the government enabled IG's overseas offices to buy up

marks quoted in Lochner, *Tycoons*, pp. 208–9. On minor military projects during
1933, see NI-5961–62/44–45, *Vorstand* meetings of Hoechst, 30.I.33 and 6.II.33;
NI-5929/44, Knipfer of the Air Ministry to Direktion, Frankfurt, 9.X.33, and reply
from Lappe and Krauch, 20.X.33; and NI-5872/44, Hoechst *Vorstand* meeting,
27.XI.33.

138 Barkai, *Wirtschaftssystem*, p. 148.
139 Bayer 4C9.29, Office of the Military Government for Germany (U.S.), I.G. Farben
Control Office, *Activities of "Bayer" I. G. Farbenindustrie Aktiengesellschaft in the
Industries of Pharmaceuticals, Sera, and Plant Protection Products* (1946), p. 143;
Bayer 15/Da 1.1, Umsätze.
140 NI-10921/90, Ivy Lee's testimony to a subcommittee of the House Un-American
Activities Committee, 9–12.VII.34.

some of the idle blocked mark accounts of foreign creditors, probably also at a discount, in order to offset the price reductions required for the concern to continue selling dyes and other products in the United States and to maintain its export quotas under the international nitrogen cartel.[141] But all of the procedures by which Farben profited antedated the Nazi regime by at least six months.[142] Moreover, official assistance did not come free in the Nazi state. IG had to kick back 1.25 million marks, some 10% of the value of the combine's dyes trade in America, as a contribution to the regime's work creation funds.[143] Nonetheless, Ilgner was not exaggerating when he told the Central Committee in October 1933 that IG's export efforts enjoyed the "excellent and very understanding" support of the government.[144]

IG's leaders were, moreover, coming to appreciate the prospective benefits of Nazi economic policies. Despite a problematic impact on fertilizer sales in the short run, the concern could not but see eventual gains resulting from the regime's measures to stabilize and reorganize the agrarian sector.[145] Above all, the state's approval of Gajewski's synthetic fibers admixture agreement in June pointed in a positive direction. From then until December, IG's sales of artificial threads rose rapidly to a figure 14% higher than at the end of 1932, and purchases of related working chemicals also increased.[146] Before the year was out, Germany's shortage of foreign exchange and the Party's emphasis on autarky, rearmament, and work creation had revived IG's hopes for several products that had significant military applica-

---

141 See Max Ilgner's draft of a lecture to the AA, 3.X.33, in Radandt, *JfW*, 7 (1966), pp. 186–95, and Radandt's findings, pp. 154–61. On the development of IG's compensation deals from 1931 on, see Verena Schröter, *Die deutsche Industrie auf dem Weltmarkt 1929 bis 1933* (Frankfurt, 1984), pp. 167–77.
142 See Alan S. Milward, "The Reichsmark Bloc and the International Economy," in Hirschfeld and Kettenacker (ed.), *Der Führerstaat*, pp. 398–9. As early as the end of 1932, the average price of German bonds on the New York market was 28.6% of par; see Harold James, "The German Reaction to the Collapse of the International Monetary System 1931–1932," in Gustav Schmidt (ed.), *Konstellationen internationaler Politik 1924–1932* (Bochum, 1983), p. 315.
143 NI-1089/11, Silcher to Helfert, 5.XII.38, summarizing the accord of 21.IX.33. Schweitzer, *Big Business*, p. 672, note 20, says that in 1933 IG paid the government 30% of the gain on a blocked mark deal that sounds rather like the one for the United States discussed here, but he provides no specific information or documentation and does not explain how he computed the 30% figure. According to Schweitzer, a 30% kickback became standard on later similar deals.
144 Ilgner's lecture of 3.X.33, in Radandt, *JfW*, 7 (1966), p. 187.
145 Bayer 186/D2, vol. 1, 6th meeting of the Nitrogen Sparte, 7.XII.33, pp. 20, 23, 33.
146 NI-14105/115, Gajewski to terMeer, 24.VI.33; Bayer 15/Da 1.1, Umsätze.

tions and that the concern could produce almost entirely from domestic resources, notably the light metal magnesium, artificial rubber, or buna, and synthetic fuel. High manufacturing costs still prevented these products from competing profitably with corresponding natural or processed materials. If, however, the Reich guaranteed a minimum market sufficient to pay off the start-up charges, the combine expected that experience would yield the necessary reductions in unit costs, as in the cases of IG's earlier major inventions. By then, the odds of extended earnings from large-scale production would have been enhanced by another supposed objective of government action: motorization. On July 27, 1933, the regime issued a law for the construction of a highway network, and by December a variety of fiscal incentives produced a doubling in the number of new automobile permits over 1932.[147]

For IG Farben at the outset of the Third Reich, then, rearmament had a primarily instrumental importance, being valued less for the profits it would bring directly than for those it might help make possible. So confident was the concern about the future of magnesium that IG swiftly seized on the Air Ministry's request in 1933 for a plant that would augment output four- or fivefold. As soon as the Finance Ministry appended an offer of twice the normal amortization rate and long before the Luftwaffe signed a sales contract, Farben began pouring 46 million marks of its own funds into construction at Aken.[148] With regard to buna, for which the necessary investments were likely to be many times higher, Fritz terMeer refused to gamble on the military. He had sharply curtailed work in synthetic rubber in 1931 after natural rubber prices dropped by 80%, and he had no intention of involving IG in a repetition of its benzin crisis. The Defense Ministry's expression of interest in the product in mid-1933 thus resulted in an appropriation of only 100,000 to 120,000 reichsmarks toward the resumption of development while Martin Mueller-Cunradi of IG

[147] Wolfgang Birkenfeld, Der synthetische Treibstoff, 1933–1945 (Göttingen, 1964), p. 23.
[148] On the early development of IG's light-metals output, see NI-7562/61, Excerpts from "The Development of the Light Metals Industry within the Four Year Plan," by Dr. Neukirch, pp. 63–80. The complete document is in BA Koblenz, R25/150–152b. On developments in 1933, see Bayer 4C9.25, unpublished manuscript by R. W. Mueller and Dr. von Knieriem, "Die IG Farbenindustrie Aktiengesellschaft. Das Schicksal eines deutschen Unternehmens," March 1951, p. 80; and NI-8317/68, Affidavit by E. Struss, 2.VI.47.

opened discussions with the Army Ordnance Office.[149] From the regime, IG wanted two very preliminary forms of aid. One, an agreement to purchase the concern's synthetic tires and test them on government vehicles, was granted in November. The other, official pressure to force German tire makers to work with the less manipulable and longer-lasting synthetic product, proved ineffective; hence, the buna project slowed once more.[150]

The bases and nature of IG's increasing economic cooperation with the new regime emerged most clearly in the case of the major business—government contract of 1933, the *Benzin-Vertrag*. By the beginning of the year, the Leuna factory had demonstrated its capacity to produce about 100,000 tons of synthetic fuel annually at a cost per liter that came to three times the world market rate for gasoline but still fell within the range of protection afforded by the German tariffs.[151] A contract with Standard and Royal Dutch Shell guaranteed the sale of any additional output via the Deutsche Gasolin AG, which the three giant firms owned. In other words, provided that wholesale fuel prices were kept above IG's costs, the way finally seemed open for large-scale production and profits on benzin. Yet IG still disliked relying on customs protection, not only because such duties discouraged consumption and clashed with the firm's interest in free trade, but, more important, because the government could alter them at will.[152] That it might do so seemed quite possible at midyear, when the führer briefly endorsed the plans of Gottfried Feder and other figures to import, refine, and stockpile American crude oil.[153] Moreover, Leuna was vulnerable from another quarter. For years the Ruhr mine owners had seen an escape from their chronic difficulties via the production of

149 NI-7241/57 and terMeer IV/186, Affidavits by E. Struss, 12.VI.47 and 30.XII.47; Bayer 13/16, vol. 1, Special Session of Sparte II, 6.VII.33, pp. 10–11. Struss's second affidavit shows that IG's development expenses for buna dropped from 2.5 million marks in 1930 to 696,000 in 1931 and still came to only 398,000 in 1933, despite the new appropriation. See also Peter J. T. Morris, *The Development of Acetylene Chemistry and Synthetic Rubber by I. G. Farbenindustrie Aktiengesellschaft: 1926–1945* (Dissertation, University of Oxford, 1982), pp. 170–3, 252–3.
150 NI-6930, IG to Army Ordnance Office, 15.VIII.33, IG to RWM, 13.XI.33, and RWM to IG, 23.XI.33, NMT, vol. 7, pp. 750–54.
151 Birkenfeld, *Treibstoff*, p. 28.
152 See Krauch's remarks in BASF, Handakten Bosch, Notiz über eine Besprechung mit Vertretern des Ruhrbergbaus, 30.VI.33, signed by C. Müller; also Birkenfeld, *Treibstoff*, p. 27.
153 Birkenfeld, *Treibstoff*, pp. 24–5.

synthetic fertilizers and fuel in conjunction with the coking process.[154] IG had managed to bring the resulting ammonia output within the German Nitrogen Syndicate in 1930, and the Ruhrchemie's potentially competing Fischer–Tropsch procedure for making gasoline had not yet matured to the point of application on an industrial scale. But by mid-1933 ever worsening sales totals were driving the Ruhr-based members of the syndicate into an attitude of every man for himself, which portended the dissolution not only of that grouping, but also of the international cartel.[155] In those events, IG's proceeds from nitrogen were bound to fall farther, as the producers fought for markets. Meanwhile, if the Fischer–Tropsch process proved rewarding, IG might face price competition and perhaps even a repetition of the overcapacity that now burdened the nitrogen industry. If the process failed, IG would be left in the unenviable position of a monopolist dependent exclusively on government protection precisely at a time when political attacks on corporate power were menacingly loud and frequent.[156]

Unless IG could both reunite the nitrogen producers and pave the way for a coordinated and profitable expansion of fuel sales, Leuna loomed by mid-1933 as an even greater liability than previously. The combine therefore offered the Ruhr mining industry technical assistance in applying IG's hydrogenation process to synthetic fuel production and more favorable terms of association with the German Nitrogen Syndicate.[157] In exchange, the concern hoped to get a broadened industrial front behind IG's now year-old efforts to persuade the Economics Ministry to sign a contract assuring gasoline producers of a minimum profit.[158]

IG's overtures to heavy industry paid off almost immediately. Joint tests on the hydrogenation of hard coal began in the summer of 1933, and in September, Albert Vögler of the Vereinigte Stahlwerke argued forcefully to the Generalrat der Wirtschaft in favor of expanding syn-

[154] D. Warriner, *Combines and Rationalization in Germany, 1924–1928* (London, 1931), p. 74; H. Wickel, *IG-Deutschland* (Berlin, 1932), pp. 135–41.
[155] See the summary of events in Bayer 186/D2, vol. 1, Report of the 6th meeting of the Nitrogen Sparte, 7.XII.33, pp. 40–1.
[156] On these considerations, see ibid., and BASF, Handakten Bosch, Notiz über eine Besprechung, 30.VI.33.
[157] Ibid; and BASF M02/1, Fischer to Krauch, 14.VIII.33, enclosing Fischer's report of conversations with LaRoche and Feder on 12.VIII.33.
[158] Tammen, *I. G. Farbenindustrie*, pp. 309–13.

thetic fuel production via this process.[159] More important, it was through Vögler that IG got an opportunity to exploit military interest in domestic fuel supplies. During August, Vögler referred Air Force General Milch's inquiries about synthetic propellants to Carl Krauch, the chief of IG's Sparte I.[160] Krauch promptly sent the general a copy of "The German Fuel Economy 1933," which either Krauch or Bosch had prepared a few months earlier.[161] In twenty pages and twelve appendixes, the document analyzed present and future German fuel demand and the possibilities and costs of satisfying it from domestic resources. Not surprisingly, considering the source, IG's paper concluded that, even assuming a 50% rise in German fuel purchases by 1937, the Reich could lift its internally produced share of gasoline consumption from 38 to 63%. The principal means to this end was to be an eightfold increase in the hydrogenation of coal, about half of it to take place at the plants of IG Farben. In order to prod the prospective producers into investing the necessary 400 million reichsmarks and thereby creating jobs for somewhere between 96,000 and 168,000 workers, the government, IG contended, merely needed to spare business the element of risk by guaranteeing a minimum price for domestic sales. Impressed, General Milch suggested that the armed services support IG's plan energetically to the responsible agencies, and in November, General Bockelberg of Army Ordnance did so at a meeting with the economics minister and his staff.[162]

Yet when IG's leaders and officials of the Economics Ministry finally gathered in Berlin on December 14 to initial the *Benzin-Vertrag*, their comments indicated that military considerations had played a quite secondary part in each side's desire for an agreement.[163] Gott-

---

159 Bütefisch III/114, 5th oil discussion, Ludwigshafen 26.IX.33; Hallgarten and Radkau, *Deutsche Industrie*, p. 288.
160 NI-5930/44, Albert Vögler to Krauch, 10.VIII.33.
161 Krauch's covering letter of 14.IX.33 is NI-4718/34. IG's report, long thought to have been lost, is in BASF, Bd. 36. On Bosch's possible authorship, see Tammen, *I. G. Farbenindustrie*, p. 440, note 599. In the covering letter, Krauch supplemented the report by noting that the Air Ministry's reported desire for an additional 700,000 tons of output would cost another 200 million reichsmarks.
162 NI-7123/55, Abschrift, Besprechung im RLM am 15.IX.33, written by Bockelberg; NI-7828/64, Ergebnis der Besprechung beim RWM am 6.XI.33.
163 BASF, Bd. 83, Abschluss des Leuna-Vertages mit dem RWM am 14.XII.33, signed by E. R. Fischer, 21.XII.33. After the war, three of the principal negotiators of the agreement, two of whom were present at the signing, swore that the bargaining proceeded from "a purely economic point of view" (Bütefisch IV/31, Affidavit by B. Mulert, 14.VII.47; IV/196, Affidavit by Ernst Fischer, 3.I.48; and IV/75, Affida-

fried Feder hailed the contract as an important contribution to civilian motorization. Carl Bosch voiced the hope that synthetic gasoline could soon compete unaided with natural fuel. More circumspectly, Hermann Schmitz stressed that new jobs and other immediate advantages to the national economy were the main reasons for IG's signature. Later, one of the negotiators of the deal remarked that the government had desired a free hand for its future tax and tariff policies concerning fuel, and it is probable that the Reich wanted to reduce the costs of importing oil from nearby Romania.[164] That IG's arguments for a price-support contract nevertheless would have arisen and very likely prevailed on their economic merits in a less militarized context is suggested by simultaneous developments in Britain. Making substantially the same case as IG, Imperial Chemical Industries obtained the chancellor of the exchequer's agreement on June 26, 1933, to a synthetic fuel guarantee the terms of which were virtually identical to those of the *Benzin-Vertrag*.[165]

If profits on rearmament had not been IG's chief concern, the terms the corporation obtained demonstrate that neither had the regime's military needs made it a compliant bargaining partner. Testifying to the length and intensity of the negotiations that produced it, the *Benzin-Vertrag* astutely balanced the interests of the contracting parties. IG agreed to triple gasoline production at Leuna to a rate of 300,000 to 350,000 tons per year by 1935, which would return the plant to the level of employment and operation at capacity last achieved in 1928.[166]

vit by Dr. Petri, 30.I.48). They were probably telling the truth; years later, Hitler, who was well informed about Farben's plans, claimed that the ministry had "sabotaged" them by delay; see Willi A. Boelcke, *Die deutsche Wirtschaft 1930–1945* (Düsseldorf, 1983), p. 161.

[164] Bütefisch IV/196, Fischer's affidavit, 3.I.48, p. 12.

[165] See the extensive discussion in W. J. Reader, *Imperial Chemical Industries: A History*, vol. 2: *The First Quarter Century, 1926–1952* (London, 1975), pp. 128–9, 171–81, and the briefer summary in idem, "Imperial Chemical Industries and the State, 1926–1945," in Barry Supple (ed.), *Essays in British Business History* (New York, 1977), pp. 233–7. Ten years later, Lord MacGowan of ICI recalled the firm's arguments for an article in *The Mining Journal* (5.II.44), which was excerpted as Bütefisch III/15. Neither Reader's accounts nor the German records suggest that the policy makers in either nation were aware of the negotiations in the other, although IG did know of ICI's plans to expand synthetic fuel production (Bütefisch III/114, Oil discussion, 26.IX.33). The German contract was kept secret for a year, and the British developments came to light only in the spring of 1934, when Parliament debated the necessary legislation. On the reasoning behind the Reich's decision not to publish its new Law for the Promotion of the German Oil Business, see the cabinet discussion of 1.XII.33 in Karl-Heinz Minuth (ed.), *Die Regierung Hitler*, Teil I: *1933/34* (Boppard am Rhein, 1983), pp. 987–9.

[166] Bayer 13/15, vol. 7, Bütefisch's report to the TEA, 15.II.34, pp. 2–4.

The Reich pledged to buy any unsold portion of that annual output from mid-1934 to mid-1944 and to guarantee that the firm's total wholesale receipts per liter would equal IG's periodically recomputed production costs, including taxes and appropriate depreciation, plus a 5% return on invested capital. Any income beyond this sum was to revert to the government.[167] IG thus got an end to the annual financial drain of the Leuna works, a sure basis for continued research on hydrocarbons, and an impetus to the deals on nitrogen and fuel with the Ruhr mining industry, but at the price of accepting a profit ceiling. Only if demand rose sufficiently to warrant the sale of licenses to other producers or increased output, to which the *Vertrag* would not apply, could the combine shorten the payback period on its accumulated plant, research, and development costs to less than about two decades. Conversely, the Reich risked a relatively small likely subsidy in return for the tax receipts on increased employment and the foreign exchange savings on reduced imports, with the possibility of substantial returns as production costs fell and demand raised prices. Since both sides thus had a stake in stimulating consumption, the secure price of 18.5 pfennigs per liter during the first year was about 3 pfennigs less than that ensured by the existing tariffs.[168]

Given Germany's importing problems, IG made a major concession by accepting the profit ceiling, as events demonstrated. The government never had to make good on its purchase agreement and subsidized the works for only two years with between 4.7 and 5.8 million marks. From 1936 to 1945, the Reich retrieved this money and skimmed off a net profit of 86.5 million marks from the excess proceeds of IG's sales.[169] But the concern had ample reason to take pleasure in the pact, both immediately and later. By the end of January 1934, representatives of IG and the mine operators were already planning the locations of new fuel plants, and a revised nitrogen syndicate agreement was nearly in place.[170] Thereafter until 1939, as a result of

---

167 NI-881/9, *Benzin Vertrag*, 14.XII.33, and accompanying letters by Feder and Finance Minister Schwerin von Krosigk.
168 Birkenfeld, *Treibstoff*, pp. 28, 234.
169 Ibid., p. 29; Bütefisch I/101, Affidavit by J. Simmler, 24.XI.47. On the size of the subsidy, compare Bütefisch IV/109 and III/344, both affidavits by E. Würth, the latter including calculations dated 6.II.37, and BA Koblenz, R2/15458, Vermerk F6523a-141V, October 1943. On the Reich's profits, see Birkenfeld, *Treibstoff*, pp. 32–3, 235; Tammen, *I. G. Farbenindustrie*, pp. 322–4; both supplemented by BA Koblenz, R2/15458, various *Vermerke*, August 1944 to early 1945.
170 Tammen, *I. G. Farbenindustrie*, pp. 324–5; Bayer 186/D2, vol. 1, 6th meeting of the Nitrogen Sparte, 7.XII.33, pp. 46–8.

the revival of German agriculture, IG's nitrogen income climbed almost without interruption, as did the concern's share of sales of nitrogenous products within Germany.[171] Though all but one of the Ruhr mining companies backed out of hydrogenation in October 1934, other licensees materialized, yielding income, insulating IG somewhat during peacetime from pressures for excessive expansion, and ending the danger of monopoly. Still, not until 1941 did Sparte I earn as much as in 1929; among the firm's product lines, only dyes lagged more.[172] Benzin alone remained through 1945, strictly speaking, a losing proposition, its accrued expenses still exceeding total net earnings.[173]

Satisfying as the trends in economic policy were to IG Farben, they reflected an intersection, not an identity, of interests between the regime and the firm. The concern remained somewhat wary, probably in part because several events during the first half of 1934 highlighted the Third Reich's tendency to take back from business with one hand what had recently been given with the other. After promulgating a labor decree (AOG) in January that assigned employers nearly complete authority to set employees' wages and working conditions, subject only to the approval of the thirteen regional trustees of labor appointed by the state during the preceding June, the government in March named an uncongenial new set of trustees.[174] In place of the previous group, of whom only seven had been party members before their appointments and nine were professional bureaucrats or former legal advisers to industrial groups, the new officeholders consisted almost entirely of "old Party comrades." The one exception, Labor Minister Seldte assured Hitler, had "understood how to win the confidence of the Labor Front and the NSBO."[175] Among those removed was Josef Klein, the former social welfare secretary at IG's Uerdingen plant.[176] During the same month, Economics Minister Schmitt dis-

[171] Bayer 15/Da 1.1, Umsätze; Bütefisch I/81, Affidavit by H. von Keler, 10.XII.47.

[172] Bayer, Da 15/1.1, Umsätze.

[173] Birkenfeld, *Treibstoff*, pp. 33–4; Bütefisch I/159, Affidavit by K. Hartmann, 12.I.48.

[174] On the AOG, see Mason, *Sozialpolitik*, pp. 107–19; Mason, in Mommsen et al. (eds.), *Industrielles System*, pp. 322–51; Schweitzer, *Big Business*, pp. 124, 367–70; Barkai, *Wirtschaftssystem*, p. 98; Schoenbaum, *Social Revolution*, pp. 86–8. The text of the law appeared in the *RGBl.* Pt. 1, 1934, p. 45, and was submitted at the postwar trial as PS-1861. A rather uninformative statement by the chief drafter of the law is NI-7015/54, Affidavit by W. Mansfeld, 7.V.47.

[175] Barkai, *Wirtschaftssystem*, pp. 99–100; see also Mason, *Sozialpolitik*, p. 107, note 26.

[176] See BDC Personalakten Klein, excerpt from *Das Deutsche Führerlexikon 1934/35*, p. 235.

closed his reservations about the need for cartels in a National Socialist economy and announced plans, pursuant to the new Law for
the Preparation of the Organic Structure of the Economy, to remodel
the nation's economic interest organizations. Implicitly brushing aside
Krupp's labors of the previous spring, Schmitt advanced a system that
emanated from the office of Gottfried Feder. The scheme dissolved the
Reichsstand der deutschen Industrie, demoted Krupp to the chairmanship of only one of twelve main economic groups, and elevated
Philipp Kessler of the electrical industry to the new post of *Führer der
Wirtschaft,* responsible to the economics minister alone. Opposed by
big business and distracted by other problems, Schmitt moved only
haltingly during the subsequent months toward enacting this program,
but he did not abandon it.[177]

The events surrounding the Röhm Purge of June 30 also had a
double-edged quality. Admittedly, two changes favorable to business
coincided with the crisis. Schmitt took leave from his office, if apparently only temporarily, on grounds of ill health, and the agreement
renewing the Adolf Hitler Spende, revealed in late June, tightened
restrictions on additional Party collections and lowered the obligatory
contribution from 0.5 to 0.3% of each firm's total wage and salary
bill.[178] And as a result of the "Night of the Long Knives," the trou-
blesome SA and NSBO were soon reduced to little more than devices
for propagandizing parts of the population and periodically exercising
their loyalties.[179] However, while disciplining those who sought to
speed the Nazi revolution, the Party leaders turned on conspicuous
figures who had tried to contain it. Among the several hundred dead
by early July were not only Röhm and his entourage, but also two

177 See NI-100/2, the law of 27.II.34; Facius, *Wirtschaft und Staat,* p. 144: Schulze,
Anfänge, pp. 341–4, and the appropriate notes; Schweitzer, *Big Business* pp. 249–
50; Barkai, *Wirtschaftssystem,* pp. 101–2; and Boelcke, *Deutsche Wirtschaft,* p.
96. For indications of business's disagreement with the economic reorganization see
Krupp HA/FAH IV C 178, *Aktenvermerk* of a meeting among Köttgen, Pietzsch,
and Schmitt, 29.XI.33; and SAA 4/Lf676, exchange of letters between Carl
Friedrich von Siemens and Rudolf Blohm, 20–23.VII.34.
178 Bayer 13/11, vol. 2, ZA Büro to Duisberg and ZA members, 25.VI.34. The author
of the letter concluded that an earlier overpayment by IG would be set off against its
obligations for 1934–5. Judging from the figures in NI-4056/29, Receipts of IG's
contributions to the Adolf Hitler Spende, October 1944, this was too optimistic,
and the firm paid almost 600,000 reichsmarks during the period.
179 On the treatment of the NSBO, see Schoenbaum, *Social Revolution,* pp. 82–3. On
the fate of the SA, see Broszat, *Staat Hitlers,* pp. 271–2; Orlow, *Nazi Party: 1933–
1945,* pp. 151, 428–9; and Jamin, in Hirschfeld and Kettenacker (eds.), *Der
Führerstaat,* pp. 343–58.

retired senior generals, including Hitler's immediate predecessor as chancellor and the two advisers to Papen responsible for his recent address at Marburg, in which the vice-chancellor had dared proclaim that "it is time . . . to avoid disturbing the labors of serious men and to silence fanatics."[180] After a spell of house arrest, Papen had to give up his office and retreat into genteel insignificance as special minister to Austria. To those who lived through it, the Röhm affair demonstrated that in the Third Reich people were either accomplices or victims, and the imprudent ran the risk of being both.

The experience of Heinrich Gattineau brought this lesson home to the leaders of IG Farben. By now a colonel (*Standartenführer*) in the SA and widely perceived as Röhm's principal economic adviser, Gattineau was arrested by the Gestapo on June 30 on suspicion of having financed Röhm's alleged plot against Hitler with Farben's money. Clapped into prison, he narrowly escaped the executions that awaited five of the eight SA commanders with whom he had associated most closely. Upon his release a few days later, he resigned from the SA and all his semiofficial or otherwise prominent posts. This self-cleansing failed to satisfy Erwin Selck, the *Vorstand* member to whom Gattineau reported. Eager to relieve IG of any taint of conspiracy, Selck declared the former SA man persona non grata at IG's offices on Unter den Linden and promised to see to his dismissal. Though Carl Bosch stepped in to protect Gattineau, he had forfeited much of his value to the concern. His Wipo office was soon subordinated to Ilgner and Kurt Krüger at Berlin NW7, and within a year, he had lost his press duties and the deputy membership on the firm's Working Committee that he had acquired in 1933.[181] Despite proof of political rehabilitation in the form of admission to the NSDAP in 1935, Gattineau's career never really recovered, and he spent the period from 1938 to 1945 managing IG's major subsidiary in Slovakia.[182]

[180] Quoted in Alan Bullock, *Hitler: A Study in Tyranny* (Harmondsworth, England, 1962), p. 300.

[181] NI-4833/35, Affidavit by H. Gattineau, 13.III.47; Gattineau, *Klippen*, pp. 116, 140–8. In a general way, the charges against IG surfaced in the *Deutsche Zeitung* for 4.VII.34. An article titled "Die gescheiten Spätlinge," preserved in SAA 4/Lf676, denounced opportunistic businessmen who had opposed the Nazis before 1933 and then "become in large part 150% National Socialists, not out of conviction but out of concern for their interests." The article asked "Whence came the money for the wire pullers of the 'second revolution'?" and answered by suggesting that such opportunistic corporate executives had continued their Weimar practice of giving to all political contenders as a form of insurance.

[182] M892/57, Gattineau's testimony, pp. 12407–14, 12420; NI-6544/50, Affidavit by M. Ilgner, 30.IV.47; NI-10044/82, Affidavit by H. Bässler, 4.VIII.47; Gattineau

Gattineau's close call and professional eclipse served as a continuing reminder to IG's leaders of what might befall those who appeared out of step with their führer. A Bosch could on occasion defy the warning, protected by his international eminence, his declining role within the firm, and the increasing quantities of painkillers and alcohol to which he turned after 1935.[183] But lesser figures felt less secure and knew that the regime could deal with real or imagined recalcitrance in numerous indirect or pseudolegal ways. Schnitzler witnessed such methods in the summer of 1934, when his friend Fried Luebbecke antagonized the Party by refusing to turn over to it a children's home run by a society he headed. In reprisal, Luebbecke recalled fourteen years later, the Nazis whipped up the local peasantry against him and "sent, together with the 'aroused population,' the riot squad to the front of my house for my delivery into protective custody." Missing arrest "by mere chance," he found asylum with Schnitzler, who later spirited him out of Frankfurt and across the Taunus Mountains, allegedly dodging Nazi roadblocks along the way.[184] The affair blew over, Luebbecke survived relatively unmolested, and in subsequent cases of arrested secretaries and subordinates IG's leaders usually were able to mobilize lawyers and contacts successfully.[185] But the outcomes were never certain, and the experiences before release always likely to be harrow-

Nachtrag III/111, a copy of Gattineau's membership file in the Party *Kartei*. Gattineau retained purely formal supervision of Wipo after 1.V.39, when Jost Terhaar was placed in effective charge of the office; see NI-7982/66, Ilgner's circular letter of 20.IV.39.

183 Bosch moved up from the chairmanship of the *Vorstand* to that of the *Aufsichtsrat* in April 1935. On his defiance of the Nazis, see his altercation with Education Minister Rust in January 1935 over a memorial service to Fritz Haber; Borkin, *Crime and Punishment*, pp. 57–58; and Beyerchen, *Scientists*, pp. 66–8. Lochner, *Tycoons*, p. 223, claims that Bosch expressed criticism openly at meetings of IG's boards. There is, however, nothing to the story that Bosch's attacks on corruption in the Party broke apart the Ruhrlade, an upshot variously dated to 1934 and 1938 in NI-11552/95, Affidavit by J. Reichert, 3.X.47; Schweitzer, *ZfN*, 20 (1960), p. 419; Manchester, *Arms of Krupp*, p. 413; and Hallgarten and Radkau, *Deutsche Industrie*, p. 292. This organization, which Bosch was invited to join in June 1935, last convened in June 1939, after which the press of wartime supposedly prevented further sessions; see GHH 40010124/15, Reusch to Bosch, 17.VI.35, Reusch to Siemens, 5.VI.39, Reusch to Vögler, 7.XI.39, and Reusch to Bosch, 11.XII.39. Quite possibly, however, the group ceased meeting at least in part because its members feared to continue after one of them, Fritz Thyssen, fled the country and had his property confiscated by the Prussian state in the fall of 1939. On Bosch's mounting depression and choice of antidotes, see Holdermann, *Im Banne der Chemie*, pp. 293–305; Duisberg, *Nur ein Sohn*, p. 149; and Lochner, *Tycoons*, pp. 46–7.

184 Schnitzler IX/161, Affidavit by Fried Luebbecke, 27.II.48.

185 For example, Schnitzler IX/160, Affidavit by H. Dubois, 23.II.48; Bütefisch II/149, Affidavit by O. Dietzel, 9.XI.47.

ing. If the humbling of the SA removed one threat to the capitalist system and the economic recovery numbed the consciences of many executives, the first eighteen months of Nazi rule also established that in the Third Reich, for individual businessmen and everyone else, "terror was the greatest of political realities."[186]

[186] Craig, *Germany 1866–1945*, p. 601. Many scholars have emphasized the paradox that the Nazi bloodletting of 1934 was taken primarily by contemporaries as a sign of the movement's desire to preserve order. I doubt that most big businessmen were so blind. Dr. Josef Klein, IG's former officer who had been removed as labor trustee for Westphalia a few months earlier, was among those who drew the proper conclusion. Shortly after the Röhm Purge, he remarked concerning the absence of legal procedures that "this is a grave development. You will see, it is only the beginning"; quoted in Paul Kleinewefers, *Jahrgang 1905* (Stuttgart, 1984), p. 80. Klein lost his seat in the Reichstag in March 1936, and on October 1943, the Supreme Party Court confirmed his expulsion from the NSDAP for "behavior damaging to the Party at his workplace, the August-Thyssen-Hütte." See M. Schwarz (ed.), *MdR. Biographisches Handbuch der Reichstage* (Hannover, 1965), and BDC, Personalakten Klein.

4. From Schacht to Göring

On August 2, 1934, when he took over the powers of the deceased President Hindenburg, Adolf Hitler selected Hjalmar Schacht to stand in for the officially ailing Kurt Schmitt. Faced with a potentially paralyzing foreign exchange shortage and perhaps eager to reassure business about his one-man rule, the führer overrode the objections of the Party's economic "experts" and reached for an established financier, albeit one whose credentials as a Hitler supporter were beyond dispute. For a little more than a year, the Old Wizard lived up to his sobriquet. While his famous "deviltries" maintained an adequate flow of raw materials to the industrially resurgent and rearming Reich, he added to his offices and power. By May 1935, he was not only president of the Reichsbank and economics minister in his own right, but also general plenipotentiary for the war economy and widely regarded as a virtual "economic dictator." He had acquired, moreover, a reputation as big business's protector in Berlin, which, though exaggerated, seemed accurate enough from the vantage point of IG Farben.

The new minister certainly lost little time putting his stamp on policy in a manner that suited the concern. Upon taking office, he removed Feder, Kessler, and Pietzsch from their economic posts and obtained Hitler's promise that the NSDAP would not further restrict the commercial activities of Jews.[1] In subsequent months, Schacht took a firm stand against the empire building of Robert Ley and the Nazi DAF and presented business with a revised version of Schmitt's reorganization scheme, shorn of its most threatening features.[2] As a result of the last-named initiative, IG regained some of its former weight in Germany's industrial associations. Georg von Schnitzler became a member of the advisory council (*Beirat*) of the RSI's successor,

---

[1] Schweitzer, *Big Business*, pp. 253–4; Schacht, *Confessions*, p. 293.
[2] The most complete discussions of Schacht's organizational "housecleaning" appear in Ingeborg Esenwein-Rothe, *Die Wirtschaftsverbände von 1933 bis 1945* (Berlin, 1965), pp. 41–6, 68–75; and Dieter Swatek, *Unternehmenskonzentration als Ergebnis und Mittel nationalsozialistischer Wirtschaftspolitik* (Berlin, 1972), pp. 134–46. See also Boelcke, *Deutsche Wirtschaft*, pp. 96–8.

the Reichsgruppe Industrie (RGI), and presided over two of its committees, and IG's representatives got seats on thirteen others.[3] The *Beiräte* of six of the eighteen regional economic chambers also included IG executives.[4] To be sure, Pietzsch's replacement as head of Main Group V within the RGI, which bracketed firms making chemicals, oils, fats, and paper, was Bernhard Pfotenhauer of the Merck pharmaceuticals house, a major competitor with close ties to the electrochemical firm Pietzsch directed. But C. A. Clemm, the leader of the Economic Group for Chemicals (Wirtschaftsgruppe or Wigru Chemie), came from Kali-Chemie, in which IG owned 25% of the shares.[5] His deputy leader was Schnitzler. Johannes Hess, the head of an IG affiliate in Munich, met with the Wigru's executive committee (*engerer Beirat*), and Ernst Fischer, Gajewski, Krauch, and Paul Müller spoke for the concern on the *Beirat*. Of the Wigru's nineteen product groups (*Fachgruppen*), those for dyes, explosives, fertilizers, fibers, and oil had chairmen from Farben, and the *Beiräte* of six more counted executives of the combine in their ranks.[6]

Owing in part to Schacht's actions, political pressure on IG abated as its access to influence revived. When the *Aufsichtsrat* convened on November 24 for its first meeting since April, there was no sign or mention of representatives from the NSBO.[7] Nor did IG have to pay much heed to the DAF during the next two years, aside from coaxing the plant leaders to join that organization in order to dilute its working-class character and comply with the Leipzig Agreement of March 1935 between Schacht and Ley.[8] Where disputes with the works councils arose, the factory or office managers generally succeeded in outmaneuvering or removing the complainants.[9] Sporadic attacks on

[3] Bayer 4B/36, vol. 2, Vowi 1678, I. G.-Vertreter in den Ausschussen der Reichsgruppe Industrie, 10.I.36.
[4] Bayer 4B/36, vol. 2, Vowi 1706, Herren der I. G. und von Beteiligungsfirmen in den Beiräten der (Bezirks-) Wirtschaftskammern, 29.I.36.
[5] Bayer 64/12, Wigru Chemie; Erich Stockhorst, *Fünftausend Köpfe* (Velbert, 1967), entries for Karl Merck, p. 291, and Bernhard Pfotenhauer, p. 323.
[6] Bayer 4B/36, vol. 2, Vowi 1708, Herren der I. G. und von Beteiligungsfirmen in der Organisation der Wirtschaftsgruppe Chemische Industrie, 29.I.36.
[7] Bayer 11/3, Aufsichtsrat meeting of 24.XI.34.
[8] NI-7245/57, Meeting of the *Betriebsführer,* 12.VII.35. On the agreement, see Mason, *Sozialpolitik,* pp. 194–5, and Schweitzer, *Big Business,* pp. 148–9; for the Party's version, see H. Biallas and G. Starcke, *Leipzig, das Nürnberg der Deutschen Arbeitsfront* (München, 1935).
[9] See Bayer 214/10 for the records of dealings with the Leverkusen and Dormagen *Vertrauensräte;* also Gajewski I/1, Hingst to Gestapo, 26.IX.39, pp. 6–10; Oster I/11, Affidavit by P. Assman, 18.II.48; and NI-7619/57, Affidavit by G. Frank-Fahle, 20.VI.47.

Jews augmented the number of endangered employees transferred to IG's overseas affiliates, but denunciations of the concern's supposed philo-Semitism waned.[10] Hence, as late as April 1935, IG dared to add a man with four Jewish grandparents, Richard Merton of the Metallgesellschaft, to the *Aufsichtsrat*.[11] Even the Party's demand for contributions slackened; expressed as a percentage of sales, the burden probably as much as halved between 1933 and 1936.[12] Only the Nazi Auslandsorganisation continued to squeeze the combine hard, with the result that increasing sums went to "various projects for Germanism" overseas. But IG could often hold up funding, consenting, for example, to contribute 500 pesos monthly to a Party propaganda office in Argentina only after it had "been in operation for three months [and] all German firms with the exception of IG had agreed to furnish financial support."[13]

Though these developments could not entirely erase the corporation's nervousness about its position in the Nazi state, they did permit IG to relax its quest for friends in high places. In fact, "well aware that IG was suspected as a big capitalistic concern with international interests and relations not at all in line with Nazi ideas about economics," the combine's chief lobbying unit, the Wipo office, generally tried to disguise the authorship of IG's proposals concerning government policy by routing them through the *Wigru Chemie* and the RGI.[14] As the regime's economic regulations grew more encompassing and intricate between 1933 and 1936, the budgets for the Vowi and Wipo offices doubled and quintupled, respectively.[15] But the two organizations concentrated on drafting written submissions for relevant agencies and interpreting their directives, not on forging links to Party bigwigs.[16] The extremely careful Hermann Schmitz, who succeeded Bosch as chairman of the *Vorstand* in April 1935, seems to have used

10 NI-5166/38, Affidavit by H. Oster, 2.V.47: NI-14000/114, Jacobi to Amchan, 3.IX.47, with enclosures; Oster II/141, Affidavit by A. Suhr; Krauch VI/49, Affidavit by R. Hasenclever.
11 Bayer 11/3, vol. 5, *Aufsichtsrat* meeting of 27.IV.35.
12 NI-9200/76 and NI-7366/59, Affidavits by H. Bässler, 30.VII.47 and 28.VI.47; Defense Basic Information II/4, Affidavit by H. Walter, 25.III.48.
13 See NI-6696/51, Siering to Bayer, 2.XII.35; NI-4613/34, Homann to Bayer, 5.VI.35; Bayer to ZA, 14.VI.35; Gattineau to Bayer, 6.XI.35; Mann III/301, Bayer to Hauser, 23.III.36; and, in general, NI-7964/66, Affidavit by H. Bässler, 16.VII.47.
14 NI-2750/20, Affidavit by K. Krüger, 31.VIII.45.
15 On the expenses, which totaled to 667,000 marks in 1936, see NI-10923/90, Affidavit by H. Muench, 10.IX.47.
16 NI-7619/62, Affidavit by G. Frank-Fahle, 20.VI.47.

his extensive connections in the capital similarly, saying little and listening for shifts in the political wind to which he might trim IG's conduct.[17] With Gattineau chastened and Ilgner ill or traveling much of the time, the firm was able to keep a low political profile during Schacht's ascendancy.[18]

Equally satisfactory to IG were Schacht's responses in September 1934 to the balance-of-payments crisis that had brought the Reich to the brink of international insolvency. For a network of political and financial reasons, he refused to take the orthodox way out and devalue the mark. Instead, he inaugurated the so-called New Plan, which established or strengthened governmental machinery for barring dispensable imports, subsidizing exports, and funneling trade toward nations that produced what Germany needed and would accept German goods in payment.[19] A few weeks later, he launched an intensified effort to reduce purchases of essential raw materials from abroad by engineering the formation of the Braunkohle Benzin AG (Brabag), a new synthetic fuel producer. Though neither of the minister's actions can be directly traced to IG Farben's influence, they interlocked with the evolution of the concern's interests during 1934.

Three months before the announcement of the New Plan, Wilhelm Gaus, a member of the *Vorstand* now associated with Sparte II, set in motion a review of the production program for that division, IG's largest (63% of sales in 1934) and most export sensitive (55% of receipts earned abroad).[20] The immediate stimulus to Gaus's action

[17] See as illustrations of Schmitz's characteristic reticence the minutes of the two meetings of Göring's Gutachter-Ausschuss on 15.V.36 and 30.IV.36, BA Koblenz, R26 I/36. In discussions stretching over six hours and concerned with export questions, Schmitz maintained complete silence. His one contribution to a third lengthy meeting on May 26 occurred in response to a direct question (NI-5380/39, the minutes of that session).

[18] According to Ilgner's travel record in IG in Abw., Personalakte Ilgner, he spent 70% of the days between July 1, 1934, and December 31, 1936, outside of Berlin and 47% of the period on trips outside of Germany.

[19] On the trading crisis, the details of the New Plan, and its multiple origins, see Gerhard Kroll, *Von der Weltwirtschaftskrise zur Staatskonjunktur* (Berlin, 1958), pp. 479, 493; Guillebaud, *Economic Recovery*, pp. 65–7; Erbe, *Nationalsozialistische Wirtschaftspolitik*, p. 71; Barkai, *Wirtschaftssystem*, p. 141; Joachim Radkau, "Entscheidungsprozesse und Entscheidungsdefizite in der deutschen Aussenwirtschaftspolitik 1933–40," *G&G*, 2 (1976), pp. 33–65; Doering, *Deutsche Aussenwirtschaftspolitik*, pp. 47–54; Schweitzer, *Big Business*, pp. 305–6; and D. Benning, "Der 'Neue Plan' und die Neuordnung der deutschen Aussenwirtschaft," *JNS*, 142 (1935), pp. 35–62.

[20] Bayer 15/Da 1.2, IG-Umsätze Gesamt 1933/37.

was a request from Wilhelm Keppler of the Reich Chancellery for a tabulation of the combine's present and expected output of potential substitutes for imported raw materials.[21] In all probability, Gaus would have contented himself with answering this limited inquiry had the general trend of the Reich's, IG's, and Sparte II's sales not been running parallel and in an unsettling direction: up within Germany since the previous year by 26, 28, and 28% respectively, but down abroad by 14, 7.5, and 4%.[22] Since IG's exports still returned more than thirteen times the cost of its imports, the firm could continue to clear its accounts quite handily through normal multilateral trading.[23] But the Reich could not, and the steady depletion of Germany's foreign exchange reserves threatened to strangle the domestic industrial customers whose purchases accounted for IG's incipient recovery. Besides, wide variation in the resurgence of the disparate product lines within Sparte II had left it with substantial pockets of costly unused capacity. Thus, while complying with Keppler's wish, Gaus asked Ilgner to have the Vowi office examine whether the current trading problems of the Reich and, particularly, of its chemical industry were likely to prove temporary or lasting. In the latter case, Gaus suspected, "one should immediately and consciously shift IG's research toward new production for domestic needs." By mid-July, the resulting study by Anton Reithinger was ready for circulation to a number of the combine's leaders for their comments.[24]

Reithinger's brief concluded unequivocally that both the nation and the concern confronted international commercial "phenomena of lengthy duration," which neither foreign financial help nor a currency devaluation could more than paper over. Given the size of Germany's foreign debts, the increasing bilateralization of international trade, and the probable rise in world prices for raw materials as a result of global rearmament efforts, the national payments balance was likely to remain adverse for some time. The consequent "conditions in the German domestic market," Reithinger predicted, "will necessitate new construction of capacities for supplying raw material substitutes

21 NI-4885/36, Gaus to meeting of Direktion at Ludwigshafen, 4.VII.34.
22 Gustav Stolper, *The German Economy 1870 to the Present* (New York, 1967), pp. 142, 145; Bayer 15/Da 1.2, IG-Umsätze Gesamt 1933/37.
23 Calculated from Bayer 15/Da 1.2, IG-Umsätze Gesamt 1933/37, and D.A. 377, Westpfahl to Kühne, 9.III.38.
24 Bayer 4/C6, Gaus to Kühne, 12.VII.34.

and, on the other hand, probably reduce the demand for the existing production of important Sparten." At the same time, the growth of closed trading blocs, the industrialization of other countries, and the decline of Germany's technical and patent advantages would make even the maintenance of the present depressed volume of German chemical exports extremely problematic. Therefore, both "duty to the national economy" and "private commercial necessity" dictated that IG reorient research and production around import substitutes and focus foreign marketing on "countries not connected to an economic sphere" and on technically sophisticated products that other nations either could not or would not strive to imitate. To carry out the detailed planning necessary for such a changeover, Reithinger suggested forming a development department composed of research chemists from the Sparten and statistical experts from the Vowi office.[25]

Lacking firm evidence, one can only speculate about the impact of Reithinger's findings on IG's leaders. The analysis no doubt sounded familiar, being merely an application to the concern's business of what had become by mid-1934 the conventional wisdom among German economic commentators. Most of them were convinced that the Reich's position as an "aging industrial nation" and its transformation by the Treaty of Versailles from a creditor to a debtor state now demanded fundamental adjustments in the country's manufacturing and markets.[26] The repetition of such views probably had disposed the majority of IG's managers to accept Schacht's specious claim that his departures from liberal principle were "hideous" necessities, forced on Germany by "structural" conditions and the actions of foreign powers.[27] For, like Schacht throughout 1934–5, Reithinger argued from external constraints that a German government more desirous of international cooperation might have tried to ease. The emergent arms race, the nation's debts, and the shrinkage of commerce among the industrial states were all alterable, at least in theory. Appreciating this, Hermann Bücher of AEG, an unreconstructed free

[25] Bayer 4/C6, Neue Ziele und Aufgaben für die Forschungs- und Produktionspolitik der I.G., 30.VI.34, pp. 1–13.
[26] For example, Institut für Konjunkturforschung, "Die Industriewirtschaft," *Vierteljahreshefte für Konjunkturforschung*, Sonderheft 31 (1933), pp. 37–45; C. Ungewitter, "Ist chemiewirtschaftliche Aktivität gerechtfertigt?" Spezialarchiv der deutschen Wirtschaft, *Der I.G. Farben-Konzern 1932* (Berlin, 1932), pp. 9–12.
[27] Kroll, *Weltwirtschaftskrise*, pp. 495–6.

trader long close to IG's chief executives, urged the regime in 1934 and again in 1935 to seek a comprehensive international settlement limiting armaments. On such a basis, Germany might then obtain a consolidation of its debt, substantial loans and new trade treaties from the United States and France in return for a devaluation of the mark and an end to controls on foreign exchange, and release from restrictions on the domestic money and capital markets as a result of a reduced need for the government to place its bills and bonds. Bücher, along with Carl Goerdeler, who also twice took issue with the New Plan in writing during these years, foresaw far better than Schacht that his program would become a vicious circle. They perceived that each attempt to rearm and recover in isolation from the other developed countries would merely reinforce the pressure to do so by aggravating international rivalries.[28] However, if any of IG's directors thought this way in 1934–5, his views went unrecorded.

Whatever the reaction within the combine to Reithinger's memorandum, immediate concerns, not market projections, decided Farben in favor of Schacht's economic program. The hard questions posed by the regime's dedication to autarky and armaments had to do, not with the direction of national policy, but with its pace and extent. Since Schacht's actions left the concern considerable leeway in these matters of execution, IG had little to fear from the measures he advanced but something to lose by their delay or failure.

This was immediately obvious with regard to the feature of the New Plan that many businessmen found most obnoxious: the need to locate purchasers and suppliers in the predominantly nonindustrial countries that were willing to enter into special trade balancing or clearing agreements with the Reich. Not all of the firm's leaders could credit the great gains that Ilgner envisioned, especially in the Balkans, from this reorientation of German trade, but the success of his convoluted "compensation" deals did provide the only bright spot in IG's dismal overseas prospects.[29] Under his supervision, the Wipo office already had demonstrated impressive dexterity in shifting some of IG's buying

---

28 On Bücher, see Schweitzer, *Big Business*, pp. 434–5; and RG242/T77/86, Frames 809800–19, his memo of 28.VII.35. On Goerdeler, see Gerhard Ritter, *Carl Goerdeler und die deutsche Widerstandsbewegung* (München, 1964), pp. 74–88; and Doering, *Deutsche Aussenwirtschaftspolitik,* pp. 223–9.
29 See Ilgner to the Working Committee, 3.X.33, in Radant, *JfW,* 3 pp. 187–92. Alfred Sohn-Rethel, *Oekonomie und Klassenstruktur des deutschen Faschismus* (Frankfurt, 1973), pp. 92–3, notes the difference of opinion within IG but contends that nitro-

toward contractors in Southeast Europe and Latin America.[30] By
1934, his most imaginative schemes, the encouragement under IG's
auspices of linseed oil production in Hungary and soybean cultivation
in Romania and Bulgaria, were coming to fruition. Over the next five
years, the soybean trade, largely guaranteed against loss by the Reich,
earned 15.5 million marks on imports of fodder and vegetable oils to
Germany and made possible exports of chemicals probably worth just
as much.[31]

More important, however, because the government recognized that
the success of its trading program depended on the contacts and skills
of major private firms, bureaucratic interference with IG's commerce
actually seemed likely to decline under the New Plan, which for a time
was the case. While the plan's groundwork was being laid in August
1934, the desperate authorities relaxed their exchange controls in
order to reanimate exports. Companies were now allowed to meet
foreign currency needs directly out of their own incomes from overseas, provided only that goods produced from the imports so funded
brought in an exchange profit of at least 20%, which had to be deposited with the Reichsbank.[32] Since IG's annual ratio of export earnings
to import purchases hovered around 10 : 1 in the mid-1930s and that
between exchange receipts and deposits averaged out to about 2 : 1,
the new procedure granted the concern exceptional commercial freedom.[33] Indeed, the lower reaches of the corporation tended to forget
in subsequent years that IG's purchases were subject to the formal
approval of the newly created Oversight Office (Ueberwachungsstelle)

gen exporters saw great opportunities in the Balkans. This is doubtful, given the
development of native production facilities and the worldwide problem of overcapacity. In fact, IG's exports of nitrogen fell steadily during the 1930s, despite
increasing trade with Southeast Europe; see Defense Basic Information II/8, Affidavit by H. Walter, 25.III.48. On the "compensation" deals, see Chapter 3.

[30] NI-2750/20, Affidavit by K. Krüger, 31.VIII.45.
[31] On the soy project, see Radant, *JfW*, 7 (1966), pp. 162–3; on the Hungarian deal,
Ilgner to the AA, 3.X.33, ibid., p. 191; and on both, Schröter, *Deutsche Industrie auf
dem Weltmarkt*, pp. 177–8. The guarantee agreement is summarized in BA Koblenz,
R2/13424, Zusammenstellung der vom Reiche übernommenen und noch laufenden
Bürgschaften . . . nach dem Stande vom 1.I.37, Item B19.
[32] Bayer D.A. 377, Ungewitter to members of the Chemie Verein, 14.VI.34; Kühne to
Industrie- und Handelskammer, Solingen, 9.VIII.34. Schweitzer, *Big Business*, p.
493, says that the government required a profit of 30% but provides no traceable
source or date for this figure.
[33] On the former ratio, see Bayer D.A. 377, Devisenverbrauch 1933, 21.III.34, and
Westpfahl to Kühne, 31.III.36; for the latter, NI-10546/87, Affidavit by G. Frank-
Fahle, 23.VII.47, with accompanying chart. See Hoechst TEA 264–65 for detailed
statements of IG's import-to-export ratios in 1933 and 1936.

for Chemicals, toward whose support IG had to pay 150,000 marks annually in fees.[34] Though the concern's central offices constantly reminded buyers at the plants that their lordly behavior was prejudicing a close and smooth working relationship with the bureaucracy and exposing IG and themselves to punishment, no real problems arose.[35] On the contrary, the government made IG the Reich's exclusive purchasing agent for such vital products as oil, benzol, sulfur, nickel, iodine, rubber, molybdenum, chromium ore, tungsten, and phosphates. By borrowing abroad against its sales to finance these imports, IG obviated any drain on government foreign exchange reserves and ensured that the concern's own raw material needs would be met. When the regime reimbursed the firm in marks or permitted it to retrieve its expenses through higher prices at home, IG probably also collected a modest commission for its services.[36]

With regard to production policy, Schacht's program also seemed to solve more important problems than it created. The foundation of Brabag as a quasi-public synthetic fuels firm provided a superficially surprising illustration. On September 21, 1934, the economics minister called representatives of Germany's brown coal producers to Berlin and announced his intention to enlist them in a compulsory corporation to construct and operate a series of plants capable of manufacturing about 500,000 tons of benzin per year from lignite. The Reich offered to guarantee sale of the output at a price that ensured reasonable depreciation and return on investment.[37] To capitalize the new enterprise, each producer of more than 100,000 tons of lignite per year was to pay 2 marks on each ton of its output and to receive shares commensurate with its proportion of total national brown coal production.[38] Anticipating disagreement, Schacht justified his plan not

---

34 Bayer D.A. 377, Westpfahl to Kühne, 20.IV.36.
35 Bayer DA. 377, Einkaufsabteilung to the plants, 15.VIII.34; Zefi to *Vorstand* members, directors, and *Prokurists*, 2.XI.35; Circular letter from Zefi, 23.IV.36. See also NI-4930/36, Affidavit by F. Ehrmann, 13.III.47.
36 NI-10679/88, Affidavit by G. Frank-Fahle, 9.IX.47; NI-4928/36, Affidavit by K. Krüger, 18.III.47. For an example, see Schmitz's report on a foreign loan for the equivalent of 30 million marks (Bayer 11/3, vol. 5, 39th meeting of the *Aufsichtsrat*, 24.XI.34, p. 4).
37 Twenty-one basic documents concerning Brabag from the files of the Flick concern are collected as NI-3975/28 and ably summarized in Birkenfeld, *Treibstoff*, pp. 37–50. Unless otherwise indicated, the following discussion rests on these sources.
38 The levy on IG proved lower than Schacht had anticipated. It was fixed at 52 pfennigs per ton of coal and 1.31 marks per ton of briquettes produced; NI-7669/62, Report of the 1st oil discussion, Ludwigshafen, 10.I.35, no signature, dated 13.II.35.

only on economic grounds, but as an attempt to prevent the development of a Party-dominated firm, intimating that Wilhelm Keppler, the führer's economic adviser, had such designs.[39] Keppler was, in fact, intent on increasing German synthetic fuel production and thus holding down increases in the 144 million marks that Germany paid for fuel imports in 1932. He also wanted to promote the use of the Fischer–Tropsch fuel manufacturing process, which could be linked to the fabrication of synthetic fats, another of his interests.[40] Nonetheless, favoring still a third production process and not wishing to tie up their liquid capital, the stunned lignite firms told Schacht that they would not participate in the new corporation voluntarily. Thereupon, he in essence drafted ten companies to finance Brabag pursuant to his decree of September 28, 1934.

Though taken by surprise by Schacht's initiative, IG, as one of the nation's principal lignite miners, readily joined in.[41] Having already decided to pursue further profits from hydrogenation largely via licensing, only to have all the privately owned Ruhr mining companies back out in the fall of 1934, the concern probably saw Brabag as a godsend.[42] On October 11–12, representatives of the Air and Defense Ministries met with Krauch, Schneider, Bütefisch, Pier, and Fischer of IG to plan two new plants, both to produce under licenses from Farben. Ten days later, delegates of the participating firms were summoned to a meeting in Berlin on October 26 and directed to bring an initial contribution of 1 million marks each. This proved to be 10% of each firm's total assessment since the stock capital of 100 million marks was divided in ten equal portions under the contract that Schacht ordered the companies to sign on that date.[43] This document placed the new firm under the control of a commissar, Robert Deumer of the Reichsbank, who selected an *Aufsichtsrat* composed of Keppler

[39] NI-6524/49, Affidavit by C. Krauch, 29.IV.47; Boelcke, *Deutsche Wirtschaft,* pp. 161–2.
[40] On the import bill, see Kroll, *Weltwirtschaftskrise,* p. 504. Clear discussions of the available technologies appear in Arnold Krammer, "Fueling the Third Reich," *Technology and Culture,* 19 (1978), pp. 396–9, and Neal P. Cochran, "Oil and Gas from Coal," *Scientific American* 234 (1976), pp. 24–9.
[41] On IG's surprise, see Bütefisch IV/268, Meeting of the AA, 9.X.34.
[42] NI-6524/49, Affidavit by C. Krauch, 29.IV.47; Birkenfeld, *Treibstoff,* p. 49, note 63 (on the Ruhr's withdrawal).
[43] IG's share began, therefore, as 10%, rising to 13.2% as of 19.IX.40, according to NI-3975 and Bütefisch I/79, Affidavit by H. Bütefisch, 15.I.48. TerMeer, however, gives 12.6% as IG's share, with no date attached (*I. G. Farben,* pp. 83–4).

as chairman, Wohltat as Schacht's representative, and seven delegates of the brown coal industry. Although no IG man served on the supervisory board, Krauch became one of four members of the *Vorstand*, indeed, its only genuine private industrialist, since the other managing directors were Heinrich Koppenberg of Junkers aircraft company, which was tied to the Air Ministry, General von Vollard-Bockelberg of Army Ordnance, and Fritz Kranefuss, a protégé of Keppler and Himmler and the Party's agent. For the next nine months, Brabag evolved precisely as IG might have hoped. Under the license agreements signed the following summer, the concern got a lump sum payment for its technical assistance in the construction and operation of two factories at Bohlen and Magdeburg and a schedule of fees on various products that added up to an annual yield of more than 1 million marks on the first new plant alone.[44] Far from resenting Brabag as a dangerous precedent or competitor, the concern was glad of the opportunity to spread the risks and costs of benzin production.[45]

The New Plan and Brabag also headed off a major threat to business created by the exchange crisis of 1934. The army's increasing impatience with economic policy making raised the possibility, to which Keppler was alive in July, that the military would seek an expanded role in this sphere.[46] Though the concern's leaders appreciated the stimulating effect of military spending on their sales volume, they continued to value rearmament primarily as a means of funding the development of particular products whose eventual commercial profitability seemed likely. Wary of the specifically military market, on which Reithinger's report had touched only in passing, the firm neither saw itself nor was regarded before 1936 as a major defense producer. IG was not among the corporate backers of one of the two front organizations employed by the regime to finance rearmament, the Metallurgische Forschungsgesellschaft (Mefo). The combine sold its four thousand shares in the other such body, the Wirtschaftliche Forschungsgesellschaft (Wifo), in November 1935, some fifteen months after its founding.[47] As yet, few of IG's researchers specialized in

---

[44] The license contracts between IG and Brabag are NI-7767/63, 14.IV.35 and 22.VIII.35.
[45] Cf. Arthur Schweitzer, "Business Policy in a Dictatorship," *BHR*, 38 (1964), p. 436.
[46] See Doering, *Deutsche Aussenwirtschaftspolitik*, pp. 232–3.
[47] On the Mefo, see Barkai, *Wirtschaftssystem*, p. 129; on IG and the Wifo, NI-6347/47, Contract between IG and the Deutsche Bau- und Bodenbank A. G., 26.XI.35.

military-related products.[48] Successes in synthesizing glycerine, producing sulfuric acid on the basis of domestic gypsum, and making gun carriage wheels and firebomb containers out of magnesium did lead to some new production for the armed forces at IG's Wolfen, Hoechst, and especially its Bitterfeld and Aken plants.[49] The Munich Camera Works also began manufacturing clockwork fuses for the army in 1935.[50] During the same year, plans for accelerated airplane construction also prompted a doubling of the firm's aluminum capacity to 17,000 tons, although IG was reluctant to expand so rapidly and consented only in order to prevent new competitors from entering the industry and to maintain the concern's share of total potential national output at about 17%.[51] And, of course, the combine continued to gain by the extraordinary growth in munitions production. The gross profits of DAG, Troisdorf alone more than quadrupled between 1933 and 1936.[52] Still, when terMeer claimed after the war that no more than 3% of IG's sales went directly to the armed forces as late as 1938, he was probably not too wide of the mark.[53] On the whole IG responded to the rearmament drive rather defensively, participating only as necessary to seize or hold a valued market position.

The relatively low profit margins offered on government contracts contributed to the corporation's reserve, but its roots were in the

[48] NI-4669/34, Verm. W. to Knieriem, 8.XI.39.
[49] EC-128, Unsigned memo re armaments, 30.IX.34, NMT, vol. 7, pp. 763–71; NI-6498/49, Müller to Kränzlein, 13.XII.35; NI-10628/88, Exchange of letters between Haefliger and Ziegler, 5 and 9.XI.38.
[50] NI-9365/78, Affidavit by A. Lingg, 1.VIII.47.
[51] See IG in Abw., Zefi 81–28, Pistor to Schmitz, 20.IX.34, enclosing his memo concerning the Bitterfeld plant of the same date; NI-7562/61, Neukirch's report, pp. 38–9. As a result of IG's influence, the international aluminum cartel agreed to the vast expansion in German capacity, provided that none of the output was exported; see George W. Stocking and Myron Watkins, *Cartels in Action* (New York, 1947), pp. 271–2.
[52] NI-10006/82, Affidavit by H. Deichfischer, 11.VI.47.
[53] M892/7, Testimony by F. terMeer, p. 6787. It is worth noting in this respect that the entire chemical industry received but 9% of the army contracts awarded during 1937 or only about 38 million marks worth of orders; see Geyer, *RVB*, vol. 45 (1981), p. 260. The only IG division for which appropriate statistics have surfaced is pharmaceuticals, which earned 1% of its sales income from the military in 1937, 6.6% in 1938, and 11.5% in 1939 (Bayer 4C9.29, Control Office, *Bayer*, p. 92). As early as 1936, however, the army was purchasing nearly two-thirds of Germany's (i.e., IG's) magnesium production (BA Koblenz, R25/150b, Fleissbild). IG's volume of sales and gross profits from gray dye for uniforms also rose by factors of 17 and 19, respectively, from 1931 to 1939 but still yielded the concern less than 1 million marks in the latter year; see Morris, *Synthetic Rubber*, p. 69.

1920s.[54] Then the predecessor firms' connections with the earlier war effort had cost the combine as dearly overseas as the retooling of the bloated explosives sector did at home. Concerning the production of poison gases, IG's leaders remained particularly skittish. In 1925, fearing that exposure would result in more lost customers abroad and Allied controls over the German chemical industry, the Little IG had protested to the Chancellery against the Reichswehr's clandestine cooperation with the Soviet Union in developing these weapons and refused to supply the necessary intermediate compounds.[55] Nine years later, when the army decided to resume domestic production of mustard gas and requested IG to exercise its patents on various preliminary products, the combine's worries about publicity were undiminished. Once more, IG turned the generals down, whereupon the High Command opted to build its own factories and induced Degea AG of Berlin and Buckau AG of Halle, parts of the Auer and Goldschmidt chemicals groups, respectively, to form an operating company, called Orgacid AG of Ammendorf. IG was directed to construct the necessary facilities and advise their operation in return for a single payment of 125,000 marks and to make the concern's patents and processes available to the new company free of charge.[56]

To avoid a repetition of this experience and "to keep control over the productive capacity of such plants and their possible effects on the relevant markets," IG went along with most of the army's other expansion plans for products whose civilian commercial prospects were dubious.[57] But the firm took care not to encumber itself. Though IG provided its construction, managerial, and technical expertise for a fee and the state's promise "not to use the plant for other purposes than

[54] NI-8925/74, Affidavit by H. Wagner, 11.VI.47.
[55] See BA Koblenz, R43 I/420, Bl. 257-58, 262-81, especially Bücher to Kempner, 1.V.25; Michael Geyer, *Aufrüstung oder Sicherheit* (Wiesbaden, 1980), pp. 152–3; Rolf-Dieter Müller, "Die deutschen Gaskriegsvorbereitungen 1919–1945: Mit Giftgas zur Weltmacht," *MM*, 27 (1980), pp. 27–30. Müller also notes, p. 32, that the Soviets specifically requested IG's participation in this work, but without success.
[56] On the army's decision, see Müller, *MM*, 27 (1980), pp. 33–4, which says nothing of the background to the founding of Ammendorf. On that, NI-6788/52, Affidavit by O. Ambros, 1.V.47; Ambros VIIA/702, Affidavit by H.-J. von der Linde, 26.XI.47, and VIA/607, Affidavit by C. Zahn, 17. VII.47; and NI-5681/42, Contract between IG and Orgacid, 10.VIII.35. NI-5682/42, Böckler to Buhl, 13.I.39, indicates that the Reich's representatives took two of the four seats on Orgacid's *Aufsichtsrat* but did not interfere with the management of the firm.
[57] NI-4669/34, Verm. W. to Knieriem, 8.VI.39, p. 12. See also the testimony of H. Diekmann, *NMT*, vol. 7, p. 1238.

those specified and above all not to use it to compete with us," the new factories remained the property, hence the liability, of a government corporation, at first called the Verwertungsgesellschaft der Montanindustrie mbH. They were maintained at "standby" status or operated with the Reich's funds.[58] Such were the arrangements with regard to the works begun in 1935–6 at Wolfen for diglycol and explosives stabilizers, at Teuschenthal for alloys, and at Vienenburg in the Harz and Döberitz for nitric acid.[59] Similar agreements governed the five plants that Troisdorf erected in 1935–6 at the behest of the army, which leased them to the special subsidiary that DAG established for this purpose, the Gesellschaft für Verwertung chemischer Erzeugnisse mbH.[60] For DAG, the rewards of this leasing system became appreciable, with gross profits coming to more than 7 million marks between 1936 and 1939.[61] But for IG proper, the new plants probably brought in little income before the war; they were small and in the nature of hedges against the consequences of a rearmament boom or bust.

IG's main problems with military intervention in the economy resulted, however, not so much from what the soldiers wanted as from how they operated. In preparing for only approximately predictable contingencies, army planners tended to inflate their needs, revise production programs and timetables abruptly, and encourage alternative suppliers, often with little regard for the efforts of corporations to maximize returns on investment and the like. Memorably demonstrated during World War I, these traits resurfaced to trouble IG's plans for precisely those products that, the firm hoped, could ride rearmament like a post horse. Thus, since the army's first tests showed that DuPont's synthetic rubber (Duprene) was superior to IG's, the military urged the concern in early 1934 to drop its research in favor of obtaining a license and constructing a factory for the American

---

[58] For the quotation, see NI-5761/43, Conference memo by G. Pistor, 20.IX.35. In general, NI-9204/77, K. von Heider's report of 30.VI.47, and terMeer's testimony, NMT, vol. 7, pp. 1239–41.

[59] On diglycol, the record is voluminous. For 1935–6 alone, see NI-5761-62/43, NI-4487-88, and NI-4490/33, all internal IG documents by G. Pistor. On the other plants, see NI-13563/111, Ritter to Krauch, 7.I.35, and file note by Schoenemann, 31.I.35; NI-14668, Meeting at Bitterfeld, 16.VIII.35, NMT, vol. 7, p. 124; NI-7135, Verm. W. to the War Ministry, 20.II.36, NMT vol. 7, pp. 1244–5; and NI-7833/64, Verm. W. to Brendel, 3.VII.36 and 6.VII.36.

[60] NI-7771/63, Omnibus agreement between DAG and the Supreme Army Command (OKH), 4.III.40.

[61] NI-10008/82, Affidavit by H. Deichfischer, 11.VI.47.

product.[62] Less than a year later, Army Ordnance helped to break IG's monopoly of German magnesium fabrication. Convinced of the commercial viability of magnesium, IG departed from its usual practice in late 1934 and took the precaution of acquiring direct title to a standby plant at Stassfurt commissioned by the air force and built almost entirely with a government credit of 44 million marks. Almost immediately thereafter, however, Army Ordnance decided to divert 30% of this installation's planned output to a new plant, which Wintershall AG proposed to construct on its own. Crying foul, since Wintershall had offered a price that exceeded IG's, the concern managed to get the air force, as the principal government purchaser, to assume exclusive control over magnesium orders. But the army's allocation stood, and the net effect of the rearmament drive in the magnesium sphere was to provide IG with both a new plant and a new competitor.[63]

Preventing a similar outcome and containing the military's zeal also characterized IG's conduct of negotiations between 1934 and 1936 concerning the manufacture of synthetic airplane fuel. In their initial correspondence of September 1933, Carl Krauch had tried to encourage Air Force General Milch's interest in hydrogenation by mentioning that IG was testing synthetic high-octane airplane fuel.[64] The firm dangled the same bait during the following year in order to persuade the government to broaden its support for synthetic gasoline and thus to clinch IG's deal with the Ruhr mining firms. Shortly after Krauch proposed a national fuel development program to General Thomas of the army in July, IG's Mueller-Cunradi informed the Air Ministry that the concern had two sorts of probably satisfactory aircraft propellants. One involved the mixing of a tetraethyl lead additive devised by Standard Oil with varieties of benzin produced at Leuna. The other was iso-octane, an especially powerful fuel already perfected by Standard and capable of being produced at Leuna on a modest scale by a

62 NI-7472/60, Report of the OKH [Supreme Army Command] "The Cooperation of the Wehrmacht in the Development and Testing of Synthetic Rubber," Autumn 1938. IG did make an unsuccessful effort to obtain the rights to Duprene; see Howard Ambruster, *Treason's Peace* (New York, 1947), p. 54, and Morris, *Synthetic Rubber*, pp. 176, 220–2.
63 NI-8317/68, Affidavit by E. Struss, 2.VI.47; NI-7562/61, Dr. Neukirch's "History," June 1943, pp. 78–93; NI-7285/57, Pistor to terMeer, 7.II.35, including notes of a conference on 6.II.35 with Bader of Army Ordnance and officials of the RLM; and BA Koblenz, ZSg 127, Bd. 836, "Magnesiumgewinnung aus deutschen Rohstoffen," *Die chemische Industrie*, no. 1 (January 1938), p. 15.
64 NI-4718/34, Krauch to Milch, 14.IX.33.

different, extremely complicated and expensive series of chemical re-actions. For the moment, IG favored the former type, since its produc-tion gave off salable by-products, whereas those resulting from iso-octane output were cumbersome and useless. But eager for supplies of both fuels, the Luftwaffe urged IG to obtain a license from Standard to fabricate the additive and to draw up plans for a free-standing iso-octane plant that could manufacture 100,000 tons per year, ten times the amount IG had envisioned.[65]

While the combine complied, Krauch set up an office at the Deutsche Länderbank, where his aide Gerhard Ritter began preparing statistical analyses of the nation's oil stocks and sources. Several cir-cumstances altered IG's calculations as he did so. The state established Brabag on the basis of licenses from Farben; among the Ruhr hard-coal miners, all but the state-owned Hibernia decided against pursuing hydrogenation in cooperation with IG; and research indicated that their coal was more suitable than Leuna's lignite for making aircraft gasoline.[66] With its interests largely secured regarding automobile gasoline, the concern had now to guard against possible competition over airplane fuel, preferably by obtaining a contract with the govern-ment as soon as possible.[67] Not surprisingly, therefore, the studies that Ritter produced between October 1934 and June 1935 expressed optimism about Germany's ability to satisfy its peacetime needs for fuel from planned production but forecast major shortfalls, especially of aviation fuel, in the event of war.[68]

Ritter's findings impressed the Reich's military leaders. In the sum-mer of 1935, Defense Minister Blomberg began urging Schacht to name a commissar to take fuel planning in hand, suggesting E. R. Fischer of IG Farben for the post, and General Milch not only appoint-ed Ritter to act as IG's liaison with the air force, but also promised Krauch an invitation to explain his ideas to Göring at Karinhall, the

[65] The letter to Thomas is cited in Schweitzer, *Big Business*, p. 672, note 29. On IG's fuel possibilities, see NI-9088/76, File note of a discussion on 20.VIII.34, dated 27.VIII.34; Birkenfeld, *Treibstoff*, pp. 63–4, 71–3.

[66] Birkenfeld, *Treibstoff*, p. 67.

[67] IG's fears concentrated on the Uhde production process, which the concern claimed impinged on its hydrogenation patents. See GHH 400 101 290 3, Bosch to Reusch, 5.XII.35, with Kellermann's significant marginalia, and Reusch's reply of 7.XII.35.

[68] Ritter's studies, dated 12/15.X.34, 1.XII.34, and 1.VI.35, along with some prelimi-nary data, are collected as NI-7295/58 and in BA Koblenz, R25/112. See Birken-feld's discussion in *Treibstoff*, pp. 54–59.

Luftwaffe chief's estate outside Berlin.[69] But the meeting did not take place, probably because several developments made it seem premature. Sparring between Schacht and Keppler prevented the appointment of a fuel czar; the Air Ministry rejected IG's plan to site the iso-octane plant at Waldenburg, southwest of Breslau and hard by the Czech border; and the American State, War, and Navy Departments delayed the concern's license for tetraethyl lead. Not until the end of the year did subsidiaries of IG and Standard Oil found an equal partnership, the Ethyl GmbH, and, with the aid of a grant from the Reich equal to about half the construction costs, break ground on a plant for the additive at Gapel near Berlin. Relieved to all but abandon what it regarded as the uneconomical production of iso-octane, IG finally produced its first standard airplane fuel in February 1936. However, the relatively high price of this product – two to three times that of imports from Romania and California – held up a sales contract with the German government for another four months.

Like its forerunner in 1933, the *Flugbenzin-Vertrag* of June 10, 1936, closely balanced the interests of the signatories. IG committed itself to a plant capacity of 200,000 tons per year. In return, the Reich promised to allot Leuna during each of the next eight to fourteen years a share in all official orders for domestic airplane fuel equal to IG's percentage of total national capacity and to pay a sum that would cover IG's operating expenses, retire its expansion costs of 3.6 million marks within nine years, and return the concern a profit of 5% annually on the funds invested.[70] In short, the contract insured IG against competitors and the regime against shortages in the event of war. During peacetime, however, the government's obligatory payments were minimal, and it was otherwise free to buy less expensive airplane fuel elsewhere (purchases came, in fact, to about 20 million marks per year in 1936 and 1937). Regardless of the quantity ordered by the Reich, the concern's profits were confined to probably about 900,000 marks over nine years and certainly no more than 200,000

69 This highly compressed summary of events in 1935–6 draws on Birkenfeld, *Treibstoff*, pp. 53–4, 63, 66–70, 73–4; Dieter Petzina, *Autarkiepolitik im Dritten Reich* (Stuttgart, 1968), pp. 37–9; Homze, *Luftwaffe*, pp. 147–8; NI-4718/34, Exchange of letters between Milch and Krauch, 23.VII.35 and 29.VII.35; and M892/15, Krauch's testimony, p. 5045.
70 NI-7836/64, Text of the *Vertrag*.

marks in any one year.[71] As with most of IG's production for the government, the firm's chief gains were the chance to develop its technology and the plant, which would be fully depreciated over the life of the contract. Thereafter, however, the factory would also have almost no value unless the nation remained on a permanent war footing or a regular, civilian demand for aviation fuel arose.

Rearmament, then, presented twin aspects to IG: opportunities to make virtually risk-free bets on the commercial future and dangers that uncoordinated planning would generate excess or competing capacity. By September 1935, recognition of both these points had proceeded far enough to prompt the concern to establish an Army Liaison Office (Vermittlungsstelle Wehrmacht or Verm. W.). This new agency consisted of one representative from each of the Sparten, who was to receive copies of all correspondence between any IG subdivision and any military-related part of the bureaucracy and to coordinate IG's dealings with the government concerning research, production, mobilization, labor assignments, air defense, espionage, patents, licenses, storage, and transport.[72] Designed above all to enable IG to "settle its problems concerning the military economy independently without influence from the outside," the Vermittlungsstelle enjoyed rather uneven success as a control mechanism.[73] Though its budget rose rapidly from 36,000 marks in 1935 to 402,300 in 1939 and its staff of six employees housed in three rooms burgeoned to thirty-three members spread over twenty-three rooms, the office's functions grew increasingly routine and clerical. Occupied mainly with hammering out IG's production program in case of mobilization, the Vermittlungsstelle was often bypassed by the Army Ordnance Office and technicians at IG's plants, excluded from major contract negotiations with the Reich, and occasionally not even informed of their outcomes.[74] But the office

---

[71] On the government's disbursements, Birkenfeld, *Treibstoff*, p. 70, note 36, and p. 226. The calculations of IG's annual return are my own.

[72] NI-4702, Krauch and Fahrenhorst to ten plants and offices, 5.IX.35, and NI-4627, terMeer to the *Betriebsgemeinschaften*, 26.IX.35, *NMT*, vol. 7, pp. 1048–51; NI-2747, Wartime report of the Verm. W. by H. Eichwede, *NMT*, vol. 7, pp. 1046–8, authenticated by NI-9261/77, Eichwede's affidavit of 30.VII.47; NI-8321/68, Affidavit by E. Struss, 30.III.47; and NI-8923/74, Affidavit by H. Wagner, 11.VI.47.

[73] For the quotation, see NI-2638, Verm. W. to IG offices, 31.XII.35, *NMT*, vol. 7, p. 1051. See also NI-7611/62, Affidavit by G. Gorr, 3.VI.47.

[74] NI-10923/90, Affidavit by H. Münch, 10.IX.47; NI-2747, Eichwede's summary, *NMT*, vol. 7, pp. 1046–8; NI-8923/74, Wagner's affidavit, 11.VI.47; Bayer D.A. 913, Verm. W. to Warnecke, Leverkusen, 5.VII.38; NI-8321/68, Struss's affidavit, 30.III.47, and his statement of 31.I.47 in Bayer 4B/36, vol. 1.

provided a platform in Berlin for its creator and commander Carl Krauch, who was becoming the leading proponent of the regime's autarky policies within IG, as well as the combine's principal link to rearmament planning via his contacts with Milch and his seat on the Armament Advisory Council chaired by Defense Minister Blomberg.[75] In this capacity, the Vermittlungsstelle briefly played a pivotal role.

Krauch's developing association with the military leadership contrasted sharply with the trend in IG's relations with the civilian makers of economic policy. Indeed, the formation of the Army Liaison Office was, in part, a response to the latter situation, for in the course of 1935, Schacht's value to the concern declined appreciably, while a more alarming figure gained influence. Appointed commissioner of raw materials creation for the Reich in the fall of 1934, Wilhelm Keppler differed with both Schacht and Farben on an issue of central importance to the combine: the development of domestic raw materials supplies. Whereas Keppler pressed for rapid production of all import-saving substitutes almost regardless of expense to the government, Schacht opposed public funding for facilities that seemed unlikely either to retain their value once rearmament leveled off and the nation's economic house had been put in order or, in the meantime, to save the government more in foreign exchange than they cost in subsidies and imports of construction materials. On this question, IG took a self-interested middle position. Fearful, like Schacht, of hasty, ultimately unprofitable investments and reluctant to become too dependent on the state, the concern wanted, according to Fritz terMeer, "to confine itself strictly to its financial capacity" and to concentrate its efforts on synthetics whose development seemed likely to spin off rewarding discoveries. Around the turn of 1934–5, therefore,

at Bosch's proposal the following conclusions were arrived at: to participate in the production of artificial fibers only with a modest share; to increase the gasoline production of the Leuna works to 500,000 tons a year . . . besides that, the hydrogenation process should be made available to other licensees; and to keep the buna field with its prospects of important and far-reaching new chemical achievements completely in hand.[76]

75 See Klaus Drobisch, "Eine Denkscrift der IG Farben über die 'Militärisierung der Wirtschaft' vom März 1935," *JfG*, 1 (1967), p. 264.
76 NI-5187/38, Affidavit by F. terMeer, 15.IV.47; repeated in slightly different form in

This limited set of objectives may explain why IG did not establish the development department that Reithinger had called for some months earlier. What can be said with greater certainty is that IG's egocentric strategy caught the combine from mid-1935 to mid-1936 in an increasingly heavy crossfire over economic policy and that the firm eventually took cover.

Though reasonably well connected to the business community and on good terms with a number of corporate executives, Keppler distrusted IG Farben. This attitude grew out of his experiences during the 1920s as manager and part owner of a small photochemicals firm, the Chemische Werke Odin GmbH, which was tied to Kodak and competed with IG's Agfa, as well as out of the concern's refusal to rally behind the NSDAP before the seizure of power.[77] His animosity toward Carl Bosch may have extended, as Hermann Bücher attested after the war, to the collection of a secret dossier for use against IG's chief at a timely moment.[78] In November 1934, Keppler recruited two other energetic small-scale entrepreneurs who shared his frustration with what they regarded as the selfishness, excessive caution, and inflexibility of giant corporations. Paul Pleiger, a self-made owner of a machine factory in the Ruhr, was soon to become prominent as the driving spirit behind the development of Germany's low-grade iron ore fields and the Hermann Göring Werke. Hans Kehrl, the manager of his family's textile business in Cottbus, had attracted Keppler's notice in mid-1934 by submitting a memorandum contending that existing types of synthetic fibers could be rapidly applied on a vast

terMeer, *I. G. Farben*, p. 82. Though terMeer dates these decisions to "about 1933–34," he links them to the moment when the first projects of Keppler's office became known to IG, which suggests the end of the latter year. The figure of 500,000 tons corresponds to the sum of Leuna's gasoline output under the *Benzin-Vertrag* plus aviation fuel production for which Krauch lobbied in 1934–5.

[77] On Keppler's background, see NG-1640, his affidavit of 25.V.47; Czichon, *Wer Verhalf*, pp. 17, 28; Matthias Riedel, *Eisen und Kohle für das Dritte Reich. Paul Pleigers Stellung in der NS-Wirtschaft* (Göttingen, 1973), pp. 15–16. IG traced Keppler's hostility at least in part to the influence of an old friend from his student days, one Waldemar Ziesser, who had left IG's synthetic rubber research staff in 1931 in a dispute over its reorganization (Bayer D.A. 913, Kühne to Brüning, 29.X.36).

[78] Schmitz I/6, Affidavit by H. Bücher, 16.XII.47; Lochner, *Tycoons*, p. 45. Bücher claimed that a Gestapo official named Zwade stole the files compiled on both Bosch and Bücher and that Bücher then destroyed them. For another indication of tension between IG and Keppler, see Radkau's reference to a letter from Keppler to IG's directors on 15.II.35, now in the files of the Deutsches Zentralarchiv (DZA) Potsdam (Hallgarten and Radkau, *Deutsche Industrie*, p. 292).

scale in order to put the textile industry back to work.[79] Toward IG
Farben, these three men pursued a consistent policy throughout their
public careers. They sought to confine the concern's activities to those
fields in which its skills and productive powers were indispensable.[80]
In 1935, the determination and effectiveness of Keppler's staff became
painfully apparent to IG in several instances.

Policy toward synthetic fibers, Hans Kehrl's specialty, occasioned
the first confrontation. In 1933, imports of cotton and wool cost the
Reich 570 million marks; by 1935, they took approximately 700
million marks, or 44% of all the foreign exchange expended on raw
materials.[81] Even before Kehrl began drafting specific expansion
plans, Keppler and Puppe, the raw materials commissioner in the
Economics Ministry, opened negotiations with Gajewski and Otto of
Sparte III concerning additions to IG's output, which already had
increased twofold since 1932. It came in 1934 to 10,000 tons of
continuous-thread artificial silk or rayon and 6,000 tons of short
staple *Vistrafaser,* soon to be known by its new generic name *Zellwolle.*[82] In order to ensure that the related financial arrangements
worked out to IG's advantage, Gajewski urged several other members
of the *Vorstand* to "try everything to prevent" the addition to Pupe's
staff of Richard Dörr, a former employee of IG's fiber division, since
he "knows everything about cost prices and previous obligations [and]
this would be most unpleasant for us."[83] However, though willing to
double *Zellwolle* production, IG doubted that the market would bear
anything like the vast expansion of national capacity to 60,000 tons
by 1936 that Kehrl favored, not to mention his eventual goal of
150,000 to 200,000 tons.[84] Since World War I, when ill-considered
applications of *Zellwolle* had yielded deficient ersatz clothing, German consumers and textile firms had shown such aversion to the fiber

---

[79] See Riedel, *Eisen und Kohle,* pp. 10–12, 21–2; and Hans Kehrl, *Krisenmanager im
Dritten Reich* (Düsseldorf, 1973), pp. 61–2.
[80] Interview with Hans Kehrl, 11.VII.78. On IG's awareness of their attitude, see, for
example, Schnitzler's remarks concerning Kehrl in NI-5196/38, Schnitzler's affidavit
of 18.III.47. It is interesting that the leading student of Thurman Arnold's attack on
America's corporate giants concluded, "The bulk of Arnold's support came not from
any uprising of consumers, but from smaller businessmen or dissatisfied business
groups unable to compete successfully with their larger rivals"; see Ellis Hawley, *The
New Deal and the Problem of Monopoly* (Princeton, N.J., 1966), p. 447.
[81] Kehrl, *Krisenmanager,* pp. 61, 87–8; Kroll, *Weltwirtschaftskrise,* p. 501.
[82] NI-1941/18, Otto and Gajewski to the ZA meeting of 22.XI.34.
[83] NI-13545, Gajewski to Selck, 5.IX.34, *NMT,* vol. 7, pp. 1271–2.
[84] Kehrl, *Krisenmanager,* pp. 87–8.

that IG had had to sell more than half of its small annual output abroad.[85] Thus, when Keppler proposed in early 1935 that IG construct two new plants at Wolfen, one for 28,000 tons of *Zellwolle* per year and the other for 35,000 tons of cellulose as the processed raw material, the combine insisted that the necessary bank loans for the project be repaid, not out of gross sales, but only out of such profits that resulted, thus pushing all the risk onto the Reich as guarantor.[86] After the Finance Ministry rejected this procedure, IG undertook a small self-funded expansion of *Zellwolle* production to 11,000 to 12,000 tons annually and put off the cellulose plant to a later date.[87]

None of this daunted Kehrl, who eagerly grasped the chance to break the German sales syndicate, the Kunstseide Verkaufsbüro GmbH, and demonstrate to IG that the Third Reich would pursue self-sufficiency with or without the concern. He recruited Richard Dörr to his own staff, along with Walter Schieber, another IG man, who later recalled having left the firm "because of technical differences with my department chief, but on a friendly understanding."[88] Together these three men planned, established, and supervised five regional synthetic fibers corporations in 1935 and five more over the ensuing five years, each owned by nearby textile companies that had to take compulsory stockholdings, each financed initially by a loan of 8 million marks from the government, and each with a capacity of 7000 to 8000 tons annually.[89] Because the textile owners thus acquired a stake in the profitability of the new firms and the state imposed a requirement that all garments for home consumption contain 20% synthetic cloth, the spinners rapidly converted to using artificial fibers, thus raising demand.[90] Not above cashing in on Kehrl's success, IG more than redoubled its rayon production, raised the output of *Zellwolle* by almost 300% to roughly 46,000 tons, and finally built the cellulose installation at Wolfen, though on a smaller scale than the government had

85 Wilhelm Jungermann and Herbert Krafft, *Rohstoffreichtum aus deutscher Erde* (Berlin, 1939), pp. 143–4.
86 See BA Koblenz, R2/15302, documents covering 12.XII.34–2.III.35.
87 NI-1941/18, ZA meeting of 26.IV.35. For Keppler's gentle but prodding reply to this decision, see NI-13576/111, Keppler to Bosch, 8.IV.35.
88 Krauch I/27, Affidavit by W. Schieber, 13.XI.47.
89 Kehrl, *Krisenmanager*, pp. 88–90; BASF T52/9, Vowi 1619, Die deutsche Zellwolleindustrie, 19.XI.35; the entries for Dörr and Schieber in Stockhausen, *5000 Köpfe*, pp. 109, 378–9.
90 Kroll, *Weltwirtschaftskrise*, pp. 503–4; also Lurie, *Private Investment*, p. 196, though he confuses cause and effect.

requested. But the concern did not try to maintain its market share, which dropped from about one-third of German synthetic fiber sales in 1933 to 21% of rayon and 29% of *Zellwolle* purchases by 1938, and then to about one-sixth of German consumption of both products during the war.[91] IG preferred to concentrate on perfecting purely synthetic fibers produced from polyvinylchloride, expecting these to supercede the cellulose derivatives that Kehrl and Keppler promoted.[92] Though Gajewski and Otto never ceased scoffing at the allegedly wasteful shortsightedness of Kehrl's program, he continued to get the better of the argument, especially after he persuaded the spinners that owned stock in IG's major syndicate partner, the Glanzstoff-Bemberg firm, to launch a palace revolt in August 1939 that toppled that corporation's *Vorstand* and led to a reconstitution of its *Aufsichtsrat*.[93]

Developments concerning fuel also demonstrated that Keppler and his staff were to be taken seriously. Though Schacht and Krauch saw to it that three of the first four factories constructed by Brabag employed IG's hydrogenation process, Keppler got his way in mid-1935 with the installation at Ruhland, where the Fischer–Tropsch process was applied. Fortunately for IG, construction problems and cost overruns plagued Ruhland and decisively set back the use of the competing process in Germany.[94] But the foundation of Brabag and the plans for Ruhland attested to Keppler's ability to force synthetic developments and on occasion to push them in a direction unwelcome to the concern. In November 1935, when Göring again aired the idea of appointing a national fuel commissar and Keppler became the front runner for the post, IG cannot have been pleased.[95] Nor did the Party

---

91 Bayer 4C9.19, Pinnow manuscript, pp. 70–71; Kehrl, *Krisenmanager*, p. 447, note 7; NI-13529/110, Gajewski to Wigru Chemie, 19.XII.38.

92 terMeer, *I. G. Farben*, p. 88.

93 NI-1295/13, Statement by G. Frank-Fahle, no date; Kehrl, *Krisenmanager*, pp. 96–7; Interview with Hans Kehrl, 11.VII.78. On the coup of 1939, see "Aufsichtsratsumbau bei Glanzstoff," *Berliner Börsen-Zeitung*, no. 382 (16.VIII.39), and "Der Verwaltungsumbau bei Aku und Glanzstoff," *Frankfurter Zeitung*, no. 419 (18.VIII.39).

94 The hydrogenation process had another advantage: Per ton of coal, it yielded about twice as much fuel and one-quarter again as much gasoline as the Fischer–Tropsch method; see Cochran, *Scientific American*, 234 (1976), p. 27. This fact, in turn, made hydrogenation more suitable for the production of aviation fuel; see Raymond G. Stokes, "The Oil Industry in Nazi Germany, 1936–1945," *BHR*, 59 (1985), pp. 267–8.

95 Petzina, *Autarkiepolitik*, p. 39.

miss the opportunity to tout Brabag as proof of Nazism's capacity to create a new form of state-controlled corporation.[96]

These events constituted the backdrop for a long wrangle between Farben and the regime over the production of synthetic rubber, or buna. Though IG's hopes for the future increasingly rode on this substance, it was also the synthetic breakthrough for which the risks seemed greatest, since, unlike benzin, metals, and fibers, its production entailed entirely new plants and unproved technologies, not extensions or imitations of existing ones. After the aborted discussions in the fall of 1933, the government briefly lost interest in the product as substitutes for more costly imports took priority. Even in the mid-1930s, the world price for natural rubber remained at only one-quarter of its level in 1925–9, and the total cost of German rubber imports was far below the bills for fuel and fibers, reaching only 25 million marks in 1935, 70 million marks a year later.[97] Despite this situation and the army's initial preference for DuPont's synthetic rubber, IG continued its work, investing another 950,000 marks in research and development during 1934 and conducting further tests in cooperation with the major German tire companies and the General Tire and Rubber Co. of Akron, Ohio.[98] In July 1934, the concern reported progress to Army Ordnance and resumed discussions over production costs and possible plant locations with E. Hammesfahr, the Reich plenipotentiary for rubber.[99] At the end of October, during meetings between Keppler, Hammesfahr, and representatives of the Economics Ministry and IG, the führer's economic adviser informed those present that Hitler wanted synthetic rubber production pushed ahead "with elemental force." IG's startled planners considered this premature. Restrained by difficulties in making buna pliable and adhesive enough for processing, IG scaled down Keppler's suggestion of manufacturing 1,000 tons monthly. Instead,

[96] See Kurt Münch, *Wirtschaftliche Selbstverwaltung* (Hamburg, 1936), pp. 63–4.
[97] Kroll, *Weltwirtschaftskrise*, p. 510. Petzina notes that in 1936 the price recovered to slightly more than one-third of the level of 1928 (*Autarkiepolitik*, p. 84).
[98] TerMeer IV/186, Affidavit by E. Struss, 30.XI.47; Charles S. Popple, *Standard Oil Company (N.J.) in World War II* (New York, 1952), p. 52. For a valuable survey of the concern's research and the various product types that resulted, see terMeer IV/187, Affidavit by E. Konrad, 8.I.48.
[99] NI-7241/57, Affidavit by E. Struss, 12.VI.47. The document supersedes and fleshes out NI-306/4, a memo summarizing conversations concerning buna with government agencies between 1933 and 1938, prepared by H. Rohdemann of IG in August 1945, as well as NI-8326/68, Struss's affidavit of 30.V.47, which certified the authenticity of the memo.

the firm agreed to a plan for producing only 200 tons per month by the end of 1935 at a plant that IG would build for up to 15 million marks of its own money. Perhaps to prod the cautious concern, Hagemann of Army Ordnance and Hammesfahr revealed to IG at conferences during November that the Chancellery harbored an "inexplicable grudge" against the firm but was prepared to shield it from further risk by providing the necessary construction capital from government funds and a levy on the rubber-processing industry, an idea later adapted to Kehrl's fibers program.[100]

During the numerous conversations that followed in 1935, however, while Keppler and Army Ordnance vied for authority over buna development, terMeer refused to be rushed into augmenting IG's plans. Since the army initially estimated its needs at only 150 to 250 tons per month and later reduced even this guess, and the tire makers protested that products made from buna would cost two and a half times as much as those fabricated from natural rubber, the concern hesitated to embark on large-scale production.[101] Nor was the combine willing to honor the army's stipulation that a rubber plant be free standing and located at Piesteritz. Instead, hoping to reduce costs by tapping into the power, brown coal, and hydrogen supplies of Leuna and linking rubber production to related operations, IG secured a large tract of land at Schkopau during the late summer of 1935.[102] Meanwhile, Hitler forced the pace of development by announcing to the Party congress at Nürnberg that Germany soon would start building a synthetic rubber factory. Keppler immediately summoned ter-Meer and Ernst Struss to meet with him and Pleiger at the Chancellery on September 19. TerMeer explained that the inability of the army and the rubber industry to use even IG's present experimental output of 20 to 25 tons monthly was raising inventories and that a plant constructed on the basis of the present four-stage manufacturing process would be rendered obsolete within two years by a two-stage process now in preparation. Keppler and Pleiger nonetheless insisted

100 NI-7241/57, Struss's affidavit, 12.VI.47; terMeer IV/187, Konrad's affidavit, 8.I.48.
101 NI-4713, parts a and b, memos of conferences on 20.I.35 and 20.II.35, *NMT*, vol. 7, pp. 778–80.
102 NI-7624/62, Grundlegenden Gesichtspunkte für die Gründung des Werkes Schkopau und den Buna Vertrag, F. terMeer, 17.II.37; terMeer IV/191, Struss to Keppler, 15.XI.35. Morris offers a slightly different chronology of Schkopau's development in *Synthetic Rubber*, p. 291.

on immediate construction. IG therefore agreed to build a suitable
plant within one year, to adapt the blueprints to the possibility of
eventually expanding production from 200–250 tons per month to
1,000 tons, and to finance the construction itself. But in return, Keppler was to arrange a military sales guarantee at a price that would
amortize the works within three to five years, compensate IG for
administrative overhead, and give the concern a return of 5% annually
on the capital invested.[103] Though General Thomas of the Military–
Economic Staff reportedly told IG two days later that he favored the
price and purchase guarantee, several officers dissociated Army Ordnance from Keppler's plans while visiting Leverkusen in late October.
Making clear their distaste for Pleiger, these men pointed out that the
army and other government offices could not absorb IG's output or
offer assurances concerning any surplus so long as Schacht refused to
let prices for natural rubber products rise to buna's level for fear of
harming German exports.[104]

By the end of 1935, IG's rubber program was caught between competing pressures. Having argued for a modest initial plant to which
different military agencies had blown both hot and cold, the concern
confronted Keppler's undiminished fervor for a large installation
soon, as well as a small one immediately, a fervor now apparently
shared by the führer. The combine saw no choice but to begin construction at Schkopau, only to find that Keppler could not deliver on
his promises of support. From November 1935 on, he wrangled over
appropriate guarantees for IG with the Economics and Finance Ministries, which calculated a likely savings of 2.2 million marks in foreign
exchange annually by virtue of the Schkopau plant as against a probable annual subsidy to IG of 5 million to 8 million marks, assuming the

---

[103] NI-4713, part c, IG interoffice memo of a conference at the Chancellery on
19.IX.35, dated 20.IX.35, NMT, vol. 7, pp. 780–2; also printed in Eichholtz and
Schumann (eds.), Anatomie, Document 39, pp. 132–3. TerMeer IV/193, File note
of a conference at the RWM, 11.II.36, makes clear that IG opposed construction of
a plant until September 1935 and gave in only in response to Hitler's statement at
the Party congress.

[104] NI-4713, part d, Conference with Army Ordnance at Leverkusen, 22.X.35, NMT,
vol. 7, pp. 782–3; NI-6194/46, Kautschuk und die Versorgungslage im Kriege by
Lt. Col. Hedler, March 1941; NI-7241/57, Struss's affidavit of 12.VI.47; and
Wilhelm Treue, "Gummi in Deutschland zwischen 1933 und 1945," Wehrwissenschaftliche Rundschau, 5 (1955), pp. 172–3. Treue's summary of the limited
proven military applications of buna as of the end of 1935 suggests why Army
Ordnance was inclined at this date to favor using available funds for stockpiling
imported rubber rather than for producing buna.

agreed-upon amortization period and investment return.[105] To the civil servants, such a deal made no economic sense.

Until actual production began, IG could afford to be patient, all the more so because it had not yet determined which of several possible buna types to manufacture. Hence, the concern betrayed no irritation at Schacht's financial reserve. In fact, in May 1936, when Göring tried to blame Schacht for the lack of progress regarding buna by asking Hermann Schmitz point-blank at a meeting of an advisory committee whether official timidity was the cause of slow development, Schmitz calmly replied that a deliberate course had been justified "in order to apply experience while enlarging the factories."[106] But Schacht had failed IG in two respects: Unable to restrain Hitler and Keppler, he refused to help the firm cope with their demands. These faults loomed larger in relation to another matter that irritated the firm after mid-1935: export promotion policy.

The Reich's export promotion procedure (*Zusatzausfuhrverfahren*, or ZAV) delighted companies like IG so long as it proceeded essentially without cost to them. Initially, with regard to the 20% of German exports that took place outside of clearing, barter, and blocked-mark accounts, the government compensated exporters for most of the differences between production costs and the reichsmark proceeds of sales made in devalued foreign currencies by providing firms with bonds, scrips, and various forms of blocked marks, all drawn on the uncollected German accounts of foreign creditors. The native seller usually lost nothing on these transactions, though he did forgo the profit he would have made by selling the exported goods at home. Since this fact tended to dull the desire to export, Schacht added various incentives, making the award of government contracts contingent on a firm's success in meeting its export quotas and allocating foreign exchange only for raw materials vital to arms or sales abroad.[107] Such measures

105 BA Koblenz, R2/15306, pp. 4–31. By February 1936, IG was asking for depreciation over five, not three, years; ter Meer IV/192, terMeer to Keppler, 4.II.36. Gottfried Plumpe, "Industrie, technischer Fortschritt und Staat: Die Kautschuksynthese in Deutschland 1906–1944/45," *G&G*, 9 (1983), p. 584, fails to point out that Keppler could not keep his end of the bargain and tends to exaggerate for both 1933 and 1935 the extent of the commitment the government would make to Farben.
106 See Morris, *Synthetic Rubber*, pp. 182, 223–4. For the quotation, see NI-5380/39, Meeting of the Gutachter-Ausschuss, 26.V.36.
107 Doering, *Deutsche Aussenwirtschaftspolitik*, pp. 196–202; Radkau, *G&G*, 2 (1976), p. 55. Schweitzer's discussion of export promotion not only confuses the

had the contradictory effects of both increasing the appeal of autarky to some German businessmen and driving companies into the export trade, where they often competed with other German firms.[108] Worse, as the volume of idle foreign funds in Germany declined, Schacht shifted the burden of export promotion onto the Reich's businesses.

After June 1935, funds for subsidizing exporters were raised from each German firm according to the size of its domestic turnover during the previous calendar year. Companies were forbidden to raise prices to pay this levy, which came to 700 million marks for 1935 and swelled to about 1 billion marks annually later.[109] The invention of Paul Pleiger, whose proposals along these lines had been discussed in the *Völkischer Beobachter,* this scheme had the fringe benefit of enabling the regime to soak up some of business's rising profits, which executives were tending to apply to acquiring other companies or retiring debts rather than to investment.[110] Much of business opposed the new arrangements, and having gotten wind of them, Hermann Schmitz expressed IG's dismay in April 1935, when he cautioned the *Aufsichtsrat* against commercial optimism because "new burdens, as in the form of the export bounty, threaten our industry."[111]

How great the threat was became apparent in June. Disclosing that the chemical industry had been assessed an obligation of 135 million marks, some 20% of the total levy, the Wigru Chemie anticipated its members' reaction and warned "that the heaviest possible punishment will be administered against anyone making any attempt to interfere with [or] evade the levy." The member firms were then instructed on how to calculate their shares of the industry's bill and directed to remit their first two estimated monthly installments within seven days.[112] As soon as IG figured its obligation under this system at 50 million to

details of the system, but is quite misleading about its administration (*Big Business,* pp. 476–85).
[108] Hallgarten and Radkau, *Deutsche Industrie,* p. 255.
[109] Schweitzer, *Big Business,* p. 479.
[110] Doering, *Deutsche Aussenwirtschaftspolitik,* pp. 218, 258; Lurie, *Private Investment,* pp. 24–5; Schweitzer, *Big Business,* pp. 444–5. The scale for computing each firm's bill appears in Ilgner VI/94, Order to the chief of the Economic Group Chemical Industry, 17.VI.35. Firms paid roughly 0.4% on the first 11 million marks of domestic sales, 0.6% on the next 15 million, 1% on the next 15 million, and so on, each additional 15 million being assessed at 0.4% more than the previous one.
[111] Bayer 11/3, vol. 5, 37th *Aufsichtsrat* meeting, 6.IV.35; Ilgner VI/90, Affidavit by G. Schlotterer, 22.I.48.
[112] Ilgner VI/94, Clemm to members of the Wigru Chemie, 18.VI.35.

60 million marks for 1935–6, Schnitzler appealed to Gustav Schlotterer of the Economics Ministry for a reduction of the burden on the
entire Wigru. In response, the ministry merely gave IG the choice
between paying 50 million marks and forgoing any returns from the
fund collected or 55 million marks minus such reimbursements to
which IG might eventually prove entitled. Ilgner persuaded his colleagues to accept the larger figure, arguing that IG could retrieve more
than 5 million marks annually as a result of the gap between production costs and foreign sales proceeds. Events, plus the concern's skill in
manipulating the new regulations, vindicated this advice. IG's net
disbursements to the government under the ZAV came to 32.4 million
marks from July 1935 to July 1936 and fell thereafter, averaging 21.2
million marks yearly for the period from 1935 to 1940.[113] Since this
still represented a new tax to fund reimbursements that seldom entirely covered IG's or other exporters' losses, the firm and the Wigru
Chemie continued to seek exemptions and to protest against the
onerousness of the new system.[114] The more export-oriented sections
of the firm, especially pharmaceuticals and photographic chemicals,
complained bitterly, not only about the direct costs of the ZAV, but
also about its effect in prompting other German enterprises to undersell IG abroad.[115] Partly as a result of both impositions, gross profits
on pharmaceuticals sales dropped from 18.1 million marks in 1935 to
16.8 million in 1936.[116] Though certain sectors of the combine, notably chemicals, derived some benefit from the subsidy system, IG's
overall exports rose by only 8% between 1934 and 1936 compared
with 19% for German industry as a whole.[117] Because the levy ema-

---

113 Ilgner VI/91, Affidavit by K. Blessing, 26.XI.47; VI/95, Affidavit by W. Dihlmann,
24.I.48; and VI/96, File memo by Dihlmann, 8.XI.40. On the specific balances for
pharmaceuticals, see Mann III/208, Affidavit by J. Belz, 9.II.48; and for dyes,
Hoechst TEA 1033, Nettoerlösrechnung Farben und F. H. Produkte Jahr 1939, p.
2.
114 See NI-355/4, Clemm to Reichswirtschaftskammer, 9.X.35; NI-357/5, Clemm to
Reichswirtschaftskammer, 12.III.37; NI-358/5, Ungewitter to Brinkmann, 20.V.36.
115 RG242/T83, Reel 89, Weber-Andreä's diary entry of 5.VI.36 concerning the meeting of the AA on that date. Schweitzer, Big Business, p. 446, says that the prices set
by the German cartels were enforced by withholding ZAV payments to firms that
undersold other German manufacturers abroad. However, he provides no date for
the alleged introduction of this practice, and IG's complaints against price undercutting continued for years.
116 Bayer 4C9.29, Control Office, Bayer, p. 140.
117 On chemicals, see Hoechst TEA 1032, Verkauf Chemikalien, 7.IV.36; on German
exports, Petzina, Zwischenkriegszeit, p. 123; on IG's exports, Defense Basic Information II/8, Affidavit by H. Walter, 25.III.48, p. 38.

nated from Pleiger of Keppler's staff but was endorsed by Schacht and apportioned by his protégé Rudolf Brinkmann, IG had yet another reason to question the economics minister's usefulness.

By late 1935, IG Farben confronted a number of alarming facts. Public spending had become the source of 55% of all German industrial investment for two years running.[118] The Reich clearly intended to concentrate this capital on import reductions and arms, and in the intragovernmental struggle over specific allocations and policies, Keppler's office carried dangerous weight. Moreover, the führer's public utterances had taken on a more menacing, impatient tone. In May, Hitler had told the Reichstag that the international trend toward autarky "can only be harmful in its result for all people" and had stressed the dangers of a centrally planned economy: bureaucratization, stifling of initiative, and a tendency to protect the inefficient.[119] But in September, he declared the Reich's policy "to make ourselves independent of imports . . . to the extent that exports do not provide the means for the purchase of raw materials and foodstuffs" and increased that probable extent by disclosing the Nürnberg racial laws.[120] Some weeks later, he reminded businessmen that the state-owned railway system was "living proof that one may operate a public enterprise very well without private capitalist tendencies and without private capitalist management," an observation the Party's *Deutsche Volkswirtschaft* gleefully picked up and found pertinent to a "whole series of companies, especially in the basic industries" that were just as monopolistic and vital to the national interest as the railroads.[121]

Finally, the combine's best assurance of respect for its interests, namely, its quasi-monopolistic position in key industries, had eroded during 1934–5. In part this resulted from the founding of Brabag and the fibers companies, in part from the still incipient emergence of the Wintershall AG as a major rival. During the first years of the Third Reich, that corporation carried out a remarkably successful diversification program, transforming itself from a potash firm into a producer of crude oil, synthetic fuel, nitrogen, chemicals, explosives, and magnesium. Largely family-owned and still small in comparison with IG,

[118] Lurie, *Private Investment*, p. 23.
[119] Meystre, *Sozialismus*, pp. 96–7.
[120] Carroll, *Design*, p. 103.
[121] H. Ruban, "Mehr Sozialismus," *Deutsche Volkswirtschaft*, 4, no. 35 (December 1935), p. 1110.

Wintershall in 1935 employed only 7,100 workers and reported capital, reserves, and profits of 137.5 million marks. But it was led by August Rosterg, a member of Keppler's circle of industrial advisers since its inception in 1932, and enjoyed equally good connections with large banks. In 1935, Wintershall flexed its financial muscles by spending 30 million marks to construct a synthetic gasoline plant at Geisenthal and then withdrawing from the German fuel sales cartel.[122]

Frequently tardy in perceiving the political consequences of his actions, Schacht, too, began to sense an erosion of his position toward the end of 1935. As the terms of trade turned against Germany, the New Plan could no longer cover the regime's growing appetite for guns and butter. Rather desperately, Schacht blamed the NSDAP, complaining in August and September 1935 about the economic damage done by infringements on the rights of Jews and by the Party's continued freedom to transfer currency, order construction projects, and otherwise upset his finely tuned financial calculations.[123] Moreover, renewed shortfalls in the German harvest during the autumn led the Agriculture Ministry to demand increased allotments of foreign exchange for purchases of foodstuffs from overseas, which could come only at the expense of industry's raw material supplies. Schacht now teamed up briefly with Defense Minister Blomberg in an effort to bring order to the Reich's trade and exchange situations. They urged Hermann Göring to adjudicate the mounting intragovernmental disagreements, with the eventual result that Hitler named him plenipotentiary for raw materials and foreign exchange matters on April 27, 1936.[124]

The choice of Göring, which proceeded entirely within the government, finally delivered German business into Nazi hands. But that is not how events looked at the time. Evidently concerned about the position of the economics minister, Ilgner reported to IG's leaders with

---

122 Bayer 91/1, vol. 8, Vowi 2008, Wintershall Aktiengesellschaft, 10. IX.36. A survey of the firm's rapid growth indicated a few months later that "building on potash, a miniature IG has arisen"; see "Die Vielseitigkeit des Wintershall-Konzerns," *Frankfurter Zeitung*, no. 294 (12.VI.37). By mid-1938, Wintershall ranked as the eighteenth largest company in Germany, according to the amount of stock capital (Bayer 84/Eur. Allg., Vowi 3003, Die grössten deutschen Unternehmungen, 25.VI.38). On Rosterg, see Czichon, *Wer Verhalf*, pp. 19, 29.
123 Schleunes, *Twisted Road*, pp. 150–5; Schacht, *Confessions*, pp. 316–21.
124 See Petzina, *Autarkiepolitik*, pp. 30–41; Amos E. Simpson, "The Struggle for Control of the German Economy," *JMH*, 31 (1959), pp. 37–45.

obvious relief at the end of April that "there are no grounds for alarm, although in substance the situation is still naturally very tense. Schacht himself wanted the insertion of Göring as the supreme authority in order to remain undisturbed in his responsibilities."[125] In fact, Ilgner's information had become misleading by the time he passed it on, for within two days of Göring's appointment, Schacht began to realize that he had created a monster and sought from Hitler a demarcation of Göring's and the economics minister's respective spheres. By May, the two men were clashing openly at cabinet meetings over Schacht's reluctance and Göring's zeal to press on with armament and synthetics production irrespective of costs.[126] However, during the preceding months, Schacht and IG both mistook Göring for the instrument of their common objective: finding a Party figure strong enough to curtail Nazi interference with the economy and to continue the development of synthetics on a more deliberate basis.[127] Hence, in April, having been recommended once more by Albert Vögler, Carl Krauch accepted appointment as head of the section for research and development in Göring's new raw materials staff. Two months later Ritter and Eckell of Krauch's Vermittlungsstelle Wehrmacht followed him into government service.[128]

To be sure, ambition may have contributed to Krauch's decision to accept a post in Berlin. Now that IG had chosen to stress licensing rather than expanded production of benzin, Schmitz had succeeded Bosch as chairman of the *Vorstand*, and terMeer's Sparte II had returned to the fore within IG, the head of Sparte I had reason to seek a new outlet for his abilities.[129] But for a man who initially assumed that his tenure would last only six to eight weeks and who had made IG's production of synthetic fuels his life's work, more immediate concerns appear to have been decisive. In March, two developments had ensured that increasing German fuel output would be the first task on the agenda of Göring's new office. Russia had embargoed further

[125] RG242/T83, Reel 89, Weber-Andreä's diary entry for 30.IV.36.
[126] Borkin, *Crime and Punishment*, pp. 65–67; Simpson, *JMH*, 31 (1959), p. 38.
[127] For Schacht's views on the latter subject, see Petzina, *Autarkiepolitik*, pp. 35, 43. Ilgner and Schacht also shared similar views concerning German economic policy toward Southeast Europe; see footnote 142 and the discussion to which it refers.
[128] NI-10386/85, Affidavit by P. Koerner, 29.VIII.47; NI-5911/44, Meeting of the Hoechst directors, 13.VII.36.
[129] Friedrich Glum, who knew most of IG's leaders and dealt with Krauch during 1936, thought he was already plotting to inherit Bosch's new role as chairman of the *Aufsichtsrat* (*Zwischen*, pp. 488–90).

Carl Krauch (1887–1968), head of Sparte I, 1933–38, and of the *Aufsichtsrat*, 1940–45; high-ranking official of the Four Year Plan, 1936–45. (*Source*: Firmenarchiv der Hoechst AG, Frankfurt-Hoechst)

deliveries of oil, and Romania had demanded payment in foreign exchange or increased quantities of marks, thus jeopardizing the supply of more than 49% of the Reich's imported petroleum.[130] Suspecting that Keppler would use this opportunity "to found a sort of state concern" in the oil sphere, Krauch set out to avert "nonsense on a larger scale" and to ensure that fields "in which we [IG] were the leading firm would remain in our hands to as great an extent as possible." Bosch released him "in order to avoid worse." In response to the objections of several *Vorstand* members, including Schnitzler, that Krauch's prominence would antagonize other firms and industries, Krauch largely ceased to exercise his corporate functions and, as his official term lengthened, offered on several occasions to resign from IG. But there was never any real question of terminating his association with the firm or his private salary during the indeterminate duration of his unpaid governmental post.[131] By 1936, the practice was well established of seconding businessmen to the bureaucracy as German versions of the American dollar-a-year men.

Faced, then, with the choice between helping steer the regime's synthetic policy or possibly being run over by it, as in the cases of fibers and, in part, Brabag, IG was willing to let Krauch climb aboard Göring's bandwagon. What differentiated the combine from some of the steel, mining, and other chemical firms that hung back, however, was not only IG's more intimate experience with the Nazi state's characteristic combination of determination and inconsistency, but also the concern's commercial evolution since 1933.

Admittedly, during the preceding three years, the core firm and its fully owned subsidiaries had made great strides: Employment had climbed to 170,869 (+52%) by the end of 1936, sales to 1.3 billion marks (+45%), gross profits to 251 million marks (+105%), net profits to 140 million (+91%), distributed profits to 55.4 million (+13%), and annual investment in the factories to 171 million (+407%).[132] Despite the large investments, liquidity had been pre-

130 Arthur Schweitzer, "Der ursprüngliche Vierjahresplan," *JNS*, 168 (1957), p. 356; William Carr, *Arms, Autarky and Aggression* (New York, 1973), p. 55; Petzina, *Autarkiepolitik*, p. 39, note 62.

131 See NI-676/7, Interrogation of Carl Krauch, 16.IV.47; M892/6, Krauch's testimony, 12.I.48, pp. 5066–83, 5115–17; NI-5168/38, Affidavit by F. Jaehne, 29.V.47; Holdermann, *Im Banne der Chemie*, pp. 291–2; Krauch I/24, Affidavit by R. Merton, 15.X.47; and NI-675/7, Schnitzler's statement of 30.VI.45.

132 NI-10001-03/82, Affidavits by H. Deichfischer, 11.VI.47; Defense Basic Information I, p. 64.

served because annual depreciation generally exceeded expenditures for the physical plant between 1933 and 1935.[133] In virtually all of these categories, IG had recovered its position as of 1926–7, but not that of the two boom years that had followed.[134] However, although the firm's growth had greatly exceeded that of its French and Italian rivals and about equaled ICI's, it had fallen far short of the gains made by DuPont and Allied Chemical since 1934.[135] Nor had IG's recovery quite kept pace with that of the economy as a whole. Taking 1928 as the base year, the value of all German industrial production reached 106.7 in 1936, whereas IG's stood at 91.1.[136] This relatively laggard performance resulted almost wholly from the collapse of international trade. As early as 1935, IG's domestic sales broke all previous records; by 1936, they had almost doubled since 1933. Exports, however, still fell slightly short of the unprecedentedly low level of that year. Moreover, the export-oriented divisions of the firm, pharmaceuticals and dyes, provided only 35% of IG's sales income in 1936, as opposed to nearly 47% in 1933.[137] The divisions that had increased in importance, especially basic chemicals and metals in Sparte II, but also Sparten I and III, exported a declining share of their total output.[138]

By 1936, the conclusion was inescapable that a restoration of IG's position as of 1929 and further growth depended, as always, on shoring up the foreign as well as the domestic market. With this in mind, Paul Haefliger of the chemicals division reverted in December to the idea of devaluing the mark.[139] But to most of his peers, the die had been cast between May and September, when Göring rejected any deviation from the New Plan and offered in Schmitz's presence the cold comfort that

---

133 Bayer 11/3, vol. 5, 37th *Aufsichsrat* meeting, 6.IV.35, p. 4. IG's high rates of depreciation provoked criticism from at least one Party organ; see BA Koblenz, ZSg 127, Bd. 838, "Anleihestockgesetz und I. G. Farbenabschluss," *NSK Wirtschaftspolitischer Dienst*, no. 86 (11.IV.35).
134 For comparative data, see Warriner, *Combines and Rationalization*, p. 118; Tammen, *I. G. Farbenindustrie*, p. 80; and Bayer 15/Da 1.1, Umsätze.
135 See BA Koblenz, ZSg 127, Bd. 838, *Die chemische Industrie*, July 1936, p. 151, and Bd. 837, *Die chemische Industrie*, July 1938, p. 182, for the comparative figures.
136 Mason, *Sozialpolitik*, p. 149; Defense Basic Information II, Affidavit by H. Walter, 25.III.48, p. 38.
137 See Tammen, *I. G. Farbenindustrie*, pp. 88–9; and Bayer 15/Da 1.2, IG Umsätze Gesamt 1933/37, from which the percentages are calculated.
138 Bayer 91/1, Vowi 2258, 25.II.37, p. 5; Hoechst TEA 1032, Verkauf Chemikalien 1935, 7.IV.36, p. 13.
139 Bayer DA. 377, Haefliger's memo, "Zur Währungslage und fortschreitenden Devisenverknappung," 4.XII.36.

the speed of armaments must under no circumstances be impaired; on the contrary, even the interests of the factories themselves should be relegated to the background. . . . After overcoming the present difficulties, ways and means will also be found to save the individual plants from collapse.[140]

Recognizing Göring's adamance as well as the value of Schacht's belated attempts to reintegrate Germany into the world economy, IG sought once again to find a "state supporting middle line." While Krauch tried to bring order to the Reich's plans for synthetics production, Max Ilgner proposed a novel solution to the nation's chronic exporting problems: "intervention in the industrialization of the world."

Ilgner's thoughts, articulated in a series of public addresses from 1935 to 1943 and in private reports to his corporate colleagues, got wider distribution via Anton Reithinger's book *Das wirtschaftliche Gesicht Europas,* which appeared in 1936 and was translated into French a year later.[141] Arguing that economic development would increase foreign demand for German merchandise, especially the high-quality producer goods that Nazi policy favored, Ilgner called on the industrial nations of the Continent, particularly Germany, to foster consumer-oriented, extractive, and agriculture-based industries abroad, primarily in the European periphery. Lacking skilled work forces, substantial home demand, and adequate communications, the developing nations would never become real rivals to sophisticated European manufacturers, and moves in that direction could be forestalled by coherent planning and a friendly attitude on the part of the developed states.[142] Such a scheme required increased international cooperation and, at home, the realization that "export encouragement, the Four Year Plan, armaments, and food provisioning can only be

---

[140] NI-5380/39, Meeting of the Gutachter-Ausschuss, 26.V.36. See also Göring's dismissal in September of Goerdeler's economic proposals as "completely useless" (Ritter, *Carl Goerdeler,* p. 85).

[141] Anton Reithinger, *Das Wirtschaftliche Gesicht Europas* (Stuttgart, 1936), translated as *Le visage economique de l'Europe* (Paris, 1937). A serialized version of the book appeared under its German title in the *Europäische Revue,* 12–13 (1935–6).

[142] M892/10, Ilgner's testimony, p. 9528, on the emergence of his conception. For its later development, see NI-1570/15, his speech in Paris on 15.III.37; Krüger, *G&G,* 6 (1980), pp. 278–9, on his speech in Kiel in 1938; and Chapter 7 on his thoughts during the war. For an illustration of the sharp contrast between Ilgner's ideas and Hitler's, see the führer's remarks quoted by Krüger, pp. 274–5, note 28. On the similarity between Ilgner's and Schacht's views, however, see Schacht, *Confessions,* p. 305.

considered in a total framework and must . . . with masterly command of the whole be reconciled with one another."[143]

Compatible on the surface with Nazi policy, Ilgner's program contained implications of a far different tendency. Some of the steel, machinery, and manufacturing equipment earmarked for Germany's own investment in arms and self-sufficiency would have to be diverted to the countries selected for industrialization, since in many cases their trade reliance on Germany made them unable to purchase the necessary materials elsewhere. Entailing increased concentration in the German economy, the elimination of many small domestic firms producing for consumers, and reduced emphasis on preparing for war, Ilgner's conception violated the regime's most cherished political and social goals: the creation of an empire built around the small producer and the barracks. From 1936 to 1939, Ilgner repeatedly restated his views, and IG kept trying to find ways of squaring synthetics development with economic rationality. These facts suggest that relatively traditional commercial and technological considerations, adjusted for the changed international environment, underlay the combine's conduct later as much as they had in 1933–6.

---

[143] Quoted in Hans-Jürgen Schröder, *Deutschland und die Vereinigten Staaten* (Wiesbaden, 1970), pp. 44–5.

PART III
The nervous years, 1936–1939

Mounting economic strains did not force Adolf Hitler into his "foreign policy of aggressive brinksmanship."[1] In the Third Reich, causation worked in the opposite direction, however mutually reinforcing the two trends became. Like Bücher's and Goerdeler's alternatives to escalating autarky, rearmament, and expansionism, Schacht's and Ilgner's counterproposals were doomed by their political, not their economic, impracticality. Nor would the unified support of German businessmen for any of these programs have altered their fate or the regime's course.[2] Flushed with his most daring foreign policy triumph yet, the remilitarization of the Rhineland in March 1936, neither the führer nor most of his compatriots saw much reason to compromise the primacy of politics. On the contrary, by the middle of that year Hitler felt sure that the diplomatic tide had turned in his favor and that he had best make ready to catch it at the flood. With the British, French, and Italians divided over the conflicts in Ethiopia and Spain, and the Russians descending into the debilitating Great Purge but also introducing conscription, Hitler would brook no interference with his most pressing task: making his military and economic resources measure up to what he considered short-lived opportunities.

The chancellor translated his determination into action over the summer of 1936. In June, almost certainly at his behest, the Army

---

[1] Karl Hardach, *The Political Economy of Germany in the Twentieth Century* (Berkeley, Calif., 1980), p. 75. Cf. Tim Mason, "Innere Krise und Angriffskrieg, 1938/39," in Friedrich Forstmeier and Hans-Erich Volkmann (eds.), *Wirtschaft und Rüstung am Vorabend des 2. Weltkrieges* (Düsseldorf, 1975), pp. 160–86; Hans Kehrl, *Zur Wirklichkeit des Dritten Reiches* (n.p., [1975]), pp. 18–21; and R. J. Overy, *Goering: The 'Iron Man'* (Boston, 1984), pp. 49–50, 89.

[2] This counterfactual observation is largely ignored by scholars who seek to explain the subsequent course of German economic and foreign policy with reference to divisions among the nation's capitalists; see the numerous orthodox and neo-Marxist works that descend from Jürgen Kuczynski's massive *Die Geschichte der Lage der Arbeiter unter dem Kapitalismus*, vols. 6, 14, 16–17 (East Berlin, 1964–72), and Daniel Guerin's *Fascism and Big Business* (New York, 1939), as well as the works of Arthur Schweitzer, especially "Business Power in the Nazi Regime," *ZfN*, 20 (1960), pp. 414–42.

High Command initiated planning for offensive operations on a large scale. At about the same time, Krauch's Research and Development Office, now subordinated to Colonel Fritz Löb of the Air Ministry, responded to the renewed foreign exchange shortage by surveying in detail the nation's raw materials needs and the possibilities of supplying them from domestic sources. During the first half of August, both organizations completed their preliminary studies. The military's contemplated fielding a force of 4.6 million battle-ready men by October 1, 1939, at a cost of just less than 27 billion marks over the intervening three years. Less exclusively keyed to wartime requirements (except in the matter of fuel), Krauch's report was also less conclusive. It estimated that an investment of about 3 billion marks in new factories would reduce the Reich's annual imports of primary products by about one-third, save Germany some 600 million marks worth of foreign exchange per year, and raise home production of oil, rubber, textiles, iron ore, fats, and ten other basic substances to levels varying between 30 and 80% of projected *peacetime* consumption by the end of 1938.[3] Probably apprised of these findings, the führer retreated to the Obersalzberg in late August. There, as he recalled to Albert Speer in 1944, he compressed his fury at "the incomprehension of the Economics Ministry and the opposition of the German economy to all bold planning" into a memorandum for Blomberg and Göring, his deputies for military and economic mobilization.[4] Declaring that the predestined struggle for existence against bolshevism and Jewry could be longer be put off, Hitler set the two generals the tasks of making the German army "operational" and the German economy "capable of war" within four years. To these ends, he forbade reduction of arms expenditures, demanded rapid and massive expansion of synthetics output without regard to technological problems or production costs, and defined the future of business in the bluntest possible terms:

[3] On the army's planning, see W. Deist, *The Wehrmacht and German Rearmament* (Toronto, 1981), pp. 45–53. On Krauch's, the surviving documents are in BA Koblenz, R25/18, and excerpted in D. Eichholtz and W. Schumann (eds.), *Anatomie des Krieges* (East Berlin, 1969), Document 46, pp. 139–42. See also Dieter Petzina, *Autarkiepolitik im Dritten Reich* (Stuttgart, 1968), pp. 44–5; Arthur Schweitzer, *Big Business in the Third Reich* (Bloomington, Ind., 1964), p. 547; and NI-9656/80, Affidavit by P. Koerner, 15.VIII.47.
[4] Quoted in Wilhelm Treue, "Hitlers Denkschrift zum Vierjahresplan 1936," *VfZ*, 3 (1955), p. 184.

The Economics Ministry has only to set the national economic tasks, and private industry has to fulfill them. If, however, private industry believes itself incapable of doing so, then the National Socialist state will know how to solve the problem itself. . . . German business will grasp the new economic tasks or it will show itself unfit for survival in this modern age, when the Soviet state is establishing a giant plan. Then, however, Germany will not go under, but at most a few businessmen.[5]

For the führer, there remained "no such thing as a commercial balance of expenditure and profit. There is only a national balance of being and not being."[6]

With the announcement of the Four Year Plan to the Party congress on September 9, Hitler hardened German economic policy into a self-fulfilling prophecy. By aiming for the highest degree of self-sufficiency as a means to conquest, he made conquest all the more necessary. During the ensuing three years, the regime manipulated the price structure, compelled savings institutions to convert their deposits into government bonds, limited stock issues and dividend payments, and raised corporate tax rates by 5% per year from 20% in 1935 to 40% in 1939, minus various exemptions for reserves reinvested in state-sanctioned projects.[7] The result was a tight lid on most firms' profits and a system of direct and "derived" public financing that drained a substantial portion of national income into capital investment in war-related industries. While exporters and potential investors in foreign industrialization thirsted for funds, new plant construction increased the Reich's bills for imports and piled up enormous productive capacity.[8] In short, the Third Reich began "strip mining the economy," and

[5] Hitler's memo was presented at the postwar trials as NI-4955/36 and is reprinted in full in Treue, VfZ, 3 (1955), pp. 204–10. Thorough summaries of the document appear in the same article, pp. 184–203; in Petzina, Autarkiepolitik, pp. 48–51; and in Gerhard L. Weinberg, The Foreign Policy of Hitler's Germany, vol. 1 (Chicago, 1970), pp. 350–6.
[6] Quoted in J. P. Stern, Hitler: The Führer and the People (Berkeley, Calif., 1975), p. 134.
[7] David Schoenbaum, Hitler's Social Revolution (New York, 1966), pp. 144–5; L. L. Hamburger, How Nazi Germany Has Controlled Business (Washington, D.C., 1943), pp. 52–9, 67–81; Alan S. Milward, "Fascism and the Economy," in W. Laqueur (ed.), Fascism: A Reader's Guide (Berkeley, Calif., 1976), pp. 396–7.
[8] Samuel Lurie, Private Investment in a Controlled Economy (New York, 1947), pp. 220–3; Peter Drucker, The End of Economic Man (New York, 1939), p. 149; R. J. Overy, The Nazi Economic Recovery 1932–1938 (London, 1982), pp. 35–7; and Joachim Radkau, "Entscheidungsprozesse und Entscheidungsdefizite in der deutschen Aussenwirtschaftspolitik 1933–1940," G&G, 2 (1976), pp. 63–5.

the public purse became the chief determinant of a corporation's growth or stagnation.[9] Opting for the former made an enterprise, nolens volens, an instrument of the state and a partner in expansionism. Moreover, as the spiral of trade crises tightened and the question of sustaining demand loomed larger, Hitler could increasingly justify a militant drive to the east as the solution to the economic problems he had largely imposed.

All of this dawned on most German businessmen – and most foreign observers – only gradually.[10] In part, the executives were blinded by gratitude for a system that rewarded sheer productivity more than efficiency. In part, their myopia resulted from the phenomenon David Schoenbaum has wittily dubbed *Kraft durch Schadenfreude*. The mix of popular compliance and complaint in the Third Reich generally depended on whose ox was being gored: Most individuals and social groups acquiesced or took satisfaction in the regime's manhandling of others and protested only when valued parochial interests were at stake.[11] So long as the labor force seemed cowed and the economy was merely reactivating slack capacity, the growing state control of economic life hardly chafed at corporate managers and their guard remained down.[12]

But the chief explanation for most businessmen's passivity lay in the regime's usual effort to lure as well as lash them into cooperation. Outside of Göring, Blomberg, and a handful of the highest-ranking civil servants, virtually no one knew of the existence, let alone the threatening content, of Hitler's August memorandum. No reference to readying the nation for war within four years accompanied the proclamation of the Four Year Plan. The führer and Göring took care to describe their program as a "political necessity," a means of ensuring

[9] Joachim Fest, *Hitler* (New York, 1975), p. 538; T. W. Mason, "The Primacy of Politics," in H. A. Turner, Jr. (ed.), *Nazism and the Third Reich* (New York, 1972), p. 187. For the instructive effects of this situation on a single industrial group, see Edward L. Homze, *Arming the Luftwaffe* (Lincoln, Neb., 1976), p. 199.

[10] On German perceptions, see Lurie, *Private Investment*, pp. 28–30; and C. W. Guillebaud, *The Economic Recovery of Germany* (London, 1939), p. 185. For the comments of one of the few foreign commentators who quickly saw through events, see Stephen H. Roberts, *The House That Hitler Built* (London, 1938), pp. 172, 180.

[11] Schoenbaum, *Social Revolution*, p. 283; Ian Kershaw, *Popular Opinion and Political Dissent in the Third Reich* (New York, 1983).

[12] Schweitzer, *Big Business*, pp. 447, 449; Avraham Barkai, *Das Wirtschaftssystem des Nationalsozialismus* (Köln, 1977), p. 178.

the nation's independence and security.[13] To the Party congress in September, Hitler held out the promise that "the new expansion of this large German raw materials industry will also usefully employ the masses of people freed after the conclusion of rearmament," thus encouraging the conclusion that "autarky did not . . . automatically commit Germany to war."[14] As always, he combined conciliation with an undertone of coercion. Denouncing those who might claim he was placing German business "in the straightjacket of our state planning," he warned that "at issue is not the freedom or profit of some industrialists, but the life and freedom of the German nation. Whoever believes that he cannot succeed within the ambit of this freedom has no justification for existence in our community."[15] Not until December did Göring let fall to a group of industrialists his convictions that "whether in every case new plants will be amortized is a matter of indifference. . . . We stand already in mobilization and war, only the shooting has not yet started," and such comments were easy to chalk up to his bluff manner of speech when compared with Colonel Löb's reassurances about the autonomy of business and the eventual relaxation of controls.[16]

Nonetheless, by early 1937 "the economic writing was beginning to go up on the walls of the Third Reich."[17] As the military budget outstripped the civilian one, businessmen began to recognize that the orderly process of rearmament for which some had hoped had turned into a program of arms at all costs and at breakneck speed.[18] Increasingly, managers grumbled about raw materials shortages, administrative confusion, red tape, and the highhanded conduct of an army of meddlesome and expensive bureaucrats.[19] The regime replied with

13 Arthur Schweitzer, "Parteidiktatur und überministerielle Führergewalt," *Jahrbuch für Sozialwissenschaft,* 21 (1970), p. 69.
14 For Hitler's remarks, see Treue, *VfZ,* 3 (1955), p. 201; NI-8459/70, Excerpt from the Munich edition of the *Völkischer Beobachter,* 10.IX.36. The second quotation, which is the judgment of William Carr, *Arms, Autarky and Aggression* (New York, 1973), p. 60, is foreshadowed in NI-8327/68, E. Struss's speech of 13.V.38.
15 Treue, *VfZ,* 3 (1955), pp. 201–2.
16 NI-051/2, Göring's speech at the Preussenhaus, 17.XII.36; Bayer D. A. 1100, Löb's speech of 24.V.37.
17 For the quotation, see Graham Hutton, "German Economic Tension: Causes and Results," *Foreign Affairs,* 52 (1939), p. 529.
18 See Michael Geyer, "Zum Einfluss der nationalsozialistischen Rüstungspolitik auf das Ruhrgebiet," *RVB,* 45 (1981), pp. 207, 214–19.
19 See "Memo by Members of Big Business in Germany 1937" forwarded by Retired

renewed attempts to coopt and corner corporate executives. Perhaps the most important of these was the new German Corporation Law published on January 30, 1937. Designed to reduce the influence of shareholders over management and to increase that of the state, the law stiffened the requirements for incorporation, stripped general meetings of the right to question an enterprise's balance sheets, and authorized governing boards to conceal information from investors if the firm's or the Reich's interests so warranted. Having thus removed legal obligations to the stockholders as a basis for refusing to allocate funds as the regime might wish, the law empowered the Justice Ministry to apply to the National Economic Court (Reichswirtschaftgericht) for the dissolution of any corporation whose *Vorstand*'s behavior "grossly violates the law or the principles of responsible business methods" or imperils the interests of "the people and the Reich."[20] Meanwhile, the files of the Reich Patent Office and the compulsory completion of questionnaires issued by the Reich Statistical Office kept the regime fully informed as to the manufacturing processes, precise composition, and necessary supplies or basic materials for virtually every large firm's products.[21] Fritz Roessler, the chairman of the supervisory board of the Degussa chemical corporation, summarized the resulting outlook under the Four Year Plan just before his death in early 1937:

The times are gone in which profits could be writ large. . . . Socialization of industry is rejected. The initiative of individual entrepreneurs is not to be restricted and leading people are to be well paid, but the profits of firms themselves will be ever more limited. Via taxes and cartel controls state officials are looking ever deeper into the books of industry. Over half of the difference between gross receipts and payments to stockholders is already taxed away, not counting the export premium and the other "voluntary" payments and deductions. . . . The executive will work in the future in the

---

Group Captain Ian Christie, the former British air attaché in Berlin, to Sir Robert Vansittart; Christie Papers, Churchill College, Cambridge. See also Marlis Steinart, *Hitler's War and the Germans* (Athens, Ohio, 1977), pp. 31–2; Drucker, *Economic Man*, p. 223; and Guillebaud, *Economic Recovery*, p. 222, note 1.

20 F. A. Mann, "The New German Company Law and Its Background," *Journal of Comparative Legislation and International Law*, 19 (1937), pp. 222–33; NI-10037–38/82, the Law and the related introductory decree of 30.I.37, excerpted from the *RGBl.* (1937), Pt. I. See also Lurie, *Private Investment*, pp. 145–6; and Maxine Y. Sweezy, *The Structure of the Nazi Economy* (Cambridge, Mass., 1941), p. 65.

21 See Bayer 4C9.25, R. W. Mueller and Dr. von Knieriem, "Die I. G. Farbenindustrie Aktiengesellschaft. Das Schicksal eines deutschen Unternehmens," March 1951, p. 81.

truest sense "for the King of Prussia," only now one says: for the people's community. Once the great private fortunes have all but disappeared and the incomes of the middle classes have undergone a strong leveling effect, the same grading off of industrial profits is to be expected in succeeding years. The Scheideanstalt [Roessler's company] still possesses good reserves. But who can say that those very reserves, insofar as they are not consumed by the Four Year Plan, will not become the object of new tax laws.[22]

Because Roessler's perceptions were hardly unique, the regime applied the combination of carrot and stick to businessmen ever more explicitly after the summer of 1937, pressuring them to join the NSDAP, offering an array of honorary posts and titles to executives, and setting in motion a number of decisive domestic and foreign policy changes.[23] In September, Hitler signaled his rising impatience by remarking, as reported in the *Frankfurter Zeitung,* "If private enterprise does not carry through the Four Year Plan, the State will assume full control of business."[24] The threat was backed up not only by the founding of the Reichswerke Hermann Göring two months earlier over the opposition of heavy industry, but also by the reorganization of the Economics Ministry that followed the acceptance of Schacht's resignation in November 1937.[25] In early February 1938, only days after the replacement of Generals Blomberg and Fritsch largely completed the long-creeping *Gleichschaltung* of the army, Göring appointed eighteen new senior economic officials "with National Socialist

22 Degussa, Biographische Unterlagen, Zur Geschichte der Scheideanstalt 1933 bis 1936 by Dr. Fritz Roessler, January 1937, Abschrift, pp. 128–9.
23 For example, on the creation of the War Economy Leaders Corps and Council, see NI-373-74/5, Announcements by the Deutsches Nachrichtenbüro, 14.XII.37 and 31.I.38; Schweitzer, *Jahrbuch für Sozialwissenschaft,* 21 (1970), pp. 70–1. On enrollment in the NSDAP by businessmen during this period, see Michael H. Kater, *The Nazi Party* (Cambridge, Mass., 1983), pp. 102–5, but note that his emphasis on an influx in 1939 ignores the equally large surge in 1937 documented by his own Table 7, pp. 252–3.
24 Quoted in Amos E. Simpson, "The Struggle for Control of the German Economy," *JMH,* 31 (1959), p. 42. See also Overy, *Goering,* p. 51.
25 See, above all, R. J. Overy, "Heavy Industry and the State in Nazi Germany: The Reichswerke Crisis," *European History Quarterly,* 15 (1985), pp. 313–40. The oft-repeated argument of G. W. F. Hallgarten and Joachim Radkau, *Deutsche Industrie und Politik* (Frankfurt, 1974), p. 255, that the HGW benefited private steel producers by relieving them of the costs of exploiting low-grade ores and by holding up prices is good for only the short run, and most of the steel makers affected were unimpressed. See also Kurt Lachmann, "The Hermann Göring Works," *Social Research,* 8 (1941), pp. 27, 29, 31, 35, 38; Gustav-Hermann Seebold, *Ein Stahlkonzern im Dritten Reich* (Wuppertal, 1981), pp. 86–92; and Overy, *Goering,* pp. 62–5. For the latest East German attempt to make the HGW a servant of private capitalism, see Lotta Zumpe, "Kohle-Eisen-Stahl 1936/37," *JfW,* 21 (1980), pp. 137–51.

convictions." Out went trusted associates of German industry like Hans Posse and Heinrich Schlattmann. In came Rudolf Brinkmann, a banker and turncoat protégé of Schacht, as state secretary; Hans Kehrl as *Generalreferent;* Wilhelm Keppler as section leader for geological research; Rudolf Schmeer from the DAF, a Party member since 1926, as section leader for economic organization, retailing, and crafts; Colonel Löb of the air force; and General Hermann von Hanneken of the army. All of this was capped a few days later by the naming of Walther Funk from the Propaganda Ministry as the new economics minister.[26] In the interval between Schacht's departure and Funk's installation, Göring launched another form of intervention in business life: Aryanization. After reducing the quotas of foreign exchange and raw materials permitted to Jewish firms, he issued a decree on January 4, 1938, defining such enterprises as ones owned or dominated by Jews or in which one personally responsible official or one *Vorstand* member or one-quarter of the *Aufsichtsrat* was Jewish.[27] A month later, such firms were declared ineligible for government contracts; by July, the presence of even one Jew on its *Aufsichtsrat* brought a company under this ban. On November 12, the government ordered "the complete exclusion of Jews from German economic life." Though commercially regrettable and personally painful to many executives, Aryanization appeared irresistible. It also made available too many positions and properties to arouse corporate protests, particularly in view of the fact that reaping the spoils depended on the approval of the economic adviser to the appropriate *Gauleitung.*[28]

Neither the regime's domestic moves nor its acquisition of Austria and the Sudetenland sufficed, however, to still businessmen's objec-

[26] Schweitzer, *Jahrbuch für Sozialwissenschaft,* 21 (1970), p. 65; NID-13629, Göring's reorganization decree of 5.II.38, *NMT,* vol. 12, pp. 484–8; Walther Funk's testimony, *NMT,* vol. 13, pp. 100–1; NI-135/2, Excerpt from the *Völkischer Beobachter* listing the new appointees, 5.II.38; Hans Kehrl, *Krisenmanager im Dritten Reich* (Düsseldorf, 1973), pp. 110–14; Willi A. Boelcke, *Die deutsche Wirtschaft 1930–1945* (Düsseldorf, 1983), pp. 181–4. On Schmeer, see Herrmann A. L. Degener (ed.), *Wer Ist's,* 10th ed. (Berlin, 1935), p. 1397. For background, see BA Koblenz, R26 I/la, Kehrl to Göring, 1.IX.37, protesting Schacht's dedication to "the liberal-capitalist system and free trade" and his consequent "sabotage of the Four Year Plan."
[27] Bayer D. A. 377, Neuberg to the *Beirat* of the Industrieabteilung der Wirtschaftskammer Düsseldorf, 10.I.38, reporting Göring's decree.
[28] See Uwe Dietrich Adam, *Judenpolitik im Dritten Reich* (Düsseldorf, 1972), pp. 172–91; Helmut Genschel, *Die Verdrängung der Juden aus der Wirtschaft im Dritten Reich* (Göttingen, 1966), pp. 139–76; NI-15171/123, Third Supplementary Decree to the Reich Citizenship Law, 14.VII.38; and Boelcke, *Deutsche Wirtschaft,* pp. 210–17.

tions to economic "pressure toward commercially unsound management."[29] Consequently, the Reich's spokesmen radicalized their rhetoric for native as well as foreign audiences. In October 1938, Göring threatened the MAN motor factory with subjection to a state commissar, told his industrial planning staff that manufacturing "which is not useful for armaments or exports must be shut down," and announced to officers at the Air Ministry that "now is the moment for private industry to show whether it still has a justification for being. If it fails, then it will be turned ruthlessly into a state economy."[30] At roughly the same time, the *Reichsmarschall* presented Wilhelm Zangen, the new head of the Reichsgruppe Industrie, with the prospect of "a state commissioner for the direction of industry" who might receive the power to "seize sectors of the economy" that in Göring's view failed to accomplish "what the state must require of them." One heavy industrialist who heard Zangen's report of this conversation concluded that "expropriation" and "socialization" were real possibilities and that "business, especially the mining industry, has never been in such danger."[31] Indeed, during the next few months, Paul Walter began his rise through the succession of government posts that gave him control from 1939 to 1941 of coal production and distribution.[32]

Göring's utterances remained relatively private, but that was not the case with State Secretary Brinkmann's speech to the representatives of the insurance and banking businesses gathered in Berlin later in the month. Taking up the "uncomfortable" subject of relations between the state and the economy, Brinkmann recited and admitted the validity of a litany of businessmen's grievances against restrictions on output and labor, "impossible" price levels, investments "which out of private motives would not be undertaken," forced loans for

29 Jost Dülffer, "Der Beginn des Krieges 1939: Hitler, die innere Krise und das Mächtesystem," *G&G*, 2 (1976), p. 454. See also the complaints of even so fervent a Nazi as Albert Pietzsch, recorded in Ulrich von Hassell, *The von Hassell Diaries 1938–1944* (London, 1948), p. 27.
30 Dülffer, *G&G*, 2 (1976), p. 454; Norbert Schausberger, *Rüstung in Oesterreich 1938–1945* (Wien, 1970), p. 37.
31 Klöckner-Archiv, Bestand Peter Klöckner, Kleiner Kreis, Bd. 1, Aktennotiz über die am 20. Oktober 1938 . . . stattgefundene Besprechung in einem kleinen Kreise, Duisburg, 20.X.38, unsigned (probably by either Poensgen or Kellermann). See also General von Hanneken's threat, quoted in John R. Gillingham, *Industry and Politics in the Third Reich* (New York, 1985), p. 61.
32 On Walter's rise and fall, see Gillingham, *Industry and Politics*, pp. 62–4, 114–5.

undesirable purposes at low rates of return, bureaucratization and its associated "dead costs," increasing economic concentration, and declining personal living standards.[33] He also conceded the need for the regime to permit business adequate profit margins and once more promised a loosening of economic regulations now that the nation's international freedom of action had been reclaimed.[34] Nonetheless, Brinkmann reminded his hearers, all sin did not lie with the government. Industry had exploited the cartel and patent systems to private advantage and engaged in a "flight . . . from open competition and responsibility" that had left the state no choice but to intervene actively in economic affairs.[35] This the regime deplored,

> for at bottom we do not seek a material but a mental nationalization of the economy. . . . Please do not forget, however, that a strong and energetic state has at all times been inclined to shift the boundaries between public and private economies in the direction of commercial activity by the state . . . and do not underestimate the capacity for endurance which has led to the fact that through all political and ideological changes, that remains state-operated which has become state-operated. Further, do not underestimate the possibility of the state managing wherever business can not produce to an adequate degree or perform creatively. . . . It does not lack professionally trained, highly patriotic forces or the capacity to plan for the long run. Also among bureaucrats are characters for whom work without rest is the stuff of life and with whom the joy of creating and the ambition to accomplish something are as strong an impulse to apply oneself as the drive for profits in other professions.[36]

In sum, the years 1936–9 brought a new and sharper tone to German business–state relations. The following chapter reviews IG Farben's reactions to the change. Before the quickening of Hitler's march toward war in the autumn of 1937, iron mining by the Hermann Göring Works and the seemingly satisfactory state of the nation's coal supplies rendered further construction for these industries unnecessary. The Four Year Plan, therefore, focused on fuel, rubber, and chemicals production and, perforce, on IG Farben.[37] Adopting a

[33] Rudolf Brinkmann, "Staat und Wirtschaft," 21.X.38, published in his *Wirtschaftspolitik aus nationalsozialistischem Kraftquell* (Jena, 1939), pp. 193, 206–7.
[34] Ibid., pp. 211, 215.
[35] Ibid., pp. 216–17, 219–21; the quoted phrase appears on p. 221.
[36] Ibid., pp. 223–4. On Brinkmann and his career in the Third Reich, see Boelcke, *Deutsche Wirtschaft*, pp. 189–92.
[37] See NI-9656/80, Affidavit by P. Koerner, 15.VIII.47; and Dieter Petzina, "Vierjahresplan und Rüstungspolitik," in Forstmeier and Volkmann (eds.), *Wirtschaft*

strategy of indispensability, the concern sought to control events by inserting its employees in the planning apparatus, to exploit IG's importance to German exports in order to blunt the ill effects of the Four Year Plan on the combine's foreign trade, and to appease growing demands from the Party for money and ideological conformity. During 1938, IG's failure on all three counts became manifest. While shortages of steel and labor hamstrung the corporation, Aryanization brought alarming brushes with the Nazis, and overexpansion atomized the firm and placed its financial stability, hence what was left of IG's autonomy, in jeopardy. Simultaneously, Carl Krauch recognized that the regime was headed toward a war that he doubted Germany could win. The upshot was a growing divergence between Krauch's efforts to prepare the country for a conflict he hoped to postpone and Farben's attempts to protect its commercial future. Caught up in "the schizophrenia typical of Nazi society" by which "revolution was both imminent and indefinitely suspended" so long as war was, IG Farben's leaders experienced a nervousness that rose along with their sales.[38]

---

und Rüstung, p. 78. The erroneous conviction that the nation's coal supplies were adequate rested on a survey of the industry in November 1935; see Gillingham, *Industry and Politics,* pp. 53–4.

[38] The quotations are from Schoenbaum, *Social Revolution,* p. 277.

5. Autarky and atomization

On October 22, 1936, the führer's new deputy for the Four Year Plan, Hermann Göring, unveiled the organization he expected to become "in the next years decisive for all economic and social policy."[1] Presided over by two largely decorative councils, the plan's central apparatus (see Appendix C) consisted of seven main divisions. Those for fats, raw materials distribution, agricultural production, and price setting were headed by veteran Nazis – Wilhelm Keppler, Bernhard Köhler, Herbert Backe, and Josef Wagner, respectively. Experienced bureaucrats directed the departments for foreign exchange and labor allocation. But the bulk of the plan's work fell to a military man, Colonel Löb of the air force, the chief of the new Office for German Raw Materials. He and two other soldiers, Major Czimatis and Major Heemskerk, assumed responsibility for the three of that office's five sections that oversaw the execution of the plan. Only the staffs for research and development, Carl Krauch's domain, and financing, under Kurt Lange, had leaders drawn from the ranks of German business. Lange, however, was closely tied to the NSDAP, as were three of the four directors of the subunits that reported directly to Löb – Pleiger and Kehrl from Keppler's former staff and Reich Forester von Monroy, a Göring appointee. Dr. Johannes Eckell took over the subunit for chemicals upon resigning from IG Farben and becoming a full-time civil servant.[2] Though the Party's presence within the plan declined somewhat during 1937, as Keppler transferred his attentions to

---

1 Quoted in Petzina, *Autarkiepolitik*, p. 57. The basic documents on the initial organization and extent of the plan are NI-12616/103 and NI-12786/105, Affidavits by H. Gramsch, 11.IX.47 and 19.XI.47. The best secondary accounts are Arthur Schweitzer, "Der ursprüngliche Vierjahresplan," *JNS*, 168 (1957), pp. 352–6, and Petzina, *Autarkiepolitik*, pp. 57–63, 78–88. Unless otherwise indicated, this paragraph rests on these sources, though I interpret the information they provide somewhat differently than either Petzina or Schweitzer.
2 Bayer 4B/36, vol. 1, Gründung der Buna Werke der I.G., unsigned and undated (1945?), confirmed by Struss to terMeer, 7.XI.36, cited in Peter J. T. Morris, *The Development of Acetylene Chemistry and Synthetic Rubber by I.G. Farbenindustrie Aktiengesellschaft: 1926–1945* (Dissertation, University of Oxford, 1982), p. 268.

Austrian matters and Köhler's distribution office was disbanded, Krauch's position remained conspicuous. From 1936 to 1938, his links to IG and his practice of selecting subordinates from industry were the targets of recurrent sniping from the NSDAP, the Economics Ministry, some army leaders, and IG's competitors.[3] These facts help explain why Krauch, always a single-minded and remote workhorse, began to behave, at least according to one man who encountered him during these months, "like a little Nazi dictator."[4]

Krauch drew fire for the same reason that IG valued his posting, at least initially. Charged with achieving the maximum degree of self-sufficiency for the Reich in some twenty-five to thirty major products, including textiles, rubber, tanning agents, resins, oil, fats, albumen, animal fodder, sulfur, phosphates, and copper, Krauch's staff rapidly became the allocator of an average of 47% of total annual German industrial investment between 1936 and 1939, exclusive of the coal and electrical industries.[5] By February 1937, when the rationing of iron and steel began, the investments contemplated by Krauch's office had risen from the 3 billion marks foreseen during the previous August to more than 8.6 billion marks, and projects costing 550 million marks were already underway. By the end of the year, Krauch's fourth draft of the Four Year Plan called for investments of 9.5 billion marks in order to save the equivalent of 2.3 billion annually in foreign exchange.[6] Fully 58.1% of this flood of capital was destined in early 1937 for fields in which IG Farben had a strong interest: oil, rubber, chemicals, nonprecious metals, and textiles. In the fourth draft of December, the figure fell to 52.2%, and the share allotted to IG's primary concerns, buna and chemicals, dropped more sharply, from 33.3 to 15.1%.[7] That last percentage, however, still represented the creation of 1.4 billion marks worth of physical assets.

The prospect of such a large infusion of capital and capacity was as

---

[3] See M892/6, Krauch's testimony, p. 5117; NI-10500/86, Affidavit by W. Lenz, 30.VIII.47; BA Koblenz, R26 I/la, Ueber die Vierjahresplanämter, 27.I.38, unsigned (probably Paul Pleiger); NI-8840/73, Krauch to Körner, 22.VII.38.

[4] On Krauch's personality, interview with Hans Kehrl, 11.VII.78; for the quotation, F. Glum, *Zwischen Wissenschaft, Wirtschaft und Politik* (Bonn, 1964), p. 490.

[5] Krauch I/87, Affidavit by C. Krauch, 29.XII.47; Petzina, *Autarkiepolitik*, p. 183.

[6] Ibid., pp. 81, 154; BA Koblenz, R2/17837, *Vermerk*, unsigned, giving construction projects as of 20.II.37; Krauch I/87, Krauch's affidavit of 29.XII.47; NI-6769/52, the fourth draft of the plan, 21.XII.37. The official *Gesamtplan* as of 1.I.38, including the various drafts of 1937, is now catalogued at the BA Koblenz as R25/19–21.

[7] See Petzina, *Autarkiepolitik*, Table 2, p. 83.

potentially damaging as it was tempting to IG. Thus, even before the full extent of the plan became clear, Sparten I and II hastened to prevent rivals from gaining heft at the public trough.[8] But Farben's chief worry about the plan was broader. From the outset, the concern feared that without stringent coordination and enforcement of priorities in distributing building and operating materials, the plan would starve more factories than it started.[9]

Hoping to contain both competition and chaos, IG complied with numerous requests to assign employees to the planning offices. Whether Köhler's staff or Army Ordnance got the assistance it sought is not clear from the surviving documents, but the concern honored Paul Pleiger's wish for an "all-around chemist" by providing a Dr. Bernhard, since he was "loyal to IG in his bones" and "it is naturally important for us that no man be chosen who for subjective reasons works against IG."[10] Farben concentrated its personnel, however, in Krauch's office and warned it against hiring persons ill-disposed to the concern.[11] How many of Krauch's aides came from IG is uncertain, since the available estimates diverge widely and rest on memory. One former official in the Economics Ministry claimed after the war that the Research and Development Office comprised largely unsalaried staffers, some 90% of whom came from Farben.[12] Probably more accurate, however, are the calculations of a former assistant to Krauch, who reckoned the share of his academically trained associates drawn from IG at 20.4% as of autumn 1939.[13] Whatever the true figure, there is no question that employees of the firm, including Gerhard Ritter, the head of Krauch's unit for chemicals, Dr. Neukirch as adviser for light metals, and one Dr. Vorländer, played an important part in formulating the details of the Four Year Plan.[14]

[8] On this and Gajewski's refusal to join in the rush, see NI-1295/13, Statement by G. Frank-Fahle, undated. For three examples of IG's maneuvering against competitors, see Bayer D.A. 1100: Besprechung am 5. November 1936 im Büro Dr. Krauch, 6.XI.36; file note of 22.III.37; Thienemann to Kühne, 24.III.37; and memo of a meeting with Keppler, 12–13.V.37.
[9] Bayer D.A. 1100, File note of conversations between IG representatives and Czimatis, Jeimke, and Sauer of the Raw Materials Office, 27.XI. 36.
[10] Bayer 64/3, Auszug aus einer Niederschrift von Herrn Weber-Andreä über Besprechung mit Herrn Dr. terMeer am 29.X.36. NI-4638/34 is a copy sent to Kühne on 2.XI.36.
[11] For an example of the warnings, see Bayer D.A. 913, Kühne to Brüning, 29.X.36.
[12] NI-4952, Affidavit by F. Ehrmann, 13.III.47, NMT, vol. 7, p. 857.
[13] Krauch I/67, Affidavit by A. Mueller, 2.XII.47.
[14] On the dispatching of Dr. Vorländer and Dr. Neukirch to Krauch's staff, see Bayer D.A. 1100, Pistor to Kühne, 6.II.37.

Nonetheless, IG Farben neither "captured the relevant governmental agencies and added them to [its] industrial empire" nor "privatized" the making of national economic policy, nor blended (*"verschmolz"*) the state's and the firm's decisions to the point of indistinguishability.[15] Both Krauch and his subordinates rapidly identified with their new tasks, not their old employers, even when private corporations continued to pay their salaries. Indeed, Otto Ambros of IG's buna program discovered that a transfer of loyalties could occur almost overnight. In November 1936, he expressed surprise at the "unfriendly attitude toward IG" shown by Johannes Eckell in the matter of producing certain spirits.[16] During the next few years, Eckell upbraided the concern for deficiencies in reporting on construction projects and held IG closely to the terms of contracts with the Reich.[17] In one instance, he intervened to prevent the concern from obtaining an unauthorized price break that amounted to a mere 14,000 marks per year on the purchase of the oxygen given off as a by-product at one of the new buna plants.[18] As for Krauch, Schmitz came to consider him "absolutely loyal to Göring," no doubt in part because Krauch proved willing to encourage Wintershall's manufacture of magnesium and not only to reproach Gajewski for resisting the regime's plans for synthetic fibers, but also to force him to license specific production processes to new producers.[19] By mid-1938, IG's Patents Committee was operating on the basis of a clear divergence of interest between Krauch's office and the concern. Predicting leaks to competitors, Carl Holdermann advised his colleagues that "internal IG reports should not be passed on to this office and that there is no reason why certain information on matters which are becoming generally known and which IG procures for itself . . . should be passed on."[20]

[15] In order, the contentions belong to Schweitzer, *ZfN*, 20 (1960), p. 441; Petzina, *Autarkiepolitik*, p. 197; and Martin Broszat, *Der Staat Hitlers* (München, 1969), p. 375.
[16] Bayer 4B/36, vol. 1, Gründung der Buna-Werke der I.G. (1945?).
[17] Bayer D.A. 1100, Raw Materials Office to Verm. W., 13.V.37, and file note by Dr. Sigwart, 23.VIII.37.
[18] See BA Koblenz, R2/15311, correspondence and draft contract, 14.IV.39–1.VI.39, pp. 158–64; R2/15308, *Vermerk*, 30.IX.39.
[19] NI-8187/67, Affidavit by F. terMeer, 15.IV.47, enclosing an affidavit by H. Schmitz, 17.IX.45. On the magnesium plant, see NI-7562/61, Dr. Neukirch's "History," 1943; on fibers, interview with Hans Kehrl, 11.VII.78, and Krauch I/27, Affidavit by W. Schieber, 13.XI.47.
[20] NI-8973/74, 35th meeting of the Patents Committee, 15.VI.38. Nine months later, the Dyes Committee of IG resolved that handing over data to Krauch's office con-

Moreover, Krauch's office was only one of several shapers of economic policy both within and outside the Four Year Plan structure. Neither Krauch nor his immediate superior until 1938, Colonel Löb, ever succeeded in gaining control over the allocation of iron and steel, a fact that repeatedly slowed IG's construction projects.[21] Nor could or would Krauch offer IG special assistance in the matter of labor supply. The Leverkusen plant's appeal to prevent local bureaucrats from assigning recently graduated engineers to weapons manufacturers rather than IG apparently went unanswered, and Syrup's Labor Assignment Office imposed a hiring ban on IG's central German factories during 1937.[22] Meanwhile, the Office of Price Control under Gauleiter Josef Wagner forced down the prices for aluminum by 8%, *Zellwolle* by 9.3%, and fertilizers by some 25%.[23] On relations with the Economics Ministry, IG's involvement with the Four Year Plan had a negative impact. Toward the end of 1936, IG calculated that Leuna would soon be earning sufficient funds to repay the government's price subsidy and exceed the 5% return on investment permitted under the *Benzin-Vertrag*. Hoping to avoid payments of excess proceeds to the state, projected at 9.6 million marks during 1937, the concern first recomputed and raised its reported investments and then sought to buy out the contract of 1933.[24] Though outwardly amenable, since IG claimed with some justice that the contracts extended by the Reich to other producers were more generous than the *Benzin-Vertrag*, Schacht had no intention of assisting Farben.[25] Instead, the refusal of Schmitz and Schnitzler to heed his warnings against participation in the Four Year Plan allegedly prompted the minister to

cerning raw materials and the value of dyes output "should be avoided" (Bayer D.A. 1100, Excerpt of meeting of 2.III.39).

21 Petzina, *Autarkiepolitik*, pp. 155–7; J. Geer, *Der Markt der geschlossenen Nachfrage* (Berlin, 1961), pp. 39–75. On IG's problems with iron allocation during 1937, see Bayer D.A. 1100, as well as note 128 below.

22 Bayer D.A. 1100, Einsler to Krauch, 15.VIII.39; Tim Mason, *Arbeiterklasse und Volksgemeinschaft* (Opladen, 1975), pp.347–8.

23 Sweezy, *Structure*, pp. 98–100; Günter Reimann, *The Vampire Economy* (New York, 1939), p. 204. Since the reduction in fertilizer prices applied to the wholesalers of trademarked goods to whom IG sold nitrogenous compounds, the concern was affected only indirectly (NI-5668/42, Nitrogen Discussion at Leuna, 22.XII.37).

24 NI-9922/82, Memo by J. Cammerer, 19.XI.36; Bütefisch IV/295, Affidavit by J. Cammerer, 27.I.48; III/344, Affidavit by E. Wuerth, 26.I.48; III/344 suppl., Fischer to Krauch and Schneider, 6.II.37.

25 On the differences among the contracts, see Bütefisch IV/10, Affidavit by K. Klinge, 2.II.48, and Birkenfeld, *Treibstoff*, p. 33.

launch stillborn efforts to form a counterweight to IG among the nation's other chemical companies and to prevent the combine from acquiring additional industrial properties.[26] Meanwhile, Schacht maintained that budget regulations barred him from altering official contracts to the Reich's disadvantage. He therefore fixed the permissible profit margin on all synthetic fuel plants at 5 to 7% of invested capital, with IG's return thus remaining at the lower end of this narrow scale.[27] After Schacht's departure from the Economics Ministry, both it and the Finance Ministry continued to keep close watch on the concern's expansion. Emblematic of this effort were not only the frequent audits of IG operations by the Deutsche Revision- und Treuhands-Gesellschaft, but also this response by Colonel Löb, after his transfer to the Economics Ministry, to IG's construction of a new installation:

I have seen from your statements with satisfaction that you do not intend to use the new production facilities of IG Farbenindustrie, which are increased by the new film factory Landsberg/Warthe, in order to decrease the share in markets which medium and smaller producers still have, particularly at home. I welcome this statement all the more because for general economic reasons we are particularly interested in seeing that capable medium and smaller film producers are maintained, and your statement relieves me of the necessity of safeguarding the market of the entire group of film manufacturers by special measures. In order to be able to dispense with such measures in future, too, I would ask you to instruct the management of your sales department with the necessary emphasis about my attitude on the continued existence of the medium and smaller film manufacturers.[28]

To be sure, IG Farben and its wholly owned subsidiaries prospered under the Four Year Plan. Between 1936 and 1939, sales rose to nearly 2 billion reichsmarks (+53%), gross profits to 377 million marks (+50%), net profits to 240 million (+71%), distributed profits to 56 million (+1%), employment to roughly 230,000 (+35%), and annual investments in the plants to 272 million marks (+59%). In each category, IG's performance surpassed its pre-Depression peaks, though exports remained well under the annual totals for 1926–31.[29]

[26] NI-9944–45/82, Affidavits by M. Kuegler, 25.VIII.47.

[27] See Birkenfeld, Treibstoff, p. 33, and United States Strategic Bombing Survey, The German Oil Industry Ministerial Report Team 78, Report 113 (January 1947), p. 20.

[28] NI-13530/110, Löb to Gajewski, 28.IX.38.

[29] NI-10001-03/82, Affidavits by H. Deichfischer, 11.VI.47; D. Warriner, Combines and Rationalization in Germany, 1924–1928 (London, 1931), p. 118; Hermann

About 41% of the increased sales, though certainly a much smaller segment of the rising profits, derived from five product lines encouraged by the Four Year Plan: gasoline, nitrogen for explosives, metals, rubber and plastics, and fibers. Their contribution to IG's aggregate turnover climbed from 28.4% in 1936 to 32.4% three years later.[30] Manufactured primarily, though usually indirectly, for the military market, these products issued largely from plants constructed or expanded under the aegis of the Four Year Plan. But the government made little direct contribution to development, aside from relatively small loans for the buna factories, and before 1939 provided only 21 million marks in tax relief to the concern, since a whopping surcharge on IG's revenue payments for 1935 nearly wiped out the assorted fiscal inducements to new construction. By 1938–9, IG was paying 34% of net proceeds (sales minus operating costs) in taxes, some 8.5% more than in 1929; as a percentage of receipts from all sources, IG's tax bill nearly doubled from 1933 (16.4%) to 1939 (30.3%).[31]

What the Four Year Plan offered the concern during 1936–9 was permission or orders to establish new fixed assets, largely with IG's own income, for which other uses were foreclosed, save the purchase of government bonds. The combine was allowed to recover the investments, generally over five to ten years, through prices charged official buyers and slightly accelerated depreciation, and then to reinvest the returns as the regime allowed.[32] It is important to recognize that this was a closed circle. For IG Farben, even more than for most German corporations, profits were reduced to a mere "bookkeeping entry," a kind of "management fee," by the system of "derived public financing."[33] The concern's attempt to influence the planning process resulted from the nature of this system. IG fought to hold onto its own and to direct funds toward purposes that served its future competitiveness.

Gross, *Further Facts and Figures Relating to the Deconcentration of the I. G. Farbenindustrie Aktiengesellschaft* (Kiel, 1950), Diagram IIb.

30 Calculated from Bayer 15/Da 1.1, Umsätze.
31 See Defense Basic Information II/4, Distribution of Total Proceeds 1926–1944; BA Koblenz, ZSg 127, Bd. 837, "Die I.G-Farben Abschluss," *Völkischer Beobachter*, no. 164 (12.VI.40). On the reassessment for 1935, see Hoechst TEA 775, Kredit-Übersicht 1938, and, as background, BA Koblenz, R2/21047. IG paid 832 million marks in taxes from 1935 to 1938. Had the concern paid the applicable annual nominal rates, the total would have been 853 million.
32 See NI-7237/57, Affidavit by P. Dencker, 7.VI.47; NI-10001 and 10013/82, Affidavits by H. Deichfischer, 11.VI.47 and 15.VII.47.
33 Drucker, *Economic Man*, p. 149.

Though large, the volume of IG's investments under the Four Year Plan hardly testified to bureaucratic clout. The plan altered neither the concern's relative position within the German chemical industry nor the trajectory of that sector's development since the turn of the century. Between 1924 and 1928, the chemical, potash, and oil industries had accounted for 21.4% of German industrial investment; in 1938–9, with the plan in full cry, the average was 24.4%.[34] The modest growth during 1936–9 in the chemical field's share of German industry's invested capital, output, and labor force also continued long-standing trends, now somewhat accentuated in comparison with the 1920s by the sharp buildup of munitions.[35] Even IG's portion of the plan funds earmarked for chemicals producers fell well below either IG's share of national chemicals output in 1936 (roughly 46%) or the firm's pre-Depression record of absorbing about two-thirds of the annual investment in the Reich's chemical industry.[36] Only in the earliest drafts of the plan, only when companies in which IG held a minority of the stock or to which the concern granted licenses are added to its totals, and only when a substantial number of as yet unallocated factories are omitted did the concern's portion of investments under the plan come to the usually cited figures of 67% of all investments, 72% of those in the chemical industry.[37]

[34] On the figures for 1924–8, see "Kapitalbildung und Investitionen in der deutschen Volkswirtschaft 1924 bis 1928," *Vierteljahrshefte für Konjunkturforschung*, Sonderheft 22 (1931), p. 46; for 1938–9, *Statistisches Handbuch von Deutschland 1928–1944* (München, 1948), p. 605.
[35] See André Leisewitz, "Die Auswirkungen der Verwissenschaftlichung der Produktion auf die Monopolbildung und auf das Verhältnis von Oekonomie und Politik dargestellt am Beispiel der chemischen Industrie," *Das Argument*, 14 (1972), p. 506; Petzina, *Autarkiepolitik*, p. 187; *Vierteljahrshefte für Konjunkturforschung*, Sonderheft 22 (1931), p. 46; and the figures on employment in the industry from 1901/10 to 1950/59 in D. Petzina, W. Abelshauser, and A. Faust (eds.), *Sozialgeschichtliches Arbeitsbuch III* (München, 1978), p. 63.
[36] On the share of output, see Bayer 4C9.19, Pinnow manuscript, p. 49, which tallies with my own estimate based on weighting IG's 41% of domestic sales in 1936, according to the ZAV computations, and its 53 to 60% of foreign sales of German chemicals, according to R. Levassort, "Quelques aperçus sur l'I. G. Farbenindustrie A. G.," in Edmond Vermeil (ed.), *Etudes Economiques Allemandes* (Paris, 1951), p. 92, and Pinnow, p. 15. On the pre-Depression share of capital investments, see above, p. 17.
[37] NI-10035-36/82, Affidavits by W. Hagert, 25.VII.47, are the usual sources cited, as by Joseph Borkin, *The Crime and Punishment of I. G. Farben* (New York, 1978), p. 71, and Petzina, *Autarkiepolitik*, p. 97, but corrected by Berenice A. Carroll, *Design for Total War* (The Hague, 1968), p. 136, and M892/4, Paul Koerner's testimony, pp. 2267–71.

As the emphasis of the Four Year Plan gravitated during 1937–8 toward fuel production, IG's relative role declined, and it continued to drop thereafter. Though hydrogenation remained the preponderant fuel production process, hence IG the beneficiary of license fees, the concern controlled only one of the ten new synthetic fuel plants begun between 1936 and 1938, that at Scholven, which was partly owned by the Prussian state's Hibernia mine. Another works, at Pölitz, was founded in cooperation with Standard of New Jersey and Royal Dutch Shell in order to employ their unrepatriable profits on gasoline sales in Germany, and IG acquired 31% of the stock. Leuna did not expand or increase production to the targeted level of 500,000 tons per annum until two years after the war began. Among the remaining eight plants, one belonged to Brabag, and the others, including four users of the Fischer–Tropsch method, were creations of Ruhr firms, which agreed in 1936 to build the factories "in order to prevent state intervention."[38] By 1938, a list of the most urgent ongoing Four Year Plan projects, from which workers had under no circumstances to be diverted, contained only 28 IG installations out of a total of 167.[39] Another compilation of 64 new chemicals factories completed under the plan during the first ten months of 1939 showed that exactly half were associated with IG or its subsidiaries.[40]

That the Four Year Plan began as or became "in practice an IG Farben plan" is one of the legends of the Third Reich.[41] During its six and one-quarter year duration from 1936 to 1942, the Four Year Plan authorized projects, in all industries other than coal and energy supply, costing some 13.25 billion marks, whereas Farben's investments in new plant (including those of majority-owned subsidiaries like

---

[38] On the Ruhr's decision, see NI-4471/33, Discussion at the Deutsche Länderbank, 6–7.X.36. On Leuna's output, see Birkenfeld, *Treibstoff*, p. 226. On the reasons for hydrogenation's predominance and its extent, see Arnold Krammer, "Fueling the Third Reich," *Technology and Culture,* 19 (1978), pp. 402–3, 406, and the sources cited in footnote 94, Chapter 4. On the other fuel producers, see Walter Silbermann, *Chemie-Industrie und Aussenhandel* (Hamburg, 1938), pp. 76–80; and Terry Hunt Tooley, "The German Plan for Synthetic Fuel Self-Sufficiency, 1933–1942" (M.A. Thesis, Texas A&M University, College Station, 1978), pp. 57–63. For a comprehensive summary, see Birkenfeld, *Treibstoff*, pp. 102–11. Birkenfeld also points out, p. 50, that the price guarantee for the Scholven plant, like that for Leuna, produced nearly 30 million marks in excess proceeds for the Reich.

[39] BA Koblenz, R25/86, 15.VIII.38.

[40] BA Koblenz, R25/89, Übersicht vom 15.XI.39, pp. 4–6.

[41] Petzina, *Autarkiepolitik*, p. 123.

DAG of Troisdorf) came to approximately 2.7 billion. These global figures convey rather accurately IG's likely share of expenditures under the plan: It probably amounted to 20 to 25%. Of course, making necessary allowance for IG's holdings in Brabag, Scholven, Pölitz, and other independent fuel producers might raise Farben's total investments to as much as 4.3 billion marks, or 32.7% of the plan total.[42] But not all of IG's capital disbursements could be booked to the plan. For the period from October 1, 1936, to December 31, 1938, the only time span for which reliable statistics have come to light, IG estimated that about four-fifths of its appropriations were so covered; projecting this ratio through 1942 reduces IG's share of total allocations to 26%. The TEA Office's figures of January 1939 indicate, however, that the combine had spent 485 million marks pursuant to the plan during the preceding twenty-seven months. That sum represents only three-fifths of Farben's outlays for new facilities and only 11.5% of the 4.2 billion marks allotted by the plan in this first third of its existence.[43] After the war began, both proportions almost certainly rose, but by how much is impossible to say precisely. Though inconclusive, this arithmetic suggests that the financial treatment of IG by the Four Year Plan was hardly disproportionate to the concern's position in the industries that Nazi policy encouraged. The calculations also lend credence to Hermann Gross's postwar statistics, which assert that the concern's relative place within the German chemical sector held fairly constant during peacetime under the Nazis.[44] Indeed, the numbers support a third iconoclastic conclusion drawn recently by Michael Geyer on the basis of other evidence. Neither rearmament nor the Four Year Plan reflected or effected a new hegemony of the chemical sector within the German economy. The chief beneficiaries of both programs were Germany's metal processors, the secondary favorites the Reich's iron, steel, and mining firms.[45] There occurred in Germany after 1936, not

---

[42] Calculated from ibid., p. 185, and NI-10001/82, Affidavit by H. Deichfischer, 11.VI.47. Deichfischer's figures for 1936–42 differ somewhat for individual years, but insignificantly for the period as a whole, from those in Hoechst TEA 393, Struss to Diekmann, 11.II.43.

[43] Calculated from the sources cited in footnote 42, as well as Hoechst TEA 393, Mittelaufwendungen: Rundfrage der Reichsstelle für Wirtschaftsausbau, 21.I.39, esp. pp. 3–5, Ausgaben auf Neuanlagen für die Z.A.-Sitzung, 25.I.39, and Erläuterungen zum Ausgabenplan der IG-Werke, 11.V.39.

[44] Gross, *Further Facts and Figures*, pp. 27, 29 (Table IVa).

[45] See Geyer, *RVB*, 45 (1981), especially pp. 211, 229–30, 245.

a Farbenization of economic policy making, but a steady militarization of IG Farben.

IG could not conquer the Four Year Plan in part because one of the consequences of this militarization was to fragment rather than focus the concern's interests. Whereas some segments of the enterprise swiftly latched on to the opportunity to amplify their importance, others sought to minimize damage from the new national priorities. Protective moves included portraying factories designed to produce for civilian markets, like the installation for color film at Landsberg, as useful to the air force.[46] IG's mobilization planning also took advantage of the sheer impenetrability of the firm's complex operations in order to maintain the output of less militarily valuable products, such as dyes and pharmaceuticals.[47] Nonetheless, the combine's central offices had increasing difficulty in keeping track of, let alone controlling, IG's development. Not only did the production of new synthetics occasionally force the concern to buy or start factories that could demonstrate to skeptical industrial buyers the proper utilization of new substances, but also individual plants or offices frequently obtained construction authorizations directly from government agencies, without clearing these plans through the firm's hierarchy, and ambitious subordinates induced military officials to impose "orders" (Auflagen) on the combine. Concurrently, the government's demands for secrecy made acquiring a comprehensive grasp of the concern's activities almost impossible.[48] "A survey of what IG really did make or not make for the Wehrmacht," Schnitzler later recalled, "became more and more pure guesswork, and one abstained from asking in order not to put one's technical colleagues in a difficult position."[49]

---

[46] See Gajewski's testimony, NMT, vol. 7, pp. 437–8.

[47] On the drafting of the mobilization plans, see especially NI-4953/36, Affidavit by F. Ehrmann, 18.III.47; NI-8925, Affidavit by H. Wagner, 11.VI.47, NMT, vol. 7, pp. 1493–5; NI-4625/34, Verm. W. to the Betriebsgemeinschaften, 23.III.47; and Bayer D.A. 913, Warnecke to Verm. W., 20.IX.37. Prosecution Document Books 7–8 for the postwar trial, M892/36, contain numerous documents relating to these plans, as well as to the military exercises that became increasingly common at the factories after September 1936.

[48] Thus, first Dr. Buhl of the legal department for chemicals in Frankfurt and then Dr. von Knieriem handled exclusively all construction contracts between IG and the army, and these were not reviewed by the concern's Central Contract Office (Knieriem V/32, Affidavit by F. Silcher, 31.III.48).

[49] See NI-5191/38, Affidavit by G. von Schnitzler, 4.III.47; Bayer D.A. 1100, Kühne and Einsler to Abteilungsvorstände of Leverkusen, Elberfeld, Dormagen, and Uerdingen, 26.X.38; and NI-5196, Affidavit by Schnitzler, NMT, vol. 7, pp. 1506–

As in earlier years, Farben tried to separate its own operations from those desired by the government for purely military purposes. Since the latter were often munitions or chemicals plants, IG's share of these reserve or "shadow" factories became large, embracing by 1939 about 36 out of a total of 62 installations.[50] Where IG's explosives affiliates, DAG of Troisdorf and WASAG, leased these plants from the Reich's Montanindustrie GmbH, their operating subsidiaries received 50 to 67% of any profits as compensation. But this system opened the way for official inspection of the factories' books. Since IG generally attempted to connect the reserve plants to the production processes for other intermediate chemicals, the concern disliked the idea of such inspection, fearing that the regime could obtain evidence for compelling reductions in the prices of these intermediates. Hence, IG contracted for shadow factories only if the compensation was based on appropriate rates of amortization and interest on the funds invested and only if the concern had an option to buy each plant after thirty years, permit its sale to a third party, or order it destroyed at the Reich's expense.[51] Neat and advantageous in appearance, these arrangements proved chaotic in practice. Negotiating agreements with the army became so time-consuming that the combine sometimes found itself haggling over construction contracts for works that had long since commenced manufacturing.[52]

The net effect of the standby plants, the Four Year Plan, and the self-promotion of shrewd subordinates was apparent in the gradual but growing militarization of Farben's investments (see Appendix D). Almost 60% of the combine's capital outlays, some 692.5 million marks by one estimate, went into the production of eighteen strategic materials during the period from 1936 to 1939. Although fuel, rubber,

11. The quoted passage, in which I have adjusted Schnitzler's ungrammatical English at minor spots, appears in the last-named document, pp. 1510–11.
50 NI-9193/76, Affidavit by M. Ziedelhack, 31.VII.47. NI-9619/80, Affidavit by H. Mureck, 14.VIII.47, lists thirty-eight plants as affiliated with IG, whereas Ambros VA/504, a compilation by Obermüller of Montanindustrie GmbH, 28.I.48, includes only seventeen IG standby plants as of 1939.
51 NI-5685/42, File note of conference at Troisdorf, 31.I.39, dated 2.III.39; NI-4491/33, Undated formula for agreements between the Reich, IG, and Montanindustrie GmbH; NI-7429/60, Buhl to IG's legal offices, 19.XII.39 and 20.XII.39. NI-4669/34, File note no. 5 of the Statistical Office, Frankfurt, 27.V.38; and testimony of terMeer and Knieriem, NMT, vol. 7, pp. 1239–43.
52 NI-5685, File note by Boeckler of a conference at Troisdorf, 31.I.39, NMT, vol. 7, pp. 1250–2; NI-4493/33, Contract between IG and OKH concerning plants at Wolfen, 18.XI.40.

Fritz terMeer (1884–1967), head of Sparte II, 1932–45, and chairman of the Technical Committee, 1933–43. (*Source:* Bayer-Archiv, Leverkusen)

and nitrogen – products with significant peacetime applications – accounted for nearly three-fifths of this sum, the concern's evolution was dictated increasingly by military needs.[53] Symptomatic of this process was the firm's gathering involvement with poison gas production, from which IG had shied away previously. Having assumed responsibility at the end of 1936 for drafting a national plan for fabricating mustard gas, IG was by 1937 supervising the construction of factories at Trostberg, Schkopau, and Hüls.[54] To these facilities, the concern added plans in 1939 to construct a plant at Dyhernfurth for a new nerve gas called Tabun, developed by IG's insecticide division. Thus, on the eve of the war, Farben controlled 8% of the existing and 59 to 65% of the intended German capacity for chemical warfare agents, though no production had yet occurred.[55]

While the Reich's policies undermined IG's cohesion, Fritz terMeer continued his uphill battle to develop buna production along lines compatible with the concern's interests. His task grew more complicated after the announcement of the Four Year Plan. Göring promptly directed that the installation nearing completion at Schkopau be geared to turning out 2,000 tons per month, twice the previously stipulated maximum, and the führer followed up by demanding construction of a second plant capable of manufacturing another 1,000 tons monthly.[56] Cutting through the long haggling over financial guarantees to the concern, Göring pledged the government to purchase the output for ten years at a price that would meet IG's construction costs plus an annual interest payment of 5% on the capital invested.[57] But he rejected IG's request for an outright grant of 31 million

---

[53] NI-10926/90, Affidavit by W. Hagert, 15.IX.47. A detailed survey of the plants in which the funds were invested appears in NI-10007/82, Affidavit by E. Struss, 21.VI.47, and further information in another of his affidavits, NI-8319/68, 9.VI.47. On one of the most important of the new factories, that for tetraethyl lead at Frose, see Birkenfeld, *Treibstoff*, pp. 63–6.

[54] NI-13521/110, Ambros to terMeer, 14.XII.36; NI-13524/110, Ambros to Krauch, 21.VII.37, and Ambros to terMeer et al., 21.VII.37; and Rolf-Dieter Müller, "Die deutschen Gaskriegsvorbereitungen 1919–1945: Mit Giftgas zur Weltmacht," *MM*, 27 (1980), p. 36.

[55] NI-6788/52, Affidavit by O. Ambros, 1.V.47; NI-12725/104, Affidavit by E. Ehrmann, 26.XI.47; NI-12678/104, Affidavit by Ehrmann, 25.XI.47; Ambros VIIA/721, Affidavit by Ehrmann, 8.I.48. IG's growing involvement in poison gas production is indicated by the documents from February 1939 printed in *NMT*, vol. 7, pp. 935–43.

[56] On the escalation of the production targets, see NI-7625/62, Göring to the TEA Büro, 16.VI.36; and NI-7241/57, Affidavit by E. Struss, 12.VI.47.

[57] BA Koblenz, R2/15306, File note of 12.XI.36.

reichsmarks toward the estimated construction costs of 180 million
for Schkopau and refused even to loan the concern half of the necessary funds. Instead, the Reich offered certain tax exemptions and
permission for IG to raise 90 million marks on the open capital market, then backed away from a promise to buy any bonds left unsold.[58]
While the combine complained that it could not possibly finance the
entire project from its own resources, the Finance Ministry had its
auditing office in Frankfurt examine the concern's books. It concluded
that IG had sufficient reserves to build Schkopau without recourse to a
bond or stock issue.[59] Caught out in this manner, terMeer had to find
a means of extracting money from the Reich without seeming to. His
solution was ingenious enough to win even Schacht's support. Proposed in December 1936, the scheme amounted to collecting a revolving loan fund for buna from a sliding tariff on imported natural rubber
destined for German domestic consumption. From the pool, IG could
borrow the necessary capital for ten years at 5% per annum.[60] With
the availability of money thus ensured, IG's wholly owned subsidiaries, the Ammoniakwerke Merseburg and Leopold Cassella & Co.,
put up 30 million marks to capitalize a new rubber-producing firm,
the Buna GmbH, in February 1937.[61]

Finding funds for the buna plants proved much easier, however,
than agreeing on the financial terms of their operation. During the two
months preceding the birth of Buna GmbH, IG demanded from the
government a package of fees, bonuses, and tax breaks that would
have yielded, the Economics Ministry estimated, an exorbitant annual
rate of return for the combine of somewhere between 14 and 31% on
its investments. This prompted the bureaucrats to hint that they might
insist on a share of the property and profits of Buna GmbH for the
Reich after the ten-year price and purchase guarantee elapsed. The
idea was a ruse, designed to reconcile IG to the ministry's own scale of
rewards, which would hold the concern's rate of return to between 4

---

[58] NI-1941/18, Z.A. meeting of 19.X.36; BA Koblenz, R2/15306, *Vermerk* of
1.XII.36.
[59] BA Koblenz, R2/15306, Memo of 1.XII.36.
[60] TerMeer IV/203, terMeer to Office for German Raw and Synthetic Materials,
17.XII.36; M892/8, terMeer's testimony, p. 7008; BA Koblenz, R2/15311, *Vermerk* of 23.I.37, memoranda of 22.II.37., 4.III.37, and 10.IV.37, Reinhardt to Finance Ministry, 14.IV.37, and accompanying letters by Löb, 29.IV.37, and Wagner,
27.IV.37. R2/21469, Kugler to Finance Ministry, 28.VII.37, explains how exporters
of goods containing natural rubber were relieved of the price increase.
[61] BA Koblenz, R2/15307 contains a copy of the notarized founding contract, 15.II.37.

and 14% annually, in part by committing the firm to minimum yearly expenditures for further research and development.[62] But the counter-demands and the prospect of indefinitely splitting profits with the state merely stung terMeer into denouncing the pettiness of the official agencies. In indignant terms, he threatened to seek all the necessary funds from private investors, a move that would either hurt the sale of government bonds for rearmament or result in the collapse of the buna expansion plans. Claiming that the regime was forcing the concern to tie up at least 50 million marks in a plant whose depreciation proceeds would go almost entirely toward repaying loans from the Reich, ter-Meer expressed incomprehension at the government's refusal to recognize the risks IG was running in manufacturing on a large scale an as yet unproved and uncompetitive product.[63]

For the next six months, as Schkopau turned out IG's first salable buna, the wrangle over pricing dragged on and "considerably endangered" the continuance of negotiations.[64] In the end, Schkopau got a tax exemption for five years (compared with the ten IG had sought); the concern received a lump sum payment for constructing the plant of 7.25 million marks (compared with the 8.1 million IG proposed); Farben accepted 4.4 million marks annually as compensation for accrued costs for research and overhead (compared with 10 million); IG got the desired annual sales fee equal to 2% of buna's proceeds; the combine was permitted to pocket 10% of any future savings on production costs as an incentive (not 20%); and only 3 million marks annually in research and development costs could be charged as production expenses in fixing the price for buna, even though IG's actual outlays for these purposes came to 5.6 million marks in 1937 and 7.7 million in 1938. In return for scaling down its wishes on all these points and expanding the Schkopau factory, IG received a loan of 90 million marks from the new pool of funds, the repayment of which over ten years, as well as the 5% annual return on investment, was ensured by the government's price and purchase guar-

[62] BA Koblenz, R2/15306, *Vermerke* of 8.XII.36, 8.I.37, 22.I.37, and 28.I.37.
[63] NI-7624/62, Basic Viewpoints on the Establishment of the Schkopau Plant and the Buna Contract, 17.II.37. The original is in the BA Koblenz, R2/15306, pp. 344–50. On the government's reasons for fearing that IG would go it alone, see R2/15307, *Vermerk* of 10.IV.37.
[64] BA Koblenz R2/15306, *Vermerk* of 7.III.37. Buna became a salable product on 1.I.37 and earned IG 12.8 million marks during that year; NI-5908/44, Meeting of the technical directors at Hoechst, 16.XII.36, and Bayer 15/Da 1.1, Umsätze.

antee. In addition, IG had to promise to license free of charge any patents, processes, and know-how developed at Schkopau during the life of the contract to such other rubber plants as the Four Year Plan required.[65] Once more, IG had narrowed its risks and the Reich had reduced the drain on foreign exchange without major costs to either party. In fact, from 1937 to 1942 terMeer's financing system took in some 345 million reichsmarks, more than twice the amount loaned for the construction of rubber factories, and reductions in production costs enabled IG to dispense with the official price and purchase guarantee for Schkopau as of January 1, 1940.[66]

Despite the outward harmony finally achieved, buna production developed slowly – too slowly to be explained solely by delays in obtaining necessary building materials.[67] Schkopau produced only 6,500 tons in 1938, about one-quarter of the projected figure and 5% of national rubber consumption. The plant did not reach full operating capacity until April 1, 1939, by which time shortfalls at the second, or Hüls, buna factory in the Ruhr kept total national output for the year at just over two-thirds of the targeted 30,000 tons.[68] When the war began, production and stockpiles of rubber were sufficient for only two months of fighting.[69] In all probability, the laggard pace reflected IG's unchanged resolve to march to the beat of technological and commercial possibilities, not Hitler's more martial rhythms.[70] Thus, though the combine acceded to Krauch's demands for a second plant well before either Army Ordnance or Kühne and terMeer thought expansion justifiable, construction did not begin until mid-1938, when IG could parlay the regime's impatience into acceptance of a site only twenty-five miles

65 On the tax exemption and IG's wily but futile efforts to widen it, see BA Koblenz, R2/15308, *Vermerk* of 18.III.38. On IG's research and development costs, terMeer IV/186, Affidavit by E. Struss, 30.XI.47, and NI-6343/47, terMeer and Buhl to Göring, 15.VI.37. On the overall terms of the contract, R2/15307, File note of 10.V.37. On the promise concerning licenses, NI-4711/34, terMeer and Buhl to Göring, 15.VI.37.
66 BA Koblenz, R2/15311, Handwritten and unsigned table of 4.IV.42; M892/8, ter-Meer's testimony, p. 7009. On average, the price for IG's three types of buna dropped by 43% between 1936 and 1940 (NI-8833/72).
67 Cf. W. Treue, "Gummi in Deutschland zwischen 1933 und 1945," *Wehrwissen-schaftliche Rundschau*, 5 (1955), p. 174; and Gottfried Plumpe, "Industrie, technischer Fortschritt und Staat: Die Kautschuksynthese in Deutschland 1906–1944/45," *G&G*, 9 (1983), p. 585.
68 Treue, *Wehrwissenschaftliche Rundschau*, 5 (1955), p. 176; BA Koblenz, R2/15308, Winner to IG Vorstand, 11.X.38; Schweitzer, *JNS*, 168 (1957), p. 379.
69 NI-6194/46, Lt. Col. Hedler's report of March 1941.
70 See Schweitzer, *JNS*, 168 (1957), p. 392.

from the Dutch border.[71] What recommended the location to IG was the opportunity to use waste gases from the hydrogenation of hard coal to produce the basic components of buna far more inexpensively than at Schkopau. Since the output of the two factories would sell at the same price but no government guarantees would circumscribe IG's profit margin at the second plant, the concern could expect to reap handsome rewards over time.[72]

Profit calculations, not military ones, remained uppermost in ter-Meer's mind, as he made clear in a letter to State Secretary Brinkmann in November 1938. After announcing his impending departure for the United States "in order to take the first steps for a utilization of our processes there," terMeer recalled telling Brinkmann on a previous occasion that

taking a long view, the production of synthetic rubber in Germany, under the protection of a tax acceptable to the economy, promises to become a sound permanent manufacture. . . . I therefore requested you not to allow the building of the buna factories to be completely or preponderantly influenced by military interests, now that the immediate danger of war has been removed.

Accordingly, terMeer now suggested that the proposed third buna plant designated for Fürstenberg on the Oder be transferred to Upper Silesia or the Sudetenland, areas whose supplies of coal, basic chemicals, and skilled labor outweighed their disadvantages as border districts vulnerable to potential enemies.[73] Equally indicative of IG's commercial priorities was the ownership of the second and third buna plants. The Prussian state's Hibernia mine held 26% of the shares in the Ruhr producer, the Chemische Werke Hüls, whereas a consortium of German rubber processors was to hold half the stock in the other plant.[74] The former arrangement would reduce manufacturing costs

[71] See NI-4626/34, Kühne to terMeer, 15.I.37, and terMeer V/227, the reply of 18.I.37. Krauch appears to have been acting on the possibility of replacing imported leather for shoes with 12,000 to 15,000 tons of buna per year. See M892/6, his testimony, pp. 5084–5; terMeer IV/180, Affidavit by R. Freudenberg, IV/181, Wulff to terMeer, 22.II.38; and Hoechst TEA 396, Kautschuk-Besprechung, 14.I.38.
[72] NI-7769/63, Report on Hüls, signed by Buhl, 22.III.38. For a history of the plant, see Franz I. Wünsch, "Das Werk Hüls," *Tradition,* 9 (1964), pp. 70–9.
[73] NI-4717, terMeer to Brinkmann, 11.XI.38. Eckell rejected IG's proposal, M892/8, terMeer's testimony, p. 7023. On Farben's dogged resistance to the Fürstenberg site, hence the failure to construct a third buna plant before the war, see Morris, *Synthetic Rubber,* pp. 304–13.
[74] On Hüls, see NI-6108/45, the founding contract of 13.V.38; and NI-6145/46, the financing contract of 8.VIII.38. On the third factory, NI-7241/57, Affidavit by E. Struss, 12.VI.47, and SAA 11/Lo806, Aktenvermerk. Betr.: Beteiligung an der 3.

by holding down charges for coal; the latter, echoing Kehrl's maneuver in the fibers field, came down to a profit-sharing incentive to the largest group of potential buyers. Both arrangements speeded the process by which IG might escape from dependence on government funding and compete unaided with natural rubber. Meanwhile, IG put off applying the long-heralded two-stage manufacturing process for buna or starting work on a third rubber factory, ostensibly because of a shortage of labor, though probably because the concern's interests were better served by increasing output, hence the economies of scale, at Schkopau and Hüls.[75]

The development of buna production from 1936 to 1939 illustrates a general proposition about IG Farben's power in the Third Reich. The concern's influence was greatest when implicit, when plans or actions had to be shaped around Farben's special skills and capacities.[76] When IG tried to assert its interests on a nontechnical matter explicitly, the enterprise almost invariably lost. Developments concerning the related issues of foreign trade policy and Aryanization redemonstrate the point.

The Reich's worsening trade situation began to impinge on Farben as early as May 1936, when the firm discovered that its "privileged position" regarding foreign exchange "can no longer be maintained."[77] In subsequent months, IG consequently searched for an escape from what Paul Haefliger now called "the sealed chamber in which we find ourselves."[78] As always, Ilgner advocated seeking advantages via ingratiation, writing to the *Vorstand:*

Because the IG is far and away the largest German exporter and hence inevitably to the greatest extent makes use of all official and semiofficial arrange-

Buna-Fabrik in Fürstenberg, 26.III.38, which shows that the rubber producers were unhappy with their proposed participation and agreed to take a one-third interest only on the condition that they not be involved in any subsequent expansion. By September 1938, a draft contract in the same file had raised their shareholding to one-half. On both Hüls and the third plant, see Schweitzer, *JNS,* 168 (1957), p. 379.

75 See BA Koblenz, R25/14, Krauch to the Generalrat, 20–21.IV.39 (also submitted at the postwar trials as EC-289); Morris, *Synthetic Rubber,* pp. 316–17. Morris attributes the subsequent neglect of the two-stage process to the danger of explosion during its operation and to Otto Ambros's preference for the Reppe, or three-stage, process; see *Synthetic Rubber,* pp. 184, 209–14.

76 Cf. Morris, *Synthetic Rubber,* pp. 386–7, and Plumpe, *G&G,* 9 (1983), pp. 586, 597, who reaches a similar conclusion beneath somewhat more sweeping formulations.

77 NI-5882/44, Kurtz to the Hoechst Vorstand, 25V.36. On that position, see above, pp. 132–3.

78 Bayer D.A. 377, his memo of 4.XII.36.

ments for export promotion, it is self-evidently necessary that we support all these agencies by all means. The more this occurs, the more we can count on understanding and support from the official offices.[79]

In the meantime, he proposed to encourage German sales in Latin America by "creating a more understanding relationship of Germany to the U.S.A." and by stepping up propaganda activities and personal exchange programs that would brighten the Reich's image.[80] But with IG's exports stagnant and the regime tightening the pressure to increase them, other leaders of the firm seem to have looked for shortcuts. Thus, Hermann Schmitz took the unusual step of issuing a directive in January 1937 reminding the *Vorstand* members of their responsibility to know and apply faithfully the regime's foreign trade and exchange regulations.[81] The wages of cooperation were not high, however. Two months later, the Economics Ministry raised the chemical industry's assessment for export promotion and tacked on a surcharge equal to 1% of domestic sales of *Zellwolle*.[82]

During the second half of 1937, the squeeze created by the regime's insistence on simultaneously expanding domestic production and exports finally forced IG into a series of unavailing pleas for relief. In August the concern informed Löb's office that IG could not continue bringing in 10.5% of the Reich's export proceeds unless the firm received 315,000 tons of iron for repairs and shipping, over and above the 160,000 tons already allocated.[83] No such extra allowance shows up in the surviving records. Two days later, the reborn Commercial Committee authorized appeals to the price commissioner to hold domestic prices constant "in all cases where there is a danger of a reduction of prices for the home market leading to a similar reduction of price levels abroad and therefore to a reduction of incoming foreign exchange." A negative reply came within the week and forced IG to all

---

[79] Ilgner's report on a trip to Latin America in August to December 1936, quoted in Hans Radandt, "Die IG-Farbenindustrie in Südosteuropa bis 1938," *JfW*, 7 (1966), pp. 157–8.

[80] NI-070/2, Schwarte to Benzler of the German Foreign Ministry, 27.I.37. For examples of the increased propaganda, much of it portraying Germany as a bulwark against bolshevism, see NI-6488/49, Hauser and Müller to Kaelble, 1.IX.37, and Muttmann to Bayer, 1.IX.37; also Hallgarten and Radkau, *Deutsche Industrie*, pp. 336–7.

[81] Bayer D.A. 377, Schmitz to *Vorständler*, 22.I.37.

[82] NI-357/5, Clemm to Reichswirtschaftskammer, 12.III.37.

[83] NI-7241/60, Jaehne and Ilgner to Hanneken, 18.VIII.37.

Georg von Schnitzler (1884–1962), chairman of the Commercial Committee, 1925–45. (*Source:* Firmenarchiv der Hoechst AG, Frankfurt-Hoechst)

but abandon exports of nitrogen under the terms of the international cartel agreement.[84]

Most importantly, Schnitzler and Ilgner decided to make their case for "participation in the industrialization of the presently undeveloped countries" directly to Hermann Göring. Their letter of August 19, occasioned by Göring's request that the concern devise additional means of increasing its exports, implicitly seconded Schacht's oft-repeated call to sacrifice arms to foreign trade. If Göring made available certain materials and machinery presently reserved for domestic use, IG's leaders advised, the Reich would earn immediate income, as well as long-term proceeds on licenses to and participations in the new companies that German business would be enabled to establish.[85] Taken up with the final stages of his long duel with Schacht, Göring did not respond until January 1938, and in the interim IG tried to strengthen its argument by documenting the extent of the corporation's previous sacrifices under the ZAV system.[86]

Göring's answer to Schnitzler and Ilgner came in the form of the Economics Ministry's General Decree Number 13/38, "Foundings Overseas and the Purchase of Foreign Participations," and it was a baited trap. Making no reference to the problem of supplying building materials and equipment, the edict offered to make foreign exchange available to fund stock purchases or construction overseas only if all resulting profits were assured of repatriation, German exports would be increased over the long run, and the sponsoring German firm was purged of Jews at home and abroad.[87] Not only were the economic conditions difficult to fulfill; the racial ones, coinciding with the ban on government contracts to "non-Aryan" firms, also placed the combine in a dilemma.

Aryanization was for IG by 1938 a matter of foreign, not domestic, concern. Most of the combine's German-Jewish employees appear to have been removed from harm's way during the preceding years, and

[84] NI-4927/36, KA meeting of 20.VIII.37; NI-4959/37, KA meeting of 10.IX.37. On the complex nitrogen problem, Oster II/55, Affidavit by E. Becker, 9.I.48, and II/56, Affidavit by E. Benn, 20.XI.47.

[85] NI-7241/60, Schnitzler and Ilgner to Göring, 19.VIII.37; NI-4927/36, KA meeting of 20.VIII.37 (also Ilgner VI/99); and NI-1570/15, Ilgner's earlier memo on export promotion, submitted to Dr. Lammers on 15.IV.37.

[86] See NI-4453/33, Memo on "the recent furtherance of exports on the part of IG Farbenindustrie," October 1937. Ilgner VI/100, Affidavit by W. Dihlmann, 8.II.48, indicates that the concern exaggerated its losses in order to convince the government that the ZAV system had reached the limit of its usefulness.

[87] Bayer D.A. 377, text of the decree, 22.I.38.

the remaining Jews on the *Aufsichtsrat* quietly resigned when Göring issued his January edicts.[88] Thus, in July, Berlin NW7 was sure that the Reich would recognize Farben as an Aryan enterprise within Germany.[89] Conversely, the concern showed little interest in capitalizing on the dispossession of Jewish proprietors. The available evidence concerning IG's corporate acquisitions between 1936 and 1939 provides no more than three possible cases of purchases from Jews in Germany, as well as one somewhat ambiguous instance in Austria after the Anschluss.[90] But overseas IG had seen nothing to gain before General Decree Number 13/38 and much to lose by dismissing Jewish employees or breaking commercial contacts with resident Jewish communities and businesses. Hence, the combine had fobbed off the Party's Auslandsorganisation (AO) with professions of compliance with its demands but continued to engage Jewish representatives and to advertise in newspapers owned by Jews.[91]

---

[88] On the Elberfeld plant, where IG's practices were fairly typical, see NI-6787/52, Affidavit by H. Hoerlein, 2.V.47. At Wolfen, which appears to have been an exceptional case, Gajewski had kept on about half a dozen Jewish engineers, but most of the victims managed to escape the country during 1938 (Gajewski I/1, Hingst to the Gestapo, 21.IX.39). Gajewski also briefly blocked the emigration of Dr. Gerhard Ollendorf, the former head of IG's film factory at Wolfen, in November 1938, because he "has knowledge of secret matters," but relented a few months later and lent the firm's support to Ollendorf's successful application to leave the country; see the documents of 25.XI.38–29.VI.39 collected as NI-13522/110. Not everyone got away, however. Gustav Pistor names three officials at the Piesteritz plant who died at Buchenwald; see *100 Jahre Griesheim 1856–1956* (Tegernsee, 1958), p. 181; Bütefisch IX/158, Affidavit by A. Baumann, 8.XI.47, reports the death of the affiant's husband, a chemist at Leuna, at Buchenwald in 1940. Of the twenty-four members of the *Aufsichtsrat* in late 1937, at least five and possibly seven were Jews (NI-7957/66, Affidavit by H. Bässler, 17.VII.47). All had retired by the *Vorstand* meeting of 28.V.38; see the minutes in Bayer 12/19.

[89] NI-5752/43, Postbesprechung 110, 14.VII.38.

[90] See the list provided in G. Keiser, "Die Konzernbewegung 1936–1939," *Die Wirtschaftskurve*, 19 (1939), pp. 222–3, which refers to the acquisitions of the Braunkohlenwerke Bruckdorf AG in Halle in 1938 and the indirect takeovers of the Weinessigfabrik L. Hirsch in 1936 and the I. F. C. Mertens K. G. in September 1938. IG did, however, also compete unsuccessfully with the HGW for the Gesellschaft für Elektrometallurgie Dr. Paul Grünfeld (Bayer 12/19, Notiz zu Punkt 5 für die Vorstandssitzung am 30.VII.38). On the Austrian case, see Chapter 6. Though Farben has a reputation as an extensive Aryanizer, I have been able to document only one such takeover before 1936, the acquisition in partnership with Degussa of the Chem. Pharm. Fabrik Homburg from one Dr. Abelmann during 1933; see Degussa, Biographische Unterlagen, Zur Geschichte der Scheideanstalt 1933 bis 1936 by Dr. Fritz Roessler, Abschrift, p. 123, and the fuller, well-documented description in "Degussa in der Zeit des politischen Umbruchs," part of the series *Von Frankfurt in die Welt* published by the Degussa-Archiv (Frankfurt, 1986).

[91] For examples of such evasion, see Ilgner's testimony, *NMT*, vol. 7, pp. 724–34; and NI-4611/34, Professor Marino's report, 20.I.38.

From January 1937 on, however, the AO's authority had swelled both at home and abroad. Ernst Bohle, its leader, became an official of the Foreign Office, and the organization built a staff of 244 *Wirtschaftsstellenleiter* to keep watch on commercial relations between German business and Jews.[92] The effect of this trend was apparent in IG's responses to the AO's criticism of the firm's hiring practices. Whereas in February 1937 Berlin NW7 politely rejected the agency's complaints against the Jewish head of IG's Soja-Gesellschaft in Romania, stressing his personal merits and expertise, by September the Commercial Committee felt obliged to order the various sales combines to prepare "lists of the non-Aryan employees working abroad, together with a proposal for the gradual reduction of their numbers."[93] At the same time, the corporation sought to blunt the Party's offensive by instructing IG's field representatives that

Gentlemen who are sent abroad should be made to realize that it is their special duty to represent National Socialist Germany. They are particularly recommended as soon as they arrive to contact the local or regional [Party] group and are expected to attend their meetings regularly as well as those of the Labor Front. The sales combines are requested to see that their agents are adequately supplied with National Socialist literature. Collaboration with the AO must become more organized.[94]

In the aftermath of decree 13/38, a new tone of urgency characterized directives from IG's home offices. Now the Bayer sales organization informed its branches that their employees should not simply "develop a positive mental attitude towards the present regime" and join in Nazi activities and fund drives, but also avoid further "advertising in journals hostile to Germany," since commercial considerations had henceforth to take second place to "the more important political point of view."[95] Moreover, "the few remaining foreign Jews have to be

---

[92] Donald M. McKale, *The Swastika outside Germany* (Kent, Ohio, 1977), pp. 108–9, 118, 126. See also Karl Dietrich Bracher, *The German Dictatorship* (New York, 1970), p. 323.

[93] Kugler I/9, AO to IG, Frankfurt, 15.XII.36; I/10 (also Ilgner IV/151), AO to Dyes Directorate, Frankfurt, 27.I.37; Ilgner IV/152, Zefi to AO, 19.II.37; NI-4862/36, KA meeting of 7.X.37. For a similar criticism of IG's staffing in Egypt, see Mann II/305, AO to IG, Leverkusen, 30.IV.37.

[94] NI-4959/37, KA meeting of 10.IX.37.

[95] NI-6489, Mann and Mentzell to Homann, 25.II.38; NI-2789/20, Bayer *Vorstand* meeting, 16.II.38. To train its personnel in that political point of view, IG began enrolling potential overseas sales representatives in "foreign policy educational courses" conducted by the Party in Berlin; see NI-1077, Mail discussion no. 131, Berlin NW7, 4.I.39.

systematically eliminated from our agencies. The department heads are responsible for the speedy execution of this order."[96] Thus, in the course of 1938, the Bayer sales combine pensioned off fifty non-Aryans in its foreign branches, and the dyes and chemical sales organizations did the same in twenty cases.[97] By January 1939, a survey of Jewish employees in IG's overseas offices identified only thirty-eight individuals, nineteen of whom the firm planned to dismiss or retire within that calendar year. Because ten of the others were directors or stockholders of subsidiaries, the combine believed that "forced dismissal cannot be taken into consideration."[98] While IG continued to contend that Aryanization was costing both the corporation and the Reich valuable business, the concern's purge of foreign agencies proceeded toward completion during 1940.[99]

Insofar as IG's Aryanization drive was an attempt to aid Ilgner's plans for "intervention in the industrialization of the world," the effort failed. Although Farben managed to divert some of its foreign deposits into twelve new or expanded productive facilities in Latin America, Finland, Italy, and England between 1936 and 1939, such developments rose or fell with the momentary winds of German foreign policy.[100] The Reich did not shift its economic priorities in anything like the direction of Ilgner's global scheme, and IG's repeated protestations that "efforts to achieve autarky are the main impediments to the expansion of our exports" remained ineffectual.[101]

The problems of Aryanization and trade policy did, moreover,

[96] NI-8428, Meeting of the pharmaceuticals sales combine, 16.II.38, NMT, vol. 7, pp. 666–7.
[97] See Case XI, Bohle I/2, Affidavit by P. Bahnemann, 11.II.48, with enclosed lists, and I/3, Affidavit by K. Krüger, 29.IV.48, with two enclosed lists.
[98] NI-4241/31, NW7 to Direktions-Abteilung Farben, Frankfurt, 6.I.39.
[99] For examples of IG's arguments, see Bayer 13/25, Gattineau's remarks at a meeting on 20.XII.38, and NI-8128/67, Wipo to Terhaar, 19.VII.39. On the gradual removal of Jews in Southeast Europe during 1939–40, see Bayer 13/25, Gattineau to Kühne, 30.III.40, reply of 15.IV.40, and Kühne to Gattineau, 30.IX.40; Kugler I/11, Affidavit by Karl Schulze-Schlutius, 28.II.48; I/16, Landwehr to Zefi, 7.IX.40; I/19, Affidavit by H. von Rospatt, 1.IV. 48; and Schmitz IV/51, Affidavit by K. Krüger, 31.XII.47.
[100] On IG's foreign undertakings, see NI-5194/43, Affidavit by G. von Schnitzler, 10.III.47; W. J. Reader, Imperial Chemical Industries, vol. 2: The First Quarter Century 1926–1952 (London, 1975), pp. 222, 414; and Arnold Ebel, Die diplomatischen Beziehungen des Dritten Reiches zu Argentinien unter besonderer Berücksichtigung der Handelspolitik (1933–1939) (Landau, 1970), p. 180.
[101] Bayer D.A. 377, Lecture by Karl von Heider to assorted executives and ministerial representatives, 9.XI.38.

provoke new worries about IG's political relations. After the NSDAP lifted its membership freeze in May 1937 and began seeking recruits from the business world, most of IG's chief executives felt advised or pressured to join the Party.[102] No fewer than fifteen of the *Vorstand* members signed on between mid-1937 and mid-1938, including all but two of the nine men promoted to the group during these years. By 1940, retirements and enlistments had left only four men on the board but outside the Party: August von Knieriem, who finally joined in 1942; Paul Haefliger, who remained exempted as a Swiss citizen; Eduard Weber-Andreä, who died in 1943; and Hermann Schmitz.[103] As far as IG's commercial and public relations officers were concerned, the wave of enlistments came none too soon. On February 10, 1938, at an unusually frank meeting of the Commercial Committee, the members told Schmitz that "Farben in its highest echelon still does not have the desired contact with the highest leadership of the Reich."[104] However, the spate of conversions and IG's contributions to the Four Year Plan did produce more favorable handling of the firm in the *Völkischer Beobachter*. In July 1938, Fritz Nonnenbruch, the economics editor, praised IG for "having exerted its own initiative in the national struggle for independence in raw materials." Diluted by only a tepid, National Socialist reproach that too few of the concern's leaders had risen from the shop floors, Nonnenbruch's article was passed on to Schnitzler by IG's press chief with the observation that "this is the first time that the legitimacy of large firms like the IG has been positively handled in this political environment."[105]

---

[102] See the testimonies of terMeer and Kühne, *NMT,* vol. 7, pp. 616–17, 636–7; and NI-8004/66, Affidavit by C. Lautenschläger, 23.IV.47.
[103] NI-12042/98, Prosecution Party membership chart, as corrected by assorted *Personalakten* from the Berlin Document Center. The *Aufsichtsrat* presented a different picture. Of the twenty-four people who served on it from mid-1938 to 1945, only four (all of whom had been on the IG *Vorstand* previously) definitely joined the Party. Fifteen members never did, and my research has not proved conclusive with regard to the remaining five.
[104] For the quotation and the characterization of the discussion, see NI-13540/110, Excerpt from Weber-Andreä's diary, 10.II.38.
[105] NI-1184/12, Excerpt from the *Völkischer Beobachter,* no. 212 (31.VII.38), and Passarge to Schnitzler, 8.VIII.38. For other signs of increasingly favorable treatment of Farben in the press, see BA Koblenz, ZSg 127, Bd. 832, "Was gibt's im chemischen Werk zu sehen?" *Der Arbeiter,* no. 176 (25.VII.38), and "Soziale Leistungen eines deutschen Grossbetriebes," *Deutsche Arbeits-Korrespondenz* (8.VI.39). Significantly, IG's plants began to win a growing number of Party commendations from mid-1938; see the list reproduced in the photographic insert to Dokumentationsstelle zur NS-Sozialpolitik Hamburg (ed.), *O.M.G.U.S. Ermittlungen gegen die I. G. Farbenindustrie AG* (Nördlingen, 1986).

But not Party memberships or increased donations to Nazi organizations and leaders or the transfer of IG's now nearly complete ownership of the *Frankfurter Zeitung* to the NSDAP's *Eher Verlag* sufficed to appease the middle- and lower-level Nazis who constituted the real political threat to IG's leaders.[106] The Party's more sophisticated captains in Berlin were not willing to change national economic and racial policy to suit IG, but they were prepared to leave its chief executives and their internal decision making largely alone, so long as both conformed broadly to the Reich's objectives.[107] Less worldly junior Nazis lacked this sense of proportion. Thus, though Bosch's distaste for the regime had become common knowledge in governing circles, the Reich acted against him only in May 1939, when he provoked an outcry from Bavarian Nazis by openly doubting the wisdom of national economic policy and the führer's infallibility during an address at the Deutsches Museum in Munich. Even then his punishment consisted merely of removal as chairman of the museum's board and a prohibition of further speechmaking.[108] Similarly mild were the consequences of a feud between IG and the Party leadership in Frankfurt. It dated from early 1938, when Gauleiter Sprenger tried to exploit the Aryanization of the Metallgesellschaft in order to advance two of his allies in the local business community, Carl Luer and Wilhelm Avieny. Not only did IG refuse to accept either man as Richard Merton's replacement on Farben's supervisory board, but Carl

---

106 NI-7366/18, Affidavit by H. Bässler, 28.VI.47. IG's contributions to the Winterhilfe rose from 1 million marks in 1936 to 1.7 million in 1938 after Hilgenfeldt, the chief of the Nazi Public Welfare Organization, complained that the concern was not pulling its weight (Schmitz V/78, Hoyer to Schmitz, 23.X.36). Schneider's testimony, *NMT*, vol. 7, pp. 624–5, provides an example, probably dating from 1939, of the increasingly common practice of making contributions to local Party potentates. On the sale of the *FZ*, see Modris Eksteins, *The Limits of Reason* (New York, 1975), pp. 303–4, and Werner Wirthle, *Frankfurter Zeitung und Frankfurter Societäts-Druckerei GmbH. Die wirtschaftlichen Verhältnisse 1927–1939* (Frankfurt, 1977), pp. 38–46.
107 Hence terMeer's remark to an American executive sometime in 1938–9: "Well, never mind the purely political aspects of the matter. I am a businessman, and I must say that so far I have not been under such specific pressure in specific cases that I feel it has become impossible for me to continue my work" (*NMT*, vol. 7, p. 1526).
108 See BASF W1, Niederschrift über die 28. Sitzung des Ausschusses des Deutschen Museum am 7. Mai 1939, which agrees in all essentials with the copy of Bosch's remarks in Deutsches Museum, Jahresversammlung 1939; see Schmitz I/10, Affidavit by J. Zenneck, 29.XII.47; I/11, Bruckmann and Zenneck to Ministerpräsident Siebert, 8.V.39; Gattineau II/12, Affidavit by E. Telschow, 14.X.47. See also Deutsches Museum, Zenneck to Bosch, 5.XII.39, and Ester to Zenneck, 11.XII.39, on the decision to publish only a sanitized version of Bosch's remarks.

Bosch managed to insert his son-in-law Rudolf Kissel on the Metallgesellschaft's *Vorstand* and thus to delay Avieny's takeover of that
firm for another two years. These maneuvers provoked bitter diatribes
from the *Gauleiter*, who excoriated Schnitzler as a "liberalist, capitalist profiteer, [and] hair-splitter," demanded his resignation, along
with Schmitz's and terMeer's, and vowed to purge the *Vorstand* after
the war. Sprenger's rage, of course, reflected his impotence, a product
of IG's threat to counter interference in its decisions by transferring
the concern's headquarters to Berlin. But he could and did continue to
harass the combine.[109]

More indicative of how individual Nazis could remind IG's executives of their vulnerability was the experience of Fritz Gajewski in
September 1939. Feisty and plain-spoken, Gajewski had never made a
secret of his conviction that the Reich's synthetic fibers development
program was burdening IG and the nation with "plants which probably one day – namely, on the reversion from self-sufficiency to a free
economy – would sink to approximately the value possessed by gun-
powder factories at the end of the World War."[110] However, when
the führer endorsed a particularly uneconomical plan to manufacture
cellulose and then paper and textiles from the skins of potato plants,
Gajewski's outrage led him into a major indiscretion. To a group of
Party officials visiting the Wolfen plant, he allegedly averred that
Hitler and Göring "were not sufficiently expert to be able to judge
something like this, and that it is shocking that a man like Staatsrat
Dr. Schieber . . . would fool them in this matter."[111] Karasek, the
Nazi *Kreisleiter* in Bitterfeld, evidently had been waiting for just such a
slip. He swiftly reported Gajewski's words to Schieber, one of Hans
Kehrl's associates, while one G. Hingst, another local Party man em-
bittered at Gajewski, denounced him to the Gestapo. Schieber com-

---

[109] See SAA 4/Lf675, Bosch to Siemens, 2.VII.38, Protocols of the 39th and 40th
Aufsichtsrat meetings of the Metallgesellschaft, 5.IV.38 and 29.VII.38, and Bus-
emann to the *Aufsichtsrat*, 21.XI.38; RG242/T83/82, Degussa *Vorstand* meeting,
4.XI.40; Schnitzler II/39, Affidavit by C. Luer, 9.III.48; IX/159, Affidavit by F.
Krebs, 16.III.48; NI-5180, Affidavit by F. terMeer, 2.V.47, *NMT*, vol. 7, p. 1529;
RG242/T83, Ernst Schwarz, "I. G. Farbenindustrie" (1947), p. 28, Frame 3460779;
and Metallgesellschaft, Privatbriefe R. Merton, R. Merton to Oliver Lyttleton,
26.II.40 A year later and in vain, Bosch protested vigorously against the Reich's
decision to revoke Merton's German citizenship; see Metallgesellschaft, Merton-
Korrespondenz, Richard Merton to Walther Merton, 9.II.40, p. 2.
[110] Quoted in Gajewski I/1, Hingst to Franke, 26.IX.39. On the provenance of this
denunciation of Gajewski, see I/2, Affidavit by F. Lampe, 5.V.47.
[111] NI-13570/111, Schieber to Struss, 3.X.39.

plained to Schmitz and terMeer and threatened to press charges against Gajewski unless he recanted within a week.[112] Since a trial could have resulted in a prison sentence for uttering "untrue or grossly distorted statements" about the Party's leaders, the head of Sparte III had to endure the humiliation of petitioning Karasek for permission to call on him and make amends. Meanwhile, he underwent the more unnerving experience of lengthy interrogation at the Gestapo office in Halle. As the affair wound down, Gauleiter Eggeling sent Gajewski a formal reprimand and warned, the businessman later recalled, that "next time he could not protect me from more serious consequences."[113]

IG Farben responded to the structural, commercial, and political problems attendant on the regime's radicalization in 1937–8 in two ways: reorganization and retrenchment. Pursuant to the new corporation law, forty-six once legally distinct subsidiaries were absorbed into the core enterprise between 1937 and 1939, the concern's complex overall organization was somewhat tightened (see Appendix E), the number of managing board members fell to twenty, that of supervisory board members fell to twenty-four, and IG removed some 80 million marks in retained stock from its books.[114] Other changes, however, were not compulsory. With the retirement or death of all but two of the other original members of the combine's Central Committee and the *Verwaltungsrat*, Schmitz moved to solidify his control of IG's manifold operations in the only way open to him: by ensuring that he alone had an overview of the firm's finances and activities. The minutes of *Vorstand* meetings ceased to be circulated to the participants

112 Ibid.
113 Donald M. McKale, *The Nazi Party Courts* (Lawrence, Kan., 1974), p. 138; NI-13570/111, Gajewski to Karasek, 3.X.39, with copies to Gauleiter Eggeling and the Gestapo office in Halle, and Gestapoleiter to Gajewski, 5.X.39; M892/9, Gajewski's testimony, pp. 8180–1. Gajewski's experience, as well as that of other businessmen documented in Sarah Gordon, *Hitler, Germans, and the Jewish Question* (Princeton, N.J., 1984), p. 234, suggests that Radkau errs in claiming that German executives operated above the level of the Party dictatorship (Hallgarten and Radkau, *Deutsche Industrie*, pp. 279–80).
114 The most thorough survey of the corporate consolidation is Robert Rippel, *Das Beteiligungssystem als Mittel zur monopolistischen Beherrschung von Produktion und Markt, dargestellt am Beispiel der IG-Farben* (Dissertation, Halle-Wittenberg, 1961), pp. 93–4, but see also Bayer 4C9.19, Pinnow manuscript, p. 45. The concern's new bylaws for the *Aufsichtsrat* and the *Vorstand* and the new basic charter of 1938 are, respectively, NI-8933-35/74. On the canceling of the stock, Bayer 12/19, Meeting of the *Vorstand*, 28.V.38. On the membership of the boards, NI-7956-57/66, Affidavits by H. Bässler, 28.VI.47.

Berlin NW7. (*Source: OMGUS – Ermittlungen gegen die I. G. Farben*, Greno Verlagsgesellschaft, Nördlingen, 1986)

after August 1938; reports on the proceeds of subsidiaries, especially of DAG, Troisdorf, were denied to board members; and IG's sales figures were concealed systematically from both the *Aufsichtsrat* and official or quasi-official bodies.[115] While IG's role in the Economic Group for Chemistry increased with the elevation of Schnitzler to the chairmanship of the Executive Committee and of Johannes Hess, the head of Wacker GmbH, in which IG owned half the stock, to the leadership of the group, IG concentrated increasingly on direct access to policy making.[116] This entailed recentralizing the splintering combine's contacts with government offices. That objective inspired the revival of the Commercial Committee in mid-1937, the expansion of Berlin NW7 (see Appendix F) a few months later, the associated doubling of its budget between 1936 and 1938, the rejection of Gattineau's proposal to divide responsibility for mobilization plans between the Verm. W. and a new agency for the sales operations, and a sheaf of directives admonishing subordinate offices to deal with government representatives only via the Verm. W. or the Wipo.[117]

By September 1938, however, administrative measures had proved inadequate to restore central direction to IG or to increase its ability to satisfy the demands posed by the Four Year Plan. Not only did labor problems and shortages plague the combine to an ever greater degree, but the proliferation of construction projects confronted IG with a liquidity crisis.[118] Since outlays for new building seemed likely to outstrip total depreciation by about 150 million marks during the year, while taxes, repair costs, stockpiling expenses, and accounts receivable were all rising sharply, Schmitz ordered the concern to pull in its horns. Foreseeing that continuing growth in IG's investments at

[115] Bayer 12/19, Hoyer to Hermann, 12.VIII.38; Interview with Curt Duisberg, 12.II.78; Bayer 64/6, Wipo to Schneider, 10.I.39; NI-15163/123, DAG of Troisdorf to Schmitz, 24.IX.38.
[116] On the Wigru, see Walter Greiling, *75 Jahre Chemieverband* (Düsseldorf, 1952), pp. 78–9; Bayer 64/12.
[117] On the KA, see NI-5169/38, Affidavit by G. Frank-Fahle, undated; NI-2778/20, Affidavit by F. Walloth, 18.VII.45; NI-653/7, Schnitzler to Bosch, 12.VIII.37. On Berlin NW7's budget, NI-10923/90, Affidavit by H. Muench, 10.IX.47, and on the extensive expansion of IG's Berlin headquarters, BA Koblenz, ZSg 127, Bd. 824, *Frankfurter Zeitung*, no. 284, 7.VI.37. On Gattineau's proposal, NI-8776/72, Memo by Verm. W., 7.XII.37, and NI-9051/75, Affidavit by H. Noack, 6.VII.47. Examples of the directives are NI-5727/42, Postbesprechung 73, 10.VIII.37, and Bayer D.A. 913, Verm. W. to Warnecke, 5.VII.38.
[118] On the labor situation, see Bayer 64/6, Memo to Wipo, 17.I.39; and Tim W. Mason, "Labour in the Third Reich," *P&P*, no. 33 (1966), pp. 132–3.

the present rate would exhaust the concern's reserves, he called for a reduction of new capital expenditures by mid-1939 to the level of annual depreciation. Only the buna plants, funded largely by government and bank loans and promising long-term profits, were excluded from this strategic retreat.[119] IG's financial situation improved somewhat during 1939, as the surplus of liquid funds over short-term obligations recovered from less than 14 million marks in 1938 to more than 73 million. But new capital outlays continued to exceed the level Schmitz sought.[120] By 1938, the concern's atomization had become irreversible, and Schmitz had lost control over the divisions of the firm represented by a new generation of managers, men like Otto Ambros and Heinrich Bütefisch, whose own advancement seemed closely tied to the regime's encouragement of autarky and the production of synthetic raw materials.

The failure of Schmitz's program of reorganization and retrenchment paralleled Carl Krauch's similar efforts with regard to the Four Year Plan. By early 1938, Paul Koerner, Göring's second-in-command for the plan, already had developed reservations about Colonel Löb's handling of his duties. Prompted by this and probably also by IG's protest against the feverish and ill-coordinated demands of the multiple agencies with which it had to deal, Krauch conducted a private review of the planning program during that spring. This convinced him that Löb had established impossible production targets in a slipshod manner and then adhered to their execution with bureaucratic inflexibility. When Koerner heard of these findings in June, he staged a confrontation between Löb and Krauch for Göring at Karinhall.[121]

[119] See Hoechst TEA 393, Auszüge aus den TEA-Niederschriften betr. Kredite, 15.IX.38 and 17.XI.38, and Hoechst TEA 775, Kredit-Uebersicht, 15–17.XI.38 and 27.II.39. In the end, IG's balance sheets showed excess depreciation for 1937–8 as 173 million marks and for 1938 alone as 90 million.

[120] BA Koblenz, ZSg 127, Bd. 837, "Der I.G.-Farben Abschluss," *Völkischer Beobachter*, no. 164 (12.VI.40); see also "Der Einsatz," *Berliner Börsen-Zeitung*, no. 264 (8.VI.39). Bayer 4C9.19, Pinnow manuscript, pp. 51–2, claims that capital expenditures exceeded depreciation by a factor of 2.6 in 1939, but my own calculations from the firm's balance sheets suggest that the excess came to only 20 million marks.

[121] M892/48, Koerner's testimony, pp. 2255–6, makes clear that he planted doubts about Löb's work in Krauch's mind, not vice versa, as misstated in NI-10386/85, Koerner's affidavit of 29.VIII.47, and generally repeated since, e.g., Schweitzer, *ZfN*, 20 (1960), p. 433, and Petzina, *Autarkiepolitik*, p. 117. Koerner's reservations probably took shape in response to NI-8590/70, Löb to Backe, 25.XI.37, enclosing a report on the already disappointing progress of the plan, dated 20.X.37.

Krauch forearmed himself with a letter from Otto Ambros formulating the combine's complaints. Proceeding from the assertion that "German industry is overburdened by the many projects of the Four Year Plan and also by the increasing of exports," Ambros concentrated his criticism on the military agencies that insisted on building excessive production capacity, locating new plants in remote areas, and neglecting the necessary financial arrangements. To remedy the situation, he argued that "in the future industry should deal with only one fully responsible, competent office." It should have plenary power to set plans, negotiate contracts and their financing, and allocate materials and labor.[122] Whether Krauch trumped Löb with this letter when they met with Göring is unknown but unlikely. The industrialist hardly needed more documentation to back up the statistical analysis with which he decimated Löb's current output projections. In any case, Göring responded by making Krauch general plenipotentiary for chemical production, a sphere that embraced fuel, explosives, and light metals as well.[123]

Even before the formal conferral of the new title, Krauch, aided by Ambros, produced a new basic planning draft, known as the Krauch or Karinhall Plan. Later, its principal author swore that his chief motive in questioning Löb's exaggerated forecasts of progress toward self-sufficiency was that "a leading person, counting on such high figures, could possibly arrive at political considerations which under the circumstances would be entirely untenable." In other words, Krauch maintained that he sought to make planning more realistic as an adjunct to the efforts of General Ludwig Beck and of Carl Bosch to persuade Göring that a war would be disastrous for Germany.[124] To a degree, Krauch's initial actions lend credence to his claims. The target dates for fulfilling the new version of the plan were immediately pushed back from 1940 to 1942–3, and Krauch decided to avoid the problems of inadequate construction materials and potentially excessive capacities by building plants capable of meeting only 60 to 85% of German needs for various sorts of fuels in the event of war and

---

122 NI-5687/42, IG Intermediates Group to Krauch, 27.VI.38, excerpted in Eichholtz and Schumann (eds.), *Anatomie*, Document 71, pp. 184–5.
123 NI-13900-01/113, Göring's decrees of 1.VIII.38 and 5.VIII.38.
124 M892/6, Krauch's testimony, pp. 5087–8; NI-6768/53, Interrogation of Krauch, 29.IV.47.

gradually stockpiling the balance.[125] Nonetheless, Krauch's pacific motives did not outlast General Beck's dismissal on August 28, if they survived that long. By then, Krauch had resigned the chairmanship of IG's Sparte I and thrown himself with characteristic dedication into the task at hand.

Two central features marked Krauch's planning: an attempt to reconcile the nation's military needs with the long-term interests of German industry and a determination to satisfy those needs as rapidly as possible. Hence, the Karinhall Plan emphasized "the closest coupling of peacetime economic manufacturing with militarily vital production" and proceeded according to the motto "What for Germany's armament is not iron, is chemistry."[126] Both principles would have delighted IG Farben but for two reasons: the liquidity crisis, aggravated in 1939 by the regime's new practice of paying for a portion of official purchases in delayed tax forgiveness, and Krauch's inability to control the execution of his designs.[127] Though he had made clear to Göring upon becoming general plenipotentiary that he would fail unless given absolute priority in the allocation of steel and workers, Krauch never got this prerequisite for success.[128] Drained of resources by competing military projects, notably the construction of the Westwall, the Karinhall Plan had met only 50% of its projected production of explosives by September 1939, and the fuel plants, to which Krauch had assigned half the plan's available funds, could cover only one-third of the Reich's military needs.[129]

Frustration took a toll on Krauch, in conjunction with the mounting international tension that followed Hitler's decision to occupy Bohe-

---

[125] Petzina, *Autarkiepolitik*, pp. 124–5; BA Koblenz, R25/83, Neuer Mineralölplan (Erläuterungen), 12.VII.38.

[126] NI-8840/73, Krauch to Koerner, 22.VII.38; BA Koblenz, R25/174, Gerhard Ritter's speech of 21.I.42, p. 15.

[127] On the payment system, see Lurie, *Private Investment*, pp. 31–5.

[128] See NI-8800/72, Memo from Krauch's Reichsstelle für Wirtschaftsausbau, 12.VII.38; NI-7858/64, Allgemeine Gründfragen der Arbeit, dated Anfang 1939. In fact, the share of German iron and steel consumption allocated by Krauch's Reichsstelle fell from 7.2% for the period of May to December 1937 to 7.0% for 1938, whereas that distributed by the Wehrmacht rose from 15.6% to 25.9%; see Geyer, *RVB*, 45 (1981), Table 12, p. 263.

[129] Petzina, *Autarkiepolitik*, p. 132; Birkenfeld, *Treibstoff*, p. 143. For the deleterious effects of the steel shortage on Krauch's plans for inorganic chemicals production, see NI-7858/64, Ritter to Krauch, 24.V.39 (also BA Koblenz, R25/13). The same source contains a *Vortragsnotiz* of 31.I.39, which conveys the intensity of Krauch's frustration at the time.

mia and Moravia on March 15, 1939. Though the plenipotentiary continued to reassure businessmen in April that his output goals were pegged to anticipated peacetime demand and to Germany's foreign exchange requirements, his remarks also began to incorporate the regime's own version of how to escape the Reich's economic impasse. Asserting that "the open encirclement policy of our enemies has created a new situation," Krauch declared that

Germany must so strengthen its own and its allies' war potential that the coalition is equal to the efforts of almost the entire world. That can happen only through new, great, and common efforts and through an improved, for the present peaceful extension, corresponding to the raw materials base of the coalition, of our economic sphere in the Balkans and Spain.

Failing this, Krauch warned German industry, the victims "in the next war" faced a self-imposed and bitter end.[130] By the time another month had passed, he and his staff were planning how best to exploit the resources of the Ukraine, and raging against "defeatism in the Economics Ministry."[131]

During the spring of 1939, IG's leaders also seem to have accepted the likelihood of conflict. Both Schnitzler and terMeer avowed later that the occupation of Prague convinced them that Hitler had embarked on "a clear course of criminal speculation."[132] Be that as it may, they and their colleagues held few illusions about the industrial might of their potential adversaries or about the likely commercial consequences of the conflict. Farben promptly bought up a large supply of tetraethyl lead from Standard Oil and began selling the concern's inventories overseas, as in earlier diplomatic crises.[133] The Legal Committee drew up plans in June 1939 for camouflaging IG's ownerships in foreign properties.[134] A month later, the *Vorstand* called in all outstanding debts from agencies abroad, collecting nearly

130 BA Koblenz, R25/14, Krauch's speech to the General Council of the Four Year Plan, 20/21.IV.39, p. 14 (also submitted at the postwar trial as EC-282).
131 BA Koblenz, R25/13, Notizen für die Besprechung mit Herrn Staatssekretär Körner, 16.V.39 (also NI-7858/64).
132 NI-5180, Affidavit by F. terMeer, 2.V.47, *NMT*, vol. 7, p. 1527; NI-5196, Affidavit by G. von Schnitzler, 18.III.47, p. 1524.
133 On the deal with Standard, see Gabriel Kolko, "American Business and Germany, 1930–1941," *Western Political Quarterly*, 15 (1962), pp. 724–5. On IG's leaders' knowledge of America's industrial might, see the article summarizing the observations of thirty-four chemists who visited the United States in October and November of 1937: BA Koblenz, ZSg 127, Bd. 41, *Die chemische Fabrik*, 11 (25.V.38).
134 NI-12796/105, Meeting of the Legal Committee, 8.VI.39.

3 million dollars from the United States alone.[135] In the meantime, a number of the plants may even have begun producing on the basis of the firm's mobilization plans.[136]

Nonetheless, the firm's leaders continued to cultivate ties to their counterparts abroad. Having long delayed in providing Standard with the know-how for producing buna – apparently in order to satisfy the German government *and* in deference to DuPont's interests in specialty rubber products – IG finally began joint testing with the American firm and its partners in the summer of 1939.[137] More important, IG's captains advocated a commercial accommodation with England. At the conference between leaders of the Federation of British Industries and the Reichsgruppe Industrie in Düsseldorf during March, Schnitzler served as one of the three chairmen of the German negotiating team and apparently supported the readiness of his colleague Ernst Poensgen to offer concessions to British sellers in markets where Germany predominated.[138] Over the summer, two of the Vowi reports, which Ilgner generally circulated to the ministries and other government offices, argued that German–British trade competition was less serious than usually perceived and that further increases in German business with the Balkans could be achieved only by an overall revival of international commerce.[139]

These efforts at international economic cooperation remained, however, beside the point. During the preceding six years, IG Farben had pursued a strategy of indispensability, hoping both to profit from the

[135] NI-14923/121, *Vorstand* meeting of 22.VII.39.
[136] NI-8925, Affidavit by H. Wagner, 11.VI.47, *NMT*, vol. 7, pp. 1494–5.
[137] Cf. Kolko, *Western Political Quarterly*, 15 (1962), pp. 721–2; NI-5180, terMeer's affidavit, 2.V.47, *NMT*, vol. 7, p. 528; Henrietta M. Larson, Evelyn H. Knowlton, and Charles S. Popple, *History of the Standard Oil Company*, vol. 3: *New Horizons 1927–1950* (New York, 1971), pp. 172–4; Josiah DuBois, *The Devil's Chemists* (Boston, 1952), p. 152; George W. Stocking and Myron Watkins, *Cartels in Action* (New York, 1947), pp. 484–5; and terMeer IV/87, Affidavit by E. Konrad, 8.I.48.
[138] On the negotiations, see A. Teichova, "Die geheimen britisch-deutschen Ausgleichsversuche am Vorabend des zweiten Weltkrieges," *ZfG*, 7 (1959), pp. 755–96; and Christel Nehrig, "Die Verhandlungen zwischen der Reichsgruppe Industrie und der Federation of British Industry in Düsseldorf am 15. und 16. März 1939," *JfG*, 18 (1978), pp. 373–416. On the background of the British industrialists' hopes for the conference, see R. F. Holland, "The Federation of British Industries and the International Economy, 1929–39," *EHR*, 34 (1981), pp. 296–8.
[139] Bayer D.A. 377, Vowi 3551, Beeinträchtigt die deutsche Ausfuhr Englands Export? 27.VI.39; Bayer 13/25, Vowi 3591, Möglichkeiten einer intensiveren Handelsverflechtung mit den südosteuropäischen Ländern, 31.VII.39.

actions of the Third Reich and to gain sufficient influence to moderate them. This latter-day, self-serving "policy of the diagonal" had helped ensure both Hitler's decision for war and his underpreparedness for it. If, as alleged, Georg von Schnitzler remarked on September 1, 1939, "The work of a lifetime is now collapsing," he cannot have known how truly he had spoken.[140]

[140] Schnitzler IX/177, Affidavit by Hans Kugler, 26.III.48.

PART IV
The Nazi empire, 1938–1944

There is little reason to suppose that IG Farben sought, encouraged, or directed the Nazi conquest of Europe.[1] If German expansionism was the "lowest common denominator" to which differences between industrial interests and Nazi ideology could be reduced during the 1930s, as much recent writing hypothesizes, Farben's leaders do not appear to have thought so.[2] To be sure, the combine's financial situation did mirror the overloading of the Reich's economic resources in 1938–9, an overloading that some scholars see as a precipitant of Nazi aggression.[3] But in partial contrast to the situation of German heavy industry, IG's stakes in autarky or military production were neither so complete nor so compelling as to have created the national crisis or militated in favor of conflict as a means of solving it.[4] In fact,

---

[1] See Klaus Hildebrand, "Innenpolitische`Antriebskräfte der nationalsozialistischen Aussenpolitik," in H.-U. Wehler (ed.), Sozialgeschichte Heute (Göttingen, 1974), p. 638; and Jost Dülffer, "Zum 'decision-making process' in der deutschen Aussenpolitik 1933–39," in Manfred Funke (ed.), Hitler, Deutschland und die Mächte (Düsseldorf, 1976), pp. 202–3. On the inability of private industry to promote a peaceful foreign policy, see Bernd Martin, "Friedens-Planungen der multinationalen Grossindustrie (1932–1940) als politische Krisenstrategie," G&G, 2 (1976), pp. 66–88, especially the concluding remarks.

[2] For examples of such writing, see David Abraham, The Collapse of the Weimar Republic (Princeton, N.J., 1981); and the works of Hans-Erich Volkmann, notably "Das aussenwirtschaftliche Programm der NSDAP, 1930–1933," AfS, 17 (1977), pp. 251–74; "Die NS-Wirtschaft in Vorbereitung des Krieges," in W. Deist and M. Messerschmidt (eds.), Ursachen und Voraussetzungen der deutschen Kriegspolitik (Stuttgart, 1979), pp. 177–368; and "Politik, Wirtschaft, und Rüstung unter dem Nationalsozialismus," in M. Funke (ed.), Hitler, Deutschland und die Mächte, pp. 269–91. But compare R. J. Overy, "Hitler's War and the German Economy: A Reinterpretation," EHR, 35 (1982), pp. 279–80; and idem, Goering: the 'Iron Man' (Boston, 1984), pp. 111–12.

[3] See Timothy W. Mason, "Innere Krise und Angriffskrieg 1938/39," in F. Forstmeier and H.-E. Volkmann (eds.), Wirtschaft und Rüstung am Vorabend des Zweiten Weltkriegs (Düsseldorf, 1975), pp. 158–88; and Jost Dülffer, "Der Beginn des Krieges 1939: Hitler, die innere Krise und das Mächtesystem," G&G, 2 (1976), pp. 443–70.

[4] On heavy industry, compare Michael Geyer, "Zum Einfluss der nationalsozialistichen Rüstungspolitik auf das Ruhrgebiet," RVB, 45 (1981), pp. 241–50, and John R. Gillingham, Industry and Politics in the Third Reich (New York, 1985), pp. 90–111.

Schnitzler and Ilgner repeatedly offered countervisions of the nation's economic future, and Krauch, like his superior Göring, thought Germany insufficiently prepared to fight. For Farben, though perhaps not for Hitler, R. J. Overy's conclusion holds: "Economic pressure was all for postponing general war in 1939, not for speeding it up."[5]

Arguments to the contrary with regard to IG generally rely on cui bono logic, which deduces the combine's wishes from what it allegedly stood to gain by Nazi expansionism or ultimately did acquire.[6] Although the Nazi empire did offer IG chances to revise international cartel agreements in its favor and to cut into undesirable competition within Europe, the foreseeable net cash value of either change has usually been assumed and exaggerated. Even critical commentators have acknowledged that the firm's commercial interests did not require the seizure of foreign enterprises or sources of raw materials.[7] When pressed, IG had merely to begin production abroad. Though less lucrative than exporting, this policy was also less costly than war. Once the regime reversed itself in 1938 and started encouraging the foundation of foreign subsidiaries as a means of collecting foreign exchange, IG gladly moved in this direction.[8] The much-cited thumbnail summaries of foreign chemical industries, which the Vowi office distributed during successive German offensives between 1938 and 1940, do not constitute evidence of aggressive intent.[9] Prompted by news bulletins

---

[5] Overy, Goering, p. 89.

[6] Josiah DuBois, The Devil's Chemists (Boston, 1952), especially pp. x, 11; Dietrich Eichholtz, Geschichte der deutschen Kriegswirtschaft 1939–1945, Bd. 1: 1939–41 (East Berlin, 1969); Hans Radandt, Fall 6: Ausgewählte Dokumente und Urteil des IG-Farben-Prozesses (East Berlin, 1970); R. Sasuly, IG Farben (New York, 1947); Janis Schmelzer, Unternehmen Südost (Wolfen, 1966); John Boylan, Sequel to the Apocalypse (New York, 1942).

[7] Eichholtz, Geschichte, vol. 1, pp. 149–52; Tim Mason, "The Primacy of Politics," in H. A. Turner (ed.), Nazism and the Third Reich (New York, 1972), p. 192.

[8] See Chapter 7, footnote 82 and the discussion to which it refers.

[9] The Vowi officers issued reports on the major chemical producers of Austria on 10.IX.37 and 31.III.38, of Czechoslovakia on 28.VII.38, 29.IX.38, and 9.XI.38, of Poland on 28.VII.39, of Norway on 1.III.40, of France on 18.VII.40 and 27.VII.40, of Holland on 13.VI.40, of Belgium on 1.VI.40, of Great Britain on 21.XI.40 and 3–17.XII.40, of Yugoslavia on 1.V.41; of Russia on 6.XII.40, 17.XII.40, 28.III.42, and 26.VI.42. All of these are available at the Bayer Archiv, 84/Europa-Oesterreich or 91/1, except the English reports, copies of which are in BASF T52/15b. For a fairly complete list of Vowi publications concerning Southeast Europe, see Hans Radandt, "Berichte der Volkswirtschaftlichen Abteilung der IG Farben-Industrie AG über Südosteuropa," JfW, 7 (1966), pp. 291–314. Radandt's list demonstrates that reports of the kind listed above were prepared routinely by Vowi throughout the 1930s and periodically updated. Bayer's Vowi files include parallel, albeit less numerous reports on nearly all IG's strongest competitors in the world and on most countries in which the firm did business. See also the lengthy lists of Vowi reports in Ilgner III/44-45.

and scuttlebutt in the capital, these reports were, at best, handy dis-
tillations of material available in several standard manuals and marginally useful in the event that diplomatic and military developments
augmented business contacts.[10] Like much of Berlin NW7's work,
such studies were probably intended to advertise Max Ilgner's alert-
ness and efficiency and to underline his eagerness to be of service to
the Reich.[11] That they were not "shopping lists" of potential booty is
indicated by IG Farben's subsequent indifference to all but a tiny
fraction of the enterprises and business fields catalogued in them.[12]

German bellicosity entailed weighty risks and costs for the concern.
Defeat meant, at minimum, a repetition of the reparations and loss of
foreign subsidiaries and markets experienced after World War I; at
most, the destruction of the firm's plants from the air and even of the
corporation by the victors.[13] Nothing in IG's commercial position in
1939 suggested the need to play *va banque*. Even peaceful accretions
to the Reich's territories or a successful war posed dangers for an
enterprise already bothered by fragmentation and with ample reason
to feel mistrusted in Berlin. In the event of conflict, Germany's gains
would have to be very great, indeed, if they were to compensate for the
export markets lost to competitors during the fighting or to new producers called into being by the interdiction of supplies from the concern. Meanwhile, each international flare-up rekindled demands that
IG transfer its main plants from the Rhineland to the German interior,
demands the firm resisted vigorously.[14] Every effort to camouflage
IG's foreign properties behind ostensibly neutral holding companies
elicited calls for explanation from the Economics Ministry and con-
demnations of IG's selfish timidity from Party agencies.[15] The repeti-

---

10 Radandt, *JfW*, 7 (1966), p. 292.
11 Testimony of F. terMeer, NMT, vol. 8, p. 87.
12 The phrase is from NI-7330/58, Affidavit by A. Reithinger, 19.VI.47.
13 In August 1940, IG estimated the value of its property losses and reparations pay-
    ments under the Versailles treaty at 203 million marks; NI-11252/93, IG's New
    Order plan, 3.VIII.40, p. 10. The fear of destruction was hardly fanciful. In the
    victor nations of World War I, where the memory of the Little IG's role in poison gas
    deployment was kept alive by reprintings of Victor Lefebure's *The Riddle of the
    Rhine* (New York, 1923), IG was the subject of persistent attacks. On German
    sensitivity to this, see BA Koblenz, ZSg 127, Bd. 825, "Stimmungmache gegen
    deutsche Chemie," *Die chemische Industrie*, 4.IV.37.
14 See, for example, NI-4954, Affidavit by F. Ehrmann, 13.III.47, *NMT*, vol. 7, pp.
    1487–8; NI-7121/55, RWM to Verm. W., 5.VII.39; NI-7124/55, reply of 7.VII.39.
15 NI-5769/43, IG to RWM, 26.VI.39, excerpted in D. Eichholtz and W. Schumann
    (eds.), *Anatomie des Krieges* (East Berlin, 1969), pp. 217–19; NI-8496/70, IG Fi-
    nance Section to RWM, 24.VII.39; NI-7078/55, IG to RWM, 15.VIII.39;

tion of crises engendered suspicion among cartel partners and foreign boycotts of German goods.[16] But isolated from the making of Nazi foreign policy and unwilling to confirm their reputation for "internationalism" in Nazi circles, the concern's leaders swallowed their misgivings and kept silent. They remained intent on making the best of what they could not and dared not try to control.

Once confronted with a series of territorial faits accomplis, however, IG Farben felt compelled to protect its interests within the new context. From the concern's standpoint, Nazi Germany's European conquests fell into two categories: those annexed to the Reich or clearly foredoomed to a semicolonial status within a German imperium, and those to be vouchsafed a degree of independence within the reorganized European economy, the so-called New Order.[17] Austria, the Sudetenland, the Czech Protectorate, Poland, Alsace-Lorraine, the Baltic states, and Russia made up the first group, which is the subject of Chapter 6. The second group of nations, discussed in Chapter 7, consisted of France, the Benelux states, Norway, Denmark, and the Balkan lands. In neither area did the concern engage in indiscriminate aggrandizement or plunder. There was no "rape of the European chemical industry."[18] Only in Austria and Czechoslovakia did IG's takeovers account for more than 5% of any subject country's chemical output. So far as was politic, Farben refused involvement in fields that did not bear on its central interests, even when prodded by the Reich or presented with obvious opportunities for profit.[19] Guided by the

---

NI-12746/104, Memo to members of the KA, 15.VIII.40; NI-1295/13, Statement of G. Frank-Fahle, no date; Joseph Borkin. *The Crime and Punishment of IG Farben* (New York, 1978), p. 190.

[16] See the cautiously phrased remarks on IG's understandings with foreign firms in the general report for 1938, quoted in Bayer 4C9.19, Pinnow manuscript, pp. 46–7.

[17] The best short guide to Nazi intentions in each of the conquered territories is Lothar Gruchmann, *Nationalsozialistische Grossraumordnung* (Stuttgart 1962), pp. 76–101. I am adopting here a modified version of the distinction among occupied areas to be found in Otfried Ulshöfer, *Einflussnahme auf Wirtschaftsunternehmungen in den besetzten Nord-, West- und Südosteuropäischen Ländern während des Zweiten Weltkriegs* (Tübingen, 1958), pp. 16–17. That IG observed this distinction is clear from NI-8454/70, Legal Position and Legal Organization of the Occupied Territories, 2.X.40.

[18] This is the title of chap. 5 in Borkin, *Crime and Punishment*. Significantly, Borkin's entire discussion contains only one indication of the size of the companies involved, a misleading remark concerning the French Etablissements Kuhlmann.

[19] On the nitrogen industry, see Oster II/36, O. Dobias to Oster, 29.I.47; II/38, Statement of M. W. Holtropp, 20.III.48; Bütefisch VII/87, Affidavit by G. Lelong, 26.II.48; Oster II/49, Statement by B. Eriksen, 28.I.47. For other representative examples, see Bayer 13/25, 7th meeting of the Southeast Europe Committee,

strategy of indispensability and concern for its postwar trading position, the combine aimed at controlling or restricting actual or potential competitors within those fields essential to its future: dyes (still operating at only 71% of capacity in 1938), light metals, rubber, plastics, and industrial gases.[20] In addition, faced with the loss of overseas markets in consequence of the war, the concern sought to compensate itself in Europe by attempting to block construction of foreign chemical plants, to reduce competition through direct private negotiations with native companies, and to strip these enterprises of most of their tariff and patent protections. However, the means to these ends, as well as their urgency, tended to differ on either side of the German customs barriers.

With regard to both acquisitions and plant closings, IG compiled a mixed record in occupied Europe. No more than in domestic policy making did the combine's motives and needs naturally coincide with those of Nazi planners; no more than at home did the concern's ability to extract advantages from the government's actions necessarily bespeak a preference for them; no more than within Germany could Farben consistently bend the authorities to its will or vice versa. Nazi planning for the Greater German Economic Sphere (Grossraum-wirtschaft), like Hitler's foreign policy, was an unstable compound of ideological visions, political interests, and strategic requirements.[21] Though the firm's desires were sometimes compatible with Nazi policy, they also frequently conflicted with the Reich's fluctuating priorities, especially the short-range needs to cultivate loyalty in the occupied and allied states and to maximize their contributions to the German war effort. Not only German political interests, but also adroit actions by the subject nations, as well as astute lobbying by competing German and foreign firms, stymied Farben's already limited ambitions almost as often as not. Because IG learned to clothe its objectives in appeals to military necessity or the Party's goals, this

---

15.XII.39, and Bayer 64/9, Weber-Andreä and Heider to Soda- und Aetzkalien Ost GmbH, 10.XI.42.

20 Capacity calculated from the statistics in Bayer 4C9.32, Control Office, *Activities of I. G. Farbenindustrie in the Dyestuffs Industry* (1946), p. 9. Only half of IG's output of 57,000 tons per year could be sold within Germany (Bayer 4C9.19, Pinnow manuscript, p. 61).

21 See among many relevant publications, Gruchmann, *Grossraumordnung;* Alan Milward, *The New Order and the French Economy* (London, 1970), pp. 33–4, 42–3, 72, 146–80; and Alexander Dallin, *German Rule in Russia 1941–1945* (London, 1957), chaps. 15 and 18.

ambiguous pattern has been easy to mistake or distort. In particular, the temptation to quote corporate documents out of context has blinded many scholars to an important reality: "The industrial expansion into Europe was carried out primarily by the Reichswerke and Four Year Plan, and not by private capitalism. . . . In fact the German economic empire . . . was firmly under the control and in large part owned and operated by the Goering economic apparatus."[22]

There is no gainsaying Farben's disregard for the property interests of foreign nationals in occupied Europe. Nor, although IG usually achieved its successes without recourse to direct pressure from German authorities, can one deny that the concern occasionally took advantage of German military preponderance. These offenses against the victims and international law do not, however, add up to the conclusion that IG conspired to capture and exploit the chemical and related industries of Europe for German military purposes. As Alan Bullock has written in another context, "There is a lot of difference between failing to stop aggression, even hoping to derive side profits from it – and aggression itself."[23] The combine reacted opportunistically and defensively to the regime's diplomatic and military triumphs, but IG did not foment them. Ironically, responding in this manner not only placed IG Farben on a criminal path, but also reinforced that mistrust of large corporations among Party and state functionaries that repeatedly attended the concern's efforts in the subjugated areas.

[22] Overy, *Goering,* p. 111; see also idem, "Goering's 'Multi-national Empire,'" in A. Teichova and P. L. Cottrell (eds.), *International Business and Central Europe, 1918–1939* (New York, 1983), pp. 269–98.
[23] Alan Bullock, "Hitler and the Origins of the Second World War," in Turner (ed.), *Nazism and the Third Reich,* p. 220.

6. Greater Germany

Nazi expansionism, with its fixation on disputed borderlands and living space in the East, concentrated on regions where IG Farben had had little previous interest or difficulty. Austria, Czechoslovakia, Poland, Alsace-Lorraine, the Baltic states, and Russia offered neither significant sales opportunities nor major competition in international markets. While outside the Reich, the present and prospective chemical industries of these nations were controllable, inconsequential, or both. The combine largely let them be. Once annexed, however, sectors of these industries threatened several of the vital monopolies on which rested Farben's indispensability, hence its influence in Nazi Germany. Given the Reich's expressed determination to place these properties under German administration and often to increase their output, IG rapidly recognized that reserve on its part might deliver protected positions to rival corporations or serve as a pretext for direct government involvement in chemical production. The concern therefore set out to defend itself. Along the way, it also came to hope that some takeovers in the lands attached to Germany would substitute for shifting the firm's production eastward or, at least, reduce the costs of doing so. This pattern of reticence and reaction, established during the prewar occupations of Austria and Czechoslovakia, held good in all the lands subsequently attached to the Third Reich. Its unfolding is worth tracing in some detail, as proof not only of its consistency, but also of Farben's subordination to Party policy in occupied Europe.

Austria

Intermittently during the decade preceding the Anschluss, IG Farben contemplated acquiring a dominant position in the Austrian chemical industry by buying into the Pulverfabrik Skodawerke Wetzler AG (SWW), the leading firm.[1] The first abortive discussions to this end

---

[1] For an overview, see NI-9289, Minutes of the special meeting of Farben officers concerning Austria, 10.IX.37, *NMT*, vol. 7, pp. 1407–8; NI-6070/45, Special meet-

were initiated by Skoda-Wetzler in 1927, when its dependence on tariff protection prompted the firm to offer a minority holding to IG.[2] The capital and technical expertise of the German concern could remedy this dependence, or in the event of a customs union between Germany and Austria, IG's investment might restrain it from competition with Skoda-Wetzler's vulnerable products. But from the point of view of IG's commercial interests, the proposed expenditure had little to recommend it. The combine already controlled two major Austrian producers, the Carbidwerk Deutsch-Matrei AG and the Dynamit Nobel AG of Vienna, through their parent company, Dynamit Nobel of Bratislava (DAG, Bratislava), which in turn belonged to Dynamit AG of Troisdorf, an IG subsidiary (see Appendix G).[3] Both Austrian satellites marketed their products through IG's sales outlet in Vienna, Anilinchemie AG. So, in large measure, would Skoda-Wetzler under the marketing agreements that IG preferred to SWW's share offer. Worked out during 1928–9, these reserved the Austrian markets for heavy chemicals to local producers and for dyes and most medicinal preparations to Farben, precluded Austrian exports to much of western Europe, and assigned Austria's chemical factories a fixed share in IG's sales to Southeast Europe.[4] Though cumbersome, these arrangements both stabilized Skoda-Wetzler's business prospects and protected Farben at virtually no cost to the concern.

ing of the KA concerning Austria, 19.IV.38. My account of relations between SWW and IG sifts the following retrospective summaries: NI-8578/70, Affidavit by H. Gattineau, 2.V.47; NI-8456/70, Statement by P. Haefliger, 1.V.47, pp. 1–3, and his testimony, *NMT*, vol. 7, pp. 1464–7; NI-10997/91, Affidavit by F. Rottenberg, 13.IX.47; NI-10998/91, Affidavit by J. Joham, 13.IX.47. Haefliger's and Gattineau's statements are obviously suspect, but so are those of Rottenberg and Joham. Employees of the Austrian Creditanstalt before, during, and after the war, they were at the time of their statements seeking restitution of SWW to the bank on the ground that the sale to IG in 1938 occurred under duress.

2 Ilgner IX/137. Pistor to IG Directorate, 11.XI.27; IX/138, Pistor's report of 26.XI.27; IX/139, Report of Dr. Kuehl, 29.XI.27.

3 NI-303/4, Report by Dr. Hans Kugler on IG's European acquisitions, 12.VII.45; for a survey of SWW and DAG, Bratislava, see Bayer 6/14, Vowi Bericht 2803, 11.IV.38. To avoid confusion, I have adhered throughout to the Czech name Bratislava rather than to the German appellation Pressburg for the firm's seat.

4 Cf. Verena Schröter, "The IG Farbenindustrie AG in Central and South-East Europe, 1926–1938," in A. Teichova and P. L. Cottrell (eds.), *International Business and Central Europe, 1918–1939* (New York, 1983), pp. 145–6, and NI-8456/70, Haefliger's affidavit, 1.V.47, p. 1; BA Koblenz, ZSg 127, Bd. 829, "Die I.G. Farben und Oesterreich," *Berliner Börsen-Courier*, 12.I.28, "Die chemische Industrie Oesterreichs," *Neue Freie Presse*, 28.V.29, "Europäische Chemieabkommen," *Industrie- und Handels-Zeitung*, 2.VI.29.

In 1932, however, the Rothschilds' hard-pressed Creditanstalt Bankverein, which owned most of the Austrian company's stock, apparently directed Isidor Pollak, who was soon to become the general director of SWW, to extricate the bank from the unwanted role of a holding company. Pollak conceived a plan to rationalize Austrian chemical production and sales and began appealing for IG's participation.[5] Though the concern snapped up a potentially profitable offer to take over a concealed majority in the Chemosan AG, a pharmaceuticals producer with plants in both Austria and Czechoslovakia, SWW remained uninteresting.[6] Eduard Weber-Andreä, chairman of the Chemicals Committee of IG, diplomatically deflected Pollak's overtures, leaving the door to agreement ajar in case a market developed in Austria for some product that it would be advantageous to manufacture there. By 1935, however, Pollak had gained the support of Wilhelm Roth, head of Anilinchemie, and of his ally in Berlin, Max Ilgner. Ilgner imagined control of Austrian chemical production as a "visiting card," an earnest of the concern's interest in cooperating with the Nazi regime's plans for Southeast Europe and his own entrée to policy making for the region.[7] Accordingly, he launched a long, seesaw battle, which did not end with the Anschluss, to transfer authority over relations with the Austrian chemical industry from the Chemicals Committee to the Central Finance Department of his Berlin NW7 office.

IG remained unwilling to commit capital to SWW until two developments gave Ilgner his opening. First, the Austrian government decided to promote domestic output of synthetic nitrogen, a product not covered by the agreements of 1928–9. Faced with a reduction in its exports, IG tried to dissuade the Austrians and, failing that, to salvage an annual payment from SWW in return for technical and financial assistance in constructing its new nitrogen facility at Moosbierbaum. Ilgner dispatched a technical adviser to the plant and Guenther Schiller, his personal assistant, to supervise IG's Austrian interests and work with Pollak.[8] Second, IG's chief challenger in East Central Eu-

[5] Ilgner IX/148, Moos von Seiler to IG Chemicals Dept., 26.II.37.
[6] NI-1941/18, ZA meeting of 24.III.32; Verena Schröter, *Die deutsche Industrie auf dem Weltmarkt 1929 bis 1933* (Frankfurt, 1984), p. 403.
[7] NI-8583/70, Affidavit by Meyer-Wegelin, 4.VI.47; also the two affidavits by Kurt Krüger: NI-4928, 18.III.47, *NMT*, vol. 7, pp. 440–2, and NI-11370/94, 2.VIII.47; and Kühne III/117, Affidavit by E. Haager, 10.III.48.
[8] NI-7619/62, Affidavit by G. Frank-Fahle, 20.VI.47; NI-8456/70, Haefliger's affida-

rope, the Aussiger Verein of Czechoslovakia, made plain its desire to buy, modernize, and expand SWW. Weber-Andreä parried by seeking an option on the 86% of SWW stock held by the Creditanstalt. This effort failed, and by early 1936 Aussig's plan "to monopolize the market of the old Danube Monarchy" had stung IG into bidding 3 million marks for outright control of SWW. When the Austrians refused to part with a majority holding, Ilgner maladroitly pressured them by withdrawing aid for the nitrogen plant. Exasperated, Pollak overtrumped him by turning to Aussig and to Montecatini of Italy and by simultaneously entertaining the proposals of the Salomon group, which had recently built a nitrogen plant for Hungary in defiance of the international cartel.[9]

Pollak's shrewd move had its intended effect. On September 10, 1937, the Commercial Committee approved a plan, developed on Pollak's initiative, to integrate SWW into IG's Austrian sales network. The shares in Farben's Anilinchemie were to be divided equally among IG, SWW, and the Austrian Dynamit Nobel AG.[10] By December, this plan gave way to negotiations aimed at forming a new production company composed of these four enterprises. In order to retain absolute control of its patents and of Dynamit Nobel, IG demanded an indirect majority in the new concern. Objections by the Austrian government quashed that idea, and IG's negotiators broke off discussions, convinced that no progress could be expected "until there are fundamental changes in the economic and political relations between Germany and Austria." This prompted one IG officer to remind the firm that its primary interest was not ownership but "to make sure that the friendly relations which already existed were kept up."[11] The result

vit, 1.V.47; Bayer 84/Eur. Oesterreich, "Die I. G. in Oesterreich," 19.III.38; and Hans Radandt, "Die IG-Farbenindustrie AG in Südosteuropa bis 1938," *JfW,* 7 (1966), pp. 182–5.

[9] Bayer D.A. 429, Notiz über eine Besprechung, 4.XII.35, signed by Weber-Andreä; Ilgner IX/142, Discussion at Berlin NW7, 10.I.36; IX/142, Schulze to Kühne and Pistor, 30.I.36; XI/182, Affidavit by G. Schiller, 4.III.48; and Bayer 84/Eur. Oesterreich, "Die I. G. in Oesterreich," 19.III.38.

[10] NI-9289, Commercial Committee meeting, 10.IX.37, *NMT,* vol. 7, pp. 1393–94 (the same document is NI-4959/37); Ilgner IX/2, Discussion on 29.V.37, dated 18.VII.37. See also NI-15605/122, the third draft of the proposed agreement among the three firms, 23.VII.37.

[11] The quotations are from NI-15195/123, Memo on negotiations with the Austrian Creditanstalt, 18.I.38. On the foregoing events, see Bayer D.A. 950, Auszug aus der Niederschrift über die Sitzung der Chema am 8.I.38, and Weber-Andreä to Kühne, 21.I.38, and Aktennotiz. Stand der Verhandlung über die Fusion Oesterreich,

was a compromise proposal to merge the Carbidwerk Deutsch-Matrei and Skoda-Wetzler into a new Ostmark Chemie AG "under the auspices and possible simultaneous participation" of IG.[12] The Creditanstalt would retain a majority of the shares, but IG would hold the deciding voice in designated matters of special importance to it. In the weeks preceding the Anschluss, negotiations proceeded over the details of this plan, which both sides had accepted in principle.[13]

In March obstacles to an agreement disappeared as fast as the German–Austrian border posts. To its Jewish ownership and management, SWW's independence lost importance, while the dangers of not acquiring the firm increased for IG. Although Skoda-Wetzler's sales amounted to a fraction of 1% of the German concern's turnover and about 2% of its chemical sales, the change of regime promised new development.[14] Göring's seventeen-point construction program for Austria of March 26, 1938, called for expansion of the arms industry and intensified exploitation of hydroelectric power; Party leaders planned to gain prestige by reducing Austrian unemployment through industrialization; and the Four Year Plan might fund the modernization of the SWW plant.[15] Self-defense required IG to obtain SWW, lest it swell the importance of another chemical company or become the nucleus of a state enterprise similar or linked to the Hermann Göring Werke.[16]

Ten days after the annexation of Austria, the Commercial Committee of IG resolved anew to purchase a majority of Skoda-Wetzler.[17] Paul Haefliger, a member of the committee, arrived in Vienna bearing a letter to the director general of the Creditanstalt, Dr. Josef Joham, which outlined a projected division of Ostmark Chemie and its sales organization between IG and the Austrian bank.[18] On March 29,

18.I.38; NI-7388/59, Pollak to Rottenberg, 5.I.38; NI-7394/59, Buhl to Pollak, 20.I.38.

[12] NI-4024, Haefliger and Krüger to Keppler, 9.IX.38, *NMT*, vol. 7, pp. 1404–05.

[13] NI-14744/120, Chemicals Committee meeting, 2.III.38; Ilgner XI/182, Affidavit by G. Schiller, 4.III.48.

[14] NI-8456/70, Affidavit by Haefliger, 1.V.47, p. 17.

[15] See Norbert Schausberger, *Rüstung in Oesterreich 1938–1945* (Wien, 1970), pp. 28, 34, 38–9; NI-8456/70, Haefliger affidavit, 1.V.47, p. 17.

[16] NI-11370/94, Affidavit by K. Krüger, 2.VII.47; NI-8578/70, Affidavit by H. Gattineau, 2.V.47. The problem of competition from the HGW was not cleared up until August, when E. R. Fischer conversed with Voss of the HGW *Vorstand*; Bayer, D. A. 1427, Aktennotiz by Fischer, 3.VIII.38.

[17] NI-9289, KA meeting of 23.III.39, *NMT*, vol. 7, pp. 1397–8.

[18] NI-3982, Haefliger to Joham, 29.III.38, *NMT*, vol. 7, pp. 1399–1400.

Haefliger, Schiller, Joham, and Pollak agreed on the sale of a controlling interest in SWW once a trustee had estimated the value of the firm.[19] Shortly thereafter, Rudolf Pfeiffer, an Austrian well connected to the NSDAP, replaced a purged Jew on the Creditanstalt's *Vorstand* and took charge of concluding the sale.[20]

Arrangements with the owners of SWW went more smoothly than with Nazi officials. Blocking IG's way stood the Reichsstatthalter's order of March 19 against the founding of new plants or enterprises in Austria by German firms. Worse, the Auslandsorganisation of the NSDAP, long bitterly critical of IG, reproached the concern for slowness in Aryanizing its Austrian subsidiaries and excessive monetary generosity to dismissed Jews. On March 24, Gauleiter Fritz Sauckel informed Göring, "I am of the opinion that IG should not have everything."[21] After ascertaining that the new Austrian trade minister Fischboeck had no objection to the Ostmark Chemie plan, Haefliger lobbied the pivotal Nazi officials. On April 2, he explained IG's intentions to Hans Kehrl, who was joined by Wilhelm Keppler, Hitler's deputy for Austrian Nazi affairs since July 1937. Neither man was sympathetic to IG, and although Keppler reacted favorably to Haefliger's presentation, he added rather gratuitously "that it was not desirable that IG should buy all the small chemical plants in Austria." Haefliger came away convinced that IG should proceed slowly.[22] A week later, he and Krüger wrote Keppler, laying out the record of IG's efforts to establish the Ostmark Chemie. They requested authorization to continue negotiations in order to integrate the Austrian chemical industry into that of the Reich "within the framework of the Four

[19] NI-8456/70, Haefliger's affidavit, I.V.47; Haefliger's testimony, *NMT*, vol. 7, pp. 1470–3. Shortly thereafter, Pollak died during a brutal search of his house by the Gestapo.

[20] NI-10998/91, Affidavit by J. Joham, 13.IX.47, p. 3.

[21] Schmitz IV/51, Affidavit by K. Krüger, 31.XII.47, *NMT*, vol. 7, pp. 1483–5; Kühne III/117, Affidavit by E. Haager, 10.III.48. Guenther Schiller claimed in 1947 that before the Anschluss only one Jew was removed from IG's Austrian enterprises, despite reiterated protests from Nazi officials; Ilgner IX/134, Affidavit by Schiller, 31.X.47, p. 2. Sauckel is quoted in G. W. F. Hallgarten and J. Radkau, *Deutsche Industrie und Politik* (Frankfurt, 1974), p. 360. The text of the order of March 19 is NI-8041/66.

[22] NI-3981/29, Haefliger's file note of 6.IV.38 on his meetings in Vienna, as printed in *NMT*, vol. 7, pp. 1401–3. See also Hallgarten and Radkau, *Deutsche Industrie,* p. 360. Haefliger's later account in NI-8456/70 distorts this conversation considerably. See also Haefliger III/40, Affidavit by H. Kehrl, 25.II.48, and III/41, Affidavit by W. Keppler, 2.II.48.

Year Plan," promising to "resubmit individual decisions for approval whenever required."[23]

Having heard Haefliger's report, a meeting at Berlin NW7 of IG officers concerned with the Austrian matter concluded on April 19 that "neither the Party nor the authorities in Germany proper and in German Austria have any fundamental objection to our long-cherished plan of uniting the chemical industry of Austria. . . . However, we cannot count on the next few weeks bringing us the necessary authorizations." For the present, IG would concentrate on buying all the shares of Skoda-Wetzler, inserting its personnel in the management of the Austrian companies, and increasing its control over DAG of Bratislava, which owned two of the firms slated to merge with SWW.[24] The new Law for the Defense of the Austrian Economy, promulgated on April 26, eased restrictions on German firms in Austria, but the establishment of new companies and plants remained dependent on the approval of Statthalter Seyss-Inquart.[25]

IG's prospects deteriorated suddenly in early May. Walter Rafelsberger, the Austrian state commissar for private enterprise, wanted assurances that IG would employ Austrians in the leading posts of the new concern and undertake a considerable investment program. Suspicious of the combine's intentions, he appointed government commissars to take over the management not only of SWW but also of the Austrian possessions of IG.[26] "Considering the antagonism within Germany toward the IG in some Nazi circles," Ilgner thought this interference with Farben's operations a dangerous precedent.[27] Almost as troubling was Guenther Schiller's embroilment in disputes with the authorities in Vienna, which jeopardized the SWW negotiations. Hence, Heinrich Gattineau, the head of the Wipo office and an old acquaintance of one of Rafelsberger's aides, was sent to Vienna to replace Schiller and aid Ernst Fischer, IG's agent in the SWW transaction. Before departing from Berlin, Gattineau obtained the approval of

---

[23] NI-4024/29, Haefliger and Krüger to Keppler, 9.IV.38, as reprinted in *NMT*, vol. 7, pp. 1404–6.
[24] NI-6070/45, Special meeting on Austria of the KA, 19.IV.38, excerpted in *NMT*, vol. 7, pp. 1407–8; see also Haefliger's affidavit, NI-8456/70, 1.V.47.
[25] Schausberger, *Rüstung in Oesterreich*, p. 30.
[26] NI-2798/20, Oesterreich Bericht für die Vorstandssitzung am 21. Oktober 1938, 19.X.38. Rafelsberger was a returned Austrian Nazi emigré; see NI-11090/91, his affidavit of 23.IX.47.
[27] NI-8456/70, Haefliger affidavit, 1.V.47.

Bergmann, the Reich Economics Ministry officer in charge of Austrian matters, for the acquisitions. In Vienna, Gattineau established contacts with Rafelsberger, Keppler, and Seyss-Inquart. He also mobilized Hermann Neubacher, the new mayor and a former employee of Berlin NW7, in IG's behalf.[28] A worried Ilgner arrived on May 10 and spent the next few days smoothing over "personal discords." By the thirteenth, he had persuaded Rafelsberger to withdraw the authority of the government commissars, both Austrian Nazis of long standing, on the conditions that IG appoint them to management posts in Austria and make no personnel changes in its Austrian plants without Rafelsberger's consent.[29]

On May 24, IG fell in behind the Nazi seventeen-point program for Austria in a letter to Rafelsberger seeking his sanction for the purchase of Skoda-Wetzler and its merger into the Donauchemie AG. The concern promised large expansion in the output of at least eleven important chemical products, pointing out that without its aid the Austrian chemical industry could not meet "the demands made by the armaments industry and the Four Year Plan." In addition, IG stressed that the high cost of transporting heavy chemicals made increased production in Austria essential "in order to work Southeast Europe intensively."[30] Within ten days, the proposal was approved.[31] However, IG decided to insure itself against a repetition of its May crisis. "For special reasons," it retained Dr. Walther Richter of the Reichsstatthalter's office "for legal advice" at a monthly fee of 1,000 reichsmarks,

---

[28] NI-8578/70, Affidavit by H. Gattineau, 2.V.47; NI-6649/50, Affidavit by M. Ilgner, 30.IV.47; Heinrich Gattineau, *Durch die Klippen des 20. Jahrhunderts* (Stuttgart, 1983), pp. 154–9. At the time of the Anschluss, Gattineau was on a trip to South Africa; Gattineau I/28, Affidavit by H. Croon, 30.XI.47. On Neubacher's Austrian career, see Radomir Luza, *Austro-German Relations in the Anschluss Era* (New York, 1975) pp. 153–5; and Harry Ritter, "Hermann Neubacher and the Austrian Anschluss Movement, 1918–40," *CEH*, 8 (1975), pp. 348–69, which establishes that Neubacher owed his post, not to his Farben connection, but to the belief in the NSDAP that his one-time association with the Austrian SPD and its housing program for Vienna would appeal to the local unions. Scarcely a year after Neubacher's appointment, Gauleiter Bürckel launched a personal campaign against him, and one Knissel of Bürckel's staff managed to reduce Neubacher's role to a largely "passive" one; see Peter Hüttenberger, *Die Gauleiter* (Stuttgart, 1969), pp. 145–6.

[29] NI-4456/33, Frank-Fahle to the KA, 7, 12, and 16.V.38; NI-2798/20, Oesterreich Bericht für die Vorstandssitzung am 21. Oktober 1938, 19.X.38; Radandt, *JfW*, 7 (1966), pp. 184–5. By the beginning of 1939, IG managed to rid itself of one of these former commissars, K. O. Schiller (Bayer 13/25, Protocol of the meeting of the SOA, 8.XII.38).

[30] NI-9631/80, IG to Rafelsberger, 24.V.38, excerpted in *NMT*, vol. 7, p. 1411.

[31] NI-9624/80, Bilgeri to IG Farben, Berlin, 2.VI.38.

"debited to the intermediate account . . . for the cost of promotion of Donauchemie AG."[32]

Detailed examination of the Austrian factories soon indicated how great a concession IG made in promising to keep them running. Carl Wurster toured SWW's Moosbierbaum plant for two hours, judging it obsolete, poorly laid out, and badly situated. Most of the output either did not suit the concern's production program or could be fabricated more efficiently at IG's existing plants.[33] On July 1, a decree reducing Austrian chemical prices to German levels rendered SWW's commercial prospects even more "disagreeable" (unerfreulich).[34] IG's Profitability Examination Section therefore concluded that only a doubling of the sales of SWW's Liesing plant could offset exceptionally high operating costs and that Moosbierbaum might just break even, assuming some shutdowns at the plant and an upturn in the Austrian economy.[35] Accordingly, Wurster sought consent from Gauleiter and Reichskommissar Bürckel to reductions in the plants. The best IG's emissary could obtain was permission to close Liesing, provided that the concern added an equivalent volume of production at its other Austrian works and either fully pensioned or transferred and housed Liesing's work force.[36]

No sooner had IG begun to count the costs of its Austrian objectives than the intervention of the Army Ordnance Office threw a new roadblock in the way of their acquisition. The sticking point was the Sprengstoffwerke Blumau AG, in which SWW owned 25% of the stock, two of its officers another 25%, and the Austrian state the remainder. Determined to assemble all the shares under government control, the German military insisted that IG obtain the privately held stock, sell it to the Reich, and guarantee raw material supplies and the technical aid of Troisdorf to the government's company. In September, IG complied, and an appropriate contract as well as the sale of SWW by the Creditanstalt to IG Farben were signed a few weeks later.[37]

[32] NI-9623/80, Mayer-Wegelin to bookkeeping department, Frankfurt, 22.VII.38.
[33] Hoechst TEA 2916, Notiz. Betreffend: Skodawerke Wetzler AG, Werk Moosbierbaum, undated (probably June–July 1938).
[34] Bayer D.A. 950, Aktennotiz für Dr. Kühne, 27.VI.38.
[35] Bayer D.A. 950, Aktennotiz by the Abteilung für Wirtschaftlichkeitsprüfung, 1.VII.38.
[36] Bayer D.A. 1427, Aktennotiz by Wurster, 28.VII.38.
[37] This account is based on NI-2798/20, Ilgner's Oesterreich Bericht für die Vorstandssitzung am 21. Oktober 1938, 19.X.38. IG paid 150% of the book value per

While the matter of the explosives plant was being settled, IG turned its attention to securing the two Austrian subsidiaries of the Dynamit Nobel AG of Bratislava. There was no question of resistance to the sale.[38] Not only did the Czech firm belong to IG through the German Dynamit AG of Troisdorf; the transaction offered both parties considerable profit. DAG of Bratislava carried the Austrian firms on its accounts at a very low book value. This ensured a low price, since sale of the plants at their real value would yield Bratislava so large a gain that Czech taxes would gobble about 66% of it. By July, in cooperation with DAG of Troisdorf, IG had agreed to pay Bratislava in twenty-five annual installments that coincided almost exactly with its yearly dividend to Troisdorf, against which they were written off.[39] This paper transaction obviated the transfer of scarce foreign exchange, which might have aroused opposition from the German government.

In its request to the Reich Economics Ministry on July 18, 1938, for a license to close this deal, IG apparently thought it necessary to justify the obvious advantages to the contracting parties. Arguing that the settlement was the best obtainable at the time, IG referred rather disingenously to the necessity of satisfying DAG of Bratislava in order to use its numerous holdings in Southeast Europe as "bases for our export policy." The document advocated consolidating the Austrian chemical industry in order to eliminate "unnecessary competition" and to facilitate "the development of the Austrian economy, its coordination with the armament plan and Four Year Plan, and the increase in cooperation with Southeast Europe." Approval came promptly; the protocol of the meeting of IG's Chemicals Committee on July 25 notes,

share for SWW, which came to 7.5 million marks (NI-7395/59, IG to Creditanstalt, 6.X.38).

38 Although the head of DAG, Bratislava, Dr. Erwin Phillipp, misunderstanding IG's defensiveness, doubted during the spring the commercial value of merging the companies (Hoechst TEA 2916, Report from Zentralbuchhaltung, 14.III.38). Moreover, IG did have to obtain the agreement of the Pester Ungarische Commerzialbank, the principal minority owner of DAG, Bratislava.

39 This paragraph relies on Bayer D.A. 1431, Gedächtnotiz über eine Besprechung am 2.VI.38 in Wien; NI-8588/70, Report of Mayer-Wegelin, 22.VI.38; NI-8349/68, Contract of 9.VII.38 between DAG, Bratislava and IG/DAG, Troisdorf; NI-9630/80, Frank-Fahle and Kersten to RWM, 18.VII.38; NI-8577/70, 54th meeting of the Chemicals Committee, 25.VII.38; NI-8633/71, Oral contract between DAG, Bratislava and IG/DAG, Troisdorf, 14.X.38: and NI-8632/71, Oral contract, n.d., between DAG, Bratislava and IG.

"We have purchased the stock of Carbidwerk Deutsch-Matrei AG, Vienna and Dynamit Nobel AG, Vienna."[40]

Formal transfer of the properties hinged on the outcome of a request from DAG of Bratislava to the Czech National Bank for permission to sell. In the aftermath of the Munich Conference, the bank refused to go along. Again IG had to appeal to state authorities, reiterating the importance of its project to German interests. In December, Terhaar and Kersten of Berlin NW7 asked Bergmann of the Economics Ministry to take up the matter with the Czech government, as "the tasks now assigned to these enterprises do not permit of their remaining under Czech influence."[41] Proceeding as if approval was forthcoming, IG, Skoda-Wetzler, and the two Austrian enterprises in question set up a joint corporation under IG's patronage on January 17, 1939.[42] After the occupation of Bohemia and Moravia in March, authorization of the sale by the new German satellite government of Slovakia seemed a foregone conclusion.[43]

Rafelsberger chose this moment to exact a final concession from IG. In late 1938, he and Gauleiter Bürckel began demanding the appointment of Nazi officials to the governing boards of Austrian corporations. Despite frequent protests to Berlin from the largest German parent firms and repeated efforts by the Reich Economics Ministry to curtail Rafelsberger's "aggressive maneuvering," some 350 corporations had bowed to the Party's wishes by March 1939.[44] Now Dr. Bilgeri, Rafelsberger's former adjutant, approached Gattineau about obtaining a seat on the *Vorstand* of Donauchemie. From Vienna, IG's Bernhard Buhl wrote to Kühne, the head of the combine's new Southeast Europe Committee, to express "the greatest hesitation about the plan," primarily because Bilgeri's salary demands "would put a heavy and unnecessary financial burden on the production corporation . . . [which] cannot bear any exaggerated expense and must work as cheaply as possible." In addition, in a veiled but unmistakable reference to the desire of IG's soberer businessmen to check Ilgner's empire

---

[40] NI-8577/70, 25.VII.38.
[41] NI-8586/70, 12.XII.38 and interoffice memo by Kersten, 13.XII.38; Bayer 13/25, 3rd meeting of the SOA, 18.II.39.
[42] NI-9625/80, Text of the protocol, 17.I.39; RG242/T83, Reel 88, Item 136, Frames 346810-28, includes numerous documents related to the execution of the protocol.
[43] The Slovakian National Bank approved on June 21; NI-8634/71.
[44] Luza, *Austro-German Relations*, pp. 211–13.

building and Party influence, Buhl ventured the reminder that "the acceptance of someone who has no closer connections with IG would strengthen certain tendencies to shift the control of the companies in Austria from Frankfurt and/or the Chemicals Committee to Berlin."[45] By return post, Kühne agreed, promising to "turn down the question completely."[46] Though Bilgeri's appointment was blocked, in June "in accordance with a request made at the last moment by Staatskommissar Rafelsberger, Herr Dipl. Kaufmann Weisshäupl, a member of the staff of Gauleiter Jury/Lower Danube" was among those elected to the *Aufsichtsrat* of Donauchemie.[47] Thus, the Party failed to insert a representative in the top management of the new company, but Nazi supervision of its operations was ensured.

On June 7, 1939, Deutsch-Matrei changed its articles of incorporation to conform to German law and elected an *Aufsichtsrat* drawn with one exception from that of Skoda-Wetzler, which on the same day renamed itself Donauchemie AG and chose an *Aufsichtsrat* "in accordance with the decisions of the Committee for Southeast Europe" of IG.[48] Nominally separate and led by an Austrian named Richard Riedl, who "enjoyed the highest respect within the Party," the two companies were actually run as a unit under Kühne from the Leverkusen plant and through Ilgner's control of credits from IG.[49] Complete merger was delayed by negotiations with the Finance Ministry for exemption from several potentially severe tax liabilities.[50] Not until the beginning of 1940 did most of the Austrian firms fuse formally into Donauchemie AG; Deutsch-Matrei came in only in December 1941.[51]

IG Farben had to pay a high price for increasing its share of Austrian chemical production from about a quarter in 1937 to just less than half.[52] The concern appointed Nazi officials to middle-manage-

[45] NI-14504/118, Buhl to Kühne, 20.III.39.
[46] NI-14505/118, Kühne to Buhl, 21.III.39.
[47] NI-9626/80, Mayer-Wegelin to SOA, 24.VI.39.
[48] Ibid.
[49] NI-8456/70, Haefliger affidavit, 1.V.47.
[50] Ibid; see also NI-9629/80, W. Richter's minutes of a conference with Mayer-Wegelin, 21.IV.39.
[51] Hoechst TEA 957, Report of the Chemische Revisions- und Treuhands GmbH on Donauchemie, 1941.
[52] Kühne II/61, Affidavit by K. Platzer, 9.IX.47. Ilgner IX/136, Affidavit by E. Hackhofer, 27.I.48, provides a much smaller, less believable estimate. Ilgner claimed after the war that SWW accounted for only 10% of Austrian chemicals production

ment and supervisory positions, a practice it resisted firmly in Germany proper, and acquiesced to Rafelsberger's demand for the right to veto all personnel changes. IG also sacrificed SWW's explosives plants, lest they stand in the way of title to the other chemical installations. Nor could Farben close most of the existing Austrian plants, as it probably would have had only economic factors been at work.[53] Instead, the state's insistence on constant or increased production demanded modernization of the factories, which led to a net loss for Donauchemie alone of nearly 225,000 marks in 1940.[54] Finally, complicated tax considerations and Nazi regulations for Austria forced the combine to maintain Donauchemie as a separate enterprise, although "this sort of concentration of power at the fringe of IG was a major preoccupation of the firm."[55]

If none of these concessions proved debilitating over time, neither did Donauchemie become Ilgner's springboard for his own and IG's influence in Southeast Europe. SWW added only minor holdings in two Romanian chemical companies to IG's stock portfolio, and DAG of Bratislava remained the preferred holding company for IG's Balkan participations. As for the plants within Austria, the discovery of oil fields near Vienna eventually made possible the development of a profitable high-octane airplane fuel at Moosbierbaum, alongside a successful new magnesium installation.[56] But the leaders of both works insisted on reporting to the heads of their respective Sparten, not to Donauchemie, and neither plant produced for export.[57]

This ironic outcome should not obscure the situation during the brief period surrounding the Anschluss. Only when the possibility of large-scale government investment underlined the need to keep the Austrian companies out of unfriendly hands and promised to offset the costs of indulging Ilgner's and the Reich's Balkan ambitions – only

(M892/10, 18.III.48, p. 9529), and Gattineau estimated SWW's share at 14% (*Klippen*, p. 159).

53 Kühne III/117, Affidavit by E. Haager, 10.III.48.
54 NI-9594/79, Annual report of Donauchemie to the *Vorstand* and *Aufsichtsrat* for the business year 1940. On the continuing losses of the Austrian subsidiaries, see Hoechst TEA 944, 957, and 2917a.
55 NI-8456/70, Haefliger affidavit, 1.V.47.
56 On Moosbierbaum's subsequent development, see Schausberger, *Rüstung in Oesterreich*, pp. 71, 75, 109; NI-305/4, Legal department file, September 1945; Bayer 13/25, 14th meeting of the SOA, 3.II.41.
57 Kühne III/117, Haager's affidavit, 10.III.48; NI-8456/70, Haefliger's affidavit, 1.V.47, pp. 17–18.

then did IG actively pursue a dominant position in the Austrian chemical industry.[58] The concern hoped that the Austrian properties would return a profit someday, but IG bought them for protection against economic competition and political intervention in an important branch of its business. To camouflage its fears, IG appealed to the authorities in terms of their interests. This response and its rationale became characteristic of Farben's conduct in Greater Germany.

The Sudetenland

Before the occupation of the Sudetenland in October 1938, IG Farben exercised greater technical than financial influence on the Czech chemical industry. It invested in three small firms and controlled three sales companies as well as DAG of Bratislava. That corporation held shares in four other Czech chemical enterprises, but with about two-thirds of its rather dilapidated plant lying idle, it earned profits of only 540,000 reichsmarks in 1938.[59] In contrast, the dominant Czech corporation, the Association for Chemical and Metallurgical Production, Aussig (Aussiger Verein), was the fourth largest chemical concern in Europe.[60] Its profits totaled 1.78 million reichsmarks in 1938, including the proceeds from its many domestic and foreign subsidiaries, and in the mid-1930s Aussig accounted for perhaps more than 60% of Czech

---

[58] Ibid., pp. 15–17; NI-8578/70, Gattineau's affidavit, 2.V.47; and Haefliger's testimony, NMT, vol. 7, pp. 1464–7. The same sorts of rationale led to IG's other Austrian acquisitions: a few small medical suppliers, an explosives-metal company, a group of mines in 1941 to safeguard raw material supplies for the magnesium plant, and four hundred gas stations in Austria purchased in 1939 from the Romanian firm Creditul Minier by the Deutsche Gasolin AG. See NI-303/4, Affidavit by H. Kugler, 12.VII.45; Bayer 13/25, Haefliger to Kühne, 24.I.41; Bayer 12/19, Niederschrift der 24. Vorstandssitzung, 5.II.41, pp. 5–6, and Notiz zu Punkt 5e, Vorstandssitzung am 30.VII.38; and G. Keiser, "Die Konzernbewegung 1936–1939," Die Wirtschaftskurve, 19 (1939), p. 224. IG also took 9.5%, later 14.5%, of the shares in a new oil exploration company, the Niederdonau Erdöl GmbH, founded in cooperation with the HGW; see Bayer 13/25, 3rd SOA meeting, 18.II.39, and NI-8266/68, 35th Vorstand meeting, 29.X.42.

[59] The three small firms are listed in Alice Teichova. An Economic Background to Munich (Cambridge, Engl., 1974), p. 294. DAG of Bratislava's holdings are detailed in NI-9593/70, Vowi 2543, 22.IX.37. On the firm's condition, see Gattineau V/81, Affidavit by K. Meyer, 30.I.48; for its profits, see Hans Radandt, "Die IG-Farbenindustrie AG in Südosteuropa 1938 bis zum Ende des Zweiten Weltkrieges," JfW, 8 (1967), p. 92.

[60] For an overview of its holdings, see Bayer 4C3, Vowi 3024, 28.VII.38, which contains a graphic representation, reproduced in Peter Hayes, The Gleichschaltung of IG Farben (Dissertation, Yale Univ., New Haven. Conn., 1982), Chart IV-3.

chemical production.[61] In the crash of 1929, control of the firm passed to an alliance of the Solvay & Cie of Brussels with 15.4% of the shares and the Zivnostenska Bank of Prague, which disposed of another 49%.[62] Although this alliance cooperated with Imperial Chemical Industries to squeeze IG out of the Czech explosives industry in 1931, it compensated the German concern with numerous cartel privileges in the Czech and Southeast European markets.[63] After 1934, increasing pressure on both the Verein and IG to export to eastern Europe placed them on a collision course, but the firms sought to avoid a confrontation.[64] IG's contribution to harmony included restricting the growth of DAG of Bratislava.[65] For the German combine, the stakes in the Balkans did not justify disrupting the stable international cartel system by seeking control over the Verein, especially while it had the backing of the British, French, and Belgian chemical giants.[66] Aside from a short-lived attempt by DAG of Bratislava to buy in early in 1937, when it seemed that British owners might withdraw, there is no trace of an IG interest in investing in the Verein before 1938.[67]

[61] Sasuly, *IG Farben.* p. 117; NI-1138/139, Vowi 4676, 17.VII.42: Teichova, *Economic Background*, p. 281; Bayer 84/Eur.-Tschechoslowakei, 2.2, p. F4. The Czech name of the firm is generally abbreviated as Spolek and that of its headquarters city is Usti nad Labem. For events before November 1938, I have used throughout the more common abbreviation Aussiger Verein for the complete German title, Verein für chemische und metallurgische Produktion, Aussig. Thereafter, in reference to that part of the firm not purchased by Germans, I have employed the new short German form, Prager Verein.

[62] Teichova, *Economic Background,* pp. 279–83.

[63] See ibid., pp. 287–9, 315–16, 321; and the same author's two articles, "Die deutsch-britischen Wirtschaftsinteressen in Mittelost- und Südosteuropa am Vorabend des Zweiten Weltkrieges," in Forstmeier and Volkmann (eds.), *Wirtschaft und Rüstung*, pp. 293–4, and "Internationale Kartelle und die chemische Industrie der Vormünchener Tschechoslowakei," *Tradition*, 17 (1972), pp. 151–6.

[64] One means to this end was the highly beneficial dye settlement granted Aussig by the Continental dye producers; see Bayer D. A. 183, Schnitzler and terMeer to Duisberg et al., 11.IV.34. See also RG242/T83, Reel 89, Frames 3462580-1, Diary of Weber-Andreä, 27.V.36, and Schröter in Teichova and Cottrell (eds.), *International Business and Central Europe*, p. 151.

[65] See Bayer D.A. 1431, Philipp to Weber-Andreä, 10.VII.35, in which the general director of the Bratislava firm protested this policy.

[66] For a list of the numerous conventions between IG and Aussig, see Bayer D.A. 183, Vowi 2000, 8.XII.36.

[67] See Teichova, *Economic Background*, p. 294. The small number of shares involved indicates that the stock dividend, not influence, was IG's goal. DAG of Bratislava apparently wanted to recover ground lost in the Czech chemical industry to Imperial Chemical Industries, namely, a 15.3% interest in Explosia of Prague, a subsidiary of the Aussiger Verein. The undeterminable British portion of the 35.65% of Aussig's scattered shares also momentarily attracted IG.

This situation changed when it began to appear as if the frontiers might. In March and April, the Anschluss touched off a widely publicized "avalanche of national feeling amongst the Sudeten Germans," culminating in Konrad Henlein's Karlsbad demands of April 24.[68] It required neither prescience nor inside knowledge of Hitler's intentions, but merely a look at a map and the newspapers, to conclude that the Sudetenland might be the next accretion to the Reich's territory. In June 1937, the Verein had moved its headquarters to Prague, but three-fourths of its production facilities remained concentrated around the predominantly German cities of Aussig and Falkenau.[69] If Germany occupied the Sudetenland, ownership of these plants might be lost; at least they would require considerable modernization to make up for the removal of Czech tariff protection. To insure against either eventuality, the Verein decided to involve IG. Antonin Basch, Aussig's director general, explored whether IG wished to exchange an unspecified number of Aussig shares for stock in DAG of Bratislava.[70]

From IG's point of view, Basch's offer was attractive but inadequate. If Germany absorbed Aussig's plants, nothing short of control over their disposition could protect IG's vital interests. Bereft of Czech tariff protection, the Verein would have to raise capital in order to improve the facilities and reduce unit costs to a competitive level. It would either sell stock to the largest foreign firms or, more likely, sell the plants to a German enterprise. Both outcomes could lead to a decline in IG's domestic market share; the second might create a powerful commercial rival to IG. Though Aussig's sales in Czechoslovakia and Germany in 1938 amounted to only 2% of IG's sales, they represented a considerably larger proportion of the concern's proceeds from organic and inorganic chemical products.[71] Worse, the Verein manufactured significant quantities of dyestuffs, the cornerstone of IG's industrial preeminence. Georg von Schnitzler later stressed that

---

[68] The British consul in Liberec, quoted in Christopher Thorne, *The Approach of War 1938–39* (New York, 1967), p. 56.

[69] NI-9632/80, Affidavit by J. Dvoracek, 12.VII.47. See also the map in Bayer 91/1, Vowi 3129, 18.X.38, reproduced in Hayes, *Gleichschaltung*, p. 316.

[70] NI-3981/29, Report by Haefliger of his conversations in Vienna, 6.IV.38, excerpted in Eichholtz and Schumann (eds.), *Anatomie*, p. 175; see also Haefliger's testimony, *NMT*, vol. 7, pp. 1474–5. Cf. NI-13556/111, Affidavit by A. Basch, 6.V.47.

[71] Calculated from NI-5194/38, Affidavit by G. von Schnitzler, 10.III.47, and Hermann Gross, *Material zur Aufteilung der I. G. Farbenindustrie Aktiengesellschaft* (Kiel, 1950), pp. 13–16.

"the main interest for the IG in this matter was the dyestuffs question. IG Farben could not and would not permit the company to pass to a third party, which would then be in a position to gain a foothold in this sphere of production."[72] As in Austria, the prospect of annexation transformed a property with which IG had reached a modus vivendi into a potential Trojan horse.

Accordingly, Paul Haefliger took the opportunity of his conversation with Keppler in Vienna on April 21 to sound out the likely response of German economic authorities to "the acquisition of influence in enterprises in Sudeten-Czechoslovakia."[73] Keppler approved in principle, so long as the costs were small, adding, however, that the economic outlook for Czechoslovakia was unfavorable. When the conversation turned to Aussig, with which Keppler did not seem particularly concerned, fear of competition from the Verein emboldened Haefliger to remark "that Aussig played a significant role in the Southeast and that it would not be enough to shut Aussig off from its market, because it would then intervene in our markets, which would mean conflict for us and a deficit in foreign exchange." The special committee of IG to which Haefliger reported on April 19 ordered "data explaining the significance of the 'Aussig' complex" readied immediately.[74]

In anticipation of a possible stock transaction with Aussig, IG acted to invalidate complaints from Party offices like those that had endangered the necessary government approval for its Austrian plan.[75] The sales subsidiaries in Czechoslovakia removed all but two non-Aryans from their staffs and gave notice of the termination of contracts at the end of the year with all firms owned by non-Aryans. Karl Seebohm, since 1935 IG's chief representative in Prague, reported these results to a meeting of sales organization leaders at Berlin NW7 on May 17, only a week after Ilgner's hurried firefighting mission to Vienna.[76] The gathering suggested other measures for bringing IG's

[72] NI-5194/38, Schnitzler's affidavit, 10.III.47.
[73] NI-3981/29, Haefliger's report, 6.IV.38; see also his testimony, NMT, vol. 7, pp. 1474–82.
[74] NI-9289/77, Meeting of 19.IV.38, NMT, vol. 7, pp. 1407–8.
[75] Similar complaints already had surfaced from Czech Nazis; see Kugler II/25, G. Kotschwar to Jacob Sprenger, Gauleiter in Frankfurt, 10.I.37, and II/26, R. Jung, Reichstag member, to Sprenger, 15.I.37.
[76] See Kugler II/24, Affidavit by K. Seebohm, 4.IV.38, excerpted in NMT, vol. 7, pp. 1575–6; NI-6221, Minutes of the conference on 17.V.38, NMT, vol. 7, pp. 1546–51; and Frank-Fahle's testimony, NMT, vol. 7, pp. 1566–74.

policy in Czechoslovakia into line with that of the Party, including locating Germans formerly employed by the Aussiger Verein and training other Sudeten Germans so that replacements for the Verein's Czech and Jewish managers would be on hand, if needed. However, during the summer nothing came of these ideas or of Basch's earlier inquiries.

No development better illustrates IG's desire to avoid a repetition of its experiences in Austria than the firm's efforts to preempt the appointment of commissars for the Verein's plants in the Sudetenland. On the day after Neville Chamberlain's first flight to Germany, the *Vorstand,* mindful of "the necessity of making quick decisions under certain circumstances and of already preparing those decisions now," appointed terMeer, Schnitzler, Kühne, and Ilgner as a special committee on the plants at Aussig and Falkenau.[77] Schnitzler and terMeer called at the Reich Economics Ministry on September 22, the morning after Czech President Benes gave in to the detachment of the Sudetenland, to apprise the permanent officers of IG's interest in the plants. They also nominated Dr. Wurster and Dr. Kugler as commissars to administer the factories pending a settlement of their status.[78] The maneuver was only a partial success. Kugler was assigned to the plant in Aussig, where he soon strove to allay Nazi doubts about IG by purging Czech and Jewish employees "under supervision of competent Party offices."[79] But the Sudeten Nazis balked at Wurster, preferring Dr. Josef Brunner, one of their own.[80] Nor did Kugler's appointment ensure for IG immediate or eventual control of the Verein's plants. As late as mid-October, the plans of the Reich Office for Economic Development foresaw Aussig continuing as an independent enterprise.[81] One may surmise that more than patriotic fervor induced IG on September 22 to donate 100,000 marks to Sudeten German organizations and on September 30 to place another half million marks at Hitler's disposal "for use in the Sudeten territory."[82]

[77] NI-15080/123, *Vorstand* meeting, 16.IX.38.
[78] NI-3721/27, Kühne to Schnitzler and terMeer, 23.IX.38, *NMT,* vol. 7, pp. 1415–16. See also Radandt, *JfW,* 8 (1967), pp. 97–8; Bayer D.A. 183, Brinkmann of the RWM to Schnitzler, 28.IX.38.
[79] NI-11264/93, IG to Regierungsrat Hoffman, RWM, 18.I.39. See also Kugler II/37, Kugler's final report as commissar, 26.V.39; and NI-11376/94, Prager Verein to personnel department, Aussig plant, 16.IX.47.
[80] NI-3721/27, Schnitzler to terMeer et al., 29.IX.38; Hoechst TEA 2911, Brinkmann of the RWM to Brunner, 28.IX.38.
[81] See BA Koblenz, R25/47, Ausbauplan Sudetendeutschland, 15.X.38.
[82] NI-2795 and NI-1318, *NMT,* vol. 7, pp. 591–3.

Immediately after the occupation, the Verein recognized that it could no longer direct the plants from Prague and should sell them. At least two German firms seriously challenged IG's claim to the Aussig-Falkenau works: the Chemische Fabrik von Heyden and Ruettgerswerke AG. In fact, during October, the Verein reached agreement in principle to sell to the Ruettgerswerke.[83] Heyden also made great progress, but through more important channels. In the spring of 1938, it agreed with the Wehrmacht Military Economic Inspectorate IV to begin hiring former employees of the plants who could keep production going for the army after Aussig and Falkenau were occupied. These men, commissioned as army officers, accompanied the German troops to Aussig in early October, only to find their importance diminished by the Economic Ministry's installation of civilian commissars.[84] Hence, Hugo Zinsser, a member of the *Vorstand* of the Dresdner Bank and of Heyden's *Aufsichtsrat,* arranged for Ferdinand Strubberg and Hans Jungel from Heyden's *Vorstand* to take their case to the ministry on October 6. Arguing that the Aussig production would now intrude on Heyden's market sphere, they complained that possession of the plants by another company would "threaten the existence of our firm and of its staff." IG posed a special danger, for Aussig would provide it with a base from which to conquer the chemical business in eastern Germany, the only section of the country in which it did not already predominate. As "one of the few large works with extensive production schedules which is still completely independent of IG Farbenindustrie," Heyden presented itself as the suitable counterweight to "the power hunger of the IG and the strengthening of its monopoly position." Jungel and Strubberg shrewdly undercut IG's position by offering an important concession: "Dyestuffs production at Aussig is not a vital necessity for the works. . . . We are prepared . . . to come to an agreement with IG whereby its interests in the field of dyestuffs, including the international field, will in no way be prejudiced."[85]

83 NI-9632/80, Affidavit by J. Dvoracek, former director of the Zivnostenska Bank and vice-president of the Aussiger Verein, 12.VII.47.
84 NI-9161/76, File notice by Ferdinand Strubberg of Heyden, 6.X.38, excerpted in Eichholtz and Schumann (eds.), *Anatomie,* Document 78, p. 191. See also NI-10402/86, File note by Jungel and Strubberg of Heyden, 13.X.38, excerpted in *NMT,* vol. 7, pp. 1420–2. For a list of the employees and a description of Heyden's business, see Bayer 91/1, Vowi 3129, 18.X.38.
85 NI-9161/76, Strubberg's file note of 6.X.38, and NI-4016/29, Jungel and Strubberg to RWM, 10.X.38, *NMT,* vol. 7, pp. 1417–19.

Aware of its unpopularity in the Economics Ministry and of the Dresdner Bank's formidable influence, IG sought a deal with Heyden. Schnitzler, terMeer, Kühne, Haefliger, and Ilgner met with Jungel, Strubberg, and Zinsser on October 13. They arrived at a possible compromise in the form of the purchase of the plants by a jointly owned company. IG would provide the technical management, thus protecting knowledge of its prized productive processes, and Heyden would conduct commercial matters, thus guarding its markets. From the new company each parent concern would "rent and administer exclusively those branches of manufacture which appear to be especially vital for it." Ilgner and Jungel agreed to inform Mulert of the ministry that agreement was in sight and to request that he "keep away, if not with finality, then for the present, other interested parties."[86] But Farben's representatives met with a cool reaction at the ministry that afternoon.[87] When negotiations resumed on October 19, Heyden set stringent conditions concerning exclusive rights to certain products, market shares for the production of others in which IG and Heyden competed, IG's payments for the color and dye manufacture, and management of the plants. With a few qualifications, IG accepted these demands the following day.[88]

In their joint petition for authorization to acquire the Verein's plants, IG and Heyden reiterated the rationales that had succeeded in IG's Austrian venture. They justified complete ownership rather than partnership with the Czech concern in order to prevent the leakage of technical secrets vital to the military economy and to weaken the rump Verein so that it would submit to German policy in the Balkans and "furnish its participations there as points of departure." Lest the Reich have second thoughts about the sale, IG and Heyden pledged to continue operations at the present level and pointed out that profits from Aussig's dye output to date had depended on provisions of the international dye cartel agreements that only IG had enough power to adjust appropriately. Because the German firms feared that Montecatini might obtain or Solvay increase holdings in the Verein, they requested a prompt response.[89]

[86] Hoechst TEA 2911, Schnitzler to terMeer, 8.X.38; NI-10401/86, Haefliger's memo on the meeting, 15.X.38, *NMT*, vol. 7, pp. 1423–4; NI-10402/86, Notes by Jungel and Strubberg on the meeting, 14.X.38, *NMT*, vol. 7, pp. 1420–2.
[87] Hoechst TEA 2911, Schnitzler to Kugler, 13.X.38.
[88] NI-13541/110, Ilgner and Kersten to Krauch, 26.X.38; cf. IG's proposals for the meeting in NI-10407/86. Schnitzler and terMeer to Jungel, 17.X.38.
[89] NI-13541/110, IG and Heyden to RWM, 21.X.38.

State Secretary Brinkmann conveyed the ministry's approval on October 26 and deputized the banker Zinsser to conduct the discussions in Prague on behalf of the Reich.[90] Zinsser pressed the Czechs hard. He disabused Jan Dvoracek, member of the *Vorstand* of the Zivnostenska Bank and vice-president of the Verein, of the notion that Ruettgers would receive permission to purchase the plants.[91] Zinsser also refused to include shares in DAG of Bratislava as part of the purchase price, to permit the Verein to maintain a minority holding in the new German company, and to pay in free currency rather than blocked reichsmarks redeemable only against purchases of German exports. Finally, the Verein had to concede that export quotas under international cartel agreements went with the plants rather than with the Verein's headquarters in Prague. While the Czechs struggled to moderate these terms, Zinsser persuaded Solvay & Cie, the Belgian parent, to advise acceptance.[92] Capitulation came on November 7 in a provisional agreement among IG, Heyden, the Dresdner Bank, and the Verein to sell the plants to a new German company, the Chemische Werke Aussig-Falkenau GmbH.[93]

The final contract, signed on December 7, 1938, embodied rather generous terms for the now-renamed Prager Verein. At 280 million Czech crowns, the price was far closer to the German offer of 200 million than to the 500 million suggested by the Czechs. However, the Czechs could keep some of the machinery of the plants, and the German firms accepted Dvoracek's request that they guarantee a minimum exchange rate of 24 million reichsmarks for the price.[94] IG and Heyden also undertook to pay over a large proportion of that sum in commodities at cost price in order to enable the Prager Verein to maintain its customers while building new plants. Most cartel restrictions on Czech production and domestic sales were rescinded.[95]

90 NI-13542/110, Brinkmann to Jungel, 26.X.38.
91 NI-9632/80, Affidavit by J. Dvoracek, 12.VII.47.
92 NI-13542/110, Zinsser to Mulert, 31.X.38; Kugler II/57, Memorandum by Ilgner, 1.XI.38; II/52, Zinsser to IG Vorstand, 8.XI.38.
93 NI-13543/110, Zinsser and Lüer to Mulert, 8.XI.38. The text of the agreement of 7.XI.38 is NI-10581/87. The new company leased the dye plants to the Teerfarbenfabriken Aussig GmbH, which IG owned through subsidiaries; see Hoechst TEA 921, report of the Deutsche Revisions- und Treuhands GmbH, TEWAG, 1939; NI-303/4, Affidavit by H. Kugler, 12.VII.45.
94 Kugler II/50, Affidavit by F. Strubberg, 11.III.48. In the end, Prager got almost 25 million reichsmarks (Hoechst TEA 2199, Zefi to terMeer, 26.V.39). On the calculation of the price, see NI-303/4, Affidavit by H. Kugler, 12.VII.45.
95 In fact, IG agreed to compensate the International Dye Cartel for Prager's new output by reducing Aussig's sales quota in Germany correspondingly. Moreover, IG

Having failed in its request for official permission to compensate the
Verein with a controlling interest in DAG of Bratislava, IG promised a
loan from that firm and further attempts to transfer some shares in it
to the Verein.[96]

Party and state oversight of the Aussig-Falkenau plants did not
cease with their sale. Brinkmann reserved the rights until December
31, 1943, to pass on any change in the 50/50 division of stock between IG and Heyden, to appoint a full member of the *Aufsichtsrat*,
and to participate in any reallocation of the plants among the partners.[97] Over IG's protests, he extended the period during which
Sudeten Germans could exchange stock in the Verein for shares in the
Chemische Werke Aussig-Falkenau until June 30, 1941.[98] Brinkmann
also refused to withdraw the commissars until February 28, 1939,
when permission was granted for the new firm to take over the factories.[99] Even then, the new owners could not wholly determine the
management personnel of their plants, since Behnke of the chemicals
section in the German Labor Front successfully intervened in their
decisions. Following complaints from the workers at the Falkenau
plant in late October, Josef Brunner had been removed as commissar.
He had won, however, the confidence of Heyden and IG as fast as he
lost that of his Nazi patron Konrad Henlein. When the companies
named Brunner plant manager at Falkenau on March 1, 1939, Behnke
protested that this action would arouse the work force and undermine
political confidence among the populace of the Sudetenland. The businessmen backed down hastily the following day, but Behnke forced a
delay in installing the successor designated by the firms because he had
been selected without consultation with the NSDAP and DAF. Brun-

favored recompensing the Verein for lost export sales under the quota during 1938,
even though ICI, the Swiss IG, and the French Dye Federation refused on the basis of
their discovery that Aussig had lied about its actual turnover when the quota was set
in the mid-1930s; see Kugler II/60, Minutes of the board of the Four Party Cartel,
21.VI.39.
[96] NI-1139/12, Notarized contract, letter of agreement, and file note, 7.XII.38;
Haefliger testimony, *NMT*, vol. 7, pp. 1474–82. The mechanics of the purchase are
laid out in Hoechst TEA 2911, Zinsser and Ansbach of the Dresdner Bank to
Chemische Werke Aussig-Falkenau GmbH, 8.II.39. The loan idea was abandoned in
February 1939 because DAG of Bratislava could not spare the funds (Bayer 13/25,
Protocol of the 3rd SOA meeting, 18.II.39).
[97] NI-13543/110, Brinkmann to Dresdner Bank, 10.XI.38; Hoechst TEA 2911, von
Hanneken of the RWM to the Chemische Werke Aussig-Falkenau, 24.II.39.
[98] NI-13543/110, Fischer and Kersten to RWM, 14.XI.38.
[99] Ibid. and NI-1445/14, Kugler to Schnitzler, 28.II.39.

ner was placed in "protective custody," and the supervisory boards of IG and Heyden withdrew his appointment at special meetings on March 8. That did not spare Schnitzler and Jungel a meeting with Henlein, after which Brunner went on vacation and then returned to Falkenau with a reduced title.[100] In the midst of this controversy, IG's Commercial Committee decided "that it would not seem expedient on the part of Farben to complain about the equalization payment of three million Reichsmarks imposed by the Reich Ministry of Economics upon the purchasers of Aussig-Falkenau."[101]

The evidence suggests that IG Farben acted in the Sudetenland to protect commercial interests menaced by the incorporation of new chemical works into the Reich and that IG responded to rather than directed German policy in the region. In the face of a direct challenge by other German firms, IG hastily deserted its initial, traditional, and complicated plan to protect itself by taking up Basch's offer of stock in the parent Verein and began to treat for the Sudeten plants themselves.[102] In doing so, the concern conceded the profits from much of the output at Aussig and Falkenau to a partner (Heyden), accepted interference in managerial appointments, made room on the supervisory board for a representative of the state, and submitted to a heavy monetary imposition – all in order to keep the dyes plants from becoming rival bastions.

Two other aspects of IG's behavior lend weight to this interpretation. First, the concern forswore the acquisition of numerous other Czech properties useful to its activities outside the dyestuffs field. For example, in October 1938, the manager of IG's light-metals production at Bitterfeld pointed out that the Aussiger Verein's ownership of 50% of the Salzbergwerk Neu-Strassfurt & Teilnehmer, an electrolysis enterprise in that city, "seems to me of essential interest for us."[103] But IG did not demand that the Verein sell this stock in 1938, and two years later the combine supported the drive of Kali-Chemie to

---

100 My summary of this matter relies on NI-1444/14, Schnitzler to members of the *Aufsichtsrat* of Chemische Werke Aussig-Falkenau, 2.III.39; NI-1443/14, Behnke to Schnitzler, 2.III.39; NI-1442/14, File note of meeting of Henlein, Köllner, Schnitzler, and Jungel, 11.III.39; and Kugler II/40, Mulert to Kugler, 15.XI.38.
101 NI-9289/77, 20th meeting of the KA, 10.III.39, *NMT*, vol. 7, p. 1427; Hoechst TEA 2911, Oberfinanzpräsident Dresden to Chemische-Werke Aussig-Falkenau, Dresden Office, 18.III.39.
102 Bayer D.A. 183, draft of Heyden/IG to RWM, 21.X.38.
103 NI-15198/123, Bürgin to Heider, 4.X.38.

purchase these shares.[104] Nor did IG contest either the Deutsche Solvay-Werke's claim to Aussig's Nestomitz affiliate or Schering AG's acquisition of assorted pharmaceutical companies in the Sudetenland.[105] Similarly, IG declined to acquire the mines and property in Brüx suitable for the production of synthetic gasoline and rubber, since the concern did not want to risk a clash with Hans Kehrl and Paul Pleiger, who preferred to assign the resources to the Hermann Göring Werke. Of course, in part this decision reflected IG's desire to refrain from new benzin production, but rubber was quite central to the concern's plans.[106] IG's only other acquisition in the Sudetenland, two hundred gas stations bought by the Deutsche Gasolin AG from the Brüder Zikmun AG of Prague, also represented an attempt to preserve an existing market position within the newly expanded Reich.[107]

Second, IG's relations with the Prager Verein after the occupation of Bohemia and Moravia continued to pivot on dyes production. In January 1939, IG offered to aid the recovery of what remained of the Verein in return for a specific concession: "The principal goal should be to see that the Verein either fully renounces the manufacture of tar dyestuffs or that it restricts its production to a small group of so-called big products."[108] Several common projects took shape in 1939–40, including the founding of a jointly owned synthetic fibers company by DAG of Bratislava and the Verein, but IG did not get its dyestuffs agreement.[109] Instead, the Verein applied the proceeds from the Aus-

---

104 NI-9289/77, 37th meeting of the KA, 12.XI.40, *NMT*, vol. 7, p. 1430.
105 Kugler III/57, Ilgner's memo of 1.XI.38; H. Holländer, *Geschichte der Schering AG* (Berlin, 1955), p. 67.
106 Hans Radandt, "Beteiligungen deutscher Konzerne an Unternehmungen in der Tschechoslowakei 1938 bis 1945," *JfW*, 10 (1969), pp. 164–5, makes light of this concession, arguing that IG decided that the facilities were unsuitable for the production of synthetic rubber and fuel. However, on 11.XI.38 terMeer received a report recommending the Brüx site for a buna plant (Hoechst TEA 863, Bericht über eine Studienreise in den Sudetengau, signed by Mack and Eisfeld) and wrote Brinkmann to suggest locating the third rubber plant in the northern Sudetenland (NI-4717, *NMT*, vol. 7, pp. 1552–4). Hans Kehrl, who also thought the resources suitable for both buna and benzin production, intervened against acquisition of the mines by one or many private firms; see Hans Kehrl, *Krisenmanager im Dritten Reich* (Düsseldorf, 1973), pp. 136–7.
107 Keiser, *Die Wirtschaftskurve*, 19 (1939), p. 224.
108 NI-15230/123, Schnitzler to Schlotterer of the RWM, 24.I.39.
109 See NI-303/4, Affidavit by H. Kugler, 12.VII.45; NI-5196/16, Affidavit by G. von Schnitzler, 18.III.47; Radandt, *JfW*, 8 (1967), pp. 98–9.

sig sale to an intensive modernization program, which extended to the construction of a dyes factory at Rybitvi capable of quadrupling the output of the lost plants.[110] At meetings in April 1939 and June 1940, IG's spokesmen conceded the Verein's right to produce dyes for the Czech Protectorate but warned emphatically against competition elsewhere with the German concern.[111] When the Czechs hinted that they intended precisely that, IG began building a syndicate of German firms, including Heyden, Ruettgerswerke, and Kali-Chemie, to take over and partition the Prager Verein.[112] By November, the group could claim the imprimatur of the Economics Ministry in order to intimidate Ernest Solvay and the Verein. This was a bluff, permitted by the ministry on the clear understanding that no real pressure on Prager's stockholders would be allowed.[113] The ruse succeeded, but even in defeat the Verein wangled concessions out of IG. In March 1941, the Rybitvi agreement fixed the Verein's dye production and export quota at a level 25% higher than that accorded Prager by the Aussig contract of 1938.[114]

This was IG Farben's last even qualified victory over the Prager Verein. Thereafter, relations between the two corporations turned on different issues, and more than once IG toyed with further takeover bids. However, Farben's stock ownership remained limited to the 2% achieved by the share exchange concerning Aussig-Falkenau in 1939–40. On July 30, 1941, the Economics Ministry put a stop for the duration of the war to attempts to purchase stock in the Verein or its subsidiaries and required purchases of shares in these companies from third parties to be deposited with a bank as trustee, pending a final decision by the ministry at the end of the war.[115]

110 See NI-1178/139, Vowi 3360, 31.III.39.
111 Bayer D.A. 183, Schnitzler and Kugler to the *Vorstand,* 8.V.39, including *Akten-notiz* by Kugler; Hoechst TEA 2915, *Aktennotiz* by Kugler and Giesler, 19.VI.40. IG's protests and the market-oriented reasons for them are clearly laid out in Hoechst TEA 2915, H. Kugler's Bemerkungen zu der Frage einer Verständigung mit dem Prager Verein auf dem Farbstoffgebiet, 7.I.41.
112 Bayer 13/25, 11th meeting of the SOA, 9.VII.40; Radandt, *JfW,* 8 (1967), p. 100; NI-9289, 37th KA meeting, 12.XI.40, *NMT,* vol. 7, pp. 1429–30.
113 See Radandt, *JfW,* 8 (1967), Anhang 3, pp. 139–41; NI-9289, 37th KA meeting, 12.XI.40, *NMT,* vol. 7, pp. 1429–30; Bayer 13/19, Schnitzler's remarks in Niederschrift über die 23. Vorstandssitzung am 12.XII.40.
114 NI-1278/13, 40th KA meeting, 18.III.41 (excerpted in *NMT,* vol. 7, pp. 1431–2); Hoechst TEA 2915, Text of the Rybitvi agreement, 15.III.41.
115 Bayer 13/25, Landfried and Kroll of the RWM to Ilgner, 30.VII.41.

Poland

On the eve of the Second World War, Farben controlled about 25% of a Polish dye market valued at approximately 20 million marks. Under the terms of the international dyes cartel, the Swiss and French accounted for another 45%. Though the foreign corporations filled their sales quotas largely through imports, two branch factories operated within the country. Of these, the larger at Pabjanice belonged to the Swiss CIBA concern and remained in its possession throughout the war; the smaller at Winnica near Warsaw was held ostensibly by the French Centrale des Matières Colorantes but in reality by that organization in secret equal partnership with IG's Swiss holding company, IG Chemie. Six native-owned Polish factories serviced the remaining third of the home market, but nearly all of their share fell to two firms: Boruta, the largest dye maker in Poland, most of whose stock was in the hands of the Polish State Agricultural Bank, and Wola, which was owned entirely by three Jewish families. Both companies survived by virtue of Polish tariffs and the cartel quotas. Altogether the stock capital of Winnica, Boruta, and Wola added up to about 3.2 million reichsmarks, the value of their output to some 6.6 million marks. In 1939, dyes amounted to perhaps 4% of Polish chemical production; Poland's portion of total world dye output came to about 1.3%.[116]

Aware that the Winnica, Boruta, and Wola plants were certain to be impounded by the invading German forces as the property of enemy instrumentalities or non-Aryans, IG Farben moved rapidly to head off potential problems and competitors.[117] At first, the combine worried only about the dyes stockpiled at the plants, lest their seizure by the army or offering on the open market cut into sales or drive down

---

[116] For details on the Polish firms and dyes trade, see NI-9151, NI-9154, and NI-9155, all of which are excerpts from Vowi 3609, 28.VII.39, *NMT*, vol. 8, pp. 4–6; NI-303/4, Report by Hans Kugler, 12.VII.45; Bayer 4C9.32, Control Office, *Dyestuffs*, pp. 11–16, 63–6; Schnitzler X/182, Contract between Boruta, Wola, and the continental dyes cartel companies, 19.XII.34; NI-2749, Schnitzler and Krüger to Mulert, 14.IX.39, *NMT*, vol. 8, p. 8; and Hermann Schwab's testimony, 29–30.I.48, *NMT*, vol. 8, pp. 36–42, 64–70. I have estimated market share from these documents and from Hoechst TEA 1082, Umsätze Farben und F. H. Produkte, 17.X.42.

[117] On the firm's motives in seeking control of the Polish plants, see NI-5196/16, Affidavit by G. von Schnitzler, 18.III.47; NI-8783/72, Affidavit by G. Kuepper, 10.VI.47; and NI-7367/59, Affidavit by A. Eckert, 13.VI.47. Their memories are substantiated by the remarks concerning Winnica in NI-1149, Wurster to Bürgin, 23.XI.39, *NMT*, vol. 8, p. 17.

prices.[118] But within two weeks of the Nazi onslaught, IG requested the economics minister to assign the three plants to the concern as trustee and nominated Hermann Schwab, the director of IG's dyes sales in eastern Europe, and Bernhard Schoener, the chief technical officer at IG's Wolfen plant, as joint managers. To strengthen its claim, IG stressed the military value of closing all the small Polish dyes factories, transferring Wola's output to Boruta, operating the latter as a partial substitute for the reduction ordered by the Reich of dyes output in the exposed Rhineland, and continuing Winnica's production of khaki for uniforms.[119]

On September 21, General von Hanneken's reply made clear that the ministry needed IG's expertise but would not entrust the factories to the concern. Though he accepted IG's plans for the use of the plants, he appointed Schwab and Schoener, not the combine, as trustees and delivered a stern admonition:

I reserve the right to alter or cancel this commission at any time and to settle the problem of management otherwise. I expressly emphasize that, through this commission, there will be no changes in the conditions of ownership of the plants concerned and that also no preparations for a change in the ownership conditions are to be seen in this appointment. In particular, no claim for a later change in the ownership conditions can be derived for the benefit of IG Farben through the appointment of members of IG Farben to the provisional management. As far as it is possible, the plants are to be operated with the present personnel and additional ethnic German personnel. The appointment of further employees of IG Farben – for the enterprise or for the administration of the plants – requires my special agreement in every case.[120]

Although throughout October and November officials of the various Sparten scouted numerous industrial facilities in Poland, recommending the closing of a number, IG's attentions remained focused on the dye plants. Now that the Reich had annexed the sites of Boruta and Wola and organized the remainder of German-occupied Poland, including the location of Winnica, into the entirely dependent Government General, the concern felt the need to create "a certain permanency of conditions" regarding these installations.[121] Accordingly, on

---

118 NI-8457, Schnitzler to Krüger, 7.IX.39, *NMT*, vol. 8, pp. 6–7; Schwab testimony, *NMT*, vol. 8, p. 75.
119 NI-2749, Schnitzler to Mulert of the RWM, 14.IX.39, *NMT*, vol. 8, pp. 7–10.
120 NI-1093, Hanneken to Schnitzler, 21.IX.39, *NMT*, vol. 8, pp. 11–12. Judging by Schwab's account, Hanneken gave such permission in perhaps a dozen cases; see *NMT*, vol. 8, p. 77.
121 NI-8330, Schnitzler and Krüger to Mulert, 10.XI.39, *NMT*, vol. 8, p. 21.

November 10, IG offered to found a holding company in Berlin to lease the three factories from the Reich for the accounts of the original owners. The combine promised to reflate the bankrupt Boruta company, close Wola, pay off all private creditors, and rent Winnica's most useful equipment for use at the Boruta site – all in return for an unspecified interest charge on IG's expenses (estimated at 3 million marks) and priority right of purchase, should the Reich decide to sell the plants upon expiration of the lease.[122] For seven months this proposal hung fire while official title to the installation was transferred to the new Main Trusteeship Office for the East and the trustees were left with the task of securing funds to operate the factories. Schwab and Schoener persuaded IG to advance more than a million marks in unsecured credits and purchases of intermediate dye products from the factories during this period. This sum, when added to Winnica's outstanding prewar debt to IG, meant that the concern possessed in mid 1940 a claim to about 1 million marks of the dye firms' collective assets.[123]

By June 1940 it was apparent that the combine could not indefinitely throw money away on the Polish plants and that the Trusteeship Office for the East could not bear the costs of running them. Therefore, the Reich authorized the appropriate leases of equipment from Winnica and Wola and invited IG to consider purchasing Boruta outright. The following month, IG submitted a draft sale agreement, and in September the concern proposed a price of 3.2 million marks.[124] The trusteeship office countered by demanding the full book value of Boruta as shown on its balance sheets, a round figure of 5 million marks. So long as neither side held a clear bargaining advantage, the negotiations dragged on.

Toward the end of the year, however, two new elements entered the picture and brought IG Farben to heel. First, the SS began to exercise its veto right over the disposition of the plants, a by-product of Him-

---

[122] Schwab testimony, NMT, vol. 8, pp. 52–3.

[123] Ibid., pp. 46–7, 66. On the latter page, the figure 503,000 is evidently a misprint. On the formation of the Main Trusteeship Office East, as well as the first outlines of the regime's economic plans for annexed and occupied Poland, see EC-410, Göring's directive to the Four Year Plan, 19.X.39, NMT, vol. 13, pp. 718–20.

[124] NI-8396, Schnitzler and Eckert to Economic Department of the Government General, 11.VI.40, NMT, vol. 8, pp. 23–4; NI-8397/69, Schnitzler and Eckert to the Economic Department of the Government General, 11.VI.40; NI-8378/69, Wola agreement, 11.VI.40; NI-2998, Schnitzler and Kuepper to Mahnke of the RWM, 10.VII.40, NMT, vol. 8, pp. 24–5; Schwab's testimony, NMT, vol. 8, p. 48.

mler's appointment as commissar for the strengthening of German nationhood. Second, and perhaps rather too coincidentally, the Gutbrod brothers, who operated a modest paint and dyes factory in Frankfurt and had "excellent connections with the SS," began seeking title to Boruta. Whether the brothers were in earnest or merely a device for shaking down IG, the concern saw them as, at best, inconvenient competition and, at worst, the entering wedge of the SS into the chemical field.[125] In January 1941, Schnitzler reported to the trusteeship office IG's willingness to comply with Himmler's expressed wish that the concern "do positive reconstruction and improvement" in the annexed territories, now styled the Warthegau:

I am authorized to confirm herewith my oral statement that IG Farben takes upon itself the obligation to invest, within the next five years, in the *Warthegau*, a total of at least five million Reichsmarks in addition to the purchase price of Boruta.

The corporation pledged not only to modernize the plant extensively, but also to take the annexed area into consideration "for any projects we may launch from time to time, as far as technical limitations permit." Hopeful that its accommodating attitude would be reciprocated, IG did not retreat from its price offer; Schnitzler merely dismissed the prevailing disagreement as "immaterial" and looked forward to a prompt resolution of the matter.[126] Although IG was permitted in January to buy equipment from Winnica and Wola for 72,000 marks, not until April did Himmler agree in principle to allocate Boruta to IG.[127] But the purchase price remained unsettled, and it required another mention of the delays occasioned by the Gutbrod brothers' requests before IG consented in July to the Reich's figure of 5 million marks.[128]

In early 1942, IG finally achieved its objectives in Poland. The

---

125 Schwab testimony, *NMT*, vol. 8, p. 48; NI-8385, File note by Dr. Kuepper, 9.V.41, *NMT*, vol. 8, p. 29; terMeer testimony, *NMT*, vol. 8, pp. 93–4; and NI-8319/68, Affidavit by E. Struss, 9.VI.47. On the early history of the Gutbrod dyes operation, see D. Warriner, *Combines and Rationalization in Germany, 1924–1928* (London, 1931), p. 170.
126 NI-1197, Schnitzler to Winkler, 16.I.41, *NMT*, vol. 8, pp. 25–8.
127 NI-8398/69, Eckert to Schwab, 12.I.41; NI-8382, Mahnke to Schnitzler, 23.IV.41, *NMT*, vol. 8, p. 28; Bayer 4C9.25, Mueller-Knieriem manuscript, pp. 203–5. Borkin, *Crime and Punishment*, pp. 98–9, traces this decision to an alliance between IG and Himmler, for which he provides a false source.
128 NI-8385, File note by Dr. Kuepper, 9.V.41, *NMT*, vol. 8, p. 29; NI-806, Schnitzler to SS General Greifelt, 19.VII.41, *NMT*, vol. 8, p. 30.

concern became the sole owner of Boruta, renamed the Teerfarben-
werke Litzmannstadt (Lodz) GmbH, on the conditions that realiena-
tion of the firm, sales of stock, cessation of work, and the introduction
of new partners all required advance approval by the authorities.[129]
Almost simultaneously, IG obtained clear title to Winnica by adding
the 50% of its stock held by IG Chemie of Basel to the other half
purchased seven months earlier from the French for the full price at
book value of 1 million marks.[130] Schwab and Schoener were formally recalled as trustees in July 1942.[131] Winnica ceased operation at
the end of the year, when the abolition of tariffs for the Government
General and the introduction of the German price level destroyed the
factory's already limited profitability.[132] IG never purchased the Wola
plant, which was officially seized from its Jewish owners in September
1942 and sold by the state for scrap metal.[133]

IG's conduct in Poland followed a now-familiar pattern. The firm
confined its activities almost wholly to the dyes field, making but three
other, comparatively minor takeovers: a French coal mine near Auschwitz, an oxygen plant at Wyrow of indeterminable ownership, and
40% of the stock in another oxygen factory in Poznan (Posen), which
had been seized from the Polish state by the city government and
handed over to one Baron von Hahn.[134] IG did not challenge the

[129] NI-6831/53, Notarized contract between Mahnke as trustee and Schnitzler and
Kuepper for IG, 12.I.42; NI-6830/53, Winkler to IG, 10.II.42; NI-6935/53,
Weisskar and Balufelder to the governor of the Warthegau, 18.II.42.
[130] Schwab testimony, NMT, vol. 8, p. 68; NI-6941, Schnitzler and Eckert to Scheidt-
mann of the RWM, 1.VIII.41, NMT, vol. 8, pp. 31–2; NI-5195/38, Schnitzler
affidavit, 17.III.47. The agreement with the French dyes group, signed by terMeer,
is in NI-6832/53, Schwab to Hirzowski, 27.X.41.
[131] NI-8389/69, Althoff to Schwab, 8.VII.42.
[132] Schwab testimony, NMT, vol. 8, pp. 68–9.
[133] NI-8388/69, Order of the governor of the District of Radom, 16.IX.42; NI-5196/16,
Schnitzler's affidavit, 18.III.47. Between 1939 and 1942, the trustees of Wola paid
the principal owner, Maurice Szpilfogel, the miserable, but legally prescribed sum of
500 zloty monthly, minus rent on his house in the Warsaw ghetto, owned by the
factory. On this matter and Szpilfogel's remarkable survival of the war, see
NI-707/7, Szpilfogel to Schnitzler, 16.I.41, Schnitzler to Schwab, 24.I.41, and
Schwab to Schnitzler, 27.I.41; and NI-10416/86, Affidavit by M. Szpilfogel,
25.VIII.47.
[134] NI-15107, 14th Vorstand meeting, 8.XI.39, NMT, vol. 8, pp. 19–20; NI-1149,
Wurster to Bürgin, 23.XI.39, NMT, vol. 8, pp. 14–19; NI-303/4, Kugler's report,
12.VII.45. On the importance of the oxygen to IG, see the discussion of Alsace-
Lorraine below. The concern also purchased machinery from various plants seized
by the German government (NI-6064/45, Invoices, 12.XII.40, and Hoechst TEA
255, Konsortialvertrag/Debica, 10.XII.40). IG also sought but seems not to have
obtained another oxygen plant at Eichenau (NI-14738/120, File note of conversation between representatives of IG and Lindes Eismaschine, 23.VIII.40). Cf.

assignment of the Polish nitrogen and explosives plant at Sarzyna to another firm, the allocation of the nitrogen plant at Chorzow to the German state's holding company, Vereinigte Industrieunternehmung-en AG (VIAG), and the distribution of several heavy-chemicals firms in Upper Silesia among various German companies.[135] Of the eighteen largest chemical enterprises in Poland, Farben took an interest in only one – Boruta – and it ranked seventeenth.[136] To retain as much as possible of its monopoly on the German dyes business, already dented by the presence of the Swiss factory, IG paid an extraordinarily inflat-ed price. The total of trusteeship costs, purchase prices, and guaran-teed investments came to more than 12 million marks, nearly four times the stock capital of the three dye companies, nearly six times that of Boruta and Winnica. Assuming a German victory and postwar sales in the Warthegau and Government General at least equal to those in prewar Poland, the payback period on this outlay was likely to be long, perhaps a decade or more. A measure of security from private and public interlopers is all IG achieved in Poland, for Boruta operated at a loss throughout the war, and pressure on the concern to shift its production eastward did not let up.[137]

Alsace-Lorraine

Although the armistice of June 1940 forbade changes in the German–French border pending a peace treaty, the Reich made clear during that summer its intention to annex Alsace-Lorraine. Each of the neigh-boring German *Gaue* incorporated one of the provinces, the customs boundary of 1871 was restored, all place names were Germanized, most appreciable French and foreign-owned businesses were expropri-ated, and German economic legislation, regulations, and currency

NI-4860/36, TEA meeting of 13.XI.40, which suggests that the concern may have taken another oxygen plant.

135 Schwab testimony, *NMT*, vol. 8, p. 71; NI-5195/38, Schnitzler affidavit, 17.III.47; see also Berthold Puchert, *Dzialalnosc Niemieckiej IG Farbenindustrie W Polsce* (Warsawa, 1973), pp. 196–7, 203–4. By 1940, however DAG of Troisdorf held three explosives plants around Kattowitz (NI-10030/82, Organization chart of DAG, Troisdorf).

136 See the list in BASF T52/15d, Vowi 3609, Die wichtigsten Chemiefirmen in Polen, 28.VII.39, p. 2.

137 Schwab stated that IG's total loss on the Boruta plant from 1939 to 1944 came to more than 1.2 million marks (*NMT*, vol. 8, p. 50). RG242/T83/87, Reports of the Chemie Revisions- und Treuhand GmbH for 31.XII.42 and 31.XII.43 give total losses for 1941–3 alone as more than 1.3 million marks.

were introduced.[138] In September 1940, Gustav Schlotterer of the Economics Ministry told German industry to treat Alsace-Lorraine as if it were part of Germany.[139] IG Farben promptly began integrating parts of the captured chemical industry into the existing power balance among German producers. Though events proceeded on the whole more smoothly than in Austria, the Sudetenland, and Poland, IG's efforts did not go unchallenged.

Of the forty chemical works listed in the Vowi office's report of July 1940 titled "The Most Important Enterprises in the Chemical Industry in Alsace-Lorraine," only two, both primarily coal tar dyes plants, touched IG's monopoly interests. Five others impinged on the concern's commercial conventions with various German firms. Three of these occupied factories manufactured liquid oxygen, the German market for which was divided between IG and Lindes Eismaschine. Another of the plants turned out titanium products, and the fifth was an electrolysis operation; in Germany, IG dominated both fields in cooperation with several other companies, the most notable being Kali-Chemie.[140] All the parties to these market agreements shared an interest in filling the vacuum resulting from the sequestration of the factories, particularly in the case of the oxygen works, since IG and Lindes could not keep up with the military demand for the gas in welding.[141]

The takeovers of the dyes, titanium, and electrolysis plants proved easiest to accomplish. All four installations were under IG's control by April 1941. Sometime shortly after the confiscation of the Société des Produits Chimiques et Matières colorantes de Mulhouse, a producer of dyes and related products owned in four equal shares by three French chemical companies and a Parisian bank, IG approached the Civil Administration of Alsace concerning the property. The result was an indefinite lease for the plant at an annual rate of 66,000 marks, outright purchase of the supplies stored there for a cash payment, and a promise of sale at the present book value "as soon as the general

---

[138] Norman Rich, *Hitler's War Aims*, vol. 2: *The Establishment of the New Order* (New York, 1974), pp. 231–5.
[139] Aktennotiz von G. Schlotterer, 16.IX.40, quoted in Eichholtz, *Geschichte*, vol. 1, p. 307.
[140] See Bayer 91/1, Vowi 4080, Die wichtigsten Unternehmungen des chemischen Industrie Elsass-Lothringens, 23.VII.40.
[141] NI-8581/70, Affidavit by Mayer-Wegelin, 5.VI.47; NI-10747/89, Affidavit by W. Hoyer, 11.IX.47.

legal regulations or general official decrees allow."[142] When these conditions were fulfilled two years later, IG bought the plant, now known as the Mülhauser Chemische Werke GmbH, for 835,581 marks, which the Reich, not the original owners, pocketed.[143] Simultaneously with the lease agreement, IG completed purely private negotiations with Armand Roesler of Basel, the owner of the Société pour l'Industrie Chimique, Mulhouse-Dornach. In return for 1.02 million marks in cash, the concern acquired 51% of the stock in a new company formed to manage Roesler's Alsatian dyes and gases plant.[144] Finally, the Reich acceded to a pact by which IG and Kali-Chemie partitioned the plants at Thann. IG took the electrolysis facility, and Kali received the titanium works on the conditions that it produce according to IG's processes and sell only to Farben.[145] Once again, the French owners were forgotten.[146]

Minor but revealing difficulties arose in connection with the three oxygen factories. Beginning in July 1940, the Vereinigte Sauerstoffwerke (VSW), an equally owned subsidiary of IG and Lindes, sought to take over the abandoned plants of Air Liquide, Strassbourg-Schiltigheim and Oxhydrique Francaise, Metz-Diedenhofen.[147] Before the Versailles treaty the Schiltigheim plant belonged to Griesheim, one of IG's constituent firms. As in the case of the Polish dye factories, the

---

[142] NI-8483/70, Lease agreement between IG and A. Braun, commissar for the plant, 8.V.41.

[143] NI-8482/70, Sales contract between Fritz Morstadt for the Reich and Kuepper and Eckert for IG, 14.VII.43. Interestingly, the price was slightly higher than that anticipated in the lease of 1941. The figure was arrived at by IG and the Chemie Revisions- und Treuhand GmbH of Berlin. Apparently IG hoped to close down the plant after the war (NI-11252/93, IG's New Order plan for France, 3.VIII.40).

[144] NI-303/4, Kugler's report, 12.VII.45. The sale was concluded on 12.VIII.41, but the minutes of the Expanded Dye Committee meeting, 17.IV.41, show IG integrating the plant's operations with those of the Mulhouse factory in early April (NI-4847/35). The Dornach transaction played no part in the postwar trial of IG's executives. Roesler retained the minority holding and complete title to the Société's other plant in Vichy France. In NI-8319/68, an affidavit dated 9.VI.47, Ernst Struss referred to the Dornach plant as one of those IG acquired in order to prevent a competitor from getting them.

[145] Bayer 12/19, Unsigned memo for discussion at the 25th Vorstand meeting, 25.IV.41. These transactions also did not come up at the postwar trial.

[146] According to ibid., French companies had held 43% of the stock in the titanium firm, which in turn owned a majority in the electrolysis facility. IG's reports assign the majority share of the parent firm to nameless private Frenchmen, but R. Stern, "Fritz Haber," Leo Baeck Institute Yearbook, 8 (1963), note 8, p. 81, mentions that a Jew named Joseph Blumenfeld owned the company. Here, then, may be one of the cases in which IG took advantage of Aryanization.

[147] Bayer 4C9.25, Mueller-Knieriem manuscript, pp. 169–70.

local Nazi administration directed IG to finance operations and some new construction at the works while negotiations over a leasing agreement proceeded. This resulted in expenses equal to the value of the property. When the state also demanded a share of the factory's profits as part of the lease agreement, VSW apparently complied but began lobbying for outright purchase.[148] Not until January 1944 did the Reich agree, charging 228,548 marks for the installation.[149]

At Diedenhofen, IG's problems were political, not financial. As early as November 1940, the chief of civil administration in Lorraine told a representative of VSW that an "unfortunate" circumstance obstructed the granting of a lease:

... in so far as this lease contract effects the first transfer of a factory of Lorraine, to IG of all people, the biggest German concern . . . the civil administration chief might be accused of favoring the large concerns. . . . It would be best to entrust factories of Lorraine to smaller German firms first.[150]

Shortly after this meeting, resistance to IG's claim stiffened with the arrival from the Main Trusteeship Office for the East of "a lawyer named Gmelch," who wanted to have the plants remain under the authority of a commissar unconnected to the concern.[151] Although the intercession of Carl Wurster of IG with the local *Gauleiter* produced official permission for VSW to lease Diedenhofen, Gmelch dragged his feet.[152] He refused to designate IG as the ultimate recipient of the property and demanded that VSW submit annual balance sheets or statements of returns on the plant to the authorities.[153] IG distrusted the motives for such a stipulation but knuckled under, and a four-year lease was signed at the end of February 1941.[154] VSW never acquired title to the plant.[155]

---

[148] Ibid., pp. 233–5.
[149] NI-8358/68, Contract of sale signed by Schuelz for the Reich and Lersner for IG.
[150] NI-8360/68, Memo by P. Pfeil, 18.XI.40.
[151] NI-8165/67, Verkaufsgemeinschaft Chemikalien to Wurster, 27.XII.40.
[152] NI-8164/67, Barth to Wurster, 13.I.41; NI-8157/67, Memo of conversation with the civil administrator for Lorraine, 21.I.41; NI-8163/67, Mayer-Wegelin to chief of Civil Administration for Lorraine, 22.I.41.
[153] NI-8162/67, Gmelch to IG, Frankfurt, 7.II.41.
[154] NI-8161/67, Bookkeeping department to Ludwigs, 15.II.41; NI-8372/69, Lease agreement, 25.II.41. Meanwhile, IG proceeded as if it already controlled Oxhydrique's second plant at Merlenbach; see NI-4860/36, TEA meeting of 13.XI.40.
[155] *NMT*, vol. 7, p. 1147.

Russia and the Baltic states

In the conquered portions of the Soviet Union three special circumstances intensified IG Farben's usual determination to control the goods, manufacturing processes, and equipment of captured plants vital to its production program. In the first place, Russia accounted in the late 1930s for 8.7% of the value of world dye production, or more than four times the corresponding figure for the Austrian, Czech, and Polish dye plants combined. Moreover, Soviet dye consumption exceeded Germany's and was worth much more than half of IG's sales proceeds within the Reich.[156] Given the state of IG's dyes business, securing this productive capacity was essential, even though the fate of demand within the Soviet Union was uncertain. Second, the extensive Russian chemical industry included at least six synthetic rubber factories, makers of the product in which IG invested more than a billion marks of its own funds under the Nazis and much of its hope for the future.[157] In light of the drawn-out and disharmonious discussions with the regime concerning buna in the mid-1930s and the uncertain prospects of the huge plant under construction at Auschwitz (see Chapter 8), IG could not confidently trust to fate to deliver it these vital installations. Such uncertainty was reinforced by the third peculiar feature of the Russian occupation: the government's decision to declare nearly all captured factories the property of the Reich at least until the end of the war and to entrust them, not to single German firms, but to state-controlled consortia, known as trusteeship companies, or *Ostgesellschaften*.

The *Ostgesellschaften* scheme attempted to reconcile the interests of the several factions and offices that competed for authority over economic policy in the occupied East. Split over the ultimate nature of German rule in Russia and over questions of expediency and timing, all these groups shared, albeit to various degrees and for different reasons, an opposition to the automatic expansion of private German corporations into the conquered lands.[158] Alfred Rosenberg, head of

---

[156] Bayer 4C9.32, Control Office, *Dyestuffs*, pp. 11–17.
[157] Ambros testimony, *NMT*, vol. 8, pp. 292–3; Hoechst TEA 2920, Vowi 4212, Die chemische Industrie der Sowjetunion, 6.XII.40, pp. 20–1.
[158] See Alexander Dallin, *German Rule in Russia 1941–1945* (New York, 1957), chaps. 1, 2, and 18.

the new and largely impotent Ministry for the East, stood apart from his colleagues only insofar as he stressed the political advisability of conciliating the Ukrainians and a few other ethnic groups. That policy could only suffer by the presence of acquisitive German businessmen. With regard to other areas, he joined the Party ideologues who took their cue from Hitler's writings, envisioning a deindustrialized Russia transformed into the agricultural and biological seedbed of the Thousand Year Reich. To such men, indispensable industrial or commercial functions ought to be reserved for German veterans or managed according to the view expressed by the German Labor Front that "colonial exploitation by private capitalist companies . . . would lead to a maldistribution of profits and benefits within the master nation. . . . [T]he State should take colonial utilization into its own hands as a monopolist in certain key branches."[159] In contrast, Göring and his supporters in the army and the Economics and Finance Ministries kept their eyes on Russia's usefulness in solving certain present, concrete problems. They intended to exploit Russian agriculture, industry, trade, and mining to the maximum advantage of the German war effort and even to retire the German war debt by accumulating vast "sluice profits" (Schleusengewinne) on the discrepancy between low production costs in the subjugated areas and high sales prices in Europe.[160] Achieving these objectives required forbearance by Göring's more radical Party colleagues, assistance from German business in reviving production, and much firmer central coordination of that assistance than had prevailed in the regions heretofore conquered by Germany. The Ostgesellschaften were designed to satisfy these preconditions by being temporary, privately owned, and directed by the government. They were a means of preventing a free-for-all among German corporations and of keeping the Reich's options open.[161]

---

[159] Quoted in ibid., p. 382; NI-8453/70, File note by Lohse, Reichskommissar for the Ostland, of a conversation with Neumann and Fischer, 16.IX.41. On the army's desire to reward demobilized soldiers in the East, see Rolf-Dieter Müller. "Industrielle Interessenpolitik in Rahmen des 'Generalplans Ost,'" MM, 28 (1981), pp. 103, 115–17.

[160] See Dallin, German Rule, pp. 38–9, 305–10, 392–3; and Roswitha Czollek and Dietrich Eichholtz, "Zur wirtschaftspolitischen Konzeption des deutschen Imperialismus beim Überfall auf die Sowjetunion," JfW, 9 (1968), pp. 154–64, 175–9. The relevant planning documents are collected as NI-10119/83.

[161] See Horst Boog, Jürgen Förster, Joachim Hoffmann, Ernst Klink, Rolf-Dieter Müller, and Gerd R. Ueberschärr, Der Angriff auf die Sowjetunion (Stuttgart, 1983), pp. 943–4, for a similar conclusion.

At the outset of Operation "Barbarossa," Göring sought to reassure business about these arrangements by announcing

that the Trustee administration, which is interconnected with strong State supervision, does not represent the final solution. It must be endeavored, at an earliest possible date, to lease the enterprises to German and . . . to local entrepreneurs. . . . The system of collective economy shall, therefore, be continued only as long as it is absolutely essential to avoid disruption in the supply of the German Army and economy from the Russian territory.[162]

Only after mid-1942, under the pressure of mounting military needs and administrative chaos, did individual firms become trustees of specific factories for the Reich.[163] However, neither individual nor collective trusteeship guaranteed the "reprivatization" of Russian plants. Indeed, the terms governing the establishment of the Kontinentale Oel AG, the first of the *Ostgesellschaften* and the only one founded as a permanent productive enterprise, belied Göring's soothing phrases.

Although the impending invasion of Russia doubtless contributed to the regime's decision to erect this new fuel company, no mention was made of the Soviets at an exploratory meeting in Berlin during January 1941 between officials of the Economics Ministry and four of the principal German banks, which were asked to participate in the undertaking.[164] Instead, State Secretary Neumann explained the desirability of constituting a holding company "that would merge all foreign petroleum interests in the areas which have recently come into the German sphere," exclusive of those participations already owned by the German firms that would hold shares in the new corporation. As the first takeovers, Neumann mentioned two French and Belgian corporations operating in Romania, another Balkan company owned by the Reich's Wifo organization, and the Hungarian oil fields IG Farben was seeking to acquire from Standard of New Jersey. But he reserved to Kontinentale the right to pass on any further oil acquisitions abroad by the subscribing German companies.

---

162 Dallin, *German Rule*, pp. 174–5, 381–3; NI-3777/27, Göring's decree of 27.VII.41, *NMT*, vol. 13, pp. 850–1.
163 Dallin, *German Rule*, pp. 383–4; Rich, *Hitler's War Aims*, vol. 2, pp. 36–42. On the motivations behind the trusteeship system, see Oster II/42, Affidavit by A. Hoffman, former chief of the chemicals section of the RWM, 26.II.48.
164 This and the following paragraph rely on NI-10797/89, File note by Hermann Abs of the Deutsche Bank, 23.I.41, reprinted in Roswitha Czollek and Dietrich Eichholtz, "Die deutschen Monopole und der 20. Juni. Dokumente zu Kriegszielen und Kriegsplanung führender Konzerne beim Überfall auf die Sowjetunion," *ZfG*, 1 (1967), pp. 66–8. Cf. Czollek and Eichholtz, *JfW*, 9 (1968), pp. 152–3.

The entire scheme was in reality an attempt to establish a sister corporation to the Hermann Göring Werke and its Sudeten synthetic fuel subsidiary, the Sudetenländische Treibstoffwerke, Brüx. This was apparent from the government's proposals for apportioning the stock and seats on the boards of the new corporation and for raising the 120 million marks it would probably need. In fact, Neumann signaled the parallel by revealing Göring's preference for Walther Funk as chairman of the supervisory board in the hope that his presence would "avoid disputes like those which emerged on the foundation of the Hermann Göring Werke." The complete board would consist of eleven deputies of the banks and subscribing corporations and eight delegates of the state, including Wilhelm Keppler as vice-chairman and Neumann. For the present, the membership of the managing board was to be left open. A temporary administrative committee of five members, at least three of whom must be counted as state representatives, would direct the firm under the leadership of Ernst R. Fischer of IG Farben "because, first, he is an expert in the petroleum field, second, the leader of the oil section of the Economics Ministry, and third, he possesses in quite special degree the confidence of the *Reichsmarschall*." The distribution of Kontinentale's stock sealed the government's authority over the new enterprise. Shares worth 50 million marks were to be issued immediately, 30 million allotted to the state-owned Borussia GmbH and the remainder divided almost evenly among seven corporations involved in oil production, including IG Farben. With fiftyfold voting rights, these shares guaranteed that Borussia could not be outvoted, even if the total stock issue grew to hundreds of millions of marks.[165] The banks were invited to purchase another 30 million marks worth of single vote shares and granted an option on further issues.

All of these provisions were embodied in the notarized documents founding Kontinentale Oel AG on March 27, 1941, except that the

---

[165] Franz Neumann's three separate and detailed discussions of Kontinentale Oel do not point out Borussia's, hence the state's, complete control of the corporation. Instead, he asserts fallaciously that "plurality votes are an absolute guarantee of the power of the capitalistic promoters"; see his *Behemoth* (New York, 1944), pp. 276–7, 356–8, 396–8 (the passage quoted appears on p. 277). On the state's control, see Bütefisch VII/58, Affidavit by E. Neumann, 30.I.48; VII/286, Affidavit by W. Diehlmann, 25.II.48. On Kontinentale as a means of "squaring" private and public interests by preventing business from obtaining excessive influence over politics while providing industry with an opportunity to give "proof of its justification for existence," see *Der Deutsche Volkswirt*, 15 (4.IV.41), pp. 995–6.

government picked up at least one additional seat on the supervisory board.[166] IG Farben collected 6% of the multiple vote stock, supplemented by limited influence over the 4% owned by Brabag. The concern also supplied the general secretary for the new corporation.[167] Immediately after the attack on Russia, Kontinentale received the exclusive rights to the extraction, refining, transport, and trade of Soviet petroleum for ninety-nine years in return for a payment to the Reich of 7.5% of total proceeds, plus Borussia's dividend.[168]

The formation of Kontinentale Oel illustrated both the advantages and the dangers for IG Farben implicit in the *Ostgesellschaft* system. On the one hand, it assured the firm of a voice in policy making for petroleum production throughout Europe. On the other, it represented Göring's determination to place that field securely under state control.[169] If the specific arrangements caused IG little concern, since the combine had years previously relinquished pride of place in the oil field, the possibilities of expanding the state's economic activity through the *Ostgesellschaft* program were disquieting.

Under these circumstances, IG Farben hastened to defend its interests once German forces crossed the Russian border. TerMeer promptly defined those interests in accordance with the strategy of indispensability, directing "that IG, which alone must take over the operation of Russian factories in some fields, like dyes, rubber, and plastics, should in other fields increasingly give precedence to other firms, all the more so because we are, indeed, quite extraordinarily taken up with all sorts of tasks as it is."[170] Other executives set in motion the same measures that had ultimately secured IG's interests in the aftermath of previous German victories. Within days of the invasion, Otto Ambros, the chairman of IG's new Buna Commission, requested official permission to follow the advancing troops in order to study the captured rubber works, and he enclosed the names of IG officers whom he recommended as managers for each plant.[171] At

166 NI-2023/18.
167 NI-10162/83, Meeting of the Kontinentale *Aufsichtsrat*, 13.I.42; Bütefisch VII/286, Affidavit by W. Diehlmann, 24.II.48.
168 Czollek and Eichholtz, *JfW*, 9 (1968), pp. 153–4.
169 Significant in this connection is the way in which the subordination to Kontinentale Oel of the extraction and refining companies for the Polish oil fields transformed these firms in 1942 from private to state-owned corporations. See Hans Radandt, "Deutsche Monopol raubten polnisches Erdöl," *JfW*, 1 (1960), pp. 305–6.
170 Bayer 64/9, von Heider to Bürgin et al., 9.IX.41.
171 NI-4446, Ambros to Krauch, 28.VI.41, *NMT*, vol. 8, pp. 256–9.

Berlin NW7, Ilgner kept particularly busy. He instructed his staff "to work out . . . suggestions for the reorganization of Russian enterprises under German leadership (on the pattern of Aussig/Falkenau)," and he stepped up his services to the army and the bureaucracy by forwarding a plethora of Vowi reports on Soviet industry, few of which had any bearing on IG's commercial interests.[172] For the rest of the year, various offices within the concern compiled lists of plastics, dyes, and rubber installations in Russia, urging IG's representatives in the field to report their captures immediately so that the combine could enter claims with the appropriate authorities.[173]

At two conferences in early July at the Economics Ministry, the regime reiterated its determination to retain title to all captured plants and merely to hire each *Ostgesellschaft* to operate them for the account and risk of the Reich. Nonetheless, IG could take comfort in the proposed distribution of the rubber plants to a company in which IG would be the only private partner, the nitrogen plants to a firm dominated by the syndicate that IG led, and all the chemical plants other than those producing soaps and alkalies to a Chemie Ost GmbH, owned by a group of private corporations, including IG, in partnership with the semiofficial Economic Group for the Chemical Industry.[174] By July 14, although the concern had not been able to begin training its prospective rubber factory managers for their assignments, it already planned to found the Russka-Betriebs GmbH to operate and finance the targeted rubber works.[175]

The actual establishment of the *Ostgesellschaften* proceeded less satisfactorily for IG than these smooth preliminaries implied. In the case of Chemie Ost, IG disliked the Economic Ministry's insistence on an internal ministerial memo, rather than a formal and legally binding contract, as the sole constitutional basis of the firm; queried the ministry's refusal to define the tasks of the new company precisely; and challenged the government's design for an administrative committee

---

[172] NI-1334, Extracts of the minutes of the Mail Conference, 7.VII.41, *NMT*, vol. 8, pp. 262–3. Many of the Vowi reports are in Bayer 91/1, vol. 7, and numerous loose copies. After the war, officials of NW7 denied that plans for taking over Russian industries were actually prepared; see Ilgner IX/161, Affidavit by H. Gierlichs; IX/162, Affidavit by E. de Haas.

[173] See NI-7468/60, Circular letter and attached lists, 14.I.42.

[174] NI-8077, Ilgner's report to the 26th *Vorstand* meeting, 10.VII.41, *NMT*, vol. 8, pp. 263–4.

[175] NI-6737, Ambros to members of the Buna Commission, 14.VII.41, *NMT*, vol. 8, p. 265.

of seven members, among whom only the business manager of the Economic Group for the Chemical Industry could be considered even a quasi representative of private industry.[176] But after brief skirmishing, the concern chose not to press its objections, consoled perhaps by the selection of Willibald Passarge, whom the Nazi AO had once driven out of IG's Paris office, as one of two senior business managers of the new company. On November 1, 1941, Chemie Ost came into being with stock capital of only 20,000 marks, half held by the Economic Group for the Chemical Industry and the remainder split equally among ten private firms, which resulted in a share of 5% for IG.[177]

Six days later a final agreement was signed to found the Soda- und Aetzkalien-Ost GmbH, after IG had failed once more to obtain revisions in the ministry's drafts. Since the state contented itself with three of the twelve seats on the administrative committee, including the chairmanship, the composition of that body was not at issue. IG protested, however, against the subsuming of chlorine electrolysis, which it controlled in Germany, under a company dominated by the Deutsche Solvay-Werke and lesser soda manufacturers. Fearing the theft of secret production processes by these competitors, the combine advocated the erection of separate trusteeship companies for the two fields and then, when the ministry rejected that idea, urged the assignment of each to an individual firm as trustee. Again the ministry refused, driving IG to its third line of defense, a proposal that its shareholding be increased from the 13% originally allotted to 25 to 29% in recognition of the concern's preeminence in the electrolysis sphere. In the end, IG got 16% of the stock and a written limitation on the operating losses the participants were required to cover annually.[178]

[176] NI-4962, Memo of the legal department, Berlin NW7, 23.VII.41, *NMT*, vol. 8, pp. 266–7; NI-4961, Schnitzler to Ungewitter, 8.VII.41, *NMT*, vol. 8, pp. 268–9.
[177] NI-4964, Mahnke to IG, 1.XI.41, *NMT*, vol. 8, pp. 272–3; NI-2996/22, Wipo report, 3.I.42; Czollek and Eichholtz, *JfW*, 9 (1968), p. 171. On Passarge, see NI-6348, Affidavit by M. Ilgner, 10.IV.47, *NMT*, vol. 8, p. 301; and Ilgner's testimony, *NMT*, vol. 7, p. 728.
[178] See Bürgin I/64, Affidavit by Karl von Heider, 30.I.48; and the complete file on the matter in Bayer 64/9, especially Heider to Bürgin et al., 9.IX.41, C. Clemm to IG, 6.IX.41, Anorganische Abteilung to Heider, 11.IX.41, Heider's Niederschrift über eine Besprechung mit Herrn Oberregierungsrat Hoffmann, RWM, 6.IX.41, and the unsigned Entwurf for Hoffmann, 23.IX.41. The only document from this collection introduced at the trial was NI-6730/51, Klebert and Bencker to Heider, 13.IX.41, a misleading expression of a minority view.

Finally, because IG received 54.7% of the shares in the Stickstoff-Ost GmbH for Russian nitrogen plants, the combine appears to have raised no difficulties concerning the allocation of three out of four seats on the administrative committee to spokesmen for the army and the bureaucracy. However, Heinrich Oster, who directed IG's nitrogen operations, doubted the new company's ability to run the distant factories and strove to minimize IG's obligations under the founders' agreement.[179]

Equally problematic for IG were the discussions over two *Ostgellschaften* that were never brought into existence: those for light metals and rubber. Inasmuch as state influence already predominated in the aluminum field through the Vereinigte Aluminium Werke, the Economics Ministry for once preferred to parcel out captured light-metal plants to specific German firms, perhaps on a regional basis, in the unlikely event that the factories returned to production.[180] "As a precautionary measure," IG filed a claim to the plants for semifinished products, pointing out that, since its competitors "have already received pertinent allocations in the West, we believe that it is our turn now."[181] Although various German companies did eventually agree on a scheme for distributing the metal plants, no trustee was ever designated for the processing works that IG wanted, and the idea of a trusteeship company faded away.[182]

Negotiations over the anticipated Synthesekautschuk Ost GmbH for the rubber factories lasted much longer than those over the other *Ostgesellschaften* and were ultimately rendered academic by the army's failure to hold even one obliterated site for longer than a few days. But given the stakes, IG took no chances. Between December 1941 and June 1942, it wrung a series of concessions from the Economics Ministry, including a five-to-four advantage for IG over the state's delegates on the supervisory board, a guarantee of absolute legal protection for any processes or know-how that IG introduced at the plants, and a pledge that the activation of Russian factories would

---

[179] NI-2996/22, Wipo report to the *Vorstand* and KA, 3.I.42; Oster II/45, Affidavit by H. Sander, 9.VII.47.
[180] NI-14530, Haefliger to Ziegler, 29.VII.41, *NMT*, vol. 8, pp. 269–70.
[181] NI-14531, Ziegler to Haefliger, 8.VIII.41, *NMT*, vol. 8, pp. 271–2.
[182] NI-14529, Haefliger to Ziegler, 9.VIII.41, *NMT*, vol. 8, pp. 270–1; Haefliger's testimony, *NMT*, vol. 8, pp. 299–300.

not in any way "prejudice the economic utilization of the German buna capacities."[183] However, as to the concern's interest in a preemptive right to purchase the rubber facilities at the end of the trusteeship period, the Reich seems to have been willing only "to bear this desire in mind" and to state that it would not subsequently operate the plants itself or lease them to a third party.[184] The decisive barrier to an agreement remained IG's demand for exclusive rights to exploit within Germany and free of charge all manufacturing methods and experiences found in Russia. Denied this repeatedly, the firm could do no better than to observe rather plaintively that "in view of the services rendered by IG Farben to the Reich we do not think it fair if the Reich were now to enter into competition with IG Farben in Germany . . . by using those methods found in Soviet Russia."[185] There the matter rested, a testimony to the concern's apprehension about the intentions of the Nazi regime.

By the end of 1941, seventeen *Ostgesellschaften* were in place; IG participated in four, counting Kontinentale Oel, with a majority holding in only one. Having surveyed the state of economic planning for Russia, the Wipo office reported to the *Vorstand* and the Commercial Committee on the intended policies of deindustrialization and "sluice profits" and on the likely future role of large concerns. Significantly, Wipo noted that the big German companies would be needed for a while, but "it is deemed desirable that, as time passes, the plants in question will not be directed by employees reporting to Germany, but by plant leaders who, in each case, will become independent and take root there." Therefore, the Wipo summary concluded, "reserve is advisable" and "industrial planning is out of the question within a reasonable period of time."[186] Accordingly, the concern undertook no

---

183 The negotiations are chronicled in NI-6735, Knieriem to RWM, 17.XII.41, *NMT*, vol. 8, pp. 274–7; NI-4972/37, Draft trusteeship agreement, 17.XII.41; NI-4975/37, Draft of an exchange of letters between IG and the RWM, 17.XII.41; NI-4974/37, File memo of a conference at the ministry, 17.VI.42. The quotation is from the last-named document. Disingenuous testimony by Ambros and terMeer appears in *NMT*, vol. 8, pp. 292–3, 296–98; see also NI-8148, Affidavit by terMeer, 23.IV.47, *NMT*, vol. 8, pp. 294–5.
184 NI-4975/37, Draft of RWM to IG, 17.XII.41.
185 NI-4971/37, Ambros and Heintzeler of IG to Reinbothe of the RWM, 3.VII.42. See also NI-6736/51, Ambros to Eckell, 3.VIII.42.
186 NI-2996, Wipo to the *Vorstand* and KA with accompanying report of the Ostverbindungsstelle, 3.I.42, excerpted in *NMT*, vol. 8, pp. 277–80, and in Müller, *MM*,

new initiatives in Russia during 1942, aside from the establishment of the Committee on the East to coordinate sales policy in the region and the related foundings of the Chemie Neukirch & Co., Riga, and the Ostland-Kontor GmbH as marketing outlets.[187]

When the Reich's military needs made it revert to its traditional policy of individual trusteeships in the summer of 1942, IG did not benefit. Rosenberg of the Ministry for the East, Koch as *Reichskommissar* for the Ukraine, and Kehrl, now the chief of Main Department II of the Economics Ministry, expressed various degrees of distaste for IG and blocked the assignment of all but insignificant trusteeships to the combine, which IG rejected. In the cases of the nitrogen factories at Kamenskoje and Dnepropetrowsk, Nazi officials went out of their way to find other firms to manage the works.[188] Nor did the concern earn any profit on the operations of the three trusteeship companies in which it participated or obtain apparatus or equipment from any of the plants within their purview.[189]

Two exceptions to IG's generally low level of activity or gain in the East had their origins in prewar business deals with private firms and the government of Estonia. The first concerned the Eestii Fosforitt AG, a producer of low-grade phosphorus ores, which had become dependent on Farben's technical, financial, and commercial assistance during the 1930s. Thus, IG was the logical choice as trustee when the Germans occupied Estonia in 1941, and the combine was ordered to send engineers to revive the plant immediately. Shortages of labor and

28 (1981), pp. 127–9. The original document is in Bayer 64/9. Because of defects in the official translation, I have provided my own. See also Bormann to Sauckel, 14.III.42, reiterating Hitler's and Himmler's view that locally based enterprises were to be preferred in Russia to branches of German corporations; see Müller, *MM*, 28 (1981), note 62, p. 134.

[187] Bayer 13/9, vol. 2, Excerpt from the minutes of the 50th KA meeting, 9.IX.42. See Hoechst TEA 253, Schnitzler to Mann, 11.XII.42, for an indication of the writer's and terMeer's determination to restrict the new Ostausschuss to a purely marketing organization.

[188] NI-303/4, Report by Hans Kugler, 12.VII.45; Oster II/45, Affidavit by H. Sander, 9.VII.47; Bayer 64/9, Weber-Andreä and von Heider to Soda- und Aetzkalien Ost GmbH, 10.XI.42. In the case of Kamenskoje, this involved replacing IG's Peter Assman, who was initially assigned as trustee, and providing the Degussa combine an opportunity to enter the synthetic nitrogen field at almost no cost; see NI-4928/36, Affidavit by K. Krüger, 18.III.47, and RG242/T83/82, Report by Retze, 20.X.42.

[189] Bürgin I/64, Affidavit by K. von Heider, 30.I.48, which provides the relevant statistics; Mann testimony, *NMT*, vol. 8, pp. 306–8.

material defeated that effort.[190] IG's second Estonian venture involved the production of oil from that nation's rich shale deposits. At the outbreak of the war with Russia, Germany was the principal market for this product, which was particularly suitable for refining into naval fuel, and IG was one of the chief suppliers of capital to two of the main producers.[191] Though never formally sold, they were absorbed in 1941 into the Kontinentale Oel's extractive and marketing subsidiaries. IG Farben appears to have contributed its technical facilities to efforts to increase the yield of oil from the shale but not to have taken part in the management of the Estonian works.[192]

In the spring of 1943, with the military tide in Russia running decidedly against Germany, two officers of IG Farben added a futile footnote to the concern's involvement in the occupation of the Soviet Union. At the instigation of an unspecified government office, Richard Riedl, the chairman of the supervisory board of Donauchemie, drafted a memorandum of more than two hundred pages on German policy in Russia. Max Ilgner advised Riedl to forward the document to the Reichskanzlei and wrote to Hans Lammers, Hitler's secretary, recommending the memo to the führer's attention. In brief, Riedl denounced the dream of colonizing Russia with Germans, argued that "one cannot condemn the Russians to the status of Helots and to political fragmentation," and reminded the regime that "contenting oneself with the attainable is here, as everywhere, the guarantee of success." His positive proposals amounted to an echo of Rosenberg's intermittent pleas that Germany capitalize on the nationalism of Russia's minorities. As such, Riedl's remarks were an attempt to get the Reich's policy toward Russia placed on the same footing of mutual interest that Ilgner consistently advocated with regard to Southeast Europe.[193]

190 Roswitha Czollek, "Estnische Phosphate im Griff der IG Farbenindustrie AG," *JfW*, 7 (1966), pp. 205–11; NI-303/4, Kugler's report, 12.VII.45.
191 See Hans-Erich Volkmann, "Oekonomie und Machtpolitik. Lettland und Estland im politisch-ökonomischen Kalkül des Dritten Reiches, 1933–1940," *G&G*, 2 (1976), pp. 487, 496; BA Koblenz, R2/16708, exchange of letters between IG and the Deutsche Revisions- und Treuhand GmbH, 2.VII.40, 19.VII.40, 23.VII.40, and 1.VIII.40; and Bayer 13/9, vol. 2, Fischer's report to the KA, 7.X.37.
192 Roswitha Czollek, "Zum Raub estnischer Oelschiefervorkommen für die deutsche Kriegswirtschaft," *JfW*, 10 (1969), pp. 109–14; Bayer 64/9, series of telegrams from Dr. Erberich on experiments in December 1943.
193 Ilgner's letter is published, along with excerpts from Riedl's report, in Dietrich Eichholtz, "Wege zur Entbolschewisierung und Entrussung des Ostraumes. Emp-

Neither Riedl's stance nor Ilgner's identification with it was likely to improve IG's standing with most Party leaders. Hitler went out of his way some weeks later to assure Rosenberg that there would be no "mild turn" in German occupation policy.[194] Nonetheless, like IG's efforts to circumvent or moderate other Nazi brutalities, from Aryanization to the construction of a factory at Auschwitz to the employment and working conditions of slave laborers, Riedl's remarks raised purely "objective," utilitarian considerations, not moral ones, and they were not repeated. Instead, sensitive to the underlying tension between corporation and state documented in this and earlier chapters, the concern adapted for the sake of its own commercial future. In Russia, that course meant responding to decisions made by a welter of administrative organs in which no representative of the combine, save the detached Krauch, occupied a decisive position.[195]

Summary

IG Farben's imperialism was the sort that followed the flag. Furthermore, the concern's driving impulse in the lands annexed by Germany was almost entirely defensive. The firms selected for acquisition, almost without exception, had two characteristics in common: (1) Their previous ownership by either state agencies or Jewish investors predestined them for resale by the Nazis, and (2) their operations included fields that Farben considered essential to its commercial and political strength: dyes, industrial gases, synthetic rubber, and fuel distribution. In nearly every instance of acquisition, the concern sought to control and shut down potential intruders on its domestic spheres of interest. As this chapter shows, neither step proved simple

fehlungen des IG-Farben-Konzerns für Hitler im Frühjahr 1943," *JfW*, 11 (1970), pp. 23–44; the originals are in BA Koblenz, R43 II/683b. On Ilgner and the Balkans, see Chapter 7. On Riedl's background as an early supporter of European federation during the interwar years, see Carl H. Pegg, *Evolution of the European Idea 1914–1932* (Chapel Hill, N.C., 1983), pp. 27–8.

[194] Quoted in Wolfgang Schumann, "Die wirtschaftspolitische Ueberlebensstrategie des deutschen Imperialismus in der Endphase des Zweiten Weltkrieges" *ZfG*, 27 (1979), p. 499.

[195] Dallin's assertion that Gustav Schlotterer of the Ministry for the East was a director of IG Farben (*German Rule*, p. 88) is false. Two junior officials of the firm, Prentzel and Schiller, were drafted into the army and assigned to the Ostministerium (NI-6713/51, Affidavit by M. Ilgner, 2.IV.47).

to execute, and at every stage the combine had to make major concessions to government representatives in order to achieve even a portion of its objectives. But IG's goals in the Greater German Reich were at least easy for the concern to define, which was more than one could say about them in the surviving subjugated or satellite nations of Europe.

7. The New Order

By mid-1940, the German Wehrmacht had overrun opposition from the North Cape to the Pyrenees, from the Channel Islands to the River Bug. Only Britain held out, and the bulk of its military equipment lay abandoned on the beaches of Dunkirk. In anticipation of complete victory, Hermann Göring began preparing for its aftermath. He directed Gustav Schlotterer, the number two man in the foreign trade section of the Economics Ministry, to draw up economic and demobilization policies that would smooth the transition to a "New Order" in Europe. Intelligent, informed, and unimpetuous, Schlotterer owed his selection to the rare combination of these qualities and political credentials – his membership in the Nazi Party dated from August 1923, before the Beer Hall Putsch. He quickly grasped both the scale of his assignment and the need for haste. Seizing on the most convenient means of compiling pertinent information, he asked numerous German business groups and firms for reports and suggestions around which he might orient his thinking, particularly in readying the German position at a possible peace conference.[1] From IG Farben, Schlotterer ordered general proposals for the reorganization of the entire European chemical industry, estimates of the direct and indirect damages inflicted on the corporation by the Versailles treaty, and surveys of the chemical business in the occupied nations, Switzerland, and England – all "in the shortest possible time."[2]

---

[1] Jean Freymond, *Le IIIeme Reich et la réorganisation économique de l'Europe* (Leiden, 1974), pp. 108, 145–6. See also Hermann Wandschneider, "Pläne der deutschen Elektrokonzerne zur 'Neuordnung der europäischen Wirtschaft' im Zweiten Weltkrieg," *JfW*, 11 (1970), pp. 219–43; and Wolfgang Schumann's articles: "Das Kriegsprogramm des Zeiss-Konzerns," *ZfG*, 11 (1963), pp. 704–28; "Die faschistische 'Neuordung' Europas nach den Plänen des deutschen Monopolkapitals. Programme der Metallindustrie, des Metallerz- und Kohlebergbaus im Jahre 1940," *ZfG*, 19 (1971), pp. 224–41; and "Neue Dokumente der Reichsgruppe Industrie zur 'Neuordnung' Europas," *JfG*, 5 (1971), pp. 379–438.

[2] NI-6842, Kufuss to IG, 19.VI.40, *NMT*, vol. 7, pp. 1437–8; NI-4897, Schnitzler to terMeer et al., 24.VI.40, *NMT*, vol. 7, pp. 1439–40; NI-4928/36, Affidavit by K. Krüger, 18.III.47; M892/7, Interrogation of Dr. Schlotterer, 27.I.48, p. 5903 (also submitted as Mann IV/649).

The Reich's initiative – and "the speedy development of the war in the West" that occasioned it – caught IG by surprise, though hardly at a loss for a response.[3] The concern had on file most of the specific data Schlotterer wanted, and the government made clear that IG's draftsmen did not have to reckon for the present with radical departures from familiar frontiers or the policies of autarky, armament, and economic direction by the state.[4] Thus, one meeting of the Commercial Committee with the chairmen of several other important corporate units sufficed to lay down the format for IG's replies. By mid-July, the rough outlines of the firm's recommendations were in place, and Jost Terhaar, the employee charged with coordinating their preparation, had ascertained that a favorable official reception depended on striking a certain tone. IG's proposals would have to take German military and strategic interests into account and "not give the impression of predilection for liberal dealings," since that would place "a weapon in the hands of those manifold circles in the Economics Ministry in which criticism of IG was prevalent."[5] In early August, just six weeks after issuing his requests, Schlotterer received the first two installments of IG's New Order program, comprising an introductory section and one on France.[6] Sequels, cut from the mold of the French segment, followed for Holland at the end of August, Belgium and Denmark during the fall, and Norway between May and September of the following year.[7] The company apparently never completed full-dress

---

[3] NI-4897, Schnitzler to terMeer et al., 24.VI.40, NMT, vol 7, pp. 1439–40. There is no evidence, let alone in the source he cites, for Borkin's claim that IG "had already prepared a 'new order' plan for the chemical industry of the world" (Crime and Punishment, p. 99), and the remainder of the paragraph containing this statement takes similar liberties with the documentation.

[4] See NI-048, Walther Funk's remarks to a conference of the kleiner Beirat, 7.VI.40, in Eichholtz and Schumann (eds.), Anatomie, p. 257; Schumann, JfG, 5 (1971), Documents 4–7, File notes by Albrecht and Hinrichs and remarks by Dr. Guth, 17.VI.40, and by Schlotterer, 19.VI.40, pp. 401–11; and Freymond, Reorganisation, pp. 114–17 and Appendix 5, Schlotterer's speech of 23.VII.40, pp. 232–6.

[5] NI-6293, Minutes of the 33rd KA meeting, 28–29.VI.40, NMT, vol. 7, pp. 1440–5; NI-9288/77, Excerpt of the minutes of the 34th KA meeting, 18–19.VII.40, p. 3; NI-4928/36, Affidavit by K. Krüger, 18.III.47. The quotation is from NI-5195/38, Affidavit by G. von Schnitzler, 17.III.47.

[6] NI-11252/93, Schnitzler to Schlotterer, 3.VIII.40, excerpted in NMT, vol. 7, pp. 1451–62. The document is printed, along with an introductory essay, in D. Eichholtz, "Die IG-Farben-'Friedensplanung,' Schlüsseldokumente der faschistischen 'Neuordnung des europäischen Grossraums,'" JfW, 7 (1966), pp. 271–327. IG also submitted a separate design for Continental patent policy (NI-4695/34, 20.VII.40).

[7] NI-10164/84 includes the reports on Belgium, Holland, and Denmark; NI-7764/63 covers Norway. Apparently, IG also drafted suggestions for peace terms governing

studies on England and Switzerland. However, IG almost certainly authored the summary proposals pertaining to those nations in the report submitted during September 1940 by the quasi-official Prüfungsstelle chemischer Industrie, whose remarks on other countries faithfully paraphrased those of IG's own papers.[8]

Though pitched to win the support of Schlotterer and his aides, these documents marked a real turning point in IG Farben's relationship to the Third Reich. As the regime approached the apogee of its success in mid-1940, Nazi economic policies took on, perhaps for the first time in the firm's eyes, an air of permanence. Thus, though consistent with Farben's pre-Nazi visions of a privately cartelized European chemical industry and a voluntary "economic block from Bordeaux to Sofia," the concern's objectives now became decidedly more Germanocentric. Old ambitions, themselves adaptations to the conditions prevailing after Germany's earlier defeat, were redefined to accord with the new commercial context apparently created by the Third Reich's triumphs. Events soon made a dead letter of most of IG's New Order program, but it marked a noteworthy step in the gradual accommodation of the corporation's traditional thinking to the ideology of the Grossraumwirtschaft.

IG built its New Order program, like most of the concern's major decisions since 1919, around an estimate of its future position in foreign markets. Hence, after paying lip service to the "economic independence" of the Continent and the "military–economic requirements of Germany," IG dwelt on the problem of overseas trade.[9] This emphasis reflected the firm's own enduring worries about overcapacity but also IG's conviction, expressed by Georg von Schnitzler later in 1940, that because of population density, climate, and shortages of indispensable minerals "the Greater German Economic Sphere, even as it will be constituted after a victorious war, can . . .

---

the concern's subsidiaries abroad that had suffered from measures taken by foreign governments upon the outbreak of the war (NI-14027/115, memo of the meeting of the Legal Committee, 2.X.40), but I have found no proof that the proposals were actually submitted.

[8] See NI-6955, Schnitzler to members of the KA, 22.X.40, *NMT*, vol. 7, pp. 1463–4; NI-2703/20, Statement by Schnitzler, 28.VII.45. On IG's provisional plans for England, see Janis Schmelzer, *Dies war ein Staatsgeheimnis* (Wolfen, n.d.), pp. 35–8. RG242/T83/94, Frames 3468489–646, Vorschläge für die Neuordnung der Chemiewirtschaft in Europa, Heft 1, September 1940, especially pp. 46–7, 56–62.

[9] NI-11252/93, pp. 1–10.

not be autarkic."[10] For both reasons, IG consistently had advised the Reich to encourage "market stabilization" by long-term international cartels and to participate "in the industrialization and development of the . . . young countries, which are rich in agricultural products and raw materials."[11] But the onset of war had hurt prospects for these efforts. While Germany was cut off from former markets and investment opportunities, the fighting stimulated foreign competitors, especially in the United States and Japan, but also in Russia and Italy, and concentrated their trade in the key areas of Latin America, the Far East, and Southeast Europe, respectively. In nations previously reliant on German goods, the conflict triggered expansion of chemical and related industries. "It will, therefore, depend," IG argued, "on the degree of order or disorder of the European economic sphere and on the creation of a determined commercial policy, how far and at what pace Europe, and more particularly Germany, will be able to rebuild, maintain, and develop its position as a regular 'trade partner.'" In other words, the immediate task of the New Order was to construct a thoroughly rationalized European economic bloc capable of negotiating and "competing with the productive forces of other major spheres in competitive markets."[12]

IG proposed to achieve this objective in the chemical industry through a mix of private and commercial actions, some of which the concern had been urging on its larger foreign counterparts for years. Mindful of its own and the regime's need for cooperation in the occupied lands, the firm explicitly renounced a restoration of its monopoly over European organic chemistry as of 1914. Instead, IG confined its claim for compensation for the losses suffered as a result of the Versailles treaty and subsequent commercial discrimination to the establishment of "a leading position commensurate with [IG's] technical, economic, and scientific rank."[13] But Farben's specific demands

---

[10] Georg von Schnitzler, "Autoritäre Wirtschaftsführung bejaht den internationalen Güteraustausch," Deutsche Volkswirt, 15 (20.XII.40), p. 481.
[11] Ibid., p. 484; Georg von Schnitzler, "Germany and World Trade After the War," Atlantic Monthly, 165 (June 1940), p. 820. The latter essay was prepared in close cooperation with the German Foreign Office; see Hans-Jürgen Schröder, Deutschland und die Vereinigten Staaten 1933–1939 (Wiesbaden, 1970), pp. 281–2, and the documents of October and November 1939 collected in NI-1418/14.
[12] NI-11252/93, Schnitzler to Schlotterer, 3.VIII.40, and the general section attached thereto, pp. 1, 8–9. The excerpt in NMT, vol. 7, pp. 1451–8, omits several of the passages relied on here.
[13] Ibid., pp. 6–9.

were extensive. The combine sought government aid in securing half-ownership of the united dyes industries of Britain and France, an echo of IG's merger attempts in the mid-1920s, and demanded a few factory closings, specifying one Dutch and one Belgian firm by name, as well as all the state-run laboratories that produced serums.[14] Existing production of dyes, pharmaceuticals, and aromatic substances was to be sold only in each occupied nation's home and colonial markets or, in a few cases, to current customers elsewhere and to be governed by price and market conventions with German manufacturers. Import needs were to be referred to German suppliers, and increases in domestic output either prohibited or subjected to licensing by German authorities. Even more far reaching were IG's recommendations for loosening the regulations of the conquered states concerning tariffs and other import restrictions, patents, taxation, the founding of German subsidiaries, advertising, and product labeling. Their enactment would have unleashed market forces powerful enough to crush all but the heartiest native producers.[15]

This design for a European bloc signaled IG's conversion from economic liberalism to the neomercantilism long advanced by Nazi economists. Proclaiming that "the times of unrestricted free trade according to the theories of Adam Smith and Ricardo are, in our opinion, past," Schnitzler now held up Germany's exchange agreements with Southeast Europe as a model of international economic cooperation and called publicly for the establishment of multilateral clearing treaties among nations.[16] Meanwhile, departing from previous practice, IG insisted on preferential tariffs in western Europe for German products. Severed by the war from the overseas outlets for fully 48% of its exports, worth some 202 million reichsmarks in 1939, the combine clearly doubted its ability to recapture these sales completely.[17] To offset the expected losses, IG counted on a virtual monopoly of European chemical exports, other than to colonial territories, and increased

[14] Ibid., section on France, pp. 27–8; RG242/T83/94, Vorschläge, pp. 56–62. IG also urged the transfer to Germany of the Dutch quinine trust and its subjection to IG's sales, price, and advertising policies. The concern did not, however, seek formal direction of the trust (NI-10164/84, pp. 11, 14, 15, 41, and 49).

[15] NI-11252/93, NI-10164/84, NI-7764/63, and NI-4695/34, passim.

[16] Schnitzler, Atlantic Monthly, 165 (June 1940), pp. 818, 821; idem, Deutsche Volkswirt, 15 (1940), p. 482.

[17] Defense Basic Information II/10, p. 24. The averages of IG's exports by country for the entire period from 1926 to 1938 result in an almost identical percentage; see Gross, Facts and Figures, p. 23.

shares of organics consumption within each occupied nation. Once more, the concern had to adapt its traditional policies to circumstances created by the autonomous actions of the Nazi state. The firm's economic interests had not animated German aggression, but they were not impervious to its consequences. By force of arms, Nazism seemed to have made economic reality fit the ideology's description of it. On the level of planning, Farben fell into line.

At the Economics Ministry, Schlotterer and his associates praised the clarity and thoroughness of IG's reports without committing the Reich to specific actions.[18] Moreover, the concern discovered that its emphasis on achieving Germany's objectives in occupied Europe through private dealings among the manufacturers and changes in national regulations did not "harmonize" with the more *dirigiste* projections of Dr. Ungewitter, the head of the Economic Group for the Chemical Industry. He envisioned the drafting by the ministry of a master plan for the entire European chemical business and the execution of that plan by continental cartels and syndicates, dominated by German managers and supervised by the Nazi state. Though such a system would not necessarily collide with IG's interests, it would complicate their translation into policy and erect a new bureaucracy. The Wipo offices, therefore, took a skeptical view of Ungewitter's conception, but did not challenge it openly.[19] Ungewitter's enthusiasm for the cartel framework continued undiminished.[20]

Whatever the official opinion of IG's program, the exigencies of war and policy disagreements within the regime soon overtook the New Order planning process. By October 1940, on the heels of the failure of the air offensive against England, Schlotterer was warning German businessmen to treat the interests of their foreign counterparts with respect. Urging tact and counseling patience, he suggested that German firms wait for the sheer strength of the Reich's economic position and the inevitable attrition attendant on the prevailing short-

18 NI-6840, File note by Terhaar, 7.VIII.40, *NMT*, vol. 7, pp. 1446–8; NI-6955, Mulert's comments, as reported by Schnitzler to the KA, 22.X.40, *NMT*, vol. 7, pp. 1463–4.
19 NI-6840, Terhaar's file note, 7.VIII.40, *NMT*, vol. 7, p. 1450.
20 See C. Ungewitter, "Industrie Organisation in Europa," *Europa-Kabel*, no. 19 (10.X.41), cited in Arno Sölter, *Das Grossraumkartell* (Dresden, 1941). Sölter's book fleshes out a program quite similar to Ungewitter's, whose emphasis on cartels is also conspicuous in the New Order report of the Prüfungsstelle chemischer Industrie, RG242/T83/94, September 1940.

ages of raw materials to do their work in the occupied lands. In the meantime, German companies could reduce undesirable competition through capital penetration, the inclusion of foreign firms in German cartels, and the facilitation of market agreements and the like with newly founded foreign business associations akin to those within the Reich.[21] These remained throughout the occupation the three principal tools for building the New Order in western Europe. Although some foreign industries were brought into German syndicates and numerous plant takeovers and shutdowns occurred across the region, no overarching cartel system came into being, and IG's proposals did not find their way into the legislative codes of the subjugated nations. After early 1942, the crush of immediate military and strategic needs forced both the Reich and IG to suspend concrete planning for the New Order.

Within the combine's "think tank," the Vowi office, Anton Reithinger continued to refine and publicize his corporation's views of the future economic shape of the Continent, but his writings were short on specifics. Instead, he discoursed on the general principles of occupation policy with that mixture of Nazi phraseology, pragmatism, and naiveté that characterized nearly all the recorded statements emanating from the firm's officials on this subject. His themes were the needs to respect cultural variety in Europe, to demonstrate to the occupied peoples the advantages of absorption into the German economic system, and to give the New Order some driving centripetal ideal, "namely the carrying over of the idea of social welfare from internal life to the companionship of peoples."[22] Whether read as

21 Schlotterer's speech to the Grosser Beirat of the Reichsgruppe Industrie, 3.X.40, reproduced in Eichholtz, *Geschichte*, vol. 1, pp. 367–74. The same document is NI-6734, and a copy circulated within IG is in Hoechst TEA 1250. In keeping with Schlotterer's policy, Farben received two weeks later authorization to expend up to 500,000 reichsmarks on the stock exchanges of Paris, Brussels, and Amsterdam; see the internal correspondence of 15.X.40–7.XI.40 in IG in Abw., Zefi 84–62, Angebot auf Beteiligung I.
22 Anton Reithinger, "Voraussetzungen und Grossenordnungen der kontinental-europäischen Grossraumwirtschaft," in *Probleme des Europäischen Grosswirtschaftsraumes* (Berlin, 1943), pp. 9–31; the phrase quoted here is on p. 14. For nearly identical wording, see his "Die Revolution der politisch-wirtschaftlichen Voraussetzungen in Europa," *Der Wirtschafts-Ring*, 14 (1941), pp. 181–2; and, in general, his "Europäische Industriewirtschaft," in Verein Berliner Kaufleute und Industrieller und die Wirtschafts-Hochschule Berlin (eds.), *Europäische Wirtschaftsgemeinschaft*, 2nd ed. (Berlin, 1943), pp. 94–116.

propaganda or self-delusion, such musings were irrelevant to the course of the Nazi occupation. If IG Farben took the concept of collaboration seriously, envisioning an integrated European economy in which the businessmen of peripheral nations would serve as junior partners, Hitler never did. However, Reithinger's ideas, like the New Order documents, argued against a ruthlessly acquisitive policy on IG's part in the defeated and satellite nations. Here, as within Greater Germany, the combine's motives were primarily defensive, but its methods had to be as varied as the barriers to their achievement.

The Benelux countries

During the summer following the conquest of the Low Countries in May 1940, the Economics Ministry had its hands full trying to restrain the rapacity of German business. Egged on by the freebooting *Reichsmarschall* and several of his subordinates within the Four Year Plan, representatives of the Hermann Göring Werke and other enterprises descended on numerous Dutch and Belgian firms to demand that they sell out immediately on pain of seizure by the Reich. General von Falkenhausen, the military commander in Brussels, held that such visits merely undercut widespread willingness to collaborate with Germany, and he asked the Economics Ministry to put a stop to them. Schlotterer did his best to oblige. Early in September, he summoned delegates of the Reichsgruppe Industrie and all thirty economic groups to a meeting in Berlin. Bluntly confronting the differences between his ministry and the Four Year Plan organization, he asserted that his office would control access to the occupied nations henceforth and denied that the ministry intended any confiscations or even reductions in the capacities of Dutch and Belgian industry except in a few instances of unprofitable or superfluous plants. As to acquisitions, tactful stock purchases were one thing, Schlotterer stated, but all discussions between German and foreign companies "are to proceed on a purely commercial basis; that is, there may be no politically based pressure exercised on any negotiating partner by a private German party." Corporations with extensive overseas interests were to be handled particularly delicately, lest Germany lose all chance of influencing their branches. As a consolation to the more avaricious of his hearers,

Schlotterer held out the prospect of gains from the Aryanization of Jewish property.[23]

IG Farben was not among the offending enterprises. In the first months of the occupation of the Low Countries, the concern steered clear of the "orgy of plundering," siding with the ministry rather than Göring.[24] As early as May 27, the Commercial Committee concluded that IG's relations with competitors in Holland would have to proceed on the assumption that the Dutch economy was to continue functioning largely autonomously. Meanwhile, the firm would place the usual array of technical advisers at the disposal of the military administration.[25] Concerning Belgium, Schnitzler informed the members of the KA on June 6 that he and Terhaar, as cochairmen of the German–Belgian Economic Committee, had been called to Brussels by the army. Though he asked the members to provide him with relevant information, he cautioned that "the special handling of IG's interests proper will be timely only at a later moment."[26] When one Herr Suhr, an IG employee attached to the German Nitrogen Syndicate, was named by the Reich to supervise the nitrogen industries of Holland and Belgium, he studiously refrained from using his position to IG's advantage.[27] The concern's circumspection was best revealed by the conduct of the Vereinigte Sauerstoff Werke (VSW), jointly owned by IG and Lindes Eismaschine, toward the conquered oxygen and acetylene plants the partners coveted. Late in August, VSW resolved "not to do anything for the time being to establish direct contact with the Dutch and/or Belgian firms" but "to intimate to" the Economics Ministry VSW's readiness to take a financial interest in the enterprises. A letter to that effect, which also acceded to the Wehrmacht's request

[23] NI-504/6, Schlotterer to managers of the Reichwirtschaftskammer, RGI, and Reichsgruppe Handel, 9.IX.40, with enclosed Bericht über die Besprechung vom 6. September 1940 über Zusammenarbeit mit holländischen und belgischen Wirtschaftskreisen; and Schlotterer's file note of meetings on 6.IX.40 and 11.IX.40, printed in Eichholtz, Geschichte, vol. 1 pp. 365–7. The quotation is from the latter source, p. 366.
[24] John Gillingham, "The Politics of Business in the Economic Grossraum: The Example of Belgium," Studia Historica Oeconomicae, 14 (1979), p. 30.
[25] Bayer 13/9, vol. 2, excerpts from minutes of the 32nd KA meeting, 27.V.40.
[26] Bayer 13/9, vol. 2, Schnitzler to KA, 6.VI.40; see also Eichholtz, Geschichte, vol. 1, pp. 164–5, which omits the comment cited.
[27] NI-4928/36, Affidavit by K. Krüger, 18.III.47; Oster II/38, Statement by M. W. Holtrop, copy dated 20.III.48.

for aid in returning the factories to operation, was drafted a few days later.[28]

The combine could afford to be patient. In the absence of plant sequestrations by the Reich, IG did not need to charge into the Benelux states ahead of potential German rivals. Moreover, the conquest itself had done away with IG's foremost problem in these lands: competition from overseas. Although Belgium and Holland doubled their chemical production between the wars, only the expansion of synthetic nitrogen output had hurt IG's exports severely. Increases in German nitrogen consumption during the 1930s more than made up for that loss. Otherwise, domestic production in both lands concentrated on heavy chemicals, a matter of indifference to the concern.[29] In 1939, IG's sales in each country exceeded the levels of 1926, both in value and as a percentage of all foreign proceeds. That the corporation had not regained the bumper export totals of 1929 was attributed more to boycotts of German goods and the consequent inroads by other suppliers, especially in the dyes field, than to indigenous development.[30] For the most part, IG could rely on wartime circumstances to take care of its commercial interests in Belgium and Holland. The concern's needs and Schlotterer's policies dovetailed almost perfectly.

In Belgium, IG therefore moved aggressively only in the dyes field. Among the more than one hundred privately owned chemical plants, the concern's sole victim was the nation's most significant prospective producer of organic dyes, a factory at Tertre. Begun in 1938 over Farben's objections and still incomplete in 1940, the Belgian-owned plant remained idle during World War II.[31] As part of the general settlement with the French dye industry in 1941, IG also got a promise that the dyes segment of the French subsidiary at Rieme-Ertvelde would be closed, but the agreement was not enforced.[32] The combine

28 NI-14738/120, File note of conversation between representatives of Lindes and IG, 23.VIII.40, and draft of VSW to RWM, 12.IX.40.
29 See Bayer 91/1, Vowi 2357, "Die Chemiewirtschaft Belgiens," 10.V.37; Vowi 3975, "Die Chemiewirtschaft Belgiens und wichtige Unternehmen der chemische Industrie," 1.VI.40; Vowi 3974, "Die Chemiewirtschaft der Niederlande und die wichtigsten Firmen der chemischen Industrie," 13.VI.40.
30 Defense Basic Information II/10, p. 24; NI-10164/84, New Order reports on Belgium and Holland, passim.
31 See Bayer 13/9, vol. 2, 19th KA meeting, 17.II.39, and NI-10164/84, p. 41.
32 NI-6845/53, Contract between the French dye companies and IG, 18.XI.41, p. 18.

left the smaller Belgian dye makers untouched, apparently expecting them to wither on the vine.

This is not to say that IG lacked more positive ambitions in Belgium, but discretion and the absence of a sense of urgency led the concern to play a waiting game. That course was particularly striking in the case of the preeminent fabricator of photographic supplies, the Gevaert firm, which had irritatingly undersold the combine within Belgium and abroad during the interwar period.[33] But the Luftwaffe appears to have protected Gevaert in order to maintain an uninterrupted supply of aerial film.[34] Between September and December 1940, IG also forswore designs on the two largest chemical manufacturers in the country, the Solvay & Cie. of Brussels and its offshoot, the Union Chimique Belge, which together dominated every sphere of local production, save nitrogen and photographic chemicals.[35] Later, IG helped Solvay fend off attempts by German firms to cut into the Belgian company's 75% share in the Deutsche Solvay-Werke, in which IG held the balance of the stock.[36] Such friendliness naturally had a firm basis in IG's self-interest. If Solvay's western European operations posed no threat to IG's products, the same could not be said for the activities of the eastern European companies jointly owned by the Prager Verein and Solvay's Swiss holding company, GEFUCIN. Probably IG hoped to trade restraint in the West for concessions by Solvay in the East. Besides, prudence dictated a hands-off policy. An assault on Solvay, with its intricate web of connections inside and outside Belgium, would not only jeopardize the Reich's program for enlisting the firm's plants in German war production, but also perhaps lead to a clash with the Hermann Göring Werke, which was eyeing the Belgian combine.[37]

In Holland, IG's immediate objectives were similarly limited. Aside from the state serum laboratories and the gases plants mentioned

[33] Bayer 91/1, Vowi 3975, p. 5; NI-10164/84, pp. 50–52. See also Bayer 91/1, Vowi 4219, Gavaert Photo Producten N.V., 9.XII.40.
[34] NI-6839/53, Memo by Terhaar, 14.IX.40, pp. 12–13.
[35] On IG's decision, see Bayer 13/9, vol. 2, 36th KA meeting, 25.IX.40; Bayer D.A. 481, Auszug aus der Niederschrift über die 78. Sitzung des Chemikalien Ausschusses, 11.XII.40; NI-10471/86, memo of conference at the RWM, 11.XI.40; NI-8080/66, Mann's report to the 23rd Vorstand meeting, 12.XII.40. On the companies, see Bayer 91/1, Vowi 2356 "Die wichtigsten Chemie-Unternehmungen in Belgien," 10.V.37; and the table of comparative capitalization in Vowi 3975, 1.VI.40, p. 5.
[36] NI-5196/16, Schnitzler's affidavit, 18.III.47.
[37] NI-6840, File note by Terhaar, 7.VIII.40, NMT, vol. 7, p. 1451.

above, only two relatively small plants among the country's more than ninety chemical installations drew IG's fire.[38] The concern sought to close down one fledgling competitor, the newly founded Neederlandsche Fotographische Industrie N.V., Soest, and gradually succeeded in driving the principal native dyes maker, the Schiedam firm of Vondelingenplaat, out of business.[39] IG played no part in the wartime management of the Unilever holdings in Holland or in the German takeover of the largest Dutch chemical company, the Algemeene Kunstzijde Unie N.V. (AKU) of Arnheim, a synthetic fibers manufacturer.[40] In 1942, the concern rejected the Dresdner Bank's tender of "Aryanized" shares in the Lijm & Gelatinefabriek "Delft."[41]

In Luxemburg, IG sought, through VSW, title to one factory, a producer of industrial gases at Rodingen. At the beginning of 1944, the concern pledged to keep the plant going even in periods of slack demand, but as in the cases of the Belgian and Dutch gases plants, there is no record that a sale was accomplished.[42]

Had Germany won the Second World War, IG almost certainly would have taken a more active role in the Low Countries. As early as October 1940, the concern concluded an agreement with Schering AG demarcating spheres of influence and possible eventual stock purchases in the pharmaceuticals field within Holland, Belgium, and France.[43] However, in the short term, IG fully accepted the comfortable argument that "the German claim to leadership in the chemicals field is so fundamentally and emphatically demonstrable that it requires no precipitate measures. On the contrary, it permits generosity."[44]

---

[38] See Bayer 91/1, Vowi 3974, 13.VI.40.

[39] On Soest, see NI-10164/84, p. 15; on Schiedam, see the fuller discussion in Hayes, *Gleichschaltung*, pp. 380–2.

[40] On Unilever, see Ulshöfer, *Einflussnahme*, p. 158; and Friedrich Facius, *Wirtschaft und Staat* (Boppard, 1959), p. 233. In general, see NG-3693, the so-called Saager Bericht, 23.IX.41, printed in Eichholtz, *Geschichte*, vol. 1, pp. 374–8.

[41] See NI-13898, printed in Ulshöfer, *Einflussnahme*, pp. 158–9; IG in Abw., Zefi 84–62, Dresdner Bank to K. Pfeiffer, 12.III.42, and Bachem and Gierlichs of NW7 to the Deutsche Länderbank, 30.III.42.

[42] NI-8585/70, Diedenhofen Branch Office to VSW, Berlin, 25.I.44. By 1940, DAG of Troisdorf also controlled an explosives producer in Luxemburg, Luxit Sprengstoff GmbH; NI-10030/82, Organization Chart of DAG, Troisdorf.

[43] NI-7656/62, Excerpt from minutes of conference between Mann and Dr. Rohrer of Schering, 16.X.40.

[44] BA Koblenz, ZSg 127, Bd. 40, "Chemie in der Grossraumwirtschaft," *Die chemische Industrie*, 63, no. 11 (November 1940), p. 148.

France

Similarly, IG set out in 1940, not to swallow the French organic chemicals industry, but to subordinate it to the firm's postwar plans. Thus, the Commercial Committee resolved in mid-July, "We . . . as a matter of principle take the point of view that the French chemical industry must maintain an individual existence under the coming New Order."[45] Behind this decision lay not only a desire to avoid the appearance of cupidity, but also worry about the concern's manageability. As Kühne wrote to Schnitzler, "We are all already abundantly burdened with every conceivable sideline, and so far as vital competing enterprises, as in the dyes field, are not involved, we should keep our hands off as much as possible."[46] Accordingly, here, too, the concern passed up a number of potential acquisitions, notably the 600,000 available shares in the St. Gobain firm, one of France's largest chemical enterprises.[47] For the most part, then, IG contented itself with the same sorts of actions as in the Low Countries: plant shutdowns, long-term market sharing agreements, export prohibitions, and assaults on the positions of foreign-owned companies. The combine sought to accomplish its ends in partnership with the larger existing French producers rather than to replace them entirely.

Nonetheless, within these limits IG pursued a more acquisitive policy with greater tenacity in France than in the other semisovereign nations of the Nazi empire. This attitude reflected a mixture of commercial calculation and accumulated bitterness. Between the wars, France developed several sizable organics firms, largely at IG's expense and, in the concern's view, on the basis of its scientific and technical achievements. At the heart of the French dyestuffs industry were the processes and subsidiaries seized from the Little IG under the Versailles treaty and updated after the war according to the terms of the Gallus Vertrag, a profit-sharing agreement that the Germans offered under duress in 1919 and the French abrogated without compensation in 1924. Almost as much as their dye-making counterparts, French pharmaceuticals firms profited by the wartime confiscation of German trademarks and the postwar imposition of virtually prohib-

[45] NI-9288/77, Annex to the minutes of the 34th KA meeting, 18–19.VII.40.
[46] Bayer 13/25, Kühne to Schnitzler, 15.X.40.
[47] See IG in Abw., Zefi 84-62, Angebote auf Beteiligung I, Berlin NW7 memoranda dated 1–21.XI.40.

itive restrictions on German imports. Meanwhile, the absence of
French patent protection for pharmaceutical discoveries freed these
companies to copy IG's creations whenever possible. Consequently,
Farben's share of French dye consumption fell from some 75–90% in
1913 to a mere 9% in 1938, its sales of medicinal preparations in
France from 1.5 million to 850,000 marks. Where once only two
native-owned dye firms were confined to about 10% of the home
market, a nine-member French dyes cartel arose to supply 66% of
domestic needs and 4 to 6% of the international dyes trade. By the late
1930s, the leading native pharmaceuticals house was outselling IG's
drugs by at least 10 to 1 in France and undercutting their prices in
other European markets. When the Third Republic surrendered, a
vengeful IG was determined to recover lost ground by regulating
"French production and its marketing for all time to come."[48]

Predictably, IG's chief target was the national dyes cartel. It consisted (after the separation of Alsace-Lorraine) of two independent firms
and two plants and four subsidiaries of the widely diversified
Etablissements Kuhlmann, and its output accounted for approximately 3% of French chemical sales.[49] Kuhlmann's dye operations
constituted about one-quarter of its total worth, which came to less
than one-twentieth of IG's.[50] Reviving the concern's rationalization
program of the mid-1920s, IG's New Order plan suggested the formation of a single national dyes company, in which IG "might be allowed
to acquire 50% of the capital" and half the seats on the governing
boards. The resulting corporation would absorb and close the smaller

[48] NI-11252/93, IG's New Order plan for France, 3.VIII.40, pp. 12–22; J. J. Beer, *The Emergence of the German Dye Industry* (Urbana, Ill., 1959), pp. 38–9; Fritz ter-Meer, *Die IG Farben Aktiengesellschaft* (Düsseldorf, 1953), p. 76; Bayer 4C9.32, Control Office, *Dyestuffs*, Annex V; NI-7658/62, Kramer to Mann, 15.I.48; NI-7629/62, Memo of discussions between IG and Rhône-Poulenc, 29–30.XI.–2.XII.40, p. 1; Milward, *French Economy*, pp. 100–1. On the Gallus Vertrag, see NI-5193/38, Schnitzler's affidavit of 7.III.47; Karl Holdermann, *Im Banne der Chemie* (Düsseldorf, 1953), pp. 167–70; and the highly colored account in Borkin, *Crime and Punishment*, pp. 32–4. Borkin's description of Joseph Frossard as IG's "secret trump card" rests entirely on a misreading of Holdermann.
[49] Kugler testimony, *NMT*, vol. 8, pp. 192–3; terMeer testimony, *NMT*, vol. 8, pp. 212, 236. A more reliable estimate is difficult to come by, since the sole scholarly work on the French chemical industry that covers the immediate prewar years, R. Richeux's *L'industrie chimique en France: Structure et production 1850–1957* (Thèse, Université de Paris, 1958) is unavailable in the United States. The figure used here was not contradicted at the postwar trial.
[50] Kugler testimony, *NMT*, vol. 8, p. 192; Bayer 91/1, Vowi 4070, ETS Kuhlmann, Paris, Konzerndarstellung, 27.VII.40.

manufacturers, monopolize the French home and colonial markets, and export only in exceptional cases.[51] It would also serve, though the concern kept this idea to itself, as the entering wedge for IG's subjugation of the entire French organic chemicals sphere.[52]

At the outset of the occupation, however, IG was unsure how and with whom to negotiate this deal. In July, the French producers, anxious to resume functioning on the basis of the interwar cartel agreements, asked for a conference with the concern under the auspices of the Franco-German Armistice Commission at Wiesbaden.[53] IG demurred, not yet certain that its reorganization scheme would have the support of the occupation authorities or even that they would leave the factories in French hands. Hence, the tentative phrasing of IG's New Order proposals of August 3 and their reference to acquiring stock in the French dyestuffs industry "from the Reich."[54] Schlotterer's reaction on that date was somewhat reassuring, however. He pronounced IG's program "not . . . excessive" and approved eventual private negotiations with the French companies once preliminary conversations had prepared them "to cede the first place to the German dye industry." But Schlotterer also directed the concern to consult first with Ambassador Hemmen, the head of the Reich's economic delegation to the Armistice Commission, and with Ungewitter, who would rule on whether IG's plan "does not run contrary to the interests of the national economy generally."[55] In the interim, the military administration in France sequestered Kuhlmann's dyes plant at Villers-St. Paul, and representatives of the Economics Ministry in Paris began "softening up" the French firms.[56]

During the next two months, Ambassador Hemmen clarified matters by deciding to use "the settlement in the dyes field . . . to a certain extent as a pattern for other industrial fields."[57] Eager to penetrate the French economy without provoking excessive antagonism, Hemmen

[51] NI-11252/93, 3.VIII.40, p. 27.
[52] See NI-6957, Extracts from the minutes of a conference at Frankfurt, 22.V.41, NMT, vol. 8, p. 133.
[53] NI-6727, Memorandum concerning the meeting of representatives of the German and French dyestuffs industries, 21.XI.40, NMT, vol. 8, p. 120.
[54] NI-11252/93, 3.VIII.40, p. 27.
[55] NI-6840, Terhaar's file memo, 7.VIII.40, NMT, vol. 7, p. 1447.
[56] NI-4894/36, Order of the chief of Military Administration in France, 7.VIII.40; NI-14224, File note by Kugler, [December 1940], NMT, vol. 8, p. 113.
[57] NI-15228, Schnitzler and Kugler to Kramer of IG's sales organization in Paris, 8.XI.40, NMT, vol. 8, p. 110.

informed IG that "the pressure required for our negotiations should develop, so to speak, from the natural course of events as the economic situation in France grew more difficult," not through "premature official intervention in the French factories." He therefore advocated accepting the French petition for purely private talks at Wiesbaden but delaying them until late autumn or early winter of 1940.[58] IG, professing "its intention to remain the object of official decisions," readily fell in with Hemmen's plan, since "it is quite obvious that our tactical position towards the French will be far stronger if the first fundamental discussion takes place in Germany and, more particularly, at the site of the Armistice Delegation; and if our program as outlined, is presented, so to speak, from official quarters."[59] For a time Schnitzler ignored increasingly desperate overtures from the French and, in his words, "let them simmer in their own juice."[60]

By October 23, the day before Hitler and Pétain met at Montoire to seal the policy of "collaboration," Schnitzler began to doubt that time was on IG's side. He feared that the common interest of the French owners and the German military authorities in returning the plants to operation would weaken IG's bargaining position since, once resuscitated, the French companies would feel less pressure to meet the concern's demands. Therefore, he requested Hemmen to schedule a parley with the French for the week of November 18 and asked to meet with Mulert and Hoffmann of the Economics Ministry to go over IG's tactics in the discussions.[61]

As a result, representatives of the French dyes companies found themselves summoned suddenly to Wiesbaden for a meeting on November 21, 1940, with their German counterparts and delegates of both governments.[62] Invited to speak first, the French proposed bas-

58 NI-6839, Memo by Terhaar on, inter alia, his conference with Ambassador Hemmen at Wiesbaden on 5.IX.40, 14.IX.40, NMT, vol. 8, pp. 105–6.
59 NI-14224, Kugler's file note, [December 1940], NMT, vol. 8, p. 114; NI-15228, Schnitzler and Kugler to Kramer, 8.XI.40, NMT, vol. 8, p. 110.
60 NI-5193/38, Schnitzler's affidavit, 7.III.47; NI-6785/52, Affidavit by G. Kuepper, 10.VI.47; NI-6161, Extract from the minutes of the 36th KA meeting, 25.IX.40, NMT, vol. 8, p. 108; NI-795, Schnitzler to J. Hess, 4.X. 40, NMT, vol. 8, pp. 108–9.
61 NI-879/9, Schnitzler to Mulert, 23.X.40.
62 On this and the subsequent rounds of negotiations, see, in addition to the sources cited specifically, the general accounts in NI-4886/36, Affidavit by G. Thesmar of St. Denis, 8.I.47; NI-4889/36, Affidavit by R. Duchemin of Kuhlmann, 9.I.47; and Milward, French Economy, pp. 100–4.

ing their future relationship with IG on the cartel agreement of 1927. At this, Hemmen pronounced himself "speechless" but recovered rapidly enough to shout them down and declare that he could not conduct conversations on so unrealistic a basis. Equally shocked by the French position, Schnitzler rejected it in calmer terms, pointing out that both the British and Swiss parties to the cartel had declared it defunct at the outbreak of the war. He then read a memorandum justifying IG's claim to leadership of the European dyes industry with reference to the advantages that France had taken of the German dye producers since 1913 and the need for a unified Continental position in postwar negotiations with overseas rivals. After Hemmen pointedly reminded the French that they were free to leave their fate to a peace conference, Schnitzler summarized the thrust of IG's plans: restriction of French dyes to the home and colonial markets, German financial participation in the French industry, and elimination of competition between IG and the French. Hemmen concluded by stressing that "there must be cooperation from production to sales" and that "he would warmly welcome the achievement of an agreement . . . which would serve as a model for further negotiations now aimed at between the more important German and French industries."[63]

The next day, the businessmen convened alone to discuss specifics. Stressing that "the German claim does not extend to all organic chemical production," but only to dyes and related products, IG outlined to the French for the first time the dimensions of and procedure for forming the proposed national dyes company. The concern then conceded that exports to Belgium and perhaps a few other countries might continue but maintained that the French could make up for the rest of their forgone foreign proceeds by cutting back on Swiss imports and the sales of a Swiss subsidiary in France. Finally, Farben claimed 51% of the stock in the new corporation as compensation for the fact that the president of its administrative board would always be a Frenchman.[64] This increased demand apparently sprang from the insistence of IG's technical leaders, especially Fritz terMeer, that only a firm majority shareholding could ensure the necessary rationalization of the French factories and protect the secrecy of the production pro-

---

[63] NI-6727, Memo by Dr. Jekel of the meeting on 21.XI.40, *NMT*, vol. 8, pp. 118–26; NI-5901/44, IG's memo to the French delegation, 21.XI.40.
[64] NI-6838/53, Memo by Schnitzler of the meeting on 21.XI.40.

cesses IG intended to introduce.[65] Angry at what they considered a "dictate," the French broke off the talks in order to confer with their government.[66] Three weeks later, René Duchemin of Kuhlmann was still fuming that "he would rather see his hand cut off than sign such an agreement."[67]

For the next four months, the French companies and government tried vainly to loosen Farben's insistence on a German majority in the amalgamated dyes firm. The concern gave ground on lesser points and sweetened its proposals by offering the companies IG's own shares rather than francs as payment and by hinting at technical aid for Kuhlmann in other chemical fields. For the benefit of the Vichy regime, IG explicitly abandoned Hemmen's idea that the final agreement would set a precedent for other industries.[68] But on the central issue, the combine's negotiators remained obdurate. As they ran out of bargaining chips, they turned to threatening. Duchemin was advised that further delays in reaching a settlement could result in outright confiscation of the French factories, as in Alsace-Lorraine, or in the seizure of the entire Kuhlmann combine under the German Aryanization decree, which took effect while Raymond Berr, a Jew, was still vice-president and general director of the enterprise.[69] Meanwhile, the French dye works stood idle for lack of raw materials.[70] With their backs to the wall, the French tried new expedients in early March, again unsuccessfully.[71]

On March 10, 1941, the struggle abruptly ended. When the German and French businessmen gathered in Paris for another round of bargaining, Schnitzler stunned his opposite numbers with the news that Vichy had capitulated to IG's demand for 51%, provided that the

[65] NI-6785/52, Affidavit by G. Kuepper, 10.VI.47; NI-5193/38, Schnitzler's affidavit, 7.III.47; NI-10263/85, Affidavit by K. Krüger, 23.VIII.47; NI-5810/43, IG's internal office memo, 31.X.40.
[66] NI-15240/123, Extract from the French minutes of the meeting on 22.XI.40.
[67] NI-3707/27, Memo by Kramer, 14.XII.40.
[68] Ibid.; NI-14224, File note by Kugler concerning conferences on 28–30.XI.40, NMT, vol. 8, pp. 113–17; NI-6947/53, Memo by Kramer, 17.I.41; NI-6949/53, Report of conference in Paris on 20–21.I.41, signed by both delegations.
[69] NI-4889/36, Affidavit by Duchemin, 9.I.47. In 1942, IG interceded with brief success to obtain Berr's release from the Gestapo, but the French executive was rearrested and murdered at Auschwitz; see Schnitzler V/192, Kuhlmann to Kramer, 23.IX.42, and Oster II/33, Affidavit by G. Lelong, 12.XI.46.
[70] NI-3708/27, Kramer's memo of 31.I.41.
[71] For details on the French negotiating positions throughout this period, see Hayes, Gleichschaltung, pp. 392–3.

new company's president would always be French, that each na-
tionality would have equal representation on the boards, and that the
Reich would certify that the agreement represented "a special case."
While the French hastily corroborated this announcement, the parties
made arrangements to fix the value of the plants destined for the new
Compagnie des Matières Colorantes et Produits Chimiques "Francolor" SA, Paris, and designated its leading personnel. Two days later,
after the German government provided the requisite assurances and
Schnitzler dropped IG's demand that Francolor possess a legal monopoly on French dyes production, Vichy formally withdrew its objections
to IG's majority holding.[72]

Though forced to accept a German-controlled dyes company, the
French salvaged a few additional concessions during the following
months. By May, IG was complaining that, in drafting the formal
convention establishing Francolor, "the French are going back on
practically all matters which are essential for us." Farben ultimately
prevented the inclusion of language in the preamble that the French
could later use to annul the deal, but the French succeeded, among
other things, in defining the president's authority quite broadly, in
retaining limited export rights in western Europe, and in frustrating
terMeer's plan to insert Francolor into other organics fields.[73] Indeed,
after the war, Duchemin boasted that the French draftsmen made sure
that "Germany did not dominate the company," since the powerful
French president could be removed only by a two-thirds vote of the
board and no German employees or technicians gained posts in Francolor.[74] Even IG's negative influence over the personnel of Francolor
remained limited to one case, the transfer out of the dyes business of

[72] NI-6950/53, Unsigned file note on German–French conference, 10.III.41, and Bur-
andt's record of the meeting on 12.III.41. In July 1941, IG and Francolor formally
pledged not to force the remaining small French dyes firms out of business at home
or abroad (Schnitzler III/64, IG and the French dyes companies to French Ministry
for Industrial Production and Labor, 24.VII.41).
[73] NI-15220, Kugler to Schnitzler, 12.V.41, NMT, vol. 8, pp. 129–32; NI-6957, Minutes of a conference at Frankfurt, 12.V.41, NMT, vol. 8, pp. 133–6; NI-15219,
Kuepper's file note, 13.VI.41, NMT, vol. 8, pp. 136–7; NI-15218, Kuepper to
Schnitzler et al., NMT, vol. 8, pp. 137–8.
[74] NI-4889/36, Duchemin's affidavit, 9.I.47; see also Schnitzler IV/78, Frossard of
Francolor to Schnitzler, 30.XII.41. NI-6845/53 contains the final contract founding
Francolor, which is excerpted in NMT, vol. 8, pp. 139–45. On the ratification, see
Schnitzler IV/73, Memo by Kramer, 12.XII.41, and Borkin, Crime and Punishment,
p. 109. NI-6886/53 is the Articles of Incorporation of Francolor, 18.XII.41.

August Rhein, an employee of BASF before 1919 who, as an Alsatian, went over to Kuhlmann after World War l.[75]

Nor were the financial advantages of the Francolor transaction one-sided. It was, of course, a bargain for IG by any reckoning. However, the French parent companies obtained a price for the new corporation's works far in excess of their probable peacetime turnover or value after depreciation.[76] IG, in addition, discounted the market value of the stock exchanged for 51% of the Francolor shares, thus partially compensating the Gallic partners for the decline in the value of the franc since 1939.[77] French investors responded by promptly bidding up the share quotations for the so-called mother houses.[78] These in turn collectively exercised a stock option in 1942, thereby perhaps outstripping Solvay of Brussels as the largest financial participant in IG Farben.[79] Though Francolor never attained more than half the annual volume of dyes production promised in the founding contract, the plants increased their output of related products and during 1942 recovered their prewar sales level. Largely as a result of IG's efforts to route military contracts to Francolor, the firm paid a dividend of 6% in 1942 and announced a similar sum for 1943.[80] Indeed, the economic rationality of IG's "dictate" was confirmed after the Second World War, when a new Compagnie Francaise des Matières Colorantes, dominated by Kuhlmann, perpetuated the fusion imposed in 1941.[81]

IG's offensive against the French pharmaceuticals business followed a similar course during 1940–2. Even before the war, Bayer, the concern's drugs and insecticides division, had resolved to outflank

[75] NI-5193/38, Schnitzler's affidavit, 7.III.47; see also NI-5810/43, IG's internal office memo, 31.X.40. Rhein was not dismissed, as Borkin would have it (*Crime and Punishment*, p. 107).

[76] Schnitzler V/81, Affidavit by H. Muench; Schnitzler X/188, Affidavit by H. Walter; NI-5193/38, Schnitzler's affidavit, 7.III.47.

[77] NI-8077, *Vorstand* minutes of 10.VII.41, *NMT*, vol. 8, pp. 138–9; Schnitzler III/54, File note by Schnitzler, 16–19.VI.41; NI-5195/38, Schnitzler's affidavit, 17.III.47.

[78] NI-5196/38, Schnitzler's affidavit, 18.III.47.

[79] NI-9288/77, 49th KA meeting, 8.VII.42; terMeer testimony, *NMT*, vol. 8, p. 219; Schnitzler V/86-89.

[80] Bayer 4C9.32, Control Office, *Dyestuffs*, Contract 29; Ambros testimony, *NMT*, vol. 8, pp. 166–9; and the five documents excerpted in *NMT*, vol. 8, pp. 145–52.

[81] Rosemarie Denzel, *Die Chemische Industrie Frankreichs unter der deutschen Besetzung im Zweiten Weltkrieg* (Tübingen, 1959), pp. 128–9; Bayer 4C9.25, Mueller and Knieriem manuscript, pp. 130–2.

official trade restrictions and rising popular sales resistance to German imports by founding a manufacturing plant in France.[82] By 1940, victory seemed to have created other possibilities for dealing with French competition. The combine's New Order proposals summarized one line of attack, calling for free access to French markets, patent protection for German products, restoration of former German trademarks, and prohibitions of new plant construction.[83] Toward the end of August, Bayer's chief, Wilhelm R. Mann, Jr., began proceeding on a second front. At Wiesbaden and Paris, he discussed with German authorities the advisability of shutting down various native producers and received offers of aid in IG's plan to acquire 51% of the capital in Rhône-Poulenc, the paramount pharmaceuticals enterprise in France.[84]

Two obstacles, however, impeded IG's efforts. In the first place, the Reich Economics Ministry emphatically informed Mann that it opposed extensive plant closings in France fully as much as in the Low Countries.[85] Though official quarters remained supportive of IG's Rhône-Poulenc project, here the concern encountered a second problem: the capacity of the French firm to wage a long defensive struggle. Not only did Rhône-Poulenc have large inventories in reserve, but most of its plants were located in the unoccupied zone, out of reach of threats of seizure.[86]

Accordingly, IG decided to scale down its initial demands. In October, it dispatched a Frenchman named Faure-Beaulieu, an old friend of the Mann family, to Rhône-Poulenc. He transmitted an offer to form a joint sales company for all the French corporation's phar-

[82] Mann IV/526, Bayer directors conference, 13.VI.39; Mann IV/327, Affidavit by R. Langguth, 19.II.48, including excerpts of minutes of the 75th Main Pharmaceuticals Conference, 19.VII.39; Mann IV/326, Affidavit by W. Schmitz, 10.III.48.
[83] NI-11252/93, 3.VIII.40, p. 41.
[84] NI-6839, Terhaar's memo of conversations on 29.VIII.40–5.IX.40, NMT, vol. 8, pp. 98–106; NI-729, Kugler to Terhaar, 12.IX.40, NMT, vol. 8, pp. 106–7. On Rhône-Poulenc and its business, see NI-7992/66, Vowi 4123, 28.VIII.40. The only published account of the Rhône-Poulenc affair is Denzel, Chemische Industrie Frankreichs, pp. 130–8, which overlooks NI-792/8, Kugler's letter documenting IG's takeover plan. For Mann's somewhat inconsistent recollections, see the following five statements recorded between 28.III.47 and 3.IV.47: NI-7991/66, NI-14495–6/137, and NI-14500-01/138–9.
[85] Mann IV/953, Unsigned file note of Mann's conference with Mulert and Hoffmann of the RWM, 28.IX.40.
[86] NI-10399/86, Memo of Mann's conversation with Kolb and Michel, government representatives in Paris, 4–5.X.40.

maceuticals exports and all of its and Bayer's products sold within France. Warning the French twice of the superiority of this settlement to any likely to issue from a peace conference, Faure-Beaulieu described compliance with IG's claim to 51% of the shares in the new firm as a means by which Rhône-Poulenc might reduce the indemnities the German concern intended to seek for previous plagiarism of its goods, use of trade names like aspirin, and price warfare abroad.[87] During the following weeks, while IG concentrated on obtaining a revision of French patent laws, Rhône-Poulenc gave the concern to believe that this proposal might be acceptable.[88]

However, in November and December 1940, the French rejected IG's plan, and Rhône-Poulenc's second-in-command, Marcel Bo, threatened to resign along with many of the firm's employees, if IG forced the common sales company on them. After "heated" negotiations, Mann noted that he would have to leave Rhône-Poulenc to the mercy of German officialdom. At this point, the French tried to propitiate IG by acknowledging its right to a portion of Rhône-Poulenc's proceeds on products to which IG claimed patent rights. On several conditions, including promises that Rhône-Poulenc would align its prices with IG's and continue discussions of an "economic interrelationship," IG agreed to the corresponding contract.[89]

The French won no more than a respite. Even as IG seemed to abandon the idea of a joint sales company, it substituted a more menacing suggestion. In order to fulfill a "sincere and urgent wish, shared also by the German authorities, to cooperate more closely with you in some direction or other," IG asked openly for the first time for a shareholding in Rhône-Poulenc itself, mentioning 25% as the goal. As in the Francolor case, Farben baited its hook with a pledge to pay with its own stock and then added a commitment to grant Rhône-

87 NI-8613/71, Faure-Beaulieu to Wendling of Rhône-Poulenc, 8.X.40; NI-8612/71, File note by Bo and Wendling, 8.X.40; NI-7651/62, Brock and Krantz of IG to Mann, 8.X.40; NI-8371/69, Statement of Marcel Bo to the French deputy public prosecutor, 26.IV.47.
88 NI-7654/62, Bruggemann and Redies of IG to Justice Ministry, 4.XI.40; NI-10471/86, Unsigned memo of conference at the RWM, 12.XI.40.
89 NI-7658/62, Brock and Krantz to Mann, 15.XI.40; NI-7629/62, Minutes of meeting between IG and Rhône-Poulenc, 29–30.XI.40 and 2.XII.40; Mann IV/627, Explanatory note by Bo, 4.XII.40; Mann IV/581, File note of conference between IG and Rhône-Poulenc, 1.III.41; NI-6944/53, License agreement between Bayer and Rhône-Poulenc, 30.XII.40.

Poulenc licenses on all IG's new pharmaceutical discoveries.[90] The Germans made good on the latter point late in March 1941, meanwhile holding out to Rhône-Poulenc cooperation in the plastics, resins, and buna fields and the prospect that Bayer would withdraw entirely from the French market upon completion of a shares agreement.[91] Tempted by IG's offers and insecure in the aftermath of the Francolor settlement, Rhône-Poulenc quickly reverted to the "lesser evil" of a joint sales company, and IG, lacking any additional leverage, made do.[92] An existing French company, Theraplix SA, provided the name and legal basis for the new enterprise. It increased its stock limit from 5 million to 50 million francs and apportioned the shares publicly, for the sake of French sensibilities, among IG, Rhône-Poulenc, and Faure-Beaulieu on the ratio of 49 : 49 : 2, with the private understanding that Faure-Beaulieu held his packet in trust for Farben and would vote with it.[93]

As finally settled in the winter of 1941–42, the Theraplix deal did IG more good than Rhône-Poulenc harm. The latter firm emerged with its right to export unscathed. Both corporations were assured of a 50 % profit margin on preparations sold through the new company, and whereas IG turned over virtually its complete pharmaceuticals line, as well as that of several associated German firms, Rhône-Poulenc supplied only those products already marketed through Theraplix plus such additional ones as the French partner chose. The new corporation accounted for perhaps as little as 1% of French pharmaceuticals sales.[94] Just one German received a managerial post in Theraplix, and Rhône-Poulenc managed to elect one of its delegates to the administrative board as president and general director in place of Faure-Beaulieu, whom IG originally nominated. But if Theraplix served IG

[90] NI-7632/62, Bayer to Rhône-Poulenc, 18.XII.40.
[91] NI-8611/71, Hoerlein and Mann to Rhône-Poulenc, 28.III.41; NI-9288/77 (also Mann V/397), 40th KA meeting, 18.III.41; Mann V/669, Borgwardt to Rhône-Poulenc, 17.IV.41; Mann V/410, Bayer to Rhône-Poulenc, 4.III.41.
[92] NI-7635/62, Conference between IG and Rhône-Poulenc/Specia, 23–4.V.41 and 28.V.41.
[93] NI-7640/62, Conference with Rhône-Poulenc, 3.VII.41; Mann V/601, Faure-Beaulieu to Mann, 15.VII.41; Mann V/602, Mann to Faure-Beaulieu, 23.VII.41; NI-6538/50, Affidavit by Mann, 21.IV.47; NI-10544/87, Statement by Marcel Bo, 1.VIII.47. This arrangement required IG to do some explaining to the Nazi AO, which demanded an open showing of the German majority; see Mann V/661, Zefi file note, 6.XII.41; and NI-7178/56, Zefi to AO, 5.I.42.
[94] M892/55, Mann's testimony, p. 10587.

immediately only as an entrée to the French market, that advantage was not insignificant. Theraplix's profits surged from 5 million francs in 1941–2 to 9 million the following year and 20 million the year after that, largely as a result of the influx of Bayer products.[95] Moreover, neither side mistook the long-range potential of their arrangement. Indeed, Rhône-Poulenc unavailingly resisted IG's desire to plow Theraplix's profits back into independent production facilities, knowing that this spelled future trouble for the French producer.[96] Still, there appeared to be lucrative trade-offs, exemplified by the contract signed in March 1942 between IG and Rhône-Poulenc for joint construction of France's first synthetic rubber factory.[97]

The Francolor and Theraplix cases do not exhaust the list of IG's gains in France. Doubtless the profits the concern drew from these new enterprises got a boost from the mutual interest of Vichy and the German occupation in eliminating inefficient producers, which led to the closing of some 400 small dyes and lacquer installations and 884 pharmaceuticals laboratories during 1942–3.[98] In the photographic field, the German branch of Kodak checked IG's hopes of driving the French Kodak into the ground, but the latter guaranteed the concern a quarter of the French film market.[99] Farben may also have taken a small portion of Germany's one-third interest in France Rayonne, an amalgam of the French synthetic fibers companies formed in December 1940, and in mid-1942 the combine acquired for its alloys operations two small mines at Chateau-Lambert and Montmins.[100] Less dramatically, the seconding of various IG officers to the Chemicals Section of the Military Administration provided the concern with useful technical and commercial information, even perhaps with po-

95 Mann V/437, Affidavit by J. Schmitz, 11.II.48.
96 NI-7640/62, Conference with Rhône-Poulenc, 3.VII.41; NI-7634/62, Conference with Rhône-Poulenc, 12.XI.41; NI-8370/69, Agreement between Bayer and Rhône-Poulenc concerning Theraplix, 19.II.42; NI-7635/62, Conference with Rhône-Poulenc, 23-4.V.41.
97 Milward, *French Economy*, p. 105. The plant was never built, however. See Peter J. T. Morris, *The Development of Acetylene Chemistry and Synthetic Rubber by I.G. Farbenindustrie Aktiengesellschaft: 1926–1945* (Dissertation, University of Oxford, 1982), pp. 348, 352–5.
98 Denzel, *Chemische Industrie Frankreichs*, pp. 30, 32; Robert O. Paxton, *Vichy France* (New York, 1972), pp. 210–20, 354.
99 NI-9288/77, 40th KA meeting, 18.III.41; NI-6839/53, Terhaar's memo, 14.IX.40, *NMT*, vol. 8, pp. 103–4.
100 Milward, *French Economy*, pp. 100, 104–5, 246–7.

tential influence in any postwar division of the spoils.[101] Finally, IG benefited from the Reich's determination to reduce the role of French capital in the rest of occupied Europe, not only in the case of Winnica or, indirectly, by the takeovers made through Kontinentale Oel, but also in Norway.

Norway

When German troops occupied Norway in April 1940, IG Farben had relatively few demands to make of the local chemical industry. No native enterprise produced dyes or photographic supplies; the dozen domestic manufacturers of pharmaceuticals and basic chemicals had neither competed with IG abroad nor prevented it from steadily expanding sales within the country during the interwar period.[102] The concern also enjoyed a well-established alliance in the nitrogen field with the cardinal Norwegian chemicals firm, Norsk-Hydro Elektrisk Kvaelstoff S/A. As a result of an exchange of shares in 1927, Norsk-Hydro's general director sat on IG's *Aufsichtsrat,* and the German corporation held 25% of the Norwegian undertaking's stock as well as a place on its managing board, occupied by no less than Hermann Schmitz. IG licensed the Haber–Bosch process to Norsk-Hydro and helped design its new synthetic nitrogen factory at Herøen; in return, the output, later limited to 90,000 tons annually, was marketed overseas through the German Nitrogen Syndicate, led by Farben.[103] Although Norsk-Hydro remained controlled by French capital and the nitrogen agreements did not preclude competition with IG in other fields, relations between the two firms evolved harmoniously. At the outset of the occupation, IG sought to freeze the Norwegian company's chemicals production in place but not to expand German financial participation in the enterprise. As usual, the concern's New Order proposals consisted of requests for restrictions on local output and removal of barriers to German imports.

Norway possessed, however, one powerful allure for IG and the Reich: an enormous potential for cheap hydroelectric power, particu-

101 See Hoechst TEA 901, Exchange of letters between Goldschmidt and terMeer, 1–19.II.43; and Denzel, *Chemische Industrie Frankreichs,* p. 58.
102 Unless otherwise indicated, this paragraph draws on NI-7784/63, IG's New Order plan for Norway, 8.V.41, especially pp. 5, 7, 27.
103 NI-7745/63, Affidavit by W. Jacobi, 7.VII.47.

larly valuable in the fabrication of light metals. Both concern and
regime immediately recognized the desirability of exploiting this resource, but they clashed sharply over the means of doing so and the
question of who should direct the effort. Of the resulting imbroglio
Alan Milward has remarked with only slight exaggeration that "no
other wartime episode is so revealing about the nature of the relationship between the National Socialist government and the industrial
circles which supported it."[104] In the end, IG Farben improved its
position in Norway, but at a price, as well as in a manner that the
concern, if left to its own devices, would not have adopted.

The Reich's plans for Norwegian industrial development grew out
of the mounting discrepancy between the performance of European
aluminum producers and the needs of the Luftwaffe. The latter projected an annual appetite for 840,000 tons of this metal by 1943 but
total output within the New Order and Switzerland of only about half
that amount.[105] Moreover, Göring believed that the Vereinigte Aluminium Werke (VAW), the manufacturer of 70% of German aluminum, was slighting the needs of his air force. Although owned by the
Finance Ministry, VAW operated largely autonomously according to
orthodox commercial canons and therefore worried as much as purely
private enterprises about potential overcapacity.[106] Göring thus resolved to expand Norwegian aluminum production rapidly and to
reserve it for his purposes through his favored device of founding "a
kind of ministerial industry" akin to the Hermann Göring Werke or
Kontinentale Oel. In May 1940, he appointed Koppenberg of the
Junkers aircraft company as trustee for the six existing foreign-owned
aluminum firms in Norway and directed him to devise a stepped-up
production program.[107] By October, Koppenberg had Göring's approval for a multistage plan to augment the Norwegian power network and to increase the associated productive capacity for alumina,

104 Alan Milward, The Fascist Economy in Norway (Oxford, 1972), p. 171. Throughout this discussion of events in Norway, I am relying heavily on Milward's thorough, generally sound, and unavoidably confusing account, pp. 171–208. There is
   a shorter, usually reliable version of this affair in Fritz Petrick, "Zwei
   Schlüsseldokumente zur faschistischen Aufteilung der europäischen Aluminiumin-
   dustrie," JfW, 18 (1977), pp. 253–6.
105 Milward, Fascist Economy, p. 172.
106 O. Klug, Konzerne in der neuen Wirtschaft (Berlin, 1936), pp. 32–4. See VAW's
   opposition to the expansion of aluminum capacity in the 1930s; NI-14674/119,
   Memo of a conference at the Raw Materials and Foreign Exchange Staff, 11.VIII.36.
107 NI-8146/67, File note by Mayer-Wegelin, 30.VI.41.

an essential intermediate, from 18,000 to 203,000 tons per year, for aluminum from 36,800 to 243,000 tons, and for magnesium from 0 to 10,000 tons – all at a cost of more than 1.2 billion marks.[108]

Although Göring wanted to exclude German industry from this project altogether, he soon recognized his technological dependence on the existing light-metals makers. The task of arranging business's cooperation in constructing and financing the necessary new factories therefore fell on Carl Krauch as head of the Reich Office for Economic Development. Informed of the *Reichsmarschall*'s determination to break VAW's quasi monopoly, Krauch strung that firm along during October while he negotiated with its only German-owned rival, IG Farben, which in partnership with the Metallgesellschaft manufactured at Bitterfeld about 20% of Germany's aluminum.[109] On October 16, he outlined to Bürgin and Moschel of the Bitterfeld plant the first stages of Koppenberg's plan, particularly as they involved Norsk-Hydro's Herøen works, and invited IG to prepare a proposal "regarding the structure of a new company in which Farben can have a controlling interest."[110]

Excited by the chance "to gain a decisive influence on European aluminum production" and convinced of "the significance of the entire light-metal field, not only for war, but also, and more particularly, for peace[time] developments," IG's representatives exhorted their superiors to "decide for participation on a large scale" in Koppenberg's plan. Besides, they noted, IG's response would very likely determine the degree to which the concern would have access to the vastly increased supply of cheap power for other purposes. And, as always, there were the perils of not acting:

We consider it quite possible that the Hermann Göring works will enter the field if Farben does not take the opportunity offered now. If that happens . . . we would once again experience the situation that existed after the World War. . . . As a result of the tendency toward socialization, the Lautawerk, the largest foundry, fell to the state and the combine had to restrict itself to 20% of aluminum production. If another state-owned firm enters this field, our share would be still further reduced. This firm would also be sure to enter the field of magnesium.[111]

---

[108] See the table in Milward, *Fascist Economy*, p. 178.
[109] Ibid., p. 196; NI-7562/61, Excerpt from Dr. Neukirch's in-house history, pp. 178–80; Petrick *JfW*, 18 (1977), p. 250.
[110] NI-8033/66, Memo by W. Moschel, 18.X.40.
[111] NI-8034/66, Bürgin and Moschel to Schmitz et al., 23.X.40.

In fact, Koppenberg's grand design posed additional dangers to the concern. The establishment of new plants for finished aluminum products would compete with IG's existing facilities.[112] More seriously, if other firms acquired a decisive voice in executing Koppenberg's scheme, they would intrude on IG's relationship with Norsk-Hydro, whose Herøen plant constituted the nucleus of the initial development effort. Outsiders might divert electric current from the concern's own goal of expanding Herøen's nitrogen output to cover all Scandinavian fertilizer needs or acquire the secrets of two precious production processes: an electrolytic smelting method for magnesium and a means of deriving alumina from Norwegian labradorite ore.[113] All these considerations made IG's leaders receptive to Bürgin's and Moschel's proposal to form a consortium of light-metals producers, dominated by IG, to take over the Norwegian plants and execute Koppenberg's plan.[114]

The concern's hopes, however, were stillborn. Krauch had seriously overestimated the price Göring would pay for industry's technical expertise. At the behest of the *Reichsmarschall*, Koppenberg founded on December 3, 1940, a new holding company to accomplish his program. Eventually named Hansa Leichtmetall, this firm was a creature of the Air Ministry, which held 51% of the stock through the Bank der deutschen Luftfahrt.[115] Two months later, the ministry went on the offensive in Norway, demanding that IG and Norsk-Hydro construct aluminum, alumina, magnesium, and cryolite plants at Herøen and allot Hansa Leichtmetall one-third of the shares in a new company that would own the entire complex. IG acceded, but not before obtaining compensation for the Metallgesellschaft in the aluminum field and for Norsk-Hydro in nitrogen, as well as promises that the Reich would supply IG with short-term credits during the early segments of the plan and reduce the official presence in Herøen once other sources of capital became available, probably after the war.[116]

---

[112] Milward, *Fascist Economy*, p. 175.

[113] Oster II/53, Affidavit by A. Hoffmann, 1.III.48; Milward, *Fascist Economy*, pp. 177, 181.

[114] NI-8034/66, Bürgin and Moschel to Schmitz et al., 23.X.40.

[115] Milward, *Fascist Economy*, pp. 183–4.

[116] NI-8144/67, Conference at the RLM re Herøen, 7.II.41; NI-8145/67, Cejka to Mayer-Wegelin, 27.II.41, transmitting Cejka's file note of the conference on 6.II.41. For the background to this settlement, see Hayes, *Gleichschaltung*, pp. 409–10.

At this point, Koppenberg's project ran up against two problems. The first was the politically inspired insistence of Josef Terboven, the German *Reichskommissar*, on adherence to Norway's strict restrictions on the exploitation of water power by foreign-dominated corporations. IG's Max Ilgner conceived a possible way out of this difficulty by forming an intermediate holding company, A/S Nordag, which would remain under the control of Hansa and the Reich but be chartered in Oslo as a Norwegian corporation. Nordag would own majorities in all the producing companies, save the power plants, in which Norwegians would hold 60% of the shares, and the Herøen factories, which would become the property of Nordisk Lettmetall, whose shares IG, Nordag, and Norsk-Hydro would divide equally.[117] IG's Wilhelm Moschel was to become chairman of the managing boards of Hansa, Nordag, and Lettmetall, as well as general director of the latter two firms, but IG dominated none of the respective governing boards.[118]

The second obstacle took longer to finesse. Backed by the Economics Ministry, VAW, adamantly refused to let itself be cut out of a share in A/S Nordag. The Air Ministry met this claim with an unacceptable counterdemand that VAW offer some of its stock to Hansa.[119] Within weeks, the two German firms were engaged in a continentwide contest to control vital raw materials for the Norwegian aluminum plants, and VAW was looking for an opening to Norway.[120] But Hans Kehrl, IG's old antagonist at the Economics Ministry, gradually engineered an armistice. Through the Dresdner Bank and an Austrian firm, he bought up a quarter of the French shares in Norsk-Hydro held in trust by the Banque de Paris.[121] Since he bruited the intention of selling these shares to VAW, both IG and the Air Ministry reacted with alarm, the former because it feared any influence by VAW's parent company VIAG in Norsk-Hydro's nitrogen production, the latter because it hoped to avoid further dependence on VAW for aluminum

117 Milward, *Fascist Economy*, pp. 187–8; NI-9360/77, Excerpts from the minutes of the 40th KA meeting, 18.III.41.
118 Petrick, *JfW*, 18 (1977), p. 254; but Moschel was not a member of IG's *Vorstand*, as Petrick states. NI-2712/20, Statement by Ilgner and Schnitzler, 12.VIII.45.
119 NI-7562/61, Neukirch's in-house history, pp. 179–80.
120 See Milward, *Fascist Economy*, pp. 189, 191–4.
121 NI-8088/66, File note by IG's Kersten, 28.III.41; Ilgner XIIA/239, Affidavit by H. Pilder of the Dresdner Bank.

supplies. Kehrl adroitly extorted concessions from each complainant. In return for his promise to sell his stock packet to Hansa instead, IG granted VAW a long-sought license to produce magnesium, and Hansa agreed to assign its shares in Nordag to VAW after the war. VAW obligingly dropped its claim to a role in Norway for the dura‑ tion.[122]

Kehrl's maneuver not only reconciled Berlin's interests in Norway, but also undercut IG's effort to strengthen its weakening grip on the development of Herøen. In order to fund its portion of the capital required there, Norsk-Hydro's board authorized a share increase of 50 million Norwegian crowns — just enough to give Farben a theoretical majority. Under the corporation's charter, the board could assign 43% of that issue to such purchasers as it chose.[123] IG intended that German interests were to acquire the bulk of this stock and buy out such subscription rights to the remaining 57% as were held by French shareholders. To force the French into selling, IG informed them that the absence of a Franco-Norwegian clearing agreement ruled out their actual purchase of the new stock. Though French representatives pro‑ tested against their exclusion from the smaller bloc of the shares and suggested a variety of means by which payment for the others might be effected, Ilgner brushed aside their arguments. In June, at a general meeting of Norsk-Hydro's stockholders, which the Frenchmen among them could not attend, the stock issue plan was approved. IG was characteristically liberal in the matter of money; hence, the rate at which the concern purchased the French subscription rights consider‑ ably exceeded their market value.[124] But by this time some of the subscription rights had fallen to Hansa via Kehrl's purchases in Paris. Upon completion of the stock issue, IG's holding in Norsk-Hydro therefore rose from 25 to only 31.5%, and the state's share came to 21.5%.[125] Moreover, in the meantime, the Reich forced IG to vote its stock jointly with the government's, thus guaranteeing that IG would

---

122 NI-2712/20, Statement by Ilgner and Schnitzler, 12.VIII.45; NI-6348/47, Ilgner's affidavit, 10.IV.47; Milward, *Fascist Economy,* p. 196.
123 NI-10163/84, Article 15 of Norsk-Hydro's Articles of Incorporation, 1932.
124 Milward, *Fascist Economy,* pp. 189–90; Bayer 4C9.25, Mueller–Knieriem manu‑ script, pp. 215–20; NI-2712/20, Statement by Ilgner and Schnitzler, 12.VIII.45; NI-13373/109, Affidavit by J. Allier, 3.XI.47; Ilgner XIIB/220, 234, 242–50, con‑ temporaneous documents concerning payment for the French rights.
125 NI-8449/69, Report of the Deutsche Revision- und Treuhand GmbH, 31.XII.41.

not have greater influence in Lettmetall than the state and that the concern would lack incentive to increase its position in Norsk-Hydro.[126]

By June 14, 1941, when the Luftwaffe presented to Terboven the organizational framework produced by all these maneuvers (approximated in Appendix I), IG had failed to prevent the outcomes feared in Bürgin's and Moschel's letter of the preceding October. The concern was now entitled to an expanded portion of Norsk-Hydro's profits and, for the duration of the war, to license fees of upward of 3.5 million marks for the plants at Herøen.[127] If the Reich kept its promises to privatize its holdings after the fighting ceased, IG would emerge with a majority in Norsk-Hydro, hence in Lettmetall. But a state-owned firm, VAW, had entered the magnesium field; IG's share of aluminum sales was likely to fall even more once VAW inherited A/S Nordag, and the concern's control of the Herøen site remained incomplete.

Koppenberg's plan came to nought well before the collapse of Nazi Germany. During the latter half of 1941, Terboven vacillated over the question of Norwegian majorities in the new corporations while other demands pressed in on the Reich's limited supplies of construction materials. In December, the planned second stage of the program was forsaken; in May 1942, the first stage was truncated; in July 1943, Speer ordered that the Herøen plants, recently bombed out by the British, not be rebuilt and charged IG with faulty planning; and in September 1944, the cancellation of work on the alumina plant at Tyin finished off the program. During the period from 1940 to 1944, annual output of aluminum in Norway failed to recover its level as of 1939.[128] The largest gainers by virtue of IG's ambitions proved, as in France, to be the native companies. After the war Norsk-Hydro retained some 268 million Norwegian crowns worth of equipment on an investment of only 86 million, and the company used these facilities to

126 NI-8086/67, Kersten to Ilgner, 18.III.41. Cf. D. Eichholtz's somewhat misleading account, "Expansionsrichtung Nordeuropa: Der 'Europäische Grosswirtschafts-raum' und die nordischen Länder nach dem faschistischen Ueberfall auf die UdSSR," ZfG, 27 (1979), pp. 20–1.
127 NI-8038/66, Contract between Nordisk Lettmetall and IG, 22.IX.41; NI-8087/67, IG to RLM, 22.V.41.
128 Milward, Fascist Economy, pp. 200–4.

complete the damaged magnesium plant as well as a related electrical installation at Marr.[129]

As Milward noted, Norway provided an illuminating test case of business–state relations under Nazism. Neither side could command the other, at least in part because neither side could achieve unity. Terboven clashed with everyone in Berlin. There the Air Ministry and the Economics Ministry were temporarily at odds, and within the Four Year Plan organization, Göring and Krauch pursued different goals. IG and VAW elbowed each other while squaring off in different fashions against the government. The officials acted on divergent conceptions of the Third Reich's political and strategic requirements, but the businessmen concentrated on their postwar commercial positions, fearing that new developments "would end up entirely under the control of the Reich government and thus weaken their position even further against the governing fascist politicians who took by no means the same view of capital and its deployment as they did."[130] Indeed, the priority IG assigned to corporate interests extended to those of Norsk-Hydro. Until the end of the war, the combine petitioned the German government to reimburse that firm for bomb damage, arguing that Norsk-Hydro had participated in the light-metals program for the regime's, not its own, advantage.[131]

The Balkans

Despite their prominence in Nazi visions of the *Grossraum*, the Balkans remained a sideshow for IG Farben throughout the Third Reich. They were, in Carl Bosch's dismissive phrase, a mere *"Hoffnungsmarkt."*[132] This status was relatively clear in the period before 1939. Although Southeast Europe's portion of IG's foreign sales rose from 15% in 1932 to 24% in 1940, the corresponding figures for all German chemical exports were 14 and 32%, for total German exports 11

---

[129] Ilgner XIIA/194, Affidavit by J. Frantz; Ilgner XIIA/205, Excerpt from Drammon's Tidende, 25.V.46.
[130] Milward, *Fascist Economy*, p. 207.
[131] Ilgner XIIA/198-204, 254, Contemporaneous documents, 1943–5, on IG's claims; Bayer 4C9.25, Mueller–Knieriem manuscript, pp. 216–17.
[132] Quoted in Hellmuth Tammen, *Die I. G. Farbenindustrie Aktiengesellschaft (1925–1933)* (Dissertation, Freie Universität, Berlin, 1978), p. 253.

and 28%. Not only did the growth rate of IG's proceeds from the region thus fail to keep pace with that of larger product groups, but the Balkans accounted for a declining proportion of IG's total sales receipts: from 6.9% in 1932 to 5.3% in 1939 to 3.7% in 1940. Since the various clearing treaties with the Southeast European governments permitted German firms to sell at inflated prices, it is doubtful that the gain in the value of IG's exports to the region from 60 million to 80 million marks represented an increase in the volume of goods sold. IG's share of regional chemical consumption in fact fell slightly, whereas that of native producers rose from 59 to 66%.[133]

Nor did the concern seek to counter this trend by pursuing an active investment and production policy in the area before the Anschluss and the Munich Pact. During the 1930s, the sales of IG's principal subsidiaries in the Balkan countries held constant at 8 million to 9 million marks; those of DAG of Bratislava actually dropped, and by 1939 only one-third of its plant was operating.[134] Whereas IG launched no fewer than twenty-one development projects in Italy, France, England, Spain, the United States, and Latin America in the five years following the Nazi takeover, the combine virtually withheld its capital from the Southeast.[135] Highly publicized undertakings, like IG's plan for soybean cultivation in Romania and Bulgaria, redounded to the benefit of a food-hungry Reich and won IG good will in Berlin, Bucharest, and Sofia but cost little and served mainly as a means of financing exports at existing levels. The mining sector, a much-touted drawing card for involvement in the regional economy, proved unattractive on close examination. In 1937, at the instigation of Wilhelm Keppler, the concern sent two technical experts to investigate seven Yugoslav ore deposits. IG's representatives advised against investing in any of the sites.[136] Just before the invasion of Poland, a report from the Central Purchasing Department to Fritz Gajewski summarized the limited importance of the Balkans to the combine as a raw materials source. Of fifty-one substances essential to IG's output, the region could supply only four; of these, the chrome, bauxite, and antimony reserves (on

---

Bayer 84/Eur. Allg., Unterlagen zum Bericht von Herrn Dr. Ilgner, 11.XI.40, p. 1; NI-10002/82, Affidavit by H. Deichfischer, 11.VI.47; Bayer 15/Da 1.1, Umsätze der Hgr. 1–3.
Hoechst TEA 1086-87; Gattineau V/81, Affidavit by K. Meyer, managing director of DAG of Bratislava, 1939–45, 30.I.48.
NI-5194/38, Affidavit by G. von Schnitzler, 10.III.47.
Bayer D.A. 1136, Jugoslawienreise 1937. Dr. Lehmann und Dr. Kolbe, 26.I.38.

which the Reich eventually had to rely) were considered so poor in quality and expensive to extract as to be usable only under wartime conditions.[137] Not surprisingly, then, IG made no appreciable additions to its Balkan holdings between 1933 and 1938. Even after the absorption of Austria and Czechoslovakia put a bit of flesh on the bones of German capital influence in the region, the combine's total stock interests in Bohemia-Moravia, Slovakia, Hungary, Romania, Yugoslavia, Bulgaria, and Greece came to under 10 million marks, or less than 3% of the total value of IG's participations. Only in Slovakia, the smallest of the countries, did IG's investments add up to even minority influence over more than 5% of the capital in the local chemical industry.[138] Then and later, this relative lack of financial penetration contrasted with even the surprisingly modest position of German capital in most other industrial sectors.[139]

The outbreak of the war and Germany's isolation from markets and suppliers outside the Continent increased the importance of Southeast Europe for IG Farben without fundamentally altering the concern's view of long-range prospects in the area. In July 1939, the Vowi section reported pessimistically on the "possibilities for a more intensive interlocking of trade with the Southeast European nations." At the end of the year, the Mitteleuropäischer Wirtschaftstag, a business association partially funded by IG and devoted to promoting close commercial ties between the Reich and the region, doubted that even complete German economic and political domination of the area would produce a rapid improvement in German sales there. The Balkan nations, both organizations concluded, simply had reached the limits of their abilities and, in some cases, willingness to absorb Ger-

---

[137] NI-13535/110, Central purchasing to Gajewski, 26.VIII.39. On Germany's dependence on these supplies, see Wolfgang Schumann (ed.), *Griff nach Südosteuropa* (East Berlin, 1973), pp. 14–15.

[138] Reckoned from the figures in Radandt, *JfW*, 8 (1967), pp. 91, 133–8; Defense Basic Information II/2, Bilanzübersicht 1939–44; Bayer D.A. 183, Vowi 3163, 9.XI.38; and from the surprisingly thin and unhelpful account in Hans Dress, *Slowakei und die Faschistische Neuordnung Europas* (East Berlin, 1972), pp. 98–100.

[139] See, for example, the data in Sergije Dimitrijevic, *Das ausländische Kapital in Jugoslawien vor dem Zweiten Weltkrieg* (East Berlin, 1963), pp. 180–1, 193–5; Teichova, *Economic Background*, pp. 278–9; idem, "Konzentrationstendenzen in der Industrie Mittelost- und Südosteuropas nach dem Ersten Weltkrieg," in H. Mommsen, D. Petzina, and B. Weisbrod (eds.), *Industrielles System und politische Entwicklung in der Weimarer Republik* (Düsseldorf, 1974), p. 146; and Hubertus Schröder-Steinegger, *Südosteuropa in der deutschen Donauraumwirtschaft* (Berlin, [1939]), p. 13.

man products, and the Reich lacked surpluses of certain indispensable goods the region had procured previously from outside.[140] Of course, once the Wehrmacht moved into the Southeast, the last traces of western competition disappeared, and the Hungarian and Romanian troops became engaged on the eastern front, IG's sales of certain lines made some strides. Pharmaceutical proceeds, for example, rose by 341% between 1940 and 1943.[141] But the concern recognized these as windfall profits, all the more so as the countries of the region seemed intent on eliminating what remained of their dependence on German chemical imports. In early 1942, a report to the *Vorstand* explained the poor outlook for German commerce in the region with reference to the same structural impediments recited in the two documents of 1939.[142]

Max Ilgner had long advanced an unconventional solution to Germany's trading problems with raw-materials-producing lands. In order for the Reich to sell sufficient goods in these countries to pay for necessary imports from them, Ilgner proposed that German firms take an active role in local economic development, thereby raising living standards to a level that would create a market for more and more German goods. Since German trade had been greatest historically with industrialized countries, the reconciliation of German needs for Balkan products and markets with native aspirations lay in intensifying regional agriculture, improving transportation, adding to local power supplies, opening up new extractive and other labor-intensive industries, and even transferring some such businesses from the Reich to the Balkans. If, in the short run, such a course seemed detrimental to certain German sellers, they should bear in mind that their true in-

---

140 Bayer 13/25, Vowi 3591, Möglichkeiten einer intensivierten Handelsverflechtung mit den südosteuropäischen Ländern, 31.VII.39; Bayer 84/Eur. Allg., Südosteuropa als wirtschaftlichen Ergänzungsraum für Deutschland, August–Dezember 1939, Allgemeine Vorbemerkungen.

141 Bayer 15/Da 1.3, Jahresbericht 1943. Umsätze der pharmazeutischen Verkaufsabteilung Bayer.

142 Bayer 13/25, Kleemann and Reithinger of NW7 to *Vorstand*, 12.II.42, enclosing Unterlagen für eine Stellungnahme der IG zur Frage der Entwicklung der chemischen Industrie in Südosteuropa, undated. Parts I and III of this document appear in Radandt, *JfW*, 8 (1967), pp. 128–46; Parts II and IV in Schumann (ed.), *Griff*, pp. 168–71. The document is also NI-15174/123. In late 1941, IG's pessimism concerning Southeast European resources also received concrete expression in a recommendation to dissolve the Erzgesellschaft, a company designed to explore for minerals in the region (minutes of the 85th Chemicals Committee meeting, quoted in Ilgner IV/54, Affidavit by K. von Heider, 9.III.48).

terests required the southeastern states "to become as rich as possible as fast as possible, in order that they can buy as much as possible as fast as possible from us." To accomplish this transformation, the Balkans needed technical and financial assistance from an unimperialist German Reich, whose good intentions Ilgner proposed to demonstrate by confining German participations in local enterprises to minority shares. Thus, he euphemized, "the term *Lebensraum* does not refer to an area in which Germany wants to settle or dwell, but to one with which Germany wants to live harmoniously and promote business."[143]

Cut off by the war from other pet projects in Latin America and the Far East, Ilgner turned all of his restless energy to translating his vision into reality in the Balkans. The compilation by his Vowi office of 547 reports on the southeastern states between 1933 and 1944 documented his mounting preoccupation with this objective; so did his creation of a cadre of contact men in each country, his constant cultivation of important political and economic figures, and his several trips to the area.[144] Not only within the concern, but also through his positions as vice-president of the Mitteleuropäischer Wirtschaftstag since 1938, head of the Southeast Europe Committee of the Reichsgruppe Industrie from November 1941, chairman of the German–Hungarian Industrial Committee, member of the German–Romanian Industrial Committee, business representative at international economic conferences, and various other posts, Ilgner established himself as one of the foremost German corporate spokesmen for the natural reciprocity of German and Balkan commercial interests on the basis of long-term, voluntary cooperation.[145]

---

[143] NI-1038/10, Ilgner's speech to the Mitteleuropäischer Wirtschaftstag, 2.IX.40. See also the work of his protégé, Hermann Gross, *Die wirtschaftliche Bedeutung Südosteuropas für das Dritte Reich* (Stuttgart, 1941), pp. 7–13, 21; and BASF T51/2, Ilgner to Schmitz, 25.III.44, enclosing Ilgner's draft memo on increasing European economic and military production. On Ilgner's basic ideas, see Ilgner VIII/122, Affidavit by A. Reithinger, 4.II.48, and VIII/127, Affidavit by Thilo Frhr. von Wilmowsky, 16.II.48. On the differences between Ilgner's and Hitler's conceptions of the *Grossraum*, see Chapter 4 and Ludolf Herbst, *Der Totale Krieg und die Ordnung der Wirtschaft* (Stuttgart, 1982), p. 141.

[144] Hans Radandt, "Berichte der Volkswirtschaftlichen Abteilung der IG Farbenindustrie AG über Südosteuropa," *JfW*, 7 (1966), p. 192; and the same author's two other articles in this journal: "Die IG-Farbenindustrie AG in Südosteuropa bis 1938," 7 (1966), pp. 171–8; and "Die IG-Farbenindustrie AG in Südosteuropa 1938 bis zum Ende des Zweiten Weltkrieges," 8 (1967), pp. 110, 112.

[145] See Hallgarten and Radkau, *Deutsche Industrie*, pp. 382–3; and Radandt, *JfW*, 8 (1967), pp. 106–9.

Ilgner's ideas bore the imprint of his remarkable political innocence, on which Chancellor Brüning commented in 1931. But they also had much to recommend them as economic analysis, commercial strategy, and devices for concealing the one-sidedness of German interests in the Southeast and rationalizing business's participation in apparently uneconomical projects demanded by the war effort. Increases in German chemical sales in the region during the 1930s indeed had been traceable largely to growing demand, not the conquest of a larger share of the market. As Germany's ability to export declined, these gains could be maintained only by the output of local subsidiaries, while the Reich's continuing demand for various raw materials invited German firms to cash in on imports from the area as well as sales to it.[146] Minority participations had the advantages of reducing political resistance to the influence of German capital, smoothing the way to local tax and other concessions, and spreading the considerable risks of doing business in the Balkans – all while satisfying the Reich's demands for increased economic penetration of the region.

Notwithstanding these factors and Ilgner's prominence, the head of Berlin Nw7 spoke for neither the Nazi regime nor his colleagues at the top of IG Farben. Party ideologues disliked his emphasis on minority shareholdings and on the equality of peoples within the German sphere; before 1942, the Reich's policy makers resisted industrialization of any sort.[147] After the military situation became adverse for Germany in that year, they strove to maximize regional contributions to the war effort, without regard to the consequences for German business. As for IG, its traditional reserve toward Southeast Europe relaxed a bit during the heyday of the New Order between 1939 and 1942, but few of Ilgner's initiatives came to fruition. In part, this resulted from IG's lack of political clout in the region, a point to which this discussion will return. But the concern also chose to concentrate, as in western Europe, not on new developments, but on securing its position within existing markets by augmenting its sales net, containing entrenched competitors (in this case, chiefly Solvay's extensive properties in the region), and stifling other potential rivals.

Thus, IG rejected a number of proffered takeovers and new departures in the Balkans and founded no new factories in Hungary, Bul-

---

[146] For an example, see Radandt, JfW, 7 (1966), pp. 162–3.
[147] Ilgner VIII/127, Wilmowsky's affidavit, 16.II.48; VIII/122, Reithinger's affidavit, 4.II.48.

garia, or Greece. Elsewhere, it established altogether but five new productive facilities: a synthetic fibers plant in Bratislava designed to supply the Reich, an explosives subsidiary in Belgrade, and three Romanian companies, namely Europetrol, a firm in which IG held 28% of the stock and that leased molybdenum mines from 1940 to 1944 to produce for military needs; Azot, a producer of synthetic nitrogen; and Sarpetrol, an oil-drilling company half of whose stock IG sold to Kontinentale Oel in 1942. Nor did the combine extensively plunder existing plants in the occupied and satellite nations. The largest acquisition, that of the Apollo refinery in Slovakia and its sales organization in Prague, transpired by uncoerced purchase from French stockholders at the beginning of 1939, months before either the German occupation of Slovakia or the start of the war. Other takeovers consisted of the following: in Slovakia, half-ownership of the Aryanized Kostolany chemicals firm; in Yugoslavia, a 25% share in the Smederevo oil refinery and minority interests in two mineral exploration companies; in Romania, a half-interest in a chemicals enterprise at Temesvar; and in Hungary, the small Thurm-Beschle lacquer and varnish plant. In Bulgaria and Greece, Farben took nothing. IG's Behring subsidiary appears also to have held briefly a pharmaceuticals installation in the portion of the Banat taken by Hungary from Yugoslavia. Among these firms, only the synthetic fibers plant, the refineries, and Azot had capital exceeding 1 million marks.[148]

The development of DAG of Bratislava, the core of IG's interests in the region, both reflected and reinforced IG's cautious attitude. At the turn of 1938–9, under pressure from the Reich, the Slovak authorities, and ethnic Germans in Slovakia, IG began replacing the predominantly Czech and Jewish administration of the company with Heinrich Gattineau, Karl Meyer, and other officials from IG and DAG of Troisdorf.[149] During the next five years, the combine sank about 26

---

[148] This summary is based on the following records at Bayer: 13/25; 84/Eur. Allg.; 84/Eur. Bulgarien; 84/Eur. Tschechoslowakei; 91/1, Vowi reports 3036 (1.VIII.38), 3828 (27.II.40), 3930 (29.IV.40), 4584 (2.III/2.IX.42), and 4797 (22.II.43). See also Dimitrijevic, *Ausländische Kapital in Jugoslawien*, p. 100. IG did attempt to obtain the oil facilities in Hungary owned by Standard Oil of New Jersey, but the proposed payment of $24 million was blocked by the U.S. government; see Howard Ambruster, *Treason's Peace*, (New York, 1947), pp. 124–5; Henrietta M. Larson, Evelyn H. Knowlton, and Charles S. Popple, *History of the Standard Oil Company (New Jersey)*, vol. 3: *New Horizons 1927–1950* (New York, 1971), p. 384.

[149] Bayer D.A. 1431, Fischer's file note of a conversation with Philipp, 14.XI.38; Gattineau's letter of 12.XI.38. Gattineau later claimed that the dismissed employees

millon marks into modernizing Bratislava's run-down plant and broadening its output, hoping to capitalize on the fact that the balances in the various international clearing accounts made the Balkan states prefer to import from Slovakia than from Germany. The number of employees rose from 300 to more than 2,000, productive capacity from 62,000 tons of chemicals annually to 121,500, stock capital from around 2.5 million to 15 million marks, fixed assets from some 6 million to 17 million marks, sales from about 2.8 million to 18 million marks, and profits from approximately 500,000 to 1 million marks.[150] But in 1941 and 1942, three-quarters of the plant's profits derived from the sale of explosives; the new works for heavy chemicals, on which the plant would have to depend in peacetime, did poorly.[151]

Bratislava proved less valuable for IG as a productive unit than as the concern's "most important administrative center" in the Southeast.[152] Using the Slovakian firm as a holding company at least reduced the appearance of German capital influence and also helped to get around the financial problems attendant on Germany's enormous debts in its clearing accounts with the Balkans.[153] But here, too, there was somewhat less than meets the eye to the indications of growth. A comparison of Bratislava's holdings and plants in 1942 with those of 1938 shows that the company almost exactly offset its losses to Donauchemie in Austria with new operations elsewhere, primarily by establishing sales organizations. The oil refineries in Slovakia and Yugoslavia and the explosives works at Belgrade accounted for most of the expansion of productive facilities. Otherwise, there was almost no change in the locations or extent of Bratislava's investments.[154] Nor does the approximate doubling of the value of these shareholdings from 7.5 million to some 15 million marks between 1940 and

were all well compensated and often clandestinely rehired as advisers or managers either in Slovakia or abroad (*Klippen*, pp. 160–1, 179–80).

[150] Gattineau V/81-82, Affidavits by H. Gattineau, 3.I.48 and 30.III.48; Radandt, *JfW*, 8 (1967), p. 92. All the figures have been converted from crowns to marks on the basis of an approximate exchange rate of 10 : 1.

[151] Bayer 6/14, Reports of the Chemische Revision- und Treuhand GmbH for 1941 and 1942.

[152] Bayer 13/25, 11th SOA meeting, 9.VII.40.

[153] See Ilgner's elliptical comments in Bayer 13/25, 17th SOA meeting, 24.X.41.

[154] See the maps in Hayes, *Gleichschaltung*, pp. 293–4, 428–9; see also the detailed data in Bayer 84/Eur. Tschechoslowakei, Gruppe A. G. Dynamit Nobel, Pressburg, [1939], and 91/1, Vowi 4797, A. G. Dynamit Nobel, Pressburg, Konzerndarstellung. Stand 31.XII.42, 22.II.43.

1943 necessarily bespeak IG's eagerness to expand in the region.[155] Splitting the stock of these subsidiaries was on occasion a means of increasing the profits that each firm could expatriate rather than reinvest.[156]

That IG's interest in the region remained somewhat halfhearted and largely derivative of Nazi expansionism is apparent from the evolution and discussions of IG's Southeast Europe Committee (SOA). Founded in October 1938, following the Anschluss and the Munich Pact and in line with the Reich's efforts to breathe new life into German exports to the Balkans, this organization was never more than an advisory body. It did not begin shaping a concrete and comprehensive regional policy for the concern until the end of the German campaign in the West. Only after the Wehrmacht moved into Romania toward the close of 1940 did the group feel obliged to regularize its lax procedures and start reporting to the Commercial Committee and the *Vorstand*.[157] By then, the SOA's activity was already waning; having met thirteen times during the first twenty-six months of its existence, it convened but nine more times during the forty-four months left before Russian troops broke into the Balkans.[158] Increasingly, the committee became the arena for a tug of war between the advocates of an active or a negative role for the concern in the region, and Ilgner ended up at the shorter end of the rope.[159]

Hans Kühne, the chairman of the SOA, took a narrower and more conservative view of IG's commercial interests than did Ilgner and his allies on the committee. Thus, Kühne raged at Gattineau and Haefliger throughout the first half of 1940 for giving in to pressure from various government offices to exercise an option on an arsenic mine at Hrmza in Yugoslavia. Convinced that IG could make nothing on the site and unwilling to trust promises of public subsidies, Kühne was unmoved by depictions of the bad impression that would be created in official quarters by IG's refusal to risk a mere 150,000 marks in order to

---

155 The figures are derived from Bayer 6/14, Report of the Chemische Revision- und Treuhand GmbH, 13.XII.40, and Radandt, *JfW*, 8 (1967), pp. 91, 133–8.
156 See Bayer 13/25, Gattineau to Kühne, 30.III.40, and the reply of 15.IV.40 concerning the Bosnische Elektrizitäts AG.
157 Bayer 13/25, Gattineau to SOA members, 3.I.39, and the 11th and 13th SOA meetings, 9.VII.40 and 14.XII.40; also NI-9289, *NMT*, vol. 7, p. 1432.
158 Bayer 13/25, list of the meetings of the SOA.
159 The turning point may be dated fairly precisely; see Bayer 13/25, Bütefisch to Kühne, 29.I.40 and 29.III.40, and the exchange of letters between Kühne and Ilgner of 3.V.40 and 9.V.40.

extract a material vital to the war effort. No more effective was Haefliger's fearful excuse that "perhaps it is unknown to you that a director Z. of the soda syndicate has been arrested by the Gestapo for a much less important mistake." In the end, Kühne forced his subordinates to wriggle out of the deal and submit a bill to the Reich for the costs incurred.[160] Though IG subsidized extensive minerals exploration between 1939 and 1943, the results confirmed Kühne's hesitancy about mining investments.[161] So did the concern's experience with one of the rare instances in which IG let military interests override its caution. The costs of extracting Romanian molybdenum at Baita-Bihor came between 1941 and 1944 to 17.5 times the prevailing German price per kilogram and resulted, despite government subsidies, in a net loss to IG of more than 2 million marks.[162] Kühne's concern for the postwar profitability of IG's Moosbierbaum plant in Austria also led him to doubt the wisdom of expanding chemicals production in the Balkans.[163] Ilgner, as the driving spirit behind IG's Austrian acquisitions, found himself hoist with his own petard.

Other members of the SOA considered Ilgner too openhanded in dealing with potential German and foreign partners in the region. The technical men, in particular, opposed offering IG's know-how and patents to these firms.[164] A similar concern for secrecy prompted Bütefisch and Heider to suggest that Ilgner's participation in the discussions of numerous committees outside the firm attracted the attention of competitors to possibly profitable projects and created the impression of IG's commitment to schemes from which the concern might want to draw back later.[165] Increasingly, IG officers responsible for undertakings outside the region spoke out against its industrialization lest that aggravate shortages of building materials.[166]

[160] Bayer 13/25, 7th SOA meeting, 15.XII.39, Kühne to Gattineau, 27.XII.39, and the exchange of letters between Kühne and Haefliger, 12–18.I.40. The quotation is from Haefliger's letter of 16.I.40. See also Bayer D.A. 1136, exchange of letters between Kühne and Gattineau, 20.V.40–21.VI.40.
[161] Roland Schönfeld, "Deutsche Rohstoffsicherungspolitik in Jugoslawien 1934–1944," VfZ, 24 (1976), pp. 224–5, 227; Radandt, JfW, 7 (1966), p. 171.
[162] See the extensive records of this operation in the files of the Finance Ministry, BA Koblenz, R2/21602.
[163] Bayer 13/25, Kühne's remarks at the 11th and 12th SOA meetings, 9.VII.40 and 3.IX.40.
[164] NI-5169/38, Affidavit by G. Frank-Fahle, undated; NI-7318/58, Affidavit by K. von Heider, 28.VI.47.
[165] Bayer 13/25, 15th SOA meeting, 25.VI.41.
[166] See, for example, Bayer 13/25, Ambros to Büro des KA, 29.XII.41.

Throughout 1940–1, Ilgner pressed IG to lay down a coherent Balkan "*Konzernpolitik*" as a substitute for the New Order planning documents that the Reich never requested for the region, but the upshot was hardly what he had in mind. In July 1941, the *Vorstand* resolved that "factories should be erected in the Southeast only in response to existing demand and the production costs should be as identical as possible with those of a factory in Germany itself."[167] Three and a half months later, the SOA directed Ilgner to avoid discussing concrete projects during his meetings with outside committees and declared that "IG should let itself be directed by the fundamental principle of pursuing only projects that touch its vital interests and leave other projects to other German firms or the Prager Verein."[168] These pronouncements virtually foreclosed further expansion in the region.

In February 1942, the SOA forwarded to the *Vorstand* a provisional report summarizing IG's experience in the Southeast, the state of the chemical business there and balance of forces within it, and proposals for the firm's future course. The document explained that the declining ability of the Balkan nations to purchase German goods and the increasing limitations on IG's capacity to deliver them added up to an unpromising outlook for exports to the region. As to participations, the concern should restrict itself to projects "that appear necessary in order to hinder existing or planned German, domestic or international competition and its harmful effects on German exports," to explosives plants and temporary undertakings indispensable to military production, and to developments that would maintain Germany's market share in the event of further reductions in the Reich's exports. Thus, when it came to specifics, the report catalogued an almost uninterrupted stream of projects that IG had derailed and participations that it had rejected. Having begun by proclaiming that "the fundamental criterion on which the commercial policy of IG in relation to Southeast Europe must be based is the adjustment of the interests of IG to the goals of the Reich's economic policy," the lengthy survey offered merely to provide technical advice to light-metals developers and to take part in the establishment of Romanian nitrogen production on the basis of natural gas.[169]

---

[167] Bayer 12/19, vol. 1, 26th *Vorstand* meeting, 10.VII.41, pp. 5–6.
[168] Bayer 13/25, 17th SOA meeting, 24.X.41.
[169] Bayer 13/25, Kleemann and Reithinger of NW7 to the *Vorstand*, 12.II.42, enclos-

More than lack of enthusiasm for the economic rewards of Balkan involvement produced this rather negative stance on IG's part. The concern found itself unable to enlist the Reich behind its struggle with major commercial rivals in the region, the Prager Verein and Italian industry, or to dominate the governments and business communities of the various satellite states. The story of these failures underlines the limits of IG's political influence and the self-interested, ad hoc, primarily defensive nature of the course the concern followed in the region.

Despite the loss of three-quarters of its productive capacity to IG Farben in the Aussig-Falkenau transaction, the Prager Verein remained a formidable industrial power.[170] In its own right or in alliance with Solvay of Brussels, Prager dominated about twenty-two manufacturing subsidiaries in Southeast Europe during the war years and held minority share packets in ten other firms. Embracing the largest chemical enterprises in Hungary, Romania, and the Czech Protectorate and the two runners-up in Yugoslavia, Prager's participations were worth more than IG's in each of these lands, as well as in the Balkans overall, throughout the conflict. Even after the expansion of DAG of Bratislava, the Verein still claimed control of 75% of inorganic chemicals production in the Southeast.[171] Moreover, the parent company recovered remarkably rapidly from the amputations of 1938. By the end of 1939, after a flurry of plant construction and takeovers, sales and net profits rebounded to their level of the previous year, and Prager tripled the book value of its stock. Proceeds kept rising so that the Verein's total worth grew by 25 million marks between 1938 and 1941, although construction costs and depreciation reduced annual net profits slightly. At the start of 1942, Prager had 54 million marks on hand for new investments.

Prager's continuing strength posed two major problems for IG. As described in Chapter 6, the possible resumption of Czech dyes production for export alarmed the concern, which considered European dyes

---

ing Unterlagen für eine Stellungnahme der IG zur Frage der Entwicklung der chemischen Industrie in Südosteuropa, undated; the same document is NI-15174/123.

[170] The figures in this paragraph are drawn from the following Vowi reports on the Verein: Bayer 13/25, Vowi 4049a, 31.VIII.40, and Vowi 4125, 31.VIII.40; Bayer D.A. 183, Vowi 3360, 31.III.39, Vowi 4247, 29.I.41, and Vowi 4281, 14.III.41; Hoechst TEA 2915, Vowi 4676, 17.VII.42, and Vowi 4681, 19.VIII.42.

[171] Bayer D.A. 183, Interne Aktennotiz über die Besprechung mit dem Prager Verein, 3.VII.42.

capacity excessive, especially in view of the probable loss of Far Eastern and Latin American markets to the United States during the war and IG's obligation to maintain and perhaps add to output at Aussig, Boruta, and Mülhausen for the sake of *"volksdeutsche* considerations."[172] And the ability of Prager's Balkan subsidiaries to expand in response to local demand for other chemical products threatened IG's attempts to both export in the face of the mounting German clearing debts and circumvent that barrier via DAG of Bratislava.[173]

Convinced that Farben had either to obtain a standstill agreement from the Verein or to take it over, IG pursued both objectives simultaneously. After Prager rejected Schnitzler's proposal in June 1940 that the Verein elect "several gentlemen from IG to the administrative board," IG's Dyes and Chemicals Main Committees came out for acquiring the Czech firm.[174] The idea never had much of a chance. Prager was protected by the importance of its two principal stockholders. The Solvay group's status as the source of the greater part of European supplies of such basic chemicals as calcium carbonate, caustic soda, and chlorine made its cooperation indispensable to the war economy; the services of the collaborationist Zivnostenska Bank earned it the favoritism of the Reich Economics Ministry.[175] Thus, in September, Ungewitter impressed on Ilgner that IG's acquisition of the Prager Verein was out of the question and that a convention governing Prager's production would have to suffice as a guarantee of German influence over the company. Quite undaunted, Ilgner set about planning the purchase of the Verein's foreign subsidiaries and the gradual conquest of the parent company through some form of community-of-interests agreement with Aussig-Falkenau.[176] His efforts provoked a curt reprimand from Schnitzler, who told Ilgner to defer to the more deliberate approaches of the Chemicals and Dyes Committees and to the decisions of the Economic Group for the Chemical Industry.[177] Meanwhile, to strengthen IG's hand in negotiations with the Verein and to prevent a squabble in the event of a takeover, the concern

172 Hoechst TEA 2915, Kugler's Bemerkungen zu der Frage einer Verständigung mit dem Prager Verein auf dem Farbstoffgebiet, 7.I.41.
173 Bayer D.A. 183, Kugler's file notes of meetings with Prager's representatives on 27–28.IV.39 and 9.V.39.
174 Bayer 13/25, Schnitzler to Kühne, 27.VI.39; D.A. 183, Auszug aus der Niederschrift über die Sitzung des Chemikalien Ausschusses am 12.VIII.40.
175 Bayer 91/1, Vowi 4704, 9.IX.42; Interview with Hans Kehrl, 11.VII.78.
176 Bayer 13/25, Küpper to Schnitzler, Kugler, and Eckert, 5.IX.40.
177 Bayer 13/25, Schnitzler to Ilgner, 11.IX.40.

arranged a coalition with Heyden, Ruettgerswerke, and Kali-Chemie, each of which desired specific Prager plants.[178] In November, Schnitzler and Ilgner, representing this group, met leaders of the Verein in Prague to discuss the delimitation of each side's production in the Southeast, pointing out that "the question of dominance of particular enterprises is not so decisive as the formation of pools, through which an effective technical and commercial cooperation would be guaranteed."[179] While negotiations concerning this cooperation continued and terMeer, Schnitzler, Kühne, Haefliger, Bütefisch, Ilgner, Gajewski, and Otto made plans to inspect Prager's works in the Balkans, Schnitzler notified the *Vorstand* that no pressure on Solvay to sell its shares in the Verein "can be exercised at present."[180] In January 1941, Prager and IG agreed to consult one another before expanding operations or participations in the fields for which the Verein's largest plants in Yugoslavia, Romania, and Hungary produced, and in March the rivals settled their dyes dispute.[181] Hence, by July, when the Economics Ministry forbade further purchases of Prager's stock or its participations in the Southeast, IG appeared to have achieved at least the beginnings of a comprehensive cartel agreement with the Verein.[182]

However, the ministry's intervention and the Germanization of the Verein's leadership a month later stripped IG of its chief weapons against Prager. As disagreements mounted in connection with new developments in Croatia, Bulgaria, Hungary, and the city of Odessa, IG proved unable to master its adversary. Decisive for the subsequent course of events was the controversy over Prager's agreement in the fall of 1941 to build and operate a sulfuric acid and superphosphates plant in Croatia and to split the stock with that satellite's regime on the ratio 48 : 52. Since the deal negated DAG of Bratislava's plans for a similar factory, which IG already had cleared with the German authorities, the concern protested vehemently. For a change, Farben initially enjoyed the backing of Ungewitter and of Hoffmann at the

[178] NI-9289, 37th KA meeting, 12.XI.40, *NMT*, vol. 7, pp. 1429–30; Bayer 13/25, 13th SOA meeting, 14.XII.40.
[179] Radandt, *JfW*, 8 (1967), Anhang III, pp. 139–40.
[180] Bayer 13/25, 13th SOA meeting, 14.XII.40; Bayer 12/19, 23rd *Vorstand* meeting, 12.XII.40.
[181] Radandt, *JfW*, 8 (1967), Anhang III, pp. 142–3; NI-9289, 40th KA meeting, 18.III.41, *NMT*, vol. 7, p. 1432.
[182] Bayer 13/25, Landfried and Kroll to Ilgner, 30.VII.41.

Economics Ministry, as well as of the German ambassador in Zagreb. Nonetheless, Prager dug in behind the claim that IG some months previously had recognized the Verein's primacy in these fields of production and behind another, more effective argument. Dr. Bernhard Adolf, the new German managing director, shrewdly aligned his firm with the Reich's reservations about Balkan industrialization. He pointed out that the Croatian contract headed off Italian competition yet permitted the Verein to delay actual construction indefinitely. This reasoning persuaded Hoffmann to shift to a more neutral stance and to warn the two parties to untangle their conflicting interests throughout the Southeast before he did it for them.[183]

The result was a meeting in Frankfurt on July 3, 1942, at which Adolf brought several of IG's leading executives up to date on the changed balance of power within the regional chemical industry. Declaring that events had overtaken IG's pretense to dominance in the area, Adolf demanded "the ordering of mutual relations and interests on the basis of absolute parity." He even dared to remind IG of its short-lived promises in late 1938 to let Prager buy DAG of Bratislava and suggested that perhaps the time had come to revive the idea. After a brief exchange on this debating point, the participants, acknowledging that they had fought each other to a standoff in the Balkans, concurred on three promises: that Bratislava was to do nothing to impair the Verein's business in the Protectorate and Slovakia; that neither side would encroach on the other's possessions, production, and present sales throughout the region; and that neither would expand its facilities for sulfuric acid or superphosphate output without mutual consultation. With regard to new projects, IG ceded pride of place to Prager in Bulgaria and Croatia and agreed that both firms would continue their applications for control over a superphosphate plant in Odessa, recently annexed by Romania.[184] Formal signatures on this compact were not exchanged until January 1943. In the interim, DAG of Bratislava got the upper hand in Bulgaria but pledged to

183 Bayer 13/25, 17th and 19th SOA meetings, 24.X.41 and 26.VI.42; Bayer 13/25, Notiz über eine Besprechung in Pressburg am 6.II.42; Bayer D.A. 183, Ilgner to members of the KA and the SOA, 19.XI.41, enclosing Kersten's file note of 17.XI.41 and Kuhn to IG, 12.XI.41.
184 Bayer D.A. 183, Interne Aktennotiz über die Besprechung mit dem Prager Verein in Frankfurt/Main am 3.VII.42; see also Verkaufsgemeinschaft Chemikalien to SOA, 23.VII.42.

abide by the agreement by making room for Prager to buy shares in the proposed new plants.[185] This gain paled in comparison with the acquisition by Prager's Hungarian subsidiary in early 1943 of the extensive former properties of the Phönix company in the parts of Romania ceded to Hungary under the terms of the Second Vienna Award. Though IG suggested that Prager compensate the concern in the Hungarian market, the documentation is silent on the outcome.[186] In sum, during 1941–3, IG had to concede equality to the Prager Verein in Southeast Europe.

By the end of 1942, IG's relations with the preponderant Italian chemicals combine, the Montecatini group, had come to a similar pass. Always dubious about Italy's economic capacities and trust-worthiness, IG's leaders resented the Balkan demands of their Axis partners, especially after the spring of 1941, when German forces had to rescue the Duce's hapless legions in North Africa and Greece.[187] In western Europe, although the two concerns arrived at a mutually satisfactory division of the Spanish nitrogen industry, Montecatini's cultivation of a "special relationship" with Rhône-Poulenc remained a bone of contention.[188] Equally vexing was the Italian enterprise's concerted effort, dating from the outbreak of the war, to expel Farben from its footholds in the Italian markets for chemicals, dyes, light metals, pharmaceuticals, and pigments. One prong of this drive con-sisted of lobbying the Fascist government for restrictions on German imports, repeated petitions for licenses to some of IG's most profitable processes, whispering campaigns against the concern's products, pirat-ing of patents and labels, and recurrent underselling.[189] In addition, Montecatini worked to undermine IG's position in several local sub-sidiaries owned jointly by the two concerns. Thus, the Italian combine used its plurality of the shares in the Società Italiana del Litopone to

[185] Bayer D.A. 183, Schnitzler to the IG Vorstand, 2.II.43, and Vorschlag für eine Vereinbarung mit dem Prager Verein als Ergänzung des grundsätzlichen Abkom-mens vom 3. Juli 1942, 13.VIII.42.
[186] Bayer D.A. 183, Pressburg Direktion to Kühne, 3.IV.43; Bayer 91/1, Vowi 4584, 2.III./2.IX.43.
[187] See Hallgarten and Radkau, Deutsche Industrie, pp. 343–9; NI-11252, General section of IG's New Order plan, 3.VIII.40, NMT, vol. 7, p. 1457.
[188] Bayer D.A. 5384, Summary of Vertrag IG/Montecatini zur Errichtung von Stick-stoffanlagen in Spanien, 11.IX.42; Niederschrift über die Besprechung mit Herrn Ing. Giustiniani am 25. Januar 1943 in Mailand.
[189] Bayer D.A. 5384, Heider and Borgwardt to Büro des K.A., 20.VII.42; memo by Schnitzler and Szilvinij, 23.VII.42; memo by Mann and Grobel, 20.VIII.42.

purge a series of allegedly pro-German chief executives, its majority in
the ACNA dyes company to prevent that firm from adopting IG's sales
and pricing policies at home or abroad, and its influence in Rome to
block the expansion of Bianchi, a smaller dyes operation in which
Farben held 51% of the stock, Montecatini the balance.[190] When IG
proposed founding another joint subsidiary for the extraction of sulfur
with a new German process, Montecatini's escalating demands for
control finally drove Farben into offering a majority in the new works
to three other Italian firms.[191] These and other conflicts contributed
to IG's decision in mid-1942 to erect a magnesium plant at Aosta in
partnership with a group of Montecatini's principal rivals in the light-
metals sphere and to turn over IG's newest aluminum production
processes to that bloc.[192]

In the Balkans, where the interests of the Italian and German combines collided virtually across the board, IG was handicapped by
Hitler's intention "to concede Italy supremacy in the entire Mediterra-
nean area" and by the long-nurtured local political art of playing off
Rome against Berlin.[193] Although the regional governments seldom
ultimately preferred Italian developers to the Reich's, the threat of
Italian competition on occasion induced IG to agree to projects more
rapidly and then to accept a more restricted role in them than the
concern might otherwise have liked. Being whipsawed by the southeastern states irked IG far less, however, than the refusal of the Nazi
regime to take Farben's side against the Italians. In Romania, Hans
Kehrl pressured IG and other German manufacturers of synthetic
fibers into assisting a local company, the Viscosa Romaneasca, and
then into relinquishing half their shares in that firm to Italian producers.[194] More irritating still were the Reich's decisions concerning
Greece and, above all, Yugoslavia. In mid-1941, the German Foreign

190 Bayer D.A. 5384, Kühne to Büro des K.A., 5.XI.42; Schnitzler and Müller to KA,
    23.VII.42.
191 Bayer D.A. 5384, Kühne to Büro des K.A., 30.X.42; see also NI-15026, Kühne to
    Schmitz, 15.V.42, NMT, vol. 7, pp. 600–1.
192 Bayer D.A. 5384, Haefliger's memo, Italien/Leichtmetall-Interessen der I.G.,
    16.VII.42.
193 Rich, Hitler's War Aims, vol. 2, p. 318; see also p. 315.
194 Ilgner to Reinhardt, 28.III.42, in Eichholtz and Schumann (eds.), Anatomie, Docu-
    ment 202, pp. 392–3; Bayer 13/25, 19th, 20th, and 21st SOA meetings, 26.VI.42,
    5.X.42, and 14.I.43. On IG's opposition to participation in the project, see also
    Bayer 91/1, Die chemische Industrie Rumäniens, unnumbered Vowi report,
    23.VI.41.

Ministry informed the concern that Slowenia and Dalmatia and with them all the properties of the largest Yugoslav chemicals corporation, a French-owned firm at Split called La Dalmatienne, fell within an exclusively Italian sphere of influence and that in Croatia and Greece only existing German interests would be protected by the Reich.[195] As a result, Italy emphatically rebuffed IG's proposals for joint participation in La Dalmatienne, thus putting an end to the concern's three-year-long quest for shares in that company.[196] Subsequently, the German Economics Ministry frustrated IG's designs on the Greek Lipasmata and Oekonomides dyes firms.[197] But the agreement had a more galling sequel for IG Farben. In February 1942, DAG of Bratislava contracted with the Croatian government to revive an idle explosives plant at Mahicno near Karlovac (Karlstadt) in which Bratislava and one of its local subsidiaries owned 38.8% of the stock. When a delegate of the Croat Military Ministry and the managing director of the new Explochemia company arrived at the plant, they encountered an Italian garrison whose commandant denied them admission. During the following summer, engineers from Montecatini brought the works back into operation and began selling the output at below German costs. Not only did the Reich decline to intercede in what amounted to an expropriation of IG's property in order to penetrate a once predominantly German market, but the Economics Ministry blandly advised the concern to meet the Italians halfway on the matter somehow.[198]

The various semisovereign countries of Southeast Europe also proved resistant to IG's objectives in the region. Even so petty a state as Slovakia increased the Swiss import quota for dyes, disregarded DAG of Bratislava's remonstrances against a law requiring each local company to purchase state bonds worth 15% of founding capital, and made the concern divide the shares in the Aryanized fertilizer and

[195] Bayer 13/25, Büro des K.A. to SOA, 26.V.41, with Anlage, and Anlage zum Rundschreiben no. 7 vom 18.VII.41.
[196] Bayer 13/25, 17th SOA meeting, 24.X.41, and the exchange of letters between Ilgner and Giordani, 12.IX.41–26.IX.41.
[197] Bayer 13/25, 21st SOA meeting, 14.I.43.
[198] Bayer 6/14, Meyer and Gattineau to Kühne, 3.III.42, enclosing the contract; D.A. 5384, Büro des K.A. to Kühne, 28.X.42, enclosing a memo on relations with Montecatini, 5.X.42; 13/25, 20th and 21st SOA meetings, 5.XI.42 and 14.I.43; Holm Sundhaussen, "Südosteuropa in der nationalsozialistischen Kriegswirtschaft am Beispiel des 'Unabhängigen Staates Kroatien,'" Südost-Forschungen, 32 (1973), pp. 246–7.

sulfuric acid works at Kostolany evenly with the Slovak union of
agricultural cooperatives and wheat warehouses.[199] From 1937 to
1942, the Bulgarians wore out IG's negotiators concerning the construction of a new sulfuric acid plant with demands for a 50% participation by the state, guaranteed minimum levels of output, and
reversion to complete government ownership after ten years. By the
time an agreement was reached, IG had lost its appetite for the concession, which the concern did not exercise.[200] Although Croatia granted
Explochemia an indefinite national monopoly on explosives production at prices set 10% above those of nearby competitors, the local
regime retained 55% of the stock in the corporation as well as five of
the nine seats on its administrative board.[201] Nor could IG dissuade
the Croats either from establishing their own sulfuric acid plant or
granting the contract to the Prager Verein.[202] In Romania, the local
government combined with the Reich and Ilgner, not to restrict IG's
expansion, but to force the combine to take an active part in developing cellulose and alumina production.[203] Farben had greater success in
evading Hungarian proposals for synthetic fibers and buna plants but
apparently failed in an effort to strengthen the concern's position in
the local explosives industry by offering to increase production in
return for a twenty-five-year extension on the monopoly held by Ipari,
in which IG owned indirectly 44% of the stock.[204] Improving on the

[199] RG242/T83/88, Frame 3460948, Door and Baumgartel to various dye warehouses, 27.X.42; Radandt, *JfW*, 8 (1967), pp. 120–2, and "Der Wirtschaftsberater
der deutschen Gesandtschaft in Bratislava – Ein Vertreter der Interessen deutscher
Konzerne im System des staatsmonopolistischen Kapitalismus," *JfW*, 13 (1972),
pp. 83–4, 87–9. In both articles, Radandt concludes that IG got an exemption from
the compulsory purchase of state bonds, since the published balance sheets for
Bratislava show no specific entry for the funds. Such a listing would, however, have
been contrary to the concern's normal accounting practice. At its meeting on
7.VII.43, the *Verwaltungsrat* of DAG, Bratislava incorporated the bond-holding
requirement into the firm's statutes; see the excerpt in IG in Abw., Jur. Abt., v.H.
5/I, Dyn. Nobel Pressburg I.
[200] This seemingly interminable wrangle is chronicled profusely in Bayer 84/Eur. Bulgarien. See also Bayer 13/25, 12th, 13th, 14th, and 20th SOA meetings, 30.IX.40–
5.X.42; and Radandt, *JfW*, 8 (1967), pp. 118–19.
[201] Bayer 13/25, 15th SOA meeting, 25.VI.41; Bayer 6/14, Meyer and Gattineau to
Kühne et al., 3.III.42, enclosing the agreement with the Croatian state.
[202] Radandt, *JfW*, 8 (1967), pp. 119–20; see above, pp. 310–11.
[203] See footnote 194; Bayer 13/25, 19th, 21st, and 22nd SOA meetings, 26.VI.42,
14.I.43, and 4.V.44; and NI-7318/58, Affidavit by von Heider, 28.VI.47.
[204] Bayer 13/25, Meeting of the German-Hungarian Industrie-Ausschuss, 12.V.42;
Ivan Berend and György Ranki, "Die deutsche wirtschaftliche Expansion und das
ungarische Wirtschaftsleben zur Zeit des zweiten Weltkrieges," *Acta Historica*, 5

Prager Verein's effective self-defense, the Chinoin pharmaceuticals firm halted IG's takeover bid by appointing two Germans to its board of directors, including Dr. Theo Morell, Hitler's personal physician.[205]

Indeed, the Hungarians dealt IG and German industry as a whole perhaps their most stunning defeat in the Balkans. In the fall of 1942, faced with ever increasing deficits in the Reich's trade balance with Hungary, Admiral Horthy's regime began demanding that the Germans pay for further deliveries of raw materials by relinquishing shareholdings in Hungarian enterprises. Despite the resolution of IG and the Reichsgruppe Industrie "that everything must be undertaken in order to prevent the execution of such plans," the Reich agreed at the end of the year to order the sales.[206] That IG complied with the order remains unproved, but its promulgation attests to the firm's limited ability to defend its most fundamental interests when those conflicted with Berlin's priorities.

All in all, IG gained little, if any, ground within the Balkan chemical industry during the Second World War. Uncertainty about the economic value of the region and about Berlin's intentions toward it combined with the skillful maneuvering of rivals and governments in the area to rule out major expansion on Farben's part. Moreover, as in western Europe and Norway, the concern found itself dependent for success on official support – and often denied it. In consequence, the firm muddled through.

Summary

The eastern orientation of Nazi expansionism neither suited IG Farben's taste nor expressed its interests. Within the New Order, the concern's ambitions abated from industrialized west to underdeveloped East. Even where strongest, IG's aspirations emerged in response to political changes. They were reactions, as in France and the Benelux states, to the new international competitive situation cre-

(1958), p. 341; Bayer 84/Eur. Tschechoslowakei, Gruppe A. G. Dynamit Nobel, Pressburg, [1939]. According to a memo to the Bratislava Managing Committee, Hans Kehrl's actions scotched the Ipari deal; see IG in Abw., Jur. Abt., v.H. 5/I, Dyn. Nobel Pressburg I, 7.VII.43.
[205] Berend and Ranki, *Acta Historica*, 5 (1958), pp. 346–7.
[206] Ibid., pp. 348–50; Bayer 13/25, 20th SOA meeting, 5.X.42.

ated by the Nazi victories or, as in Norway, to government initiatives
that infringed on long-standing corporate interests. Of course, further
German triumphs would have brought other developments that quite
probably would have prompted additional acquisitions on Farben's
part. The defensive pattern of the combine's behavior offered little
consolation to those victimized by it in 1940–4 and would not have
shielded their successors. But that pattern does clarify, at least, the
problem of distinguishing between cause and effect in the Nazi conquest of Europe.

PART V
The nature of war, 1939–1945

Administrative chaos was as endemic to Germany during the war years as to occupied Europe. To be sure, by 1939 the Nazi regime had acquired such dominance over the economy that "one can scarcely speak any longer of any sort of equal relations or even of the existence of a still intact sociological unit called 'industry.'"[1] If the primacy of politics reigned, however, an amorphous and unpredictable Behemoth ruled.[2] In economic affairs, the diffusion of governmental authority nearly matched that of industrial interests. As of 1939, the contenders for control over parts or all of German production included the Ministries of Economics and Labor, the Four Year Plan organization and its five principal subdivisions, the ordnance offices of the three armed services, and the Military Economy and Armaments Staff of the High Command under General Thomas. During the ensuing six years, the names of the claimants to power changed, the lack of coordination among them persisted. A new Ministry of Armaments under Fritz Todt and his successor, Albert Speer, gradually subordinated the organizations led by Thomas, Funk, and Göring, only to encounter increasing rivalry from those headed by Fritz Sauckel (labor allocation), Heinrich Himmler (the SS), and Martin Bormann (the Party hierarchy). Moreover, the chronic "war of each against all" within the Nazi system characterized as well as resisted Speer's initiatives. The devices by which he tried to streamline decision making – the main committees and rings that synchronized the output of armaments and component parts, respectively – were in fairly constant flux, and they

---

[1] Dietmar Petzina, "Hitler und die deutsche Industrie," *GWU*, 17 (1966), p. 483.
[2] Here the classic account is Franz Neumann, *Behemoth* (New York, 1944), especially pp. 459–67. The interpretation has been strengthened by much recent work on "polycracy" in the Third Reich and by the new, functionalist group of German historians; see Martin Broszat, *Der Staat Hitlers* (München, 1969), pp. 363–402, 423–42; and Tim Mason, "Intention and Explanation: A Current Controversy about the Interpretation of National Socialism," in G. Hirschfeld and L. Kettenacker (eds.), *Der Führerstaat* (Stuttgart, 1981), pp. 23–41. But compare the sensible observations of Eberhard Jäckel, *Hitler in History* (Hanover, N.H., 1984), pp. 28–32.

grew up in addition to, not in place of, the existing network of economic groups, regional chambers, and supervisory bodies. Not even "total war" could cure Nazism's congenital inclination to multiply competencies, confuse lines of authority, and ordain competing objectives.[3]

This inability to fix and enforce binding priorities constituted one of two major handicaps imposed on the German military effort. The other was the prematurity of Hitler's decision to fight.[4] In 1939, unfinished but essential plants littered Berlin's drawing boards and the Reich's landscape.[5] Neither the stockpiles of munitions and supplies nor the capacities to produce more were up to the demands of an extended campaign. Industry had not been automated sufficiently or otherwise adequately prepared to cope with the withdrawal of millions of soldiers from the labor force. An economy already hamstrung in peacetime by constant shortages of men, materials, and money henceforth had both to complete its industrial infrastructure and to turn out vastly increased quantities of operational equipment. From 1939 to 1941, the spoils of blitzkrieg and the availability of supplies from Russia masked the Reich's weaknesses. During the comfortable intervals between defeating Poland and attacking the West, between the fall of France and Hitler's move east, the nation could restore its depleted reserves and press the most vital factories toward completion without unbearable exertion. But the Reich never entirely made good its industrial deficiencies, and these came home to roost after December 1941. Though Pearl Harbor and the battles before Moscow put an end to most illusions, recurrent shortages and habitual infighting continued to reinforce one another. Together, they held the well-known productive feats of 1942–5 below not only Germany's needs, but also its potential.[6]

---

[3] On the disorganization of economic administration in wartime, the best guides are Burton H. Klein, *Germany's Economic Preparations for War* (Cambridge, Mass., 1959), pp. 147–72; Berenice Carroll, *Design for Total War* (The Hague, 1968), pp. 191–249; and Ludolf Herbst, *Der Totale Krieg und die Ordnung der Wirtschaft* (Stuttgart, 1982), especially pp. 111–17, 255–75.

[4] See, for this observation and much of what follows, the argument in R. J. Overy, "Hitler's War and the German Economy: A Reinterpretation," *EHR*, 35 (1982), pp. 272–91. Also pertinent is Williamson Murray, "German Army Doctrine, 1918–1939, and the Post-1945 Theory of 'Blitzkrieg Strategy,'" in Carole Fink, Isabel Hull, and MacGregor Knox (eds.), *German Nationalism and European Response* (Norman, Okla., 1985), pp. 90–3.

[5] Even after the Four Year Plan suspended all projects that could not be completed within a year from the outbreak of the war, 283 remained in process; see Dieter Petzina, *Autarkiepolitik im Dritten Reich* (Stuttgart, 1968), p. 145.

[6] See Klein, *Economic Preparations*. For an early recognition of all this, see J. K.

Shortly after Germany's collapse, one Farben official compared the wartime situation for businessmen to "that of people who have to cover themselves with too short a blanket: the more one succeeds in his attempts to be well covered, the more the other must suffer."[7] The image understates the case. For the tug of war took place on a roller coaster, one created by economic policies that repeatedly changed direction, speed, and pitch.[8] In vain, corporate leaders, including several of IG's, pleaded almost from the outbreak of hostilities for a single authoritative office to govern economic activity.[9] So long as Germany appeared ascendant, however, they received more criticism than cooperation. Party periodicals attacked their allegedly inflated administrative organizations; government agencies whittled away the functions of the economic groups; Hitler railed against corporate opportunism and ridiculed parasitical directorships; additional taxes on dividends and controls on the stock market expressed the regime's animus toward this "oasis of profiteers and financial wire pullers"; Price Commissar Wagner imposed strict profit ceilings on firms; and the Party's dormant Nationalsozialistischer Wirtschaftsdienst reemerged in 1940 with plans to obtain a decisive voice in the promotion and personnel decisions of companies.[10] The resulting uncertainty about the future in corporate circles was mirrored in the accumula-

Galbraith, "Germany Was Badly Run," *Fortune*, 32 (December 1945), pp. 173–200. One should add, however, that the military's procurement policies contributed significantly to this situation; see R. J. Overy, *Goering: the 'Iron Man'* (Boston, 1985), pp. 158–62.

[7] NI-2750/20, Affidavit by Kurt Krüger, 31.VIII.45.

[8] The best illustration of this situation is provided by munitions production. See BA Koblenz, R25/191, Zur Entwicklung des Pulver-, Sprengstoff-, K-Stoff- und Vorprodukte-Programms seit 1937, 21.IV.42.

[9] See Carroll, *Design*, p. 212; Dietrich Eichholtz, *Geschichte der deutschen Kriegswirtschaft 1939–1945*, vol. 1: *1939–41* (East Berlin, 1969), pp. 116–18; and Hans-Erich Volkmann, "Zum Verhältnis von Grosswirtschaft und NS-Regime im Zweiten Weltkrieg," in W. Dlugoborski (ed.), *Zweiter Weltkrieg und sozialer Wandel* (Göttingen, 1981), p. 89.

[10] See H. W. Singer, "The German War Economy in the Light of German Economic Periodicals," *Economic Journal*, 50 (1940), pp. 536–7; (vol.) 51 (1941), pp. 400–01, 419; and (vol.) 52 (1942), pp. 19 and (for the quotation) 36. On the control of profits, in particular, see the same source, (vol.) 50 (1940), p. 540; (vol.) 51 (1941), pp. 205, 400, 410–11; and Arthur Schweitzer, "Fixing of Cost Prices: An Experiment of World War II," *Journal of Business*, 23 (1950), p. 229. On Hitler's demagogic pronouncements, see Case X, Bülow I/203, a speech to arms workers on 10.XII.40, printed in his collection of speeches, *Der Grossdeutsche Freiheitskampf*, vol. 2, pp. 160–62; another example, a speech of 30.I.42, is quoted in Max Seydewitz, *Civil Life in Wartime Germany* (New York, 1945), p. 406. Finally, on the Nationalsozialistischer Wirtschaftsdienst, see Dietrich Orlow, *The History of the Nazi Party: 1933–45* (Pittsburgh, Pa. 1973), pp. 284–5.

tion of reserves and a general reluctance to invest, which in turn prompted the massive stock issues of 1941–2.[11]

With the turning of the military tide and the appointment of Speer in 1942, businessmen's stature and influence rose once more. Price Commissar Wagner departed, and his restrictive pricing and profits policies were replaced by a combination of excess profits taxes and efficiency-based pricing groups. These maintained the flow of revenue, yet introduced incentives that permitted Germany's most productive firms to retain more of their earnings than heretofore.[12] The need to boost corporate morale, hence output, also inspired Economics Minister Funk to promise businessmen repeatedly during 1943–4 that central control of the economy "can only be considered a transitory necessity occasioned by the war."[13] Even SS General Otto Ohlendorf pledged the eventual restoration of entrepreneurial autonomy, though he could not help appending a barb: "What we want is a free economy, free also from monopolies, cartels, and syndicates."[14] Moreover, under Speer, energetic technical experts came to the fore as special commissars for various aspects of production, and the regime's intermittent dedication to the "self-administration of the economy" got a new lease on life.[15]

But these corporate satraps acted as representatives of a state power that remained at once expansive and fractious. Only on rare occasions, and then only by threatening to resign, could they affect major economic decisions.[16] Nor were they an antidote to local-level political encroachments on firms. Whatever reassurance and rationality seemed provided on the national scene by the rise of veteran businessmen was offset by the growing powers of the *Gau* economic ad-

[11] Samuel Lurie, *Private Investment in a Controlled Economy* (New York, 1947), pp. 127–8, 135–6. On the extent of the stock issue, see Singer, *Economic Journal,* 53 (1943), p. 138.

[12] Ernst Doblin, "The German 'Profit Stop' of 1941," *Social Research,* 9 (1942), p. 378; Schweitzer, *Journal of Business,* 23 (1950), pp. 228–36; and Singer, *Economic Journal,* 52 (1942), pp. 196, 202–3.

[13] Quoted in Seydewitz, *Civil Life,* p. 416; and see Wolfgang Schumann, "Die wirtschaftspolitische Ueberlebensstrategie des deutschen Imperialismus in der Endphase des Zweiten Weltkrieges," *ZfG,* 27 (1979), p. 505.

[14] Schumann, *ZfG,* 27 (1979), pp. 505–6.

[15] See Volkmann in Dlugoborski (ed.), *Zweiter Weltkrieg,* pp. 98–9; Edward R. Zilbert, *Albert Speer and the Nazi Ministry of Arms* (Rutherford, N.J., 1981), pp. 108–21; Singer, *Economic Journal,* 52 (1942), pp. 186–9, 377; and Fritz Blaich, *Staat und Verbände in Deutschland zwischen 1871 und 1945* (Wiesbaden, 1979), p. 111.

[16] See the two instructively contrasting examples mentioned by one such executive, W. Rohland, *Bewegte Zeiten* (Stuttgart, 1978), pp. 88–9.

visers, who were ultimately responsible to Bormann.[17] They and the *Gauleiter* proved quite effective in neutralizing the pressures for industrial concentration created by the military situation.[18] Finally, though Himmler was gradually forced to concede that "during the war a fundamental change in our totally capitalist economic system is not possible," his influence over the Economics and Armaments Ministries grew from mid-1943 on, and his long-range intentions continued to worry businessmen.[19]

All in all, the authority of prominent executives, like that of individual firms, remained a tenuous matter of relative autonomy, and their collective influence over the system continued to be small. Overborne by the victories of 1940, businessmen were intimidated after 1942 by the recrimination attendant on the impending defeat – exemplified by the ouster of Ernst Poensgen and Paul and Hermann Reusch from their positions in heavy industry, by Ernst Kaltenbrunner's desire to indict alleged "defeatists" like Hermann Bücher of AEG, Albert Vögler of the Vereinigte Stahlwerke, and the elder Reusch of the Gute Hoffnungshütte, and by Goebbels's and Bormann's attacks on "reactionary captains of industry."[20] For executives, as for the rest of the country, what held the regime together after Stalingrad in January 1943 "was neither common interest nor a consensus, but fear – fear of 'the Russian hordes,' and of the now indiscriminate terror of the Gestapo."[21]

This was the environment in which Farben operated during the years surveyed in Chapter 8, when the concern's leaders made decisions that blackened its name for all time.

---

17 Orlow, *Nazi Party 1933–45*, pp. 375–6, 438; Albert Speer, *Inside the Third Reich* (New York, 1970), p. 211. But compare Volkmann in Dlugoborski (ed.), *Zweiter Weltkrieg*, pp. 96–7.
18 See Peter Hüttenberger, *Die Gauleiter* (Stuttgart, 1969), pp. 182–7.
19 Himmler is quoted in Rolf-Dieter Müller, "Industrielle Interessenpolitik im Rahmen des 'Generalplans Ost,'" *MM*, 28 (1981), p. 113, and more extensively in Herbst, *Totale Krieg*, p. 270. On business fears of the SS, see Fritz Blaich, "Wirtschaftspolitik und Wirtschaftsverfassung im Dritten Reich," *Aus Politik und Zeitgeschichte*, Beilage 8 (1971), p. 17. For a summary of recent research on Himmler's growing influence over Speer, Pleiger, and the RWM during the war, see Wilhelm Treue, "Wirtschaft im Dritten Reich," *Zeitschrift für Unternehmensgeschichte*, 29 (1984), pp. 131–49.
20 GHH 400 10 128/59, Reusch to Julius Dango, 12.VI.42; Speer, *Inside the Third Reich*, pp. 212, 397. See also Alan Milward, "Towards a Political Economy of Fascism," in S. Larsen, B. Hagtvet, and J. P. Myklebust (eds.), *Who Were the Fascists?* (Oslo, 1980), p. 63.
21 T. W. Mason, "The Primacy of Politics," in H. A. Turner, Jr. (ed.), *Nazism and the Third Reich* (N.Y., 1972), p. 196.

8. Commerce and complicity

Almost inevitably, the Third Reich's apogee was also IG Farben's. As an American businessman turned military officer later observed,

When Germany entered the war, it was natural that IG should emerge as Germany's Number 1 producer. They had the factories, they had the great engineering and technical skill, and, of course, they had the vast line of products so essential to modern war.[1]

Consequently, the work force of the combine increased by about 45% in the first four full years of fighting, cresting in 1943 at 333,000.[2] According to IG's accountants, the core concern's external sales swelled during the same interval to 3.1 billion marks (+57%), its gross profits to 549 million (+46%), and its net profits to 300 million (+25%).[3] Despite steeply rising tax rates, Farben added more than 1.1 billion marks to its retained earnings between 1939 and 1944, twice as much as in the preceding thirteen years.[4] The firm also sank some 2.5 billion marks into new plant, about 38% of it financed by government loans, credits, subsidies, and tax breaks.[5] Though much of this investment was depreciated rapidly, the book value of the concern's assets exceeded 3 billion marks in 1944, or roughly double the sum reported annually from 1932 to 1938.[6] That figure made very conservative allowance for a network of shareholdings and other forms of influence that extended to some 400 corporations in Germany and more than 600 enterprises in 101 other countries.[7] Moreover, it omitted the

---

[1] NI-307/4, Control of IG Farben in Germany, Speech by Colonel Edwin Pillsbury, 29.III.46.
[2] Hermann Gross, *Further Facts and Figures Relating to the Deconcentration of the IG Farben Aktiengesellschaft* (Kiel, 1950), p. 35, Table VIa.
[3] NI-10002-03/82, Affidavits by H. Deichfischer, 11.VI.47.
[4] Calculated from Defense Basic Information II/4, p. 29.
[5] Calculated from NI-10001/82, NI-10004/82, and NI-10016/82, Affidavits by H. Deichfischer, 11.VI.47 and 21.VI.47. Deichfischer's figures indicate that for the entire period from 1932 to 1944, IG's total investments came to slightly more than 4 billion reichsmarks and identifiable government assistance to some 1063 million, or 26% of the total.
[6] See the balance sheets in Defense Basic Information I, pp. 70–1, and II/2, pp. 23–4.
[7] The fullest compilations of IG's holdings are NI-9763/16, World map of IG Farben's

potential worth of at least fifty-nine war factories constructed by the
government at a cost of 3.2 billion marks and then leased to the
concern or its subsidiaries with the possibility of eventual acquisition.[8]
By 1945, the combine provided perhaps 50 to 55% of chemical production in Germany.[9] So diverse were the activities of IG's 334 plants
that they were represented in sixteen of the nation's thirty-one industrial economic groups at the height of the conflict.[10]

War and conquest also furthered the transformation under Nazism
of for whom, what, and where the firm produced. To a mounting
degree, the concern became a mere executor of government orders,
and technical possibilities, not financial or commercial considerations,
dominated the *Vorstand*'s decisions.[11] A division like pharmaceuticals, which traditionally served civilian markets, sold almost half of
its output to the armed forces during the war years.[12] More important, such sectors continued their decline in relative significance to the
firm. Dyes, drugs, photographic materials, and fertilizers accounted
for only 31% of Farben's sales in 1943, compared with 70% a decade

participations and agencies, and NI-9540/16, Affidavits by W. Dagne and H. Wolff-
sohn, 12.VIII.47 and 15.VIII.47. Less comprehensive lists appear in NI-9286/16
(also NI-2518); Bayer 4C9.19, Pinnow manuscript, p. 53; Bayer 6/1; and Hartmut
Raupert, *Rolle und Bedeutung der IG-Farben im Rahmen der nationalsozialistischen
Wirtschaftspolitik* (Diplom-Arbeit, Bochum, 1976), p. 24. A postwar study of
Farben's foreign participations estimated their value in 1939 as 1 billion marks; see
Bayer 4C31.13, K. Timm, "Die Entwicklung des Auslandsvermögens der I.G.
Farbenindustrie A.G.," p. 13. On the leased plants, see Ambros VA/504, Affidavit by
Strube and Obermüller, 28.I.48.

[8] Calculated from NI-10004/82 and NI-10016/82, Affidavits by H. Deichfischer,
21.VI.47, which incorporate and supersede numerous other estimates of government
aid (e.g., NI-10011 and 10022, Affidavits by E. Struss, 12.VI.47 and 21.VI.47;
NI-10012, Affidavit by K. Hartman, 19.VII.47). Counting prewar investments,
Deichfischer gives the total public outlay for government plants run by IG as 3.7
billion marks. Concerning IG's voice in the eventual disposition of the plants, see
NI-4491/33, Undated summary of Montan agreements. Their future value should not,
however, be exaggerated. Substantially more than half the government monies went
into explosives plants, whose superfluity was expressed by the unwillingness of Farben
to purchase them when asked to do so in August 1943; see Ambros VA/505, Affidavit
by H. Schmid-Lossberg, 27.I.48.

[9] NI-687/7, U.S. Intelligence estimate, 21.VI.45. The estimate must be used with
caution. A contemporary German estimate, which may also be doubted, placed
Farben's share of German chemical production at one-quarter to one-third; see BA
ZSg 127, Bd. 40, "Zu Neuen Wirtschaftsformen," *Berliner Börsen-Zeitung*, no. 49
(30.I.43).

[10] NI-8325/68, Affidavit by E. Struss, 29.V.47; Hoechst TEA 1351, Memo by ZA
Büro, 12.VI.42; Neumann, *Behemoth*, p. 242.

[11] See Karl Winnacker, *Nie den Mut verlieren* (Düsseldorf, 1971), pp. 120–1.

[12] Bayer 4C9.29, U.S. Control Office, *Activities of "Bayer" I. G. Farbenindustrie
Aktiengesellschaft* (1946), p. 92.

earlier. For heavy chemicals, light metals, technical nitrogen, and synthetic fibers, fuel, and rubber, the proportions were nearly reversed. Benzin and buna alone, which had provided none of Farben's earnings in 1933, brought in more than 20% of the combine's proceeds ten years later.[13] More than one-third of the concern's wartime capital expenditures went toward the manufacture of these two products, and a second third was devoted to producing sixteen other industrial raw materials deemed vital to the war effort (see Appendix D).[14] The military's dependence on IG's production of these eighteen goods ranged from 8% for aluminum, about 25% for artificial fibers, and 33% for fuel to 100% for synthetic greases, buna, tetraethyl lead, methanol, and stabilizers for explosives.[15] Via three subsidiaries – DAG, WASAG, and Wolff & Co. – and their equally large leasing firms for government plants, Farben made most of the Reich's explosives by 1942, though the share tended to fall thereafter.[16] Even more than before the war, the regime insisted on siting installations for all these products in central or eastern Germany. Thus, the firm's historic center of gravity in the Rhineland contained fewer than half of IG's plants and only 42% of their book value at the end of 1944. The territory that later belonged to Poland or the German Democratic Republic (DDR) housed virtually all of the remainder.[17]

In direction, though not quite in degree, IG's development paralleled the wartime experiences of the company's principal foreign counterparts: Imperial Chemical Industries and DuPont. The militarization of the British firm began as early as 1937, when it undertook to construct and operate eighteen government-owned factories and, like Farben, grasped the chance to expand aluminum production at its own expense. During the war, the number of ICI's government plants

13 Calculated from Bayer 15/Da 1.1, Umsätze der Hauptgruppen 1–3.
14 NI-10007/82, NI-10020/82, and NI-10025/82, Affidavits by E. Struss, 12.VI.47, 20.VI.47, and 21.VI.47; NI-10926/90, Affidavit by W. Hagert, 15.IX.47.
15 N-10010/82, excerpted in Hans Radandt (ed.), Fall 6: Ausgewählte Dokumente und Urteil des IG-Farben-Prozesses (East Berlin, 1970), p. 111.
16 See Raupert, Rolle und Bedeutung, pp. 169–70; and Wolfram Fischer, WASAG: Die Geschichte eines Unternehmens 1891–1966 (Berlin, 1966), pp. 105–20, 146–53.
17 Hermann Gross, Material zur Aufteilung der IG Farbenindustrie Aktiengesellschaft (Kiel, 1950), p. 7. Werner Reichelt, Das Erbe der IG-Farben (Düsseldorf, 1956), p. 43, provides a less complete tabulation. Raupert, Rolle und Bedeutung, p. 24, divides the book value of IG's stock participations in 1944 as 37.8% in the territory that became the Federal Republic, 45.7% in what fell to Poland and the DDR, and 16.5% in foreign countries.

increased to twenty-five, their cost hit 58 million pounds ($278.4 million), and they supplied nearly all their nation's explosives, incendiary bombs, ammonia, chlorine, metal alloys, and basic chemicals.[18] ICI put another 19 million pounds ($91 million) into its own plants, and by 1941 the government was buying half of their output as well.[19] Most of the new construction occurred in the western half of Great Britain, particularly Lancashire and South Wales.[20] In addition, like IG, ICI released many of its employees for state service, including two members of the board of directors, five heads of production groups, and thirty-three middle managers and chemists sent to ministries, along with 3,345 trained personnel assigned to run the government installations.[21]

The returns on ICI's assistance were ultimate survival and short-run influence over particular matters, such as agricultural policy affecting fertilizers. But the former colleagues in state employ also frequently dealt quite severely with the firm, as did the Inland Revenue. Though sales rose by 79% between 1939 and 1943, net profits dropped by nearly one-quarter.[22] The government plants hardly paid in any immediate sense, since the construction fees were soon fixed at 1% of costs and the management fees descended from 1.5 to 0.5% of fixed capital expenditure as that sum rose toward and exceeded $10 million.[23] In the words of the firm's historian, "ICI became a government agency, on a very large scale, for investment, construction, research, development, and production."[24]

DuPont's involvement in war production commenced somewhat later, but in the roughly eighteen months preceding Pearl Harbor, the company expended almost $222 million on factories commissioned,

---

[18] W. J. Reader, *Imperial Chemical Industries: A History*, vol. 2 (London, 1975), pp. 256, 260, 265, 272–3.
[19] Ibid., pp. 256–7, 279, 501.
[20] Ibid., p. 263.
[21] Reader, *Imperial Chemical Industries*, vol. 2 pp. 252–3.
[22] W. J. Reader, "Imperial Chemical Industries and the State, 1926–1945," in Barry Supple (ed.), *Essays in British Business History* (New York, 1977), p. 240. On ICI's tax payments, see Reader, *Imperial Chemical Industries*, vol. 2, pp. 280–1, and compare the figures there with the pretax totals on p. 497. In 1943, for instance, a gross operating profit of 15.7 million pounds became a net income of only 4 million after depreciation and taxes.
[23] Reader, *Imperial Chemical Industries*, pp. 254–6. The later value of the plants is another matter, since ICI spent more than $28 million in 1947–8 alone to acquire several of them from the British government (ibid., p. 501).
[24] Reader in Supple (ed.), *Essays*, p. 238.

paid for, and owned by the United States government.[25] Most of these
were munitions works, from which DuPont anticipated no long-term
competition, but the construction or leasing contracts governing new
chemicals facilities generally included an option to purchase for the
lettor and a standard insurance clause forbidding the government to
"use the plant or any part thereof for business or commercial purposes" within twenty years of completion.[26] By the end of the war, the
firm had participated in erecting fifty-four installations scattered primarily across the relatively unindustrialized South and West. The $1.1
billion spent on them equaled one-sixteenth of the public outlay for all
industrial facilities during the war.[27]

Explosives, ammonia, methanol, and neoprene rubber were the
chief products of the twenty-five government plants that DuPont managed.[28] They included, however, the nation's principal mass producer
of plutonium, the huge Hanford Engineer Works in Washington State,
which covered 600 square miles, cost $350 million, and required
45,000 construction workers as well as an operating staff of 6,000.[29]
All told, roughly half of the 180,000 or so employees of DuPont and
its subsidiaries worked at such factories in 1943; their output that year
was sold at cost for $247 million.[30] The enterprise earned only $1.65
million in fees for its assistance during the war, but its own external
sales more than doubled between 1939 and 1943, and retained earnings increased by $79 million, a gain of 31%.[31] Despite having invest-
ed more than $200 million in its own works since the fall of Poland,
DuPont emerged from the fighting with a cash fund exceeding $196
million.[32] Meanwhile, the company had won 128 military commendations for productivity, and its research laboratories had made major
contributions to the development of plastic and other forms of ex-

25 E.I. DuPont de Nemours and Company, *Annual Report 1945*, p. 13.
26 See Gerald T. White, *Billions for Defense* (University, Ala., 1980), pp. 20, 62–3. For
   expressions of the business fears behind this clause, see pp. 26, 32.
27 E. I. DuPont de Nemours and Company, *DuPont: The Autobiography of an American Enterprise* (New York, 1952), p. 113; Louis Cain and George Neuman, "Planning for Peace: The Surplus Property Act of 1944," *JEH*, 41 (1981), p. 129; White,
   Billions, p. 123.
28 E. I. DuPont de Nemours and Company, *Annual Report 1944*, p. 17.
29 DuPont, *Autobiography*, pp. 116–17; idem, *Annual Report 1945*, p. 17–18.
30 DuPont, *Annual Report 1945*, pp. 12, 25.
31 Fees calculated from DuPont, *Autobiography*, p. 113, and idem, *Annual Report
   1945*, p. 12.
32 Ibid., p. 13.

plosives, gun and rocket propellants, chemical warfare agents, and the atomic bomb.[33]

These brief summaries suggest the comparable ways in which Farben, ICI, and DuPont became components and beneficiaries of their nations' war efforts. Stimulated by patriotism and public pressure, the firms traded their skills and some of their autonomy for victory, good will, and growth. Indeed, in purely statistical terms, they developed basically apace during the entire period between the onset of the Depression and the beginnings of severe bomb damage to IG's plants (Table 8.1).[34]

Though comparisons of this sort are notoriously difficult, one may reasonably conclude that neither the Depression nor the respective national recovery and armament programs greatly altered the relative standing of the three chemical giants. Farben remained the biggest, most ramified operation, primarily by virtue of its commitment to benzin and buna, yet was losing ground in more strictly chemical fields. The German concern also retained more of its wartime earnings, a fact that mirrored not only greater agility in dodging taxes, but also the constraints on investment exerted by the Reich's chronic shortages of materials and labor and its preference for forced loans over taxation in order to pay for the war. All in all, however, allowing for shifting exchange rates and differences in the corporate financial reports, the 1930s and early 1940s seem to have favored the companies similarly, and for similar reasons. In peacetime, the firms gained by the revival of domestic industrial customers and by a remarkable burst of inventiveness – DuPont, for example, estimated in 1937 that 40% of its products had been unknown eight years before.[35] During the war, all three firms profited by the urgent tendency, common to the procurement agencies of the belligerents, to concentrate contracts on a small number of the largest, most experienced, and efficient suppliers.[36]

[33] DuPont, *Autobiography*, p. 114; W. A. Noyes, Jr. (ed.), *Chemistry: A History of the Chemistry Components of the National Defense Research Committee 1940–1946* (Boston, 1948), pp. 46–7, 90, 92–4, 136, 173–4.

[34] The figures for IG are derived from Defense Basic Information I, pp. 64, 70–1; Defense Basic Information II, pp. 22–3. Those for ICI are calculated from ones provided by Reader, *Imperial Chemical Industries*, vol. 2 pp. 497–9, and the estimate of ICI's wartime workforce in Defense Basic Information II/17, pp. 54–5. For DuPont, see the annual reports for 1933, 1939, 1944.

[35] Robert Sobel, *The Age of Giant Corporations* (Westport, Conn., 1972), p. 151.

[36] John Morton Blum, *V was for Victory* (New York, 1976), p. 123; Cain and Neu-

Table 8.1. *Growth of IG Farben, DuPont, and Imperial Chemical Industries,*
1929–1943 (1929 = 100)[a]

Year	Employment			Assets			Sales		
	IG	DP	ICI	IG	DP	ICI	IG	DP	ICI
1932	68	80	63	83	110	na	62	61	96
1938	138	120	116	89	150	na	116	116	151
1943	204	180	236	155	203	na	219	302	318

Year	Gross operating profit[b]			Net operating profit[c]			Dividends		
	IG	DP	ICI	IG	DP	ICI	IG	DP	ICI
1932	49	68	111	38	48	108	50	50	84
1938	169	161	161	153	158	146	57	68	114
1943	350	577	291	470	241	108	85	91	114

Note: The net profit and dividend figures for ICI are based on estimates of the totals for 1929.
[a]Core or parent firms only.
[b]Sales minus operating and administrative costs, wages, and benefits.
[c]Gross operating profit minus depreciation, research and development, and taxes.

But if what the corporations made – and what they made by doing so – were similar, the atmospheres in which they worked were not. To be sure, all three companies operated in a system of adversarial cooperation, with each firm and each state seeking both to exploit and to guard against the indispensability of its partner. All the governments accepted the force of Henry Stimson's dictum that "if you are going to . . . go to war . . . in a capitalist country, you have to let business make money out of the process or business won't work."[37] At the same time, each regime endeavored to discipline corporate power: witness the nearly identical excess profits tax schemes enacted by the United States, Britain, and Germany, the antitrust suits the American government briefly suspended and then renewed with a vengeance against ICI and DuPont in 1944, and the Nazi practice of founding

mann, *JEH*, v. 41 (1981), pp. 132–4; Sobel, *Age of Giant Corporations*, pp. 153–77.
[37] Blum, *V was for Victory*, p. 122.

state-controlled concerns, such as Kehrl's fibers companies, Hansa Leichtmetall, the Hermann Göring Werke, and Kontinentale Oel.[38] In this context, the size of the chemical firms proved a weakness as well as a strength. Size conferred visibility, even presented an inviting target; hence, the evasion of official requests and regulations appeared particularly imprudent to DuPont, ICI, and Farben.[39] Still, three elements made IG's situation distinct during the war: the political setting, the labor shortage, and the increasing desperation of the Reich's and the firm's prospects after December 1941.

These factors account in large measure for Farben's participation in the sordid aspects of the tale told in this chapter. The Nazi regime applied the concern's efforts to purposes morally beneath comparison with those served by DuPont and ICI and made Farben one of the Reich's largest employers of conscript and slave labor. At none of these developments did the combine's leaders draw the line. There are many possible explanations for this. Fear is one, obtuseness another. Both undoubtedly played a role, as did the distorting effects of propaganda and patriotic feeling. Even the tribunal that later convicted several IG executives of war crimes noted that "we cannot say that a private citizen shall be placed in a position of being compelled to determine in the heat of war whether his government is right or wrong, or, if it starts right, when it turns wrong."[40] Moreover, men of

---

[38] On the U.S. excess profits tax, see Thomas Cochran, *American Business in the Twentieth Century* (Cambridge, Mass., 1972), p. 147; DuPont, *Annual Report 1945;* and Sobel, *Age of Giant Corporations,* p. 165. On the German procedures, see Singer, *Economic Journal,* 51 (1941), pp. 410–11. The British system may be gauged by comparing the pretax and post-tax figures in Reader, *Imperial Chemical Industries,* vol. 2 pp. 280, 497. One should bear in mind here that the appearance of relative leniency in German taxation is false. The Reich soaked up untaxed funds by forcing banks to turn deposits into bonds and companies to do likewise. See Alan S. Milward, *War, Economy and Society 1939–1945* (Berkeley, Calif., 1979), p. 107, for a comparison of British, American, and German tax policies. On the antitrust suits, see Reader, *Imperial Chemical Industries,* vol. 2, pp. 419–44; Blum, *V was for Victory,* pp. 132–39; and DuPont, *Annual Report 1945,* pp. 22–4.

[39] On the incentives to comply, see J. K. Galbraith, *A Theory of Price Control* (New York, 1945), the argument of which is summarized in his *A Life in Our Times* (New York, 1981), pp. 173–4. Cf. Hugh Rockoff, "The Response of the Giant Corporations to Wage and Price Controls in World War II," *JEH,* 41 (1981), especially p. 128. Another indication of corporate reluctance to incur public displeasure was Standard Oil's handling of its rubber patents; see Henrietta M. Larson, Evelyn Knowlton, and Charles J. Popple, *History of the Standard Oil Company (New Jersey),* vol. 3: *New Horizons 1927–1950* (New York, 1971), pp. 431, 507–8.

[40] James Morris, "Major War Crimes Trials in Nürnberg," *North Dakota Bar Brief,* 25 (1949), p. 107, quoting the judgment.

affairs often take a perverse pride in doing what has to be done, in biting the bullet. Such pride in one's unsentimental decisiveness can outweigh distaste for the actions that result. Something like this was at work among IG's leaders. They behaved primarily in response to specific situations and insistent problems, which skewed their apprehension of what they were doing. Delineating how this happened helps, not to minimize what Farben did, but to throw the moral meaning of the firm's actions into sharper relief.

From September 1939 to mid-1940, Farben's leaders seemed to match the Wehrmacht victory for victory. At Leuna, output climbed as production shifted smoothly from automobile fuel to the high-octane and diesel grades required by the air force and army.[41] Similarly rapid changeovers occurred at Landsberg and Ludwigshafen, Wolfen and Wuppertal, Munich and Marburg. In Austria, the combine began turning its run-down Moosbierbaum facilities into a modern complex of chemicals, light metals, and oil refining works.[42] Meanwhile, a steady stream of resource-saving inventions reduced IG's bills for imported raw materials to only 31 million marks in 1940, one-half the level of 1938.[43] The tricky question of preserving the concern's distance from purely military operations was settled by January 1940 with the foundings of Luranil GmbH to construct government-owned factories and Anorgana GmbH, a companion managing firm for the manufacture of chemical weapons.[44] Directed by a supervisory board composed of four IG executives and three representatives of the High Command, Anorgana broke ground almost immediately for two new works at Gendorf and Dyhernfurth. They were to produce mustard gas and the singularly toxic nerve agent called Tabun, which IG's insecticide division had happened upon four years earlier.[45] Simul-

---

[41] Wolfgang Birkenfeld, *Der synthetische Treibstoff, 1933–1945* (Göttingen, 1964), p. 226.

[42] On Moosbierbaum and its costs, see NI-305/4, File folder on Moosbierbaum, Griesheim plant, September 1945.

[43] For examples of such inventions, see BA Koblenz, ZSg 127, Bd. 825, "Schwefelsäure aus deutschem Rohstoff," December 1939. For the import figures, Bayer D.A. 377, Zentraleinkauf to *Vorstand*, 22.VI.40, and Zentraleinkauf to Einkaufsabteilung Leverkusen, 3.VI.41.

[44] NI-4988, Memo on first discussion of Luranil, 29.I.40, *NMT*, vol. 7, pp. 1254–6; Ambrose VA/506-07, Affidavits by G. Dilthey, 16.I.48; and Ambros' testimony, *NMT*, vol. 7, pp. 1260–3.

[45] See NI-6788/52, Affidavit by O. Ambros, 1.V.47; Robert Harris and Jeremy Paxman, *A Higher Form of Killing* (London, 1982), pp. 53–6.

taneously, Luranil commenced work on a huge installation for iso-octane and related products at Heydebreck on the Oder, and the government pledged to pay half the total expected costs of nearly 600 million marks.[46] Instances of administrative confusion arose, of course, as when the chemicals sales combine refused supplies of a vital compound to a subsidiary and shipped them to one of its competitors instead.[47] On the whole, however, the corporation mobilized for war in clockwork fashion.

Equally successful at first were the combine's efforts to insulate its international connections from the European conflict. Maintaining a flow of goods to branches and clients overseas proved easy enough for the time being. IG simply directed its American subsidiaries to provision customers in the British Empire and Latin America.[48] But the longer-run problem of protecting these buyers and sellers from impoundment by enemy or neutral governments posed more serious difficulties. A solution entailed camouflaging IG's ownerships, which the Nazi Party Foreign Organization continued to reject as defeatist. Even the more pragmatic officials in the Economics Ministry qualified their consent to such subterfuge, announcing at the outset of the war that any failure by a German parent corporation to keep repatriating foreign profits "will be prosecuted as sabotage of the economy."[49] Hemmed in by these constraints, the concern once more found a way to trade its services for a bit of maneuvering room. Farben authorized its agencies abroad to act, in effect, as bankers for the Foreign Ministry. As discreetly as possible, they transferred their surplus earnings to the accounts of local German legations, consulates, Party offices, or purchasing organizations, whereupon the Reich deposited equivalent sums in marks with the combine's Central Finance Office in Berlin. The scheme became increasingly obvious to host governments as the war wore on, but it relieved Germany's foreign exchange shortage while bringing IG into compliance with the repatriation requirements. Moreover, in 1939–40, the procedure gave the Party and the Reich an interest in permitting the concealment of IG's external assets.[50]

[46] NI-305/4, File folder on Heydebreck, Griesheim Plant, 27.VIII.45.
[47] NI-6345/18, Mueller of DAG to Ludwigs, 30.IV.40.
[48] Joseph Borkin and Charles A. Welsh, *Germany's Master Plan* (New York, 1943), pp. 117–18; Howard Ambruster, *Treason's Peace* (New York, 1947), pp. 254–68.
[49] See NI-300/4, Schlotterer to Devisenstellen, 9.IX.39.
[50] Among the numerous relevant documents, see NI-4928/36, Affidavit by K. Krüger,

In fact, during the first nine months of the war, IG managed to salvage its most valued foreign properties: the firm's American holdings and its nonaggression pact with Standard of New Jersey. To hide its control of the affiliates, IG sold its sales outlet, the General Dyestuffs Corporation, to an American front man, had the name of the production holding company changed from the American IG Chemical Corporation to General Aniline and Film (GAF), withdrew Hermann Schmitz and Carl Bosch from that organization's board of directors, and began the complicated process of masking the concern's control of GAF's owner, IG Chemie of Basel. In June 1940, having persuaded the German Economics Ministry that IG's real possession of the Swiss firm remained unimpaired, the combine completed this specious divestiture. However transparent, it bid fair to protect IG's U.S. operations until Farben could hire a trustworthy and credible American "purchaser."[51]

The deal worked out with Standard Oil concerned the only two of IG's American properties not subordinated to GAF, the Standard-IG Corporation, and the Joint American Study Company (JASCO). Since 1930, these partnerships had held the rights outside Germany to all but the purely chemical applications of hydrogenation.[52] Fearing that, if America entered the war, an alien property custodian would seize IG's shares and perhaps resell them to an unfriendly party, Standard bought IG out of the former firm on September 1, 1939, and began considering how to acquire the German corporation's 50% of the latter enterprise. Its assets included the patents for buna rubber. Within the month, Standard's Frank Howard and IG's Friedrich Ringer met at The Hague and initialed a memorandum recasting the decade-old market division between the two giants. Farben gave up its stock in JASCO and rights to two thousand patents in the United States and the British and French Empires in return for Standard's surrender of claims to these rights elsewhere. Each side agreed to keep close tabs on the proceeds from specific markets and to compensate the other for any financial shortfall in comparison with the returns that would have accrued under the old arrangements. Since JASCO already owned the

---

18.III.47; NI-062/2, Embassy in Buenos Aires to Foreign Ministry, 30.IV.41; Nl-068/2, Embassy in Madrid to Foreign Office, 6.IV.41.

51 Joseph Borkin, *The Crime and Punishment of I.G. Farben* (New York, 1978), pp. 185–95.

52 See Chapter 2.

buna patents, and hence their eventual exercise in the United States was virtually unavoidable, the German government agreed in October to authorize the new pact, provided that IG did not include the know-how gathered during the translation of the patents into actual production. By December, the Hague memorandum had been executed. IG had recovered some of the rights sacrificed during the fuel crisis of 1929–30 and been guaranteed against any resulting monetary loss. In exchange, the concern had released control over patents that could not have been withheld in time of war anyway.[53]

Bankrolling German missions overseas was only one of several ways in which IG had to compromise its foreign interests in order to hang on to them. At the outbreak of the war, both the German Intelligence Organization (the Abwehr) and the Military Economy Staff of the High Command hinted at taking over Farben's Vowi section, the nexus of the combine's foreign connections. To preserve a measure of privacy and independence, the firm met the Reich halfway once again. Reithinger and Krüger culled their files for the army and set up a special staff to handle requests for information from that source.[54] Erich von der Heyde, the Abwehr's delegate in Berlin NW7, was allowed to assemble pertinent reports and to turn IG's contact men overseas into sources on such matters as foreign attitudes toward Germany, stockpiles of raw materials, shipping arrivals and departures, and propaganda or economic warfare activities by the United States and Britain.[55] If these arrangements, like the financial ones, ran mounting risks of exposure, they at least headed off the outright conscription of one of the concern's central offices.

Even on the more explicitly political front, Farben had grounds for satisfaction during the early months of World War II. To be sure,

[53] Borkin, *Crime and Punishment*, pp. 83–8; Larson et al., *New Horizons*, pp. 405–7; Bennett Wall and George Gibb, *Teagle of Jersey Standard* (New Orleans, La. 1974), pp. 305–6; Ambruster, *Treason's Peace*, pp. 57–8; and Frank Howard's disingenuous account in *Buna Rubber* (New York, 1947).
[54] See NI-4875/36, Affidavit by A. Reithinger, 3.II.47; NI-6544/50, Affidavit by M. Ilgner, 30.IV.47; NI-9512/79, Affidavit by H. Noack, 12.VII.47; NI-9827/81, Affidavit by R. Huehnermann, 14.VIII.47; and Gerhard Woithe, "Zur Zusammenarbeit zwischen Wehrmachtführung und IG Farbenindustrie AG bei der Aufrüstung Hitler-Deutschlands (1933–1939)," *Zeitschrift für Militärgeschichte*, 6 (1965), p. 82. NI-7978/66 is a four-page list, dated 14.I.44, of reports prepared by the Vowi office since 1939 for the Army High Command.
[55] See NI-9634/80, Affidavit by E. Mueller, 6.VIII.47; NI-8149/67, Affidavit by H. Bannert, 19.V.47; NI-6646/50, Affidavit by J. Saxer, 20.III.47 and 18.IV.47.

Gajewski's troubles with the Party at Wolfen took some forgetting. And Hans Kühne, the manager of the Leverkusen plant, had his own run-in with the NSDAP in early 1940. In fact, he lost a fight to prevent the local *Gauleitung* from posting new instructions for workers to report grievances directly to their Nazi shop steward rather than to the factory administration. But Labor Minister Seldte answered the firm's protests reassuringly, pointing out that the placards announced merely procedural changes and that the regional labor trustee would take care of any misuse of the new system.[56] Because the Leverkusen shop steward was a conciliatory fellow named Schwarz, the nephew of the Nazi Party treasurer, the issue soon became moot.[57] Several months later, the combine adroitly navigated the dangers presented by the death of Carl Bosch, chairman of the *Aufsichtsrat*. Fearing political interference in the choice of a successor, IG quickly elected Carl Krauch to the post and resolved, supposedly as an economy measure, to let his seat and subsequent openings on the *Vorstand* lapse for the duration of the war.[58] Lest the overburdened Krauch balk at the strategem, the combine voted him not only the usual director's fees, but also an extra monthly allowance of 5,000 marks and a one-time payment of 400,000 marks "in consideration of your premature departure from the *Vorstand*."[59]

In addition, during this period Farben established ties to the rising stars in the Nazi firmament: Heinrich Himmler and the SS. Via Fritz Kranefuss, the *Reichsführer*'s protégé in the Brabag corporation, Heinrich Bütefisch of the IG *Vorstand* became a regular participant in Himmler's "Circle of Friends." This successor to the Keppler circle of 1932 had by 1939 some thirty-six members drawn from industry and various government and Party offices. About half of them held honorary SS ranks, including Bütefisch, who entered the Black Shirts as of April 20, 1939, with the title of lieutenant-colonel.[60] Between the

56 Bayer 64/6, Kühne to Seldte, 11.I.40 and reply of 15.II.40.
57 Curt Duisberg, *Nur ein Sohn* (Stuttgart, 1981), pp. 191–2.
58 NI-5184/18, Affidavit by F. terMeer, 29.IV.47, pp. 16–17; NI-6120/18, Affidavit by C. Krauch, 28.III.47. Given this decision, made at the height of the Third Reich's success, I am inclined to discount the story current among IG veterans that Ulrich Haberland, who became head of the Lower Rhine Betriebsgemeinschaft in 1943, was not also named to the *Vorstand* in order to protect him from punishment by the Allies after the war and thus to ensure continuity in the concern's management.
59 IG in Abw., Personalakten Krauch, Schmitz to Krauch, 31.V.40.
60 Michael H. Kater, "Heinrich Himmler's Circle of Friends 1931–1945," *Marab*, 2

outbreak of the war and early 1943, the group convened thirty-eight times to trade thoughts and hear lectures on matters of interest to Himmler, though he seldom attended. Bütefisch seems to have missed few if any of the sessions, despite his ever growing responsibilities for IG's and Germany's fuel production.[61] That he played an active role in the meetings seems doubtful, however. He did serve on an informal committee that assessed the contributions of the members' firms to the *Reichsführer,* among them IG's own payments of 100,000 marks per year from 1941 to 1944.[62] But postwar accounts by participants rarely mention his name, and a security report prepared by the SS for Himmler's adjutant in January 1943 cautioned that he "possesses a mentality geared to international cooperation and exchanges of experience, for which it is self-evident that a concern is a state within a state possessing its own laws and rights of existence."[63] Nevertheless, in 1939–40, access to and good will with the SS leader were valued commodities, and Bütefisch apparently had secured them for Farben.

This contact perhaps seemed all the more desirable because the economic bureaucracy continued to bargain hard with the concern. On the surface, Farben remained ascendant within the Four Year Plan apparatus. As general plenipotentiary for chemicals and head of the recently renamed Reich Office for Economic Development, Krauch was reaching the high point of his authority under the Third Reich. To aid him in awarding contracts for new plants, he drew increasingly on IG's personnel. By the end of 1940, at least six section leaders in Krauch's offices and perhaps one-third of their total managerial staff

(1965–6), pp. 74–93; Reinhard Vogelsang, *Der Freundeskreis Himmler* (Göttingen, 1972), p. 161. Exactly when Bütefisch enrolled in the SS is impossible to say. The fall of 1939 seems likely, since the Freundeskreis became increasingly active after the war began and the coincidence of his membership date with Hitler's birthday suggests backdating. Cf. Bütefisch X/201, Affidavit by E. R. Fischer, 25.IX.47.
61 See Kranefuss to Himmler, 21.IV.43, reprinted in Vogelsang, *Freundeskreis,* pp. 145–8.
62 Ibid., pp. 82, 111, 158. IG's contributions are firmly documented only for 1943–4, but the totals for earlier years suggest that IG began giving in 1941.
63 On his inconspicuousness, see his absence from Vogelsang's account; and NI-5514/41, Affidavit by K. Lindemann, 28.II.47, which comments on twenty-eight members but says almost nothing substantive about Bütefisch. NI-10624/88, RSHA to Himmler's adjutant, 11.I.43, for the quotation. In December 1944, when asked to comment on an intended award of the Knight's Cross of the War Service Cross, with swords, to Bütefisch in recognition of his war service, the *Gauleiter* of Halle apparently proffered no political objections but balked at the distinction with swords (BDC, Personalakten Bütefisch).

were the combine's employees.[64] But only a few of these men notice-
ably favored Farben; most of them displayed sufficient evenhanded-
ness to win the confidence of rival chemical firms.[65] On one occasion
in 1939, Dr. Neukirch, the IG executive who supervised light-metals
production for Krauch, demonstrated his independence by rejecting
proposals to double the capacity of IG's plants for the recovery of
aluminum from scrap. Instead, he chose competing processes and
companies to provide the additional output.[66]

As before the war, negotiations over buna typified IG's relationship
with the state. By January 1940, Farben had attained the revised
annual production target of 40,000 tons at Schkopau and was nearing
the goal of 30,000 at Hüls. What is more, production costs at the
former plant had fallen well below the price of 3 marks per kilogram
fixed by contract with the government in 1936. Excess profits had
begun, therefore, to accrue to the Reich. With most of the technical
problems of buna production now solved and the government propos-
ing expansions of output at both plants plus the construction near
Breslau of a third rubber factory, IG sought an escape from the limits
on buna's profitability. The concern suggested that the Reich loan it
75 million marks of the 133 million required for augmenting the
existing plants but offered to fund the third installation itself, provided
that prices for all buna output were made uniform and lowered in
stages only so far as to allow a continuing excess return sufficient to
pay for the new installations.[67] In other words, IG hoped to make
artificial rubber pay as it went and to shorten the period of dependence on direct government aid, but all without risking any of the
concern's capital. Moreover, the firm wanted the Reich to promise
that any sudden decline in demand would affect all three plants equally, not work discriminatorily against the third one, in which the government would have no financial interest.[68] During the first half of

[64] Bayer 4B/36, vol. 1, Memo on Verm. W. as of January 1940, 23.V.47; Krauch I/67,
Affidavit by A. Mueller, 2.XII.47, which gives IG's share by 1944 as 31.2%.
[65] See RG242/T83, Reel 82, Protocol of conversation between representatives of
Henkel and Degussa, 25.X.40, *Anlage* to the Degussa *Vorstand* minutes of 3.XI.40,
p. 9.
[66] BA R25/105a, Neukirch's in-house history, p. 109. The light-metals sphere was a
constant source of frustration to Farben during the war, and the extent of its failure
to expand its position is chronicled in R25/151–52a.
[67] BA Koblenz, R2/15308, Copy of IG's letter of 8.I.40.
[68] Ibid., Memo of discussion at Price Commissar's Office, 6.III.40.

1940, the combine won the agreement of both the Economics Ministry and the price commissar to the scheme of phased price reductions but got almost nowhere on the other points. The Reich refused to commit itself on the protection of the third factory and rejected any additional loans to the concern, offering instead only a two-year delay on repayments of part of the money borrowed earlier for the first plant at Schkopau. In addition, the Reich set the bill for excess profits due through early 1940 at 7.3 million marks.[69] The revised rubber contract signed in mid-1940 reflected the same balance of power as before the war. In the give and take between the firm and the state, the parties made sure they came out even.

By mid-1940, then, Farben's leaders could breathe somewhat easier than in the preceding September. Production was burgeoning, but manageably so; abroad, the combine had walked the tightrope between the demands of home and host governments; new opportunities to improve relations with the NSDAP had emerged; and the concern seemed to be at least holding its own in the continuous pulling and hauling with the economic policy makers in Berlin. Furthermore, as explained in an earlier chapter, the triumphs on the western front promised some compensation in Europe for the loss of overseas exports occasioned by the war. Yet amidst the rampant euphoria of victory, IG's leaders remained cautious. Earlier in the year, Gustav Frank-Fahle of Berlin NW7 had spoken for a general undercurrent of public opinion when he told Ulrich von Hassell of his pessimism about Germany's ultimate prospects and his horror at atrocities perpetrated against occupied, presumably Polish, populations.[70] Now the ever understated Schmitz confined his comments at IG's meeting of stockholders to the hope that "it may be granted to our führer and Wehrmacht to achieve soon a real peace, which will make good the great injustice of Versailles and thus finally give Europe its long sought satisfaction."[71] When Hitler sent out peace feelers to the British over

---

[69] Ibid., Memo of discussion in RWM, 6.III.40; memo of discussion at Price Commissar's Office, 6.III.40; *Vermerk* of 29.V.40. NI-6344/47, Contract between Reich and Buna-Werke GmbH, 24.IV.40, signed by IG on 21.VI.40, by the RWM on 8.VII.40, and by the Finance Ministry on 25.VII.40. The documents of R2/15309–10 make clear that IG fought so long and hard to reduce the excess profits bill that the matter was finally closed on 20.VII.42 with the payment of only 2 million marks.

[70] Ulrich von Hassell, *The Von Hassell Diaries 1938–1944* (London, 1948), pp. 115, 121. On the general public mood, see Marlis Steinert, *Hitler's War and the Germans* (Athens, Ohio, 1977), pp. 59–65.

[71] BA Koblenz, ZSg 127, Bd. 837, contains a report of Schmitz's remarks on 21.VI.40.

the summer, Farben's leaders probably rejoiced, feeling that their and Germany's interests would be best served if the Reich quit while it was ahead. If so, they were prescient, for the regime was about to lead IG to ruin – and worse.

In the ensuing four years, Farben found its interests undermined, first by the Reich's military successes, then by its declining prospects. The former invited arrogance in Berlin, the latter scapegoating. Victory emboldened the AO to make its anticamouflage policy stick, so that for the six months around the turn of 1940–1 the concern had to reverse course overseas.[72] The resulting failure to transfer GAF's stock from IG Chemie to the hands of a bona fide American owner led to the freezing of the firm's U.S. assets in mid-1941, thence to their complete seizure after Hitler declared war on the United States.[73] In the meantime, the growing adamance of Price Commissar Wagner had prompted the *Vorstand* to impose a moratorium on requests for price increases and to withdraw those that were pending.[74] Most fatally, the regime's self-confidence in 1940–1 fostered wishful thinking about the nation's central economic weakness: the labor shortage.

Nazi labor policy grew out of a self-imposed dilemma. Compelled to call even many skilled workers to the colors, the regime hesitated to replace them on the assembly lines with German women. Even after the Battles of Britain and Moscow shook, then shattered Hitler's faith in impending victory, anxiety about German morale reinforced the führer's conviction that women belonged at home, where they could attend to children, cooking, and the church. As a result, the Reich clung throughout the war, despite nominal changes in official decrees, to a contradictory policy. It encouraged women to volunteer for work but granted generous allowances to soldiers' dependents and allowed shirkers to go unpunished.[75] Thus, between May 1939 and September 1944, the number of working German women rose by only 300,000.

---

[72] See NI-14027/115, Meeting of the Legal Committee, 2.X.40.

[73] See Borkin, *Crime and Punishment*, pp. 193–8, though his chronology is muddled, and he does not see that IG's behavior reflected the shift in policy under pressure from the AO established by the document cited in note 72; see also Ambruster, *Treason's Peace*, pp. 122–31.

[74] Bayer 12/19, 24th *Vorstand* meeting, 5.II.41. Schnitzler later estimated the cost of this and other price concessions by Farben at more than 120 million marks in the course of the war (NI-5196/38, Affidavit by Schnitzler, 18.III.47).

[75] For a good summary of and introduction to the large literature on this subject, see Leila Rupp, "Women, Class and Mobilization in Nazi Germany," *Science and Society*, 43 (1979), pp. 51–69.

Into the breach the Reich thrust increasingly involuntary foreign laborers, as well as prisoners of war and a growing population of concentration camp inmates. By late 1944, the 7.5 million such workers
constituted 21% of the Reich's work force, 29% of its industrial
laborers.[76] Predictably, their health and motivation compared un-
favorably with those of the men they replaced; hence, productivity fell
as their number rose.

For Farben's leaders, the labor crisis and the solutions adopted to it
were sources of intense irritation. In the initial phase of the war, IG
had joined the chemical industry's effort to automate production in
order to facilitate the use of women.[77] Consequently, the number of
women employed in the industry climbed by 30,000, or 67%, between
1938 and 1940, whereas the figure for German industry as a whole
went up by only 12.6% and the actual count of working females held
nearly constant.[78] But the increase proved impossible to sustain, and
the army's needs made it prone to draft skilled personnel, especially
metal and chemical workers, in greater proportions than service employees.[79] As anywhere from one-quarter to one-half of the prewar
work force at any given Farben plant was gradually called up, the firm
turned to foreign substitutes. The first of them appeared on the roster
of the Wolfen factories in May 1940, when more than 1.1 million non-
Germans were already at work in the Reich.[80] By March 1941, IG had
partially offset the loss of 18,000 men to the armed forces by engaging
12,366 foreigners, including 2,162 prisoners of war.[81] In view of their
deficient performance Hans Kühne proposed to close the remaining
gap by shutting down small producers of chemical goods for which
Germany possessed excess capacity, such as lithopone, thus freeing up
native skilled laborers.[82] But Dr. Ungewitter, the Reich commissioner
for chemistry, favored adjusting IG's demand for labor, as well as its

---

[76] Dietmar Petzina, *Die deutsche Wirtschaft in der Zwischenkriegszeit* (Wiesbaden,
   1976), p. 153.
[77] See the *Deutsche Volkswirt* of 8.IX.39, as cited in Singer, *Economic Journal*, 50
   (1940), p. 538.
[78] Singer, *Economic Journal*, 51 (1941), p. 407.
[79] Petzina, *Zwischenkriegszeit*, p. 154.
[80] On the proportions drafted, see NI-2564/19, a chart of 1.VIII.43; Bayer, "Listen,"
   Stand der Gefolgschaftszahlen, 1.XII.44; Gustav Pistor, *100 Jahre Griesheim 1856–
   1956* (Tegernsee, 1958), pp. 131–2. On the Wolfen plant, NI-14135, *NMT*, vol. 8,
   p. 330. On the national totals, Edward L. Homze, *Foreign Labor in Nazi Germany*
   (Princeton, N.J., 1967), p. 24.
[81] NI-7107, Minutes of the *Unternehmensbeirat*, 11.III.41, *NMT*, vol. 8, p. 371.
[82] See Bayer D.A. 1100, v. 3, Kühne to Krauch, 18.III.41.

supply. In the spring of 1941, he began directing IG to relinquish some of its output to competitors in occupied Europe, specifically Rhône-Poulenc and Gevaert. Since the products involved, aspirin and film, ranked among IG's most prized and since one of Farben's principal objectives abroad was to weaken precisely these rivals, the concern protested vigorously. Allocating excess munitions contracts to under-worked foreign enterprises was one thing, in IG's view, but this prac-tice was quite another. In reply, Ungewitter merely repeated his in-structions "with all emphasis" and said he awaited reports of the firm's compliance.[83]

By mid-1941, then, Farben's leaders were boxed in once more by policies they regarded as irrational. Given the regime's demands for expanded output and refusal to push women into industry, the con-cern could either tap the pool of foreign and/or forced laborers or watch the Reich farm out commercially significant but militarily ex-pendable sectors of the combine's business. To the pragmatic *Vor-stand* members, the issue presented no contest; they never even de-bated it.[84] By August 1942, they had appropriated more than 106 million marks for enough barracks to house 114,076 predominantly non-German workers.[85] Over the next twenty-six months, the number of such laborers within the core concern grew from 22,300 (17% of the work force) to 83,300 (46%), and the latter figure encompassed 9,600 prisoners of war and 10,900 concentration camp inmates.[86]

The concern never considered the use of forced labor as anything but the best alternative in an unnecessary situation. Indeed, frustration with the practice set off in October 1941 a heated exchange reminis-

---

[83] Hoechst TEA 252, Ungewitter to Elberfeld plant, 19.IV.41 and 19.V.41; Ungewitter to Wolfen plant, 26.III.41 and 14.VI.41. Ungewitter was here anticipating Speer's own efforts from mid-1943 to transfer consumer goods production to the occupied areas; see Homze, *Foreign Labor,* p. 218.
[84] Knieriem Document 35, Affidavit by C. Jacobi, 24.I.48.
[85] NI-10942/90, Minutes of TEA meeting, 10.IX.42.
[86] Homze, *Foreign Labor,* pp. 236, 239; NI-11411A, Affidavit by K. Hauptmann, 17.XI.47, *NMT,* vol. 8, pp. 310–11. Hauptmann's figures are as of October 1944. Bayer, "Listen," Stand der Gefolgschaftszahlen, 1.XII.44, gives a total outside labor force of 84,200 (43%), including 9,500 prisoners of war and just less than 7,000 inmates. In contrast, 38% of the work force at the Ruhr coal mines in June 1944 consisted of foreign laborers, some two-thirds of whom (93,668 people) were Rus-sian prisoners of war; see John R. Gillingham, *Industry and Politics in the Third Reich* (New York, 1985), p. 125. As of the same date, the corresponding figure for the main plants of the Reichswerke Hermann Göring was 58.7%; see Dietrich Eichholtz, *Geschichte der deutschen Kriegswirtschaft, 1939–1945,* vol. 2: *1941–1943* (East Berlin, 1985), p. 548.

cent of Gajewski's outburst against the excesses of autarky. At a social gathering with a group of Rhenish businessmen, Paul Pleiger cited declining industrial productivity to justify one of his usual diatribes against the inefficiency of large corporations. An incensed Hans Kühne responded by blaming the downward trend squarely on the government's coddling of German women. Their comfort, he contended, made them unwilling to work and thus drove business to sign up less competent foreign help. So vehemently did Kühne press his case that he forced Pleiger to except IG from his criticism of large-scale industry, and Walther Funk, who was also present, chimed in to the effect that the war could not have been fought without IG's services. Kühne thought the altercation worthy of a rather proud note to Schmitz, but the meeting brought Farben no relief with regard to labor policy.[87]

As nearly always under Nazism, IG contrived to make the most of given conditions. Despite the influx of putatively inferior foreign workers, Farben's sales income per worker in the core corporation was 580 marks higher in 1942 and 806 marks higher in 1943 than in 1939; expenditures for wages, insurance, and social services had fallen by 407 and 194 marks per head, respectively. Thus, at the height of the war, the enterprise was making roughly 1,000 marks more per worker annually before deductions for general overhead than when the fighting began.[88] Employing German women would quite probably have been even more profitable, since prevailing wages for females were appreciably lower than for males, whereas foreign workers, aside from prisoners of war and inmates, nominally earned the same wage as their German counterparts.[89] Moreover, native labor would not have imposed as many costs for recruitment, housing, food supplies, supervision, entertainment, and the like. But optimization was not an option. Only in 1944 did the combination of heavy air raids and a strong national effort to improve the lot of foreigners drive sales per worker below the level of 1939 and remuneration per head above it. For all its defects, the Nazi labor system paid, both for Farben and for the Third Reich in general.[90]

---

[87] NI-15027/122, Kühne to Schmitz, 18.X.41.

[88] Calculated from the data provided by Gross, *Further Facts and Figures*, Tables Ia, Va2.

[89] On the wage rates, see Homze, *Foreign Labor*, pp. 42, 48, 78, 125–7.

[90] Ibid., pp. 172, 247–9; Hans Pfahlmann, *Fremdarbeiter und Kriegsgefangene in der deutschen Kriegswirtschaft 1939–1945* (Darmstadt, 1968), p. 235.

Nevertheless, the course of profit did not run smoothly, and the factory managers in the heat of war worried more about the quantity of output than the income per worker on it. Such men complained ceaselessly about the labor system. In part, their discontent sprang from the fact that, despite its importance to the war economy, Farben could never get as many foreign workers as it claimed to need, and certainly not through official channels. Thus, the concern's central labor office in Berlin may have thought in March 1943 that "on the whole the present [labor allocation] organization may be said to meet the requirements of present conditions," but the view from the Leverkusen factory was quite different.[91] Officials there reported in August that "up till now none of our applications for the allocation of labor resulted in our being given assistance from any agency"; hence, they had "helped themselves" by launching independent recruiting drives in the occupied countries.[92]

Furthermore, applying and retaining foreign workers proved as difficult as obtaining them. The skilled and relatively well treated western Europeans tended to slack off on the job or desert in numbers that by late 1943 and early 1944 equaled or exceeded those of their replacements.[93] The so-called Eastern workers from occupied Poland and Russia were at first comparatively willing but also unskilled and, pursuant to government orders in the period from 1940 to 1942, to be treated as "subhumans." Firms received more than six hundred pages of regulations governing the "special conditions" for such workers.[94] These and other directives required companies to provide housing of "barrack type" at their own expense and out of existing supplies of construction materials, to eliminate "all frills" while so doing, to maintain strict separation between the Easterners and Germans, to exclude Poles and Russians from a host of miscellaneous social benefits, and to provide them with food, clothing, and medical facilities inferior to those of German employees.[95] Recognizing that such mea-

---

[91] NI-681, Bertrams to Krause, 10.III.43, NMT, vol. 8, p. 513.
[92] NI-8965, Conference of Leverkusen officials with plenipotentiary for construction of Military District VI, 29.VIII.43, NMT, vol. 8, pp. 530–1.
[93] Homze, Foreign Labor, pp. 253–6; NI-5765, Directorate conference minutes, Leverkusen, 14.IX.42, NMT, vol. 8, p. 365.
[94] Homze, Foreign Labor, p. 169.
[95] Ibid., pp. 247, 265–6; Singer, Economic Journal, 52 (1942), p. 32; idem, Economic Journal, 53 (1943), pp. 134–5; NI-7066, Popp to department heads, etc., Leverkusen, 29.XII.41, NMT, vol. 8, pp. 410–16.

sures were counterproductive in the plants and the workers' homelands, Farben began in 1942 to introduce job placement tests and
performance incentives, such as leaves, wage premiums, special food
and monetary bonuses for exceptional output, and in at least one
instance the establishment of a brothel.[96] But by the time the government came around to this milder course between mid-1943 and early
1944, the nation's manifold shortages of food, building supplies, foot-
wear, and apparel hamstrung efforts to ameliorate the workers' often
wretched conditions. The concern resorted increasingly to severe discipline and punishment, only to find that this practice and continuing
deficiencies in the treatment of what were now called "guest workers"
provoked the ire of the newly virtuous labor agencies, as well as the
SS.[97] To Farben's plant leaders, Nazi labor policy seemed consistently
backward, harsh when gentleness was in order, placating when only
severity remained.

The continuous labor shortage prompted IG to employ a growing
complement of captured soldiers and concentration camp prisoners:
about 1,600 in 1941, more than 6,000 in 1942, around 18,000 during
1943, and approximately 21,000 in 1944.[98] As with all foreign workers, the percentage of these conscripts in the work forces of IG's
individual plants tended to rise from west to east, hence from Farben's
oldest to its newest factories, whose locations the Reich often dictated.[99] Where there were fewer Germans to begin with, the concern
had to rely more heavily on forced labor, especially for construction

[96] NI-8995, Fürst to Warnecke, 26.I.43, NMT, vol. 8, pp. 502–5; Homze, Foreign
Labor, p. 241; NI-7064, Popp to supervisory employees, Leverkusen, NMT, vol. 8,
pp. 443–6; NI-7604/62, Affidavit by C. Schneider, 22.IV.47; Falk Pingel, Häftlinge
unter SS-Herrschaft (Hamburg, 1978), p. 132.

[97] On the shift in national policy, Homze, Foreign Labor, pp. 247–9, 264, and
NI-10883/89, Merkblatt über die allgemeinen Grundsätze für die Behandlung der im
Reich tätigen ausländischen Arbeitskräfte, 15.IV.43. For examples of increasing
disciplinary actions, see NI-5765, Technical Directorate conference minutes, Uer-
dingen, 10.VII.44, NMT, vol. 8, pp. 366–7; NI-6151, Minutes of the Technical
Management meeting, Hoechst, 24.I.44, NMT, vol. 8, p. 557; NI-14560, Lang and
Frey to Bürgin, 14.VII.44, NMT, vol. 8, p. 564. On IG's disputes with the government,
see NI-8999, Exchange of correspondence between Gebechem commissioners in
Belgium and northern France and Leverkusen, 20.IX.43–4.X.43, NMT, vol. 8, pp.
545–9; NI-12018/98, Minutes of interrogation of Wodniak, 15.II.44; NI-12017/98,
SS to Fürstengrube, 28.VII.44.

[98] NI-11411A, Affidavit by K. Hauptmann, 17.XI.47, NMT, vol. 8, pp. 310–11. The
figures for 1943–4 are monthly averages, those for 1941–2 apparently refer to a
single, but unspecified date during the year.

[99] NI-11412A, Affidavit by K. Hauptmann, 17.XI.47, NMT, vol. 8, pp. 311–12.

work. Ironically, however, these cheapest of available hands proved the most expensive. The prisoners of war, many of whom arrived at the factories ill or malnourished, cost the firm two-thirds to three-quarters of the wages for comparably employed Germans but performed at about half their level. This discrepancy scandalized even Göring and Milch of the Luftwaffe. They dubbed the funds collected by the German military for the captured soldiers' services "the biggest racket" in the Reich.[100] Camp inmates generally cost and produced even less. At a rate of just 3 to 6 marks per worker per day, depending on his or her skills and paid directly to the SS, Farben could make a profit only when the prisoners lived on the factory grounds.[101] Thus, despite the acuteness of the labor shortage and the eagerness of the SS to rent out its captives, the core corporation's slave labor force peaked in August 1943 at 13,700.[102] This relatively small total in comparison with IG's needs and the camp populations, its subsequent decline, and its increasing concentration around Auschwitz suggest that Farben made use of inmate labor only as a last resort.[103] Indeed, the exceptional case – Auschwitz – proved the rule.

IG Farben arrived at Auschwitz on a road paved with buna rubber but broken by several detours. Since 1937, drafts of the Four Year Plan had destined at least one of up to four German synthetic rubber factories for the eastern part of the Reich. Not until October 1939, however, after four promising locations had been tried and found wanting, was an appropriate site firmly identified. Clearing and grading the ground at Rattwitz, near Breslau, actually began early in 1940.

[100] On the conditions of the prisoners of war, see, for example, NI-13551, IG Landsberg to Command of the Armament District, Air Force Group, Frankfurt a.d. Oder, 24.I.42, NMT, vol. 8, pp. 419–23; and NI-13544, Hofmann to Hermann, 13.III.42, NMT, vol. 8, pp. 430–1. See Homze, Foreign Labor, pp. 172, 259–60, for both the quotation and the wage and productivity fractions.
[101] NI-4182, summarized in Berthold Puchert, "Aus der Praxis der IG-Farben in Auschwitz-Monowitz," JfW, 4 (1963), p. 207.
[102] NI-11411A, Affidavit by K. Hauptmann, 17.XI.47, NMT, vol. 8, pp. 310–11.
[103] The other significant concentrations of camp labor were at Leuna (2,070 inmates in December 1944; see Bayer "Listen," Stand der Gefolgschaftszahlen, 8.I.45), Wolfen (some 650 women in the latter half of 1944 from Ravensbrück and Buchenwald; see NI-091/3, Affidavit by F. Suhren, 17.VI.46, and NI-4185/31, SS report of 3.I.45), and the Munich Camera Works (451 women from Dachau in 1944; see NI-4038, Schulze to Dachau camp, 2.XII.44, NMT, vol. 8, p. 572). Each of the two government-owned plants for poison gas, Dyhernfurth and Falkenhagen, employed around 500 camp inmates from Auschwitz and Sachsenhausen, respectively (see NI-14291, Bauer to Haaf Construction Co., 31.VII.43, NMT, vol. 8, pp. 535–7, and NO-1905, 15.I.44, NMT, vol. 8, pp. 553–4).

But in July, IG petitioned Krauch to halt the work. Buoyed by Germany's military successes, the concern foresaw an early peace, a "shift of the entire economy to the west," and "the early possession of a colonial empire." Therefore, "the creation of further rubber factories seems inadvisable."[104] Behind this position stood some simple calculations. By the summer of 1940, the combine's Schkopau and Hüls units had contracted to produce 115,000 tons of buna per year at a manufacturing cost of 2 marks per kilogram. The output virtually equaled total German consumption of rubber during that war year, while the cost came to about twice the international price for natural rubber.[105] Buna had reached the limits of its protected market but could not yet compete in an open one. To add 60,000 tons of capacity, as projected for Rattwitz, risked wasting considerable quantities of scarce resources and burdening Farben with superfluous plant. Over the objections of Johannes Eckell, IG's former employee, Krauch concurred, and the Rattwitz project died.

With the failure of the German air offensive against Britain in September, however, IG's scenario collapsed. The prospect of a long war strengthened Eckell's case for increased output and returned the concern's buna program to a familiar bind. Once more, Farben had to contain growth in capacity without tempting an impatient Reich to intrude on the company's monopoly. At a series of conferences during the fall, IG, the Military High Command, and the Economics Ministry worked out an acceptable compromise. The firm undertook to create a third rubber factory, with an annual run of 25,000 to 30,000 tons, but at Ludwigshafen, where various advantages ensured the earliest possible completion date. To offset this addition to plant in the exposed Rhineland, IG abandoned the latest round of expansion at Hüls and agreed to erect promptly a new works of equivalent size "in Silesia." Thus, the Reich would get its facility in the East and increased output, but IG got the scale of that installation halved in comparison with

104 For the quotation and the preceding narrative, see NI-8842/73, Memo on Buna-Erzeugung 1940/41, 12.XII.41, and Peter J.T. Morris, *The Development of Acetylene Chemistry and Synthetic Rubber by I.G. Farbenindustrie Aktiengesellschaft: 1926–1945* (Dissertation, University of Oxford, 1982), pp. 321–6.
105 See Fritz terMeer, *Die IG Farben Industrie Aktiengesellschaft* (Düsseldorf, 1953), p. 93. Gottfried Plumpe's figures for average buna and natural rubber prices vary slightly from mine because his cover the entire period from 1936 to 1944; see his "Industrie, technischer Fortschritt und Staat: Die Kautschuksynthese in Deutschland 1906–1944/45," *G&G*, 9 (1983), pp. 564–97.

Rattwitz.[106] Almost immediately, three potential sites for the new factory came to the fore: Heydebreck, Emilienhof near Gogolin, and Auschwitz. In mid-December 1940, Otto Ambros of IG visited the former two locations, among others, seeming to prefer Emilienhof until the German firm that owned the land declined to make it available. Only then did Ambros take an interest in Auschwitz, a railroad depot near the confluence of the Sola and Vistula Rivers that was also under consideration by an oil firm as the possible location of another new hydrogenation works. Since the preceding June, the village had possessed one special feature. Across the river to the west, in an old Austrian cavalry barracks, the SS had opened a "transit camp" to hold up to 10,000 Polish political and military prisoners pending their deportation farther east; by the end of the year its population had come to include Jews and perhaps to exceed the projected size slightly.[107]

Judging from the SS's preliminary surveys, Auschwitz's marshy and malarial ground offered an inauspicious setting for a concentration camp, let alone a large factory.[108] But Farben soon got wind of a far superior site on a flat, elevated plain along the rail line about three miles east of the town. By mid-January 1941, Ambros was convinced that the alternatives were unsuitable and that the topographical and transportation advantages of the spot, along with its proximity to supplies of water, lime, and coal, offered some compensation for the fact that building there would probably cost three times as much as expanding at Hüls. Though assembling the requisite labor force presented a formidable challenge, housing it would not, since the municipal administration promised that the Jews and Poles who constituted most of the 12,000 inhabitants "will be turned out, so that the town will then be available for the staff of the factory."[109] From this decision, it was a short step to the suggestion a week later by another eager

[106] See NI-7241/57, Affidavit by E. Struss, 12.VI.47; NI-11112/92, Memo by F. ter-Meer, 10.II.41; NI-11781, Hanneken to terMeer, 8.XI.40, NMT, vol. 8, pp. 330–1; NI-11114/92, terMeer and Dencker to Römer of RWM, 22.II.41; NI-8842/73, Memo on Buna-Erzeugung 1940/41, 12.XII.41; and Morris, Synthetic Rubber, pp. 327–8. On IG's concerns about hasty expansion, see August von Knieriem, The Nuremberg Trials (Chicago, 1959), pp. 518–21.
[107] NI-11110/92, Ambros's report of his visit to Silesia, 15–18.XII.40; NI-11783, Report on the conference of 10.XII.40, NMT, vol. 8, pp. 334–5. On the origins of the camp, see Raul Hilberg, The Destruction of the European Jews (Chicago, 1967), pp. 563–4.
[108] Konnilyn G. Feig, Hitler's Death Camps (New York, 1979), pp. 340–1.
[109] Ambros Document 308, Gutsche to Ludwigshafen, 9.I.41; NI-11783, Mineralöl-

local official that the displaced residents be considered as construction workers.[110] Still, when the die was cast for Auschwitz at a conference between Krauch, Ambros, and terMeer on February 6, 1941, the participants envisioned solving the labor problem by "an extensive settlement program . . . to induce German workers to settle in Auschwitz" and planned to arrange the details with Himmler in his capacity as *Reichskommisar* for the strengthening of German nationhood in the border regions.[111]

IG's planners promptly estimated, however, a construction period of two to four years, far longer than Krauch wished.[112] He therefore mobilized Göring to request Himmler to provide the "largest possible number" of camp inmates for work on the site.[113] While awaiting the *Reichsführer*'s assent, Krauch also tried to impress his sense of urgency on Farben. In a letter of February 25, he directed Ambros to spare no expense or effort in getting production started and warned that "it must never happen that, for some reason, you show delay in employing the workers assigned, either because they do not include as many skilled workers as you wish or because of lack of housing." Lest Ambros miss the point, Krauch added that the new plant would be exempted from labor regulations governing rations, working hours, and the employment of women.[114] Having indulged Farben's objections to an eastern site once too often, Krauch thus made clear that he would brook no more delay.

Farben's selection of Auschwitz may not have hinged on the presence of the concentration camp. The surviving records suggest that the

Bau GmbH to Ambros, 11.I.41, and NI-11784, Report of conference between IG and Schlesien-Benzin, 18.I.41, *NMT*, vol. 8, pp. 332–8. The quotation is from NI-11784, p. 337.

110 NI-15258, Faust to Santo, 25.I.41, *NMT*, vol. 8, p. 339.

111 NI-11113, terMeer's notes of conference with Krauch and Ambros, 6.II.41, *NMT*, vol. 8, pp. 349–51. The chief issue on this date was financing the plants through the sales price for buna made elsewhere; see NI-11112, terMeer's note of conference at RWM, 6.II.41, *NMT*, vol. 8, pp. 346–9; and NI-11114/92, terMeer and Dencker to Römer of RWM, 22.II.41. On Himmler's importance to IG as *Reichskommissar*, see also Ambros IIIA/312, Minutes of the 5th meeting of the K-Committee, 30.I.41, dated 17.II.41. On his and the Reich's resettlement policies in the annexed portions of Poland, see Hans-Erich Volkmann, "Zwischen Ideologie und Pragmatismus," in U. Haustein, G.W. Strobel, and G. Wagner (eds.), *Ostmitteleuropa* (Stuttgart, 1981), pp. 433–8.

112 NI-11782, Eisfeld's memo, 13.II.41, *NMT*, vol. 8, p. 351.

113 NI-1240, Göring to Himmler, 18.II.41, *NMT*, vol. 8, pp. 354–5.

114 NI-11938, Krauch to Ambros, 25.II.41, *NMT*, vol. 8, pp. 358–9. Krauch informed Ambros of Himmler's agreement in NI-11086, Wirth to Ambros, 4.III.41, *NMT*, vol. 8, p. 356.

regime's insistence on an eastern location and specific geographic assets won Ambros over before the possibility of employing inmates
emerged. Even later, the concern came to regard the camp as a source
of, at most, about one-quarter of the 16,000 workers IG expected to
need during construction.[115] Himmler was important to Farben at the
outset more as a supplier of resettled ethnic Germans than as a pro-
vider of prison labor. Nor did the combine enter into complicity with
mass murder at this early date. In February 1941, the decision to
massacre the Jews was still several months away, the first experimental gassings more than half a year off.[116] By the time the initial rail
shipment of doomed Jews arrived in 1942, IG had passed the point of
no return at Auschwitz. The Reich was engaged on multiple fronts and
against two new enemies, the United States and Russia. The concern
had appropriated more than 100 million marks out of an eventual
investment of 776 million for a factory complex covering roughly 20
square kilometers and including units for methanol, iso-octane, carbide, and other chemicals, as well as buna.[117]

But these observations do not reduce Farben to a merely passive
victim of Auschwitz's tragic history. The combine's decision to occupy
the site, however unintended and unforeseeable the consequences,
contributed mightily to the camp's expansion and its eventual evolution into a manufacturer of death. As on other occasions under the
Third Reich, Farben's response to politically ordained choices accelerated the dynamic that produced them.[118]

What Farben did was to focus Heinrich Himmler's attention on the

---

[115] See NI-15148, Dürrfeld to Ambros and Bütefisch, 27.III.41, and NI-11116, Dürrfeld's report, 1.IV.41, NMT, vol. 8, pp. 373, 382; and NI-4184/31, Affidavit by W.
Dürrfeld, 18.II.47. For an excellent treatment of Farben's selection of the Auschwitz site, see Morris, Synthetic Rubber, pp. 328–42. Cf. Borkin, Crime and Punishment, p. 115, where the assertion that the decision for Auschwitz resulted from the
labor supply at the camp rests on a document that does not even mention the use of
such labor, NI-11784.

[116] On dating the decision and the first murders, see Martin Broszat, "Hitler und die
Genesis der 'Endlösung,'" VfZ, 25 (1977), pp. 739–75; and Christopher Browning, "Zur Genesis der 'Endlösung,'" VfZ, 29 (1981), pp. 97–109, an English
version of which appears in the Simon Wiesenthal Center Annual, 1 (1984), pp.
113–32.

[117] See NI-1435, Heidebroek to Speer, 21.II.42, NMT, vol. 8, pp. 457–8; NI-7241/57,
Affidavit by E. Struss, 12.VI.47. Hoechst TEA 403 contains virtually complete
records of the appropriations for the plant, 1941–4. For the camp's dimensions, see
NI-305/4, File folder from Griesheim records.

[118] See in this connection, Hans Mommsen, "Die Realisierung des Utopischen: Die
'Endlösung der Judenfrage' im 'Dritten Reich,'" G&G, 9 (1983), pp. 381–420.

Upper Silesian camp. To be sure, he had already begun to see Auschwitz as the location of an extensive agricultural experiment station. In Göring's appeal for labor of February 18, however, the *Reichsführer* SS quickly recognized a chance to advance two larger, previously frustrated ambitions. Since 1935, when a contingent of industrialists, including representatives of IG, had visited Dachau, he had been trying without success to interest business in contracting for his captive labor force.[119] Partly in consequence of this disappointment, the Black Corps had developed by 1939–40 an alternative system of exploiting about one-third of its then nearly 100,000 inmates. Through a complex of firms owned by the organization and manned by prisoners, the SS had begun to aim at economic self-sufficiency. But the deficient commercial experience of Himmler's cadres limited the success of this venture. Thus, cooperation with Farben offered the *Reichsführer* an important double precedent. It would lay the basis for further private uses of slave labor and for partnerships that would provide the SS access to the managerial and technical skills it sorely lacked.[120]

Early in March 1941, Himmler therefore not only acceded to Göring's request, but also visited his transit camp and ordered its transformation into a permanent installation, one conceived as the hub of a kind of industrial park. Dismissing the objections of the regional *Gauleiter* and the leader of the district civil administration, Himmler directed Camp Commandant Rudolf Höss to prepare for a "peacetime" population of 30,000 prisoners and to earmark 10,000 of these for the purposes of IG Farben.[121] To conduct immediate negotiations with the firm over the details of the SS's assistance, Himmler assigned his right-hand man, SS Lieutenant General Karl Wolff.

By the time of the founders' meeting for the new rubber factory on

[119] Raul Hilberg, *Destruction*, p. 590.
[120] See Christian Streit, *Keine Kameraden* (Stuttgart, 1978), pp. 217–19. The basic work on the SS economic empire is Enno Georg, *Die wirtschaftlichen Unternehmungen der SS* (Stuttgart, 1963). On the camp population and the numbers working for the SS, see Jan F. Triska, "'Work Redeems': Concentration Camp Labor and Nazi German Economy," *Journal of Central European Affairs*, 19 (1959), p. 7, and Falk Pingel, "Die Konzentrationslagerhäftlinge im nationalsozialistischen Arbeitseinsatz," in W. Dlugoborski (ed.), *Zweiter Weltkrieg und sozialer Wandel* (Göttingen, 1981), p. 157. Himmler's growing interest in the economic return on his captives did not immediately crowd out, however, his enduring insistence on their punishment. At least through 1942, he sought both to exploit his prisoners and ultimately to work them to death; see Triska, especially pp. 9–10, and Pingel, pp. 157–9.
[121] NI-034/2, Affidavit by R. Höss, 20.V.46; Rudolf Höss, *Kommandant in Auschwitz* (München, 1963), pp. 179–80.

April 7, 1941, Farben and the SS seemed on their way to an excellent working relationship. Höss and his superiors had promised to furnish gravel and other basic materials, to supply, train, guard, and help feed up to 1,500 skilled inmates during 1941, to at least double their number during 1942, and to construct a bridge and rail spur linking the camp with the construction site, all in return for Farben's paying the SS 3 to 4 marks for each worker's nine- to eleven-hour shift. For its part, IG already envisioned a construction force of 12,000 other workers housed in barracks and an eventual operating staff of 15,000 quartered in a model workers' settlement extending from the little town.[122] So heady were the prospects to Otto Ambros, whose expertise in the buna field had now brought him to the front ranks of IG at the age of only 41, that he got quite carried away. The founders' meeting heard him declare IG's intention "to make this industrial foundation a strong cornerstone for a virile, healthy Germanism in the East."[123] Five days later, he reported to terMeer how well everything was going, noting in particular that "our new friendship with the SS is proving very beneficial [segensreich]" and that Eckell had demonstrated his worth in removing petty bureaucratic obstacles (perhaps a reference to the speed with which IG acquired 51% of the stock in the nearby Fürstengrube coal mine).[124] Within a few more months, Commandant Höss was paying visits to IG's Leuna and Ludwigshafen operations "so that I would be in a better position to utilize the labor of concentration camp inmates in such a plant."[125]

But over the next twelve months, the problems that were to bedevil the Auschwitz site began to mount. Inability to complete a fence around the work area held the number of inmates to less than one thousand during 1941 and made them employable only during daylight and in inefficient clumps. Security-conscious guards, or Capos, mostly professional criminals furnished by the camp, administered ever more frequent beatings to the prisoners, which had "a demoralizing effect on the free workers (Poles), as well as on the

122 NI-15148, Dürrfeld to Ambros and Bütefisch, 27.III.41, NMT, vol. 8, p. 373; NI-11115-16, Minutes of the 1st Auschwitz Construction Conference, 24.III.41, and Dürrfeld's report, 1.IV.41, NMT, vol. 8, pp. 377–86.
123 NI-11117, Ambros' remarks to the founders' meeting, 7.IV.41, NMT, vol. 8, p. 386.
124 NI-11118, Ambros to terMeer and Struss, 12.IV.41, NMT, vol. 8, p. 389; NI-12011/98, Contract between IG and Fürstliche Plessischen GmbH, 8.II.41.
125 NI-034/2, Affidavit by R. Höss, 20.V.46.

Germans."[126] Their productivity also suffered from overcrowding as a result of shipping delays that slowed the construction of barracks. By the turn of the year, Dürrfeld and Faust, the IG officials responsible for construction, faced a major labor shortage and contemplated an appeal to the Organization Todt for relief. While the nearby Heydebreck and Blechhammer fuel plants received priority in the allocation of Polish and German labor, the camp had to reduce its buna detachment to only about one hundred men in order to construct a huge pen for incoming Russian prisoners of war.[127]

Briefly in the spring of 1942, Farben's builders got a respite. The total work force swelled from 5,000 to 11,200, the number of inmate laborers rose toward its peak for the year of 2,000, barracks materials flowed in, and the Organization Todt took over the construction of a railroad station, dump, waterworks, and the smaller military factories attached to the buna plant. Undersupplies of iron and lumber continued to impede building, however, and these were aggravated from May to July 1942 by a ban on the transport of all nonmunitions products on German railways.[128] Equally debilitating was the loss of energy and time caused by having to march the prisoners to and from the construction site each day. IG's proposed solution to the latter problem, the establishment of a branch camp at the works, surfaced just as an outbreak of typhus at Auschwitz began to deprive the concern of slave labor between July and November.[129]

In consequence, by mid-1942 Farben's Auschwitz project had fallen badly behind schedule. From the concern's point of view, the fault lay with the Reich, which had failed to provide or transport essential materials and labor. In particular, the camp's performance had been deficient, all the more so now that the SS had decided to change the makeup of Auschwitz by transferring Polish prisoners to camps in

[126] NI-14543, Auschwitz weekly report 11, 19.VIII.41, and NI-11127, 12th Auschwitz Construction Conference, 13.X.41, NMT, vol. 8, pp. 392–6.
[127] NI-11129-32, 13th–16th Auschwitz Construction Conferences, 18.XI.41–16.XII.42, and NI-15256, Auschwitz weekly report 33, 5–11.I.42, NMT, vol. 8, pp. 401–19.
[128] NI-11132, 16th Auschwitz Construction Conference, 6.III.42, and NI-11137, 19th Auschwitz Construction Conference, 30.VI.42, NMT, vol. 8, pp. 427–33, 441. On the number of prisoners, see the charts in Dürrfeld Document 1505. On the railroad stoppage, Singer, Economic Journal, 53 (1943), p. 124.
[129] NI-15424, Auschwitz weekly report 56, 15–21.VI.42, and NI-14524, Auschwitz weekly report 57, 22–28.VI.42, NMT, vol. 8, pp. 436–7. See also NI-4182/31, Affidavit by H. Bütefisch.

Germany and replacing them with Jews culled from the numerous boxcars that began to converge on the village and a new sister camp at nearby Birkenau. A parallel increase in the severity shown inmates assigned to Farben now reached such proportions that Dürrfeld and Faust felt compelled to order their subordinates to report incidents of maltreatment immediately so that the two men could intervene.[130] Whether Himmler knew of or accepted these explanations for the plant's slow progress is unclear, but he ascribed at least some responsibility for the delays to Farben's self-interest. During a visit to the plant on July 18, he challenged IG's practice of constantly altering the design of the buna works to improve on that of its three predecessors. To his way of thinking, "if this meant a loss of time it would be preferable to build more quickly in accordance with the same plans and to put up with certain disadvantages in manufacture." The firm's manager countered by promising to commence operations within about a year.[131]

But Farben could not afford to take any shortcuts, since two developments during the preceding year had undermined the plant's commercial prospects. In the first place, the three existing installations for buna now appeared equal to the Reich's needs, even on the Eastern front.[132] Keeping a fourth plant afloat would depend on maximizing efficiency. Moreover, it was becoming clear that World War II would do to buna what World War I had done to dyes: create overseas competitors and reduce future markets. By mid-1942, Standard of New Jersey had licensed its buna patents to all comers in America without fee, and the U.S. government was pouring the first of more than 700 million dollars into the manufacture of synthetic rubber. Farben could not yet foresee the extent of this investment or the fact that by 1944 it would be yielding four and one-half times as much buna as Germany's maximum production target. But the concern could apprehend that its dream of dominating the international buna market had vanished, that only a continental *Grossraum* could assure Farben of a firm sales base, and that, even then, buna's profitability hinged on the creation of the most up-to-date of factories.[133]

---

130 NI-14512, Auschwitz weekly reports 58–9, 29.VI.42–12.VII.42, *NMT*, vol. 8, pp. 438–9.
131 NI-14551, Auschwitz weekly reports 60–1, 13–26.VII.42, *NMT*, vol. 8, p. 448.
132 See Plumpe, *G&G*, 9 (1983), pp. 592–3; terMeer, *IG Farben*, p. 92.
133 On the American program, see William M. Tuttle, Jr., "The Birth of an Industry:

In other words, once more Farben's rubber program was caught between the regime's priority (immediate output) and the combine's objective (ultimate competitiveness). But now the situation of both parties had grown more desperate; hence, their readiness to go for broke had risen. Though proved right about the superfluity of a plant they had not wanted, terMeer, Ambros, and the other *Vorstand* members were too committed economically and politically to reverse course. At the site, the nerves of Dürrfeld and Faust, already strained by the tension between the needs for haste and quality work, were gradually rubbed raw by repeated interruptions of supplies. What followed was a steady barbarization at IG-Auschwitz, as the increasingly illogical buna plant partook more and more of the brutal madness that ruled its setting.

A more frantic and impatient tone characterized Dürrfeld's and Faust's biweekly reports from Auschwitz almost from the moment Himmler departed. Though finally, by September, the labor force had nearly caught up to the intended totals, its efficiency remained subpar, and the concern estimated the shortfall of skilled mechanics and machinists at seven thousand. Similarly, the "catastrophic situation as regards barracks" improved gradually over the summer, but many of the seven thousand available beds could not be occupied because latrines, baths, and kitchens remained absent. Finally, the "wretched" clothing of the foreign workers was alleviated somewhat by the purchase from the camp of what IG's managers recognized as "presumably the civilian clothes of the admitted inmates." Shoes and socks however, were not included; hence, the factory had to continue making wooden shoes the standard issue. Under these conditions, it was no wonder that the voluntary foreign laborers grew restive. IG's leaders felt compelled to send 160 Belgian and French "shirkers" home in August, then began threatening would-be imitators with transfer to the concentration camp. Such harshness merely inflated the number of desertions among the foreigners, which came to 23% of their total

The Synthetic Rubber 'Mess' in World War II," *Technology and Culture*, 22 (1981), pp. 39–44, 62; White, *Billions*, pp. 77–8. For terMeer's high appraisal of it, see the summary of his conversation with Mulert and Eckell at the RWM on 15.V.42 in Morris, *Synthetic Rubber*, pp. 238–9. Like terMeer, other IG experts doubted during the war that buna could compete with America's synthetic output in peacetime, let alone with natural rubber, and events in the immediate postwar years bore them out. See Douglas Todd, "Synthetic Rubber in the German War Economy," *Journal of European Economic History*, 10 (1981), pp. 161, 165.

IG's buna plant at Auschwitz. (*Source: OMGUS – Ermittlungen gegen die I. G. Farben*, Greno Verlagsgesellschaft, Nördlingen, 1986)

complement by the end of September.[134] As of November 3, 1942, nineteen months after the founders' meeting, the assembly of IG's factories had just begun, and only 55% of the necessary earth moving, 61% of the road construction, and 25% of the track laying had been accomplished.[135]

---

[134] See NI-11138, 20th Auschwitz Construction Conference, 8.IX.42, NI-14553, Auschwitz weekly reports 62–3, 27.VII.42–9.VIII.42, NI-14489 and NI-14514, Extracts from Auschwitz weekly reports 70–1, 20.IX.42–4.X.42, *NMT*, vol. 8, pp. 453–63. That IG bought the clothing, paying 100,000 marks during 1943 alone, is established by the affidavits cited in Klaus Sator, *Grosskapital im Faschismus: Dargestellt am Beispiel der IG-Farben* (Frankfurt, 1978), pp. 74–6. IG's inability to procure shoes reflected the national shortage; see Singer, *Economic Journal*, 51 (1941), pp. 210, 414; idem, *Economic Journal*, 52 (1942), p. 199.

[135] NI-11139, 21st Auschwitz Construction Conference, 3.XI.42, *NMT*, vol. 8, p. 483.

Neglected by the Speer ministry, which considered the camp a more than adequate source of labor, but unable to use more inmates for want of sufficient guards, the plant management saw its only hope in completing the long-delayed branch camp on the factory site and introducing incentives for better work performance.[136] To the latter end, Farben proposed that the SS sanction systems of bonuses and extra rations, a house of prostitution, and offers of early release for particularly productive inmates. Only the last suggestion was rejected.[137] These changes, along with the shift in national policy toward building European solidarity against bolshevism, led to improvements in the treatment and efficiency of foreign laborers at IG-Auschwitz during 1943.[138] Despite continuing short-handedness and a mounting incidence of sabotage to nearby rail lines, the methanol plant came on line in June 1943, three months ahead of schedule, and all the other units except buna started operating by April or May 1944, which was still nearly a year later than promised Himmler.[139] By then, foreigners composed 40 to 50% of the 27,000 to 29,000 workers at IG-Auschwitz and ethnic Germans only some 20 to 30%. The remaining 30% or so consisted chiefly of camp inmates, who fared far worse during 1943–4.[140]

Intensified exploitation of these slaves after Farben's subcamp opened in late 1942 had much to do with the gathering pace of work on the factories. This was not, however, the immediate effect. For several months around the turn of the year, 30 to 40% of the approximately 3,000 employed inmates were either assembling the camp, which became known as Monowitz, or in sick bays, partly as a consequence of severe cold and brutal handling by foremen pressing to

---

136 Ibid., p. 484; NI-15256, Auschwitz weekly reports 76–7, 2–15.XI.42, NMT, vol. 8, pp. 487–9.
137 NI-15254, Auschwitz weekly reports 72–3, 5–18.X.42, NMT, vol. 8, pp. 470–1; Pingel, Häftlinge, p. 132.
138 See, e.g., NI-10883/89, Merkblatt über die allgemeinen Grundsätze für die Behandlung der im Reich tätigen ausländischen Arbeitskräfte, Gestapo Aussendienststelle Auschwitz, 15.IV.43.
139 Dürrfeld Document 1505, Chart IV; NI-10821/89, Ambros to IG-Auschwitz Construction Conference participants, 22.IV.44. NI-11143, 25th Auschwitz Construction Conference, 9.IX.43, and Dürrfeld 1408, Auschwitz weekly reports 108–9, 14–27.VI.43, NMT, vol. 8, pp. 541–3, 523–5.
140 Estimated from comparing the charts in Dürrfeld Document 1505 and in NI-11412A, Affidavit by K. Hauptmann, 17.XI.47, NMT, vol. 8, pp. 311–12, where the totals for Auschwitz are incomplete.

complete the installation.[141] By late winter of 1943, the wasting away
of the inmates was conspicuous enough to provoke, probably at IG's
instigation, the first systematic "selection" at Monowitz. With Dürrfeld at his side controlling for valuable skills, SS Captain Heinrich
Schwarz reviewed the 3,500 prisoners and consigned roughly half of
them to the return journey to Auschwitz.[142] Thus began the rolling of
a grisly human conveyor belt between the SS's rail sidings and Monowitz. Able-bodied Jews were brought from Auschwitz, billeted three to
a bed in stifling and verminous barracks, provided minimal food and
clothing supplements to the standard camp issue, subjected to lengthy
predawn roll calls in all sorts of weather, and put to work on eleven-
hour shifts hauling or carrying heavy loads at a trot. Within three to
four months of their arrival, such treatment literally consumed the
inmates, reducing them to walking skeletons. Those who did not drop
dead were sooner or later reclaimed by the SS and gassed. Either way,
they were replaced, and the cycle resumed.[143] In this manner, some
35,000 people passed through Monowitz during 1943–4; the toll of
confirmed deaths came to about 23,000, or an average of 32 per
day.[144] At IG's mines in the neighborhood, the Fürstengrube, Jan-
inagrube, and Gunthergrube, where the concern employed another
6,000 inmates during 1942–4, the mortality was even more frightful.

[141] NI-14532, Auschwitz weekly reports 80–1, 31.XI.42–13.XII.42, and NI-11140,
22nd Auschwitz Construction Conference, 21–22.I.43, NMT, vol. 8, pp. 490–2,
501.
[142] NI-15256, Auschwitz weekly reports 90–1, 8–21.II.43, and 94–5, 8–21.III.43,
NMT, vol. 8, pp. 489–90, 510–17; NI-12069/99, Affidavit by G. Herzog,
21.X.47; Otto Kraus and Erich Kulka, The Death Factory (New York, 1966), pp.
21–3.
[143] Cf., for example, Kraus and Kulka, Death Factory, pp. 18–24; NI-4184/31, Affidavit by W. Dürrfeld, 18.II.47, which includes the almost certainly spurious claim that
menus for the workers provided 2,800 calories per day; NI-11692-11706, Numerous affidavits by British prisoners of war interned at Auschwitz; NI-12070/99,
Affidavit by S. Budziaszek, 27.X.47; and Primo Levi, Survival in Auschwitz (New
York, 1961), p. 113. On the life expectancy, see NI-4830/35, Affidavit by R. Vitek,
who gives three months as the maximum figure. The employment and death figures
for 1943–4, however, suggest a complete turnover of the work force at slightly
longer intervals (see footnote 144 and Dürrfeld, Document 1505).
[144] NI-7967/66, Affidavit by E. Schulhof, 21.VI.47, the prisoner who compiled the
card catalogue of inmates for Monowitz, and NI-12070/99, Affidavit by S.
Budziaszek, the head physician at Monowitz, 27.X.47, provide the generally accepted figures. Estimates ten times as great appear frequently in accounts of Auschwitz but do not rest on the firsthand knowledge of Schulhof and Budziaszek; e.g.,
Josiah DuBois, The Devil's Chemists (Boston, 1952), pp. 220–1, and Jürgen
Räuschel, Die BASF. Zur Anatomie eines multinationalen Konzerns (Köln, 1975),
pp. 18–19.

Despite relatively high food allowances, the life expectancy there dropped late in the war to only four to six weeks.[145]

Though individual foremen and managers occasionally sought to alleviate the plight of the prisoners, compassion typically took a back seat to the drive to finish the factories.[146] Besides, most of the German employees lived on short rations and under a Spartan regime that dulled their sense of sympathy, and the intermingling of the semidead with fresher inmates and more robust foreign laborers helped insulate IG's officials from what was happening.[147] So long as Auschwitz maintained the flow of warm bodies, Farben's managers could excuse themselves by ascribing the prisoners' fate to the policies of the SS and the general shortage of supplies. When rationalization failed, such men behaved like Albert Speer and relegated their misgivings to the realm of mere sentiment.[148] For the record, the general consensus, summed up at the Twenty-fourth Construction Conference in June 1943, was that "the allocation of inmates is now working much better."[149] The SS largely concurred, not least because it collected on the order of 20 million marks in "wages" from Farben over the life of the Monowitz camp.[150] Yet as the death toll rose and the Russian lines closed in during 1944, the buna plant remained unfinished.

---

[145] On the number of inmates, see NI-034/2, Affidavit by R. Höss, 20.V.46, and NI-7966, Affidavit by E. Orlik, a prisoner and physician at Janina, 18.VII.47. On the probable life spans, compare Orlik's affidavit and NI-11652/96, Affidavit by Dr. W. Loebner, inmate surgeon. So bad were the conditions at the mines that the refusal of British prisoners of war assigned there to work won the support of the German military authorities responsible for them. See NI-10525/87, Guard unit to Janina management, 11.VIII.43; NI-12019/98, File note re inspection of the mine camps, 16.VII.43. For examples of the punishments meted out to inmates, see NI-11038/91, IG Auschwitz to SS Obersturmführer Schoettl, 11.IX.44, and reply of 14.IX.44, and NI-11043/91, Labor Camp Janina to SS, 15.VII.44.

[146] Hermann Langbein, *Menschen in Auschwitz* (Wien, 1972), pp. 507–11; NI-7184/56, Affidavit by G. Alfine, 5.VI.47.

[147] Interview with Frau Dietze, a former secretary at Auschwitz, 18.XI.82; NI-838/9, G. Burth to Dr. Küpper, 30.VII.42.

[148] See Speer, *Inside the Third Reich*, p. 375, but compare Matthias Schmidt's evidence that Speer had a hand in creating some of the conditions he professed to deplore, *Albert Speer. Das Ende eines Mythos* (Bern, 1982), pp. 224–8. Nor do I mean to imply here that Speer's portrayal of his relation to the persecution of the Jews is entirely honest or accurate. See Erich Goldhagen, "Albert Speer, Himmler and the Secrecy of the Final Solution," *Midstream*, 17 (1971), pp. 43–50.

[149] NI-11142, 24th Auschwitz Construction Conference, 22.VI.43, *NMT*, vol. 8, p. 537.

[150] NI-9542, Affidavit by O. Ambros, as quoted in Kazimierz Smolen, "The Concentration Camp Auschwitz," in K. Smolen (ed.), *From the History of KL-Auschwitz* (New York, 1982), pp. 14–15. The estimate seems credible on the basis of

Gathering feelings of guilt and panic no doubt strengthened "the silent hostility between the SS command and the civilian authorities" of the buna plant noted by an Italian-Jewish chemist assigned to Monowitz in 1944.[151] In turn, those feelings fed on the general awareness at the site, and the growing perception among Farben's senior officers, of what had been going on upwind from the factories. Certainly no one at IG-Auschwitz can have mistaken the SS's murderous intent toward the Jews employed there. As early as July 1943, Georg Burth of the factory staff informed one of his superiors back home that the "diet and treatment" of the Jewish inmates were "appropriate to the purpose [zweckentsprechend]," since they never gained weight, were shot on trying to escape, and often "disappeared" as a result of "heat stroke."[152] But knowledge of the systematic annihilation of the Jews in gas chambers came later, more haltingly, and with less clarity.

That the scales fell but slowly from the eyes of Farben's leaders may seem difficult to believe. After all, it was Zyklon B, a granular vaporizing pesticide, that asphyxiated the Jews of Auschwitz, and a subsidiary of IG, the Deutsche Gesellschaft für Schädlingsbekämpfung mbH (German Vermin-Combating Corporation), or Degesch, that controlled the manufacture and distribution of the Zyklon.[153] IG's 42.5% of the stock in Degesch translated into three seats on its Administrative Committee, occupied by members of Farben's own Vorstand, Heinrich Hoerlein, Karl Wurster, and Wilhelm R. Mann, who acted as chairman. But this body ceased to meet after 1940. Though Mann

extrapolations from the documented amounts paid for October 1943 (489,000 reichsmarks for about 6,500 laborers; Danuta Czech, "Most Important Events in the History of the Concentration Camp Auschwitz-Birkenau," in Smolen (ed.), From the History, p. 204).
151 Levi, Survival, p. 96.
152 NI-838/9, Burth to Küpper, 30.VII.42.
153 Degesch did not actually manufacture or sell the Zyklon. Instead, it provided the necessary apparatus, carrying material, odor additive, stabilizer (purchased from Farben's Uerdingen plant), and packing material to two licensed producers, the Dessauer Werke and the Kali-Werke of Kolin. These shipped the finished product directly to customers, once their orders had been received by either of two sales companies, Heerdt-Lingler (Heli), which covered the south and west of Germany, and Tesch & Stabenow (Testa), whose territory was the east and north, and then cleared by Degesch against the official allocations among categories of consumers authorized by the Working Committee of the Ministry for Armaments and Production. See NI-12217/100, Affidavit by K. Amend; NI-11937/98, Affidavit by A. Zaun; NI-11393/94, Contract between Degesch and Testa, 27.VI.42; and Hilberg, Destruction, pp. 567–70.

Table 8.2. *Production and sales of Zyklon B, 1938–1945*

	1938	1939	1940	1941	1942	1943	1944
1. Sales (thousands of marks)	257	337	448	366	506	533	
2. Percentage of total Degesch earnings	30	38	57	48	39	52	
3. Production (short tons)	160	180	242	194	321	411	231
4. Volume ordered by Auschwitz (short tons)					8.2	13.4	2.2*
5. Percentage of production ordered by Auschwitz					2.5	3.3	1.0*
6. Volume ordered by Mauthausen (short tons)					0.9	1.5	

Note: The figures marked with an asterisk are incomplete. One ton of Zyklon was sufficient to kill roughly 312,500 people (Friedländer, *Gerstein*, p. 185). According to one estimate (cited by Hilberg, *Destruction*, p. 570, note 70), only 5.6 of the 23.8 short tons ordered by Auschwitz were required for actual fumigation, leaving enough to gas more than 5.6 million people. For slightly different figures and kill ratios, see Smolen (ed.), *From the History*, p. 31.
Sources: 1, 2: NI-15060/122, Degesch income statements, Special Dept. F, Leverkusen, certified 31.III.48. 3, 4: Friedländer, *Gerstein*, pp. 183–4. 5: Calculated from 3–4. 6: NI-7963/66, Ledger card from Heerdt-Lingler, Degesch's sales outlet for western and southern Germany.

continued to review the monthly sales figures for Degesch, he could not necessarily have inferred from them the uses to which the Auschwitz camp was putting the product (see Table 8.2).[154]

Developed during World War I as a powerful delousing agent and still employed principally as such for submarines, barracks, rolling stock, and prison camps, Zyklon was bound to yield rising returns in wartime.[155] Its very prevalence and toxicity were what led one of Commandant Höss's assistants to first test the substance on about 850 Soviet prisoners of war and sick inmates in September 1941.[156] Even had Mann troubled to note that the quantities purchased by the con-

154 On Farben's shareholding, see NI-12073/99, Affidavit by P. Haehni, 28.X.47; NI-6363/48, the contract among IG, Th. Goldschmidt, and Degussa, 1936–7. On IG's representation and Mann's role, DuBois, *Devil's Chemists*, pp. 213–15.
155 See NI-9098/76, Lectures by G. Peters and H. Sossenheimer, 27.II.42; BA Koblenz, ZSg 127, Bd. 827, "Gas zur Seuchenbekämpfung," *Die chemische Industrie*, April 1942, p. 56; NI-10185/84, Klebe to Degesch, 16.VIII.44.
156 NI-7183/56, Affidavit by R. Höss, 29.I.47; Smolen (ed.), *From the History*, p. 20.

ventional concentration camp at Mauthausen came to only about one-tenth of those ordered by Auschwitz in 1942–3, he might very well have written this ratio off to the relative size of the camps and their satellites. And the SS apparently consulted no one associated with either Farben or Degesch concerning the construction of the gas chambers.[157] After learning in June 1943 from Kurt Gerstein of the SS that Zyklon had been used to liquidate "large numbers of people . . . criminals, mental cases, and so on," the general manager of Degesch, Gerhard Peters, allegedly kept an oath of secrecy. He persisted even after Gerstein added a request on "humanitarian" grounds that the Zyklon be delivered without its usual and noxious warning odor.[158] More talkative was Bruno Tesch, the owner of Degesch's sales agency for eastern and northern Germany. He reportedly told one of his secretaries in about June 1942 of gassings with Zyklon and recorded revelations by Wehrmacht officers to this effect in a report seen by two other employees a few months later.[159] But in all the postwar trials of Tesch, Peters, and Farben's officers, no proof emerged that this first-hand information passed up the ladder to the concern's *Vorstand*. And Allied radio broadcasts could not have alerted the firm before July 1944, when evidence of the camp's murderous activities finally made an impression on the Allies and led to mentions of Auschwitz by name.[160]

Nor did Farben's leaders ever confront the machinery of death face to face. When senior executives like Ambros, terMeer, Knieriem, Schneider, Jaehne, and Krauch visited Auschwitz at various intervals between 1942 and 1944, they did not tour Birkenau, where the trains disgorged their human cargo for the infamous sorting between tenuous life and immediate death.[161] Located behind a stand of trees

---

[157] Ibid.

[158] See NI-9113/76, Affidavit by Peters, 16.X.47; Pierre Joffroy, *A Spy for God: The Ordeal of Kurt Gerstein* (New York, 1971), p. 208; Saul Friedländer, *Kurt Gerstein: The Ambiguity of Good* (New York, 1969), pp. 189–91. Peters was tried three times after the war and eventually escaped punishment; see Jan Sehn, *Auschwitz-Birkenau Concentration Camp* (Warsawa, 1961), p. 129, and Hilberg, *Destruction*, p. 702.

[159] United Nations War Crimes Commission, "The Zyklon B Case," *Law Reports of Trials of War Criminals*, 1 (1947), pp. 93–103. Tesch was convicted by the British military tribunal and hanged, along with Karl Weinbacher, one of his aides.

[160] See Martin Gilbert, *Auschwitz and the Allies* (New York, 1981), pp. 233–4, as modified by Richard Breitman, "Auschwitz and the Archives," *CEH*, 18 (1985), pp. 369–71.

[161] For confirmation of the presence of these men at Auschwitz, see NI-14889, Ausch-

about two miles west of the main camp, Birkenau was not visible from there or from the more distant Farben factory. Those outsiders conducted around the main installation saw something of a "showpiece . . . deliberately designed to allay suspicions. . . . The twenty-eight one- and two-story brick buildings with spacious washrooms and the careful land-scaping did not conform to normal camp appearance."[162]

Yet rumors accumulated – to the point that the desire to remain ignorant replaced the real thing. At Monowitz the pervasive stench emanating from the crematoria of Auschwitz and Birkenau simply overwhelmed the official explanation that the camps' continuous battle with typhus forced the burning of dead bodies.[163] By 1943, Monowitz's inmates were well aware of the destiny prepared for them, in part because some of IG's supervisors at the site not only spoke openly of the gassings, but wielded them as an incentive to work harder.[164] Having heard such talk, Dürrfeld finally asked Commandant Höss directly "whether it is true that the Jews were cremated in the Oswiecim [Auschwitz] camp." Höss's reply that he could not discuss the subject can hardly have been taken as anything but an admission. Indeed, thereafter Höss assumed that Dürrfeld understood "the destination of those selected and transferred for extermination in Oswiecim."[165] When Christian Schneider learned some months later of the gassings, the conduit was probably Dürrfeld, either directly or via Ambros and Bütefisch.[166] The word had by then spread relatively widely within the top ranks of Farben. Friedrich Jaehne gathered enough from a police official while traveling on a train to Auschwitz

witz weekly reports 70–1, 21.IX.42–4.X.42, *NMT*, vol. 8, pp. 160–1; NI-15256, Auschwitz weekly reports 76–7, 2–15.XI.42, ibid., p. 489; NI-7604/62, Affidavit by C. Schneider, 22.IV.47; NI-5168/38, Affidavit by F. Jaehne, 29.V.47. Bütefisch swore he never went to Auschwitz (NI-4182/31, his affidavit, 19.II.47), but Borkin places him there seven times (*Crime and Punishment*, p. 147).

162 Feig, *Death Camps*, p. 342. See also the testimony of H. W. Muench, *NMT*, vol. 8, pp. 312–17, and the maps showing the relations among the three sites in Gilbert, *Auschwitz and the Allies*, p. 193, and Borkin, *Crime and Punishment*, following p. 114 (which is a photostat of NI-7968, Affidavit by M. Faust, 24.VII.47).

163 Testimony of H. Muench, *NMT*, vol. 8, p. 315.

164 NI-11694/96, Affidavit by Frederick Davison.

165 NI-7183/56, Deposition by R. Höss, 29.I.47.

166 See NI-7604/62, Affidavit by C. Schneider, 22.IV.47, which claims he cannot definitely identify his sources, hence retracts an earlier tracing of his knowledge to Dürrfeld, Ambros, and Bütefisch. The retraction seems somewhat too convenient for his fellow defendants.

to ask his son, an engineer in the boiler house of the buna plant, whether gassings were taking place: "He answered that this was the rumor. Henceforth I considered it as an exaggerated rumor, which was quite incredible."[167] Perhaps; but IG's Martin Mueller-Cunradi informed Georg von Schnitzler that Ambros and other IG directors knew of the murders, and Ernst Struss later claimed to have told Ambros and terMeer of them in 1943, after talking with Dürrfeld. Carl Lautenschläger heard of the killings from personnel at faraway Ludwigshafen, Auschwitz's parent plant.[168] Establishing certain knowledge on the part of Schmitz, Farben's chief executive, is impossible. But clearly enough conversation was going on to have reached his ears, and the prevalence of rumors must have strained the Vorstand's capacity for denial to its outer limits.

Could Farben's leaders have done anything meaningful once the machinery of murder started to roll? The very size of the firm worked against the success of clandestine efforts to save Jewish laborers, such as those of Oskar Schindler. A Moravian-German manufacturer of enamelware, Schindler knew how to ingratiate himself with pivotal SS men and thus managed to preserve about one thousand inmate workers from the maw of Auschwitz. But even his remarkable combination of bribery, charm, and daring prevailed by a narrow margin. He was jailed and interrogated twice by suspicious Nazi warders.[169] Other cases suggest the chanciness of businessmen's opposition or any deviation from harshness toward Jewish prisoners. Passive resistance and outright refusals to take part in camp atrocities resulted for SS Dr. Franz Lucas in first his demotion by one rank, then his transfer from Auschwitz to Sachsenhausen, and finally the threat of a court martial, which the end of the war headed off.[170] Eduard Schulte, a managing director of Georg von Giesche's Erben, who passed information to the Allies concerning the gassings and German troop movements, barely escaped arrest by fleeing to Switzerland in 1943 on a tip from an

[167] NI-5168/38, Affidavit by F. Jaehne, 29.V.47.
[168] NI-5197/38, Affidavit by G. von Schnitzler, 27.III.47; NI-9811/81, Affidavit by C. Lautenschläger; Borkin, Crime and Punishment, p. 142, quoting Struss.
[169] See Benjamin B. Ferencz, Less Than Slaves (Cambridge, Mass., 1979), pp. 191–2; and the fictionalized account of Schindler's heroism in Thomas Keneally, Schindler's List (New York, 1983).
[170] Bernd Naumann, Auschwitz (New York, 1966), pp. xvi, xxvi, 20–1, 313, 322–3, 408.

official in the military intelligence organization under Admiral Canaris.[171]

And one must remember that not even the army could slow or halt the killings with rational arguments. When generals protested against deportations of productive Jewish laborers from the ghettos, Himmler brushed aside their objections with the remark that "it is the Führer's wish."[172] Had Farben's leaders stood up against the further use of inmates near Auschwitz, they would doubtless have heard the same reply – and risked their monopoly over rubber as well. In 1944, Himmler gave proof of his long-suspected desire to annex for the SS certain fields of production. Over Speer's objections, he obtained control of the factory at Falkenhagen for N-Stoff, "an inextinguishable burning chemical mass, similar to the legendary Greek fire," as a preliminary to seizing the output of Sarin, the nerve gas manufactured at the same plant.[173] For the executives of a conspicuous corporation, whose employees included many fervent Nazis, the potential penalties for evasion or opposition were always large and real, the potential benefits of either always marginal and remote.

Yet none of Farben's leaders ever provided proof of having *wanted* to act. None spoke even later of having spent sleepless nights trying to find an exit from the dance of death. In part, this reflected a hard reality of the postwar trials in 1947–8. In the atmosphere created by the horrible revelations concerning Auschwitz, the defendants rapidly realized that an admission of knowledge would be treated as an admission of guilt. They concluded that safety lay in pleading absolute ignorance, not extenuating circumstances or force majeure. Hence, most of those quoted above about the gassings promptly withdrew their confessions. Having taken this stance in court, they were locked into it ever after.

There was, however, another reason for the absence of evidence of emotional turmoil. At bottom, Farben's leaders were pragmatists, not revolutionaries, living demonstrations that "the holocaust is a horrify-

171 James M. Markham, "An Unsung 'Good German': Fame Comes at Last," *New York Times* (November 9, 1983), p. 2. See also Richard Breitman and Walter Laqueur, *Breaking the Silence* (New York, 1986).
172 Hugh Trevor-Roper, "The Will to Exterminate," *Times Literary Supplement* (25.I.83), p. 75.
173 Albert Speer, *Infiltration* (New York, 1981), pp. 199–200. Borkin, *Crime and Punishment*, pp. 131–3, errs in confusing N-Stoff with Tabun, which was not manufactured at Falkenhagen.

ing example of the seductability of otherwise normal individuals."[174]
They were "responsible men" of the sort described by Milton Mayer:

Responsible men never shirk responsibility, and so, when they must reject it,
they deny it. They draw the curtain. They detach themselves altogether from
the consideration of the evil they ought to, but cannot contend with.[175]

They thus got in the habit of letting themselves off easily, and any
lingering discomfort they felt merely fortified their sense of innocence
against the ruthlessness of their deeds. Lacking the courage of moral
conviction almost as a condition for professional success, they shut off
their consciences, which was tantamount, in this instance, to having
no consciences at all. One German emigrant later asked, "What good
does it do to claim a conscience if one doesn't use it when it makes the
difference between someone's living or dying? Is a conscience just for
self-flagellation?"[176] Because the conduct of Farben's leaders left them
no answer to these questions, nothing can ever excuse their quies-
cence. Understanding their motives, even conceding the probable
hopelessness of anything they might have done, is not, in the end, the
equivalent of pardoning them.

Throughout 1944, then, the Auschwitz project continued on its
gruesome course, more impeded by continuing labor shortages than
by the Allied air strikes that hit the plants on August 20, September
13, and December 18 and 26.[177] No rubber had flowed by the time
the SS ordered evacuation of the site on January 19, 1945. While some
nine thousand inmates of Monowitz marched west toward Gleiwitz,
where the war had begun, IG's employees began dismantling or destroying the factories. Eight hundred and fifty ill inmates remained

174 Mommsen, G&G, 9 (1983), p. 420.
175 Milton Mayer, They Thought They Were Free (Chicago, 1955), p. 76.
176 Daniel Lang, A Backward Look (New York, 1981), p. 106. My comments are not
   meant to deny that Farben officials frequently acted to protect endangered individuals in Germany, usually the Gentile spouses or children of mixed marriages,
   during the war. In 1947–8, many people came forward to attest to such shielding.
   See, for example Ilgner I/28–9, Affidavits by H. Fuhrmann and O. Jaques; Kühne
   I/31, Affidavit by K. Florey, 17.III.48; I/32, Affidavit by I. Gusdorf, 9.IV.48; and
   I/34, Affidavit by R. Berliner, 20.II.48; Krauch VI/59, Affidavit by A. Ernst, and
   VI/105, Affidavit by A. Suhr, 24.XII.47; and Schnitzler IX/169, Affidavit by B.
   Reifenberg, 8.III.48.
177 For examples of transfers of laborers from Auschwitz to other plants, see
   NI-13512, File note by Ritter and Dürrfeld, 3.II.44, NMT, vol. 8, pp. 558–9, and
   NI-7572/62, Ritter to Speer, 12.V.44. On the air raids, see Gilbert, Auschwitz and
   the Allies, pp. 307, 310, 315–17, 322, 331–3, 335.

behind to receive the Russians.[178] Two hundred died in the week
before the arrival of the Red Army, but the survivors escaped at least
the final horror visited on the sick at Fürstengrube, who were burned
in their huts.[179] Having descended to the very depths of complicity
with Nazism, IG Farben came away from Auschwitz still showing a
net loss on its books for the development of buna.[180]

Farben's role at Auschwitz cannot have been irrelevant to the steady
deterioration of Hermann Schmitz's health. According to his personal
physician, as the war progressed the chairman of IG's managing board
became a nervous wreck, and his habitual secretiveness began to
border on the abnormal.[181] Certainly he suffered under the mounting
uncontrollability of the combine's willful Sparten and overlapping
committees, which competed with one another not only for authority,
but even, in at least one instance, for the same parcels of land.[182] Like
the combine's technical leaders, he resented and thought foolish the
regime's steady demands to shift production east and, later, underground.[183] Moreover, by late 1943 or early 1944, he knew the war
could not be won. To be sure, since the various postwar planning
groups in which Schmitz or Ilgner participated during the final two
years of the fighting were all organized under the auspices of the
Economics Ministry and supervised by SS General Otto Ohlendorf,
their reports proceeded from the apparent assumption of a negotiated
peace with a surviving Third Reich. There was thus much written of a
postwar "foreign trade offensive" and of a "European economic community" in which Germany would act merely as the "flag-bearer" and
predominate by "elastic political methods . . . not with brutal
power." But the real agenda of these planning bodies soon turned into
a highly circumspect effort to gather information about likely Allied
policies later on and to work out some of the technical economic
problems of the transition to peace, with or without the survival of a

---

178 NI-11956/98, Report by Dürrfeld, 7.II.45; Czech in Smolen (ed.), *From the Histo-ry*, pp. 46–7.
179 Sehn, *Auschwitz-Birkenau*, p. 153.
180 Plumpe, *G&G*, 9 (1983), p. 595.
181 Schmitz V/173, Affidavit by Dr. Singer.
182 See Winnacker, *Nie den Mut verlieren*, pp. 120–1; Bayer 13/25, Exchange of
correspondence between Haefliger and Kühne, 14.I.41–24.I.41, and Kühne to
Bütefisch, Haefliger, and Ilgner, 21.I.43.
183 See Winnacker, *Nie den Mut verlieren*, pp. 117–18; BA Koblenz, R25/6, Wehr-
wirtschaftliche Bauvorhaben und Produktionsprogramme bei einzelnen Grossunternehmen . . . , 25.II.43 (also NI-8828).

Nazi regime.[184] As the Reich crumbled these groups probably continued to function because no one dared betray defeatism by suspending them. For Schmitz, the realities were clearly summarized in various
Vowi reports, such as the two of late May 1944 that discussed the
imminent invasion of Europe and the enormous growth of American
military production "despite the maintaining of civilian supplies to an
extent unknown in the other warring nations."[185]

Schmitz's response to these realities and to the firm's own disorganization was typical of the man — cautious, complicated, and ultimately unexecuted. To insulate investors from the fate of the German
currency and to preserve IG's civilian-oriented operations from the
taint of its military ones, Schmitz got the *Vorstand* to authorize a
convertible debenture issue of up to 500 million marks. He probably
envisioned carrying out a division of the concern and the apparent
divestiture of certain plants on the model of what was done with
WASAG's holdings during 1944.[186] But fear nullified the plan — the
same fear that, above all his difficulties, accounted for his declining
emotional state throughout 1944–5.

More and more, Schmitz was gripped by a terror of impending
persecution at the hands of either the Nazis or the Allies, whichever
came first. That the coalition fighting Hitler intended to exact retribution for association with the crimes of the Third Reich was a staple of

184 The remarks cited are quoted in Joachim Piskol, "Zur Entwicklung der aussenpolitischen Nachkriegskonzeption der deutschen Monopolbourgeoisie 1943–
1945," *JfW*, 10 (1969), pp. 331, 333, 341. On the postwar planning process, see
the rest of Piskol's essay, as well as Wolfgang Schumann's three articles:
"Nachkriegsplanungen der Reichsgruppe Industrie im Herbst 1944," *JfW*, 13
(1972), pp. 259–96; "Politische Aspekte der Nachkriegsplanungen des faschistischen deutschen Imperialismus in der Endphase des Zweiten Weltkrieges,"
ZfG, 27 (1979), pp. 395–408; and "Die wirtschaftspolitische Ueberlebensstrategie
des deutschen Imperialismus . . . ," *ZfG*, 27 (1979), pp. 499–513. Certainly the
best treatment of the subject to date is Herbst, *Totale Krieg*, pp. 341–452, which
depicts the planning process as a battleground between the SS's "socialistic" version of Germany's future economic organization and the efforts of big business
both to counter this in case the Nazi regime survived and to lay the groundwork for
capitalist reconstruction in the event of defeat.
185 BASF, T51/2, Vowi 5014, Die wirtschaftliche Entwicklung der Vereinigten Staaten
von Amerika seit 1943, 30.V.44, from which the quotation is taken; and Vowi
g144, Vierteljahres-Bericht zur Entwicklung der Wirtschaft in der Welt, 25.V.44.
186 See Schmitz V/72, Affidavit by H. J. Abs; NI-5191/16, Affidavit by G. Schnitzler,
4.III.47; Duisberg, *Nur ein Sohn*, pp. 196–7; NI-8258/68, Minutes of the 43rd
Vorstand meeting, 2.III.44; and Forschungsstelle zur NS-Politik (ed.), *O.M.G.U.S.
Ermittlungen gegen die Deutsche Bank* (Nördlingen, 1985), pp. 116–19. On
WASAG's split, see Fischer, *WASAG*, pp. 154–63.

Western broadcasts, and Farben's vulnerability weighed heavily on the board chairman. He may have known that the combine risked exposure for even more than involvement with Nazi labor policies and the manufacture of Zyklon B. Since 1942, IG's pharmaceutical and sera divisions had been supplying antityphus drugs and sleeping pills for testing by SS doctors on several hundred inmates of Buchenwald and Auschwitz.[187] Other prisoners had been made guinea pigs for nerve gas experiments designed by Farben employees.[188] Without question, Schmitz had grounds to fear the Western powers, let alone the anticapitalist and justly vengeful Russians.[189]

His apprehension of the Nazis was no less real or justified. Forty years later, Schmitz's son could still recall how his father used to place a blanket or tea warmer over the family telephone for fear of eavesdropping by the Gestapo.[190] He knew of Hitler's periodic threats to make an example of one or two alleged industrial saboteurs atop the internationally minded enterprise.[191] No doubt the faithful in the Foreign Organization, which continued to criticize IG's personnel overseas, encouraged such fits of pique on the part of their führer.[192] So did the *Gauleiter* and their man in the Chancellery, Martin Bormann. Krauch became the recipient of renewed demands by Gauleiter Sprenger of Frankfurt for the removal of Schmitz, Schnitzler, and terMeer from IG's management, as well as of Bormann's assertions that the concern was "unreliable" and the object of "a number of complaints . . . from the Gauleaderships."[193] And after Schmitz and

---

[187] Eugen Kogon, *The Theory and Practice of Hell* (New York, 1975), pp. 143–9; Alexander Mitscherlich and Fred Mielke, *Doctors of Infamy* (New York, 1949), pp. 42–9; DuBois, *Devil's Chemists*, pp. 123–32; Hilberg, *Destruction*, p. 602; Smolen (ed.), *From the History*, p. 17; Feig, *Death Camps*, p. 354 (though the extent of experimentation is here overestimated); NI-12070/99, Affidavit by S. Budziaszek, 27.X.47.

[188] Feig, *Death Camps*, p. 348; Borkin, *Crime and Punishment*, p. 132.

[189] Since Schmitz was generally kept well informed about Allied postwar planning, he probably also knew of the conviction abroad that "the industries engaged in the production of synthetic raw materials have to be stamped out"; see Paul Einzig, "A Plan for Germany's Economic Disarmament," *Economic Journal*, 53 (1942), p. 180.

[190] Interview with Harald Schmitz, 27.XI.82.

[191] Schmitz VI/107, Affidavit by H. Hoffmann, 11.III.48.

[192] See Schnitzler II/4, Exchange of letters between G. Christian and Waibel, 10–13.VIII.43. On the background to Waibel's appointment as point man in fending off the AO, see Ilgner's testimony, *NMT*, vol. 7, pp. 729–30.

[193] NI-5184/18, Affidavit by F. terMeer, 29.IV.47, p. 20; Krauch I/27, Affidavit by W. Schieber, 13.XI.47.

Krauch persuaded Himmler to release IG's Arthur von Weinberg from Theresienstadt, it was a *Gauleiter* who held up the order for nearly nine months during 1942–3, long enough to kill the eighty-two-year-old man.[194] In the summer of 1942, Reichsstatthalter Eigruber of the Upper Danube region allegedly ventilated his hostility toward the concern to two Farben officials in no uncertain terms:

> I do not want the I.G. in my *Gau*. I have just been to see the Führer. He is terribly furious about the I.G. because it is a state within a state. He has firmly decided to smash that whole racket completely after the war. He would love to do it right now, but that is not possible at the moment. But, after the war, they will not be spared anymore; there will be a thorough cleaning up.[195]

Sensitive to the Party's suspicions, Krauch's office circulated a memo to Farben's directors in June 1944 advising them how to respond to charges that IG's international connections had led it to betray important production processes to foreigners.[196] Shortly after the failed attempt on Hitler's life in July set off a fearsome wave of reprisals, the *Gauleiter,* now encouraged by Goebbels and Bormann, returned to the offensive, "muttering threats about 'another July 20 in industry.'"[197]

Even had Schmitz been cool enough to dismiss this sort of talk as familiar and empty, there remained the economic challenge posed by the SS, as well as Hans Kehrl's penchant for establishing rivals to the concern. In August 1942, the Vowi section reported that "a new chemicals combination seems to be underway" in the form of the Schlesische Chemie AG, recently founded at Kehrl's instigation. The new firm, whose emergence had been "pretty confidentially handled," constituted a 50/50 partnership between the Economics Ministry and three private firms to manufacture various chemical products, including clay, sulfuric acid, synthetic fibers, and the related raw materials. In the Vowi's judgment, it was "certain that the enterprise cannot get

194 NI-13678/111, Krauch to SS Obergruppenführer Wolff, 7.VI.42; Schmitz IV/53, Affidavit by Rudolf Graf von Spreti, Weinberg's son-in-law.
195 Schmitz VI/104, Affidavit by W. Steinle, 5.II.48, corroborated by VI/105, Affidavit by M. Naumann, 5.III.48, and VI/106, Affidavit by H. Violet, 21.I.48.
196 See NI-10551/87, File note, 6.VI.44; and Birkenfeld, *Treibstoff,* p. 186, note 20. For indications that IG already was readying its defenses, see Borkin, *Crime and Punishment,* p. 131.
197 Homze, *Foreign Labor,* pp. 227–8.

along without large subsidies" from the government; hence, IG "should follow developments very carefully."[198]

That Schmitz could not simply shake off these verbal and implicit threats was related to another circumstance, one that also had much to do with the concern's inability to complete the plant at Auschwitz. Carl Krauch may not have been Farben's servant in high office, but he and his staff at least provided access to influence. From 1942 on, they steadily lost power.

Albert Speer administered his first defeat of the general plenipotentiary for chemical production (Gebechem) almost immediately after replacing Todt in February of that year. The new minister rejected Krauch's pleas for higher priority in the allocation of essential materials and made clear that the chemical sector would have to live within its existing quotas of fuel, iron, and labor.[199] When Krauch protested that this rendered efforts to increase production nugatory, Hans Kehrl, who was now entrenched in the Economics Ministry and the new Central Planning Committee, began suggesting a reassignment of some of the Gebechem's responsibilities to more "appropriate" agencies.[200] By early 1943, his principal means of embarrassing and pressuring Krauch had become the issue of shifting production eastward, which burdened the Gebechem with reconstruction needs despite an already inadequate supply of material for new building.[201] Krauch coped by suspending numerous projects, concentrating resources on the most pressing installations, and pillaging plants in occupied western Europe for machines and iron transferable to the East.[202] But he could not perform magic. Though some spheres of production under his purview suffered more than others – light metals, for instance, had shortfalls of 30% of needed iron and 70% for fuel during 1942 – all lagged.[203] As of October 1944, not a single sector of the chemical

---

[198] Hoechst TEA 253, Vowi to Struss, 14.VIII.42, enclosing a short summary, dated 13.VIII.42, of the new corporation's evolution.

[199] See BA Koblenz, R25/92, Krauch to Körner, 27.IV.42; R25/151, Neukirch's in-house history, pp. 319–20.

[200] BA Koblenz, R25/90, Notiz. Betrifft: Weiterführung des chemischen Erzeugungsplans, 29.X.42.

[201] BA Koblenz, R25/98, Vermerk. Besprechungen mit den Herren Wurster und Ambros, 19. and 23.III.43, and Zusammenfassung des Ergebnisses der Besprechung . . . am 25.II.43.

[202] BA Koblenz, R25/39, Eckell to Krauch, 8.II.43; R25/9, Krauch's circular letters of 2.IV.43 and 5.IV.43.

[203] BA Koblenz, R25/151, Neukirch's in-house history, pp. 332, 337, 350–1.

production program had reached its targeted output, and the failures were not attributable solely to air raids.[204]

Nor did Krauch's expedients suffice to shake off Kehrl's challenge. That required an armistice in the form of an exchange of letters during March 1943 that demarcated the respective spheres of authority of the two men. The new arrangements left Krauch responsible for all research, development, and construction related to the output and processing of industrial raw materials. But he lost any control over actual production at the chemical plants, some of which now fell under Kehrl's command, others under the direction of Speer's ministry or the Wehrmacht.[205] About half of Farben's plants were henceforth subordinate to an authority other than Carl Krauch.[206] Although this meant in practice greater autonomy for IG in some cases, such as the light-metals and sulfuric acid fields, the new system also had its dangers.[207] Kehrl lost no time in getting Dr. Kolb from the Degussa Corporation's *Vorstand* named, first, head of the department for the complete direction of chemistry within the Economics Ministry and, a few months later, chief of the chemical sector within Speer's ministry.[208] In turn, Kolb moved quickly to explore Degussa's willingness to undertake buna production and thus to break Farben's monopoly. Though rebuffed, Kolb's suggestion underlined the perils to IG of Kehrl's rising power.[209]

By 1944, Carl Krauch was a beleaguered man. Pinned down by the bureaucratic guerrilla warfare of Berlin, spied on by Dr. Fritz Baur, Himmler's agent in Krauch's Reich Office for Economic Development, aware that the SS leader ascribed to him an "inactive if not negative attitude to the policy of the Third Reich," Krauch now lost the small remaining protection afforded by Hermann Göring's patronage.[210] At a meeting with Hitler on May 20, 1944, the Luftwaffe chiefs tried to

---

[204] See BA Koblenz, R25/73, Stand des chemischen Erzeugungsplanes vom 1.X.44. One can trace the progress of Krauch's plans from 1939 to September 1944 in R25/101–10.

[205] NI-820, Kehrl to Krauch, 30.III.43, *NMT*, vol. 7, pp. 971–7. The original is in Bayer 64/3.

[206] NI-6506/49, Verm. W. to Hoechst, 8.VI.43.

[207] On the advantages to Farben, NI-5196/38, Affidavit by G. von Schnitzler, 18.III.47.

[208] RG242/T83, Reel 82, Degussa *Vorstand* minutes, 5.IV.43 and 4.X.43.

[209] Ibid., 7.VI.43.

[210] See Krauch I/82, Affidavit by G. Ritter, 10.XII.47; I/27, Affidavit by W. Schieber, 13.XI.47.

divert attention from the deficiencies of air defense over the Reich's fuel plants by blaming Krauch for designing them without adequate camouflage, earthworks, and protection against shrapnel. Reminding his accusers that most of these factories were conceived in peacetime, Krauch insisted that he had been right to construct them solely with an eye to economic competitiveness and hence low building costs. Hitler let the matter drop, but Krauch prudently detailed several subordinates to compile a white book on his efforts during the war to improve the works' defenses.[211] Defenses – his own and his plants' – took up virtually all of Krauch's energies from 1943 to 1945. Probably only Speer's respect for his efficiency kept the man in office until the bitter end.[212]

All in all, Farben's influence within other organs of economic administration remained roughly constant during the war. Bütefisch held his post as head of the Economic Group for the Oil Industry throughout the conflict, as did Otto and Müller as chiefs of the trade sections for photographic products and munitions within the Economic Group for Chemicals; and Gajewski's retirement as leader of the Product Group for Fibers was offset by Kugler's appointment to direct the group for dyes.[213] The major personnel changes that surrounded the reorganization of the Economic Group for Chemicals in 1942–3 proved similarly inconclusive. Johannes Hess, the manager of an IG affiliate in Munich, stepped down as leader of the group in favor of Hermann Schlosser of Degussa, but Fritz terMeer became the vice-president of a new six-man directing committee.[214] Only the continuing rise of Claus Ungewitter within the chemical organization marred the satisfactoriness of these arrangements. This dedicated convert to Nazism, who died in Russian captivity in 1946, spent the final year of the war denouncing to the SS the defeatism and selfishness of the nation's industrialists.[215]

211 Birkenfeld, *Treibstoff*, pp. 186–7; cf. Borkin, *Crime and Punishment*, pp. 128–9.
212 Carroll, *Design*, p. 243.
213 NI-6713/51, Affidavit by Ilgner, 2.IV.47; *Gliederung der RGI 1941*, pp. 151–6; BA Koblenz, ZSg 127, Bd. 825, *Neue Mannheimer Zeitung*, 16.I.42 (on Gajewski); Hoechst TEA 1197, Fachgruppe Farben und Teerfarbenzwischenprodukte. See Radandt, *JfW*, 8 (1967), p. 114, on several lesser appointments.
214 NI-5188/38, Affidavit by F. terMeer, 14.IV.47; Greiling, *75 Jahre Chemieverband*, pp. 72–4.
215 See BA Koblenz, ZSg 126, "In Memoriam Claus Ungewitter," *Die chemische Industrie*, no. 4 (April 1958); Bachhaus to Brandt, 26.VIII.44, in D. Eicholtz and W. Schumann (eds.), *Anatomie des Krieges* (East Berlin, 1969), p. 459.

Within IG Farben, there was little evidence of such defeatism or of efforts to ride out the gathering catastrophe. Otto Ambros did discourage Hitler from employing nerve gas in 1943–4, but his argument that the Allies could retaliate in greater strength may have been as sincere as it was untrue.[216] Though Wilhelm R. Mann claimed after the war to have begun warehousing pharmaceutical goods during 1943 in order to finance the concern's postwar revival, he was probably merely complying with the Brandt Reserve Plan of 1943–4, by which the regime directed all drug firms to stockpile an extra inventory equal to demand for two, later six, months.[217] In the final days of the war, Mann refused to be dissuaded from repeatedly complying with Hitler's orders to evacuate production toward the German interior.[218] Ilgner's proposals to transfer IG's patent rights to a holding company in neutral Sweden were rejected by the Commercial Committee, whose only appreciable response to the impending collapse was to order subsidiaries in the rest of Europe to sell off goods on hand.[219] Otherwise, only minor traces of corporate preparations for the transition to peace have ever been discovered.[220]

IG's passivity is not particularly surprising, given not only the pervasive Nazi terrorizing during 1944, but also the uneven effects of the war on Farben's plants. Leverkusen, Elberfeld, Marburg, and Hoechst, to name only the principal examples, suffered very little damage in the course of the fighting, hence saw little need to draft designs for reviving production.[221] At the benzin factories, the frequency and severity of the air raids had the opposite effect, leaving no time for speculation about the future.[222] This was especially true at Ludwigshafen, where sixty-

---

216 See Borkin, *Crime and Punishment*, pp. 131–3.
217 Interview with Mann, 13.VII.78. His claim is echoed by Duisberg, *Nur ein Sohn*, pp. 211–12. On the reserve plan, see Cortez F. Enloe, Jr., "The War and the German Drug Industry," *Chemical and Engineering News*, 24 (1946), p. 3048.
218 Duisberg, *Nur ein Sohn*, p. 218.
219 NI-1323/14, Affidavit by Küpper, 26.VI.45.
220 For one example, dating from March 1945, see Raymond G. Stokes, *Recovery and Resurgence in the West German Chemical Industry: Allied Policy and the I.G. Farben Successor Firms, 1945–1951* (Dissertation, Ohio State University, Columbus, 1987), chap. 1.
221 Duisberg, *Nur ein Sohn*, pp. 217–18; BA Koblenz, R25/113, unsigned letter on rubber production to Kolb, 6.VI.44; Bayer 4C9.29, Control Office, *Bayer*, pp. 38–9.
222 See BA Koblenz, R25/36, Die Produktionsentwicklung . . . , 1.V.45. The oil factories absorbed in 1945 slightly more than 10% of the total tonnage of bombs dropped by the American and British air forces during the war; see Zilbert, *Albert Speer and the Nazi Ministry of Arms*, p. 29.

five attacks on the plants by April 1945 had inflicted 400 million marks worth of damage and left unscathed only 6% of the 1,470 buildings on the factory grounds.[223] Overall, however, Farben emerged remarkably intact. Inspectors told a U.S. Senate committee in 1946 that the combine's "installations could be brought back to 90% capacity within three months if the necessary input of raw materials was released."[224] This estimate, of course, applied only to the plants in the western zones of occupation, where most of the managers had remained at their posts. In the Russian zone, most fled in the general panic, and reconstruction was likely to prove move difficult. As the Reich caved in, the pressing concern before Farben's leaders was the survival not of their firm but of their persons.

[223] BASF, *Im Reiche der Chemie* (Düsseldorf, 1965), pp. 110–11.
[224] Subcommittee of Committee on Military Affairs, Hearings, 1946, p. 621, quoted in Lloyd C. Gardner, *Architects of Illusion* (Chicago, 1970), p. 237.

Epilogue

The fate of IG Farben after 1945 mirrored that of Germany. Both were partitioned, "denazified" according to the lights of the respective occupiers, then collectivized in the East and decentralized in the West. By the early 1950s, some 300 million marks worth of the concern's assests in eastern Germany and Europe had become the property of People's Own Factories and approximately 90% of what remained in West Germany had devolved upon three independent successor firms: BASF, Bayer, and Hoechst.[1] Few of the combine's managers remained for the Russians to deal with, since most had retreated from the Soviet zone west of the Elbe with Eisenhower's troops in July 1945, at the latest. But the nineteen surviving members of the *Vorstand*, along with the head of the *Aufsichtsrat* and three more junior corporate officers, went on trial before an American tribunal at Nürnberg during 1947– 8, charged with five counts of crimes against peace, membership in criminal organizations (e.g., the SS), plunder and spoliation in occupied Europe, and the use of slave labor. After a nine-month trial, the court convicted eight defendants on spoliation in Poland, Norway, and France, four on slave labor at Auschwitz and Fürstengrube, and one on both charges and acquitted the remaining ten businessmen. The prison sentences ranged from one and a half to eight years, with time in confinement before and during the proceedings counted as time served.[2] By 1951, when the last incarcerated executive was freed, the combine's erstwhile leaders were returning to prominence and

---

[1] "Ungeheure Geschäfte," *Der Spiegel*, 20 (7.II.66), p. 52; Hans-Dieter Kreikamp, "Die Entflechtung der I. G. Farbenindustrie A.G. und die Gründung der Nachfolgegesellschaften," *VfZ*, 25 (1977), pp. 220–51.
[2] The charges are detailed in *NMT*, vol. 7, p. 2, the verdicts in vol. 8, pp. 1206–9. Those convicted and the duration of their sentences were as follows: on spoliation, Bürgin (2), Haefliger (2), Ilgner (3), Jaehne (1.5), Oster (2), Kugler (1.5), Schmitz (4), and Schnitzler (5); on slave labor, Ambros (8), Bütefisch (6), Dürrfeld (8), and Krauch (6); on both charges, terMeer (7). Acquitted completely were Gajewski, Gattineau, von der Heyde, Hoerlein, Knieriem, Kühne, Lautenschläger, Mann, Schneider, and Wurster.

prosperity as advisers or officers in numerous German corporations, though not, with three exceptions, to managerial roles in any of Farben's corporate descendants.[3] Of the once mighty concern, only the small staff of the IG Farben Corporation in Dissolution remained, its tasks reduced to managing the firm's pension funds, keeping alive its claims to lost properties in the East, and arranging, somewhat grudgingly, restitution in the amount of nearly 28 million deutschmarks to 5,855 Jewish survivors of work on the Auschwitz plant.[4]

These outcomes departed considerably from the Allies' intentions when they brought Hitler down. All but the French had believed that a somewhat curtailed Germany should remain united but that its economy required remodeling if a third German war in the twentieth century was to be avoided, and all had set out to smash IG Farben. Indeed, the Allied Control Council Act of November 1945, which sequestered IG's property and ordered its dissolution, may be taken as a high point of Four Power cooperation in Germany. Why their plans unraveled is a much told, still controversial tale that reaches beyond the scope of this book. Suffice it to say that in 1946–7, economic and security interests tugged the Soviets toward nationalization of wealth in their zone and the British and Americans toward using theirs as "the spark plug" for a general recovery in western Europe. Haltingly but inexorably, a "race for Germany's favors" began, and the nation's chemical industry and its leaders proved among its beneficiaries.

Precisely because the resolution of Farben's and its leaders' futures owed so much to political expediency, the question of the fairness of the settlements has remained a burning one. To the concern's loyalists, the trial and dissolution were instances of victors' justice, unfair applications of ex post facto laws to people who had functioned under duress and by powers whose own wartime and postwar deeds com-

---

[3] See Joseph Borkin, *The Crime and Punishment of IG Farben* (New York, 1978), p. 162; Willi Kling, *Kleine Geschichte der IG-Farben – Der Grossfabrikanten des Todes* (East Berlin, 1957), pp. 208–13; Berthold Puchert, "Aus der Praxis der IG-Farben in Auschwitz-Monowitz," *JfW*, 4 (1963), p. 211; Josiah DuBois, *The Devil's Chemists* (Boston, 1952), pp. 358–9; and Heinrich Gattineau, *Durch die Klippen des 20. Jahrhunderts* (Stuttgart, 1983), pp. 218–19. The exceptions were Wurster, who became chairman of the BASF *Vorstand;* Gajewski, who took a seat on the managing board of DAG, Troisdorf; and Gattineau, who did likewise for Wasag-Chemie.

[4] See Benjamin B. Ferencz, *Less Than Slaves* (Cambridge, Mass., 1979), pp. 35–7, 42–52, 66, 210–11. The payments were not handsome, since the largest award of compensation came to only $1,250, but the total restitution, Ferencz's figures show, came to more than half the funds ever disbursed by German industry to the victims of the Third Reich's labor policies.

promised their right to sit in judgment.[5] To the victims of Nazism and
critics of big business, the punishments meted out to the firm and its
managers were mockingly light, proof that capital is thicker than
blood or water.[6] How, in light of this book, ought we to assess the role
of IG Farben in the Third Reich, the actions of its chief executives,
and, by implication, the decisions of those who judged them?

It should by now be clear that the leaders of IG Farben became in
the Third Reich both indispensable and inconsequential. Their desire
to be the former made them the latter. It placed them at the service of a
regime that always regarded them as it did everything and everyone
else, including the state and the populace: as mere means to an end. At
its inception, the strategy of indispensability was an instrument of
survival, a way of keeping the product cycles that propelled the firm
turning. As such, it succeeded until 1945. By other measures, it failed
earlier. In no sphere of policy outside their narrow technical expertise
could Farben's leaders make their interests prevail – not in preventing
Hitler's accession, not in evading Aryanization, not in opposition to
autarky, not in controlling the Four Year Plan, not in avoiding the
war, not in designing the New Order, not against the desires of German allies or client states in Europe, not with regard to labor policy,
not even in the matter of setting the maximum desirable output of
buna. Yet in each of these instances, IG's chiefs learned to live, usually
profitably, with the consequences of their failures. In doing so, they
contributed not only to the power of the Third Reich, but also to its
criminality. They became not so much guilty of the Nazi horrors, since
they lacked Hitler's intent, as co-responsible for them. Why did they
continue to conduct themselves so?

One common answer stresses tendencies inherent in the capitalist
system, and it is partially correct. In a sense, Nazi economic policy
rested on the recognition that so long as a state displays its determination but permits businessmen to make money, they will let themselves
be manipulated as to how. The Nazis knew that commercial interests
are not immutable objects, but definitions capable of restatement according to context. As Hitler once remarked, "Experts can always

[5] See August von Knieriem, *The Nuremberg Trials* (Chicago, 1959); Bayer 4C9.25,
Müller/Knieriem manuscript, pp. 172–200; and Louis Lochner, *Tycoons and Tyrant*
(Chicago, 1954), pp. 248–9.
[6] There are a host of East German publications in this vein. See also Ferencz, *Less Than
Slaves*, p. 35; DuBois, *Devil's Chemists*, p. 355.

think differently than they did at first."[7] To induce them to do so, he monopolized the instruments of power in the state, subordinated the protections of law to the demands of ideology, built an arbitrary and confusing political edifice in which influence mattered far more than office, and extended his sway to most of Europe. Moreover, as this book has demonstrated at length, his regime proved far cleverer than has commonly been supposed at rigging the economy to make private interests serve Nazism's purposes. Farben's leaders chose to behave in this situation like businessmen, not revolutionaries. This is not to say that the Gestapo operated as the regime's trump card with them. To be sure, the prospect of arrest seemed menacing enough on occasion, and the führer himself knew the importance of terror, boasting once that it had largely staved off inflation in the 1930s. "The primary cause of the stabilization of our currency," he claimed to have told Schacht, "is the concentration camp."[8] But national loyalty generally proved a sufficient incentive to cooperate – and not only for corporate executives. The Ruhr coal miners produced prodigiously under severe circumstances during the war, largely out of patriotism.[9]

Above all, Farben's managers became prisoners of the process they prized most: competition. This accounted primarily for the fear that often animated them. Fear may seem an unlikely motive for barons of such a firm. Citizens of liberal societies habitually assume that size and wealth confer power, forgetting David Schoenbaum's insight that "in the wonderland of Hitler Germany . . . there were no longer reliable indications of what was up and what was down."[10] And size and wealth attract attention and animosity. The genius of the Nazi regime, as well as one source of its eventual defeat, lay in its creation of a "road race of organizations" (*Wettrennen der Ressorts*) backed by "the threat in cases of recalcitrance to entrust doing the dirty work to another."[11] Kontinental Oel, the Hermann Göring Werke, Hansa Leichtmetall, Kehrl's fibers companies, the rise of Wintershall, and the

---

[7] Quoted in Avraham Barkai, "Sozialdarwinismus und Antiliberalismus in Hitlers Wirtschaftskonzept," *G&G*, 3 (1977), p. 408.

[8] Quoted in Willi A. Boelcke, *Die deutsche Wirtschaft 1930–1945* (Düsseldorf, 1983), p. 132.

[9] See John Gillingham, "Ruhr Coal Miners and Hitler's War," *Journal of Social History*, 15 (1981), pp. 637–53.

[10] David Schoenbaum, *Hitler's Social Revolution* (New York, 1966), p. 281.

[11] Hans Mommsen, "Zur Verschränkung traditioneller und faschistischer Führungsgruppen in Deutschland beim Übergang von der Bewegungs- zur Systemphase," in W. Schieder (ed.), *Faschismus als soziale Bewegung* (Hamburg, 1976), p. 176.

offer of buna plants to Degussa illustrated the possibilities. Though the desire to preserve the concern's international connections functioned as a countervailing fear before 1939, this restraint fell away with the outbreak of the war. Thereafter, the business struggle acted out a terrible logic, in which IG Farben was caught up. The firm's conduct reminds us that, when political changes condition profit making in ways that tend to have immoral results, a capitalist system will prove strikingly malleable.

And yet the dynamics of capitalism do not entirely explain the Farben case. They did not, after all, set the agenda for the Third Reich. And referring to them comes perilously close to restating the "naive belief," which Hannah Arendt denounced, "that temptation and coercion are really the same thing, that no one can be asked to resist temptation."[12] People can be more than asked; they can be expected to do so. Behind obedience to the impersonal imperatives of competition or technology, as even that foremost pleader of the latter excuse, Albert Speer, admitted before his death, lies an "ethical hardening."[13] It permits decision makers and those who would succeed them in all socioeconomic systems to reason only within the demands of efficiency. Its presence explains why the question of whether Farben's leaders were or were not Nazis gradually became superfluous. To serve the Party's ends, they did not have to be members or believers in its doctrines. What Michael Geyer has written of the German military holds for its civilian counterparts: "One just needed to be an ordinary, ambitious young officer . . . with no particular philosophy at all. Indeed, one had to be a very committed and dedicated anti-National Socialist with very strong convictions in order *not* to fit into that movement."[14] One merely had to want success and to dismiss any other measure of one's actions. Richard Merton, the member of IG's supervisory board driven out of Germany in 1938 because of his Jewish descent, made this point after the war in an unusual letter to Lily von Schnitzler:

That I in the years after 1933 did not, like so many others, slide into the sins of National Socialism was . . . not a special accomplishment on my part; I owe it to the fact that I was protected by my four Jewish grandparents from damag-

---

[12] Hannah Arendt, *Eichmann in Jerusalem* (New York, 1965), p. 295.
[13] Albert Speer, *Infiltration* (New York, 1981), p. 8.
[14] Michael Geyer, "Etudes in Political History," in Peter Stachura (ed.), *The Nazi Machtergreifung* (Winchester, Mass., 1983), p. 111.

ing my soul. I was *forced,* as I said already then many times, to make a virtue of necessity. Others, like you . . . had the option to cooperate, to make compromises, to build bridges. The great majority did that under the compulsion of maintaining their positions. . . . To be sure, toward all of those who were not in this situation but still wanted to take part, I always felt a certain skepticism, but also understanding. One *wants,* indeed, to take part. The drive for prestige is a very powerful impulse in all people of all social classes.[15]

That drive had much to do with the unwillingness of Farben's leaders ever to draw the line, to say, as a later generation sometimes did, *ohne mich* – "Count me out." We may, like Merton, understand this attitude, but we ought not to forget that its basis is egotism and, sometimes, sheer indifference.

Ambition, achievement, and the avoidance of punishment were guiding elements in the behavior of the men who ran IG Farben, but so was professionalism. It insulated them from their actions; more than that, it transmogrified in their eyes the ethics of their deeds. Faced with political and economic conditions they had little role in creating, Farben's leaders acted as they thought their calling required. They disagreed cautiously with the trend of events from time to time but sooner or later sought to benefit from it. Their sense of professional duty encouraged them to regard every issue principally in terms of their special competences and responsibilities, in this case to their fields and stockholders. In obeying this mandate, they relieved themselves of the obligation to make moral or social judgments or to examine the overall consequences of their decisions. Of course, people could do only so much. Of course, a principled refusal to cooperate, which was the one political action within reach of all, might have resulted in fruitless oblivion. Of course, such a stance required weighing dangers to family and friends. But the professional spirit, with its glorification of partial, even tunnel vision, helped Farben's leaders to evade these difficulties. That spirit operates in all highly organized societies and among all managers, whether corporate, bureaucratic, or political, and irrespective of the prevailing relationships to the means of production. That function is one reason why professionalization has triumphed in the modern world – it excuses opportunism while enjoining adherence to standards. It has thus contributed significantly to "the nature of modern sin, the withdrawal of moral concerns from public roles in our lives."[16]

---

[15] Metallgesellschaft, Privatbriefe R. Merton, Merton to Lily von Schnitzler, 18.II.55.
[16] Rainer C. Baum, *The Holocaust and the German Elite* (Totowa, N.J., 1981), p. 266.

To depict the actions of Farben's managers as products of these processes is not to relieve them of responsibility. It is, instead, to connect their world with ours. Any society or part of one that ceases to grapple with the old preoccupation of history and philosophy, the problem of power and its proper use, and succumbs to an amoral, fatalistic historicism, as did the leaders of the firm here described, will surely end as they did – momentarily prosperous and ultimately discredited.

Appendixes

Appendix A. Manufacturing plants and mines of IG Farben, 1929.
(*Source:* Bayer, Appendix to IG Farben *Geschäftsbericht 1929*)

386

Products manufactured:

dyes	insecticides	nitrogen
organic & inorganic chemicals	photographic materials	benzin
solvents & varnishes	fibers	oxygen
light-metals	celluloid & cellophane	other
pharmaceuticals	plastics & explosives	

The subdivisions of the circles are not scaled to relative volumes of output.

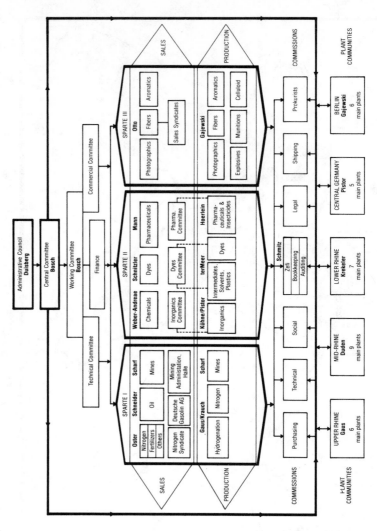

Appendix B. Organization of IG Farben, 1931. (*Source:* Bayer 13/2)

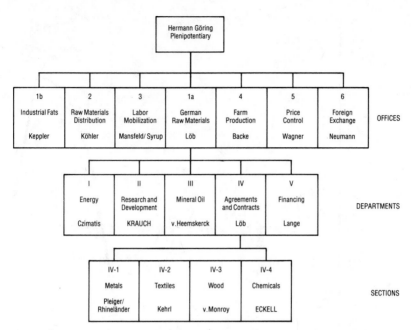

Appendix C. Initial structure of the Four Year Plan, 1936. (*Source:* NI-4706)

389

450
million
RM

Investments in
18 strategic materials

400

300

Investments in
all other products

200

100

1932 1933 1934 1935 1936 1937 1938 1939 1940 1941 1942 1943 1944

Appendix D. Militarization of IG Farben's investments. (*Source:* NI-10926/90, Affidavit by Werner Hagert, 15.IX.47)

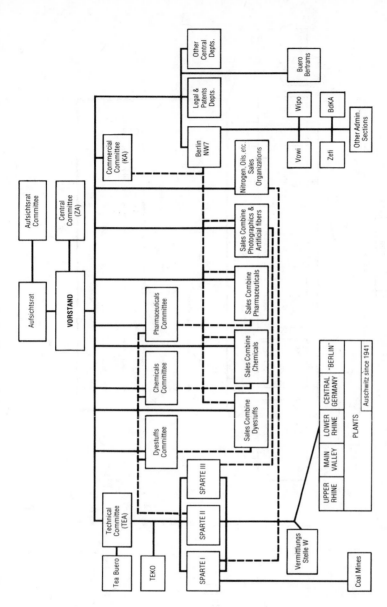

Appendix E. Organization of IG Farben, 1938–1945. (*Source:* NI-10042, 24.VII.47)

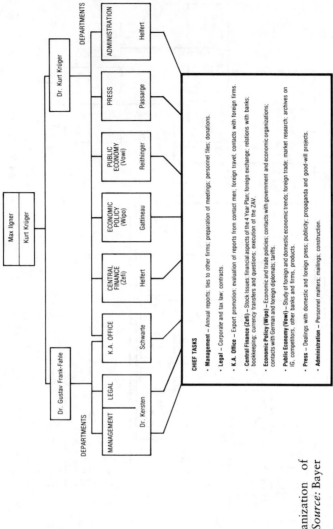

DEPARTMENTS

Max Ilgner
Kurt Krüger

Dr. Gustav Frank-Fahle | Dr. Kurt Krüger

DEPARTMENTS

MANAGEMENT | LEGAL | K.A. OFFICE | CENTRAL FINANCE (Zefi) | ECONOMIC POLICY (Wipo) | PUBLIC ECONOMY (Vowi) | PRESS | ADMINISTRATION

Dr. Kersten | Schwarte | Helfert | Gattineau | Reithinger | Passarge | Helfert

CHIEF TASKS

- **Management** – Annual reports; ties to other firms; preparation of meetings; personnel files; donations.
- **Legal** – Corporate and tax law; contracts.
- **K.A. Office** – Export promotion; evaluation of reports from contact men; foreign travel; contacts with foreign firms.
- **Central Finance (Zefi)** – Stock issues; financial aspects of the 4 Year Plan; foreign exchange; relations with banks; bookkeeping; currency transfers and questions; execution of the ZAV.
- **Economic Policy (Wipo)** – Economic and trade policies; contacts with government and economic organizations; contacts with German and foreign diplomats; tariffs.
- **Public Economy (Vowi)** – Study of foreign and domestic economic trends; foreign trade; market research; archives on IG, competitors, other banks and firms, products.
- **Press** – Dealings with domestic and foreign press; publicity; propaganda and good-will projects.
- **Administration** – Personnel matters; mailings; construction.

Appendix F. Organization of Berlin NW7, 1937. (*Source:* Bayer 4C3)

A.G. DYNAMIT NOBEL, BRATISLAVA

HUNGARY

'Terrachemica' A.G. Budapest

Chemische Fabrik Graf Batthyany A.G. Budapest

55%

'Ipari' A.G. für industrielle Sprengstoffe, Budapest

32%

20%

ROMANIA

3.7%

'Nitramonia' A.G. Bukarest

84.5%

Erste Rumän. Sprengstoff-Gesellschaft, Bukarest

20%

YUGOSLAVIA

29.6%

'Titanit' A.G. für chemische Industrie, Zagreb

96.7%

Bosnische Elektricitäts-A.G. Jajce

9.2%

73.6%

Mostar Lack- und Farbenwerke A.G. Zagreb

'Aga-Ruse' A.G. Ruse

37.1%

Kalkwerk Celje G.m.b.H. Ruse

100%

40%

Stickstoff-Werke A.G. Ruse

Dynamit A.G. vorm. Alfred Nobel & Co. Troisdorf

51.1%

A.G. DYNAMIT NOBEL, BRATISLAVA

24%

CZECHOSLOVAKIA

Nobel-Bickford A.G. Bratislava

75%

A.G. zur Verwertung von Industriegasen. Bratislava

Chemische Industrie A.G. Bratislava (Geschäftsbetrieb ruht)

100%

31%

'Olea' A.G. Bratislava (in Liqu.)

AUSTRIA

100%

Österreichische Dynamit Nobel A.G. Wien ✱

100%

Carbidwerk Deutsch-Matrei A.G. Wien ✱

83.3%

Anilin-chemie A.G. Wien (in Liqu.)

35.4%

Öster. Pflanzenschutzgesellschaft A.G. Wien

68.3%

Contin. Gesellschaft für Angew. Elektrizität. Wien

Schrottverband G.m.b.H. Wien

4%

4%

1.73%

Ferro-silicium G.m.b.H. Wien

3.46%

1.73%

3.46%

'Pyrochemie' Flammschutz-G.m.b.H. Wien

100%

Öster. Kunstdünger- Schwefelsäure- und chemische Fabrik A.G. Wien

45%

Kalk Stickstoff-Verkaufs-G.m.b.H. Wien

45%

10%

37.9%

Enzesfelder Metallwerke A.G. Enzesfeld

1.2%

Pulverfabrik Skodawerke-Wetzler A.G. Wien

Karbid G.m.b.H. Wien (in Liqu.)

Key:

○ Sales firm

☐ Production firm

✱ The Austrian Dynamit Nobel and the Carbidwerk transferred by contract of October 14, 1938 to IG and DAG, Troisdorf.

→ Minority or unknown holding

➡ Majority holding

⟶ Contractual Connection

Appendix G. Holdings of DAG, Bratislava, showing the transfers following the Anschluss. (*Source:* Bayer 4C₃, Vowi Bericht 4797, 22.II.43)

393

Appendix H. Locations of plants of SWW and DAG, Bratislava. (*Source*: Bayer 6/14, Vowi Bericht 2803, 11.IV.38)

394

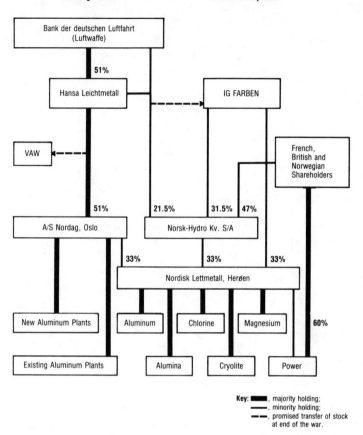

Appendix I. Reich's plan for Norwegian light-metals development, June 1941.

Index

Praise for the Jack Reacher series

"This series [is] utterly addictive."
—Janet Maslin, *The New York Times*

"Reacher [is] one of the century's most original, tantalizing pop-fiction heroes."
—*The Washington Post*

"One of the great many things about Jack Reacher is that he's larger than life while remaining relatable and believable."
—James Patterson

"Jack Reacher is the thinking reader's action hero."
—*The Seattle Times*

"Jack Reacher is a wonderfully epic hero; tough, taciturn, yet vulnerable. . . . Irresistible."
—*People*

"Child is a superb craftsman of suspense."
—*Entertainment Weekly*

"Tight, sinuous, and addictive."
—*USA Today*

"Easily the best thriller series going."
—NPR

"Shows no signs of slowing down . . . You need Jack Reacher."
—*The Atlantic*

"Reacher is Marlowe's literary descendant, and a 21st-century knight—only tougher."
—Minneapolis *Star-Tribune*

"The strongest brand in publishing."
—*Forbes*

BY LEE CHILD AND ANDREW CHILD

The Sentinel
Better Off Dead
No Plan B
The Secret

By Lee Child

Killing Floor
Die Trying
Tripwire
Running Blind
Echo Burning
Without Fail
Persuader
The Enemy
One Shot
The Hard Way
Bad Luck and Trouble
Nothing to Lose
Gone Tomorrow
61 Hours
Worth Dying For
The Affair
A Wanted Man
Never Go Back
Personal
Make Me
Night School
No Middle Name
The Midnight Line
Past Tense
Blue Moon

Short Stories

Second Son
Deep Down
High Heat
Not a Drill
Small Wars
The Christmas Scorpion

By Andrew Grant

Even
Die Twice
More Harm Than Good
RUN
False Positive
False Friend
False Witness
Invisible
Too Close to Home

The Secret

LEE CHILD and ANDREW CHILD

Bantam | New York

The Secret

A JACK REACHER NOVEL

2024 Bantam Books Trade Paperback Edition

Published in the United States by Bantam Books, an imprint of Random House, a division of Penguin Random House LLC, New York.

BANTAM & B colophon is a registered trademark of Penguin Random House LLC.

Originally published in hardcover in the United States by Delacorte Press, an imprint of Random House, a division of Penguin Random House LLC, in 2023.

This book contains an excerpt from the forthcoming book *In Too Deep* by Lee Child and Andrew Child. This excerpt has been set for this edition only and may not reflect the final content of the forthcoming edition.

LIBRARY OF CONGRESS CATALOGING-IN-PUBLICATION DATA

Names: Child, Lee, author. | Child, Andrew, author.
Title: The secret / Lee Child and Andrew Child.
Description: First Edition. | New York: Delacorte Press, 2023. |
Series: Jack Reacher; 28
Identifiers: LCCN 2023033072 (print) | LCCN 2023033073 (ebook)
| ISBN 9781984818607 (Trade paperback) | ISBN 9781984818591
(Ebook) | ISBN 9780593871454 (International)
Subjects: LCSH: Reacher, Jack (Fictitious character)—Fiction. |
LCGFT: Thrillers (Fiction) | Novels.
Classification: LCC PS3553.H4838 S43 2023 (print) | LCC PS3553.
H4838 (ebook) | DDC 813/.54—dc23/eng/20230720
LC record available at https://lccn.loc.gov/2023033072
LC ebook record available at https://lccn.loc.gov/2023033073

Printed in the United States of America on acid-free paper

randomhousebooks.com

9 8 7 6 5 4 3 2 1

Book design by Virginia Norey
Title page art: gokturk_06/stock.adobe.com

For Larry, with thanks

The Secret

Chapter 1

Keith Bridgeman was alone in his room when he closed his eyes. The morning medical rounds were over. Lunch had been delivered and eaten and cleared away. Other people's visitors had clattered along the corridor in search of relatives and friends. A janitor had swept and mopped and hauled off the day's trash. And finally a little peace had descended on the ward.

Bridgeman had been in the hospital for a month. Long enough to grow used to its rhythms and routines. He knew it was time for the afternoon lull. A break from getting poked and prodded and being made to get up and move around and stretch. No one was going to bother him for another three hours, minimum. So he could read. Watch TV. Listen to music. Gaze out of the window at the sliver of lake that was visible between the next pair of skyscrapers.

Or he could take a nap.

Bridgeman was sixty-two years old. He was in rough shape. That was clear. He could debate the cause—the kind of work he had devoted his life to, the stress he had suffered, the cigarettes and alcohol he had consumed—but he couldn't deny the effect. A heart attack so massive that no one had expected him to survive.

Defying odds that great is tiring work. He chose the nap.

These days he always chose the nap.

Bridgeman woke up after only an hour. He was no longer alone. Two other people were in the room with him. Both were women. Maybe in their late twenties. They were the same height. The same slim build. One was on the left side of his bed, nearer to the door. The other was level with her on the right, nearer to the window. They were standing completely still. In silence. Staring at him. Their hair was pulled back, smooth and dark and tight. Their faces were expressionless like mannequins' and their skin shone in the harsh artificial light as if it were molded from plastic.

The women were wearing white coats over hospital scrubs. The coats were the correct length. They had all the necessary pockets and badges and tags. The scrubs were the right shade of blue. But the women weren't medics. Bridgeman was sure about that. His sixth sense told him so. It told him they shouldn't be there. That they were trouble. He scanned each of them in turn. Their hands were empty. Their clothes were not bulging. There was no sign of guns or knives. No sign of any hospital equipment they could use as weapons. But Bridgeman still wasn't happy. He was in danger. He knew it. He could feel it as keenly as a gazelle that had been ambushed by a pair of lions.

Bridgeman glanced at his left leg. The call button was where the nurse had left it, lying on the sheet between his thigh and the safety rail. His hand darted toward it. It was a fluid movement. Smooth. Fast. But the woman was faster. She snatched the button then dropped it, leaving it dangling on its wire, almost to the floor, well out of Bridgeman's reach.

Bridgeman felt his heart quiver and tremble in his chest. He heard an electronic beep. It came from a piece of equipment on a stand near the head of the bed. It had a screen with a number in the center of the top half and two jagged lines that zigzagged across the full width of the lower half. The first line showed his pulse. It was spiking wildly. Its peaks were surging closer together like they were chasing one another. The number showed his heart rate. It was climbing. Fast. The beeps grew louder. More frequent. Then the sound became continuous. Insistent. Impossible to ignore. The number stopped rising. It began to flash. It changed direction. And it kept going down until it reached 00. The lines flattened out. First at the left of the screen and then all the way across until both were perfectly horizontal. The display was inert. Lifeless. Except for the desperate electronic howl.

It told of total cardiac failure.

But only for a moment.

The second woman had grabbed Bridgeman's right wrist when the alarm began to shriek. She had yanked a square blue clip off the tip of his index finger and attached it to her own. The screen flashed twice. Then the sound cut out. The heart rate started to climb. The two lines began to tick their way from left to right. None of the values were quite the same as Bridgeman's. The woman was younger. Fitter. Healthier. Calmer. But the readings were close enough. Not too high. Not too low. Nothing to trigger another alarm.

Bridgeman clutched his chest with both hands. Sweat was prickling out across his forehead and his scalp. His skin felt clammy. He had to make an effort to breathe.

The woman with the clip on her finger lowered herself into the visitor's chair next to the window. The woman on the left of the bed waited a moment then looked at Bridgeman and said, "We apologize. We didn't mean to startle you. We're not here to hurt you. We just need to talk."

Bridgeman said nothing.

The woman said, "We have two questions. That's all. Answer them honestly and you'll never see us again. I promise."

Bridgeman didn't respond.

The woman saw him glancing past her, toward the door. She shook her head. "If you're hoping the cavalry's going to come, you're out of luck. Those clips slip off people's fingers all the time. And what do they do? Stick them right back on. Anyone at the nurses' station who heard the alarm will figure that's what you did. So. First question, OK?"

Bridgeman's mouth was dry. He did his best to moisten his lips then took a deep breath. But not to answer questions. To call for help the old-fashioned way.

The woman read his play. She put a finger to her lips and took something out of her coat pocket. A photograph. She held it out for Bridgeman to take. It showed a gloved hand holding a copy of the *Tribune* next to a window. Bridgeman could read the date on the newspaper. Tuesday, April 7, 1992. It was that day's edition. Then he saw two figures through the glass. A woman and a child. A little girl. Even though they were facing away from the camera, Bridgeman had no doubt who they were. Or where they were. It was his daughter and granddaughter. In the home he had bought them in Evanston, after his wife died.

The woman took hold of Bridgeman's arm and felt for his pulse. It was fast and weak. She said, "Come on, now. Calm down. Think of your family. We don't want to hurt them. Or you. We just need you to understand how serious this situation is. We only have two questions, but they're important. The sooner you answer, the sooner we're out of here. Ready?"

Bridgeman nodded and slumped back against his pillow.

"First question. You're meeting with a journalist the day after tomorrow. Where is the information you're planning to give her?"

"How do you know about—"

"Don't waste time. Answer the question."

"OK. Look. There is no information. We're just going to chat."

"No credible journalist is going to believe a whistleblower without ironclad proof. Where is it?"

"Whistleblower? That's not what this is. The reporter's from a little weekly rag in Akron, Ohio. Where I was born. The story's about my heart attack. My recovery. It's a miracle, according to the doctors. People back home want to read about it. They say I'm an inspiration."

"Heart attack? That's what you're going with? When you're sitting on a much bigger story?"

"What bigger story?"

The woman leaned in closer. "Keith, we know what you did. What you all did. Twenty-three years ago. December 1969."

"December '69? How do you know . . . ? Who are you?"

"We'll come to who we are. Right now you need to tell me what information you're planning to give this reporter from Akron."

"No information. I'm going to tell her about my recovery. That's all. I will never talk about December '69. Why we were there. What we were doing. What happened. Not to anyone. I swore I wouldn't and I keep my word. My wife never even knew."

"So you don't have any documents or notes hidden in this room?"

"Of course not."

"Then you won't mind if I take a look around."

The woman didn't wait for an answer. She started with the locker next to the bed. She opened the door and rummaged through Bridgeman's spare pajamas and books and magazines. She moved on to a leather duffel on the floor near the door. It held a set of clothes. Nothing else. Next she checked the bathroom. Nothing significant there, either. So she moved to the center of the room and put her hands on her hips. "Only one place left to check. The bed."

Bridgeman didn't move.

"Do it for your daughter. And your granddaughter. Come on. I'll be quick."

Bridgeman felt his pulse start to speed up again. He closed his eyes for a moment. Took a breath. Willed himself to relax. Then pushed back the sheet, swung his legs over the side of the mattress, and slid down onto his feet. He looked at the woman in the chair. "Can I at least sit? I'm older than you. I have one foot in the grave."

The woman held up her finger with the clip attached. "Sorry. The cable's too short for me to move. You want to sit, use the windowsill."

Bridgeman turned and looked at the windowsill. Considered sitting on it. But taking orders from one of the women was bad enough so he settled on leaning against it. He watched as the other woman finished her search of the bed. Again she came up empty.

"Believe me now?" Bridgeman said.

The woman took a piece of paper out of her pocket and handed it to Bridgeman. There was a list of names. Six of them, handwritten in shaky, spidery script. Bridgeman's was one of them. He recognized all the other five. Varinder Singh. Geoffrey Brown. Michael Rymer. Charlie Adam. Neville Pritchard. And beneath the final name there was a symbol. A question mark.

The woman said, "A name is missing. Who is it?"

Bridgeman's heart was no longer racing. Now it felt like it was full of sludge. Like it didn't have the strength to force his blood into his arteries. He couldn't answer. It would mean breaking his oath. He had sworn to never reveal a single detail. They all had, twenty-three years before, when it became clear what they had done. And the missing name belonged to the flakiest of the group. Better for everyone if it remained off the list.

The woman handed Bridgeman another photograph. Another shot of his daughter and granddaughter, on foot this time, halfway across a crosswalk. The picture had been taken through a car windshield.

Bridgeman was channeling all his energy into trying to breathe. It was only a name that the woman wanted. What harm could come from telling her? Plenty, he knew.

The woman said, "Bonus question. What happens tomorrow? Or the next day? Is the driver drunk? Do his brakes fail?"

Bridgeman said, "Buck. The missing name. It's Owen Buck."

The woman shook her head. "Buck's dead. He died of cancer a month ago. Right after he wrote that list. So his isn't the name I need. He said there was an eighth name. He didn't know what it was. But he was certain one of you others do."

Bridgeman didn't answer. He was struggling to make sense of the information. Buck's conscience must have gotten the better of him. He was always mumbling about doing something stupid. But that didn't explain why he told this woman there was an extra name. Maybe his mind had gone. Maybe whatever cancer drugs they gave him had fried his brain.

The woman said, "Maybe the driver will be distracted? Maybe he'll be asleep at the wheel?"

"Maybe there is another name." Bridgeman closed his eyes. "Maybe someone knows what it is. One of the others might. But not me. I don't think one exists."

The woman said, "Maybe there'll be enough of your granddaughter left to bury. Maybe there won't."

Bridgeman was struggling for air. "Don't. Please. I don't know. I swear. I gave you Buck's name. I didn't know he's dead. I've been sick. I've been in here. No one told me. So if I knew of some other name I'd tell you it, too. But I don't. So I can't."

"You can. You don't have to say it. You can do what Owen Buck did. Write it down. He gave me six names. You only need to give me one."

She pulled a pen from her coat pocket and held it out. Bridgeman stared at it for a moment. Then he took it and added *Owen Buck* to the top of the list.

He said, "That's the only name I know. I swear."

The woman said, "Have you ever seen a child's coffin, Keith? Because if you haven't I don't think anything can really prepare you for how tiny it will seem. Especially when it's next to the full-sized one your daughter will be in."

Bridgeman's knees started to shake. He looked like he was ready to collapse.

The woman's voice softened. "Come on. One name. Two lives saved. What are you waiting for?"

Bridgeman's body sagged. "Buck was wrong. There isn't another name. Not that I know of. I was there three years. I never heard of anyone else getting brought on board."

The woman stared at Bridgeman for ten long seconds, then shrugged. She took the pen and the paper and slid them back into her pocket. "I guess we're done here." She stretched out and touched Bridgeman's forehead. "Wait a minute. You feel awful. Let me open the window. Fresh air will perk you up. I don't want to leave you like this."

Bridgeman said, "You can't. The windows don't open in this hospital."

"This one does." The woman leaned past Bridgeman, pushed down on the handle, and the window swung out on a broad arc. Then she scrabbled under the collar of her scrubs and pulled a fine chain up and over her head. The key to the window was hanging from it. "Here." She dropped the chain into the breast pocket of Bridgeman's pajama top. "A present. Something to remember us by, because you're never going to see us again. As promised. There's just one last thing before we go. You asked who we are." The woman stood a little straighter. "My name is Roberta Sanson."

The woman with the finger clip climbed out of her chair. "And I'm her sister. Veronica Sanson. Our father was Morgan Sanson. It's important you know that."

Morgan Sanson. The name was an echo from the past. An unwelcome one. Four syllables he had hoped to never hear again. It took a fraction of a second for the significance to hit him, then Bridgeman pushed off from the wall. He tried to dodge around Roberta Sanson but he never stood a chance. He was too frail. The space was too cramped. And the sisters were too highly motivated. Roberta shifted sideways and blocked his path. Then she grabbed his shoulders with both hands and drove him back until he was pressed against the sill. She checked that he was lined up with the open window. Veronica bent down and took hold of his legs, just above the ankles. She straightened and Roberta pushed. Bridgeman kicked. He twisted and thrashed. Roberta and Veronica pushed one more time. Two more times, to make sure there was no room for error. Then they let gravity do the rest.

Chapter 2

Jack Reacher had never been to the Rock Island Arsenal in Illinois before, but he was the second Military Police investigator to be sent there within a fortnight. The first visit was in response to a report of missing M16s, which proved to be false. Reacher was the last to join his unit, following his demotion from major to captain, so he had been allocated a less interesting allegation. Inventory tampering.

The sergeant who had filed the complaint met Reacher at the main entrance. There were maybe ten years between them. They were about the same height, six foot five, but where Reacher was heavy and broad, the older man was skinny and pinched with pale skin and thin, delicate features. He couldn't have been more than 180 pounds. That would be sixty pounds lighter. His uniform hung off his shoulders a little, causing Reacher to worry about the guy's health.

Once the usual courtesies were taken care of, the sergeant led the way to Firing Range E, near the base's western perimeter. He locked the heavy steel door behind them and continued to a loading bench that jutted out from the rear wall. Six M16s were lying on it, neatly lined up, muzzles facing away, grips to the right. The weapons weren't new. They had spent plenty of time in the field. That was clear. But they were well maintained. Recently cleaned. Not neglected or damaged. There were no obvious red flags. No visible indication that anything was wrong with them.

Reacher picked up the second rifle from the left. He checked that the chamber was empty, inspected it for defects, then slid a magazine into place. He stepped across to the mouth of the range. Selected single-fire mode. Took a breath. Held it. Waited for the next beat of his heart to subside and pulled the trigger. A hundred yards down range, the red star on the target figure's helmet imploded. Reacher lowered the gun and glanced at the sergeant. The guy's face betrayed nothing. No surprise. No disappointment. Reacher fired five more times. Rapidly. Sharp *crack*s rebounded off the walls. Spent cartridges rattled onto the cement floor. A neat T shape was hammered into the figure's chest. It was textbook shooting. There was no sign of any problem with the gun. And still no response from the sergeant.

Reacher pointed to the magazine. "How many?"

The sergeant said, "Sixteen."

"Vietnam?"

"Three tours. No misfires. If it's not broke . . ."

Reacher slid the fire selector to its lowest position. Full auto. The model was old, from before the switch to three-shot bursts. He aimed at the target's center mass and increased the pressure on the trigger. The green plastic torso should have been shredded. The ten remaining bullets should have torn through it in less than a second. But nothing happened. Because the trigger wouldn't move. Reacher changed back to single-shot mode and lined up on the target's face.

The crude contour representing its nose split in half under the impact. Reacher toggled to full auto. Again, nothing happened. Which left no doubt. The trigger would not move in that position.

He said, "They all like this?"

The sergeant nodded. "All of them. The whole case."

Reacher crossed to the bench and set the gun down. He removed the magazine, cleared the chamber, pushed out the takedown pins, separated the lower receiver, and examined its interior contours. Then he held it out toward the sergeant and said, "The trigger pocket's the wrong size. It won't accept the auto-sear. And there are only two trigger pinholes. There should be three."

The sergeant said, "Correct."

"This isn't military spec. Someone's switched out the original with a civilian version. It makes the gun semi-auto only."

"Can't see any other explanation."

"Where did these come from?"

The sergeant shrugged. "Admin error. They were supposed to be sent for destruction but two crates got mixed up and these wound up here by mistake."

Reacher looked down at the guns on the bench. "These would be considered end-of-life?"

The sergeant shrugged again. "I wouldn't say so. Ask me, the condition's acceptable for weapons that would generally be held in reserve. Nothing stood out when the crate was opened. Only when a malfunction was reported. Then I stripped the first one down. Saw the problem right away. Just like you did."

"Who decides which weapons get destroyed?"

"A dedicated team. It's a special procedure. Temporary. Lasted a year, so far. Result of Desert Storm. The war was a great opportunity for units to reequip. Assets that are designated surplus as a result come back from the Gulf and get sent here for evaluation.

Firearms are our responsibility. We test them and give them a category. Green: fully serviceable, to be retained. Amber: marginally serviceable, to be sold or allocated to civilian gun safety programs. Doesn't apply to fully automatic weapons, obviously. And red: unserviceable, to be destroyed."

"You got sent a red crate when you should have gotten a green one?"

"Correct."

Reacher paused for a moment. The account was plausible. There wasn't a kind of equipment the army owned that hadn't been sent to the wrong place, some time or other. Which was usually totally innocent. Like the sergeant said, an admin error. But Reacher was wondering if there could be a broader connection. Something to do with the recent report of stolen M16s. Someone could designate good weapons as unserviceable, fill their crates with the right weight of whatever trash came to hand, send that to the crusher or the furnace, and sell the guns on the black market. Officially the weapons would no longer exist, so no one would be looking for them. It was a feasible method. A loophole someone needed to close. But it wasn't what had happened here. Reacher had read the report. The inspection was unannounced. A full crack-of-dawn, shock-and-awe operation. And it had been thorough. All the weapons crates on the entire base had been opened. All had the correct number of weapons inside. Not so much as a pocket knife was missing.

Not so much as a *complete* pocket knife . . .

Reacher said, "When did these guns get delivered to you in error?"

The sergeant looked away while he did the math, then said, "Fifteen days ago. And I know what you're going to ask me next. You're not going to like the answer."

"What am I going to ask?"

"How you can trace which unit owned these weapons in the Gulf. Before they were sent back."

"Why would I want to know that?"

"So you can figure out who's stealing the lower receivers. Someone is stealing them, right? And selling them. So that gangbangers or whoever can make their AR-15s fully automatic. The Gulf's the perfect place to swap parts out. Officially every last paperclip is tracked. But in reality? Different units have different systems. A few have switched to computers. Most are still paper-based. Paper gets lost. It gets wet. It gets ripped. Digits get transposed. People have handwriting that's impossible to read. Long story short, you'd have a better chance of selling bikinis at a Mormon convention than tracking that crate."

"You don't think I have a future as a swimwear salesman?"

The sergeant blinked. "Sir?"

Reacher said, "No matter. I don't care who had these guns in the Gulf. Because that's not where the parts were stolen."

Roberta and Veronica Sanson heard the impact all the way from the street outside. They heard the first of the screams over the background grumble of traffic. Then the cardiac monitor at the head of the bed started to howl again. Its lines had slumped back down to the horizontal. Its display read 00. No heart activity. Only this time the machine was correct. At least as far as Keith Bridgeman was concerned.

Roberta turned left into the corridor and made her way to the hospital's central elevator bank. Veronica went right and looped around to the emergency staircase. Roberta reached the first floor before her sister. She strolled through the reception area, past the café and the store that sold balloons and flowers, and continued out of the main exit. She walked a block west then ducked into a phone booth. She pulled on a pair of latex gloves and called American Airlines. She asked for information about their routes and schedules. Next she called United. Then TWA. She weighed the options. Then she tossed the gloves in a trash can and made her way to the public parking lot in the center of the next block.

The sergeant led the way to a storeroom that was tacked onto the side of a large, squat building near the center of the site. The wind had picked up while they were at the range which made it hard for him to heave the metal door all the way open, and after Reacher had gone through the guy struggled to close it again without getting blown over. He finally wrestled it into place then locked it. Inside, the space was square, eighteen feet by eighteen. The floor was bare concrete. So was the ceiling. It was held up by metal girders that were coated with some kind of knobby fire retardant material and flanked by strip lights in protective cages. There was a phone mounted by the door and a set of shelves against each wall. They were made of heavy-duty steel, painted gray. Each had a stenciled sign attached—*Intake, Green, Amber, Red*—and a clipboard with a sheaf of papers hanging from its right-hand upright. There were no windows and the air was heavy with the smell of oil and solvents.

The shelves held crates of weapons. Short at the top, long at the bottom. There were fourteen crates on the Red shelves. Reacher pulled one of the long ones out onto the floor and cracked it open. He lifted out an M16. It was in much worse shape than the one he had fired earlier. That was for sure. He field-stripped it, checked its lower receiver, and shook his head.

He said, "It's original."

The sergeant opened another crate and examined one of its rifles. It was also pretty scuffed and scraped. He said, "This one's the same."

Each crate had a number stenciled on the side. Reacher took the Red clipboard off its hook and turned to the last sheet. It showed that the crate he'd picked had been signed off by someone with the initials UE. The crate the sergeant had chosen had been initialed by DS. Reacher could only see one other set: LH. He picked a crate with a corresponding number, removed the lower receiver from one of the guns inside it, and held the part up for the sergeant to see.

The sergeant said, "Jackpot."

Reacher said, "LH signed off on this. Who's LH?"

"Sergeant Hall. In charge of the inspection team."

"Sergeant Hall's a woman."

"Yes. Sergeant Lisa Hall. How—"

"UE and DS are men?"

"Yes. But—"

"There are no other women on the team?"

"No. But I still—"

Reacher held up his hand. "Fifteen days ago you received a Red crate by mistake. Fourteen days ago we received a report that M16s had been stolen from this facility. We checked. They hadn't."

"I heard about the raid. I don't see the connection."

"The report was anonymous, but the voice was female. I read the file."

"I still don't—"

"Sergeant Hall realized a Red crate was missing the day after it got mishandled. She knew it could be traced back to her so she made a bogus accusation. A serious one. Stolen weapons. The investigators came running, just like she knew they would. They opened all the crates, including hers. They were looking for M16s. Complete ones. That's what they found, so they closed the case. No crime detected. Then if the missing receivers came to light, Hall had just been cleared of theft. She was hoping an investigator would make the same jump you did. That the doctored weapons arrived that way, from the Gulf."

"No. I know Lisa Hall. She wouldn't do something like that."

"Let's make sure. Where is she today?"

"Don't know, sir."

"Then find out."

"Sir." The sergeant shuffled across to the phone on the wall. Thin clouds of dust puffed up around his feet. He dialed slowly, made the inquiry, and when he was done he said, "Not on duty, sir."

Reacher said, "OK. So where's her billet?"

Veronica Sanson was waiting for her sister, Roberta, on the fourth floor of the parking garage. She was standing at the side of a blue minivan. They had stolen it from the long-term lot at O'Hare when they arrived in the city, two days before. Roberta nodded a greeting and opened the van's rear door. They took turns, one keeping watch, one hunkering down between the back seats and changing their clothes. Off came the hospital outfits. On went jeans and sneakers and shirts and jackets. All plain, anonymous items. When they were dressed the sisters hugged, retrieved their plain canvas duffels from the van's narrow cargo area, wiped the vehicle clean of prints, then made their way to separate exits. Roberta threaded her way west. She pushed through knots of shoppers and tourists, past the wide storefronts and cafés and offices, until she reached the

Clark/Lake El stop. Veronica walked south and kept going to Roosevelt, where the Orange Line emerged from its underground section.

Reacher liked the armory sergeant at Rock Island. He figured the guy was reasonably smart. Reasonably street wise. Reasonably capable of anticipating the kind of trouble he'd be in if Hall somehow got word that she was under suspicion. But Reacher was a cautious guy. He'd learned a long time ago that it can be dangerous to overestimate a person. That unit loyalty can run deeper than deference to a stranger. Especially when that stranger is an MP. So he made sure that the sergeant was clear about the consequences of any phone calls he might be tempted to make. He left no room for doubt. Then he requisitioned a car from the base's motor pool and found his way to Hall's address.

Hall lived in the last of a little knot of houses stretched out along a river about four miles east of the Arsenal's main gate. Her home was small and neat. Set up for efficiency, Reacher thought. No fancy décor to maintain. No complicated yard work to stay on top of. There was no answer at the door when Reacher knocked. No sign of anyone through the windows, front or back. Just an array of budget furniture laid out as if someone had tried to re-create a picture from a low-cost catalog. There was nothing personal. No photographs. No ornaments. None of the knickknacks people use to impose their identity on a place. Reacher understood that. Aside from his four years at West Point he had spent his life bouncing from one base to another. Six months here. Six months there. Different countries. Different continents. Never anyplace long enough to feel at home. First as a kid, because his father had been an officer in the Marines. Then as an adult, as an officer himself. Maybe Hall had the same experience. Maybe she was anticipating her next change of station and didn't want to waste effort on a place she knew she was soon going to quit. Or maybe she had another reason to be ready to leave in a hurry.

Reacher walked back to his borrowed car and settled in to wait. He wasn't worried about how long it might take. He was a patient man. He had nowhere else to be. And he was naturally suited to two states of existence. Instant, explosive action. And near-catatonic stasis. It was the in-between he struggled with. The sitting through pointless meetings and reviews and briefings that made up so much of army life.

Chapter 3

The phone rang at 9:00 P.M. Eastern. That was 8:00 P.M. Central, where the call originated. Which was right on time.

It was answered immediately.

The guy who had dialed said, "Another one's dead. Keith Bridgeman. Massive blunt force trauma resulting from falling out of his hospital room window. United Medical, Chicago. Twelfth floor. Had been recovering from a heart attack. Not out of the woods but was expected to pull through. Fine when the nurses did their rounds a couple of hours earlier. No reported visitors or calls or outside contact. The police are fifty/fifty, suicide or accident. He must have unlocked the window himself—the key was still in his pocket—but there was no note. All for now. More at 0800."

"Understood." The guy who had answered hung up.

Officially the telephone line they had used didn't exist. It was one of the Pentagon's ghost circuits. There were hundreds of them in the building. Maybe thousands. They generate no records, incoming or outgoing. The call that had just ended could never be traced. It could never be correlated with the next call made on the same line, but the Pentagon guy walked through to the outer office anyway. Old habits die hard. He picked up a different phone and dialed a number from memory. A number that was not written down anywhere. Not listed. Not officially in service.

The Pentagon guy's call was picked up in the study of a house four miles away, in Georgetown, D.C. By Charles Stamoran. The Secretary of Defense of the United States of America.

The Pentagon guy repeated what he'd been told a minute earlier. Word for word. Neutral tone. No summarizing. No editorializing. The way Stamoran insisted it was done.

"Understood," Stamoran said when the Pentagon guy stopped talking. "Wait one."

Stamoran laid the handset down on the worn leather desktop, crossed to the window, and peered out from around the side of the closed drapes. He stared across the lawn, toward the pond and beyond that the wall, picturing the sensors and tripwires and hidden cameras, and he weighed what he'd just heard. He received briefings on all kinds of subjects, all the time. It was part of the job. One regular report he got was a list of significant deaths. Foreign leaders. Key military figures, friend and foe. Terrorist suspects. Essentially anyone who could upset the geopolitical status quo. Dry stuff, on the whole. But a perk of the job was that he got to add a few extra names for himself. Nothing official. Just people he had a personal interest in. One of these was a guy named Owen Buck. He had died of cancer four weeks ago. Nothing suspicious about that. On its own. Then another guy on his list had died. Varinder Singh. Electrocuted in his bath. A tape player had wound up in the water with him. Its cord was still plugged into the wall. Fifty/fifty, suicide or accident, the police had said. And now Keith Bridgeman had died. Also on his list. Also fifty/fifty. Not the kind of coincidence that was ever going to pass Stamoran's smell test. That was for damn sure.

Stamoran returned to his desk and picked up the handset. "I'm going to give you three names. Geoff Brown. Michael Rymer. Charlie Adam. They're already on my list. I want them under surveillance, twenty-four/seven, effective immediately. Send our best people. Someone looks at these guys funny, I want them in a cell before they can blink. In isolation. No one gets access until I send someone to question them."

"Covert surveillance, sir? Or can the watchers make contact? Make it known what they're doing?"

"Covert. Strictly hands-off. These guys are Company lifers. If they cotton onto the fact that we have reason to watch them, they'll disappear faster than a politician who's asked to keep a promise."

"Understood."

"And there's a fourth name. Neville Pritchard. He's also on my list. I want him in protective custody. The most secure place we have. The most remote. Now. Tonight. No delay."

Stamoran dropped the receiver into its cradle and walked back to the window. Three guys were dead. Three would be watched. One would be put on ice. Which left one last name. Not on the list. Stamoran knew it, of course. So did Pritchard. But no one else did. Stamoran needed to keep things that way. The secret he had hidden for twenty-three years depended on it.

Stamoran turned his attention to Pritchard. Tried to picture his face. It wasn't easy after so many years. He could remember more about the guy's temper. He wasn't going to be happy about getting dragged out of bed and bundled off to some distant safehouse. Not happy at all. But that was too bad. When you're forced into a game of Russian Roulette you have no time to worry about people's feelings. There's only one move to make. Ensure the bullet that could kill you is removed from the gun.

Sergeant Hall showed up a whisker after 8:30 P.M. She parked her car—a small, clean, domestic sedan—directly outside her house and walked up the path to her door. She was around five foot six and was wearing civilian clothes. Jeans, white sneakers, and an Orioles sweatshirt. Her blond hair was tied back in a ponytail and she moved with fluid confidence, like an athlete. She wasn't in a rush. She wasn't glancing around to see if she was being watched. Reacher was pleased. It showed the armory sergeant had listened. He gave her a couple of minutes to get settled then made his own way up the path.

Hall answered the door right away. She looked surprised to see a huge guy in woodland BDUs on her doorstep, but not worried. "Help you, Captain?" she said.

Reacher showed his Military ID card then slid his wallet back into his pocket. "I need a minute of your time. To follow up on the missing weapons case."

Hall's expression was blank. "There aren't any missing weapons. The MPs searched the entire base. They confirmed it."

"The weapons aren't missing. But something else is."

Hall looked away. She scratched the side of her face then tucked a loose strand of hair behind her ear. "I don't—"

Reacher said, "Some of our paperwork. A couple of pages got lost. Someone screwed up. I need to fix it before our CO finds out. Just need a few details. I was told you were the person to talk to."

"Paperwork?" Hall blinked, twice. "Oh. OK. Sure. What . . . wait. You don't have a briefcase or a clipboard or anything."

"Don't need one." Reacher tapped his temple. "I'll remember what you say. Then I'll call my base and pass the information along to the right person. He needs to do the actual form-filling. Otherwise the handwriting won't match."

Hall didn't respond.

Reacher said, "It won't take long. And we're in a time crunch here . . ."

"Oh. OK. What do you need to know?"

"Mind if I come inside? It's been a long day. I could use a glass of water while we talk."

Hall paused. She looked Reacher up and down. He was practically a foot taller than she. Probably twice her weight. But he was an MP and MPs don't like to be told no. Nothing good ever comes of it. So after a moment she nodded and gestured for him to follow her down the hallway. There were framed pictures on the walls. Three on either side. Prints of animals and birds and scenes from nature. Hall pointed to the door on the right then continued to the kitchen. Reacher followed her direction and found himself in her living room. He stood just off center to avoid hitting his head on a light that hung from the ceiling and waited for Hall to catch up. She appeared a minute later with two plain glasses of water. She put one on a side table next to the couch and then perched at the front of a matching armchair.

"So," Hall said. "Details?"

Reacher sat in the center of the couch, took a sip of water, then said, "The weapons that come back from the Gulf. The ones designated surplus. You're responsible for testing them. Deciding which are kept and which are disposed of?"

"My team is. Not just me. But none of those weapons is missing. The MPs searched and—"

"Who decides who tests which crates?"

Hall paused for a moment, then said, "It's basically random. No method to it."

Reacher said, "Who decides?"

"I do, I guess. From a record-keeping point of view."

"I think you do have a method. And it has nothing to do with record-keeping. You make sure the guns that come to you to test are in good shape. And are older ones. With full-auto capability."

"Why would I do that?"

"Where do you get the civilian-spec lower receivers?"

"Civilian-spec? You must be confused. We have nothing to do with civilian weapons."

Reacher said, "Full-auto capable lower receivers are valuable things. They can turn an AR-15 that any bozo can buy into a military grade weapon. So you swap them out, sell them, then send the complete-looking guns to be destroyed. No one ever finds out. *Should* ever find out. But you heard that a crate of doctored weapons had gotten lost on the base. An admin screwup. That could be a big problem. You had to cover your ass. So you called in a bogus report. You said M16s were being stolen. They weren't, so you knew everyone at Rock Island would be cleared. Including yourself. Then if the doctored weapons came to light, you figured the suspicion would be deflected up the chain, to the original owners in the Gulf. Who would never be traced because the systems are all out of whack."

Hall jumped to her feet. "Doctored weapons? I don't know what—"

"Sit down." Reacher's voice was loud enough to have knocked her over.

Hall sat. She wriggled back into the chair, looking small and deflated.

Reacher said, "You're in a hole. So you know what you should do?"

Hall shook her head. Just a tiny, nervous motion.

Reacher said, "Stop digging. You're only making things worse for yourself. Now's the time to be honest. Tell me everything, right now, no more bullshit, and I'll see what I can do to help you. Maybe I can limit the damage a little. But only if you stop being a pain in my ass."

Hall covered her face with her hands and curled up even smaller. When she emerged a moment later, a tear was running down one cheek. "OK." She sniffed. "I'm not admitting to anything. It wasn't me. But I know things. I'll tell you. Make you look good with your CO. Just let me use the bathroom first. I'll be quick. I need to get my head straightened out."

Reacher said, "Fine. But use the one upstairs."

Hall unfolded herself from her chair and scuttled to the door.

Reacher heard light, fast footsteps on the stairs. He heard Hall's bedroom door slam shut and a couple of seconds later he heard her bathroom door close, more quietly, on the far side.

Sergeant Hall knew Reacher would have heard the doors. She wanted him to hear them. Needed him to, for authenticity. But she prayed that he did not hear the next sound she made. The slight, unavoidable squeak as she eased her bathroom window open.

Susan Kasluga was in the kitchen, waiting for the kettle to boil, when Charles Stamoran found her. It was a wide rectangular space with an island in the center. The countertops were plain white, polished to a high shine. The cabinets were also white, with smooth fronts and no ornamentation. The backsplashes were made from sheets of stainless steel, and the few appliances that were on display were organized into logical groups. Kasluga had specified every detail herself and when a journalist had once described the place as feeling like a laboratory, she had been delighted.

Stamoran said, "Got a minute, Susie? We need to talk."

Kasluga crossed her arms. "Better not be about my *tea*." Her tone was fierce, but a smile was playing around the corners of her eyes.

The pair had been together twenty years and married a month shy of seventeen. They weren't a typical couple. She was ten years younger. Six inches taller. She had wild red hair that reached her waist when it wasn't tied up for work—to match a suit or, less often these days, a lab coat. She had high cheekbones and bright green eyes. When she walked into a room, people noticed. They couldn't help it. They couldn't avoid staring, even now that she was on the wrong side of fifty. Physically, Stamoran was the opposite. The wrong side of sixty, short, compact, forgettable face, hair innocuously cropped—what was left of it. He could be by her side throughout a party or a reception or a dinner and people would have to check the press photos the next day to tell if he'd been there at all. They worked in different worlds. They had different interests. Different hobbies. Different tastes in food and books and movies. But when it came to brains and guile, they were a perfect match.

"This has nothing to do with your . . . drink." Stamoran smiled, too, but there was no warmth in it. He was a precise man. Pedantic, even. He couldn't stand that she called a bunch of foul-smelling herbs infused in hot water *tea*, because there wasn't any tea in it. He hated the lack of accuracy and thought that as a research scientist she should know better. It was one of the few things about her that rankled with him, even after two decades. "I have some news. Not good. Three people who worked at Mason Chemical when you were there have died. All in the last month." He paused. "Owen Buck. Varinder Singh. Keith Bridgeman."

The kettle managed a first feeble hint of a whistle, but Kasluga didn't wait for it to get louder. She picked it up and poured hot water into her mug. She knew she didn't need the full 212 degrees for that kind of *tea*. And she had no problem with switching between precision at work and vernacular at home. Her husband's single-track rigidity drove her crazy.

She said, "Those names ring a bell. They were in India, in '69, right? They were part of some special development team. Their work was kept separate. Some kind of a secret project. Those guys must all be pretty long in the tooth by now. What happened? Old age catch up with them?"

"Buck, cancer got him. The others, not so clear-cut. The police say fifty/fifty, suicide or accident."

"Both of them?"

Stamoran nodded.

Kasluga said, "They can't both have had fatal accidents, one after the other. So suicide? Really?"

"No. I think someone killed them."

"Killed, as in murdered?"

Stamoran nodded again.

Kasluga shook her head. "Why would anyone want to murder a couple of retired scientists? That makes no sense."

"Susan, there are some things you should know about what happened in '69. Things I didn't tell you before, for reasons that will become obvious. But I need to fill you in now, because I think you're in danger."

"Danger? Me? How? I had nothing to do with whatever work those guys were doing."

"I know."

"It was the 1960s, for God's sake. It was hard enough as a woman to get any kind of research job. No matter that I was smarter than every man who had applied to Mason Chemical in the previous ten years. Probably the previous twenty. And that I could run rings around every man who was already there when they did finally hire me. The assholes wouldn't let me near anything halfway interesting."

"Which is why you took the position in India. I know. And that was a wise move."

"It wasn't. I thought if I got away from corporate HQ I'd have more freedom, but no. I was still stuck on the sidelines. Only over there I was caught in the million-degree heat with no amenities and nothing to do. Not until the shit hit the fan, anyway. Then they wanted a pretty face to stick in front of the cameras until the fuss blew over. Pretty and naïve. I went from unwanted hanger-on to flavor of the month, overnight. Suddenly they couldn't get enough of me. And boy, did I pay the price for that, the minute they didn't need me anymore."

"You were taken advantage of. Used as a PR mouthpiece. That's clear. But it's not why I'm worried."

"So what's the problem? A couple of guys I had basically no connection with, more than twenty years ago, might have been murdered. If anyone should be looking over their shoulders, it's the other members of that team, surely? Maybe you should be talking to them. Maybe someone has a grudge. Maybe one of the surviving scientists."

"I don't think so. This is the work of an outsider. And I'm taking the appropriate steps. The surviving members will all be . . . taken care of."

"You really think someone's going after the rest of the team, then? All of them? Why? What did they do?"

Stamoran didn't reply.

Kasluga glared at him. "And why is someone so upset about it now, after all this time?"

Stamoran took a moment, then said, "There were seven people on that team. On the face of it, all legitimate scientists. But that's not all they were. Two were employed by the army. Five, by the CIA. Their civilian credentials were a cover."

Kasluga lifted her mug, then set it back down on the countertop. "You're joking. The place where I worked was crawling with soldiers and spies? How long have you known?"

Stamoran said, "That's not important."

"The hell it isn't. Why didn't you tell me before?"

"It was on a need-to-know basis. You didn't need to know. Now you do."

Kasluga shrugged. "Explains the secret squirrel vibe, I guess. What were they working on?"

Stamoran shook his head. "That's not important, either. There are only two things that matter right now. First, I do believe someone is going after the whole team. Two dead in suspicious circumstances, one after another, is too big of a coincidence. Second, technically there weren't seven people involved. There were eight. Someone else was connected to that project, indirectly. But significantly."

Kasluga reached for her mug, then pulled her hand back and pressed it against the outside of her thigh. "An eighth person? You sure?"

Stamoran nodded. "Certain."

Kasluga took a breath. "You know who it is?"

Stamoran nodded again. "I do."

Kasluga rested her palms on the countertop and leaned all her weight on them. Her voice dropped to barely a whisper. "Charles? If you have something to say, say it."

"OK." Stamoran paused. "The eighth person? It's me."

Chapter 4

Reacher did not just hear Hall's bathroom window open.
He also saw it.

The moment her bedroom door closed he jumped up from the couch and moved silently down the hallway. He opened the front door. Left it open to avoid making a sound. Hurried along the front of the house until he got to the left-hand corner. Lined up so that the reflection in the driver's window of his borrowed car gave him a clear view down the side of the house. And waited. A moment later Hall's head appeared. She glanced both ways then stretched for the drainpipe that ran down just to the side of the casement. Gripped it with one hand. Then the other. She wriggled out backward until she was sitting on the sill, facing the wall. Pulled her right foot up so she was squatting on it. Did the same with her left. Braced herself, pushed back, and stepped her right foot across to the other side of the pipe. Then she started to lower herself, hand over hand, soles flat against the wall, leaning out almost horizontally, like she was rappelling down a rigid iron rope.

Reacher let her get halfway down before he moved. He stepped around the corner and started in toward her. She spotted him right away. Changed direction. Tried to climb up. To dive back through the window. But before she got close Reacher stretched out and grabbed her belt.

"Want to come here, nice and slow and secure?" he said. "Or risk falling on your head?"

Hall climbed down. Her feet hit the path and she slumped back against the wall.

Reacher stepped in close and said, "It's safe to say the confession phase of this interview is done, yes?"

"Asshole. What happens now?"

"Depends on you."

"What do you want?"

"You took the lower receivers?"

"Obviously."

"How many?"

"Forty-eight."

"Hear that?"

Hall looked left and right. "No. What?"

"That's the sound of the window for you helping yourself slamming shut."

"Wait. Ninety-six."

"You sold them?"

"I didn't take them as souvenirs."

"Who did you sell them to?"

Hall shook her head and sighed. "Be honest with me. How much trouble am I in?"

Reacher said, "My guess? A lot."

"Anything I can do to improve the forecast?" Hall pushed away from the wall and looked Reacher in the eye. "Anything you need? Any way to make the outlook a little sunnier?"

"Maybe," Reacher said.

"Wait a minute." Kasluga stepped back, away from the kitchen counter. She was holding her right hand out in front, palm upright, like a cop stopping traffic. "You were at the Mason plant in India in '69? The same time as me? No way. I would have known. I would have seen you."

Stamoran shook his head. "I didn't say I was there, in India. I was based in the States. At Langley. I was in charge of the program those seven guys were working on at Mason Chemical. And five other projects kind of like it in other countries."

Kasluga's hands switched to her hips. "You were in charge? So it's down to you that I got hung out to dry?"

"No. My number two, the point man on the ground, he was responsible for that. He was authorized to act independently if there was an emergency. And this was all long before you and I met. Before I even knew you existed."

"Who was this guy? Your number two?"

"That's not important."

Kasluga snatched a chef's knife from a block next to the stovetop. "Say something I ask you about is *not important* again and I'll stab you. Now, come on! Pritchard, right? Neville Pritchard? He was your number two. He's the guy we're talking about."

Stamoran didn't reply.

Kasluga set the knife down next to her mug. "Pritchard reported to you. So he knows your name?"

Stamoran nodded.

"Does anyone else?"

"Only him. The structure was compartmentalized. For security."

"So he could give you up. If whoever is killing his team members catches up to him, trying to put names in all the frames."

"Theoretically."

"Then this murderer could come after you, too? Oh no, Charles. I don't like that. I don't like it at all." Kasluga moved around to Stamoran's side of the kitchen island and stretched to touch his arm.

Stamoran said, "I'm in no danger. It's you I'm worried about."

"Why? I wasn't involved with that team. I was just a *PR mouthpiece.* You said so yourself. And what I did is hardly a secret. There's no reason for Pritchard to point a finger at me. Or for any of the other survivors to."

"You're not seeing the bigger picture, Susie. Singh was an old man, living alone. Bridgeman was in a hospital bed, half dead from a heart attack. Getting to those guys was easy. But me? After the president, I've got to be the best protected man in the world."

"So what do you think? This guy will come after me to get to you?"

"That's what I'd do in his shoes."

"That's not very nice." Kasluga let go of Stamoran's arm.

Stamoran shrugged.

Kasluga moved back to the other side of the island. "Can't you do something? Catch this guy before he gets to anyone else? Before he even finds out about you?"

"It's in hand."

"'In hand'? What does that mean? What are you doing, exactly?"

"That's not . . . Suffice it to say, this guy won't be on the loose for long."

"Is it safe to leave the others out there, while he's roaming around, hunting them down? Can't you lock them up somewhere where they'll be protected?"

Stamoran said nothing.

"So that's a no?"

"I can't get into the specifics. You know that. You also know I'm not someone who leaves anything to chance. So I'm going to ask you to do something for me."

"Of course. What is it?"

"Stay here. At the house."

"When?"

"Tomorrow. The next day, too. Don't go to the office. Don't go anywhere. Not till this guy is behind bars."

"You cannot be serious."

"I'm completely serious."

"That's the dumbest thing you've ever asked me to do. I have meetings scheduled all day tomorrow. All day the next. Aside from me, only three women head up a top 500 company. Versus 496 men. You know that. So if I don't show up, what are all those men going to say? She's flaky. Unreliable. Not up to the job. Weak. The knives would be out for me before the sun was halfway up."

"What would people say about your job skills if you got electro-cuted? That's what happened to Singh. Or if you *fell* out of a twelfth-floor window? Like Bridgeman. Susie, think about it. You can't be CEO of anything if you're dead."

"Goddamn it!" Kasluga picked up her mug and flung it into the sink. It shattered, spraying rivulets of pale greenish-brown liquid all over the stainless-steel backsplash. "I'm going to work out. We'll talk about this later."

* * *

Roberta and Veronica Sanson caught up with each other at the New Orleans Airport Hilton, as planned. They had arrived on separate flights, from different airports. They were traveling under fake IDs. They took courtesy shuttles twenty minutes apart. The only unexpected detail was that Roberta got to the hotel first. The airline schedules had her a quarter hour behind her sister, but the baggage handlers at Midway were working slowly that day. They were causing all kinds of delays. But the wrinkle was a minor one. Roberta figured it didn't call for any major recalibration, so she slid straight into her next task. She bought an iced tea at the hotel's ground-floor café, carried it outside to a seating area behind a cutesy white picket fence, and settled in to watch the valet parking station at the side of the curb.

When Veronica arrived she made the valet station her first port of call. She sauntered up to the guy behind the stand and said, "Evening. How are you doing today?"

The valet shrugged. "Fine, I guess. Thank you for asking. You collecting your car?"

Veronica shook her head. "Not me. I don't drive. I'm on my way to check in. But here's the kicker. I hear this is a great party town, and I'm only here for one night. I don't want to waste my time in some lame-ass dive. So, I was wondering, do you live around here?"

"Born and bred."

"That's what I was hoping you'd say. What's your name?"

"Riccardo."

"Nice to meet you, Riccardo. I'm Stephanie. And here's my question. If you had a good friend coming to visit who knows how to enjoy herself but has no time to waste, where would you take her?"

"Enrico's. A block away from Bourbon Street. All the fun but a lot more class. Can't go wrong there."

"What if this friend wanted to . . . go wrong?"

Riccardo smiled. "In that case, The Vault. A person can get into all sorts of trouble there."

Veronica smiled back. "Sounds like you're speaking from experience."

"Maybe. But we've just met. Maybe I should take the Fifth."

"Or maybe we should meet there, later, and you could show me what's up. Given that I'm a stranger here and you have all this . . . experience."

Riccardo's smile grew wider. "Sure. We could do that. I get out of here at eleven."

"Excellent. See you there around midnight?"

"Count on it."

Veronica walked away, feeling the valet's gaze on her ass, and headed for the hotel entrance. She twisted her hair into a tight knot at the back of her head, approached the desk, and booked herself a room. Just for one night. She paid cash. The ID she used showed the name Cailin Delaney. She signed all the forms the clerk handed her, took her change and her room key, and walked back outside. She threaded her way through a gap in the fence around the café's seating area and paused next to an empty table. She scanned the space like she was looking for someone. She leaned down and rested the tips of three fingers on the tabletop. She didn't look at Roberta. She knew her sister was watching. After a moment she curled her ring finger up, leaving two fingers showing, then a moment later she flexed her hand so that all four fingers were touching the table. She stayed still for a moment. Then she shrugged like the person she'd hoped to find hadn't showed up, headed inside, and made her way to room 324.

*　*　*

Outside, Roberta continued to watch the valet station. She let a black convertible come and go. Three domestic sedans. A Jeep. Then she drained the last of her tea and stood up. A minivan had stopped by the curb. Its passenger door opened and a woman climbed out. She looked stiff and tired and irritated. She would be in her mid-thirties, Roberta guessed, and was wearing white shorts, a pink blouse, and sandals. The blouse had a large oval stain on it. Her hair looked like it hadn't seen a brush in days. She stretched her back, grunted, then turned and rolled open the rear door. Four kids instantly spilled out. The oldest was maybe twelve. The youngest, six. They were all boys and right away they were chasing and yelling and shoving. Roberta had seen packs of wild dogs fighting over a prize carcass that were calmer. The mother started herding the boys toward the hotel, arms outstretched, shaking her head. A man appeared at the back of the van. Presumably the father. He swung up the load gate and began hauling out a bunch of bright, multicolored suitcases. The valet helped him load them onto a baggage cart. Then he handed the father a claim ticket and looped around to the driver's door.

The father seemed in no hurry to catch up with his family. He slipped his valet ticket into the back pocket of his baggy shorts and started to push the cart with one hand. It was a halfhearted effort. The cart barely moved. It was rolling so slowly that Roberta had to adjust her own pace. She changed her angle slightly then pulled a notebook out of her bag. Pretended to be checking something written inside it as she walked. Made out like she didn't realize she was on a collision course. And bumped right into the guy. Her knee wound up brushing against his inner thigh. She shrieked and dropped her book. It landed right in front of him. He let go of the cart and stepped aside. Took a moment to gather himself. Then leaned down, retrieved the book, and handed it back to Roberta.

She said, "Thank you so much. You're very kind. And I'm sorry I was so clumsy."

The guy grinned and straightened the front of his crumpled shirt. "Don't worry about it. That was the most exciting thing that's happened to me all week." *You say that now,* Roberta thought. *Wait till you try to get your minivan back . . .*

Chapter 5

Two cars were stopped at the side of a road south of Annapolis, Maryland, between Back Creek and the Chesapeake Bay. They were tucked in together, right after the crest of a tight bend, in darkness. Not the safest place to park, but the drivers had no choice. The road was narrow and it was lined with trees, already in leaf, which restricted the view of the old, peaceful houses that were scattered along either side. Soft lights twinkled faintly through the ancient shrubs and bushes that filled most of the gaps between the trunks, making it harder still to observe the buildings.

The first car was empty. Two men were sitting in the second. They had partial sight of one of the houses. They'd brought binoculars, a camera with a long lens, and a pair of portable radios. One of the men was writing in a log book. He had a flashlight in one hand. His fingers were covering a chunk of the lens which smothered most of the beam and turned the little light that did escape a subdued pink. He had a cheap ballpoint pen in his other hand. He jotted down the time. The place. His initial observations. Stuff he would need later for the report he would have to write. He had just finished recording what he could see when his radio crackled into life. It was one of the guys from the other car. They had made their way around back, behind the house, and were reconnoitering on foot.

The voice on the radio said, "Pritchard's here. Positive ID. I saw him through the kitchen window, clearing dishes. Over."

The guy with the pen said, "Is he alone? Over."

"Affirmative. There's no one with him. And he washed only one plate and one wineglass."

"Is he still there?"

"Negative. He's gone upstairs. The first-floor lights went off. The bathroom light came on. Wait. It just went off. Now his bedroom light is on."

"He's getting ready for bed?"

"Looks that way. Wait. His bedroom light just went off as well. So do we grab him now? Or wait for him to get settled?"

The guy with the pen took a moment to think. This wasn't his first rodeo. He liked his targets dopey and compliant. He'd learned the hard way what could happen if they weren't. Pritchard had drunk at least one glass of wine, which was a good start. Then it takes the average person between forty-five minutes and an hour to reach deep sleep. So experience dictated that they should wait ninety minutes. To be on the safe side. To give themselves a good chance that Pritchard would be away with the fairies. Then pick his locks and approach his bedroom with maximum stealth. Nine times out of ten the cuffs would be on before the target's eyes were even open. But this operation was different. The orders came right from the top. Which meant the result would be under the microscope. His performance would be, too. And the word *immediate* had been used. Even if the arrest went like clockwork a delay could take some of the shine off it. And if something went wrong, it would be blamed on his decision to wait. He was under no illusions about that.

The guy with the pen hit the Transmit button on the side of his handset and said, "Egress points at the rear?"

The voice on the radio crackled back, "Seven, as expected. Three windows, second floor. Two windows, one personnel door, first floor. One personnel door, rear of garage."

"OK. Form up. Watch them in case he tries to bail out. We're hitting the front door in ninety seconds."

Charles Stamoran was in his study, rereading one of the day's reports, when his wife found him. She was wearing a white bathrobe, knotted in the front, and her hair was still wet from the shower. Her feet were bare and her skin was glowing from the recent heat and steam. She smelled of all kinds of shampoos and conditioners and lotions. Stamoran found the combination a little overpowering, although he had never admitted that to her. He said, "Well?"

Kasluga crossed the room, perched on the ottoman in front of her husband's armchair, and stretched out to touch his knee. She said, "Charles, I'm sorry about before."

Stamoran didn't reply.

She said, "Two days."

Stamoran frowned. He hated it when his wife dangled an unfinished comment and clammed up until he coaxed the rest of the information out of her. He tried to resist the follow-up, but as always, he failed. He said, "What about two days?"

"I'll lay low, like you asked. Stay here. Keep away from the office. Give you time to catch the guy."

"Why two days? Why set a timetable? Why not stay safe until he's in custody?"

Kasluga shrugged. "It was you who said two days. And I've found a way to turn a two-day absence into an advantage. Any longer and it won't work."

"Two days was just a sensible starting point. Not a maximum duration. And what won't work?"

Kasluga leaned in closer and lowered her voice like she was afraid of being overheard. "I've been working on something. An acquisition. A major one. A game-changer. I've been keeping it under the radar so that if it doesn't pan out, I won't lose face in the industry. I figured I'd wait till the ink was dry then claim credit for it as a fait accompli. But just now I made some calls. Looks like we're home and dry. The lawyers have cleared the final obstacle and swear the papers will be signed within forty-eight hours. So I've whispered in a couple of ears. Seeded some rumors. Made out like the deal is on life support. A bunch of the asshole men will be getting hard-ons, thinking I'm going to publicly crash and burn. And when the result is a triumph, it's going to look like I dropped out of sight to personally intervene. I'll be the hero. But if I stay away any longer, it'll look like I had nothing to do with it. I can't have that."

Two days, Stamoran thought. Maybe enough time to make an arrest. Maybe not. It was out of his control. The remaining targets were being watched. The traps were set. The guy who was picking off the scientists from '69 might try to strike again within forty-eight hours. Or he might not. Stamoran had no idea what was driving the guy's schedule. But he wasn't too worried about it, because Susan was off the money in one important respect. The arrest wasn't the crux of the matter. The key was removing Pritchard from the game. Stamoran checked his watch. The team he had sent should already be at Pritchard's house.

Stamoran looked at his wife. He nodded and said, "Two days will be enough."

The guy with the pen in the car in Annapolis was named Paul Birch. He put his pen away, took out his gun, and turned to his partner, Simon Stainrod. Birch nodded. Stainrod pulled the lever that popped the trunk and the two men climbed out. Stainrod retrieved a tactical battering ram—a heavy metal cylinder nine inches in diameter and eighteen inches long, with two articulated handles fixed to its center line—and they crossed the road, side by side, Birch a couple of feet ahead, six feet apart. They ignored the gate and stepped over the two-foot-high wall. Walked parallel with the path, one on either side, feet in the flower bed, churning up the damp dirt and crushing the shrubs that were growing there. They reached the house and stepped up onto the porch. Stainrod swung the ram back then heaved it forward, hard, waist high, parallel with the ground, gaining momentum as it passed through the air. It slammed into the door near the keyhole for a heavy-looking lock. The wood splintered. The screws tore away from the hinges. The frame ripped off the wall and the door careened back into the hallway like a punch-drunk boxer reeling from a knockout blow. Then it flopped over, landed horizontally, and slid until its top edge was pressed against the foot of a grandfather clock. Stainrod dropped the ram, pulled his gun, and took up a position tucked in tight against the wall near the ruined doorway. Birch ran past him. He left a trail of muddy footprints over the remains of the door, along the hallway, and up the stairs. He knew where the bedroom was. He knew where all the rooms were. He'd memorized a faxed copy of the house's original design before leaving the Pentagon that evening. He found the right door. Held his flashlight parallel with the barrel of his gun. Kicked the door open. Burst through. And lined up his gun on the head of the bed.

Paying for a night in an airport hotel and only using the room for a couple of hours was not strictly necessary. Not an optimal use of funds. Not the kind of thing Roberta and Veronica Sanson would have considered doing even a month before. But under the circumstances, they figured they could justify it. There were some definite benefits. They could hang out without anyone seeing them together. They could order food from room service and eat without the risk of other restaurant guests remembering either of them. And very soon—maybe in only a few days' time—they were going to be rich, so the cost aspect was essentially a nonissue.

How rich they were going to be was yet to be determined. But when Owen Buck's investigator had tracked them down, and they had verified his bona fides, and Buck had tried to salve his dying conscience by revealing what had happened in India back in '69, he had left them with no doubt. A heap of cash was out there. The way they saw things, it had their names on it. They were entitled to it. They were going to take it. And that would be a fitting way to round off what was needed to right the wrong that Buck swore had been done to them.

It took Birch a moment to register the fact, but the bed was empty. He checked all four corners of the room. The bathroom. Under the bed. Inside the closet. And found no one. He cleared the other upstairs rooms. There were two more bedrooms and another bathroom, but no sign of Pritchard and no indication that anyone else lived there. So Birch went back downstairs. He stopped in the hallway and shot a glance at Stainrod. Stainrod shook his head. Birch moved on and searched the living room. The dining room. The kitchen. A tiny laundry room. And finally the garage.

There was no sign of Pritchard in any of them.

Birch returned to the hallway and used his radio to call the pair who were watching the back of the house. He said, "Anything?"

The reply was loud and clear. "Nada."

"Are you certain?"

"One hundred percent."

"OK. One of you come inside. Help me search. Pritchard must be hiding. He must have a bolt-hole somewhere. In the crawl space. The attic. A hollow wall. Somewhere. And he must still be here. His bed hasn't been laid in. His closet is full of clothes. I saw a bunch of suitcases still in there, too. His car is in the garage. And we know he didn't leave on foot. So we need to find him. Immediately."

The sisters ate, and talked, and watched TV, and took turns showering, and were ready to leave the hotel by 11:30 P.M. That gave them a half-hour cushion in case Riccardo's shift finished late. Veronica left first. She walked down the stairs, strolled through the deserted lobby, crossed to the courtesy bus stop, and waited ten minutes for a ride to the airport's departure terminal. Then she made her way straight to arrivals and found the passenger pickup area.

Roberta stayed in the room another five minutes then headed outside, to the valet stand. She smiled at the new guy on duty and handed over her stolen collection ticket.

The guy returned with the minivan after fifteen minutes. Roberta gave him an average tip—not memorably big, not unforgettably small—and climbed in behind the wheel. She drove away from the hotel and followed the signs to the airport, and then the arrival terminal. She drifted to a stop by the curb at the far end of the pickup zone and immediately Veronica stepped out from behind a pillar. A moment later she was in the passenger seat. A minute after that Roberta was speeding toward the city, following a route to an address she had memorized before they had arrived in Chicago.

Chapter 6

The phone in the Pentagon rang at 9:00 A.M. Eastern, the following morning. That was 8:00 A.M. Central, where the call originated. Right on time.

The guy who answered listened in silence then hung up, switched to an internal line, and dialed the extension for an office that was one floor higher up and one ring closer to the center of the building.

Stamoran picked up immediately. He said, "Is it done?"

"Neville Pritchard is not in custody," the guy recited. "Repeat, not. He was positively identified, alone, at his home, but in the short time between confirming the sighting and the team gaining entry, he disappeared. How he evaded capture is unknown. His current whereabouts are unknown. Records indicate he received no phone calls prior to the raid. No other signals were observed or detected. Therefore he is believed to be acting alone. Attempts to locate him are ongoing with the utmost urgency."

Stamoran laid the receiver down, leaned back in his chair, closed his eyes, and silently cursed. He should have sent snipers, not nursemaids. Especially not nursemaids who somehow tipped their hand in the middle of a simple snatch job. Which they must have done. There was no other explanation. Pritchard had been alone. No one had contacted him. The report made that clear.

Stamoran took a long, slow breath. He tried to view the situation rationally. The news wasn't great. They didn't have Pritchard. But equally, the news wasn't terrible. There was no reason to believe that Pritchard had been captured. He was just in the wind. So whoever was going after the scientists from '69 didn't have him, either. The secret was safe. For now.

Stamoran opened his eyes and picked up the phone. "I want the team from last night to understand they have one chance to redeem themselves. I want two additional units assigned. The best we have. I want Pritchard found. Like, yesterday. And when he is found, if he tries to run again, I want him stopped. By any means necessary."

Sergeant Hall was already at her post at Rock Island Arsenal. She was set for a busy morning. A truck was due in from Little Rock Air Force Base, Arkansas. Paperwork was going to be involved, followed by some manual labor. It was a process Hall was familiar with. She had gone through it more than seventy times in the last year. She knew exactly what to expect so was already at the guard post at the base's main entrance, waiting, when the M35 Deuce and a Half rumbled into sight, looking tired and worn in its faded desert-sand paint job.

Hall waited for the gate to clank back into place behind the truck then climbed into her Humvee and led the way to the storeroom Reacher had visited the previous day. It was a step called for by regulations, not necessity. The sergeant who was driving the truck had pulled that duty more than fifty times. He could have followed the route with his eyes shut but was required to have an escort for as long as he was on-site. He didn't mind. And neither did Hall. It was an arrangement that worked very well for both of them.

Hall drove slowly until she reached the front of the building, then parked well clear of the storeroom's steel door. She walked back, unlocked it, and waited for the truck to grind to a halt. She watched the driver jump out. His name was Chapellier but she privately called him *Ape* because of his short body, long arms, and hunched gait. He rolled up the flap at the rear of the truck's canvas cover and opened the metal cage that had been bolted to the load-bed floor. Then together they started to haul out the crates of weapons that had been sent back from the Gulf and stack them up on the storeroom's Intake shelves. They worked steadily and efficiently and when the truck was empty, they moved straight on to refilling it with the crates from the Red shelves. The ones that held the weapons Hall's team had earmarked for destruction.

When the final crate had been squared away and the records had been updated and signed and the doors to the storeroom and the truck's cage had been locked, Hall got back into her Humvee. Her forehead was prickling and she could feel a drop of sweat inching its way down her lower back. She shifted in her seat and watched in her mirror as Chapellier climbed into the truck. She could have made him turn around in the narrow roadway but instead she set off the way they were already facing, planning to loop around and circle back to the guardhouse from the opposite direction. That was the way she always did it. No one watching—in person, or on a screen fed by the site's network of security cameras—would have been remotely surprised.

Hall's chosen way out was a little longer than the route they had followed on the way in. It involved passing through a kind of tunnel that had been formed when a set of classrooms had been extended out over the road due to a lack of space on the site. The covered section was more than 150 feet long. Cameras were lined up along its entire length. There wasn't an inch that escaped observation.

There wasn't an inch that hadn't escaped observation when the cameras were installed. But two of those cameras had been moved. Very gradually, over the course of ten weeks. The pair nearest the center, either side of an alcove formed by a fire escape that provided a convenient marker. They had been moved by Sergeant Hall, far enough to leave a blind spot twenty-three feet long. That was enough space for an M35 truck to stop with five inches to spare, front and rear.

Hall watched for the alcove, made sure there would be room for the truck to pull up alongside her, then stopped and climbed out. She hustled around to the rear of the Humvee and lifted out a crate. A plastic one. Olive green, but not army issue. She carried it into the gap between the vehicles. Waited for Chapellier to open his door then heaved the crate up higher so he could pull it into his cab. The guy balanced it on his knees and loosened the lid. He looked inside. Pulled out a metal object. An M16 lower receiver. He checked its holes and contours. Smiled. Dropped it back into the crate and reattached the lid. Placed it on the cab floor to the side of the gear lever and passed Hall an identical crate from the passenger side footwell. She wedged it against the top step and examined its contents. A wad of cash, which she counted, as she always did. And another stack of gun parts. Civilian spec.

She looked up and said, "You need more? Already?"

Chapellier frowned. "Is there a problem?" Then he heard a sound, behind him and to the side. A metallic screech. Primitive hinges that were starved of oil after a long stint in the desert. He spun around in his seat and saw the passenger door opening. A head appeared. And a torso. Belonging to a man he didn't recognize. A huge, broad man with a ferocious scowl on his face and a gun in his hand.

"Problem?" Reacher said, leaning farther into the cab. "Guess you could put it that way. If you're big on understatement."

Roberta and Veronica Sanson's night had not gone as planned.

It had started out OK. They completed the drive from New Orleans airport to Geoff Brown's house without incident. But when they slowed to look for a suitable spot to stop and keep watch, they saw another car parked at the side of the road. A Ford Crown Victoria. Plain blue. Poverty spec. An extra antenna on the roof. Another on the trunk lid. And two men inside. Neither one was making a move to get out. This wasn't a worn-out detective's car repurposed as a cab. It wasn't someone getting home late after too many beers and fumbling with his wallet so he could pay his fare. The car was positioned deliberately. The guys inside were waiting, perfectly relaxed and still, like they knew they were there for the long haul. Like that was something they were used to.

Roberta figured they could afford one pass-by. They needed at least some idea of what they were dealing with—and in any case, continuing in the same direction was less suspicious than abruptly turning around and slinking away. Brown's house was set back about fifty feet from the road. The area around it was somewhere between rustic and overgrown, like the owner had once been on top of his yard work but in recent years had started to let it slide. Nature was gaining the upper hand. That was clear. The house itself was long and low. It had a deep porch running along the front and the white paintwork was neat and crisp. Brown was keeping up with his property maintenance, at least.

Veronica gestured toward the house and said, "Windows."

All of Brown's shades were drawn. Maybe against the heat that would start building the moment the sun came up. Maybe for privacy. But either way, it meant no one could see in. Not from any of the neighbors' houses. Not from a car parked on the street. And not by anyone prowling around the grounds.

Roberta nodded. "We can work with this."

Roberta had kept up a slow, steady speed until she reached the next intersection, where she took a left and made her way back toward the southeast side of the city. She remembered seeing some kind of abandoned industrial site there. It looked like the place was being set for demolition. A security fence had been thrown up around the perimeter and a handful of portable offices had been dumped in a cluster outside. No vehicles had been parked nearby. No lights were on. There was nothing to suggest it was a twenty-four-hour operation. But there was plenty of scope to conceal their stolen minivan until the morning.

They took turns sleeping and when Veronica woke for the second time she nudged her sister. "The guys watching Brown's house? Could mean he's the one. He could have the name we need."

Roberta shook her head. "Buck said one guy on his list knew the name. The security doesn't mean anything. Someone's connecting the dots. That's all. Former CIA assets start dropping like flies, someone at Langley's going to notice. They'll be watching all the survivors from '69."

"I guess you're right."

"You know I am." Roberta clambered back into the driver's seat and fired up the engine. "Come on. I'm starving. We need breakfast. And supplies. And then you have a call to make."

* * *

Reacher climbed up into the truck's cab and settled into the right-hand seat. He said, "OK. There are two ways we can play this."

Sergeant Chapellier sat for a moment with both hands on the wheel. Then he lunged to his left. He grabbed Hall by the front of her tunic and dragged her up and into the truck and kept on pulling until she was sprawled across his lap. He said, "No. Only one way. Get out."

Hall thrashed and struggled. She twisted around onto her back and stretched up and tried to gouge Chapellier's eyes out. Reacher didn't move.

Chapellier pinned both of Hall's arms with one of his and slid his other hand up to her throat. He turned to Reacher and said, "Get out. Now."

Reacher said, "Get out? Is that it?"

"Get out or I'll break her neck."

Reacher checked the guy's name tape. "You're not one of the world's deep thinkers, are you, Chapellier? She already gave you up. I don't need her anymore. Kill her and I can nail you for murder. Much easier than rolling up whatever kind of a racket you've got going on."

Chapellier tightened his fingers around Hall's throat. She wriggled her arms free and grabbed his wrist with both hands. She strained to pull it clear but she couldn't get the leverage. Her legs were hanging out of the open door and her weight was pulling her harder into Chapellier's grip. She was also kicking and squirming like crazy. It was an instinctive response. There was nothing she could do to stop it, but it only made her problem worse.

Reacher stretched out his left hand and flicked the truck's master switch to Off. Its engine rattled to a stop. He waited for the last raucous echo to fade away then said, "First you're going to let her go. Then you're going to tell me who you're selling those gun parts to. Or we're going to step out of the vehicle, pieces of you are going to get broken, and then you're going to tell me."

Chapellier was still for three seconds then he hauled Hall up so that she was sitting. He shoved her in the back with his right hand, launching her out of the truck, then he sprang across toward Reacher. His arms were stretched out. He was trying to grab Reacher's gun. Reacher leaned to his left and raised his elbow. Chapellier plowed into it, hard, face-first. Reacher didn't wait to assess the damage. Instead he heaved his door open and jumped down. He slid the gun into its holster. Then he leaned in and grabbed Chapellier by his right arm. He dragged him sideways. All the way to the door. He kept going until Chapellier slithered off the edge of the truck's seat and bounced down its metal steps and slammed onto the ground. Reacher rolled him over onto his back. Stepped on his neck. And twisted his arm until his shoulder and elbow and wrist were all a hair's breadth away from breaking.

Reacher said, "This is the end of the road, Chapellier. Give it up."

Chapellier whimpered and a bubble of blood billowed out of his nose. His voice was strained and husky. He croaked, "Screw you."

Reacher kept up the pressure on Chapellier's arm. He said, "Tell me something. Did you pick this spot because, A, a lot of cameras are focused on it? Or B, because no one can see what happens here?"

Chapellier grunted. He managed a faint, "Asshole."

Reacher said, "Something else for you to think about. Those gun parts are US Army property. No civilian should ever get their hands on them. So I want whoever you're selling them to behind bars. I'll need your help with that. If you cooperate, I can't hurt you. I'll need you in one piece. Or reasonably close to one piece. But if you don't help me I can do as much damage as I like. *Injuries sustained while resisting arrest.* My word against yours. And you can forget about Sergeant Hall as a friendly witness."

Veronica Sanson pulled a file from her bag, checked a number, and fished a quarter out of her pocket. She was wearing leather gloves, which made snagging the coin more difficult than usual. She finally got hold of it, dropped it into the slot on the front of the payphone, dialed, and waited. It took ten rings for her call to be answered.

"Yes?" It was a man's voice on the line, quiet and slightly breathless.

Veronica said, "Dr. Brown? Geoffrey Brown?"

"Who's asking?"

"Sir, this is Special Agent Holbeck with the Federal Bureau of Investigation. I have some news for you. Bad news, I'm afraid. And I need to ask for your assistance in a very urgent matter."

Brown took a moment to reply. "Go on."

"Sir, I'm sorry to have to tell you this, but two of your former colleagues are dead."

"Owen Buck I know about. Cancer, right? Who else?"

"Dr. Buck died of natural causes, as you say, but I'm calling about two others. Varinder Singh and Keith Bridgeman."

"Bridgeman and Singh? Dead? When? How?"

"Dr. Singh was electrocuted. Dr. Bridgeman fell out of a window. Reports in the press are suggesting their deaths may have been accidental. Those reports are wrong."

"There was foul play? You're sure?"

"One hundred percent. The Bureau wouldn't be involved, otherwise."

"Who killed them?"

"That's where I need your help. Our sketch artists have put together a likeness. I need you to take a look. Tell me if you recognize the person."

"How would I recognize him?"

"He's killing members of your former research team, Doctor. There must be a connection. And he's not going to stop until we catch him. We believe you will be his next target. That's why I've come here, now. So please, take a look at the sketch. It'll only take a minute and it could save your life. I could come to your house and—"

"No. But I'll meet you. Somewhere public. Forgive me. Old habits."

Veronica smiled. "I understand. I'm working out of the local field office while I'm in town. There's no safer place than that, right? I'll give you the address. And if you could come right away, that would be in everyone's best interests. Particularly yours."

Chapter 7

It took Dr. Brown thirty minutes to reach the FBI field office. And another thirty seconds to discover that Agent Holbeck didn't exist.

Brown knew what he should do next. Run. His go-bag was in the trunk of his car. Old habits. He could take it and disappear. Stay out of sight until he figured out who was coming after him. And how to stop them. That's what he would have done at any time during his career. And when he was newly retired. But now there was a problem. Without the human contact that comes with work, for the first time in his life, he had started to feel lonely. He didn't have any friends in the city. He wasn't a sociable man so he wasn't likely to make any new ones. He didn't get on with his neighbors. And he knew no one would ever want to live with him. So he adopted a cat. Hercules. Another creature that no one had wanted. Who was still at his house. With no way to get out. No way to get food. No way to get water.

It took Brown twenty-five minutes to get back to his street. He slowed down and drove past his house. It looked the same as when he had left it. The drapes were all drawn. The door was closed. There were no cars parked at the curb. No strangers loitering on the sidewalk or poking around his yard. That allayed one of his fears, but he was still worried about something else. A couple of times while he was driving home he'd thought he was being followed. He'd thought it, but he wasn't certain. So he took a left. Then a right. Then he stopped dead. No cars steered desperately around him. None screeched to a halt behind him. There was no one in sight in his mirror. He shook his head. Chalked it up to rusty instincts. And too much adrenaline. He was out of practice. That was all. With that concern put to bed he figured it was safe enough to loop around and pull up onto his driveway. Dart inside. Grab Hercules. And race back out. A couple of minutes, max.

Brown opened his front door and paused. He listened. He couldn't hear anything. Couldn't smell anything. But he could feel something. A subliminal disturbance in the silent vibrations he was accustomed to the house giving out. Someone was there. Waiting. For him. Rusty or not, Brown's instincts told him to get out. Immediately. He started to turn. Then he heard a muffled squawk. From the living room. It was Hercules. He was in distress. Brown crept forward. Stopped at the threshold. Listened. Heard another squawk. More anguished this time. He reached for the door handle. Took a breath. And burst into the room.

A woman was standing next to Brown's favorite armchair. Her dark hair was pulled back. She was holding Hercules tight to her chest. Another woman was on the other side of the chair. Same height. Same build. Same hair. They were completely still. Their faces were expressionless, like statues. Neither of them spoke.

Brown took a step forward. "Let go of my cat."

The first woman's face cracked into a smile. She said, "Dr. Brown, we're glad you're back. Your cat doesn't seem to like us. Please, sit. I'll drop him on your lap."

Brown stayed where he was. "I recognize your voice. You called me. Pretended to be from the FBI. Why?"

"I apologize for the subterfuge. We didn't mean to mislead you. We just need to talk. Privately. And two men were watching your house so we couldn't just knock on your door. We figured they would follow you if you went somewhere. Give us a chance to get in, unobserved."

Brown crossed to the window, peered around the side of the drapes, then turned back. "The blue sedan? What the hell's going on?"

"What I told you on the phone? Aside from me being an agent, it's true. Particularly the part about you being in danger. We're here to help you."

"Help me? How? Who are you?"

"We'll come to that. But we need a piece of information first. Please sit. Let me explain."

Brown shuffled across to the chair and lowered himself into it.

The woman handed over the cat. "Your research team in India, in 1969. There were eight people on it."

"India? Never been there."

"Don't waste time. The threat against you is imminent. Believe me. So, eight people."

Brown shook his head. "Seven."

"Eight." The woman took the handwritten list out of her pocket and passed it to Brown. "We know seven names. You need to tell us the one that's missing. So that we can protect the surviving members who were involved."

Brown glanced at the piece of paper. Owen Buck's name was written in a different hand. He must have given up the rest of them. He always had been the weakest. Always talking about coming clean. But he must have been slipping if he could no longer count. "There were seven people. Their names are all here."

"There were eight. See the question mark? One name is missing. You need to tell us who it is."

"There were seven. I was there. You weren't. So I know what I'm talking about. You don't. And you shouldn't be asking questions about '69. No one should. It's time to close the book. Time for you to leave."

"You live in a nice neighborhood, Dr. Brown. Although there are a lot of busy roads around here. Lots of drivers in a hurry, not concentrating, not looking where they're going. It would be very easy for a person to get run down. Even easier for a small animal. Like a cat."

"I'm not going to listen to this. You need to leave. Now."

Brown held Hercules to his chest with one hand and used his other arm to start hauling himself out of the chair. He made it halfway then the second woman darted around behind him and leaned on his shoulders, forcing him back down. His elbow shot out to the side, almost knocking his pipe and tobacco pouch off his side table.

The first woman said, "If a cat did get hit by a car, would it be killed right away? Maybe, I guess. But maybe not. Imagine finding yours, all crushed and bleeding. Scooping him up. Racing to the veterinarian's office."

"No."

"Waiting outside the operating room door. Praying he can be saved. Worrying that the damage is too severe."

"I swear, there are only seven names. Anyone tells you otherwise, they're wrong. You want to cause pain to prove I'm not lying, hurt me. I don't care. Just leave my cat alone. He hasn't done anything to you."

The woman took the list back and slid it into her pocket. "OK. We're done here. I believe you. And I apologize. This is important so we had to be sure. I'm sorry we upset you." She paused for a moment, then said, "You know, you're looking very pale all of a sudden. Can I get you some coffee before we go? Tea? Something stronger?"

"Are you kidding? You break into my house and threaten to kill my cat and think I'm going to drink anything you give me? Forget it. You can show yourselves out."

The women made it as far as the door then stopped and turned around. The first one said, "Where are our manners? We forgot to introduce ourselves. I'm Veronica Sanson. This is my sister, Roberta."

Brown didn't answer. He hugged Hercules a little tighter.

Veronica said, "Our father was Morgan Sanson. It's important you know that."

Brown didn't need to be told. He knew who Morgan Sanson was. He took a deep breath and listened to the footsteps in his hallway. They approached the front door. It opened. Closed again. And there was silence. He breathed out. Gave Hercules a stroke and reached for his pipe. His nerves were shot. He packed the bowl. Brushed away a stray strand of tobacco. Held his lighter so its flame flickered and the tobacco began to smolder. He took a long, deep drag. Gulped down the smoke. Held it in his lungs. Exhaled, slowly. Sucked down some more. Kept the routine going until his head settled against his chair. His eyes rolled back in their sockets. Then globs of off-white foam started to dribble out of his mouth.

| 65

Veronica and Roberta stepped back into the room. They had never left the house. They watched as Brown's back arched. The cat jumped down and ran behind the couch. Brown jerked and grabbed his stomach. Then his chest. He vomited, a long greenish watery stream. It soaked the front of his shirt and his pants and sprayed across a wide arc of carpet. He jerked again. His whole body spasmed. Twice. Three times. Then he flopped back and lay completely still.

Veronica and Roberta waited for five minutes, to be certain. Then they moved into the hallway. Brown's telephone was sitting on a low, square table. Veronica put her gloves on and took an object from her pocket. A small tape recorder. She worked its buttons until she found the place she wanted, then picked up the phone. She dialed 911. Waited for the emergency operator to answer. Then she held the recorder up to the mouthpiece and pressed Play.

"Help me?" Brown's voice said, a little muffled but easy enough to make out.

Reacher gave Sergeant Chapellier a couple of minutes to stem the bleeding and stretch his sore joints. He checked that Sergeant Hall wasn't too much the worse for wear after getting flung out of the truck. Then he climbed back into the cab and made Chapellier drive behind Hall's Humvee as far as the Arsenal's guard post. He had formalities to complete. Medical attention had to be arranged. Escorts organized. Paperwork filled out. But first he had to make a phone call. Time was suddenly of the essence. Special arrangements needed to be made and Reacher knew how the machine worked.

The regular cogs would grind too slowly. Shortcuts were called for; otherwise, a golden opportunity was going to slip through their fingers. Meat Loaf may have thought that two out of three ain't bad, but Reacher didn't agree. That was for damn sure.

Roberta and Veronica had expected there to be vomiting. They had researched the side effects carefully when they were deciding what kind of substance would be best to add to Geoff Brown's tobacco. They just hadn't realized how much there would be. And they hadn't anticipated that Brown would put his keys back in his pocket when he arrived home. They'd imagined that he would set them down on a table in the hallway or hang them on a convenient hook. The reality only dawned on them when Veronica dropped the receiver back onto its cradle after she ended the 911 call. Roberta had picked the lock on the front door when they broke into the house but they couldn't leave that way because the agents who were watching the place were on station again, outside. They couldn't climb out of a rear-facing window because there would be no way to lock it and they figured that a single unlocked, accessible window would be suspicious. So they needed the key to the back door. Only now it was on a ring that was encased in vomit-soaked cotton and attached to a corpse. Retrieving it was not an appealing prospect.

Veronica said, "Maybe there's a spare?"

Roberta glanced at her watch. "Go look. Quickly."

Veronica ran to the kitchen. She checked the walls near the door. There were no hooks or shelves with keys on them. She opened the nearest drawers. The cabinets beneath them. Looked inside the refrigerator. And found nothing that seemed like a viable hiding place. She figured she'd used up two minutes. They had maybe two more before the police would arrive, so she ran back to the living room. Roberta was standing six feet away from Brown's body. She looked like she was ready to puke, herself. She said, "Anything?"

Veronica shook her head, then held up her hands. She said, "My gloves are leather. Yours are disposable. You do it."

As soon as everything was squared away at Rock Island, Reacher set out to drive east, to Chicago. He made good time, so when he left the highway and saw a line of large, soulless buildings crammed around three sides of a square, open-air parking lot, he pulled over. He had no civilian clothes with him and he knew he was going to need some later in the day. He figured he might as well get the task out of the way as quickly as possible, so he headed into a sporting goods store and picked up the first things he saw that would fit. Black sneakers. Beige pants with all kinds of extra pockets sewn onto the legs. A blue T-shirt with a logo he'd never seen before. And a lightweight, blue, waterproof jacket.

Reacher paid for the clothes and changed in the store's fitting room. He folded his BDUs, placed them in the bag the clerk had given him, and stowed them in his trunk, alongside his duffel. Then he continued toward the west side of the city, slightly south of the center, which he figured put him closer to the White Sox than the Cubs. He found the building he was looking for without difficulty. The FBI field office. A mid-rise tower of glass and concrete. It had a bowed front but otherwise looked like a child had designed it with a construction set that only had square-shaped parts.

Roberta and Veronica Sanson heard the siren at the same moment. They listened to it draw closer. Crossed to the window and peered around the side of the drapes. Watched a patrol car barrel down the street and slide to a halt outside the house. And saw the two agents jump out of their Crown Victoria and intercept the cops before they made it halfway up the path.

That was their cue. The watchers were occupied, so Roberta and Veronica hustled to the back door. Roberta had already unlocked it. They hurried out into the yard, relocked the door, and retraced their steps to their stolen minivan. They'd left it three streets from Geoff Brown's house, facing away. Veronica climbed up into the passenger seat. Roberta dropped her gloves and Brown's key down a grate in the gutter and slid behind the wheel.

Veronica waited until they were under way, then said, "Where next?"

It was an important tactical decision. They couldn't work their way down the list in order, or whoever had noticed that the former CIA agents were dying would know where to focus their resources. Roberta and Veronica wanted their opposition spread as thin as possible, which meant picking their next target at random. But nothing is truly random. All kinds of studies have been done. Subliminal influences shape people's choices in diverse, subtle ways. So they resorted to a technique they'd learned years ago.

Roberta said, "Three names left to pick from." In her head she allocated a number to each remaining one. "Give me three colors."

"Red. Silver. White."

The next car they saw was white. The third color Veronica had named. The third name on Roberta's mental list was Michael Rymer, who lived in northern Colorado.

Roberta said, "Get ready for some altitude. We're going to Denver."

* * *

Reacher dumped his car in the lot and headed inside to the reception desk. He asked for Agent Ottoway, who did exist. She was small and wiry with long black hair and she arrived to collect him after only a couple of minutes. She used a plastic card to let him through a turnstile and escorted him to a bank of elevators and then on to a meeting room at the end of a corridor on the third floor. It was a small, stale space with no windows. It smelled of cigarette smoke and sweat, like half its air was piped in from a bar and the other half from a locker room, and its contents made it look like a dumping ground for redundant furniture. There were half a dozen chairs. Two tables, one balanced on the other, upside down, with its legs pointing at the ceiling. And a handful of squat bookcases that were all missing half their shelves.

Reacher wasn't surprised by the place. He knew the score when it came to interagency cooperation. Choosing a room like that was a way of expressing a lack of enthusiasm on the part of the hosts. Reacher could understand their position. He was on their turf. His request hadn't come through the proper channels. And it had come with next to no notice. It had probably stretched their resources thin on one of their other operations. But if this one worked out, it was going to be worth the inconvenience. He was confident about that.

Agent Ottoway's supervisor arrived hard on their heels and he kept the briefing mercifully short. Just the three of them, huddled together on dilapidated chairs under a flickering fluorescent light. No need for notes or diagrams. No unnecessary complications, which was the way Reacher liked it. Just confirmation of the objective. The time and place. The principal players. And the code word should it become necessary to abort.

When all the details were set, Agent Ottoway led the way back to the elevator. She hit the button and while they waited for the car to arrive, she said, "Captain, can I ask you one question?"

Reacher said, "Shoot."

"What are you planning on wearing tonight?"

Reacher glanced down at his shirt and pants. "What I'm wearing now."

"That's what I was afraid you'd say."

"Is there a problem?"

"You might as well hang a sign around your neck saying *Undercover Cop*. All right. This is what's happening. If you have plans for the afternoon, cancel them. I'm taking you shopping."

Chapter 8

The phone in the Pentagon rang again at 1:02 P.M. Eastern. Not a scheduled time for a call.

The guy who answered it listened, hung up, then moved to his outer office and dialed another number. It was for a cellular phone mounted in a car that was traveling southeast on Pennsylvania Avenue.

Charles Stamoran picked up after one ring. "Tell me Pritchard's been found."

"Sorry, sir," the Pentagon guy said. "This is about Geoffrey Brown. He's dead. The cause is pending confirmation from the lab, but a New Orleans PD officer who attended the scene was confident he recognized the symptoms. Brown suffered a fatal reaction to the venom of the Sonoran Desert toad. He smoked the dried secretions mixed with tobacco in a pipe that was found at his side. People do this for its psychedelic effect, and to combat psychological conditions such as PTSD. If Brown was new to the practice, he could have used too high a concentration. The source of the substance is being traced but is most likely one of the stores in the city that caters for pseudo-religious ceremonies. Brown had no visitors and received no deliveries. He called 911 himself, so the police think his death is likely an accident, but cold feet following a suicide attempt cannot be ruled out."

Stamoran lowered the receiver to his lap and glanced out of the car window at the swarms of people rushing in and out of one office building after another. He felt himself getting angry. He could think of an explanation that couldn't be ruled out. Toad venom? Seriously? Brown did smoke a pipe. Had smoked one for years. And after some of the things he'd done, it would be a miracle if he never had some kind of psychological reaction. But there was no way he would involve himself in New Age hippy designer-drug bullshit. Not voluntarily. A generous pour of bourbon and branch? Yes. Smoking secretions harvested from poisonous amphibians? No. Not in a million years. Someone was adding insult to injury.

Stamoran lifted the handset. "Waiting to catch this guy when he strikes isn't working. We need to get proactive. Leave the agents watching Rymer and Adam in place but I want a task force set up, as well. By tomorrow. Reps from the army, CIA, FBI, Treasury, and any other agency this guy could be from based on his performance and obvious training. I want him identified. I want a focused suspect pool our people in the field can work with. And I want him stopped."

At eight o'clock that evening Reacher was in a bar in River North, Chicago. He was wearing the second set of new clothes he'd bought that day. A pair of black jeans, a dark green shirt, a leather jacket, and black ankle boots that were secured with straps. Agent Ottoway was sitting opposite him across a low, round table. She was wearing a plain black dress and her hair was curlier than it had been earlier.

The bar was fashioned out of an old factory. The walls were brick. They were pitted and stained and riddled with holes and sockets and brackets where all kinds of equipment must once have been secured. Like industrial petroglyphs, Reacher thought, telling the story of the people who spent their lives working there. He spent a few minutes trying to decipher them, then glanced across to a stage that was set up in the far corner. A three-piece band was midway through its set. The performance was competent from a technical standpoint but it was nothing Reacher would call exciting. Nothing that was going to knock Howlin' Wolf or Magic Slim off his list of favorites.

Ottoway nudged Reacher's foot with her own under the table and nodded almost imperceptibly toward the entrance. Sergeant Chapellier had walked in. He was wearing stained jeans and a Metallica tour shirt. He paused for a moment like he was looking for someone then made his way across to an empty table. It was six feet away from Reacher and Ottoway's, in a section that was separated from the rest of the space by a line of vertical iron pipes. There were a dozen of them, three feet apart, four inches in diameter, rusted almost black. Ten were lit from above. They all should have been. But the lamps over two of them had failed and that left them lost in the gloom.

Reacher pretended to be watching the bartender prepare drinks but he kept one eye on Chapellier. He was fidgeting, drumming his fingers on the tabletop, and glancing repeatedly at the door. No one came through. One of the waitstaff picked up a tray of drinks. He was aiming to deliver it to a table at the back. It was made out of an old beer keg with things that looked like upturned buckets as seats. Two twenty-something guys were perched there along with two women who looked a little younger.

One of the guys gestured for the waiter to hurry up. Maybe he was thirsty. Maybe he was trying to show off. But whatever the reason, he wasn't helping. The waiter was doing his best. The space was crowded. The furniture was jammed in at all kinds of crooked angles. There was no set path for him to get through. There was no point trying to make him go faster. A couple of times he nearly dropped the tray. Once he skidded on a wet patch on the floor. And finally, when he was almost at the right table, he knocked into another customer.

The man was hard to miss. He was six foot six with a huge beard, a baseball cap worn backward, baggy jeans, and a plaid shirt with buttons that were struggling to contain his gut. He glanced around. He was checking to see if anyone was looking. He saw that plenty of people were. So he shoved the waiter in the chest. Hard.

The waiter stumbled back a couple of steps then lost his balance. The tray slipped out of his hands. Four drinks hit the floor. Three beers and some kind of fancy cocktail with an umbrella in it. The waiter tumbled over backward and hit his head on the base of another table.

Chapellier paid no attention to the altercation. His gaze was now fixed on the door. No one came through. There were a couple dozen people already in the railed-off section of the bar. None of them lifted a finger to help the waiter. Not even to haul him back onto his feet. He finally rolled over then crawled forward to retrieve his tray. The fat guy pushed it farther away with his foot. Still no one did anything. Still no one came through the door.

The waiter came back a couple of minutes later with a mop and a broom and a bucket. He started to clean up the mess. The fat guy took every opportunity to nudge and jostle him. No one in the bar did anything to help. Then Reacher stopped watching the sideshow. Because someone had finally come in. A man, late thirties, loose shirt, baggy jeans, and a battered leather messenger bag slung over one shoulder. He was scrawny with lank, unwashed hair and a week's stubble on his face. Reacher recognized the look. A dollar would get a dime that the guy was a former soldier. A drug habit had led to stealing had led to a dishonorable discharge. A pattern Reacher had seen play out a thousand times.

The scrawny guy hustled across to Chapellier's table and sat down. The waiter appeared and Chapellier said something, then held up two fingers. The guys sat in silence until the waiter came back with two beers. They nodded, clinked glasses, and both drained their drinks in a single gulp. The scrawny guy belched, then set his bag down on the empty seat next to him. Chapellier picked it up. Glanced inside. Then took a vehicle key from his pocket and placed it on the table. The scrawny guy nodded again, took the key, got up, and headed for the door.

Ottoway turned away and took a radio from her purse. She held it close to her mouth and said, "He's coming out. He'll be heading for a vehicle. Wait till he's in it, then take him."

A minute passed then Ottoway's radio crackled back into life. A man's voice said, "We have him. The contraband, too. It's a wrap."

Susan Kasluga hung up the phone and closed her eyes. She breathed out slowly and felt the knots in her shoulders ease, just a little. She was sitting at her desk in her home office. It was a small room but it was quiet and its view over the pond and the trees made up for its lack of size.

"Trouble at work?" Charles Stamoran said.

Kasluga opened her eyes and saw her husband standing in the doorway. She said, "Are you spying on me?"

"If I were, you'd never know."

"Maybe this is a double bluff?"

"It isn't. So what was up? Wrong number?"

Kasluga picked up a bright pink stress ball and flung it at his head. "None of your business. Now get out. I'm working."

Ottoway left the bar first. Reacher was last, and Chapellier was sandwiched between them. The street outside was a blaze of red and blue. Four Bureau cars were lined up with dome lights flashing on their dashboards. The scrawny guy was in the backseat of the last car. Behind it was an old, dented Toyota Corolla. Its driver's door was open. So was its trunk. An agent was standing next to it, and as Reacher watched, a plain white box van pulled up next to it and a pair of technicians climbed out. Ottoway made her way to the lead car and leaned down to talk to someone in the passenger seat. Then two men emerged from the shadows near the wall. They were trim. Lean. Dressed all in black. Like French avant-garde philosophers who had become obsessed with exercise, Reacher thought. Although he knew what they really were. He could recognize soldiers in and around bars in his sleep. Years of experience had honed his instinct. And MPs were even easier to spot. No one else ever hung out with them. They were too unpopular. The only thing Reacher couldn't figure was what they were doing there. He hadn't requested backup.

The MPs stepped forward. The taller one said, "Captain Reacher?"

Reacher nodded.

"Could you verify that, please, sir."

Reacher took out his wallet and showed his Military ID card.

"Thank you, sir." The MP pulled an envelope from his jacket pocket and handed it over.

Reacher tore the envelope open. Inside was a single sheet of paper with the Military Police crest at the top. It stated that he was to relinquish custody of Sergeant Chapellier and report to an address in Washington, D.C., at 11:00 A.M. the following day.

Reacher looked at the MP. "What do you know about this?"

"Nothing, sir."

"What have you heard?"

"We've been told nothing, sir."

Reacher smiled. It was clear that these guys were NCOs. The backbone of the service. And Reacher knew from experience that the NCO scuttlebutt was the most efficient communication medium in the world. "I didn't ask what you've *been told*. I asked what you've *heard*. And if you tell me you've not heard anything I'll have you locked up for impersonating a member of the US Army. So let's start with this. I'm being sent to D.C. How come?"

The MP glanced at his buddy then said, "Word is, a couple of people died."

"Who?"

"Don't know."

"Ours?"

The MP shook his head. "Retired scientists. One got electrocuted. One fell out of a hospital window."

"Fell out?"

The MP shrugged.

"So they were CIA. What's our angle?"

"Word is, it's part of a bigger thing. CIA, plus other agencies. Orders from the Pentagon."

"Then why are they sending me?"

"They wanted an O-3 or higher. No one from HQ would touch it. I guess you must have pissed off the wrong guy, sir."

* * *

Susan Kasluga tapped gently on Charles Stamoran's study door, pushed it open, and took a small step into the room. Stamoran was sitting in his armchair. He was reading a book. A biography of George Meade. He glanced up, then went back to his Civil War history.

Kasluga saw her stress ball sitting on a low table beneath the window. It was leaning against a decanter of whiskey. A pair of cut-crystal tumblers sat on either side. She made her way across to the table and poured two measures. She went heavier on one, which she carried over and handed to Stamoran.

"I'm sorry," she said. "You took me by surprise. That call—"

"You don't have to tell me," Stamoran said.

"I know. It's just . . . it's nothing you need to worry about. Just business."

"Your takeover deal?"

"A vulnerability. Something that could have derailed everything. But it's fixed now. That call was confirmation. Which is why it was so short."

"I've never known a lawyer to be so brief."

"Who said it was a lawyer?"

"Maybe I'm better off not knowing about this."

"See? Another reason I married you. Impeccable instincts. Now let's leave work till tomorrow. It's getting late." She took a long sip of her drink. "And there are much better ways to spend an evening together."

Ottoway watched the MPs lead Chapellier away then crossed to Reacher's side. She said, "What was that all about?"

Reacher shrugged. "New orders."

"Anything good?"

"More likely the opposite."

"Oh. I'm sorry to hear that. So are you shipping out?"

Reacher nodded.

Ottoway said, "When?"

Reacher said, "Tonight, I guess, if I can get a flight. Otherwise first thing tomorrow."

"I vote for tomorrow. Stay in Chicago tonight. That was a job well done. We deserve to celebrate."

"You have a point." Reacher was quiet for a moment. "And there's something else I wouldn't mind taking care of before I leave."

Reacher led the way back inside the building and strolled across to the bar. The bartender looked up then took a step back. He hadn't noticed Reacher approach. He wasn't expecting to see anyone right in front of him. Certainly not anyone who looked like Reacher. Six foot five. Chest like a refrigerator. Arms like other people's legs. Cropped hair. Head tipped quizzically to one side.

On the far side of the bar there was a metal tub about ten inches high and a yard across. At the start of the evening it had been crammed with ice and bottles of beer. Now it was mainly full of water with a few residual cubes floating around. Reacher pointed to it and said, "That thing? Give it to me."

The bartender blinked and said, "Why?"

Reacher said, "I want to borrow it."

"No," the guy said. "But you can rent it. Twenty bucks for a half hour. Driver's license for security. No questions asked. Do what you want with it."

Reacher shook his head. "I borrow it. For two minutes. You

watch what happens. And when I return it, if you still think I should pay, I'll give you forty."

The bartender thought for a moment then called his buddy to help him heave the tub across to a spot close to Reacher. Reacher picked it up and headed toward the fat guy who'd messed with the waiter, earlier. The guy made a point of turning his back. Reacher closed in, paused to make sure the waiter was close enough to see what was happening, then lifted the tub and dumped the icy water over the fat guy's head.

He screamed. He howled. He flailed his arms and danced up and down on the spot. He huffed and gasped and finally spun around to face Reacher. His cap had been washed off. His beard was drenched. His shirt was clinging to his torso.

"The hell was that?" the guy spluttered.

Reacher said, "Training."

"What?"

"Like with a dog."

"You're saying I'm a dog?"

"I read somewhere, you have a dog and it misbehaves, you do something it doesn't like. Then it'll learn to mend its ways. Now, you're clearly not as smart as an average dog. Probably not as smart as a stupid dog. Probably a dog that started out really dumb and then had half of its brain removed is still smarter than you. So maybe I should stick around. Become your personal trainer. Put this tub to work whenever you act like a jackass."

The guy frowned and shook his head. Droplets of water flew in a wide circle like he was a poodle that had been caught in the rain. He was quiet for a moment. Then his frown turned into a scowl. "Enough," he barked. "I'm going to kill you. I'm going to crush every bone in your body."

"You think?" Reacher was holding the tub low in front, base toward him, angled at about forty-five degrees.

"I know."

Reacher glanced down at the tub then ghosted across about a foot to his left. "You sure you're not going to break your own hand?"

"No. I'm going to break your face."

"Are you?" Reacher took a half step back and said, "Are there any bookies in the house? My money's on the lobotomized dog. That's for sure."

The guy flung himself forward and launched a punch straight at Reacher's face. No technique. No finesse. Just a whole lot of weight and momentum and fury. In some circumstances, that could have served him well. But not that night. Because Reacher stepped aside. Away from the unlit iron pipe he had been standing in front of. The guy's fist slammed right into it. His knuckles shattered. His fingers broke. All kinds of little bones in his hand and wrist and forearm were smashed. Tendons tore. Ligaments ripped. And this time he didn't make a sound. The pain took care of that. It caused him to faint, right there on the spot. His knees buckled. His legs folded. He flopped backward and landed on the ground with his head six inches from the little umbrella that had fallen from the drink he had made the waiter spill a few minutes earlier.

Reacher carried the tub back to the bar and set it down.

The bartender said, "No charge."

Reacher didn't let go of the tub right away. He was thinking about a similar situation that had led to him getting busted back to captain. He said, "Anyone asks, who hurt that guy?"

"No one. He hurt himself."

"Correct answer."

Chapter 9

Michael Rymer ate breakfast on the deck behind his house, alone, as usual. He didn't hurry. He had no need. His hurrying days were behind him. He was retired. Happily so. He had no family. No one to mold his days around. Not since his fourth wife had left him nearly a decade ago. All he had to do was soak up some early-morning sun along with his oatmeal and coffee then make his way down to his boathouse and unmoor *Pegasus*. His pride and joy. A day's fishing in the lake lay ahead of him, followed by a bottle of wine and a movie on his VHS player to fill his evening. It hadn't always been this way. Far from it, in fact. But these days life was treating him well. He was under no illusions about that.

Rymer was halfway to his favorite spot to drop anchor—where he could be sure the largemouth bass would bite and the view of the Rockies never failed to take his breath away—when he saw something he wasn't expecting. Another boat. A forty-footer. The owners of the other half-dozen properties scattered around the lakeshore generally only used their houses—and boats—in the summer, and occasionally for the holidays. The rest of the year he could pretty much guarantee he would be alone on the water. The way he liked it. He considered changing course. Finding a more secluded spot. But something about the other boat bothered him. The way it was moving. It seemed to be drifting aimlessly. Not under way. And not at anchor. For a moment he wondered if it could somehow have broken loose from a neighbor's dock during the night and been blown all the way out there by the wind. Then a person appeared from its wheelhouse. A woman. She started waving. But not in a friendly way. Both arms were windmilling wildly over her head. She was clearly in some kind of trouble. Rymer leaned on the throttle and moved in to investigate.

As he drew closer, Rymer recognized the boat. *The Duchess*. It belonged to a couple from Denver. He had never bothered to learn their names. He thought they might be doctors. But he didn't recognize the woman who was on board. She looked like she could be in her late twenties. She was slim, like she kept herself fit, and her dark hair was pulled back in a practical, no-nonsense style. A relative of the doctors, maybe? Or a family friend? Presumably someone who had permission to be there, anyway. Rymer had gotten caught up in a lot of crazy things in his life but he'd never heard of anyone joyriding in a leisure boat on a mountain lake that was so remote it was virtually impossible to find unless you already knew where it was. He dropped a row of fenders over the gunwale, tied them to the cleats, and eased *Pegasus* up alongside the stricken vessel.

Rymer called out, "Everything OK?"

The woman clutched her head in her hands. She said, "Oh my goodness, I'm so embarrassed. I don't know what to do. The engine just stopped and I can't get it to start again and I don't know how the anchor works and the boat keeps floating around all over the place. Can you help me? Please?"

"You're out here on your own?"

The woman nodded. "Claudia and Andreas are letting me use their house for a couple of weeks. They said I could take *The Duchess* out anytime I wanted. But then they also said it was easy to drive. I feel like a total idiot."

"Don't worry." Rymer took a coil of line from the bow of *Pegasus* and tossed it so that it wound up lying across the raised prow of *The Duchess*. He took another from near the stern, handed it to the woman, jumped over, and landed next to her. He took the rope and secured it to a cleat, then did the same with the line at the bow. "I'm sure it's no big problem. We'll get you up and running in no time."

The Duchess was older than *Pegasus*. It had probably started life as a fishing boat, hauling in loads of lobsters or crabs in shallow coastal waters. Now its wooden hull was painted white with blue stripes here and there and comfy chairs had been added to the open section behind the wheelhouse where the catch would have been carried. A red life buoy stood out against the bright paint near the wheelhouse door and a mess of ropes and lines was strewn around all over the deck. Rymer shook his head at the chaos and took a step toward the trapdoor that covered the engine compartment. Then some of the ropes started to move. They seethed across the shiny surface like they were alive. Wrapped themselves around his feet. Whipped up around his ankles and cinched in tight. His ankle bones ground together. He almost lost his balance. He recovered. But a moment later he crashed down onto his back. Something had heaved on the rope, hard. It felt like he'd somehow gotten hitched to a stampeding horse. Most of the breath was knocked out of his body. He struggled to lift his head and saw it wasn't *something* that was in control of the rope. It was *someone*. Another woman. Almost identical to the one who had asked for his help, but maybe two or three years older. She must have been crouching on the far side of the wheelhouse.

The new woman moved in close, gripped the rope with both hands, and heaved Rymer's legs off the deck. The first woman leaned down and slid her hands under his armpits. She lifted his torso. Moved him around so that his head was pointed away from *Pegasus*. Rymer was struggling for air. He didn't understand what was happening. Then the women bundled him toward the vacant side of the boat. The original woman hauled his head a little higher then dumped him down with his shoulders on the gunwale. She rolled him so that he was facing down, staring at the water. And both women pushed and jockeyed and shoved. He slid across the wooden rail until it reached his waist. Then he pivoted forward, slamming his palms against the outer hull to avoid smashing into it face-first and winding up with the top of his head an inch above the water line.

Roberta Sanson gave the rope a sharp tug to make sure she had Rymer's attention, then said, "Michael, can you hear me? And more important, can you understand me?"

Rymer didn't respond.

Roberta took a large step forward. Rymer's legs tipped up. His torso pivoted down. His head was dunked into the freezing water. Roberta let it stay there for ten seconds then started to pull back. The physics were against her so Veronica had to reach over the side and tug on his belt before he could resurface.

Roberta said, "Michael . . .?"

Rymer spluttered and coughed. "Are you nuts? What are you doing? I'm no kind of threat. I stopped to help you!"

"You want to help? That's good. All you have to do is give us one name. One name, and this will be over. You'll never see or hear from us again."

"What name?"

"Your research team in India. In 1969. We know seven names. Including yours, obviously. You need to tell us the eighth."

"What? No. There is no eighth name. There were only seven of us. I swear. Me. Owen Buck. Varinder Singh. Keith Bridgeman. Geoffrey Brown. Charlie Adam. Neville Pritchard. No one else."

"There were eight. I need the other name. You have to tell me."

"There is no eighth name! Why do you—?"

Roberta plunged Rymer's head back into the water. She left it submerged for fifteen seconds this time. Again she needed Veronica's help to pull him clear.

Roberta said, "This isn't pleasant, is it? The only way it stops is for you to give us the name. Come on. It's not hard. Two words. First name, last name. That's better than drowning, surely. You don't doubt that I will drown you, right?"

Rymer was gasping for air. "Can't. Only seven names. Swear to you."

Roberta looked at Veronica, shrugged, and said, "OK. Your choice. But at this point it's important you know our names. I'm Roberta Sanson. This is my sister, Veronica. Our father was Morgan Sanson."

Rymer groaned.

Roberta said, "Any last minute inspiration?"

Rymer was silent.

Roberta shrugged again and lowered Rymer back down. She

braced her feet against the deck and held on tight to the rope. Rymer thrashed and kicked and struggled. His movements were hard and desperate. Then they softened and waned. The tension ebbed out of his body. His energy almost gave out altogether. He arched his back and clawed at the water one last time then he slumped down deeper into the darkness. A final few bubbles floated to the surface and he was left hanging there on the rope, heavy and slack, slapping against the hull in the slight swell.

Roberta switched her grip to the strand of rope that led away from the knot around Rymer's ankles. She pulled. The knot released itself and Rymer's body slid silently the rest of the way beneath the surface. It bobbed back up a moment later and settled, floating facedown, arms and legs stretched wide, hair spread out around his skull like pale seaweed.

Reacher had also woken that morning with a view over a lake. In his case it was Lake Michigan, through a floor-to-ceiling window, thirty-two stories up in a clover leaf–shaped building near Navy Pier in Chicago. It was Agent Ottoway's bedroom.

"Don't worry," she had said when they got back after a night of blues music on Halsted Street and she saw the expression on Reacher's face. "This is not the product of ill-gotten gains. I got it in my divorce."

Reacher and Ottoway drank coffee in bed, then took a shower together. Soap was involved. So was hot water. And steam. But given how long the process took, not a whole lot of cleaning took place. It left them with no time for breakfast. They got dressed, hurried down to the underground garage, and collected Ottoway's car. She drove to the FBI field office and while Reacher retrieved his duffel from the trunk of the vehicle he'd borrowed from the Rock Island Arsenal, she scribbled on a scrap of paper.

"Take this," she said, and handed the note to Reacher. There was a phone number written at the top. It had a 312 area code. "This is my home number. Anytime you're in town, call me."

Reacher said nothing.

The walk to the El stop and the train ride to O'Hare were uneventful. There was time at the airport for a cup of coffee before the flight to Washington National, then Reacher found his way to the cab line and gave the driver the address from the orders he'd received the day before. The route took them across the Potomac then away from the city, nose to tail in a lingering cloud of exhaust fumes for all but the final ten minutes of the journey. They were heading for some kind of business district. The buildings were long and low, no more than twenty years old, all pale brick and mirrored glass, separated by rectangular open-air parking lots and set back behind glossy green hedges. The cabdriver pulled up outside the last building on the street. There were three cars in its lot. All domestic sedans. Two Fords and a Chevy. One green, one blue, one black. All sprouting more antennas than they'd had when they rolled off the line in Detroit.

Reacher gave the driver a respectable tip then made his way through the building's main entrance. Inside, he found cheap, durable carpet, new inexpensive furniture, and walls covered with fresh, bland paint. Which told him two things. The place was owned by the government. And it was up for sale. Reacher had no idea why, but he'd noticed that the government never spent money on buildings it was planning to keep.

There was no one behind the reception desk so Reacher pushed through a pair of double doors and found himself at the head of a long, bright corridor. The first door on the left was marked *Board Room*. Reacher looked inside. Three people were already there, each on a different side of a rectangular table that seemed too large for the space. Two men and a woman. All looked like they were in their thirties. All seemed a little tense, like they didn't know why they were there but assumed whatever the reason, it was certain to not be good. There were a dozen chairs, arranged in two fours and two pairs, and the only other piece of furniture was a table under the window. Two shiny pump-action flasks were sitting on it, along with a stack of upside-down Styrofoam cups and a bowl that was overflowing with cartons of creamer and sachets of sweetener.

Reacher helped himself to a cup of coffee and then squeezed his way around to the chair at the corner of the table that gave him a view of the window as well as the door. He placed his bag on the floor and sat down. The woman was on the same side of the table, midway along. She had short blond hair and was wearing a navy suit coat over a crisp white blouse and a tan leather briefcase was set, closed, in front of her. One of the men was opposite her. He also had on a navy suit, but his could have been slept in. His hair looked like it had won a fight with a comb that morning, and probably did every morning. His face was plump. His eyes were bloodshot and his nose was a mesh of fine, cracked veins. The final guy was at the corner diagonally across from Reacher. His eyes were cold and blue and he had neat, tidy hair like a banker or an accountant. He was wearing a sport coat and staring intently out of the window like he thought if he concentrated hard enough, he could physically transport himself out of there.

No one spoke. Two minutes crawled past then footsteps echoed in the corridor. The door opened and a man bustled through. He was tall, maybe six foot six, with a long face and neatly combed silver hair. He paused, looked at each person in turn, then took one of the chairs at the head of the table.

He cleared his throat and said, "Let's get started, shall we? First things first. Introductions. My name is Christopher Baglin, Department of Defense. Let's go clockwise."

That meant Reacher was next up. He said, "Jack Reacher. US Army."

The woman followed. "Amber Smith. FBI."

The sport coat guy said, "Gary Walsh. Treasury Department."

The scruffy guy went last. "Kent Neilsen. Central Intelligence Agency."

Baglin nodded, clasped his hands on the table in front of him, and continued. "Lady, gentlemen, thank you for being here. I say that on behalf of the secretary himself. I know you were summoned at short notice, but believe me, we would not have done that if your mission here was not of the utmost importance. We—and by *we* I mean the United States of America—have a problem. A serious one. And we need your expertise to solve it."

Baglin paused, as if he was expecting someone to ask what that problem was.

No one spoke. No one was that naïve, which Reacher found encouraging.

Baglin shifted his hands onto his lap. "By way of background, I need to take you thirty years into the past. Now, as we know, the evils of the Soviet Union have finally been consigned to the garbage can of history, but for decades its empire was a formidable enemy. Back in the 1960s the reds were coming at us from all angles. Nukes, of course. Satellites. Submarines. Sleeper agents. Spies. The list goes on, and at the top was something particularly nasty. Chemical and biological weapons. Newly devised strains and variants designed to kill and blind and incapacitate in the most ghastly ways imaginable. And that's where Project 192 originated from."

Again Baglin left an implied question hanging in the air. Again no one took the bait.

Baglin's hands appeared back on the table. "Before I go on, I must stress two things. First, the secretary insists on complete transparency. He feels that you won't be able to operate with the utmost effectiveness unless you are armed with all the facts. Nothing will be held back, so secondly nothing you learn in this room can leave this room. Are we clear?"

"Crystal." "Yes, sir." "Of course." "One hundred percent." Reacher's and the other three voices overlapped.

Baglin said, "Good. Now, Project 192 was an initiative designed to protect us against these diabolical Soviet weapons. Its purpose was to understand their full effects and develop effective antidotes that could be manufactured rapidly and in huge volumes. This was no mean feat. It required cutting-edge equipment and the latest techniques, and it had to be done in absolute secrecy. The fear was that if the Soviets learned we could counteract their weapons, they would develop new ones, which we may have been unaware of or not immediately able to respond to. So, what happened was that we partnered with the best American industrial research corporations. We built discreet, partitioned facilities within their laboratories. But . . ."

Baglin paused. Again no one bit.

Baglin said, "But this was done outside the realm of direct governmental control. It was done in close proximity to civilian workers. In some cases in close proximity to significant civilian populations. And more often than not, in other countries. Sometimes very poor countries. Countries that would have struggled to say no to that kind of work being done on their soil. Now, I stand

behind these decisions. So does the secretary. It was right for America at the time. But as you know, times change. Attitudes change.
We've weathered the storm caused by all the reporting on Agent
Orange and VX gas since then. Lived through the debacle of the
final days of Vietnam. Through Watergate. Through the Contra
scandal. Et cetera, et cetera. Our concern is that, particularly with
the Soviet Union no longer a threat, people would be less likely to
accept the necessity of what we did. If details of the Project became
public, it could foster unrest. Our remaining enemies could use the
information to embarrass the United States and harm our standing
on the world stage."

Another pause was left unfilled.

Baglin lowered his voice. "Which leads us to the nub of the issue.
In the late sixties, a team of seven scientists worked on neutralizing
a particular Soviet nerve agent. They were based within a civilian
laboratory owned by a company called Mason Chemical Industries.
It was located in India. Recently, one of the team fell victim to cancer, and three of the others have died in extremely suspicious circumstances."

Smith cleared her throat and said, "How suspicious?"

Baglin said, "One was electrocuted. One fell out of a window.
One ingested a fatal dose of toad venom."

Reacher said, "Poison."

"What was that?"

"If it was ingested, it was poison. Venom is introduced through a
bite or a sting."

"You think that's the relevant fact, here?"

"It's accurate. And I think accuracy is always relevant. Especially
when lives are on the line."

Baglin glared at Reacher for a moment, then turned away and
said, "Our working hypothesis is that a hostile agent killed these

men in an attempt to uncover information that could be used against the United States. Three men from the team are still alive. Precautions are being taken to ensure their safety, but the secretary is not satisfied with a passive response. He wants the perpetrator identified and stopped. That's where you all fit in. The identification of suspects. The army and the CIA because those organizations were jointly responsible for the research operations in the sixties. The FBI in its counterintelligence capacity, in case the initiative is being driven by a foreign country. And the Treasury Department in case we're off the mark and someone is merely trying to steal industrial secrets. An office has been prepared for each of you, with a phone, fax machine, and stationery supplies. Accommodations are being provided at a local hotel for as long as necessary. Any questions?"

Reacher raised his hand. "Have any ransom demands been received?"

Baglin shook his head. "No."

"Have any scientists who worked on other bioweapon programs been targeted?"

"Not that I'm aware of."

"Will you find out?"

"I'll ask the question. Now—"

"One last thing. You said precautions are being taken to safeguard the remaining scientists from Project 192. What kind of precautions?"

"They're being watched, twenty-four/seven, by experienced agents."

"Were any of the victims being watched?"

"Captain, this is not the time for finger pointing or interagency point scoring."

"That's not my intention. If we're going to cast a net, we need to know how fine to make it. So we need to know what we're fishing for. The different methods of killing tells us something. But not enough. The first guy was electrocuted, right? Killing someone that way is one thing. Doing it under the noses of experienced agents is another. It would indicate a higher degree of competence, and confidence, which in turn would imply a certain kind and level of training, and motivation."

"I see. OK. Yes. Dr. Brown. He was at home when he was *poisoned*, and his house was under observation."

"He was the third victim?"

"Correct." Baglin paused for a moment. "Does anyone else have a question?"

The other three stayed silent.

Baglin nodded. "All right, then. We will reconvene here at 0900 tomorrow, at which time I expect you to furnish the names of the first suspects you think should be investigated."

Chapter 10

Roberta and Veronica Sanson gathered up all the ropes from the deck, coiled them, and put them back in their rightful places. They guessed it would be quite a while before the owners would see the boat again. They didn't know how observant those owners would be. But even so, they didn't want to leave any signs that the boat had been used. Especially given what it had been used for. Operating unseen was a habit. It was ingrained in them. Years of intense, arduous training had made sure of that.

When they were happy with the state of *The Duchess* they turned their attention to *Pegasus*. They took every piece of rope they could find and left them strewn around all over the place. Then, with just the stern line attached, Roberta worked the controls until the boat was pointing roughly in the direction of Rymer's house, which by now was just a dot on the distant shoreline. She set the throttle to just above stalling speed. Waited for Veronica to jump back onto *The Duchess* then leapt across after her. Cut the remaining line.

And steered toward the property they had borrowed the boat from that morning.

The sisters had stolen a pickup truck this time. An F-150. So ubiquitous as to be practically invisible. They hoped. But they took no chances. They didn't risk the most direct route back to Stapleton airport because that would involve passing the agents watching Rymer's house for a second time in a few hours. Instead, they started by heading north, then east, and finally turned south for a straight shot back to Denver.

"There are two men left," Roberta said. She was driving with one hand on the wheel. Her right palm was stinging from a friction burn she'd gotten from the rope the first time she'd lowered Rymer into the water. "So it's fifty/fifty the next one will know the name we need."

Veronica said, "I'd rather it was a dead cert."

Roberta smiled. "Nice."

"Who's the next lucky contestant?"

"Give me two car brands. Not Ford. Not Chevy."

Veronica thought for a moment. She said, "Dodge. And Honda."

A minute later Roberta pointed through the windshield. "There. A Honda Civic." Honda was the second brand Veronica had picked, so Roberta matched it with the second name on her mental list. "Charlie Adam. Initials, CA. Lives in California. Symmetry. I love it."

Reacher spent the afternoon in the building outside D.C., closed away in a room farther down the corridor that had been allocated as his office. Its décor was as bland as the reception area's. The desk was small and the chair was a tight fit for someone as broad as Reacher. A window looked out onto an empty section of parking lot, and beyond that a row of pale shrubs that separated the site from the road. It wasn't the kind of place he would choose to spend time, but he wasn't about to complain. Over the years the army had sent him to a lot of places that were much less pleasant. That was for damn sure.

Reacher was pretty certain that Christopher Baglin, the Defense Department guy, hadn't been entirely on the level. He didn't think the guy had been lying, necessarily. What he'd said was likely to be close to the truth. It just wouldn't be the whole truth. Reacher's general position when it came to briefings from the top brass was that they were incomplete unless proved otherwise. That went double for top brass he didn't know. And double again for politicians. But he also knew that made little difference when it came to the task at hand. Some scientists had been murdered. There was little doubt about that. Based on what he'd been told, there was a chance that a soldier was responsible. And three potential victims were still alive. Reacher wanted to help keep it that way, so he picked up the phone. His first call was to the US Army Chemical Corps at Fort McClellan, Alabama. His second was to the Office of Administration at the Department of Veterans Affairs, which was just down the road, also in D.C., a stone's throw from the White House. He needed to make a third call, to the army's National Personnel Records Center in St. Louis, Missouri, but he couldn't do that until the list he'd requested from Fort McClellan came through.

Reacher inspected the fax machine. It wasn't doing anything. He hoped there wasn't anything he was supposed to set or switch on or program to make it work. He checked it from all sides and saw two cables leading out of its rear. A thicker one that was connected to a power outlet, and a thinner one that was plugged into a phone socket. That seemed reasonable, so Reacher picked a button on the front of the machine at random and pressed it. A little gray screen lit up and a shrill electronic tone pierced the air. Reacher guessed that meant the thing was all set. There was nothing he could do to make the information he wanted appear more quickly, so he turned back to the phone. He called Agent Ottoway in Chicago. He left a message on her machine asking if she could find anything out about Amber Smith. He called a buddy in the CIA and asked him to dig into Kent Neilsen. He called his brother, Joe, who worked at the Treasury Department, and left a message about Gary Walsh. Then he grabbed a blank piece of paper and a pen. He wrote down three names. All belonging to soldiers who were AWOL. Low-level offenders who were likely to skulk at the bottom of his unit's nuisance list for the foreseeable future. Then he picked up the phone again. Called a few other MPs who had helped him over the years, or who he owed favors to. Asked if they had any names stuck on their own lists. If it was true that the Secretary of Defense was personally involved in the operation, they were going to throw the kitchen sink at it. That's the way the world works. There was bound to be plenty of spare manpower. Enough to round up a few additional miscreants, and there was no point in letting all those tax dollars go to waste.

The phone in the Pentagon rang again at 3:13 P.M. Eastern. Not a scheduled time for a call.

The guy who answered it listened, hung up, then dialed the number for Charles Stamoran's private extension.

Stamoran answered after one ring. He said, "Go."

The guy recited the message he had memorized a minute before. "Michael Rymer is dead. He drowned. His body was recovered from the lake behind his house at 11:38 A.M. The security detail watching his house was alerted when they saw his boat run aground a couple of hundred yards from his dock. They investigated, found it empty, and called a rescue helicopter. An initial examination confirmed there was water in Rymer's lungs. He had a bruise across his chest consistent with falling against the side of the boat, and there was chafing on his ankles consistent with getting tangled in a rope. There were ropes scattered all across the deck, so his death could have been accidental if he tripped, fell, and went overboard. Or the injuries could be coincidental if he had become despondent and jumped into the water in an attempt to commit suicide."

Stamoran took the receiver away from his ear for a moment. Michael Rymer was the most fastidious man he'd ever met. There was no way he would have left ropes lying around on his boat. No way he would have gotten tangled in them and tripped. There was a zero percent chance of that happening. Which meant someone else had been on the boat. Someone who murdered him there. Stamoran felt an unexpected flash of relief. It only lasted a moment then a flood of guilt chased it away. It had occurred to him that if someone was in Colorado killing Rymer, they couldn't be anywhere else tracking Pritchard down and forcing him to reveal his secret. Not yet, anyway.

Stamoran lifted the handset again. He said, "The second someone on the task force comes up with a name, I want it followed up. Vigorously. Resources are not an issue. I don't want any stone, big or small, left unturned."

At ten after five there was a knock on Reacher's door. It opened before he said anything and Amber Smith, the FBI representative in the group, stepped into the room.

Smith tucked a loose strand of hair behind her ear and said, "I'm calling it a day. Going to head to the hotel. See what kind of a place they've stuck us in. Want a ride? Looks like you don't have a vehicle with you."

Reacher looked at the fax machine. No new pages had come out since he'd called the army's National Personnel Records Center a couple of hours earlier and he couldn't make any more progress without the list he'd asked for. He said, "Sure. Thank you."

One of the cars had already gone by the time Reacher and Smith got to the parking lot. The black Impala. That left the two Crown Victorias. Kent Neilsen, the CIA guy, was leaning against one of them. The blue one. His suit was so crumpled it looked like he'd just been run down by it.

Neilsen said, "Either of you hungry? I am. I know a place near the hotel. How about we get squared away with our rooms then go and grab a bite?"

Smith shrugged. She said, "Don't see why not."

Reacher worked on the principle that you should eat when you can so that you won't have to when you can't. He said, "I'm in."

Neilsen pushed himself away from the trunk of his car and made for the driver's door. "Meet in the hotel lobby at six?"

The hotel was a hair over a mile away from the office building. Reacher had spent more nights than he cared to remember in hotels. Mainly in the course of hunting down fugitives or digging up evidence or following leads. And mainly in places with rates that wouldn't cause heart attacks when the army saw the bills. Which tended to define the kind of facilities the establishments had on offer. It was fair to say he was used to his accommodations being on the plain and simple end of the scale. But the place the task force had picked was the equal of the blandest building he'd ever seen when it came to functional design. It had absolutely nothing that wasn't one hundred percent necessary. It was four floors high, built of pale brick, with small windows and a flat roof. There was no cover above the entrance. No valet parking stand. Even the signs lacked illumination. They had to make do with reflective paint.

Smith turned into the lot, spun her Ford around, and backed into a parking spot near the building, next to Neilsen's car. On the far side of the lot Reacher could see a line of much larger bays. The right kind of size for tour buses. He doubted they would be for rock bands or sports teams. So maybe for school parties, he thought. He had heard that it was common practice for kids to visit D.C. when they were in eighth grade. That seemed like a good idea. He'd learned about the nation's capital when he was younger than that, but all the information came from the dog-eared pages of a book in a humid classroom on the other side of the world. That was fine for absorbing facts. Not so good for capturing scale and atmosphere.

They sailed through check-in without a hitch, so Reacher took his key and carried his bag to his room on the second floor. He used the stairs and as he was working the lock on his door he saw Smith emerge from the elevator. She had the room next to his.

Inside his room Reacher found that the bare-minimum approach had been maintained. The essential bases were covered. There was a bed. A dresser. A chair. A kind of flap attached to the wall that could be used as a desk, if you were desperate. A closet with hangers that were fixed to the rail to stop people from stealing them. And a bathroom with soap and shampoo in dispensers in brackets on the wall. Reacher guessed it would be cheaper to top them up a little than to provide fresh miniature bottles for every guest.

* * *

Neilsen was already waiting in reception when Reacher got there at a minute to six. Smith caught up two minutes later and Neilsen started for the exit without saying a word.

Reacher said, "What about Walsh? The Treasury guy."

Neilsen kept moving. "No idea. He was gone when we decided to leave the office and there's no sign of his car outside. Guess he's staying somewhere else."

The bar Neilsen had in mind was a couple of hundred yards from the hotel, heading farther away from the city. They decided to walk. It wasn't the most pleasant evening. The air was heavy with exhaust fumes from all the traffic in the neighborhood and it had started to drizzle, but Reacher didn't mind. He'd been cooped up all morning in trains and planes and cabs, and all afternoon in meeting rooms and offices, so he was glad to be able to stretch his legs.

The building they were aiming for had two floors. The higher level was shared between a nail salon and a wig maker. Two places Reacher had zero interest in visiting. The whole of the first floor was taken up with the bar. Its gimmick was that it looked like it was still under construction. A thick plastic sheet with a zipper down the center hung in the entrance in place of a door. The bar itself was made of scaffolding, with roughly formed shelves and nooks and niches for the bottles and glasses. The kitchen was on the other side of a wall with a jagged hole in it that was supposed to seem like it had been smashed with a sledgehammer. The tables were fashioned out of giant cable drums and instead of regular chairs there were a bunch of wooden crates.

Smith paused near the entrance. There were no other customers in the place. She said, "You sure about this?"

Neilsen looked serious. "Wait till you taste the food. And they make a mean Old Fashioned. Trust me."

They took a table in the corner farthest from the bar and a server approached them after less than a minute. She was wearing denim coveralls and giant, unlaced work boots, and she had a red paisley bandanna in her hair. Reacher figured she was going for the Rosie the Riveter look, and wondered if that was her choice or if it was required by the management. Neilsen ordered a glass of champagne. Reacher and Smith asked for beer.

"You celebrating?" Smith said after the server had retreated to the bar.

Neilsen said, "I guess. I mean, I still have a pulse. I'm still upright. Those things have to count for something, right?"

The server brought their drinks. Neilsen took a sip and said, "So, what do you think? Are we going to save the country from a blackmailing fanatic?"

Smith shrugged. "We're going to try, I guess."

Reacher said nothing.

Neilsen set down his glass. His expression suddenly became overbearingly earnest. "Listen. Here's how I see our situation. We need to trust each other. We need to pull together. If we do, we might just get through this. If not, we're screwed."

Smith said, "How do you figure?"

Neilsen said, "We all have skeletons, right? That's why we're here. Why whoever got the call from the Department of Defense put our names forward. They didn't just pick us out of a hat. We're expendable. This whole thing is a train wreck waiting to happen. When it goes off the rails, we need to make sure we don't crash and burn along with it. We need to decide, right now. Are we going to trust each other? Or not?"

Smith and Reacher stayed silent.

Neilsen said, "You know I'm right. Tell me the first thing you did in your little hutches this afternoon wasn't to pick up the phone and ask questions about the other three. See what dirt you could find."

Smith said, "It wasn't the first thing . . ."

Neilsen said, "But you did do it."

Smith nodded. Reacher gave nothing away.

"Good." Neilsen smiled again. "We may be late for happy hour at the last chance saloon but at least you're not total idiots." He turned to Reacher. "Think the blackmailer is one of yours?"

Reacher said, "I don't think there is a blackmailer."

Neilsen nodded. "That's why you asked Baglin about ransom notes and attacks on people from other projects. But if our guy isn't digging for blackmail material, what is he doing? What does he want?"

"Revenge. The murders? They feel personal."

"I came to the same conclusion."

"If someone who was involved with the project is behind the murders, then it's definitely not about blackmail. They would know what happened, because they were part of it. They wouldn't have to force the information out of other people."

Neilsen nodded again. "Right. And it would be impossible to get away with it. If the killings stop with only one guy left alive, he might as well print a confession in *The New York Times*."

Reacher said, "Agreed. Which is why I think it's a relative of someone who was harmed by the project. Some kind of long-term damage or disability."

"And this could be a soldier?"

Reacher breathed out slowly. "Could be. Think about the training the guy must have had. Kill someone in a hospital and none of the staff notices you were even there? Then get in and out, and murder a guy, while his house is being staked out by professionals? Those aren't things that just anyone could do."

Neilsen said, "Could be army, I guess. Could just as easily be CIA. How are you going to find him?"

"Start with everyone who served in those research units. See who has a son or a grandson or a nephew in green. Or who was in green. Then prioritize by those old-timers who've died recently or who just got a terminal diagnosis. Anyone who had or has a reason to set the record straight at long last."

"That's a sound method. Our records are kept differently but I'm doing basically the same. I wonder if either of us will hit the jackpot."

"You won't." Smith swallowed the last mouthful of her beer and set the bottle down. "You're both wrong. The Soviets are behind this."

"They can't be," Neilsen said. "There aren't any Soviets anymore. They lost."

Smith snorted. "Of course there are. The Soviet Union closed for business, sure. But the KGB didn't. The name it uses will make no difference. You'll see. And their agents are still here. These guys are fanatical. True believers. They'll continue the fight till the end of their days, no matter what else is happening in the world."

"Maybe."

"Definitely. Look at the deaths. No one can prove they weren't accidents or suicides, but come on. Anyone with a brain can see those scientists were murdered. The whole thing screams KGB. It's what they do. They even have a term for it. *Assassination by purported suicide.* They're sending a message. They're making clear they can kill anyone, anywhere, anytime, and no one can do anything about it. They'll pick off the rest of the scientists, one by one, in bizarre, eye-catching ways, then whatever dirt they picked up about the project along the way, they'll release it. Could be years from now when they do that. Whenever they think it'll cause the most harm. You have no idea how long a game these guys play."

While Reacher and the rest of the task force were talking, Roberta and Veronica Sanson were driving. They were in California, south of L.A., right on the coast, in a stolen Jeep Grand Cherokee, and they were going with their new MO. Taking one pass of their target's house before withdrawing out of range of the watchers and finding somewhere to spend the night. Only this time they spotted two government cars parked in strategic places.

Roberta glanced across at Veronica as she steered down the twisty road that led away from Charlie Adam's house. "Lights were on. They were home. Which is good."

Veronica said, "But you saw the cars?"

Roberta nodded.

"Adam was home. And so was his wife."

"That's unfortunate."

"What do we do? Wait?"

"No. Waiting multiplies risk."

"What, then?"

"Make it a murder/suicide this time, I guess."

Reacher ordered steak and had one more beer before switching to coffee. Smith had a salmon salad and three more beers. Neilsen had a burrito stuffed with every available option, three more glasses of champagne, and then switched to whiskey. A lot of whiskey. The conversation came in fits and starts as they ate and drank and waited on refills. Mostly superficial details about places they'd been posted and hints of highs and lows in their personal lives. Smith and Neilsen revealed more than Reacher. And they both seemed to have had more lows than highs. Reacher began to think that Neilsen had been right about why they'd been selected for the assignment. If things went south and targets were needed to pin the blame on, they all had bull's-eyes already drawn on their backs. In fluorescent paint.

Susan Kasluga was standing in her dressing room. She had a clothes hanger in each hand. One held a navy blue suit. One held a black suit. She was trying to choose between them. She always liked to pick the next day's outfit before she went to bed. She believed it helped to counter decision fatigue. She knew most people scoffed at the concept but she didn't care. She would do pretty much anything to give herself an edge.

Charles Stamoran appeared in the doorway before she'd reached a verdict. He said, "What are you doing?"

She said, "What does it look like? I can't go to the office in my pajamas."

"You shouldn't go to the office at all. Not for a couple more days."

"We agreed I'd stay home for two days. I've done that. No more."

"Susie, it's not safe."

"You haven't caught the guy?"

"Not yet."

"That's your problem. Not mine."

"It'll be a problem for both of us if you get yourself caught by this maniac."

"He killed more scientists?"

Stamoran nodded. "Geoffrey Brown. Michael Rymer."

"That's a shame, I guess. I didn't know them very well. But he didn't get Neville Pritchard. So you're safe. So I'm safe. End of discussion."

"He could get Pritchard tomorrow. Tonight."

"He won't."

"You can't know that."

"Call it intuition. Call it anything you like, but I'm going back to work."

Stamoran could hear the steel in her voice. He'd known her long enough to realize there was no point in arguing so he said, "All right. Back to work. But you're going to need a guard detail."

Kasluga dumped the black suit back on its rail. She said, "Already taken care of."

The sky had cleared by the time Reacher, Smith, and Neilsen left the bar. Neilsen went first, weaving slightly and almost tripping on cracks in the sidewalk a couple of times. Smith hung back. She stayed by Reacher's side. She was tucked in a little closer to him than she had been before. Reacher put it down to the beer. When they arrived at the hotel, they saw that Walsh's car was in the lot, two spaces away from Smith's.

Neilsen's room was also on the second floor, on the other side of Smith's. He mumbled something that could have been *good night*, took out his key, and dropped it on the floor. Reacher picked it up. He worked the lock, nudged Neilsen through the doorway, and tossed the key in after him. Reacher turned back and saw Smith standing in her own open doorway. She smiled, then said, "Sleep well."

Chapter 11

Reacher woke himself at 6:00 A.M. the following morning. Two minutes later he heard footsteps in the hotel corridor. Someone treading slowly and carefully, trying not to make much sound. Then a note slid into view between the base of the door and the carpet. The footsteps padded away, faster than before. Reacher slid out of bed and looked through the spyhole in the door. He saw a woman's back, distorted in the little lens. But clear enough to recognize. It was Amber Smith, and she was carrying her shoes.

Reacher picked up the piece of paper and unfolded it. Smith's handwriting was jagged and bold. She said she couldn't drive him to the office because she needed to make an early start. She was expecting an update on some hares she'd set running the day before. She thought something important was about to break. So she suggested Reacher hit up Neilsen for a ride instead of her and signed off with her initials.

Reacher tossed the note in the trash, took a shower, dressed, and headed downstairs in search of breakfast. He ate two bagels with cream cheese, drank two cups of coffee, and left the hotel without setting eyes on Neilsen. It took him fourteen minutes to walk to the commandeered building, and when he arrived he found a security guard had been installed since the day before. He showed his ID then made his way down the corridor and unlocked the door to the room he'd been allocated.

Inside, Reacher saw that two things had changed overnight. A new page had emerged from the fax machine, and the light on the answering machine was no longer solid red. It was flashing. Three blinks and a pause, three blinks and a pause, like it was repeating S in Morse code. Reacher squeezed into the chair and turned one of the dials on the machine to Play Message(s). The first voice he heard belonged to Agent Ottoway, from Chicago. She had found someone who'd worked with Amber Smith a year or so ago. Smith had been a good agent, apparently, but had gone off the rails due to some kind of family tragedy. Reacher's CIA friend was up next. He had learned that Kent Neilsen was once a rising star. He'd done enough stellar work to earn a lot of slack with his bosses, but the word was that he was rapidly approaching the end of that particular rope. People were rooting for him, but not many expected him to find his way back. Last was Reacher's brother, Joe. His was the shortest message, which didn't surprise Reacher. Joe simply said he couldn't find any trace of a Gary Walsh at the Treasury Department, then advised caution before hanging up.

Reacher wasn't too surprised by the first two reports. Not after what he'd seen and heard at the bar, and again after they left. Joe's information was more troubling. He was a thorough guy. If Walsh's record was there to be found, there was no way Joe would have missed it. Reacher would need to dig deeper. But not just then. He

LEE CHILD and ANDREW CHILD

had work to do before the morning's meeting. He picked up the new fax. It was from the army's National Personnel Records Center. He set it on his desk next to the two reports that had come through the day before and began scanning the names, looking for connections that might unmask a murderer.

It was the dog that saved Lucy Adam's life. Sophie. A golden retriever.

Lucy and Charlie ate breakfast together on their patio, tucked between the glass railings at the top of the cliff and the back of their house. Yogurt, fruit, coffee, and orange juice. Charlie would have preferred an omelet or something involving bacon and sausage, but given the struggles he'd been having recently getting his pants to fasten, he figured he needed to make some changes. He wasn't happy about it. He was never at his sunniest in the mornings and his new diet did nothing to improve his mood. He scowled his way through the meal, hunched and grumpy and silent, and when Sophie dropped her toy at his feet he just kicked it away.

"Come on, girl." Lucy stood up and glared at her husband. "Ignore Mr. Personality. Let's go for a nice walk."

Charlie waited for his wife to find her shoes and fetch the leash and disappear to the north along the cliff path, then he pushed his bowl away. He struggled out of his chair and went into the kitchen. He came back out a minute later with a bag of croissants in his hand but he didn't sit down. He paused by the table, straining his ears. He thought he'd heard a voice. Then it came again. A little louder. From somewhere on the clifftop. It was female and it said just one word. "Help!"

Charlie dropped the pastries on the table and rushed toward the railing. He leaned over, looked down, and saw someone. A few feet below. A woman. Maybe in her late twenties. Slim and fit with dark hair. She was lying on one of the narrow, natural ledges that the wind and water had cut into the rock face over the last several millennia. She must have climbed up from the beach, far below. It wasn't easy, but it could be done. Charlie had plotted a couple of different routes, years ago, when they had first bought the house. When he was much younger. And much lighter. There were some sketchy places, for sure, but they were all much lower down. The woman was safe where she was. There was no danger of falling from there. Not unless she rolled off deliberately. Charlie looked her over, scanning for injuries. As far as he could tell, there was nothing wrong. No blood on her head or seeping through her clothes. No limbs bent into unnatural positions. He said, "You need help?"

The woman said, "No. But you do."

Something slammed into Charlie's back. The force threw him against the railing. His hips crunched against the top edge and his torso jackknifed over it, leaving him bent double and scrabbling for grip. He tried to straighten up but he couldn't move. A weight was pushing him. Two weights, he realized. A pair of hands planted squarely between his shoulder blades.

Roberta Sanson sat up. She said, "Only one person can help you now, Charlie. Yourself." She took a piece of paper from her pocket and held it in front of Charlie's face. "Read these names. Tell me whose is missing."

Charlie said, "I can't. I don't have my glasses."

Roberta shook her head and put the list away. "OK. Recite for me. The names of everyone connected to your research team. India, 1969."

Charlie didn't respond.

Roberta grabbed his wrists. Veronica took the pressure off his back, took hold of his ankles, and started to lift.

"No!" Charlie kicked and wriggled. He was trying to free himself but all he did was grind his pelvis against the narrow glass rim. "Let me go!"

Roberta said, "We will. As soon as you tell us the missing name. We'll let you go and you'll never see us again. I promise."

Charlie was silent for a moment longer. The pain in his hip bones was becoming unbearable. He whimpered, then reeled off six names.

"And?"

"And what? That's everyone."

"No. You're missing one."

"I'm not."

"You are. Come on. Complete the set."

"There's no one else. I should know. I was there from the start."

"Owen Buck told us there was."

"Buck was crazy. He was paranoid. He was always going on about secrets and running to the authorities. But he never did. You know why? Because there was nothing to tell."

"There was plenty to tell. He told us. We believed him. So now we want the name."

"I don't know any other name."

"Last chance."

"There's no one else!"

"OK. If that's how you want to play it."

Veronica pushed Charlie's legs higher until he slithered down and his hands touched the ground. Roberta stood and wrapped her arms around his knees. Veronica vaulted over the railing and took his right leg. Roberta kept hold of his left. She looked at her sister and mouthed, *One, two, three.* Then they heaved his legs forward, toward the ocean. The momentum carried him over the little ledge Roberta had been lying on and out, away from the cliff. He plunged down, cartwheeling and picking up speed and bouncing off the rocks until he hit the beach. He landed headfirst, drilling a couple of inches into the sand and snapping his neck clean in half.

Christopher Baglin opened the meeting with the news of Michael Rymer's drowning.

No one spoke after he had finished. The air in the room felt heavy. Gary Walsh stared out of the window. Amber Smith looked like she was angry. Kent Neilsen looked like he'd slept in a hedge and wasn't sure how he came to be inside.

Baglin said, "The fact that another man was killed despite being kept under close observation shows the kind of threat we're up against. So, I need names. Reacher, you first. What have you got?"

Reacher slid a piece of paper across the giant table. It had five names on it. Four of them came from the lists he had correlated in his office along the corridor. He had expected more, but that was all the data would support. There had been 3,798 officers and men in the Chemical Corps in 1969. Of those, 157 had kids who followed them into the army. And only one of those kids had been AWOL at the time of the murders, plus another three who had left the service.

Baglin said, "Confidence level?"

"Low to very low."

Baglin nodded. "Smith?"

Smith handed over a page, folded in half. Baglin straightened it out and Reacher saw six names laid out in an orderly column. They were scrawled in the same jagged script he'd read at the hotel.

Smith said, "Due respect to the other people here, sir, but I believe their approach is wrong. My investigation suggests that we're not dealing with one individual who has committed multiple murders. We're dealing with a number of killers who work for the same organization. Same head, different hands. This explains the inconsistent MOs that are reflected in the crimes."

Baglin sat a little straighter. "Interesting theory. And the organization?"

"These men are KGB lifers. Same game, different name."

"Confidence level?"

"High to extremely high."

"Good. They will be checked first. Now, Walsh?"

Walsh dragged his eyes away from the window and said, "Nothing from me."

"Nothing? Not one name?"

"Nothing. The kind of work those guys were doing, the kind of material they were involved with, it doesn't really have a civilian application. Safe to say my well is dry."

Baglin glared at Walsh, then moved on. "Neilsen?"

Neilsen took a sheet of paper from his jacket pocket and held it out. It was surprisingly smooth and crisp, and four names were neatly written in cobalt blue ink. "Confidence? Also low to very low. I wish I could say otherwise but the facts just aren't there."

Baglin stacked the three pages, straightened their edges, and got to his feet. He said, "Keep working. Wrack your brains. Think laterally. Read tea leaves or cast chicken bones if you have to. Just get me more names in case none of these pan out. I'm going to have pagers delivered to you this afternoon. Wear one at all times. If anything breaks out of hours, you're to be back here within fifteen minutes. Any questions?"

Reacher said, "Any word of attacks on scientists from other projects?"

Baglin shook his head. "No. This is the only one."

The phone in the Pentagon rang again at 11:21 A.M. Eastern. Not a scheduled time for a call.

The guy who answered it listened, hung up, then moved into his outer office and dialed the number for Charles Stamoran's car phone. Stamoran had just settled into the car's backseat after a meeting at the White House, which had not gone as well as he'd hoped. He picked up the handset and said, "This better be good news."

The Pentagon guy took a breath, then said, "Charlie Adam is dead. He fell off a cliff from the patio behind his house. His wife returned from walking their dog and found he was missing. She thought he'd gone to the store but his car was still in the garage. Then she noticed more gulls than usual circling and swooping toward the beach. She looked down and saw his body. It was in bad shape. The ME confirmed he died from injuries sustained in the fall. A safety rail that meets the local construction code is in place, so the fall could not have been an accident. Not unless Mr. Adam climbed over voluntarily, then slipped or lost his balance. The agents confirmed that no one entered or exited the property, so foul play is unlikely. Mrs. Adam admitted that her husband had recently exhibited signs of depression but rejected the idea that he committed suicide."

Stamoran leaned his head back against the soft leather. Charlie Adam was the guy from the project he knew least well. He'd always found him prickly and a little vain. He couldn't offer an informed opinion about what Adam would or wouldn't do in any given situation. Except this one. He was sure Adam hadn't jumped. And he was sure he hadn't fallen. However *unlikely*, this was foul play. He had no doubt. Because this wasn't about Adam. It was about whoever was picking the scientists off, one by one. Now there was only one left. Pritchard. And Pritchard was still missing. Which was a circumstance that might play in their favor. But equally, it might not. Much as Stamoran hated to admit it, maybe it was time to think about contingencies.

Stamoran straightened up and said, "There's an upside here. We know where the guy will strike next. We know Pritchard won't be there. We can make sure a surprise is in store. But I want something to fall back on, if it becomes necessary. Baglin is running the task force?"

"Yes, sir."

"Tell him to keep mining for names. If we can identify this asshole before he gets to Pritchard's house, so much the better. But also tell him to shift his focus. There's something else I want him to find."

A pager was delivered to Reacher's office at 1:00 P.M. He had seen doctors and businesspeople wearing pagers clipped to their belts but he didn't want to do that, himself. He thought it would look pretentious, so he shoved it into his jacket pocket. At 1:05 it started to beep. Quietly at first, but by the time he'd fished it out and found a button to press, it was loud and angry. Reacher put it back in his pocket. He figured the sound must have been some kind of a test procedure, or confirmation that the device was activated.

Then he heard doors slamming and footsteps hurrying down the corridor and realized the alert must be for real.

Christopher Baglin was already in his seat at the head of the table when Reacher got to the boardroom. The other three were getting settled. Reacher made his way around to his place, sat, and folded his arms. He could see from Baglin's expression and the stoop of his shoulders that more bad news was on its way.

"We've lost another one." Baglin looked at each person in turn. "Another scientist from Project 192. Charlie Adam. Officially, he jumped, or fell, off a cliff behind his home in California. But let's be realistic. No one's buying that kind of coincidence. He was murdered by the same person who killed his colleagues."

"Or by another person from the same organization," Smith said.

Baglin glared at her, then said, "I guess we can't rule out a team effort, at this stage. But here's the thing. Only one scientist is still alive. Obviously efforts to protect him will be ramped up to the max. But we've already seen that our perp is pretty adept at getting around security. It's like he's a ghost. It would be far safer to intercept him before he gets close. To do that, we need to identify him. So I need you to cast your nets wider. To think more creatively. In short, I need more names. And I need them yesterday. Understood?"

Four heads nodded around the table.

Baglin said, "Good. If you come up with anything hot, page me. Failing that, we'll reconvene at 0900. Now, one more thing. Reacher and Neilsen, you've been looking for relatives of scientists from the sixties in your services. Anyone who died very recently, or who is seriously sick. I like that. It's sound logic. But I want you to expand on it. It doesn't follow that the scientist and the killer have to be related. They could be friends. Comrades in some kind of counter-culture movement. Hell, the current guy could be getting paid by the older one. So I want you to stop worrying about the precise connection for a moment. We can piece that together afterward. Just look at anyone connected, however loosely, to the program in the sixties. Understood?"

Roberta and Veronica Sanson did the closest thing possible to making their stolen Jeep disappear. They parked it in the long-term lot at LAX, wiped it for prints, just in case, and walked away.

There was no debate about where to go next. No need to pick at random from a list of targets. They knew exactly what their destination was. And they had a plan to get there without attracting attention. Roberta took a Delta flight to Washington National. Veronica flew United to Dulles. Both used cash and fake IDs. And then, to mix up their routine, they figured on staying one night at an airport hotel, each stealing a car the next morning, and making their way toward the coast.

The meeting wrapped up and Reacher's afternoon played out much like it had the previous day. Phone calls and faxes and lists of names. Nothing to get his pulse racing, but nothing to complain about. Not directly.

Smith knocked on his door at ten after five and offered a lift to the hotel, which Reacher accepted. Neilsen was waiting in the parking lot. He suggested dinner at the same place as the night before, which Smith and Reacher didn't object to. They met in the hotel reception at 6:00 P.M. and again they walked. Again the drizzle started to fall. The bar wasn't crowded, so they took the same table as before. The same waitress came to take their order.

Neilsen skipped the champagne and went straight to the whiskey. Reacher and Smith stuck to beer. Reacher waited until the food had arrived and the others were on their second drinks, then he said, "One of the names I gave Baglin was for an AWOL soldier. Nothing to do with the task force. I did it to save myself the trouble of tracking him down later."

Neilsen drained his glass and set it down. "Why are you telling us about it? You were Mr. Cagey last night."

"Because of something you said. About the importance of trusting each other. It's even more important now."

"Why?"

"I met a navy guy, years ago. He had this expression. He said if you don't know which port you're heading for, every wind is an ill wind."

"Do you get that?" Smith said to Neilsen. "I don't follow."

Reacher said, "It's like if you don't know what you're aiming for, you're always going to miss. Like with this detail we're assigned to. How can we draw valid conclusions when we don't know what's going on?"

Smith said, "Have you not been listening? Bioweapon research, dead scientists, revelations that could embarrass the country. That pretty much covers it, right?"

"Wrong. The dots don't connect the way Baglin says they do. Think it through. Someone claims the United States did some secret research to find antidotes to bioweapons? So what? Why deny it? Of course we did it. We had to. It would be embarrassing if we hadn't. It would be worse. It would be criminal."

"You're being too logical. We're talking about the general public.

Civilians. They're weirded out by bioweapons. They think of people bleeding out of their eyeballs and babies with two heads."

"That's why we need antidotes."

"Again, forget your logic. This is about emotion."

"It's about something we're not seeing yet. Think about the last thing Baglin said today. He wants names of scientists from the sixties. Why? They can't be behind a plan to find out what was done. They know, because they were the ones who did it."

"I guess."

"And there were a bunch of these bioweapon antidote projects. None of the others has been targeted. Why this one? What's special about it?"

"I don't know. Does it matter?"

"The tide is about to turn. I can feel it. If that last scientist buys the farm, or if some other kind of secret gets revealed, the whole focus is going to switch to blame. The thing itself won't be the problem. Us not containing it will be the problem. And like Neilsen said, we all have some dings on our records right now. Do you have people lining up to go to bat for you? Because I don't."

"So what do we do?"

"We start by getting the truth about Project 192."

"How? Turn inward? Do some digging? Twist some arms?"

"No. That's not going to get the job done. If we're going to save that scientist, and our own asses, we need to go off-base a little bit. Together. Hence, trust."

There was silence for a moment, then Neilsen said, "Two of the names I gave were for my own reasons. Bad guys, sure enough. The world will be better with them behind bars. Or in unmarked graves. But they have nothing to do with the task force."

Smith said, "Same goes for all six of mine. All murdering assholes, but nothing to do with the dead scientists." She paused. "So.

Project 192 was a joint army/CIA thing. Are you suggesting you and Neilsen lean on some people? Cut some corners? Break some rules? Is that what you mean?"

"No. There's no point. We would only come across two kinds of people. Ones who don't know anything. And ones who do know but won't tell us. If we want accurate information about what our side was doing in the sixties, there's only one place to get it. That's where you come in."

"The FBI?"

"No. The KGB."

Chapter 12

The odds were that they would walk into a trap before
the morning was out, and Roberta and Veronica Sanson knew it.
There was only one name left on their list. Neville Pritchard. The
last guy who had worked in the lab in India in '69. Whoever was
responsible for keeping him alive would know they were coming.
Would focus their resouces. It would be crazy to expect anything
less. The smart move would be to walk away. To be content with
what they had already achieved. But there was a problem with that.
Pritchard was the only one who knew the identity they needed to
discover. The key to the secret they needed to unlock. So dumb move
or not, they were going to take a trip to Pritchard's house. Their decision was set in stone. But that didn't mean they had to go in with their
eyes closed.

Roberta and Veronica rendezvoused at first light at an abandoned
gas station five miles outside Annapolis, as planned. Roberta was
driving a white Toyota Corolla she had stolen at Washington National airport. Veronica was in a Dodge Caravan she had taken from

an off-airport hotel at Dulles. Previously they had done their drive-bys together, but with the likely extra surveillance in mind they decided to keep both vehicles. Make two passes, one from each direction, then compare what they had seen.

Roberta went first, heading south toward Back Creek, sticking close to the speed limit and obeying every stop sign and red light she came to. Veronica followed, sometimes five cars behind, sometimes six, and when she was two streets away from Pritchard's she coasted to the side of the road and stopped next to a stretch of tall, ancient hedge. Three minutes later she saw Roberta's Toyota coming back toward her. She gave no sign that she recognized it. She sat for another minute then pulled out and made her way to Pritchard's house. Drove past it, slowly enough to get a good look, quickly enough to not attract attention, then made for a stretch of scrubby grass that overlooked the water and pulled up alongside her sister. She wiped the interior of the van for prints, jumped down, and slid into the Toyota's passenger seat.

Roberta said, "I saw four cars watching."

Veronica said, "Same. Four cars, but one way in. We're going to need costumes. Props. And a different kind of vehicle."

Reacher was awake, dressed, and sitting on his bed when Amber Smith knocked on his hotel room door. It was 8:00 A.M. Right on time.

Reacher let Smith in. Her eyes were wide and she was bouncing on the balls of her feet. She said, "We're getting somewhere. I had people working on it all night. They've hit on three possibilities. Three KGB defectors. I'm still waiting on the details."

Reacher and Smith rode down in the elevator together. They took a detour via the breakfast room to pick up coffee and bagels, then

Smith drove them the mile to the building the task force was using. She spent the remaining three-quarters of an hour in her office, staring at the phone, willing it to ring. Reacher was happy for his not to. He picked up a couple of pages that had spilled out of the fax machine, ran through the names listed on them so that he would have some ammunition for Christopher Baglin at the morning meeting, then settled back in his chair, closed his eyes, and let Magic Slim loose in his head.

Baglin was late. Not catastrophically, but enough to leave him red-faced and out of breath when he finally bustled into the boardroom. The other four were in their customary places, in silence. Reacher was on his second refill of coffee. They each handed over their next tranche of names, except for Walsh. He had drawn another blank. Reacher was beginning to wonder if the guy was trying to get returned to the Treasury. If that was really where he was from. He made a mental note to follow up with his brother, Joe.

No new information was forthcoming, and no new orders were issued, so Reacher was back in his office inside ten minutes. Five minutes after that Smith knocked on his door and rushed in without waiting for an answer. She said, "I've heard from my people. One option is a dead end. Literally. The guy got killed while he was training for a dogsled race up in Alaska. He should have known better, at his age. The other two leads are promising, though. One guy is based in Oregon. The other's here, in D.C."

Reacher said, "What do you know about the local guy?"

"He runs a Russian-themed café. And honestly, he sounds like a complete headcase. He was a KGB colonel. Defected in '74. Declined the whole new name, relocation package in return for more money and the chance to stay in town and build his own fake identity. And earn a fortune feeding politicians weird shit they'd never eat at home. He goes by—and I checked this to make sure I was getting it right—His Royal Highness the Prince Sarb of Windsor."

"As in Windsor, England?"

"It's a nod to a legend he supposedly created before he bailed on the Soviets. He claimed he was stationed in London in the late fifties and MI5 picked up his scent. They were closing in fast, his escape routes were blown, so he went to the Brits and pretended to be the illegitimate son of an aristocrat who had been living in Hungary. He said he was on the fringes of the intelligence community there and he had a line on the Russian spy they were chasing. Said the Brits took the fact that he knew who they were looking for as a sign he was legit, and they bought it. So effectively he got them to hire him to catch himself. Which he clearly did not do. If his story is true. Which I doubt."

"What was his specialty?"

"His last two postings were in Southeast Asia. He had a lot to say about chemical and biological stuff when he was debriefed, post-defection."

"Sounds like he's worth a shot."

"I guess. Although . . . Reacher, are we crazy? Is this guy really going to talk to us if we just show up on his doorstep? Normally this sort of thing takes months of negotiating to set up."

"Oh, he'll talk. Strangers always open up to me. I'm a people person. Haven't you noticed?"

Eight pairs of eyes watched the UPS truck as it dawdled along Neville Pritchard's street. It was moving erratically, speeding up and slowing down like the driver was searching for an address. The agent in the lead car picked up the handset of the phone that was mounted between his front seats. He called a number at the Pentagon. Asked his control to find out which UPS depot covered the area, then check whether the truck was one of theirs. The truck drew level with Pritchard's driveway. It turned and crept toward the house. The agent's phone rang. It was his control. He confirmed that the local UPS manager had vouched for the truck. The agent was happy with the news but not completely satisfied. Pritchard hadn't received any other deliveries the whole time they'd been watching his house, and he wasn't home now so it didn't make sense for him to be expecting anything. The agent swapped the phone for his radio. He pressed the Transmit button and said, "Possible contact. Stand by. Over."

The truck made it all the way to Pritchard's garage, then stopped. It sat for a moment, shaking slightly and rattling and pumping exhaust fumes into the morning air. The driver didn't get out. Then the truck began to turn around. It sawed back and forth, back and forth, lurching and swaying each time it changed direction. It paused when it had gotten halfway, perpendicular to the driveway, like the driver was taking a breath. Then it started moving again, even more abruptly, like the driver's patience with the whole situation was wearing thin.

The truck finally got back to the road and turned so it was heading the same way as before. It drove another ten yards then stopped again. It was right in the line of sight of the third agents' car. The only one with a view of Pritchard's garage door. The agent in the driver's seat wound down his window. He saw the UPS driver was a woman. He nudged his partner as if to say, *that explains it*, then waved and yelled at her to move. She may have said something back but it was hard to tell because the side of her face was covered with a large square of gauze bandage, like she'd recently been in an accident. She did return his wave, though. Only she used fewer fingers than he had done.

Roberta Sanson crouched inside Neville Pritchard's garage and leaned against the door. She was wearing a balaclava that covered her ears as well as her face, but she could still hear the truck's engine. She listened to it wheeze and groan and then run and stop and she pictured each step of its progress. Each step they had carefully mapped out. The truck was stationary out on the road for longer than she'd expected. She held her breath. Pictured agents from the watching cars swarming around it. Sliding back the door. Pulling Veronica out. Ripping off her disguise. She held her breath. Then the truck puttered away. It kept going this time. There was no sound of squealing tires. Nothing to suggest pursuit. She relaxed. Just a little. She could see the door that led into the house, but she had no idea what was waiting on the other side.

Roberta inched her way along the side of Pritchard's car until she reached the connecting door. She took hold of the handle, gathered herself, then twisted, pushed, and dived through the gap. She rolled. Pushed back onto her feet. Spun around 360 degrees, fists raised, ready to block or strike. And saw no one. No sign of Pritchard. No sign of any agents.

Roberta moved forward, slowly, planting her feet carefully, making next to no sound. She didn't know Pritchard. She wasn't familiar with his habits but she figured it was probably too late for him to be asleep. There was no sound of water running so he wasn't taking a shower. No sound of kitchen equipment being used so he probably wasn't cooking. Based on the window configuration she'd seen from outside, she guessed the last door in the corridor would lead to the living room. She decided to start there. She kept moving. Passed the first door. Which opened. A man came out. Late twenties, cropped hair, stocky. Dressed in black. Holding a gun.

Not Pritchard.

The guy sneered at Roberta then took a radio from his belt and held it to his ear. He said, "Contact. You owe me fifty bucks. He did show up. Only get this—he's a she. Hold your positions. We'll bring her out in a minute."

Roberta thought, *Of course I showed up. Why would he think I wouldn't? Because they've got Pritchard in custody?* Then she punched the guy in the throat, knuckles extended. He fell back. His gun and his radio rattled against the shiny wooden floor and he grasped his neck, gurgling and gasping as he fought to suck air through his crushed windpipe.

Two more doors opened. Two more men appeared. Both young and fit. Both with guns.

Roberta thought, *Why would they think I'd expect Pritchard to be in custody? None of the others were.*

Another guy appeared at the top of the stairs.

Roberta thought, *Wait. Maybe Pritchard's not in custody?* She darted forward. The guy closest to her stayed still. He let her get close. Which was a mistake. She shaped up like she was going to throw another punch but instead she smashed the side of her foot into the guy's knee. Weight wasn't on her side but she did have strength and momentum, and they were enough. The guy shrieked and fell sideways. He bounced off the wall and whimpered and tried to wrap his arms around his injured leg. Roberta kicked him in the side of his head. Hard. After that he was still and quiet.

Maybe Pritchard ran? Got a tip-off? Heard about the others?

The third guy took a step toward Roberta. He raised his gun. Aimed it at her chest. She grabbed his wrist with her left hand.

Twisted, to stress his elbow. Crashed her right forearm into it, shattering the joint. Punched him in the solar plexus, knocking the wind out of him. Punched him under the jaw to rattle his brain. Then she let go of his wrist, took a half step back, swung her leg up and around, gaining speed and power all the way, and kicked him in the temple. She wasn't exceptionally tall but she was flexible and she was fast. The guy was out cold before he hit the floor.

Maybe they assumed I know his location. Maybe they don't know it themselves? I'll have to be careful how I play this. There are still four cars outside . . .

The fourth guy was already at the bottom of the stairs. He turned to face Roberta. He raised his gun but stayed well out of her reach. He said, "I've got to thank you, miss. These fellas are never going to live this down. Getting their asses handed to them by a girl? The fun I'm going to have? Priceless. But today's fun is over. You're a skinny little thing but no one could miss you from this range. Especially not me, because I'm a hell of a good shot. So give it up. Turn around. Hold your hands out behind your back."

Roberta was still for a few seconds like she was weighing up words of such profundity she could barely grasp their full meaning. Then her head slumped forward, her shoulders sagged, and she turned so that she was facing away from the guy. He wasted no time. He didn't want her changing her mind or pulling any tricks so he stepped in close, wrapped a PlastiCuff around her wrists and pulled it tight. He leaned in so close that Roberta could feel his breath on her neck and said, "That really was quite a performance. I never saw that coming, I'll be honest. Was it you who put an end to the other five guys, too?"

Roberta said, "They never saw it coming, either. But then men have a long history of underestimating women, don't you? If you didn't, maybe more of you would be alive."

"Maybe so. Maybe not. Either way, it's time to go." He pushed Roberta toward the door. "There's someone who wants to talk with you."

"I'm not saying a word. Not unless you tell me something first. I have to know. Did you find it? Was it here? Or was Pritchard lying?"

"The hell you talking about?"

"Pritchard's black book. With the dates and the times and the places, all written down. It's what I came here for."

"Bullshit. You came to kill Pritchard, like you did the others. You admitted it. Only you're behind the curve. You didn't know Pritchard's gone. You don't know where he is."

"I know exactly where he is. He's where I left him."

The guy spun Roberta around. "You have him?"

Roberta winked at the guy.

He said, "He's alive?"

"For the time being. Until his book is safely in my hands. You know how much money I could make off of that thing? A king's ransom. We could split it . . ."

"Where is he?"

"Safe. For now. But if I don't get back to him sometime soon, that could change."

"Tell me where."

"How can I make this clearer? No."

The guy glared at Roberta. "You don't get how this works, do you?" He touched the muzzle of the gun against her chin, held it there for a moment, then slid it down over her neck. He kept it going, across her chest, between her breasts, over her stomach, all the way to the tops of her thighs. "This operation is being run from the top. The very top. I could tear you into a dozen pieces and they'd give me a separate medal for every one of them. And if I felt like doing anything else to you before then, nobody would ever be the wiser. Same goes for my buddies, when they wake up. I don't think you're top of their Christmas card lists. Do you?"

Roberta's eyes opened wide. Her voice shot up an octave. She said, "Go back to town. Head east on 450, then north on 2. Just past mile marker 17 you'll see a boathouse on the right. It's blue. He's in there. In a sail locker. Tied up and gagged."

The guy patted Roberta on the cheek. He said, "See, that wasn't hard." He took his radio and repeated her directions, then said, "Go. All cars. Everything's under control in here. I'll take her for questioning, myself. Out."

Roberta waited until the sound of the cars' engines had faded into the distance. She said, "Under control?" Then she sprang forward and drove her knee into the guy's groin. She put every ounce of strength and fury into it. She would have left the ground without his bulk to stop her. He screamed. His knees buckled. He toppled forward, clutching himself. He puked, spat, rolled onto his side, and settled into a drawn-out, shrill howl. Roberta looked at him and said, "There you go. Underestimating a woman, again. Will you never learn?"

Chapter 13

Amber Smith dropped the car in a loading zone a block from the Soviet defector's café. She climbed out, Reacher and Neilsen joined her on the sidewalk, and together they walked the rest of the way. The place they were looking for was called the Tsar's Tearoom. It took up the first floor of a small, low-rise office building on the edge of a fashionable part of town. A red awning jutted out over its entrance and its facade was covered with garish paintings of onion domes and fairy-tale cathedrals and double-headed eagles. It was a look. There was no doubt about that. Reacher was no design expert but he was pretty sure it wasn't a good one.

Smith went in first. There was a waiting area near the door with green velvet armchairs lined up along the wall. A coat check closet. A lectern for a maître d'. And plenty of tables. Four-tops in the center of the space, neatly set out like squares on a chessboard, and rectangular six- and eight-tops around the edge, all laid with white tablecloths and shiny silver cutlery and delicate cups and saucers. Reacher shook his head. The owner wasn't re-creating a slice of his past. He hadn't experienced anything like this in the Soviet Union. That was for damn sure. What he was selling was pure fantasy.

There were three customers in the place, spread across two of the smaller tables, and one waiter was on duty. He strolled across to the lectern and said, "Table for three? Breakfast or brunch?"

Reacher said, "We want to see the owner."

The waiter looked startled. He said, "He's not here."

"We'll wait."

"OK. I guess. As long as you place an order and don't block a table if other guests—"

"We'll wait in his office."

The waiter shook his head. He said, "That will not be possible."

Reacher said, "Are you sure?" He started toward the back of the room. The waiter set off after him, fussing and flapping in his wake like an anxious child. Smith and Neilsen followed a few steps behind. Reacher weaved through the tables until he got to an embroidered red and gold curtain that was hanging across a doorway in the back wall. It was between two giant paintings of old guys in antique military uniforms sitting astride docile white horses. Reacher pulled the curtain aside. He saw a tiny vestibule and a staircase, leading up. A guy was by the bottom step, perched on a wooden stool. He stood up. He was the same height as Reacher but his chest was so wide that his arms couldn't hang straight down at his sides. He glared, but didn't say a word.

The waiter hustled up and said, "I'm sorry, Sergei. This guest is . . . lost. He didn't mean to trespass, I'm sure." The waiter went up on tiptoes and leaned over, closer to Reacher. He lowered his voice and said, "Come on. Let me take you to a table. If you place a large enough order—champagne, caviar, a suckling pig perhaps—then this little mistake can be overlooked. Sergei will stay here. You can leave. He won't hurt you."

LEE CHILD and ANDREW CHILD

Reacher said nothing. He had hoped someone like Sergei would be waiting there. It confirmed that the stairs led somewhere important. With luck, to the owner's office. In which case there would be more bodyguards. Probably the same size, or bigger. Probably armed. Ready to rush down and snuff out any threat at the first sound of trouble. Which was bad luck for Sergei. It meant there was no time for Reacher to offer him the opportunity to surrender. He had to get straight down to business, so he tipped back his head. Just a little. Just enough to provide some leverage. He engaged the muscles in his neck and chest and abdomen. Then he flung himself forward, jackknifing at the waist and driving his forehead straight into Sergei's face. It was a brutal, primitive, devastating move. The kind Reacher liked best. Sergei had no warning. No time to react. No chance to defend himself. His nose and cheekbones shattered. Cartilage was crushed and torn. Teeth showered down onto the carpet. Blood gushed onto his shirt and he fell back and landed crumpled, inert, half on the floor, half on the staircase.

Reacher turned to the waiter, wiped a trace of blood from his forehead, and said, "We're going upstairs. If anyone's waiting for us, I'll come back down—and what I did to Sergei, I'll do to you. Are we clear?"

Reacher picked his way around Sergei's immobile limbs and led the way upstairs. It took Smith and Neilsen a moment to catch up. Reacher's outburst of violence had wrong-footed them. Reacher stepped out into a corridor that ran perpendicular, the whole width of the building. There was a window at each end, six doors on one side, and four on the other. The walls were painted a dull almond color with scuffs and dents scattered all the way along at various heights. Light came from naked bulbs in plastic holders at intervals on the ceiling. One was flickering and hanging down on its wires. Outside of the public area the place fell somewhere between dump and fire hazard, Reacher thought. Maybe the café wasn't doing so well, after all. Maybe the Soviet guys weren't too familiar with high standards of decoration. Or safety. Or maybe they just didn't care.

Smith and Neilsen arrived in the corridor behind Reacher and straightaway the nearest door flew open. A guy strode through. He could have been Sergei's twin. He was the same height. The same weight. He had the same bulked-up stance. Only this guy didn't stay still. He put his head down and started to charge.

Reacher pointed to the other half of the corridor and said, "Move!" He glanced to his right to make sure Smith and Neilsen were at a safe distance, then he stepped the other way. Toward the onrushing guy. He squared up. Waited until impact seemed inevitable, then danced aside and flattened himself against the wall. The guy was level. Almost past Reacher. On course to demolish the other two. Reacher stretched out. He grabbed the guy's collar and belt, planted his feet, and pivoted, hard. He felt like his arms were getting wrenched out of their sockets but he held firm. He waited until the other guy had swung through 90 degrees. So he was no longer in line with the corridor. He was facing down the stairs. Then Reacher let go. The guy's velocity had dropped a little but he still had plenty of momentum. Enough to carry him half the length of the staircase in midair. When he finally made contact, his arms were stretched out above his head. It was an instinctive response. An attempt to break his fall. Which it did in the extremely short term. It also broke his wrists and his collarbones. It slowed the front half of his body. But not his legs. It caused them to flip up, over his head, and sent him cartwheeling down onto the floor beyond the bottom step. He landed in a solid heap, half on top of his doppelganger.

More bad news for Sergei, Reacher thought.

* * *

Reacher checked both ways along the corridor. Nothing was moving. He had ten doors to pick from. The guy they needed to find would be behind one of them. Assuming he was in the building. And the presence of the heavies suggested he would be. Reacher figured the kind of guy who used fake titles and grandiose made-up names must have quite an ego, and a guy with an ego would want his bodyguards close, to show how important he was. So Reacher closed in on the door that Sergei's lookalike had rushed out of. It was still open, but just a crack. Reacher listened. He heard papers rustling. A creaking sound like someone shifting their weight in a stiff leather chair. And breathing. Calm. Relaxed. No sense of tension. And from more than one person.

Reacher nudged the door with his shoulder and strolled casually through like he was returning home from a boring day at the office. Like he wasn't expecting to face any kind of a challenge. The room was rectangular with a window at the far end and dark wood paneling on the walls. There was a desk three-quarters of the way in. A man was sitting behind it. He had broad shoulders. His head was large and square. He was bald, and he had narrow eyes that were set close together beneath a giant slab of a forehead. There were four other men in the room. Two were sitting on plain wooden chairs in front of the desk. Two were on identical chairs near the left-hand wall. All were wearing expensive suits and ties but they looked child-sized compared to the last two guys Reacher had faced. Even though they were sitting down, he could tell they were not very tall. He guessed maybe five feet eight. Five feet ten at the most. They had shaved heads. Their eyes were bright and constantly moving. They looked lean and rangy. The kind of guys who could run all day and all night with huge packs on their backs. Special Forces types. Probably former Spetsnaz operators. The big lunks who were now at the bottom of the stairs were just window dressing. Their job was to scare people who didn't know better. These guys were the ones who would get the job done if a threat got serious.

Or so someone hoped.

Reacher stopped in the center of the room and looked at the man behind the desk with an expression that said he'd been more impressed with the contents of his Kleenex the last time he'd blown his nose. Smith and Neilsen had followed Reacher in but hung back near the doorway. The two guys near the wall got to their feet. So did the pair by the desk. They shifted around so the four were in a square. None had their backs to Smith or Neilsen. Reacher was boxed in. It was a promising position for them. Their numerical advantage and the close quarters negated Reacher's natural strengths—his weight, and the length of his arms and legs. Had it been one against one, or two against one, with more room to maneuver, they wouldn't have been able to get anywhere near him. If they tried to get in range for a punch or a kick he could pick them off at leisure. But here they could swarm in from all sides. One or two of them would take some damage, most likely severe, but if the others sustained the attack, there was every chance they would succeed. And the way they were formed up was smart. Two of them were behind Reacher, outside his field of vision. The odds were against him. That was for sure. But the odds had been against him before. Countless times. All the way back to his childhood when he and his brother, Joe, had been forced to slug it out with the local tough kids the first day of every new school they attended, all around the world. Reacher knew what was going to happen. He didn't need to see the guys in his blind spot. One of them would be the first to attack. It didn't matter which. Not as long as Reacher moved before he got hit. So he spun to his left. He raised his arm as he turned. Brought it up to horizontal. The side of his fist was like the face of a sledgehammer and it was accelerating as it swung around. It caught the first guy under his chin and lifted him off his feet. The force threw him back. His head hit the wall and he slid down to the floor, out cold.

Reacher pushed off his back foot, reversed direction, twisted at the waist, and launched the same fist at the guy in the opposite corner of the square. He was aiming for his face. Going for power rather than placement. But the guy was fast. He anticipated Reacher's move. Given the weight difference he opted to block with both forearms. It was effective. He knocked Reacher's fist off target. Deflected it so it was set to sail harmlessly past his ear. Only the moment they made contact, Reacher bent his arm. His elbow shifted sideways and the tip crunched into the guy's nose. He fell like a suit slipping off a hanger and before he hit the floor Reacher had reversed course again. He was back in the first corner. The guy who'd started to the right of that was moving, too. Going forward into what was now empty space. Their roles had flipped. Now he couldn't see Reacher. For a moment he was defenseless. And Reacher had a rule. You get the chance to put your enemy down, you take it. Every time. No hesitation. No pearl clutching about whether that's a gentlemanly thing to do. No Marquess of Queensberry rules. So Reacher stepped in close. He punched the guy in the right kidney, hard and fast, middle knuckle extended to multiply the force. He did the same to his left kidney. And when the guy collapsed forward onto his knees, Reacher kicked him in the head like he was trying for a sixty-yard field goal.

One guy was left standing. He had shifted across, directly in front of the desk, and was pulling something out of his pants pocket. A knife handle. He hit a round brass button and a blade snapped into place, bright and sharp and mean.

Reacher said, "Bring that thing near me and I'll make you eat it."

The guy held the knife out in front and moved it from side to side in a slow, fluid, mocking motion.

Reacher said, "Don't say I didn't warn you." He stretched to the side and picked up the chair the guy had been sitting on. He flipped it around so that its legs were pointing straight out, then charged. He drove the guy back. The guy's arms were flailing and his knife was nowhere near finding a target. Reacher kept going. The guy bumped into the edge of the desk and fell, sprawling onto its scratched wooden top. Reacher dropped the chair, pinned the guy's wrist with one hand, and used his other forearm to crush the guy's throat. He lifted the guy's wrist then hammered it down, dislodging the knife from his grip. Swung his leg up and planted his knee on the guy's chest. Picked up the knife. Folded away the blade. And pinched the guy's nose.

The guy held his breath for thirty seconds. Forty-five. His face turned red. His eyes started to bulge. He finally opened his mouth. He spluttered and gasped. Reacher shoved the knife so far in it jammed against the guy's tonsils. Then he lifted the guy up and flung him headfirst into the wall.

The man behind the desk had rolled his chair back to avoid getting slashed. He waited a moment then stood up and came around and set the fallen chair back on its feet in its place by the wall. He stared at each unconscious body in turn, then turned his attention to Reacher. This guy was a good five inches shorter but must have been fifty pounds heavier. His legs were relatively short and his waist was narrow, which made his chest and shoulders look cartoonishly big. He was still for a moment, then he launched himself forward, arms spread wide, straight toward Reacher. He was trying to grab him and wrestle him to the floor. Reacher moved at the same moment. Straight toward the guy. One arm rising. Elbow out front like the tip of a steel bar. It connected with the bridge of the guy's nose. His head stopped dead. His legs kept moving. His feet left the floor and he crashed down, flat on his back, still as a rock.

Smith moved up alongside Reacher. She jabbed him in the arm and said, "The hell have you done? How can we talk to him now?"

Reacher said, "Don't worry. This isn't the guy we want. He can't be. It was too easy."

Roberta Sanson wanted the agent to suffer for as long as possible so she left him writhing on the floor, grasping his groin, until she heard the UPS truck pull up outside Neville Pritchard's house. Then she kicked him in the side of the head, made sure he was out, lay on the rug, and pulled her arms as far apart as the PlastiCuffs would allow. She slid her wrists down the back of her legs and out from beneath her feet. Stood, and went to let Veronica in through the front door.

Veronica took out her knife and freed Roberta's hands. She gave her a hug, then looked at the agents' bodies slumped in the hallway and said, "You OK?"

Roberta said, "Fine," and peeled off her balaclava. "You?"

Veronica pulled the bandage from her cheek. "Did Pritchard give up the name?"

"He's not here. It was an ambush."

"Where is he?"

"He's missing. They don't know where he is. We need to figure out where he went. And we don't have much time. I sent the surveillance guys on a wild-goose chase but they'll be back soon. Ninety minutes, max."

"He ran?"

"Must have heard about his old buddies' accidents."

Veronica was quiet for a second then she turned and looked at the doorframe. She opened the door and ran her fingers over a patch near the lock. She said, "I'm not sure about that. This door's been busted in, then fixed. Recently. I think they came to snatch him up, botched it, and he slipped away somehow."

"Maybe. But *why's* not important right now. It's *where* that matters."

"He was a career agent. A cautious guy. He would have had a go-bag ready. Is his car here?"

"In the garage."

"So he left on foot, or he had another vehicle nearby. Something untraceable."

"Must have had a vehicle. He's no spring chicken and he'd need to carry supplies. And if he was seen walking or running, that could be suspicious. Especially if they came for him at night."

"So what kind of vehicle? Where would he have kept it? How would he have gotten to it?"

"If they hit the house from the front, they'd also have been watching the back. The east side is pretty exposed. Not a great place to bail out from. What about the west? We need to check the garage."

Roberta led the way, retracing her steps from when she had snuck into the house. The garage was small by modern standards. There was room for one car plus just about enough space for a workbench at the far end and some shelves running along the side walls. The workbench was kept clean and a whole assortment of tools was laid out on a pegboard on the wall above it. The shelves were sagging under all the stuff that was piled on them. Years' and years' accumulation of car parts and tools for yard work, and redundant kitchen gadgets and cans of dry food. And the car was a beauty. A blood-red 1969 Camaro with a black stripe down the hood. It looked well cared for. Pritchard was clearly conscientious when it came to its upkeep. Cosmetically, it was flawless. Its paint was gleaming and there was not a scratch or a ding to be seen. A maintenance pit stretched the whole length of the floor so the sisters figured maybe he handled the mechanical stuff himself, too.

They inspected every inch of the walls. Roberta made her way around clockwise. Veronica, the opposite way. They pushed and pulled and prodded every plank and board and panel. Nothing gave an inch. They even poked the ceiling with a broom but it was rock solid, too.

Roberta started toward the door. She said, "Come on. We're wasting time."

Veronica stayed where she was. She said, "Wait. I have an idea. Have you seen a flashlight in here?"

"I don't think so."

Veronica nodded and made her way around to the Camaro's hood. She crept down the steps to the maintenance pit. A moment later, an inspection lamp flickered to life beneath the car. Veronica was out of sight for more than two minutes. When she climbed back up, she had a smile on her face. She said, "This is it. The pit branches off to the side and comes up under a fake coal hatch on the other side of the garage wall. It's how he got out. It has to be. So follow me. Quick. We need to figure out where he went next."

Chapter 14

Reacher crouched down and started to work his way through the guy's pockets. He pulled out a wallet and opened it. He held it up for Smith to see. There was a driver's license in the center section behind a clear plastic window. It gave the name Valery Kerzhakov.

Reacher raised his voice and said, "I wonder what the Russian community in D.C. would do if they found out that Maksim Sarbotskiy is such a pretentious freak he doesn't just make up names, he also hides behind a body double? Laugh, I bet. Certainly stop coming to his little café."

There was a scraping sound from the side of the room. A section of the wood paneling on the wall behind the pair of chairs slid to one side. A man appeared in the gap that had been created. He was wearing a suit with a telltale bulge under the left armpit. His head was shaved. He was tall, but not giant. Broad, but not imposing. Somewhere in size between Sergei and the whippy guys who were now lying unconscious on the floor.

Reacher said, "Got any buddies in there? Because no offense, friend, but you're not going to get very far on your own."

The guy said, "I'm not here to fight you. If I were . . ." He patted the bulge in his suit coat. Then he stepped back and gestured for Reacher to follow him. "Please."

Reacher stepped through the hidden doorway. Smith and Neilsen followed. It led them to another room, the same size and shape. This one also had a window and a desk with a pair of chairs in front of it. It had a leather couch off to the side. Paintings of nineteenth-century battle scenes on the walls. And a console in the corner with a bank of small, square TV screens. There were six. All black and white. They showed live feeds from the room Reacher had just left, the corridor, the stairs, two from the café, and one from the side-walk outside. Reacher turned to the guy who was sitting behind the desk. He said, "Enjoy the show?"

The guy looked remarkably like Kerzhakov, except that he was still capable of sitting upright. He had the same barrel chest and wide shoulders. The same kind of square head and beady eyes and neolithic forehead. He stared back at Reacher and shrugged as if to suggest he'd seen better.

Reacher said, "You're Sarbotskiy?"

The guy prickled. "I am His Royal Highness the Prince—"

"Cut the crap," Reacher said. "This is America. Son of a king or son of a whore, it's all the same here."

Sarbotskiy scowled. He said, "And you are?"

"Jack Reacher. US Army."

"Army? All of you?"

"Close enough."

"What do you want?"

"I'm here to do you a favor."

"What kind of favor?"

"Not burning this place to the ground."

"Not the most generous of favors."

"Best offer you're going to get."

"Undoubtedly. And I assume you want something in return."

"Not much. A little information."

"Why would I trust you?"

"Why would you not?" Reacher gestured toward the TV monitors. "You've seen this isn't a social call."

"You can't force me to cooperate. I have protection."

"You do?" Reacher looked around the room. "Where is it?"

"From the US government. We have an agreement. A contract. It's watertight."

"Watertight. Huh. But is it fireproof? Does it make this property and everything else you own impossible to burn down?"

Sarbotskiy didn't answer.

"Is it soundproof? Does it guarantee that word of your whereabouts won't spread to the guys back home? The ones you no doubt sold out to get this agreement?"

Sarbotskiy crossed his arms. He didn't reply.

"I hear your homeland is falling apart. Collapsing like a house of cards. I bet a lot of those guys are planning to relocate. Looking for a cozy little business to buy into. Only not by using money."

Sarbotskiy leaned back and steepled his fingers. "Maybe I could help you with this *information* you want. But I can't just give it to you. I have principles. I'll need something in return."

"What?"

"A wrestling match would have been nice. You and a couple of my guys. It's one thing watching a bout on a screen, but nothing beats violence up close and personal, does it? I love wrestling." Sarbotskiy sighed. "Tell you the truth, I miss it."

"I never had time for it. Never saw the point. Too many rules."

"All right. Then we drink." Sarbotskiy opened a drawer, pulled out a cut-crystal decanter full of clear liquid and a pair of glasses. Also cut crystal. Tumbler-sized, not shot glasses. He plonked everything down on the desk, filled the glasses, and pushed one toward Reacher. "Come. Sit. The first is for good faith. Then you can ask your question."

Reacher moved toward one of the chairs. Reluctantly. He would have preferred the same kind of approach he'd used with the army driver at Rock Island Arsenal. He wasn't much of a drinker. But not because of some moral scruple. It was a practical thing. Alcohol degrades performance. He'd seen the effect a thousand times. So going shot to shot with a giant Russian wasn't an ideal solution. Especially when the shots were super-sized. That was for damn sure. On the other hand he had a lot of experience with interrogations. Some subjects crumble, given the correct incentive. Others would die before they talked. His gut was telling him that despite his bluster, Sarbotskiy was from the second category.

Reacher kept going, slowly. Neilsen was faster. He darted forward, dropped into the nearer chair, picked up the glass, and downed it in five long, thirsty gulps. He smiled and said, "I believe this is my area of expertise."

Sarbotskiy shook his head. "No." He pointed at Reacher. "The deal's with him."

Neilsen said, "Forget him. You want to loosen someone's tongue with this stuff? Maybe pick up a few secrets, quid pro quo? Then he's not your man." He tapped his forehead. "There's far more interesting stuff in here. Believe me."

Sarbotskiy thought for a moment, then he refilled Neilsen's glass. He said, "The rate's double for you."

Neilsen drained the glass again. "Very generous. We could be friends. Now, we want to know about Project 192. It was a thing in the sixties."

Sarbotskiy drained his own glass then refilled both. He said, "That was your project. Not ours." Then he blinked and started to laugh. His whole belly shook. "You know you can't trust your own government, so you come to the KGB when you need the truth. I like you people. OK. Project 192. I assume you know the basics. It was a program to make antidotes against our chemical and biological weapons."

Neilsen nodded and drained his glass.

Sarbotskiy said, "Your government probably even admits that, in private at least. Yes? But you suspect there's more. You can sense it." He drank, then poured refills for both of them. "Well, your instincts are correct. There was more."

Sarbotskiy gestured for Neilsen to drink.

Neilsen downed the drink in one gulp, again, and slammed the glass down on the desk.

Sarbotskiy emptied his own glass and said, "There was a parallel project. A secret within a secret. We never even learned its official designation. Moscow called it *Typhon*. The deadliest of the mythical monsters. And who says communists don't have a classical education?" He laughed again, as deeply as before.

Neilsen said, "And the purpose of this second project was?" His voice was growing a little slurred.

Sarbotskiy refilled both glasses and said, "One ninety-two was defensive. Countering our weapons. The ones you knew about, anyway. Typhon was the opposite. It was one hundred percent offensive. Literally and figuratively. America was brewing up newer and nastier weapons to attack us with, and all the time pretending to be a passive victim of Soviet hostility." He took another drink. "Western hypocrisy in overdrive."

"Is there any proof? Or is this the potato juice talking?"

"Proof exists. I've seen it. I don't personally have it."

"Who does?"

"A guy named Spencer Flemming." Sarbotskiy took a pen and a pad of paper from a drawer and wrote down an address. "He's a journalist. He has everything. Even pictures."

"Bullshit. If a journalist had pictures like that, it would have made his career. He'd have sold them for a fortune. They'd have been all over the front pages."

Sarbotskiy leaned forward and tapped his forehead in an exaggerated imitation of Neilsen's earlier move. He said, "There can't be much interesting stuff in there if you're so naïve. He has copies. Your government took the originals. They thought they'd taken everything. And they made it clear there was a jail cell with his name on it at that so-called secret facility you guys have in Cuba, in case any of those pictures ever saw the light of day."

Reacher stepped forward and said, "And you know this, how?"

"We communicate."

"You put this Flemming guy onto the story?"

"I may have nudged him in the right direction. The truth can be elusive, sometimes."

Reacher picked up the piece of paper Sarbotskiy had written on. "We're going to visit this guy. Soon. When we do, will he be expecting us?"

Sarbotskiy said, "Do I look like I have a crystal ball?"

"Remember what I said about this place burning down? If Flemming doesn't faint with surprise when I knock on his door, that's what's going to happen. You're going to be inside when it does. You're going to be wide awake. And you're not going to have a drop of vodka to dull the pain."

* * *

Veronica Sanson held the lid of the coal hatch open until Roberta had climbed out, then the sisters stood together and surveyed the area to the west of Neville Pritchard's house. The garage wall was behind them. The street was to their left but they couldn't see it because of a line of shrubs. They had been planted close together and laid out carefully to look like they happened to have sprung up there, naturally, on their own. Over the years they'd grown thick and tight and impenetrable. They formed a perfect screen. Impossible to see through. They were standing right there in the open and yet a thousand people could walk by and not realize their purpose. It was the same story to their right. There was another set of bushes, sprouting apparently at random but totally blocking the view from the rest of Pritchard's yard. Someone could be watching the back of the house with binoculars and they'd still have no idea what was happening in that space. The ground was covered with some kind of short, wiry grass. It was silent to walk on and didn't reach high enough to leave suspicious damp patches on the cuffs of anyone's pants. Ahead was a fence separating Pritchard's property from his neighbor's. It was a standard affair, six feet tall, with vertical planks attached to horizontal rails strung between sturdy posts. Veronica and Roberta moved across to take a closer look. At first the planks looked uniform, but Roberta noticed a set of five that had an extra row of nails. She pushed near the top of the central one and the lower edge of the group swung up and away from the fence frame. It left plenty of room to crawl through.

The neighbor's yard was tidy, but plain. It suggested older residents, happy to pay a college student or grandchild to go through the place occasionally and do just enough to stop the trees and shrubs from getting out of hand. Nothing was neglected, but there was no sign of any new planting or recent attempts at cultivation. A house sat on the far side of the lot, away in the distance. Another structure was much closer. A standalone garage. Which was strange given that all the properties on that street had been built with garages attached. Roberta and Veronica crept closer. There was a window in the side wall. They peered through. There was no vehicle inside. The space looked like it was empty.

There was a personnel door next to the window. Roberta took hold of the handle but Veronica grabbed her arm before she could turn it.

"Stop." Veronica pointed to the top corner of the window. A pair of wires was just visible through a wad of cobwebs. Part of a security system.

Roberta pulled her arm free. She said, "I bet that it's connected to Pritchard's house. Not the police. Not the neighbors. I bet Pritchard built this place. Probably pays rent, or does them some other kind of favor."

"You can't be certain of that."

"Only one way to find out." Roberta pushed on the handle. The door didn't give. It was locked. She turned around, raised her knee, then drove her leg back. Her foot hit the wood, the frame split, and the door swung open. No bells rang. No siren sounded. Not anywhere in their earshot, anyway. Roberta darted inside. She said, "Come on. We're burning daylight. The watchers will be on their way back."

The garage was just as empty on the inside as it had seemed from the outside. There was no workbench. No tools. Nothing hanging on the walls. Nothing stacked in the corners. Nothing shoved in the rafters. But there were two things dangling from the roof trusses. An electric cable and a hose. The cable was thick. It was heavy gauge and it had an elaborate cylindrical plug at the end. The hose had a brass connector attached and faint white writing stamped along its length. Roberta turned her head sideways and read it. She said, "Approved for potable water. This is a hookup for an RV."

Veronica pointed at the floor. Four tires had left dark traces where the vehicle had been parked. They looked wide and splayed out. She said, "Right. And it was heavy. Carrying a full load. Pritchard was ready to disappear for quite a while."

The sisters went back outside and around to the front of the garage. The vehicle door opened onto a driveway. The other houses they'd seen nearby all had driveways made of gravel. This one was made of compacted dirt. It would be silent to drive on. It sloped down toward the street. And its curve led away from Pritchard's house. A heavy RV could roll down and coast a considerable distance without needing to start its engine. A near perfect setup for a covert getaway.

Roberta said, "I'm starting to like Neville Pritchard. I like his style."

Veronica said, "Me too. Shame we'll have to pump him full of LSD and let him loose in rush-hour traffic."

"If we can find him. He could be anywhere."

"I have an idea about that. We're going to need a phone. And the Yellow Pages."

Reacher let Neilsen go down the stairs first. He felt that was a sensible precaution, given the quantity of vodka Neilsen had sucked down. He was still moving on his own, but unsteadily. He took each step slowly and kept his palms pressed against the walls on either side. He made it to the bottom without falling. Sergei and the other guy were no longer lying there. That was fortunate. Their tangled limbs and outsized torsos could well have been one obstacle too many.

Neilsen fought his way through the curtain, took a moment to catch his balance, and started for the exit. Reacher and Smith followed close behind. The waiter stopped in his tracks when he saw them. He stood and stared with an expression of half shock, half admiration on his face. Neilsen plowed on, weaving between the tables, and the three of them got to the sidewalk unscathed. They walked around the corner to where they'd left the cars. Both had tickets on their windshields. Smith tore them off and dropped them into her purse.

"I'll take care of those," she said.

Neilsen stumbled past her, heading for his driver's door. He pulled out his keys. Reacher stretched across and took them.

"Hey!" Neilsen scowled. "I'm fine to drive."

Reacher said, "What you think you can do and what you're going to do are two different things. Go around. Get in the other side."

Neilsen didn't move.

Reacher said, "Or walk. Your choice."

Reacher followed Smith's car through the downtown traffic and back to the hotel. She drove fast. He had to work hard to get close to keeping up. She was already parked in her regular spot when he pulled into the lot. He stopped by the hotel entrance and kept the engine running. Smith opened the passenger door, leaned in, and unfastened Neilsen's seatbelt.

Neilsen said, "Why are we here? We should be at the office. There's no reason I can't work."

Reacher said, "There's no way Baglin won't notice something's up if he calls a meeting. Is that something you want?"

Neilsen struggled forward in his seat. "Maybe I'll just spend some time here, in my room. Meet at six for dinner?"

"Sure. Take it easy. And thanks for doing the heavy lifting back there."

"Please. You know me. And you know the two best words in the English language. *Free alcohol*. Not to be confused with the worst two words. *Alcohol free*."

Reacher and Smith took both cars to the task force building in case Neilsen got any bright ideas about trying to drive someplace. They showed their IDs to the guard and parted ways in the corridor. Reacher let himself into his office. Three new faxes had arrived. He gathered the pages, selected one, and dropped the others onto the desk. He scanned the list of names. Then he squeezed into the chair, picked up the phone, and dialed the number for the Chemical Corps at Fort McClellan. His call was answered quickly but he spent the next twenty minutes bouncing from one desk to another, listening to one feeble attempt at stonewalling after another. When he finally hung up he figured he had accomplished two things. He had beaten plenty of bushes. He hoped enough to rattle anyone who knew about Typhon. The offensive counterpart to Project 192. Maybe cause a little panic. Maybe bring them out into the open. And he had identified a couple of people who had been on the fringes of the work in the sixties and who were big enough assholes that he wouldn't lose sleep if Baglin tried to stick them with some blame if everything went sideways.

Reacher tried his brother's number again and this time his call was answered.

"Reacher," Joe said.

"Joe."

"You OK?"

"Fine. You?"

"Fine. Listen, I've got an update for you. This guy Gary Walsh. Turns out he's using a cover name. He just got through with a spell undercover. A long one. It was rough. He came back with his head bent out of shape a little, plus there's a suspicion the group he infiltrated had picked up his trail. I guess he got sent to your task force partly as therapy, partly as a safe haven. Aside from that, I'm hearing he's a solid guy."

They shot the breeze for another couple of minutes, mainly about music, then Reacher hung up. He leaned back in his chair, closed his eyes, and filled his head with Howlin' Wolf. A pleasant hour passed and then the music was interrupted by a beeping sound from his pocket. It was his pager. He was being summoned again.

Christopher Baglin was already in his place when Reacher walked into the boardroom. Smith got there right after him, before the door had swung all the way shut. Walsh was sitting at the far end of the table, staring out the window, looking like he hadn't moved since the morning.

Reacher lowered himself into his seat and said, "No need to wait for Neilsen. He's out sick. He had to go back to the hotel."

Baglin frowned. He said, "Names from the sixties?"

Reacher handed him a page with two names. Smith had nothing. Neither did Walsh.

Baglin folded Reacher's piece of paper, slid it into his pocket, and said, "OK. Listen up. We've had a major development. The perp showed up this morning at the house of the final scientist, Neville Pritchard. Got past the watchers, all the way inside."

Reacher said, "So Pritchard's dead?"

"No. Pritchard wasn't there. Four agents were waiting inside, in his place."

"So was the guy captured? Killed?"

"Neither. The agents inside the house attempted to make an arrest but were unsuccessful."

"The guy got away?"

"Correct."

"Did the agents get a good look? Do we have a description?"

"A partial. But the big news is that our guy is actually a girl. A woman. Not a man. So your new top priority is to recalibrate your search parameters."

No one moved.

Baglin said, "What are you waiting for? Go!"

Smith stood up. Walsh struggled to his feet a moment later. Reacher stayed where he was. The news made no difference to him. It had never occurred to him to exclude women from the equation. Instead of moving he said, "Question. Pritchard. Is he in protective custody?"

Baglin hesitated. "Not at present."

"So an attempt was made to bring him in?"

"It was."

"Where is Pritchard now?"

"That's not known. He's proving hard to find. Which is our only silver lining right now. The killer didn't know Pritchard was missing or she wouldn't have come to his house. Therefore she doesn't know where he is, either. Which gives us a reprieve. Maybe only a short one. We need to find her before she finds him. And kills him."

Chapter 15

Reacher, Smith, and Neilsen met in the hotel lobby at 6:00 P.M., as agreed. They walked to the same restaurant as before and sat at the same table. Reacher and Smith ordered beer. Neilsen started straight in on the whiskey.

"What?" he said when he saw the others' expressions. "You think I should stick to vodka?"

Smith cupped her hand to her ear. "What's that I hear? Oh. It's your liver. It thinks you should stick to water."

Reacher and Smith brought Neilsen up to speed on the outcome of the afternoon's meeting while they waited for their food. When it was delivered, Neilsen ordered another drink and said, "Covering up the existence of a secret nerve gas factory is a much stronger motive than keeping antidote testing under wraps. I like that much better. I made some calls this afternoon. Shook some trees. We'll see if anything falls out."

Reacher said, "I did the same."

"This new information about Neville Pritchard means he must be key to potentially exposing the whole illicit program. That's why he's the only one they tried to take into protective custody. My guess is that he was more spy than scientist. Langley's point man on the ground. Or the Chemical Corps'. Whoever's pulling the strings now must have been in overall charge then. Because he has the most to lose if the lid gets blown off. With public opinion the way it is these days this could be career-ending stuff. Legacy destroying."

Reacher said, "Whoever's pulling the strings is a cynical bastard. He could have had all the vulnerable guys taken into custody. But he didn't. He was happy to leave the other scientists out there in harm's way, like bait. He tried to use them to catch the killer before she caught up with Pritchard."

Neilsen breathed out, slowly. "That's cold, man. You can see how this guy got to the top."

Smith said, "Right, but what I don't get is this. Look at it from the killer's point of view. If Pritchard is key to revealing the secret, why leave him till last? I'd go after him first. Get the info I needed. Move on to stage two—embarrassing the USA, blackmailing the government, whatever. Then I wouldn't need to kill the others. I'd save time. Avoid risk."

Neilsen took a large swig and said, "Maybe she deliberately left Pritchard till last to ramp up the tension he was under. She would need him stressed to make him cooperate."

"I guess."

Neilsen said, "Or maybe she didn't know all the names up front. She might have had to start at the bottom and work her way up the food chain, getting a new name out of each victim in turn."

Smith shrugged. "Possible."

Reacher said, "Maybe she did know all the names, but not which the important one was. It could have been chance that Pritchard was last."

Smith shook her head. "Surely he couldn't just randomly be last."

Reacher said, "Sure he could. It's a version of the gambler's fallacy. It's just as likely for Pritchard to be picked last as in any other position. Hitting on his name doesn't get more likely after each failure."

"You certain it works that way?"

"Absolutely. But that might not be relevant. The murders still feel personal to me. Killing everyone on the list could be the whole point. If she just wants to kill all seven, the order won't matter. And if she knows Pritchard's significance, leaving him till last would make sense because his security is the highest. Right now she's batting a thousand. If she went for Pritchard first, she could have struck out right away."

Neilsen said, "Right. But that's academic. Maybe she wants to expose Typhon. Maybe she's just on a homicidal spree. But whether she wants information or to complete her set of corpses, she'll still go after Pritchard. She has to. So we have to find him, to stop her, and avoid the blame landing on us."

"No." Smith put her empty glass down. "You're missing something. If she wants information, she doesn't need Pritchard. Someone else knows about Typhon. Someone who allegedly has proof. Photographs. A secondhand source, but maybe good enough. Maybe better."

Neilsen said, "Flemming. The journalist."

"She could change tack. Go after him instead."

"If she knows about him."

"We know about him, and we've only been involved in this for two days. How long has she been researching? She seemed to know plenty about all her other victims."

"We'll visit Flemming tomorrow. As soon as Baglin's morning briefing is over."

Reacher said, "No. Tonight. Now. Tomorrow could be too late."

The address Sarbotskiy had given them for Flemming turned out to be an abandoned building perched on a narrow strip of land between I-295 and the Potomac. It was three stories high, built of strangely orange bricks, and it was a wildly irregular shape. Sections bulged out here and dropped back there in a way that suggested some kind of complex hidden purpose behind the design. The tops of the walls had a series of bites taken out of them like an ancient European castle. All the windows were blocked up with sheets of rusting metal and the whole place was surrounded by a fence like contractors use to secure construction sites.

Smith pulled her car over at the end of the building's driveway. She didn't switch off the headlights or kill the engine. Neilsen was next to her in the front. Reacher was sprawled out in the back.

Neilsen said, "Whatever is this place? It looks evil. Like an asylum in a horror movie. Maybe Jack Nicholson's in there."

Smith said, "I think it is a kind of asylum. Or was. An annex of St. Elizabeth's. It closed in the sixties. The main site is still open. It's notorious. It was one of the first psychiatric hospitals in the country. Every bad thing happened there. Electroshock treatment. Forced lobotomies. Trials of truth serums during the Cold War. All kinds of stuff they can't do anymore. The operation's much smaller now. Rumor is, they're going to close it soon, too."

Neilsen said, "It gives me the creeps. Let's go. We're clearly on a wild-goose chase. We should buy a can of gas and some matches and pay that prick Sarbotskiy another visit."

Smith shifted into Drive but before she lifted her foot off the brake, Reacher said, "Wait." He could feel a prickling sensation at the base of his neck. An instinctive response. A signal from his lizard brain. The part that was hardwired to sense when he was being watched. The kind of signal Reacher had learned not to ignore. "We're here. It can't hurt to check."

Smith and Neilsen stayed silent. Neither of them moved.

Reacher said, "Stay in the car if you like. I'll go."

"No." Smith turned the ignition key, pulled it out, stretched up and switched off the dome light, then opened her door. "I'll come. Let's just stick together, OK?"

Neilsen fumbled for his door handle. "Guess I better come, too. Keep an eye on you guys."

Reacher led the way around the perimeter of the site on the outside of the fence. He moved slowly. His gaze was constantly switching from the ground in front of him to the sides and top of the building. He was looking for wires, or the glint of metal or glass. He saw nothing. It was too dark to make out much detail. But he could almost feel the presence of the hulking structure like it was some kind of giant prehistoric creature, alive, but asleep.

They completed their circuit without incident and wound up in front of what must have been the asylum's main entrance. A giant portico jutted out from the wall. It was supported by ornate columns, originally to protect new arrivals from the rain or the sun. Reacher checked the join between the nearest sections of the fence. All the others he'd seen were secured with two clamps shaped like butterfly wings with a nut and bolt through the center of the body. This one only had a single clamp, and the nut was missing. The bolt was just pushed through its hole. There was nothing to hold it in place. Reacher pointed down at the concrete base that supported the fence's metal posts. One was scuffed. Something had carved a portion of an arc into its rough surface. Reacher popped out the bolt and opened the clamp. He lifted the post. He pushed and it moved. The clamps holding it to the next section of fence were acting like hinges. And they were silent. They had seen some oil in the recent past.

Reacher squeezed through the gap he'd made in the fence and crossed to the portico. Smith and Neilsen followed. He continued to a pair of double doors. They were huge, made of dark wood, shot through with black metal studs and divided into panels covered with intricate carving. The workmanship had been high quality. That was clear, even though now the surface was dull and rough. The result of years of neglect and damp air, Reacher guessed.

Neilsen was staring at a padlock that secured one door to the other with a hasp and eye. It was a substantial item. Designed to exude strength, and discourage wannabe trespassers from wasting their time trying to pick it. But it was old. It was caked in rust. It couldn't have been opened in years. Neilsen shook his head and turned to go. Reacher grabbed his arm and stopped him.

"What are you doing?" Neilsen whispered. "This is a waste of time. That lock's seized solid. We'll never get it open."

"We don't need to," Reacher replied. "That's not the way anyone gets in or out. Think about it. You can't work a padlock from the inside."

Reacher crouched down and inspected the doors' lower panels. The bottom edges were in the worst shape. He figured that was due to rain splatter so he switched his attention to the next row up. He pressed one of them. It was solid. So was the next one he tried. But the third gave a tiny bit. He tried its opposite edge and it swung back, under tension from some kind of spring. It left a gap about six inches by eight. Reacher stretched his arm through. The surface was contoured and uneven. More carving, Reacher thought. Then his fingers brushed against something smooth and straight and narrow. A small plank. Reacher pushed and pulled and twisted until it came loose. He dropped it, pulled his arm out, and pressed on the next panel. This time a whole section swung inward. Nine panels by nine. Like a tiny door within a door.

It took a lot of squirming and wriggling and struggling but Reacher managed to squeeze his body through the hole. He stood up and stepped to the side, sliding his feet and stretching his arms into the empty darkness. Smith joined him. Then Neilsen. They all stood still and waited for their night vision to kick in. After a couple of minutes a few details started to emerge. The floor was covered with black and white tiles. They were submerged under a thick layer of dust. The cornice around the ceiling, high above them, was crusted with dirt and cobwebs. Hunks of plaster were hanging off the walls at random intervals. There was the indistinct outline of a piece of furniture ahead of them. Maybe a reception desk.

Smith said, "Close your eyes for a second."

Reacher heard rustling, then a click. He opened one eye and saw Smith was holding a slim flashlight. She had pinched the beam down to a narrow shaft and was playing it around the space. A chandelier was hanging from the center of the ceiling. There was a pair of double doors on each side. Ahead was a wall of glass, now obscured by layers of grime. It felt like a grand hotel gone to seed. Reacher could imagine it with uniformed bellhops ferrying fancy luggage and gussied-up guests flitting between dining rooms and ballrooms and the formal gardens that lay outside. Though he knew in reality living there could hardly have been more different. Being forced to live there. There could have been few worse places in the country if Smith's recollection was correct.

Smith lowered her flashlight beam to the floor. The extra illumination revealed multiple sets of footprints going back and forth along a path through the dust. She started to follow them.

Reacher said, "Stop."

He was too late. He had seen a small break in the line of footprints. A narrow patch that hadn't been stepped on. That meant one thing. There was a tripwire above it. Then the flashlight confirmed it. The line was colorless. As fine as a hair. It ran the whole width of the room. And Smith caught it with her right shin. Immediately the room filled with light from somewhere above them. It wasn't harsh and bright, like it would be in the movies. It wasn't enough to blind them. Or to blind the guy who stepped out from the doorway on the right. He was maybe six feet tall, but he was stooped. His hair was long and gray and thin and it hung down on either side of his face in no particular style. His skin was pale. His feet were bare. He was wearing jeans with huge bellbottoms. A bright paisley shirt with a massive collar. And he was holding a shotgun. An old one. A Winchester Model 97. A Trench Broom, as the infantry in the First World War used to call it. He was aiming it at Smith but Reacher and Neilsen were so close behind that they would get torn to shreds along with her if the guy pulled the trigger.

Chapter 16

The guy with the shotgun said, "Stop. Who are you? Why did you break into my home?"

Reacher drifted to his right. He wanted to put some distance between himself and the others. He kept his eyes on the guy's trigger finger and raised his hands to shoulder height. He said, "We're looking for Spencer Flemming. Is that you?"

"Stop moving. What do you want?"

"Are you Flemming?"

"Who's asking?"

"My name's Jack Reacher."

"Are you police? FBI? CIA? What?"

"US Army."

"For real?"

"For real. My ID's in my pocket." Reacher started to lower his right hand.

"No. Stay still. What's the army doing here? You can't operate on US soil."

"We're here to help you. If you're Spencer Flemming."

The guy didn't reply.

Reacher said, "Come on. What's the harm in telling us your name? You're the one with the gun. Are you Flemming?"

The guy nodded. Just the tiniest of gestures. "Might be."

"Then you're in danger. Someone's out to kill you. We're looking to stop that from happening."

"Kill me? Impossible. They'd have to find me first. No one knows I live here."

"We know."

"Yeah." Flemming hitched the shotgun up a little higher. "You do. How come?"

"A friend of yours told us. Maksim Sarbotskiy."

Flemming was quiet for a moment. Then he said, "Who?"

"Maksim Sarbotskiy. He said you were a journalist."

"Oh. That guy. Short, skinny. Albanian. Remind me—which arm is his tattoo on?"

"He's Russian. We didn't see his arms. And he's not short and skinny. He's huge, like a wrestler."

"He goes by a French name now. What is it?"

"It's English. Or it's supposed to be. Prince Sarb. But I doubt anyone takes it seriously."

"OK." Flemming paused. "Go on. Why does someone want to kill me? And why do you care?"

"Because of Project Typhon."

"What do you know about that?"

"Not enough. Which is why we care. It's why we're here. We want you to tell us about it. That will help us stop the person who's coming after you. But if you don't want our help, fine. We'll leave. We won't bother you. We'll just watch for your name in the obituary columns."

Flemming didn't respond.

Reacher lowered his hands and turned away. "Fine. See you. But you should know the person we're talking about has already killed five people."

Flemming said, "Random people?"

"Specific people. All scientists who worked on the project."

"Then why should I worry? I'm not a scientist. I wasn't on the project."

"The killer wants information about Typhon. The only remaining scientist who has it is MIA. The only other person who knows about it is you. Go ahead. Do the math."

Flemming took a step back. "I'm not leaving this place. I won't run. I won't hide."

"Help us and you won't have to."

"How do I know this isn't a trap?"

"How could it be a trap?"

"I've been here twenty-two years. You know why?"

"You have an eccentric taste in décor?"

"Because of the piece I wrote about Project 192. In '69, going on '70. I was a reporter back then. A damn good one. The article was dynamite. The best thing I ever did. It was locked and loaded, two days from going to press. We were all set for a big splash on a Sunday. Going for maximum impact. I was walking home from a date, happy, dreaming of promotions and Pulitzers and book deals. I saw a van waiting outside my building. A blue Ford. I thought nothing of it then. I'll never forget it now. And I'll never forget the smell of the hood they pulled over my head. My world went black. And it stayed black for what felt like weeks. It was actually three days. First I was in the back of the van. Then in a tiny room. I don't know where it was. Somewhere cold. The floor and walls were hard concrete. There was no bed. No chair. No toilet. They gave me hardly any water. No food. Then finally a light came on. It hurt my eyes. A guy came in. He stood. I lay on the floor. I couldn't move. He gave me a choice. Hand over all my notes and early drafts and photos and never tell a soul what I knew, or spend the rest of my life in a room like that. In the dark. Cold. Hungry. Alone."

"And Sarbotskiy helped you with the article?"

"He was a source, sure. He thought he was using me, I expect. I thought I was using him. The truth? A bit of both, probably. But I never printed anything that wasn't true. I triple-checked every detail. I wasn't a Soviet asset. I'm no traitor."

"So you gave this guy in the room what he wanted, then you came here?"

"Damn straight I gave him what he wanted. And I didn't come here right away. I tried to go back to work. But it was no good. The guy said they'd be watching me. If I ever made a nuisance of myself, if I poked my nose where it didn't belong, if I attracted attention in any way, all bets were off. He said they would keep the room ready for me, just in case. He said they had already hung a sign on the door with my name on it. I'll be honest. That messed with my head. I couldn't write a story without thinking about how it could be interpreted. Couldn't walk down the street without having a heart attack every time I saw a van parked at the curb. I figured it would be best to disappear."

"You think we're here to test you. See if you're ready to make waves again."

"In my life, when people show up out of the blue it's to hurt me, not help me. Why should this time be any different?"

"What if someone vouched for us?"

"Who?"

"Sarbotskiy. You know him. And he's already done his deal with the government. He's got what he wants. There's no mileage for him in selling you out."

Flemming took a moment to think, then said, "OK. I guess that could work."

Reacher said, "We'll take you to him. You guys talk. We'll bring you right back."

"I'm not leaving. I told you that. We'll call him."

"How?"

Flemming gestured to a door in the glass wall at the far end of the space. "You three go first. Don't try anything."

The door led into a square courtyard. It was totally enclosed by the four sides of the building except for a vehicle-sized gate that was now barricaded with old tires. Reacher figured the gate had originally been for deliveries, and the space for allowing light into the inner side of the wards. It could also have been a place for patients to exercise. Maybe there had been gardens and paths and benches. Maybe conscientiously maintained. But now there was nothing growing on the ground apart from a few weeds that peeped out from between hunks of rubble. The center of the area was empty. There was nothing against three of the walls apart from graffiti. But against the west wall there were three travel trailers tucked in close to the brickwork. Their skin was aluminum. It was dull, but Reacher guessed it would have been shiny when they were new.

Flemming pointed toward the one on the left. He said, "That one's my office. The center one's my living room. The other's where I sleep."

He folded back the office trailer's door and latched it open. He leaned in, flicked a switch, and a light came on. He gestured for the others to climb in ahead of him. There was a desk under the window. It was plain and utilitarian, with a metal frame and plain wood surfaces. A chair on wheels, which had seen better days. Its fabric was torn in multiple places and stuffing was spilling out in dirty orange clumps. And a leather armchair which wasn't in much better shape. The rest of the area was stuffed with shelves. They looked homemade. They were crammed with books and files and sheaves of papers and piles of magazines. One wall was covered with things in frames. Diplomas. Awards. Reprints of articles. And a single picture. It was of Flemming when he was a much younger man. He was thinner and his hair was dark brown. He was on a boat crossing a river in a jungle. It looked like Vietnam.

Reacher nodded toward the heap of papers on the desk and said, "You still working?"

Flemming shrugged. He said, "I keep busy. I don't write anymore. Not under my own name. That's too risky. But I help a few folks out with things. Research. Copyediting. Like that." He moved some papers around on the desk, uncovered a phone, and lifted the receiver.

Smith said, "That thing works?"

Flemming said, "You think I'm going to have a pretend conversation? Of course it works. Everything works. You spend as much time as I did working in some countries I could tell you about, you get pretty good at borrowing things. A little power here. Some water there. A bit of dial tone in between. I've got cable hooked up in the other two vans."

Flemming kept hold of the shotgun, wedged the phone between his shoulder and his chin, and dialed a number from memory. Reacher could hear the slow, lazy ringtone. Then a deep rumbling voice. He couldn't make out the words.

Flemming said, "Sorry, man. Yes, I do know what time it is. But this is an emergency. I've got three guys here who say you sent them." He described Reacher, Smith, and Neilsen, then listened for a few moments. Then he said, "Thanks. I'll let you know how it goes."

Flemming dropped the receiver back into its cradle and lifted the gun. He braced it against his shoulder, pointed it at Reacher, and said, "Sarbotskiy doesn't know you."

Reacher said, "Call him back. Remind him about the fire. I was very specific about where he's going to be when I start it."

Flemming lowered the gun. A tiny hint of a smile flashed across his face and he said, "Sarbotskiy told me if you came back with that, you're OK. So. What do you want to know?"

Reacher moved closer. He said, "Is it true that there was a program running parallel with Project 192? One that created offensive bioweapons? Project Typhon?"

"Yes. Absolutely. Although that name came from the KGB. It was never official."

"How do you know about it?"

"Research. I was good, once, remember. I put in the hard yards. Here, and in India. I know partly because of the facts I pieced together. The kind of chemicals that were shipped to the site. The equipment that was used. The protective clothing that was brought in. The precautions that were taken. Snippets I picked up from lab techs and cleaners. But mainly because of the bodies."

"People died?"

Flemming nodded. "'Fraid so."

"They were experimented on?"

"No. There was an accident. A leak. One night in December '69."

Reacher said, "An accident? Are you sure? Because I hear about an accident and I know the CIA was involved, and my bullshit meter goes off the scale. No offense, Neilsen."

Neilsen said, "None taken. I was thinking the same thing."

Flemming paused. "Let me back up a minute. I'm not explaining this right. The incident that caused the deaths was sabotage. One hundred percent. There's no doubt about it. But it was aimed at Mason Chemical Industries. The civilian corporation that was used to shelter the covert operation. The guy who did it was just a disgruntled employee. Morgan Sanson, he was called. He had no idea Project 192 even existed. Let alone a parallel project to produce offensive weapons. He impacted those by accident."

"So what was his story?"

"It was sad, really. He had all kind of beefs. You name it. Pay. Conditions. Not enough vacation days. Lack of opportunities for promotion. No one in management would listen to him. There was no union so he couldn't get any traction as an individual. So he had the genius idea to mess up some equipment. Cost the company some money. Get attention that way. One night he switched off the water supply that fed a cooling system. He thought it was something minor. It was actually totally critical to 192 and Typhon, but obviously there were no signs saying so. Nothing in the site manual about it. The increase in temperature caused an over-pressurization in a storage tank, which burst, and a bunch of gas leaked out. A lot of people died. Civilians. Locals. It wasn't pretty. I was there. I took pictures."

"How many casualties are we talking about?"

Flemming held up his finger. "This is where it gets interesting." He crossed to one of his shelves and stared at all the stuff piled up there for a second. Then he pulled out a binder, blew some dust off it, leafed through until he found the right page, and handed it to Reacher. Smith and Neilsen closed up on either side and together all three read the article. It was from *The New York Times*. Its date was January 13, 1970. The paper was yellow and it looked thin and fragile inside its protective plastic sleeve. There was a photograph of a woman in a lab coat at the top of the page. Her hair was tied back. She was wearing glasses. She looked young and earnest and pretty. The text that surrounded her picture reflected some of what Flemming had said. It told of a radical employee. Vandalism. A gas leak. An experimental disinfectant that would bring major benefits to underprivileged communities as soon as it gained regulatory approval. It mentioned seven fatalities, and stressed that the toll would have been much worse if not for the rapid response from the company's emergency team. A second photograph showed the bodies. They were lying in a field of long grass and flowers. They were dressed in clean, pale-colored clothes. Their faces looked calm. Almost serene. It was like they were returning home from a stroll in the countryside and had decided to take a nap in the afternoon sun.

Reacher looked at Smith and Neilsen in turn. That was not what he'd expected to read or see. He could tell from their expressions that they were surprised, too. And not in a positive way. He felt like the ground had shifted a little beneath his feet. The article told of a tragedy. That was for sure. But it was pretty light on shock value. It didn't establish much of a motive for multiple murders. He could feel their theory begin to wobble.

Flemming took the binder and said, "That's what appeared in the *Times*. It's not what I wrote." He took a different binder from the shelf and passed it to Reacher. "My piece is in here. Remember, I'm not supposed to have this. I swore I'd handed everything over. You can't tell anyone you've seen it."

This binder didn't contain newsprint. Just regular letter paper covered with double-spaced, typewritten text. It told a story that was similar in some respects. It included a saboteur. A gas leak. Dead civilians. But in other ways it was very different. It involved secret government research. The CIA. Nerve agents. A corporation panicking over a potential PR disaster. A cover-up operation. But the most dramatic discrepancy came in terms of the death toll. This version didn't tell of seven fatalities. It claimed that 1,007 people had lost their lives.

"Turn the page," Flemming said when he saw from their faces they had finished reading. "But only if you have strong stomachs."

The next plastic sleeve held a photograph. It was ten inches by eight. This one was in color and it was sharper than the newspaper image. It showed a different kind of field. There were no flowers. No plants. Nothing living at all. Just dust and rocks and corpses. It was a wide shot to establish the scope of the scene. It captured a huge expanse and the whole space was filled with bodies. They were twisted into alien, distorted shapes like the victims had been convulsed in unspeakable agony at the moment of release.

"Turn again," Flemming said.

The next sleeve held another photograph. A close-up of a victim's face. Her eyes were screwed shut. The flesh was pulled tight over her cheekbones. Her mouth was stretched open in an eternal scream. Her skin was stained with weird purple blotches.

"Again."

There were thirty-four more pictures in the binder. All of corpses. Some on their own. Some entangled. All having clearly perished in hideous pain.

"Awful," Smith said. "Just awful. I can see why the government was desperate to stop the story getting out. That doesn't justify what they did to you, though."

"Thank you." Flemming took the binder back and replaced it on the shelf.

Reacher said, "I want to know more about the saboteur. This guy Sanson."

"There's not much else to say. He was a scientist. Frustrated at work but content at home, by all accounts. He was married. His wife's name was Alisha, I think. They had four kids. Robbie, Ronnie, Ritchie, and what was the other boy's name? Ryan, maybe?"

"What happened to him after the incident?"

"He got crucified in the press. His role didn't come out for a couple of days but when it did, things got ugly, fast. Even when people believed he only had seven deaths on his hands. Whether it was the vilification or whether he knew the truth about the numbers and that was too much to bear, I don't know. But two weeks later, back in the States, right before Christmas, he killed himself."

Reacher said, "I hear suicide, the CIA's involved . . ."

"I know, I know. But there was no Company connection. I checked long and hard when I was researching the article. Plus it would make no sense for the CIA to kill him. They wouldn't have derailed their own project. Maybe he knew the truth about the death toll, but so did I. So did my editor. They didn't kill me. Or her."

"Could he have been KGB?"

Smith said, "No way. The KGB is loyal to its agents. If one of them had spiked a major US weapons program, they'd have been taken back to Moscow, a hero. Given a medal. Maybe a slightly larger-than-average apartment with a marginally less depressing view. Sanson still might have killed himself, but not in the States, and not for that reason."

Reacher said, "What about the victims? Do we know their IDs?"

Flemming shook his head. "And you'll never find out now. It was too long ago. Too far away. It wasn't in the corporation's interest to keep records of them. It certainly wasn't in the CIA's. Or the army's. And the families were all paid off to keep silent, so there's no way in there."

"What about witnesses. A thousand is a lot of corpses to hide."

"Hide? You're thinking like a westerner. We're talking about a place where famines regularly kill millions of people. Plus a large proportion of the population believe in pre-ordained destiny. And for anyone who was looking to make waves, there was always good old-fashioned hush money."

"One other thing's bothering me," Reacher said. "The woman in the photo in the *Times*. I didn't see a name. Why does she look familiar?"

Flemming said, "That was a very young Susan Kasluga. It was her first job out of college."

"Susan Kasluga, as in Charles Stamoran's wife?" Reacher said. "The Secretary of Defense?"

"Right." Flemming nodded. "She came back from India after the incident, quit her job at Mason Chemical, and founded AmeriChem Incorporated. She grew it into one of the largest companies in the world. She still works there. She's the CEO."

"Anyone else find that weird?"

"What's weird about it?"

Reacher said, "Stamoran set up the task force to stop Project 192 from getting exposed, and now we find his wife was part of it? That's got to be self-interest, at the very least."

Flemming said, "But Kasluga wasn't part of Project 192. Or Typhon. She worked for Mason Chemical, which was purely civilian. The government was using the inevitable overlap between weapons development and civilian research to conceal the covert programs they were running. No Mason employees knew anything about the secret work. Look at Sanson, the saboteur."

"Kasluga's picture was in the paper. She was part of the cover-up."

"Don't believe everything you read in the papers. I checked her out for the article. Everyone said the same thing. It was the sixties. She was a woman, fresh out of college. The closest she'd have gotten to the lab where they did the secret stuff was if they let her in to clean it. If they hadn't needed a pretty face to stick in front of the cameras, she wouldn't have gotten a mention. The original version had her take an active role on the emergency team. By the time it went to press, she was just a talking head. She was no more part of Project 192 or Typhon than those bodies in the *Times'* picture were the actual victims. Wait a second. Let me show you something else."

Flemming went back to his shelves and searched through a pile of manila envelopes. He pulled one from near the bottom, tipped the contents onto his desk, and selected a sheet with a kind of flow chart traced out on it. "This is an organizational diagram I made when I was researching another article about a chemical plant in Sri Lanka. It was the same deal as in India. A public-facing civilian plant hiding a secret government laboratory. The secret lab had two missions. To develop antidotes to Soviet weapons. And to create weapons of our own. The local point man coordinated both of these, and he reported to a control in the States. There were no leaks or fields full of bodies, so the story got bumped to the back burner by 192 and Typhon."

Reacher took the diagram from Flemming and studied it. The names of the scientists were all different, which didn't come as a surprise. But the box representing the head of the program was empty. No name. No rank. No job title.

It wasn't going to stay that way for long, Reacher thought.

Chapter 17

Reacher's third full day in D.C. started in pretty much the same way as the previous two. He took a shower, dressed, ate a quick breakfast, grabbed an extra cup of coffee to go, and covered the short distance to the task force's office. That day he chose to walk. He hadn't slept well and he hoped that a little exercise combined with caffeine and what passed for fresh air in the capital would get him going. All night he had been plagued by a recurring image from something he'd heard about in Flemming's RV. He pictured a guy, creeping furtively in the shadow of a complex piece of machinery. Shutting off a valve or a faucet. Looking to make some kind of a point. Not trying to hurt anyone. And waking up to the news that he'd killed a thousand innocent people. Now, decades later, on the opposite side of the world, five more people were dead. It had to be part of the same picture, but something was missing. Reacher was sure of it. He felt like all the elements were there in front of him but he couldn't quite see some of them. Like he was looking at a distant panorama through a blanket of patchy fog. He knew it would clear, and that when it did, the connections would come into focus. There was nothing he could do to speed up the process. He knew that from experience. But that didn't mean he was happy about it.

Christopher Baglin started the morning meeting with another announcement.

He said, "Listen up. The agents who were involved in yesterday's debacle at Neville Pritchard's house have finally completed their after-action reports, now that they're all out of the hospital. One further piece of useful information has emerged. The killer is not working alone. She had a partner, or an accomplice. Another woman. She drove a stolen UPS truck that deposited the killer outside the house. She then blocked the view of the corresponding watcher while the killer gained entry. We presume she was also involved in the killer's escape. It's not clear at this stage whether she was involved in the other murders, but personally I'd be surprised if she wasn't. The two clearly have a rapport. The exact relationship or dynamic between them is not known. It is still important information, clearly, so you'll need to update your search parameters again. This should help to narrow the field considerably."

Reacher said, "Not in the army's case, unfortunately. There were no female soldiers AWOL within the relevant time frame, so it makes no difference whether we're looking for one or two. And I found no record of any female veterans with relevant experience or training who are related to anyone involved with Project 192 in the sixties, either by blood or marriage."

Neilsen said, "Same. We're looking at a dead end, from the Agency's perspective."

No one else spoke up.

Baglin said, "Agent Smith?"

"I'm getting no hits for anyone currently on our radar," Smith said. "It's conceivable that there's a sleeper—a pair of sleepers— that we didn't previously know about who've now been activated. Or a pair of clean skins recently infiltrated. But both those scenarios are highly unlikely, in my opinion."

Baglin nodded and said, "Walsh, is there any point asking you?"

Walsh looked away from the window. He said, "None." Then he turned back and carried on staring into the distance.

Baglin said, "OK. You all know what we're trying to find. Go look. Hard."

The time Veronica Sanson spent on the phone proved fruitful. She had started with the premise that Neville Pritchard would have wanted to spend as little time on the road as possible. A basic principle of escape and evasion. Minimize your exposure. She also assumed that given Pritchard's state of readiness, he would have prepared a safe haven in advance. So she called all the RV parks and campsites within a fifty-mile radius of his home. That was made easier by the fact that he lived so close to the coast. Almost half the potential area was discounted by the ocean. She explained to each person she spoke to that she'd recently moved to Annapolis with her husband and was keen to find a place where they could enjoy regular weekend getaways. They had no kids or dogs so would prefer somewhere without too many young families. In fact, the more private and secluded, the better. They were experienced RVers so didn't need a ton of facilities. And they weren't big on change, so if they liked the place they'd want to make a long-term booking to make sure the same plot was always available to them. Two places ticked all the boxes. They decided to try the nearer one first.

* * *

Reacher had been back in his office for less than ten minutes after the morning meeting finished when there was a knock at his door. It opened before he said anything and Smith walked in. Close up she looked pale and there were dark circles under her eyes.

She said, "Reacher, can we talk?"

He said, "About what?"

"I think we need to tell Baglin what we know. What we learned from Flemming last night."

"You do? Why?"

"The way I see it, our goal hasn't changed. We need to stop the killer. Save Pritchard. Keep Project 192 a secret. There's no reason to assume the killer's motive has changed. It's still revenge, exposure, maybe both. But what has changed is the subject pool. It's been transformed out of all recognition. We're not talking about a handful of KGB holdouts any longer. Not a few soldiers or spies with relatives who were harmed by the project. No. We're talking about the relatives of a thousand bereaved families. That could be, what? Five thousand people? Ten thousand?"

"Could be."

"That's way too many. And think of the logistics. We'd need to liaise with the civilian company, Mason Chemical, if it's still in business, and if it keeps records so far back. We'd need cooperation from the Indian government. The Indian army, too, if we're right about the military training. Which we probably are."

"Which is another problem. The Indian army only just started admitting women. No time for our suspects to have gotten trained."

"So we'd have to look for families or individuals who had emigrated to countries with armies that have accepted women for at least, what, five years? More complication. And then we'd need help from INS, to confirm who was in the States at the relevant

The Secret

time. Three people can't do all that. It's just not possible. Especially from thousands of miles away. And when we can't work the way we normally would. The families were paid off, right? Well, we can't follow the money because it was paid by the CIA, in a foreign country, so no doubt it was funneled through a bunch of shell companies and cutouts. We'd have more chance of finding Bigfoot."

"We could look for the effect the money had. Families that suddenly bought big new houses. That set up businesses, flush with cash. Or left the village and moved to the city. Or abroad."

"All good suggestions. But again, all things we can't find out on our own. Which is why we should hand it off to Baglin. We should brief him, then he can make all the approaches and line up the resources."

"Makes sense. But there's yet another problem. There's no way to do that without revealing that we know about Typhon. The thousand dead. Which didn't work out too well for Flemming."

"True. And it's not like I want to live in a dark cell, or in a bunch of ruins like a rat. But there's a moral obligation here. A man's life is on the line. The reputation of the country as well, potentially."

There was another knock at the door. Neilsen came in. His eyes narrowed when he saw that Smith was already there. He said, "What are you guys talking about?"

Reacher said, "Last night. What we learned. What we should do about it."

Neilsen said, "What we should do? That's obvious. Pass the buck to Baglin. Let him earn his corn. Look, if we keep doing what we're doing, we'll continue getting what we're getting. In other words, nowhere. Neville Pritchard's going to turn up dead sooner or later, or word of 192 will leak, or both, and we'll be left sitting here with *Blame Us* tattooed on our foreheads. I don't know about you, but I don't want that."

Reacher said, "OK. But there's no way to involve Baglin without

| 183

burning Flemming. Is that what you want to do? Seems like the guy's had enough bad luck for one lifetime."

Neilsen shrugged. "I don't want to burn him, no. But hey. Omelets. Eggs. And look, they might lock him up, I guess. But it's not like he's living like a king now. And as long as the story doesn't go public, I can't believe they'd throw him in the hole."

"There might be implications for us, for knowing what we know."

"I don't think so. We're professionals. Not reporters looking to shout scandal from the rooftops. We know how to handle secrets. We do it all the time."

Smith said, "So, Reacher, what do you think? Do we tell Baglin? Or not?"

Reacher said, "I think there's another dimension we need to consider before we decide. A thousand people were killed. Innocent people. Their deaths have been swept under the rug. Feels like there could be a moral obligation here, too. We know what happened. We've seen the pictures. Would it be right to turn a blind eye?"

"It would be right to let sleeping dogs lie. No crime has been committed. No one has profited. Justice has not been cheated. We can't bring the dead back to life. What happened was that sabotage led to an accident. The saboteur is dead. The victims' families have been compensated. So we should focus on the problem in front of us. Not on digging up the past. Especially when the past is buried in a minefield."

Smith said, "I'm not so sure. I agree with Reacher. We need to think about it more. I mean, what if it wasn't sabotage?"

Neilsen said, "What else could it be? The Agency didn't rain on its own parade. You can be sure of that. And it wasn't the KGB. You said so yourself."

Reacher said, "It could have been negligence. Or corner cutting. Or something that was just inherently dangerous. Look at the location they chose. American lives weren't at risk. If it was safe, why didn't they do it in New York or California?"

Smith nodded. "We need more data before we make a decision. We should start with Morgan Sanson's family. He had a wife. Four kids. What kind of a guy was he? Happy? Depressed? Did he keep a diary? Is it true he was in dispute with the chemical company?"

Reacher said, "Good. Can you make a start on tracking them down? In the meantime we should talk to Neville Pritchard. If the structure was the same as the site in Sri Lanka that Flemming looked at, Pritchard could have been on point for Typhon as well as 192. He could tell us who his control was in the States."

Neilsen said, "Are you forgetting? Pritchard's missing."

"Then we'll find him."

"How?"

"I need to see his house. Figure out where he went."

"You can't. His whole neighborhood will be swarming with agents in case he comes back."

"I don't need to physically go there. A satellite photo will be good enough. The CIA has those, right?"

"Maybe."

"I need you to get a copy of the latest one for the area."

Neilsen shrugged. "I can try."

"I'll need a map, too. Maryland and the surrounding states."

Smith said, "I have one in my car."

Neilsen said, "We're wasting our time. Even if we find him, he won't talk."

Reacher said, "Sure he will. If we ask nicely."

Roberta and Veronica Sanson figured that a Ford Explorer would fit the bill. The kind of vehicle that outdoorsy people use for towing trailers and carrying bikes and transporting kids and dogs. Versatile, but not flashy. So they stole one, twenty years old or so, from the parking lot at a Walmart, five miles outside of town. Then they turned north and west and drove for another thirty miles until they found the entrance to the Whispering Pines campsite and backwoods resort.

The site covered a hundred acres. It was mainly forest, but there were a couple of ponds for fishing, some rocks for scrambling, and plenty of tracks for walking and trails for riding. In the center there was a cluster of buildings known as The Oasis. There was an office. A store that sold food and basic maintenance items for RVs. A restroom block. And a shower block. Spread out to the east were the full service RV plots with hookups for power, fresh water, and drainage. Roberta and Veronica ignored those. They were too close together. Too near the buildings that would attract other people. Maybe nosy people. Maybe people with good memories. Instead they drove around the site looking for remote plots. The more isolated and inaccessible the better. Any time there was a choice, they took the smaller, less obvious road.

After twenty minutes of circling around and crisscrossing back and forth, Veronica spotted a glint of white paint through a distant stand of trees. Roberta continued for a quarter of a mile then pulled off the road. They jumped down from the Ford and made their way back on foot. They slowed right down as they approached the gap Veronica had glimpsed the vehicle through. They crept close. Took a good look. It was definitely a promising candidate. An RV. White with green and brown stripes. A dated, angular shape. Windows dotted along the side and a sleeping pod bulging clumsily out over the cab. It was sitting low on its springs. So it was heavy. With tanks full of water, like they were sure Pritchard's would be.

They worked their way around through the undergrowth so that they could approach the RV from the front. They figured that Pritchard—or someone else if this wasn't Pritchard's vehicle—would be in the living accommodation in the back. Not lurking in the cab. Roberta crept ahead. Veronica followed. They closed in, staying low, placing each foot carefully, steering clear of dead branches and dried-up twigs. When they were ten yards out they split up, with Roberta on the left, Veronica on the right. They covered another five yards. Then Roberta stood up and ran straight forward.

"No, no, no," she yelled. "Don't you dare."

She had spotted a hosepipe like the one they'd found in the garage Pritchard had been using in his neighbor's yard. Only this one wasn't attached to a water inlet. It was connected to the RV's tailpipe. It hung down from there, ran along the ground, then went up and in through a neat hole in the bottom corner of the main door.

Veronica caught up with her sister. The vehicle's engine wasn't running. Roberta laid her hand on the hood. She shook her head and said, "Stone cold." Then she took off her sweater and wrapped it around her head. She took hold of the door handle and pulled. The door swung open. A faint gray-blue mist drifted out from the interior. Roberta hesitated for a moment then climbed inside. She found a kitchen area with a tiny sink, a single burner cooktop, and a mini-fridge. A flimsy table with a bench seat on either side. A narrow door that opened into a basic bathroom. And a couch at the very back of the space. It took up the RV's whole width. Neville Pritchard was sprawled out on it. His eyes were open, unfocused, completely still. Everything in the place was coated with a thin, oily film. Including Pritchard's skin, which made him look more like a ghost than a man.

Roberta jumped down onto the ground outside and broke the news to Veronica.

Veronica screamed and stamped her foot. She said, "This can't be happening! It ruins everything." She was quiet for a moment, then said, "Do you think he did it to himself?"

Roberta said, "No way. No one escapes and then kills themselves. People kill themselves because they *can't* escape. No. The eighth man did it. To keep his ID secret. There's no other explanation."

Veronica slumped against the side of the RV then slid down until she was sitting on the ground. "It was all for nothing. Pritchard's dead and our only chance of learning the eighth name died with him. Shoot me now."

Roberta gave Veronica's leg a gentle kick. "It's not for nothing. Not even close. Seven of the assholes are dead. That's all but one of them. We swore we'd make them pay for keeping quiet and letting Dad take the blame. We've done that. In style. And aside from Buck with his cancer, their deaths stink of suicide. Reek of it. So it's their families' turn to live with that, now. How different would our lives have been if we hadn't had to? If Mom hadn't felt like she had to flee the country? Richard would be alive. Ryan wouldn't be in jail. We wouldn't have had to join the army to escape the madness. We could have done anything we wanted. Plus, I'm not giving up on getting the eighth name. Or the money the asshole made out of Dad's misfortune. I have an idea. Maybe there is another person who can help us figure it out."

"Who?"

"We'll talk about it when we're back on the road. We need to find a phone. Call 911. There's no point Pritchard being dead if no one knows about it."

Chapter 18

It took two hours and cost a dozen favors but Neilsen came through with the satellite photo. Or a faxed copy, at least. Which was the best anyone could hope for under the circumstances. He collected Smith, who had already fetched her map from her car, and together they went back to Reacher's room.

Neilsen placed the picture on Reacher's desk and said, "I have to duck out for a while. I heard from a buddy. He has information about 192. Something important going back to the sixties. He wouldn't discuss it on the phone. If I'm not back before you wrap up here, I'll see you in the bar."

Smith stood by Reacher's shoulder and tapped the center of the photograph with her finger. She said, "That's Pritchard's house. Does it tell you anything?"

Reacher studied the image for a minute, then said, "If you want to find someone, you have to think like they do. So imagine you live here. You're a little paranoid. Worried that hostile agents could come for you in the night. What would you do? You know the house is vulnerable from two directions. The front and the back. There's nothing you can do about that. Attackers could hit the front and watch the back. Or they could hit the back and watch the front. Or they could hit both simultaneously. So you would create an escape route out of one of the sides. Not the east. It's too exposed, and you'd have nowhere to go from there. So you'd use the west. Construct some kind of concealed exit leading out of the garage."

"How?"

"Doesn't matter. Lots of ways you could do it. The important point is that it would bring you out, here." Reacher's fingers were too thick so he pointed at the picture with the tip of his pen. "You'd be invisible. You'd be screened by the vegetation, here and here. And from there you'd have clear access to the fence. It would be easy to rig an unobtrusive way through. Then you'd be in the neighbor's yard. The hard part would be done. And then, what's this?" He pointed to a small rectangular structure.

"Looks like a shed? No. It has a driveway. It's a garage."

"All the houses in the subdivision have attached garages. What's an extra one doing there? It's nowhere near the house. Not very convenient. If the neighbors needed more space, why didn't they build an addition? My bet is that Pritchard leased the space and had the garage built. No. I bet he bought the whole property and rented the rest back to the occupants. And uses the extra garage to store a getaway vehicle. See how the driveway sweeps away from his own house? It's way longer than it needs to be. Why pay for that? So that he could coast down to the road, almost in silence. No wonder those agents missed him."

"The getaway vehicle will be registered in a false name. You can be sure of that. But what kind will it be? How do we find it?"

"Depends on what his goal is. If he was looking to flee the country, it'll be a car. Something comfortable. Nondescript. Dependable.

With a gas tank big enough to get to an airport, or a seaport, or even over the border. If that was his plan, he's long gone. We'll never find him. He'll be holed up on a beach someplace in a country with no extradition treaty."

"That doesn't sound promising."

"On the other hand, fleeing the jurisdiction is a young man's game. It's stressful. Physically demanding. You have to move fast, and carry lots of stuff, and airports are natural pinch points. They have security. Cops. A limited number of exits. And Pritchard's old. He's retired. The kind of guy who's more likely to use his experience than his muscles. Let his brain do the heavy lifting. I can see him tucked away by a quiet lake somewhere pleasant, fishing, waiting for the fuss to blow over. Or for his buddies to pull enough strings to nix whatever caused the danger. In which case he'd pick an RV. The garage looks big enough for one."

"The RV gets my vote. So where would he go in it? Could be anywhere in the country. Canada, even. Or Mexico. RVs are mobile. That's the whole point of them."

Reacher thought for a moment. He had no experience with RVs but he figured they would be similar in principle to army infantry fighting vehicles. Designed to provide shelter and mobility. So maybe like a Bradley but with more home comforts and fewer guns. Able to carry a certain quantity of supplies. Water. Fuel. And food, in a civilian context. But there would be a limit. Pritchard would need the ability to resupply. Reacher assumed specialist facilities existed to meet that kind of need. He took the map from Smith and spread it out next to the photograph.

He said, "How fast can an RV go?"

Smith shrugged. "I don't know. Sixty?"

"I figure Pritchard would want to be on the road for less than an hour. So here's what we need to do. Find every place that could supply a vehicle with fresh water within a forty-mile radius of his house. Contact the local cops. Fax them the most up-to-date picture of Pritchard you can get your hands on. Have them send an officer to each potential location and find out if anyone there has seen him. Tell them to be discreet. If they get a confirmed sighting, to report it. Not to make an approach. Pritchard's paranoid. He's in flight mode right now. But that could easily change."

"The businesswoman, scientist person? Why her?" Veronica Sanson settled back in her seat.

"Because she was there." Roberta shifted into Drive and lifted her foot off the brake.

"In India? How do you know?"

Roberta eased out into a gap in the traffic. "I guess you're too young to remember the press conferences on TV. Her picture was all over the newspapers at the time, too. She was the spokesperson for the chemical company."

"That was her? I didn't realize. Didn't make the connection. But she was a civilian. Not CIA. Not army. How can she help?"

Roberta leaned on the gas. "When I was in Pritchard's house I let the fourth agent cuff me. I put myself at a total disadvantage. So how was I able to send the watchers away? How come he was on the floor, unconscious, when you arrived? Because he underestimated me. A woman. Men are always underestimating women. And now what are you doing? Susan Kasluga is smart. Capable. Resourceful. Probably curious and inquisitive, too. She must be, to have achieved everything she has. Who knows what she saw over there? What she heard? What dots she was able to privately join? I bet no one bothered to ask, because she's a woman. She was young. And even if she doesn't realize the significance of it, she could have the secret locked away in her brain. We can't call this thing quits until we at least find out."

"OK. I see the logic. But how do we get close enough to ask? She's the CEO of a gazillion-dollar corporation. Her husband is the Secretary of Defense. We can't just stroll into her office. We can't just knock on her front door."

"We'll do what we always do. Watch. Wait. And when we see an opportunity, we'll take it."

The phone in the Pentagon rang at 2:27 P.M. Eastern. Not a scheduled time for a call.

The guy who answered it listened, hung up, then dialed the number for the study at the rear of Charles Stamoran's home.

Stamoran was sitting in his armchair, lost in thought, when the jangling sound disturbed him, so it took him several rings to move across the room and pick up. He cleared his throat and said, "What now?"

The guy recited the message he had memorized a minute before. "Neville Pritchard is dead. The cause was carbon monoxide poisoning. He was in an RV and a hosepipe had been attached to its exhaust, presumably by himself, though no note has been found. His body was recovered following an anonymous call to 911. The ME provisionally estimates that he's been deceased for four days."

Stamoran stood still and held the receiver down by his side for a moment. This wasn't suicide. If Neville Pritchard was going to kill anyone it would have been the agents who broke into his house, or the women who were gunning for him. Not himself. And something was off with the timeline. If he had been dead for four days, he'd have had to be killed the same day as Geoff Brown, down in New Orleans. That had been an intricate affair. All decoy phone calls and toad venom. It would have taken time to set up. And it was too far away. The logistics wouldn't work. The ME must have been out with his conclusion. Just by a few hours. Pritchard must have been killed the same night he bolted from his house. The women must have followed him. It's hard to outrun someone in an RV, after all. It must have been the women who spooked him. Not the agents he'd sent to bring Pritchard in. But that was a minor wrinkle. The real question was whether Pritchard had talked. Whether he had revealed the secret. Probably not, given that the women went on to kill the other scientists. *Probably* not. Which was very different from *definitely* not. And it would make a kind of sense for them to leave the biggest prize till last.

Stamoran raised the handset. He said, "Three things. Find out if there were any signs of torture or coercion on the body when Pritchard's autopsy is done. Stand down the agents at his house. And leave the task force in place. Tell them to redouble their efforts at identifying these women."

Stamoran didn't like to waste resources. But if there was a chance a pair of killers was coming for him, it wouldn't hurt to know who they were.

Reacher and Smith finished pulling together their list of places where Pritchard could be hiding in his RV. It ran to two sheets of paper. Smith tucked them inside her map and started toward the door, then her pager began to beep. So did Reacher's. His was a semitone lower and it was a fraction out of sync.

Christopher Baglin was standing, looking out of the boardroom window. His back was to the table. Reacher and Smith took their places. Walsh followed them in. Baglin turned and glared at the door. The expression on his face was somewhere between anger and fear.

He said, "Is Neilsen joining us?"

Reacher said, "He's following up on a lead. Could be out for a while."

"Then we'll start without him. I'll keep this brief. Neville Pritchard is dead. He was found in an RV at a campsite thirty-five miles from his house. A hosepipe had been hooked up to the exhaust."

Smith said, "So our killers are six for six and the other team is fresh out of hitters. Do we get to go back to our day jobs now?"

Baglin scowled. "You're lucky to have day jobs. You've all been as effective as toupees in a hurricane. So, no. Not yet. We have a pair of serial killers on the loose. We couldn't stop them, but we can damn well catch them. You know what to do. Go."

Walsh raised his hand. A moment of awkward silence followed, then he said, "I have something."

Baglin was halfway out of his seat. He paused, then lowered himself back down. Reacher and Smith exchanged a glance.

"I know I haven't made much of a contribution when it comes to identifying suspects and I feel bad about that. And I was getting bored of the view out of the window, so I did what I do. I went sniffing for money. I did a deep dive into all the victims' affairs. They were all pretty messed up. Poor balance between income and expenses. Inconsistent approach to assets and debts. Which is to say, normal. Except for Pritchard. To use a technical term, the guy was loaded."

Baglin said, "How loaded?"

"Seriously loaded. I can get you the numbers if you want them."

"Yes. Do that. Where did the money come from?"

"That's the second interesting thing. The superficial answer is

interest and dividends from a bunch of fairly conservative investments. But that's chicken feed compared to what the original seed
money must have looked like. And where that originated I haven't
found out yet."

"OK. Good. Keep working on that. See where it leads. Reacher
and Smith—get me an ID on our killers."

Reacher said, "A question first. Pritchard's body. Did it have any
physical injuries? Any sign of electrocution? Any drugs in his system?"

"No. Why do you ask?"

Reacher shrugged. "What can I say? I have a thirst for knowledge."

Smith tore up their list of campgrounds the moment she walked
into Reacher's room.

"That'll save the police a heap of trouble," she said. "And
Pritchard's dead, too. What do you make of that?"

"Reminds me of a time when I was a kid and my dad got posted
to the Philippines. Our quarters were a bit shabby, I guess, so my
mom decided to grow potted plants. Make the place more homey.
Except that one kind she liked kept dying. Whatever she tried to
keep them alive, it made no difference. Plant after plant wound up
shriveled and thrown in the trash. Getting one to survive became an
obsession. Eventually she came across a book about horticulture in
the base library. She looked in the troubleshooting section. It covered the exact problem she was having. It said the cause was too
much water, or too little water."

"So it's impossible to say what his death means."

"Could bring the sky crashing down. Could make no difference
at all."

"What about Walsh springing to life? I didn't see that coming."

"I'm glad, actually. I got a call from my brother. He also works at the Treasury Department. Apparently Walsh was just undercover. A long stretch. Another of these counterfeiting cases that keep cropping up. It didn't end well. Seems he's suffering from PTSD as a result."

"I didn't realize. Poor guy. I thought he was just a lazy asshole. Let's hope he's turned a corner. But what about all this money he says Pritchard had? Significant, do you think?"

"Have you ever investigated anyone, found out they had a secret stash of cash, and it turned out not to be significant?"

Reacher and Smith stayed at the office until their regular knocking-off time. Ten after five. Neilsen hadn't come back by then. He wasn't in reception at the hotel when they passed through at six, and he wasn't waiting for them at the bar when they claimed their usual table.

Smith took the seat opposite Reacher at their table, leaned forward with her elbows on its wooden top, and said, "You're not married, are you, Reacher?"

Reacher smiled. "Me? No. You?"

Smith looked away and right then the server appeared at her side.

"Just the two of you today?" she said.

Reacher said, "For now." He saw a flutter of disappointment cross her face. Her tip was going to be a lot smaller without Neilsen's bar tab to build on.

"Can I get you started with some drinks?" she said.

They ordered beer, and their food, as they knew the menu down pat by then, and when the server stepped away Smith held up her left hand for Reacher to see.

She said, "No ring."

Her statement was true, but Reacher felt like he could make out a slight depression around her finger, where one recently could have been.

Smith leaned forward again and said, "Any thoughts for tomorrow? I heard back from my guy who's checking into the Sansons. The wife moved the family to Israel after Morgan's suicide. They didn't fare too well, it seems. One of the boys, Richard, died. A drug overdose. Ryan's in jail. For dealing. And there's no trace of Robert or Ronald yet. I told my guy to keep digging."

Their food arrived and when they were done eating, Reacher said, "What do you make of Susan Kasluga?"

Smith shrugged. "I don't know much about her. Just a few things I've read in the papers."

The server came by to collect their empty plates, and when she was out of earshot Reacher said, "I keep thinking, Kasluga was in India. She might have known Sanson. She might have information that could help us. Then I remember she's married to the Secretary of Defense."

A scowl spread across Smith's face. "I don't see how her husband's job is relevant."

"He ordered up the task force that ties back to some kind of wrongdoing at a chemical plant. And she worked at the plant. I don't like coincidences."

"Sometimes a coincidence is just a coincidence. And anyway, she didn't work at the secret part of the plant. She was with the civilian company. Mason Chemical. And I read a profile on her once. She didn't meet Charles Stamoran until '72. They didn't get married until '75. He was a big noise in the CIA back then. Imagine the security clearance she must have gone through. She's probably the most honest person you could ever meet."

"Then why did she lie?"

"When did she lie?"

"In '69. She said seven people died in that accident. She left out the other thousand."

Smith was quiet for a moment. "It's only a lie if you know what you're saying isn't true. How would she have known about the real death toll? I doubt the CIA and the army gave guided tours of the scene. They probably just stuck her in front of the cameras because she was young and pretty, and trusted she was naïve enough to read out what they told her to read."

"Maybe."

"I think it's a good idea to ask her about Sanson. I think we should do it."

"Let's take—"

There was a loud ripping sound from the doorway, then a crash. Neilsen had arrived. He'd gotten tangled up in the plastic sheet that hung from the frame and overbalanced in the course of freeing himself. He stood up, brushed off his crumpled suit, strolled across, and took the seat next to Reacher.

He said, "Where's the server. I need whiskey. Immediately."

Smith said, "Looks like you've already had plenty of whiskey."

Neilsen tipped his head to the side. "Correct. *Had.* Past tense. Which is why, now, I need more."

"Your informant had a thirst on, I guess."

"Not an informant. And no. Frank doesn't drink. This," Neilsen gestured to his loosened tie and a stain on his shirt, "all happened after he left."

"You've been drinking all afternoon?"

"If I'd met him for breakfast I'd have been drinking all day. So lighten up."

Reacher said, "He had bad news?"

Neilsen said, "Bad? Such an inadequate little word. Here's what he told me. He said the Agency has no record of Project Typhon. Nothing to say it ever existed. It's been buried. That's what they do with time bombs. But he's a thorough guy, Frank. See, I'd asked him who was in charge of it. And when he couldn't answer that, he moved on to what he figured was the next best thing. Who was in charge of the 19x projects. All of them. And all their spin-offs. So including 192 and Typhon. Care to guess?"

Smith shook her head.

Reacher said nothing.

"Charles Stamoran."

Chapter 19

Neilsen got his whiskey. A double. Smith had a glass, too. A single, with water. Reacher switched to coffee. Black, with a sidecar of espresso.

"There's one tiny silver patch in this cloud," Neilsen said. "The question about whether we dig into Typhon? That's answered. It was the Secretary of Defense's baby. We don't touch it with a ten-million-foot pole." He drained his glass. "Here's another thing that sucks. Our fate is out of our hands. It's down to those killer women now. And Neville Pritchard. If he can disappear, we'll be OK. If they catch him and only want to kill him, we'll be OK. But if they catch him and he blabs, we're screwed. No way is Stamoran going to stand still and take the blame for all those dead bodies. He'll be deflecting, left and right. Onto us, or some poor schmuck from the sixties. Wait. That's a good point. We need to give him a schmuck from the sixties. First thing tomorrow, we find one. Or another KGB guy. Smith, got any up your sleeve? Not that you're wearing sleeves, but you know what I mean."

Reacher said, "You might want to order another whiskey."

"Of course I do. Wait. Why?"

"Pritchard's dead."

"He is? When?"

"We found out this afternoon."

"Did he blab?"

"That remains to be seen."

Neilsen signaled for the server to come over.

Smith took a sip of her drink, then said, "There's one other thing to take away from this. We can forget about talking to Susan Kasluga. She either knows about this, or she doesn't. And if she knows, she's not going to say a word. Not with her husband's neck on the block."

Neilsen took exaggerated care navigating the exit from the bar and then stayed a few yards ahead of the others. He was swaying slightly as he walked but he made it back to the hotel without injuring himself. They all rode up to the second floor together in the elevator. Then they made their way along the corridor, Neilsen in front again, and when they got close to his door he pulled out his keys. And dropped them. Reacher started to lean down to retrieve them but Neilsen waved him off.

"Go," he said. "It's only a door. I've got this."

Smith let herself into her room and Reacher continued to his. He shrugged off his jacket and put it on a hanger. Then he heard a tap on the door. Light, but insistent. He turned, checked the peephole, and opened it. Smith was standing in the corridor. She was barefoot. She'd shed her purse. Her key was in one hand. Her gun was in the other.

She said, "My room's been searched. Has yours?"

Reacher gestured for her to come in. He took a look around. His duffel was on the floor beneath the hangers. Maybe an inch closer to the door than where he'd left it. His spare clothes were laid out on the second queen bed. Maybe not quite as straight. In the bathroom, his toothbrush was standing in the glass by the sink. It was leaning a little. Not quite as vertical as it had been.

He said, "A couple of things have moved, I guess. But searched? I don't know. Housekeeping could have done it."

Smith shook her head. "Not with me. Things have been disturbed inside my suitcase. That's deliberate."

"You haven't unpacked?"

"I repack every morning. It's SOP for me. I need to leave in a hurry, I grab my bag and go. No time wasted."

Reacher shrugged. He figured there was nothing in his room valuable enough to come back for in a pinch. He said, "You check with Neilsen?"

Smith shook her head. "I came to you first."

They hurried back out into the corridor and Reacher tapped on Neilsen's door. There was no answer. He knocked again, a little louder. There was no response. He banged, loud enough that he half expected other guests to come out and yell at him, but still Neilsen did not make a sound.

"What do you think?" Smith said. "Passed out?"

Reacher said, "Probably. But we should make sure. I'll get a passkey."

Reacher used the stairs both ways and was back outside Neilsen's room a couple of minutes later. He had a key on an extra-large brass fob in his hand. He worked the lock. Pushed the door. And saw Neilsen's feet. Still in his shoes. Sticking out through the bathroom doorway. Reacher moved in closer. Smith followed. Neilsen was facedown on the floor. He wasn't moving. His head was by the shower tray. There was a smear of blood on the white porcelain and a neat round puddle on the tiles. It was like Neilsen had rested his cheek on a scarlet dinner plate. Reacher leaned down and pressed two fingers against his carotid. He held them there for a full minute. Then he turned to Smith and shook his head.

"Seriously?" There was fury on Smith's face. "The same day he finds out who was running a top secret government program he falls and winds up dead? How stupid do they think we are?" She crouched down and brushed a strand of hair away from Neilsen's open, unseeing eyes. Her voice was suddenly soft, almost on the edge of breaking. "You know, this is worse. Stalin was right. The thousand deaths in India is just a number next to the body of one person you knew."

Reacher was thinking about something else. About how the killer must have been waiting in the room when they said good night to Neilsen. *Goodbye*, as it turned out. About how he was going to find whoever sent that person. And when he did, how they were going to get more than a tap on the head.

Reacher and Smith moved out of the bathroom and closed the door to the corridor. They didn't want any onlookers gathering around.

Reacher said, "How are your acting skills?"

Smith said, "Not great. Why?"

"It's time to sharpen them up. We need to play dumb. Do everything by the book. Make sure whoever had Neilsen killed thinks his knowledge died with him."

"You mean Stamoran."

"Looks that way. So here's the story. We didn't see Neilsen tonight. He didn't come to the bar. We had dinner, came back, found our rooms had been turned over, knocked on his door, and when he didn't answer we got worried. Because of his drinking. We borrowed the passkey, checked, and found him dead. That's all. Agreed?"

"I guess. But what about the bar? The server saw us together."

"I'll talk to her. Remind her about the story of the golden goose. Make sure she gets the reference."

"So we should call the police?"

"No. Baglin. He can deal with the police. The CIA. Stamoran. Whoever. But first we need to get Neilsen's phone records."

"How?"

"The front desk will have them, so they know how much to bill to his room."

"Why does that matter?"

"It doesn't. But we need to find his contact, Frank, and warn him. And see who else he was in touch with. He said he'd been shaking the trees. He might have said the wrong word in the wrong ear. The alarm could have gotten raised that way. You don't get to the top by being overly trusting. Stamoran will have tripwires out there. All kinds of defense mechanisms. We just don't know how many. Or where they are."

Christopher Baglin was on the scene half an hour after Reacher spoke to him on the phone. He assessed the situation then called the chief of the D.C. police. Two detectives arrived within another twenty minutes. A crime scene truck was hard on their heels. Yellow and black tape sprouted all over the place, running between doorframes and across corridors. A fresh-faced uniformed officer was set up with a clipboard to record everyone who came and went. Designated paths were marked for entering and leaving. Photographs were taken. Guys in paper suits and elasticated booties got busy with all kinds of powders and sprays. At some point two guys in dark suits showed up. They poked around everywhere but didn't introduce themselves to anyone. They didn't need to. Everyone there recognized CIA agents when they saw them. Finally, a pair of paramedics wheeled Neilsen's body away on a gurney and the detectives set to work taking statements from Reacher and Smith.

They were moved into separate, makeshift interview rooms. There were no panic strips or one-way mirrors, but the rest of the detectives' repertoire was in play. They tried every trick. Saying the other one had flipped and it was time to get out ahead of the inevitable charges. That there were witnesses. That there was only one deal to be done and the other one was wavering. Nothing worked. And the whole time a CIA guy was lurking in the corner, leaning against the wall, saying nothing.

When the dust had settled and the majority of the emergency personnel had dispersed, Baglin pulled Reacher and Smith aside. He said, "Are you folks OK? It can't have been pleasant, what you've been through."

Smith said, "I can think of better ways to spend an evening."

Baglin said, "Your rooms were searched by the same guy?"

Reacher said, "Our rooms were searched. We assume it was by the same guy. There's no proof, but it would be a hell of a coincidence otherwise."

"I'm sure the detectives asked you this, but can you think of any reason why someone would come after Neilsen? Maybe after all of you?"

Reacher shook his head. "None. It's hard to see how the attack connects with the task force in any way. We know that two women have committed a string of murders, and we have a good idea why, but that's all. We have no IDs. No descriptions. No physical evidence. They're clearly well trained and proficient, so if they believed the net was closing in, the smart play would be to go back to their regular lives. They could serve us coffee every morning at the café on the corner and we'd be none the wiser. They had no need to kill any of us. It would be a tactically retrograde move to try. Very out of character for them."

"So what happened tonight?"

"My guess? A burglary gone wrong. Hotels get robbed all the time. And look at the sequence of our rooms. The guy started with mine. Found nothing worth taking. Moved on to Agent Smith's."

Smith said, "Nothing valuable in mine."

"So the perp moved on to Neilsen's. He was in the process of rummaging around, looking for goodies, when Neilsen stumbled in. It's safe to say from the smell that he'd been drinking tonight. The intruder might not even have been trying to kill him. Maybe he just pushed him, trying to make a run for it."

Baglin crossed his arms and Reacher got the feeling he wasn't buying the story at all. No one spoke for a moment, then Baglin said, "I should apologize. Placing you all in the same hotel, let alone in adjacent rooms, was a tactical error. It exposed you to unnecessary risk. That has been remedied. You're being moved to new hotels. Separate ones, in different parts of town. Effective immediately."

Reacher said, "I don't have a vehicle."

"One has been arranged. It may have been delivered already. Check with reception on your way out."

Smith said, "Thank you. And what about tomorrow morning?" She checked her watch. "This morning, I guess."

Baglin said, "What about it? Be at the office, usual time. We now have three killers to catch."

* * *

A car was waiting in the lot for Reacher. It was a rental. A Ford sedan. A tinny thing with thin seats and too many buttons on the dash and not enough room behind the steering wheel. Reacher wasn't worried about its design flaws, though. He wasn't planning on spending much time using it.

The hotel Reacher had been allocated to was pretty much at the opposite end of the scale from the original. If the first had been designed with hordes of raucous Midwest schoolkids in mind, the second was aimed squarely at the political and diplomatic end of the market. His room was enormous. It was two rooms, really. One with a bed and a bathroom and a walk-in closet. And the other with separate sitting and dining areas. There were full-sized bottles of various washing products he didn't recognize set around the sink and basin. The kind of things he would never dream of using. There were giant towels. Fluffy robes. Enough scatter cushions that if you had to escape the building in a fire you could throw them out of the window and they'd break your fall from ten floors up. Reacher wasn't interested in any of those things, though. He just wanted to put the day behind him and start fresh in the morning. He made his way around, switching off lights and closing drapes, and he noticed the door to a little cabinet wasn't closed all the way. It was a mini-bar. Neilsen would have liked that, he thought. He looked inside. Took out a miniature of Maker's Mark, popped the cap, and drank a silent toast to absent friends.

Chapter 20

Reacher and Smith pulled into the parking lot outside the task force's office within a minute of each other the following morning. Reacher came from the south. Smith from the north. They walked into reception together and saw that two extra security guards were on duty. The stable door's been locked, Reacher thought, and showed his ID. He followed Smith down the corridor and into the boardroom. She sat and he poured himself a mug of coffee.

She said, "Do you think they'll send a replacement for Neilsen?"

Reacher said, "I doubt it. Sending someone from the Agency was a gamble for Stamoran. A misstep, with hindsight. Neilsen was only able to get to the truth because he could tap up his buddy. The guy would never have spoken to us. Or Walsh, now that he's woken up. Stamoran probably figured it would look more suspicious if the Agency wasn't represented. Eyebrows would have been raised then, for sure. He probably hoped a drunk like Neilsen wouldn't be able to do him any harm."

"You know, that makes me sad. We never got the chance to find out what Neilsen's story was. He was a good agent. That was obvious. Even when he was four sheets to the wind. He couldn't have been drinking like that from the start of his career. His liver wouldn't have survived. And if he didn't get killed he would have been kicked out. Something must have happened to him. Something traumatic. I wish I'd known him well enough for him to share what that was."

Reacher said nothing.

Smith stifled a yawn and said, "Did you sleep?"

Reacher said, "I could have gotten more." The truth was that his eyes had closed a minute after his head hit the pillow and he hadn't stirred until a minute before it was time to get up, but he'd learned over the years that people aren't generally looking for a positive answer to that kind of question.

Smith said, "I hardly got a wink. I'm wiped. This is really bad, Reacher. Neilsen's death, Charles Stamoran, Typhon, a thousand corpses—I just kept thinking, what are we going to do with it all?"

"We'll do what we would do if we were investigating any other person for any other crime. Follow the evidence. If it confirms that Stamoran's guilty, then we take him down."

"But he's the Secretary of Defense."

"Like I told Sarbotskiy, this is America. The law applies to him the same as everyone else."

"Makes going after him harder, though."

"So we work smarter."

"Any thoughts?"

"My gut tells me Neilsen's death starts with someone he spoke to at the CIA. He likely mentioned Typhon. Asked if it existed. If there was any proof. Who had run the program. Something that touched a raw nerve. From there I see three possible paths. One, Neilsen's contact came and did the deed himself. Two, he sent someone else to do it. Three, he reported Neilsen's questions to another person and they arranged the murder."

"Stamoran would fit scenario three?"

"Right."

"How do we prove it?"

"We find out who Neilsen spoke to. I'll contact them. I'll let them know I worked with Neilsen and that I know what he knew. Then I'll wait for someone to come snooping around my hotel room. And instead of me winding up on the bathroom floor, whoever shows up will give us a name. Then we'll rinse and repeat as necessary until we get to the top of the food chain. We already know who Neilsen called from the hotel. Now we need a list of his calls from here. Do you think the Bureau could get that for us?"

Smith stretched out and grabbed the phone from the center of the table. She dialed a number, gave a couple of quick instructions that were mostly in jargon and acronyms that Reacher didn't understand, then hung up. She pushed the phone back and just then the door opened. Gary Walsh hurried in. His face was flushed. He started toward his regular seat near the window then turned back and shuffled awkwardly on the spot for a moment. Then he said, "I heard about what happened. I'm really sorry. I guess you were getting close. If there's anything I can do . . ."

The door opened again and the original security guard appeared. He said, "Message from Mr. Baglin. He can't be present at the meeting this morning. He says you all know what you need to do."

Walsh waited for the door to close then sat in Baglin's place. He said, "What happened to Neilsen—was it to do with why he missed the meeting yesterday?"

Reacher and Smith exchanged a glance.

Walsh said, "I know I haven't given you any reason to believe this, but you can trust me. I haven't really been present because I've been processing some stuff but I want to put that right. Please, let me in. I can help."

Reacher said nothing. Smith looked down at the table.

Walsh said, "Reacher? I know your brother. In passing, at least. Call him. He'll vouch for me. And Amber? Two years ago my team did some number crunching for Phil on a sting he was running. He told me—"

Smith said, "Neilsen went to meet a contact. He wasn't back before we left and when we got to the hotel after dinner we found our rooms had been searched. We tried to check in with Neilsen but he was dead. It was staged to look like he'd fallen, but we're not buying that."

"The meeting with his contact. Was it about the Project?"

Smith didn't pick up on the question. She was staring at the side wall.

Reacher said, "It seems that way."

"Then the cops will do some window dressing but they'll be kept well away from the business end. You're trying to find Neilsen's killer yourselves?"

Reacher nodded.

"Made any progress?"

"We have a list of numbers he called from the hotel." Reacher explained his theory about Neilsen causing panic at Langley and the need to figure out who he'd spoken to.

Walsh said, "Can I see the list? Numbers are kind of my thing. Even without dollar signs in front of them."

Smith didn't respond. Reacher nudged her arm. She said, "Sorry. What?"

Reacher said, "Show Walsh the numbers from the hotel."

Smith passed him the page the receptionist had printed for her the night before when she flashed her badge.

Walsh studied the paper for a minute then said, "OK. One number crops up over and over. The one with four zeros at the end. That'll be a switchboard number. Langley? And all these numbers where only the final four digits are different? Direct dial extensions. They'll be Langley, too. Then there are a few with the same area code. Langley people's home numbers, I would guess. And a few outliers. I don't know about those. Friends, maybe? Except for this one. 1-800-266-9328. He called that a couple of times." Walsh grinned and shook his head. "He was out of control."

Smith said, "I don't get it. What's the significance?"

Walsh said, "I guess it will be advertised alphanumerically . . ."

Reacher did the transposition in his head. "1-800-BOOZE 2 U. A delivery service, presumably. Liquor stores across the Eastern Seaboard are going to mourn Neilsen's passing. That's for sure."

Smith said, "What a world we live in. OK. We should focus on the Langley numbers. How do we prioritize? The switchboard number's no good without knowing who he asked for."

Walsh said, "Maybe if we knew if he also received calls from any of the numbers. That would suggest a back and forth interaction. Not just a brush-off or a message left on a machine. It won't be possible for the hotel—calls to the room phones go through the switchboard—but here it should be."

Smith picked the phone up again and made another call. She hung up and said, "They're on it. It'll take a while, though. Anything we can do in the meantime? We should build on the panic. Try and get them to send another hitman tonight. If you're cool with that, Reacher."

Reacher said, "The sooner, the better. Send him now."

"There's maybe something we can do." Walsh sounded hesitant. "It's a long shot, but it wouldn't hurt to try. Anyone know if Neilsen was the kind of guy who was uptight about deleting his messages?"

* * *

Roberta and Veronica Sanson decided not to steal a car this time. They knew they were going to be up to their armpits in law enforcement of all different flavors so they figured renting a vehicle would be a sound investment. They thought a Suburban would look the part. It would blend into the kind of environments they were anticipating operating in, but it took them a while to find a place that didn't quibble when it came to doing the deal in cash.

Their outlay proved worthwhile inside ten minutes. That's as long as it took to observe Susan Kasluga leaving the house she shared with her husband. She was sitting in the back of a black Town Car. It nosed out of their fortified gate and merged into the slow morning traffic. Kasluga was reading that morning's *Wall Street Journal.* A chauffeur was driving and there were two other people on board. Men in cheap suits with earpieces and curly wires disappearing beneath their collars. Bodyguards. From a private agency, by the look of them. Perfect, from the sisters' point of view.

Roberta eased away from the curb. She was four cars behind Kasluga. She varied the interval as the traffic sped up and slowed down. Sometimes she was three cars behind. Sometimes five. A couple of times when they were on longer sections with no turnoffs she briefly pulled ahead then let the Town Car retake the lead before it reached a point where it had a choice of directions. She kept up the same rhythm for twenty minutes, then the Town Car pulled off to the right onto the top of a ramp that led down to a garage beneath an office building. It was twenty stories high, mirrored blue glass over a steel frame, rectangular sections, relentlessly symmetrical. The headquarters of AmeriChem Incorporated. The company Kasluga founded when she returned from India.

Roberta continued straight, then took two lefts in quick succession. No one was following them. She didn't expect there to have been, but it pays to take precautions. The street they were on was quiet so she pulled over and turned to Veronica. She said, "What do you think?"

Veronica said, "In an ideal world we would watch her for a week, minimum. But they know there are two of us now. And there are no scientists left. They could start piecing things together. So good now is better than perfect later. Let's check her schedule. If she's in the office tomorrow, and we can pick up what we need this afternoon, I say we do it in the morning."

Roberta shifted back into Drive. She said, "Agreed."

Neilsen's office was locked. Smith took a slim leather wallet from her purse and selected two slender, metal picks. She inserted the flatter one into the keyhole and held it down low. She slid the pointier one in above it, raked it back and forth, and thirty seconds later the door swung open. Walsh went in first. Reacher followed and the feeling of trespass he always experienced when he entered a dead person's room soon descended on him. Smith closed the door behind them. Walsh crossed to Neilsen's desk and hit a button on his answering machine. A smoked plastic lid popped open. There was nothing under it. He turned to the fax machine. Its output tray was empty.

Walsh said, "Well, looks like the Agency cleaned house already. Damn. Although there's one other thing . . ."

Walsh tapped a few digits on the fax machine's keypad. The mechanism began to whirr and a few seconds later a sheet of paper cranked out. Walsh held it out for the others to see. There were columns with dates and numbers and times and durations. He said, "It's the transmission log. Shows us all the faxes Neilsen sent and received." Then he turned to Smith. "Can I grab that call list again for a second?" He checked a detail and nodded his head. "Yes. Look. The same number shows up on both."

"Does that help us?" Reacher said. "Murderers don't generally fax their plans ahead of time."

Walsh said, "I don't think he sent a fax. Look. Duration: one second. Pages received: zero."

"So what did he do?"

"In the office they gave me the phone and the fax numbers are one digit apart. Yours?"

Smith said, "Same."

Reacher nodded.

Walsh said, "Safe to assume it's the same for Neilsen, then. So I think someone called his fax machine by mistake. Then hung up right away."

Reacher said, "Why would they do that?"

"If Neilsen left a message, he could have given the wrong number. Or the caller could have misdialed."

Smith picked up the phone list and the fax log. "The timing works. Neilsen called the number from the hotel right after we'd been to see Sarbotskiy. He'd sucked down all that vodka, remember? Easy to get one digit wrong when you leave a message and you can hardly stand up straight. And the call back came that evening, when we were at the bar."

"So Neilsen leaves a provocative message. The recipient tries to reach him, but can't. And does what? Escalates? And whoever's above him sends someone to take care of the problem?"

Whoever being Stamoran, Smith thought, but she didn't say it out loud.

"It's plausible," Reacher said. "Worth following up. But why did you say the guy would hang up right away?"

Walsh said, "You've never called a fax machine by mistake?"

"How would I know?"

Walsh pointed to Neilsen's phone. "Try it. Call yours, now."

Reacher punched in the number. The call connected. And his ear was instantly assaulted by a howling, screeching electronic cacophony. He slammed the handset down. "The hell was that?"

Walsh smirked. "Sorry, Reacher. That's how fax machines talk to each other. You can see why the guy wouldn't stay on the line."

Smith leaned over and picked the handset back up. She dialed and when she was answered she reeled off the same succession of acronyms she'd used earlier and requested a list of any other calls the number that had tried to reach Neilsen had made. Then she asked to be transferred and gave instructions for the number to be run through a reverse directory. She was silent for a few seconds, then shook her head and hung up. She said, "The list of calls will be faxed to me later. The number's registered to a John Smith. No relation."

Chapter 21

The reception area at AmeriChem's headquarters was an opulent space full of high-end materials and museum quality art, but boil it down to its bones and it was there to do one thing: Keep people out. Unless they had a pass to operate one of the turnstiles. Staff members had them. Legitimate visitors could get them. Veronica Sanson was neither. So her first step toward gaining access to the building started next door, in a Starbucks. She got in line and while she waited she took a lanyard out of her pocket. She'd bought it years ago in a tourist store in Tel Aviv. It was yellow with cartoon monkeys printed all over it. She slung it around her neck and tucked its clip inside her jacket as if she had a pass card but didn't want to display it to the world on her commute to work. She reached the counter and ordered four venti lattes. That was the largest size of drink available. She asked for a cardboard carrier, wedged the giant cups into the cutouts in each corner, and loaded a bunch of sugar packets and stirring sticks into the space in the center.

Veronica made her way out of the coffee shop and through one of AmeriChem's revolving doors. She was holding the drink tray out in front and moving cautiously, as if the whole thing was about to collapse and scald her. She crept all the way to the nearest turnstile. And then she was stuck. She couldn't hold the drinks with one hand. She couldn't free her lanyard with no hands. People were coming up behind her, pinning her in. She was getting flustered. She tried to rebalance her load and almost dropped it. She tried to hold it level and lean down close enough to the sensor to activate the machine without undoing her jacket. Three packets of sugar slid off and hit the floor. She tried to wriggle one forearm under the tray and one of the cups almost fell. Her face turned scarlet. She looked like she was close to tears. Then a guy in a suit with silver hair and a mustache stepped up alongside her. He leaned down and used his own pass to release the turnstile. She tiptoed through and made for the elevators.

"Thank you so much," she said when the guy caught up to her. "I thought I was going to die of embarrassment back there. It's only my second day. I won't forget to have my card ready ever again." She lowered her voice. "You couldn't hit the button for me when we get in, could you? I don't want a repeat of that debacle. I need Ms. Kasluga's floor."

Susan Kasluga had the largest corner office on the twentieth floor. A perk of being the big boss, Veronica figured. She figured another perk would be having the most qualified assistant so she ditched the milky coffees in the women's bathroom near the elevator lobby, rushed down the corridor, and burst into Kasluga's outer office. A woman in a sleek black pantsuit looked up from behind a wide antique desk, alarmed. She had gray hair pulled back from her face, fine bones, and stern blue eyes.

Veronica said, "You're the one they meant, right? You know CPR?"

The gray-haired woman was on her feet immediately. "Someone's having an arrest?"

"Downstairs. One floor. By the elevators. Someone called 911, but you know how long those guys can take to come."

Veronica made as if to follow, but as soon as the older woman was through the door she turned back. She looped around the desk. A computer monitor took up almost half the real estate. It was beige, hulking, bowed at the front, with a thick tangle of wires hanging down at the back. There was a telephone. A big, complicated thing with all kinds of lights and buttons. A leather desk pad. A pair of trolls, three inches high, with wild fluorescent hair. A gift from a grandchild, Veronica thought. There was a pad of paper and a pen. A Rolodex. Veronica wondered how much she could get for some of the names and numbers it must contain. And at the side, on its own, a leather-bound executive diary. Veronica opened it. Flicked through to the current week. Looked at the following day's entries. Saw they started at 6:00 A.M. with *Serge, Press Conference Prep, Boardroom,* and ran through to 6:00 P.M. without a break.

Sorry, Serge, Veronica thought. *You're going to be getting up early for nothing.*

Reacher and Walsh followed Smith out of Neilsen's office. Smith used her picks to relock his door then led the way to her own office. That felt less ghoulish than hanging out in a dead person's space, and it meant they were near Smith's fax machine. The one the information about the phone calls she'd requested would be sent to.

Reacher and Walsh ducked out briefly to fetch the chairs from their offices, then the three of them sat in a loose triangle and waited. The fax machine became the center of attention, despite being completely inert. Smith made a couple of attempts to kick-start a conversation. Walsh offered a few snippets about his take on the country's financial prospects. Reacher said nothing.

After forty minutes the display on the fax machine began to flash and a few moments later a single piece of paper slid into its output tray. Smith grabbed it, took a look, then held it up for the others to see.

"Calls made by the number Neilsen was in touch with," she said. "Only one was made after he dialed Neilsen's fax. A minute after he hung up. Let's see who it was."

Smith picked up the phone and spoke to the reverse directory guy again. She listened. Asked him to repeat what he'd told her. Then she thanked him and hung up. It was a long moment before she turned and looked at Reacher and Walsh.

"The person Neilsen's contact called?" she said. "Charles Stamoran. A private line at his house. His name's on the bill."

Roberta pulled the Suburban over to the side of the road and Veronica jumped down. She ducked into a phone booth and used directory assistance to get the number for the fire department's central office. When she was answered there she introduced herself as a journalism major from Johns Hopkins. She said she was writing a piece on public infrastructure in contrasting urban environments and so she needed to know which firehouses covered certain buildings in the city. She reeled off her list. The National Cathedral. The Dumbarton Oaks Museum. The Library of Congress. The Kennedy Center. And the headquarters of AmeriChem Incorporated.

The firehouse they were interested in was set on a triangular lot where two streets met in a V shape. That made for an efficient configuration. It meant the fire trucks and ambulances could drive in one side and out the other without ever having to turn around or back up. The tall, wide exit doors were standing open when Roberta and Veronica arrived. They had been told that such buildings are considered *public* in the United States and are mainly open, allowing people to walk right in, but it still seemed strange to them.

Roberta parked on the street out of the way of the firehouse's broad apron and led the way inside. There were four vehicles on the equipment floor. Three fire trucks and an ambulance. The trucks were different sizes. One had a giant ladder that ran its whole length. One had a water cannon mounted on its roof. The other looked more like a regular delivery truck, painted red. They were all parked neatly between lines painted on the floor. Boots and helmets and other pieces of personal equipment were set out in parallel groups. Three sets of double doors in the wall to the left led to an inner area. Roberta and Veronica figured that's where the offices and the kitchen and sleeping quarters would be. And the waiting area. The sisters could hear the rumble of voices and the frenzied commentary that accompanied some kind of televised sporting event.

Veronica took up a position where she'd be seen immediately if anyone came through the doors. Roberta hurried around the front of the ladder truck. She stretched up, opened its passenger door, and hauled herself into the cab. She ran her fingers along under the dashboard, below the banks of switches and dials. And found the edge of a stiff, waterproof pouch. It was held in place with Velcro. She pulled it free. Took a knife from her pocket and cut through the cable tie that held it closed. Shuffled through the papers inside, checking each in turn until she found the one she needed. She took a breath. Focused on the information that was printed there. Committed it to memory. Then replaced the papers and fixed the pouch back in its place.

Roberta took the spot near the doors and Veronica crossed to the other side of the space. To where the ambulance was parked. She made her way between it and the wall and suddenly the sound of cheering and yelling became much louder. Just for a second. Two people had come out of the waiting area. A man and a woman. They were both wearing black and green uniforms. They spotted Roberta and changed direction.

"Help you?" the woman said. Her expression was hovering halfway between friendly and suspicious.

Veronica checked over her shoulder. Whoever had come out couldn't see her so she continued until she was standing in front of a large notice board.

"Are you two paramedics?" Roberta said.

The man and the woman both nodded.

"Fantastic. That's why I'm here. I want to sign up. Start my training. So I came to find out what the score is. There'll be forms to fill in, I'm sure. What about minimum educational requirements? How high is the bar?"

"Wait here," the man said. "There's a pack. It lays everything out. You can take it home. Study it. And if you're really up for it, you can get the ball rolling."

* * *

Veronica scanned the pages that had been tacked up on the board. Most were trivial or officious. Some were out of date. But the one she wanted was right in the center. A list of addresses with a history of callouts related to gun violence. There were fourteen, each with a set of checkmarks next to it. The idea was to warn the crews to take extra care if they were dispatched to one of those places. To call for police backup at the first sign of trouble. Veronica compared them for a moment, then memorized the three with the most marks.

The man returned and held out a sheaf of photocopied pages for Roberta. He said, "Good luck," but he didn't stay to talk any more. Neither did the woman. They moved toward the far side of the ambulance. The same way Veronica had gone. And she was still there.

"Hold up!" Roberta took a big step forward. "This is amazing. Thank you. Let me just ask you one more thing. Are there any physical requirements? Do you have to run a mile in a certain time, or carrying some specific weight?"

Veronica dropped to the ground and rolled under the ambulance.

"It's all in the book," the man said. He kept going. The woman had barely slowed down.

Veronica rolled out on the near side of the ambulance. She got to her feet. Checked that no one had seen her. Then collected Roberta and strolled back to their SUV.

* * *

"It's a mistake," Walsh said. "It has to be. Charles Stamoran?"

Smith shook her head. "It's no mistake. My guy triple-checked. It's Stamoran's number. There's no doubt. He even made sure it's not a different Charles Stamoran."

"It's unbelievable."

"You don't want to believe it," Reacher said. "There's a difference."

"The Secretary of Defense set up a murder? That's ridiculous."

"Is it? Why? Only people with certain job titles can be killers? I catch murderers for a living. Believe me, they come in all different shapes and sizes."

"You really believe it's true?"

"I believe it's plausible. There's a clear sequence of events. Neilsen called this *John Smith* guy to *shake the tree*, as he put it. John Smith tried to call Neilsen back but got his fax by mistake. John Smith next called Stamoran. And Neilsen wound up dead. John Smith passed it up the tree when he hit a dead end and Stamoran took no chances. It actually makes sense for the Secretary of Defense to do that. You don't get the top job if you can't make ruthless decisions."

"You're—"

Smith's phone rang. She answered it, listened for a moment, and said, "Why?" Then, "Bullshit. Someone must be able to." And finally, "OK, then. Thanks for trying."

Walsh said, "That didn't sound encouraging."

"That was my phone records guy," Smith said. "We can't get any details about calls to or from the office lines. They're some kind of special Department of Defense spec. There's no data, incoming or outgoing."

"So we only have one lead to go on?"

"We only need one," Reacher said. "If it's the right one."

"The timing works for it," Smith said. "Neilsen's movements—and his drunkenness—tie together, no mistake."

"There's only one way to find out." Reacher stretched out, took the phone, and began to dial. "Now it's my turn to shake the tree."

Roberta Sanson found the way to the first address that Veronica had taken from the ambulance notice board at the firehouse. She pulled over to the curb and kept the engine running. The street number corresponded to a single green door in the long blank side of a single-story brick building. There was no sign of any activity. Not at that time of day.

"Gambling den?" Roberta said.

Veronica said, "Most likely. I don't like it. One entrance. No way to see what's inside. I vote, *pass.*"

"Agreed." Roberta pulled smoothly away and drove to the second address on the list. Right away she could see why gunshot wounds were so frequent in that neighborhood. The windows of the house in question were painted black on the insides. There was a heap of plastic bottles by the front door. Empty cat litter sacks. A stack of buckets, all warped and twisted. And even from inside the vehicle they could smell ammonia. The place was a meth lab. That was clear. And the houses on either side must have been, as well, before they burned down.

The Suburban had been sitting for less than a minute when a man appeared from one of the neighboring houses. He approached slowly from the opposite side of the street. He was tall. Gaunt. He was wearing a Mets cap. A generic baseball jacket. Ripped jeans. And sneakers that might once have been white. Veronica opened her door a crack and slipped out. The guy didn't notice. He only had eyes for Roberta. He kept coming, all the way up to her window. She wound it down, just a couple of inches.

The guy sneered. "You lost, little girl?"

"Spiritually?" Roberta said. "Geographically?"

"What?"

"I'm not lost. I'm here to do business."

"What kind of business you think we do around here?"

Roberta nodded toward the house. "I'm thinking, a little cooking?"

"You a cop?"

"I'm the opposite of a cop."

"Whatever you are, I don't like you. Time for you to leave."

"But I only just got here. And the neighborhood is so charming."

"You're leaving."

"What if I don't want to?"

The guy straightened up and opened his jacket. He had a pistol tucked into both sides of his jeans, butts facing forward so he'd have to cross his arms over his body to draw them.

Roberta raised her voice a little and said, "Two guns, huh? Guess the area's not so great, after all."

The guy said, "Are you on—"

Veronica stepped out from behind the Suburban. She moved toward the guy. Her left arm was out wide. It was swinging around. She was holding a tire iron. She closed in and planted her feet and twisted from the waist for extra power. The flared end of the tool caught the guy in the temple. His head wobbled to the side. His eyes rolled back. His knees turned to pulp. And he flopped down onto the pavement right at Veronica's feet. She leaned in and took the guns. Checked his pockets for additional ammunition. Found two spare magazines. Took those, too, then looped around and climbed back into her seat.

Roberta said, "That's our community service done for the day. Now it's time for some shopping. We need clothes and radios. And some props, just in case she won't play ball. Which do you want to get first?"

Reacher and Walsh were still in Smith's assigned office when all three pagers went off. They made their way down the corridor together and filed into the boardroom. Christopher Baglin was already at the head of the table. Reacher and Smith took their places. Walsh made for the window. They all did their best to avoid looking at Neilsen's empty seat.

Baglin said, "I'm sorry to have abandoned you this morning, but I'm sure you appreciate there were certain arrangements to be made. I trust you've had a productive day, regardless. What do you have to report?"

Reacher had nothing. Smith shook her head. Then Walsh raised his hand. He said, "I have more on Neville Pritchard. How he amassed his capital. I had to dig back a long way but I got there in the end. I found multiple records of him selling, then buying, large quantities of obscure foreign currencies."

Baglin said, "Explain, please? How is that significant? Keep it at a level for the non–financially literate."

"It's called the foreign currency loan scheme. Not a snappy name, but highly efficient. It has the effect of covertly transferring funds and simultaneously establishing provenance."

"So, smuggling money and laundering it at the same time?" Reacher said.

"Kind of. Only it's legal. And there is some skill to it. You have to accurately predict which currency is about to lose a lot of its value. Here's how it works. Imagine I bought a million dollars' worth of Venezuelan bolivars and lent them to Reacher. He could immediately sell them, and he'd have a million dollars. Right?"

No one objected.

"Now imagine the value of the bolivar falls by twenty percent. Reacher could buy back the same quantity he just sold, but it would only cost him $800,000. He could return the bolivars to me, discharging the loan in full. And he'd be $200,000 better off. Yes?"

Smith said, "I guess."

Baglin said, "Ingenious."

Reacher said nothing.

Walsh said, "Not only would Reacher have the two hundred grand, it would be clean. He *earned* it through currency speculation, which is legal. He'd have a legitimate paper trail for all the trades he made. Much better than trying to account for money made by selling drugs or guns."

Baglin said, "Pritchard was doing this? You're sure?"

"Pritchard did it. Back in the early seventies. And yes, I'm sure."

"Any of the other scientists?"

"I've found no evidence."

"Keep looking. Good work. And Reacher? Smith? I can appreciate you having a slack day today. But tomorrow? No. Be back here in the morning with your heads on straight. Understood?"

Walsh waited for Baglin to leave then he moved closer to Reacher and Smith. He hesitated for a moment, then said, "Guys, there's something I didn't mention just now. I didn't know if it was safe, or sensible, with Baglin in the room."

Reacher said, "What is it?"

"The loans that Pritchard benefited from? They were all made by the same company. AmeriChem. So I also looked into it. Before Susan

Kasluga established it, she set up another corporation in Grand Cayman, with a partner out of the Virgin Islands. Its stated purpose was to compete for a contract to build a chemical plant in Pakistan. That was unsuccessful so the company was dissolved. Kasluga got her money out, and she also sued her partner. She came out of it with a huge settlement."

"So was that good luck? Or bad luck?"

"It was another way to bring money into the country and also legitimize it. It happened right before the business with Pritchard and the foreign loans. And guess who one of the directors was? Charles Stamoran. Which isn't illegal. He stepped down in '79 when his political aspirations started to bear fruit. And AmeriChem has never had any iffy government contracts. But still. Given our suspicions . . ."

"You were right to be discreet. That was smart. And there's that name again. Kasluga."

"What do you mean?"

"Her name's cropped up a couple of times recently. Maybe I'm just more tuned in to it, with everything that's going on with Stamoran. Do you know anything about her? I bet there's a file over at Treasury."

"I don't know about a file. I've read a few interviews with her, though. A few articles and profiles. She's a major figure in the industrial world. A trailblazer. Her career path's been almost flawless."

"Almost?"

"She started small, grew enormous, and pretty much everything she touched along the way turned to gold. The only blip was when her company was still quite new. It got sued. Some issue with a product it was developing. Not unusual, really. I can't remember the details. I could find more out though, if you'd like?"

"Definitely. Please do."

"Give me twenty-four hours."

"Perfect. Now, anyone hungry?"

Smith said, "Sure. But let's find somewhere else to eat, OK? I don't ever want to set foot in that wacky half-built bar again."

Chapter 22

Reacher was a fan of symmetry. Someone had left Neilsen's body on a bathroom floor, so Reacher naturally wanted to leave that person's body on the same bathroom floor. The problem was, that floor was in a hotel. And not only had Reacher moved hotels, breaking the potential pattern, but hotels have people in them. People hear things. They report things to the police. Like sounds. The kind that might get made if the guy who had killed Neilsen proved uncooperative. So when Reacher spoke to *John Smith* on the phone and told him he knew everything that Neilsen had known, he said he'd be waiting in an abandoned church, two miles outside the city, at 10:00 P.M. that night.

Reacher got to the church at 8:00 P.M. His golden rule of ambushes is to always get there first. That gave him the chance to learn the lie of the land. The old building was in a sorry state. Its roof was entirely missing. Some of its walls were crumbling. It had one stained-glass window left above what would have been the altar.

Two parallel rows of columns ran alongside the overgrown nave. And there were a few disconnected stubs left where the buttresses used to prop the structure up from the outside. Reacher found a place where a heap of fallen masonry cast a good, deep shadow and settled in to wait.

Neilsen's killer arrived at 9:00 P.M. He was also early. Just not early enough.

Reacher considered himself a fair man. He made an effort to avoid jumping to conclusions. And he always gave his opponents the opportunity to surrender. Almost always. That night turned out to be one of the times he didn't. Because from minute one the other guy made his intentions known. They were crystal clear. He had come prepared. He had a flashlight strapped to his head, like the kind miners wear on their helmets. He had brought a stepladder. And a rope. He fashioned the rope into a noose then took a moment to survey the ruin. He selected a surviving arch between a pair of columns. It was right where a pair of headlights would pick it out if someone arrived by car. A striking image, no doubt. Which was no doubt his intention. The guy was hoping to win the battle before the fighting even began.

The guy draped the rope around his shoulder and wrangled his ladder into place. He climbed three-quarters of the way up and started to swing the rope back and forth, preparing to toss the noose over the arch. He was looking up. Reacher emerged from the shadow. He inched forward, careful to avoid the debris and any loose stone slabs. He closed to within a couple of feet. Then leaned down, grabbed the base of the ladder, and jerked it into the air. The guy flew forward like a bike rider crashing over his handlebars. He hit the ground. His flashlight fell and landed pointing upright, casting weird shadows. He rolled, struggling for air. Reacher stepped forward and placed his foot on the guy's neck.

Reacher said, "There's one reason I haven't crushed your larynx. Yet. You know what that is?"

The guy tried to squirm away. Reacher increased the pressure with his foot and said, "Because you need to be able to talk. So you can answer my questions. Ready? Here's the first one. Did you kill Kent Neilsen last night?"

The guy stopped moving but he didn't reply.

Reacher said, "I might not crush your larynx for a while, but you have plenty of other body parts." He lifted his foot then stamped on the guy's left hand.

The guy howled.

Reacher moved his foot back to the guy's neck. "Tell me about Neilsen."

"I was sent to kill him. I did. What's to talk about?"

"Who sent you?"

"Same guy who sent me to kill the science freak. Don't know his name. Haven't worked for him very long."

"How do you get your instructions?"

"Phone."

"How do you get paid?"

"Dead drop. Cash."

"How did you meet?"

"We've never met. Friend of mine said he knew someone who was looking for help. I was looking for work. It's all done at arm's length."

"You said you killed a science freak. Neville Pritchard?"

"Yeah. Sounds right. I don't really care about names."

"Two in one day?"

"No. Pritchard was five days ago."

"You sure?"

"Dates are the kind of thing I remember."

"How did you find him?"

"I was told where he'd be."

"At his house?"

"At an RV camp. In his RV. That's how I knew to take a hose."

The shapes and patterns in Reacher's head were shifting and rearranging themselves like the shards in a kaleidoscope. Charles Stamoran was already in the frame for Neilsen's death but they'd chalked Neville Pritchard's up to the two women. Now this guy was admitting he'd killed them both. On the same person's orders. So that put two murders at Stamoran's door. Not one. And Pritchard had been dispatched days earlier than they'd realized. Stamoran hadn't just used the other scientists as bait. He'd used them as cover. He was even colder than Reacher had thought.

Reacher said, "I'm going to give you a choice. You can repeat what you told me to a detective. Or you can die right here, right now."

The guy was looking at his crushed left hand, and he was waving it around as if he was trying to cast out the pain. But his right hand was also moving. It was creeping toward his waist. To his pocket. Through the shadow cast by his fallen flashlight. That made Reacher late seeing it. He was slow to lift his foot. The guy's hand had reappeared. He was holding something. A piece of metal, round, with vicious spikes sticking out in all directions. He bent his wrist. He was shaping to flick his hand up and launch the thing. He had plenty to aim at. Reacher's thigh. His groin. His stomach. Even his face or his neck. Plenty of major arteries in those places. Lots of critical organs. A wound from that kind of weapon could be serious. Maybe fatal. So Reacher stamped down. Harder than he'd intended. He caught the guy's hand square on. Drove it back down.

Straight into his abdomen, along with the razor-sharp disc. Reacher couldn't see the resulting damage. The shadow was too deep. But right away he could taste a telltale bitter, metallic tang at the back of his throat.

The guy looked up and grunted in pain. He whispered, "Guess you know what you can do with your detective now."

It was almost midnight when Reacher got back to his new hotel. Smith and Walsh were waiting for him in the bar. Reacher didn't feel like being around strangers so he suggested they reconvene in his room. He took a cup of coffee with him. Smith brought a whiskey. Reacher got the impression it wasn't her first. Walsh was sticking with water.

When they were all settled in the living room side of Reacher's suite he told them what had happened at the ruined church. He couldn't hide his frustration. He'd been hoping to convert their suspicions into facts but all he'd come away with was more theory. And it was a theory that made Stamoran look worse, not better. Neilsen's killing could still be seen as a panicked reaction to an imminent threat but given the timing, Pritchard's was looking more like a cold, calculated maneuver.

"I'm just glad you're OK," Smith said. She shivered. "A noose? He was going to hang you? My God."

Reacher said, "That was never going to happen."

Walsh said, "He gassed Pritchard."

"I'm not Pritchard," Reacher said.

Smith said, "At least the guy from tonight can't kill anyone else."

"He's just a foot soldier. It's the general I want. And I'm running out of patience. It's time to shake things up."

"What have you got in mind?"

"I'm going to talk to Stamoran. Show him the phone records. Look him in the eye and see how he reacts."

"You can't be serious." Smith stared at Reacher. "Oh shit. You are serious."

"You can't do it," Walsh said. "He's the Secretary of Defense."

"And that puts him above the law?"

"No. That puts him behind a bunch of bodyguards. You can't just walk up to him and start making accusations. And how would you find him? They don't print his schedule in the *Post*."

"I'll wait outside his house. Then it doesn't matter where he's heading. And I've got an idea that will take care of his security de-tail."

"You can't—"

"In a non-harmful way. And don't worry. I'll be acting alone. If there's any blowback, it won't touch either of you."

The conversation rambled on for another ten minutes then Walsh finished his water and stood up to go. He paused on the way to the door and pulled an envelope out of his satchel. He set it down on the counter near the minibar and said, "Here's that information you asked for. About Susan Kasluga. Let me know if you need any-thing else."

Smith got up and went to use the bathroom. She was gone long enough for Reacher to start worrying that she'd had too much to drink. When she finally did come out she went back to the couch but she wouldn't meet Reacher's eye. She rocked back and forth for a moment then curled forward until her face was almost pressed against her knees. She wrapped her arms around her head and Reacher saw her whole torso begin to heave. He heard her sob, deep and hard and raw.

Reacher didn't know what to say. The best he could come up with was, "Amber? Are you OK?"

Smith didn't respond for a minute then she straightened up and wiped her cheeks and said, "The other night at the bar, you asked if I was married. I said no. Which is true. If you go with the whole till-death-do-you-part thing."

"Your husband died?"

"His name was Philip. He was killed. By a KGB agent. Danil Litvinov. Who's now back in Moscow. Where I can't get to him."

"That's why you fed all those agents' names to Baglin?"

She nodded, which set another plump tear careening down her cheek. "It happened a year ago. Everyone says that's long enough. That I should move on. My mom. My sister. My friends. I figured they might be right. Told myself the next guy I meet who I like . . . But the only one I can think about is Philip. I'm stuck. I don't know what to do. My personal life's turned to stone. My professional life's turned into a disaster. I . . . I'm sorry. I don't know why I'm telling you this."

Reacher sat on the couch next to her and put his arm around her. "You have nothing to be sorry for. You can't put a clock on these things. They take as long as they take. And they're no one else's business. Maybe one day you'll feel ready to move on. Maybe you won't. Either way, you're not doing anything wrong. The asshole who killed your husband was the one who did wrong."

Smith leaned against Reacher's chest. He felt her start to sob again, silently this time, then after ten minutes her body went slack. Reacher picked her up and carried her to the bed. He laid her down and folded the comforter over so that she was covered up. Then he went to the other half of the suite and picked up the phone. He called the duty sergeant at his base and gave an order for his Class A uniform to be delivered to his hotel before 6:00 A.M. that morning.

Then he lay down on the couch and closed his eyes. He wondered what kind of machine down in the bowels of the building would have made a record of his call. And he wondered if that sort of record would ever be used as a clue if he was found bled out on a bathroom floor.

Chapter 23

Four hours later, at 5:00 A.M., Roberta and Veronica Sanson coasted down the ramp that led to AmeriChem's parking garage. Roberta stopped at the barrier and entered the override code she'd found in the pouch in the fire truck the day before. Nothing happened for a long moment. Her pulse spiked. There was no guarantee that the fire department kept its emergency access information up to date. If they couldn't get the vehicle into the garage their whole plan would be left in tatters. But she needn't have worried. The barrier rose and she drove through. She parked the Suburban as far away from the elevators as possible. Then they settled down to wait.

Susan Kasluga didn't read in the car on the way to the office that morning. It was unlike her to waste twenty minutes when she could be doing something productive—ten minutes, at that hour—but she was exhausted. She was stressed. She hadn't slept because she'd been waiting for a phone call that never came, and she had a grueling session ahead of her with Serge, the media coach. She was going to announce her new, groundbreaking merger deal in the next few days, with her in the starring role, and she needed to be at the top of her game to prepare. Needed to be. But knew she wasn't. And now that she had lost the chance to sleep, the only thing she wanted to do was shut her eyes.

Roberta and Veronica watched the Town Car enter the garage. It stopped at the bottom of the ramp and the two bodyguards got out. They made a show of scanning the area, then Susan Kasluga joined them and they headed to the elevator. Roberta and Veronica waited ten minutes after the shiny door closed, just in case, then Veronica dribbled some chloroform onto a rag. Roberta fired up the engine, drove toward the ramp, and stopped next to the Town Car. Veronica climbed out. She gestured for the chauffeur to lower his window. He did, and she leaned in and clamped the rag over his mouth and nose. When he stopped struggling Roberta helped her wrestle his body around the side of the car and into the trunk. They gagged him, tied his wrists and ankles, and Veronica took his place behind the wheel. She drove up the ramp. Roberta followed in the Suburban. Ten minutes later they drove back down, together. The Town Car was now on the top deck of a public garage three blocks away.

Veronica used the chauffeur's security pass to activate the elevator then hit the button for the twentieth floor. They rode up, stepped out into an empty corridor, and Veronica led the way to Susan Kasluga's corner suite. Roberta opened the door to the outer office. Veronica moved aside in case the assistant worked the same hours as her boss. She didn't. The only people there were the two guards. One was sitting behind the desk, playing with the trolls. The other was sprawling on a two-person couch.

Roberta stepped through the doorway and said, "Fellas, thank goodness we've found you. We've got a problem. Two guys, Middle Eastern–looking, clean shaven, carrying backpacks. They just went in the men's room by the elevators. Come on."

Roberta darted back into the corridor. The guards followed. She led the way to the bathrooms then stood aside. The guard who'd been sprawling said, "Thanks, ladies. We can take it from here."

The guards pushed the door to the men's room and rushed inside. Roberta and Veronica went in after them. The first guy spun around. He said, "I told you. We can handle this."

Roberta said, "Can you? Can you handle him?" She nodded toward the far corner of the room.

The guy turned to look and Roberta punched him in the side of the head. One hit was all it took. He went down like a switch had been thrown. Veronica took a two-step approach with the other guard. First she kicked him in the balls. Then when he doubled over she drove her elbow down into the base of his neck. Twice the number of blows, but the same end result.

Roberta stood outside the inner door in Susan Kasluga's office suite and held up three fingers. Then two. Then one. Then she pushed down the handle and burst through. Kasluga was sitting behind her desk. It was a cantilevered glass-and-chrome affair with nothing on it except for two stacks of index cards. Her chair was chrome and green leather and it looked like it had sprouted an exoskeleton.

Roberta said, "Ms. Kasluga, we need to get you out of here, ma'am. Right now. This is a tactical evacuation."

Kasluga dropped the card she was holding onto the left-hand pile and said, "The hell it is. I have work to do. And who exactly are you?"

Roberta said, "Ma'am, please. This isn't a subject for debate. You need to come with us, now. We're going to take you home. Mr. Stamoran has been briefed and he's waiting for you there."

"I said, who are you? And where are my regular guards?"

"My name is Erica Halliday. My colleague is Caroline Burton. We've rotated in for the duration of the emergency. It's standard operating procedure. Rules out the possibility of collusion with hostile parties."

"What kind of emergency?"

"There was an incident in the area in the early hours of the morning. A man was killed. Your name was mentioned by an individual who was taken into custody. Further details are still emerging, but we feel it's wise to take every precaution. So, ma'am." Roberta gestured toward the door. "Please."

Susan Kasluga took a long look at Roberta, and then Veronica. They were wearing gray pantsuits. Unflattering, medium quality, but appropriate. They were armed. They had earpieces with curly wires like the ones her regular guys had. And they had ID cards clipped to their jackets, even if the photographs were too small to make out properly. Also just like her regular guys. A voice at the back of her head started to speculate about how she could play this to her advantage. *Industry titan survives assassination attempt. Foreign rivals running scared of new powerhouse forged by audacious takeover.* She hesitated for another moment then scooped up her index cards and dropped them into her purse. She said, "All right. Let's go. But you bring me back the moment the panic's over, OK?"

Smith left Reacher's room at a little after 5:30 A.M. He was already awake. He heard her leave then got up and took a shower. He shaved and did what he could to tame his hair. He dressed and went downstairs and checked with reception. There were no deliveries for him. He ate breakfast—bacon and a full stack plus two mugs of coffee—then went back and inquired again. A canvas suit-carrier had just been dropped off. He signed for it and returned to his room to change.

Traffic was light that morning so Reacher got to his destination ahead of schedule. Charles Stamoran's residence. A gate covered a driveway to the right of the house. It was armor-plated and eight feet tall. Reacher circled around the block to make sure there were no other ways for vehicles to leave, and when he was satisfied he returned to the main street and pulled up near to the curb. The river was to his left. He rolled down his window, did his best to get comfortable in the cramped space, and settled down to wait.

Susan Kasluga didn't balk when Roberta and Veronica Sanson ushered her into the backseat of their Suburban. She'd ridden in vehicles just like it more times than she could count. Roberta drove smoothly and cautiously. The seats were soft and supportive. The heat was cranked high and Kasluga found herself fighting the urge to close her eyes. She rested her head and let the familiar landmarks drift by as they closed in on her home. The trees were welcoming and Kasluga knew the river was close. She could feel it. She found it reassuring. Then Roberta took a sudden right onto a short, steep hill. Kasluga had never driven that way before. There were brick buildings on both sides with a special sloping design to accommodate the gradient. Roberta turned right again onto a service road. There was a dead end ahead and blank, featureless walls on both sides. She leaned on the brake, shifted into Park, killed the engine, and swiveled around in her seat. Veronica jumped out and scrambled straight into the back. Kasluga reached for her own door handle but Roberta was too quick for her. She hit the button on the center console that locked it out.

Kasluga blinked. She said, "The hell's going on? Are you kidnapping me? It had to happen eventually, I guess. But let me tell you, you're making a big mistake. You'll get your money. For sure. But you won't live to enjoy it."

Roberta said, "This is not a kidnapping. We just need to talk to you."

"You ever heard of making an appointment?"

"Would you have agreed to see us? I doubt it. Especially when we told you what we need to talk about."

"Which is?"

"India. In 1969."

Kasluga was silent for a moment. Then she swallowed and said, "India. I was there, of course. In a very minor capacity. There's not much I can tell you."

"There might be more than you realize. We need you to write down the name of everyone you can remember from that time. Everyone. No matter what job they did. No matter where they were based. Please. It's important."

"Why is it?"

"Because one of those people murdered our father."

Kasluga was silent for a moment. Then she said, "I'm sorry. I don't know how to react to that."

"By grabbing some paper and starting to write."

"OK. Sure. Of course I'll try to help. But I have to ask. I haven't been in India for more than twenty years. If your father was murdered that long ago, why are you looking for names now?"

"His murder is new information."

"You think the murderer worked at the Mason Chemical plant?"

"Worked at, or was connected with it in some way."

"A lot of people worked at that plant. And staff turnover was sky high. They'll be all over the world now. Some will be sick. Some will be in seniors' homes. Is there any way to narrow the field? Give yourselves a better shot?"

"Actually, yes. Because there was this one particular research team. I'm sure you saw them around the plant. They mingled with everyone else in the normal way. But the work they did was secret. The regular team members all knew one another, but there was one extra person associated with them in some kind of a detached role. A supervisor, maybe, or a support person, or a technical specialist. And due to all that paranoid Cold War obsession with secrecy, only one team member knew who this associate was."

"You don't know which team member it was who had the contact?"

"We have an idea."

"Could you ask him?"

"Tricky. He's dead."

"Could you try the other team members? Just in case?"

"They're all dead, too."

"Then how did you find out about this whole thing?"

"One of the team members told us before he died. Owen Buck. Did you know him?"

"Never heard of the guy."

"He knew at the time that this extra associate killed our father but he did nothing. Then he found out he had cancer and he had a sudden attack of conscience."

"That sucks. It's a shame he didn't act earlier. Like, right away. So listen, I'll write my list. And I'm still in touch with a few others. I could ask around, if you like? Discreetly? I wouldn't have to fake any office emergencies or impersonate any security personnel."

Roberta shook her head. "Thank you. But I think we'll start with what you know. Then go from there."

"Sounds like a plan. I do have to ask one other thing, though. Sorry if it's insensitive. Am I right to assume your father worked at the plant?"

Roberta nodded.

"Mind if I ask his name? Maybe I knew him."

"I'm sure you knew of him, at least. His name was Morgan Sanson."

Kasluga didn't say anything. She just stared.

"I'm Roberta. This is Veronica."

Kasluga felt like she couldn't breathe. Her chest was tight. She told herself it was just the stress. The lack of sleep. She said, "Robbie and Ronnie? I heard your names. I always assumed you were boys."

"Most people did."

"I remember all the things they said about your dad." Kasluga was feeling light-headed. Maybe if that phone call had come when it was supposed to, she would be more in control. "I can see why it's important to set the record straight."

"The record is straight," Veronica said. She opened her satchel and took out a dog-eared manila folder. "This is his personnel file. It confirms everything about his character. Our father's only concern was safety. He found out that someone was stealing money. Maintenance standards were slipping as a result. That's what caused the leak that killed those people. Not sabotage. Dad was going to blow the whistle so someone had to shut him up."

Kasluga took the folder and pressed it against her lap. "How the hell did you get this?"

"Owen Buck gave it to us. He took it when he left the plant. Said it was proof he always meant to help."

"I'll help. And I don't *mean to* do things. I do them." Kasluga's heart was beating so hard it felt like it might break a rib. She was feeling hot. She was worried she was going to faint. "But listen. All the same, don't get your hopes up. There's a lot of time gone by. A lot of water under the bridge. Finding this eighth guy will be no kind of cakewalk. It might not even be possible. You should prepare yourselves for that. Now, could we get going? I really need to be back at the office."

Chapter 24

After more than an hour Reacher saw the big heavy gates twitch then slowly begin to pull apart. He fired up his engine, pulled forward, stopped, and jumped out. Then he stood in the mouth of Stamoran's driveway with his car parked directly behind him.

By any reasonable measure it was a reckless thing to do. Reckless, and stupid. The Secretary of Defense is one of the best protected people in the world. Anyone executing a hostile maneuver directed at him is likely to get shot. Or tackled to the ground at the very least. And the secretary's official limousine could brush a lightweight rental car aside like a bug. But that morning none of those things happened. The Class A uniform did its job, just as Reacher had gambled it would.

Stamoran's car slammed to a halt and rocked on its springs. Reacher stepped forward and approached its left-hand rear door. For a moment he could see nothing because of the heavy tint on the glass, then the window purred down about four inches. Stamoran glared through the gap and said, "This had better be a dire national emergency, Captain."

Reacher said, "I believe it is, sir. On the grounds that it pertains to the task force that you yourself established. I have a document that calls for your urgent review."

Stamoran wasn't expecting that. He didn't like surprises. He was inclined to send the MP away with a note of reprimand to pass on to his CO. But if he was there on task force business, that could mean the killers had been identified. Or that some indication had been found that Pritchard had given up what he knew. Either way, it was ridiculously overzealous for the captain to show up in person. And either way, it wouldn't hurt to see what he had brought.

Stamoran opened his door. He said, "Whatever you've got, pass it here."

Reacher took a sheet of paper from his jacket pocket, unfolded it, and handed it over. It bore a single line of text. One call record. The one from *John Smith* to Stamoran's private line. The one that preceded Neilsen's murder. Reacher kept his face completely dispassionate. Stamoran didn't betray even a flicker of recognition.

Roberta shifted into reverse and began to back out from between the blank brick buildings. She made it halfway then put her foot on the brake. She turned to look at Veronica. She could see that the penny had dropped for her, too. Veronica pulled her gun. Roberta shifted into Drive and nosed forward again, off the street.

Roberta swiveled around and said, *"This eighth guy?"*

Kasluga said, "What? Don't shoot the messenger. I was just being realistic. I don't want you to be disappointed after everything you've been through. Twenty-three years is a long time. It might not be possible to find the guy you're looking for by now."

"Why did you say *eighth,* specifically?"

"Because I can count?"

"For the extra guy to be the eighth, there would have to be seven on the regular team."

"Obviously."

"There were seven. Only we didn't tell you that."

"Yes you did."

"We didn't."

"I thought you did. But anyway, you didn't need to. I remember the team you're talking about. I knew there were seven people on it."

"Bullshit. You said you didn't know who Owen Buck was. He was on that team."

"I don't remember all the names. Sure. But I know there were seven guys."

"You knew there were eight guys. You know who the eighth guy is. You better tell us."

"I do not know. How could I? You're defying your own logic. You said only one person on the team knew who the eighth guy was. I wasn't on the team. Ergo I don't know."

"Veronica?"

Veronica shook her head. "All these frantic denials don't pass the smell test. You hit the nail on the head. She knew there were eight. She knows who the eighth is."

Kasluga said, "How many times do I have to say it? I do not."

Veronica said, "There's another way of looking at this. If she really doesn't know who the eighth guy is, then she's no use to us. No one knows she's with us. No one saw us leave together. She's trash. We should throw her in the ocean."

"You can't make knowledge magically appear by threatening me, you know."

"Or here's another idea. She's a big-shot scientist, right? Scientists like experiments. So we could do some experiments on her. See what impact that has on her knowledge."

"Bluster all you want but I'm not going to bite. Look, I get that you're hurting. Losing your father and thinking he'd killed himself and hearing all the smack the knuckleheads were talking about him—that must have taken a toll. Pushed you to do crazy things. But you haven't crossed a line yet. So let's say no more about this eighth guy nonsense, and my promise to help you find the name you need still stands. What do you say? Deal?"

Charles Stamoran handed the piece of paper back to Reacher. He said, "When I hear about a document to review, I'm expecting a hundred pages, minimum. Often two hundred. Always a bunch of jargon and buzzwords and empty verbiage that sets my teeth on edge. So in a way I applaud your brevity. But here's some free advice. Next time you write a report, you're going to need to use some words. Include an argument of some kind. A conclusion. A call to action. This—what is it? A prank? A joke? A little act of rebellion against your recent demotion?" Stamoran gestured toward Reacher's car. "Now get that piece of junk out of my way before I have my driver crush it. Then return to your unit. You're off the task force. You may well be saying goodbye to your silver bars as well as your oak leaves. I'll be having a full and frank discussion with your CO in the very near future."

* * *

Susan Kasluga was hanging upside down.

Veronica Sanson had made her sit on her hands and she kept her covered with her gun while Roberta drove. She backed out from between the sloping brick buildings and navigated to a water pumping station on the east bank of the Potomac. It was a twenty-foot-tall rectangular structure that dated back to the 1930s. An era when public buildings were made to last. Pipes were strong. Walls were thick. Sound waves produced by all the engines and machines and other pieces of equipment had a tough time getting through them. So did the sound of people screaming.

Roberta got out of the Suburban first. She took a pair of bolt cutters and a rope from the trunk and crossed to the building's double doors. She cut the hasp of the lock and went inside. Veronica led Kasluga to a spot almost in the center of the main space. They were beneath a six-inch water pipe that was suspended from the ceiling on stout metal brackets. Roberta tied a loop in the rope and laid it on the floor. Veronica maneuvered Kasluga back a couple of steps so that she was standing in the middle of the loop. Roberta yanked the rope, hard, jamming Kasluga's ankles together. Veronica shoved Kasluga in the chest and she pitched back onto the floor. She screamed. Part pain. Part surprise. Part indignation. Cement dust puffed up all around her. She tried to roll onto her stomach and lever herself upright but there wasn't time. Roberta tossed the rope up and over the thick water pipe. Veronica helped her to pull and together they hauled it up until Kasluga's fingertips could no longer touch the ground.

Roberta pushed Kasluga and set her swinging slowly like a pendulum in a giant clock. She said, "One name, Susan. That's all we need. Give it to us and you'll never see us again."

"I don't know the name."

Roberta took a piece of paper out of her pocket. "See this? It's our list. Seven names. You can write the eighth one down if you like. Then you can always say you didn't *tell* us."

"I don't know the name. Please. You have to believe me."

"Why do we have to? Because you're rich?" Roberta put the list back in her pocket. "Because you're used to getting anything you want? To buying your way out of trouble? OK. Here's an idea. Imagine that eighth name is money. It's the last currency that exists in the world. It's the only thing you can use to pay for your freedom."

"OK. Fine. I'll tell you. It's Ernst. Richard Ernst. Now let me down."

Roberta shook her head. "Really, Susan, I thought a businesswoman would be a better liar. Do you think we don't read the papers? Richard Ernst won last year's Nobel Prize in Chemistry. So here's what we're going to do. We're going to leave you to think for a little while. To get your priorities sorted out. And while you're doing that, we're going to get a little device ready. See, we thought we might be in a position where we're dealing with someone who needs a little persuasion. We just didn't bank on it being so soon."

Roberta and Veronica returned a quarter of an hour later. Kasluga was still swinging. Faster than before as a result of trying to break free. Her face was red. She was struggling for breath. Veronica was carrying a large goldfish bowl. It was full of clear liquid and an olive green spherical object was rolling around on the bottom. She placed the thing on the floor near Kasluga's head and stepped well back.

Roberta said, "Have you heard of the Sword of Damocles, Susan?"

Kasluga said, "Long time ago."

"Good. Then you'll get the principle. We call this the Grenade of Damocles. It should maybe get a nod to Molotov as well. The branding needs work, I guess, but as a scientist I think you might like it. See the liquid? That's ordinary gasoline. And the green globe? A standard M67 grenade. Only we've removed the spoon and stretched an elastic band around it to hold the striker in place. Now, what happens to rubber when it's bathed in gasoline?"

"It dissolves."

"Correct. And when there's nothing to stop the striker from activating the fuse?"

"It explodes."

"Correct. The only thing we're not a hundred percent clear on is how long the elastic band will hold out. It's not a very thick one, to be honest. Not very good quality. We're thinking twenty minutes? Half an hour, tops? But we may be wrong so we're going to the other room now. It's very unpleasant having to wash body parts out of your hair. Believe me. We've done it. Oh, one other thing. The kill radius of the M67 is sixteen feet, so if you do decide to take the name with you to the grave, at least you won't suffer. No matter how high you swing."

Kasluga tried to bend at the waist and pull herself up, but her stomach muscles just weren't strong enough. She tried to squeeze her ankles tighter together and slip one free, but the rope was too tight. All she did was increase the agony. She started to swing again. Tried to grab a cluster of vertical pipes. They were too far away. She craned her head, searching for something she could use as a weapon. There was nothing in sight. She looked for her purse, then remembered it was in the Suburban. It was no good to her there. She could feel the despair building throughout her body. Overwhelming her. The pressure behind her eyes was building. Becoming unbearable. Her ankles felt like they were on fire. She held out for another seven minutes then gave up the fight. She called for Roberta and Veronica. She said, "You win. I'll tell you. I'll give you the name. The eighth man? It was Charles Stamoran. My husband."

Chapter 25

Reacher didn't move. He stayed standing next to Charles
Stamoran's car and said, "Understood, sir. But let me clarify one
thing before I leave. These phone numbers. You're saying you don't
recognize them?"

"Correct. I do not recognize them. Why should I? Do I look like
a walking telephone directory?"

"One belongs to a suspect in a murder case. The other terminates
in your house. As you can see, a call was made from one to the
other."

Stamoran snatched the page back and scanned it again. He said,
"I've never seen either of these numbers before. Let alone owned
one or taken a call from one. You don't know what you're talking
about. You've been given bad information. Now, conversation over.
I've wasted enough time on you."

* * *

Roberta and Veronica Sanson lowered Kasluga to the ground, loosened the rope, and gave her a minute to catch her breath and regain her balance. Then they took hold of an elbow each and led her to a room at the side of the building. It was small and square. One wall was covered with all kinds of gauges and valves and levers and indicators. And on another there was a small red cabinet. *Emergency Use Only* was stenciled on the side in bold white letters. Roberta opened it. A telephone was inside.

Roberta said, "Call your husband. Tell him you're a hostage. Tell him we'll kill you if he's not here, alone, inside thirty minutes."

Kasluga folded her arms.

"Or I could shoot you in the head and call him myself."

Kasluga said, "You could. But I wouldn't recommend it. He'd send every SWAT team on the Eastern Seaboard to storm this place. The only way he'll come is if I call. We talked about situations like this. Made a plan. We have a code."

"So go ahead."

"I will. On three conditions."

"You're in no position to negotiate."

"I'm in the best position. Strength. I have something you need. Something you can't achieve your goal without."

The sisters looked at one another, then Roberta said, "Conditions?"

"First, you can't hurt Charles. He's a good man. He didn't kill your father intentionally, I'm sure. It must have been part of something bigger. Part of his job. Defending the United States. You've got to find some way for him to make amends that doesn't involve violence."

"OK."

"Second, I don't want to be hung upside down again. I don't

want my hands tied, or my feet. If I'm going to be a Judas goat I'm at least going to do it with a little dignity."

"Done."

"Third, I need the bathroom. Which means I need to get my purse from your car."

Stamoran slammed his car door in Reacher's face but before the window had wound all the way up his car phone began to ring. He picked it up and Reacher heard the first couple of snippets of his conversation. He said, "Susie? My God. Have they hurt you? Where . . . ?"

Reacher ran to his car. He jumped in, fired it up, and reversed rapidly out of the way. Stamoran's car lurched forward then took a right, as tight as the great heavy barge could manage. Reacher jammed his into Drive and chased after it. Return to unit be damned. He could worry about explanations later.

When Reacher saw Stamoran's car arrive at what he assumed was their objective his heart sank. It was some kind of old industrial building on the bank of the river, to the east of the city. It was a generous single story high, like it had been designed for machines, not people. The walls looked solid. They were well maintained. There were no windows. No skylights in the roof. And worse still, there was only one way in. A double door. It was made of solid-looking wood. And it was closed. There was no view inside.

Outside, there were no surveillance teams. No support vehicles with additional troops or armor or weapons or ventilators. And there were no helicopters in the air. It was your basic nightmare scenario. Disaster was written all over it. No competent commander would let his troops within a hundred miles of the place. There was no way an entry should be attempted without knowing the occupants' numbers and weapons and disposition and morale. Even then any assault would need to be carefully planned and launched at an optimum time with suitable decoys and diversions.

The only saving grace was that Stamoran was still in his car. It looked like he was arguing with his bodyguards. Then Reacher's heart sank further. Stamoran got out. Alone. He started walking toward the door. He was reckless as well as ruthless, Reacher thought. And then he was inside.

The bodyguards jumped out the moment Stamoran disappeared. They ran to the entrance. One opened the door. The other covered him. The first guy went inside. The second followed. The door swung shut.

Reacher heard a gunshot. A second. Then silence.

Reacher leaned on the gas and his car lurched forward. He steered past Stamoran's and swerved around the Sansons' Suburban. He kept going until he was as close to the entrance as he could get. Then he slid out. Drew his gun. Ducked low and weaved across the last of the open ground until he got to the door. He slipped inside and right away he saw the bodyguards. They were sprawled on the ground in the entranceway. There was no need for him to check their vitals. Neither of them had enough of their heads left. Big chunks of their skulls had been blasted away and blood and bone and shiny gray slime lay glistening on the wall and floor. Someone inside the building liked to do their wet work up close and personal. That was clear.

Reacher took cover behind four blue water tanks that were fixed to the floor. The space was surprisingly bright given the absence of windows. There were lines of giant lights running along the ceiling. They threw weird shadows through the forest of blue and red pipes that sprouted up and branched out at all different heights and angles. There was a constant, low throbbing sound from some kind of nearby equipment. The air was heavy and stale and had a slight odor of oil and chlorine.

Reacher listened. He heard nothing so he left his cover, darted forward, and took up a more advanced position behind a long gray equipment cabinet. Then he heard more shots. There were three this time. They were loud and echoey in the enclosed space and it sounded like they'd been fired close together. There was the rattle of metal against concrete. A gun had fallen. Then a solid, heavy thump. A body had hit the ground. Then two more thumps, similar but lighter. A second body. And a third.

A woman's voice shrieked, "Charles!"

The echo died and silence returned. Reacher risked peering around the cabinet. At twelve o'clock he saw Susan Kasluga. She was standing with a rope around her waist, secured to a pillar. Her purse was at her feet. Her hands were empty. Her eyes were wide and desperate.

Charles Stamoran was at two o'clock. He was lying on the ground, on his back, his right leg folded under his body. His shirt was soaked with blood. His hands were empty, but a Ruger pistol was lying on the ground in front of him.

A woman was on the ground at four o'clock. She would be in her late twenties. She was slim and her dark hair was pulled back tight. She had a Sig Sauer pistol in her hand, but she wasn't moving. A bullet had hit her in the forehead. It had left a gaping hole there like a third, sightless eye.

Another woman, almost identical, was at five o'clock. She was on her back, immobile, eyes blank, with a diagonal swathe of blood cutting across her white blouse from her neck to her hip. A bullet had torn a jagged hole at the tip of the stain, dead in the center of her chest. She also had a pistol in her hand. An identical Sig Sauer.

Reacher straightened up and came out from behind the cabinet. He kept his gun angled down, covering the bodies, just in case. He stepped forward and kicked away their weapons. Then he crouched to check Stamoran's carotid. There was no pulse. He waited until he was certain then he got back to his feet.

"Stop!" Kasluga yelled out. "Where are you going? Leave those others. Help Charles. You've got to save him."

Reacher said nothing. He moved across to the first of the women and leaned down to press his fingers against her neck. He couldn't feel even the faintest flutter of blood flowing in her artery. She was dead, too. That was no great surprise. He straightened, ready to pivot around and examine the second woman. Then he heard a hard metallic click, close behind him.

Kasluga yelled, "Watch—"

White-hot pain exploded in the back of both Reacher's legs. It felt like a thousand volts had been blasted into his joints and ligaments. His legs buckled and he dropped forward. One knee crashed into the hard concrete floor. The other slammed into the dead woman's sternum. A part-formed thought flashed through his mind— *Odd, that doesn't feel like bone*—then he twisted around sharply from the waist so he could look back. He was suddenly angry. Someone had landed a blow from behind. He should not have allowed that to happen. He couldn't remember the last time he had. And he wasn't going to let it happen again. That was for damn sure.

He raised his gun as he spun around, searching for a target to fire at, and at the same time he pushed up from the ground with his left hand. He got halfway onto his feet and caught sight of someone. The second woman. She was alive. She was standing up. He saw a glint of metal against a rough black background peeping through the tear in her shirt. It was the remains of a bullet, mushroomed against Kevlar. The blood on her clothes must have come from someone else. One of the dead agents, probably. She must have been hit after she killed them, but only wounded. Because she was wearing a vest. So was her lookalike. That's what he'd felt under his knee. Good against a shot to the chest. No help at all against a hit to the head.

The woman was holding something in her right hand. It was slender. Made of metal with a ridged grip and a matte black coating. It was two feet long with joints every six inches, and its diameter stepped down slightly at each one. So it was telescopic. Easy to carry and conceal. Easy to extend. All it would take was the flick of the wrist. And it had a rounded tip, half an inch in diameter, which would concentrate the force of impact. Destructive against glass or wood or metal. Devastating against flesh and bone. A hit on the chest would fracture some ribs. A blow to the neck could be fatal. Or to the side of the head.

The woman brought the baton slashing down. She was aiming for Reacher's right wrist. Looking to shatter the joint. Trying to make him drop his gun. Reacher twisted faster. He hauled his arm out of the woman's range. Just. The round metal tip cut through the air. It was close enough for Reacher to feel its draft on his skin. It scythed all the way down to the ground, kicking up a faint blue spark. Reacher grabbed the woman's wrist with his left hand. He squeezed. His fingers dug into her skin, mashing the tendons and ligaments until she screamed. Her grip slackened and the baton clattered to the concrete. Reacher kicked it away. The woman jabbed at his face with her free hand. Her first two fingers were spread wide. She was trying to gouge his eyes. At the same time her right knee was jerking up, aiming for his groin.

Reacher lowered his shoulder twelve inches and launched himself forward. He slammed into the woman's chest. It was a heavy contact. The woman was thrown back like she'd been hit by a dump truck. She landed on the ground and slid away in a thin cloud of dust.

Reacher said, "Roll over. Face down. Hands behind your head."

The woman coughed but she didn't move.

Reacher raised his gun. "I'm trying to think of a reason not to shoot you but I've got to admit, I'm coming up empty."

The woman rolled over.

Reacher said, "Who are you?"

"My name is Veronica Sanson." She jerked her head toward the other woman's body. "That's—" She brought her right arm up and clamped it over her face so that her eyes were buried in the crook of her elbow. She didn't move for a moment. Didn't breathe. Didn't make any kind of sound. Then she raised her arm and dropped it back down at her side. Her eyes were red. She blinked away a tear and said, "That's my sister, Roberta. Our father was Morgan Sanson."

Roberta and Veronica, Reacher thought. Robbie and Ronnie. Two of the four kids taken to Israel by Mrs. Sanson after her husband's death. He said, "You were in the Israel Defense Forces?"

Veronica nodded. "Combat Intelligence Collection Corps."

"Your sister, as well?"

Veronica nodded again. "We came to avenge our father. But listen, please. I was a captain. Same rank as you. So I'm asking as a courtesy from a fellow officer, let me stand up. Explain our circumstances. Maybe we can—"

"Oh my God!" Susan Kasluga's eyes were wide and her face was suddenly deathly pale. "Where is it? What did you do with it? How long till it goes off? You—army person—you've got to do something."

Reacher said, "What are you talking about?"

"The crazy sisters. They made a bomb. An improvised thing. A grenade, a bowl, gasoline, an elastic band. They used it to force me to give up Charles's name. It could blow up any second. It'll kill us all."

Reacher did not like what he was hearing. He had seen photographs from Vietnam. Guerrillas would sneak up to parked US Army jeeps and drop grenades wrapped with elastic bands into their fuel tanks. It turned the vehicles into moving time bombs. The results were not pretty. Even less pretty if anyone was on board or close by when the elastic finally gave way. He looked at Veronica and said, "Is this true?"

Veronica lifted her chin. "Roberta invented it. She called it The Grenade of—"

"Where is it?"

"I'll show you. On one condition."

"There's no time for bargaining. Get it now."

"If it goes off now, you two are dead. There's no escape for you. But down here? I might survive. I'm happy to roll the dice. Are you?"

"And if I shoot you in the head? How do you like those odds?"

"You'd shoot an unarmed prisoner in front of a witness? Hello, court-martial. Plus you'd still have to get out of here. How much time do you have before, boom?"

"What do you want?"

"If I make the device safe, I want you to listen. I want you to know the truth about my father. I want everyone to know. I want you to tell them."

Reacher nodded. "Go."

Veronica stood up. She moved across to a spot where three large pipes rose out of the floor, turned 90 degrees, and were fixed to another set with heavy bolts and flanges. Reacher covered Veronica with his gun. She leaned over, stretched down into an obscured area, and lifted out the goldfish bowl. She tiptoed toward Reacher. She was holding the bowl out in front. The grenade was still inside. The elastic band was intact. She crept closer. Then when she was ten feet away she flung the bowl at Reacher's face. He stepped back. Gasoline sloshed over the front of his tunic. Veronica dived to the side. She hit the ground, rolled, scooped up the Sig that Roberta had been holding, and scrambled onto her feet. Reacher caught the bowl. He trapped it between his chest and right forearm. Thrust his left hand inside, into the dregs of the gasoline. It was a tight fit, like trying to cram a baseball mitt into a cookie jar. He pushed harder. Scrabbled for the grenade. Brushed it with his fingertips. And snapped the elastic band.

Chapter 26

Reacher shook his head and set the bowl down. Veronica Sanson threw herself over another tangle of pipes and disappeared from view. Susan Kasluga started to scream.

"The hell are you doing?" Kasluga yelled. "The kill radius of that thing is only a few feet. Get it out of here. Get it outside. Or throw it as far as you can. Or there's a control room. Over there. You could—"

Reacher stepped across so that he was standing between Kasluga and Veronica's concealed position. "There's no need. The grenade's made of plastic. It's a toy. You were tricked."

"What? No." Kasluga started to cry. "I thought it was real. I believed them. That's the only reason I gave Charles up. They're such liars. They promised not to hurt him. And now . . ."

"Don't beat yourself up over it. Those women were not playing games. They'd have made you talk some other way if you had seen through their bluff."

"Correct," Veronica called from behind her cover. "We're not playing. I'm not. So stand aside, Captain. I have no argument with you."

Reacher figured it made sense for Veronica Sanson to need to kill Kasluga. She'd used her to lure her husband. Kasluga knew what had happened to him. Probably saw it happen. It would be crazy to leave a witness. So by the same token Reacher didn't believe for a second that Veronica planned to let him walk away.

Reacher said, "You want to tell your father's story? I can help you. Make sure people listen. But only if you put your gun down. Surrender now."

"You don't understand. Step aside."

Reacher didn't move.

The Sig's muzzle poked out from between a pair of valves and Veronica fired. Dust kicked up a couple of inches from Reacher's right foot. The bullet whined up and away past Kasluga's head. There was a clank as it slammed into a pipe. Then silence.

The muzzle disappeared. Reacher couldn't see Veronica. He couldn't get a shot. But she could pick him off at will. Then there would be nothing to stop her from getting Kasluga. Reacher knew how many people Veronica and her sister had killed. He knew how ruthless she was. How relentless. Reacher had served temporarily with IDF personnel and had great respect for them. She would have been well trained so would have a degree of patience. But there would be a limit. She had no way of knowing if reinforcements were on their way. Any delay could compromise her chances of success. Which told Reacher he couldn't afford to wait very long.

Reacher heard sounds behind him. A hiss, then a gushing noise. He glanced over his shoulder. The pipe that had been hit by Veronica's ricochet had now burst. It was blue. And it was leaking water. Which gave Reacher an idea.

He turned back. There was still no sign of Veronica. Nothing to aim at. Not even a foot or an elbow or an ear. So he picked a different kind of target. A red pipe. He pulled the trigger. The pipe shattered. And the surrounding space was engulfed in clouds of scalding steam.

Veronica screamed. She dived out into the open, rolled to the side, and came up half sitting, half kneeling. She had the Sig lined up on Kasluga's chest. Reacher could see tension in the ligaments of her wrists.

Reacher stepped closer. He said, "Stop. Don't do it. Shoot her and your father's story will never be told."

He could see in her eyes that Veronica was not going to stop. She raised her Sig a fraction higher. Her ligaments tightened a notch more. Reacher pulled his trigger. He was never going to miss at that range. The bullet hit her in one temple and burst out from the other. All the electrical activity in her brain was shorted out. The signals to her nerves shut down. Her muscles relaxed and her tendons sagged and she tumbled sideways, landing like a mirror image of her sister.

Reacher kicked Veronica's gun away and checked for a pulse, although that was just a formality. She was way beyond saving. He crossed to Kasluga and untied the rope from around her waist. She pushed past him and threw herself toward her husband. She knelt beside him and her tears flooded his chest and mixed with the blood on his shirt.

Reacher heard a sound from behind him. Footsteps. There were two sets. He spun around, gun raised, ready.

"Blue on blue." It was a man's voice. "Federal agents. Reinforcing Secretary Stamoran's protection detail."

"Clear," Reacher called.

The agents stepped into view and stayed still, trying to make sense of the scene. The first one said, "Stamoran?"

Reacher shook his head. "I guess you'll be needing another secretary to protect."

Susan Kasluga stood up. Her tears were still flowing and she was trying to control her voice. She said, "I think the danger's passed, don't you? So I would like a moment alone with my husband now."

Chapter 27

An aged TV on a tall stand had been wheeled into the meeting room at some point during the night. Christopher Baglin used it to get the task force's final meeting under way with a VHS recording of the previous night's press conference from the White House. A suitably somber spokesman announced Stamoran's death. He spent a couple of minutes running through a bunch of weasel-worded platitudes, then signed off with the minimum of details.

Smith said, "They won't get away with that for very long. Questions are going to be asked."

"They'll be hoping things heat up in Serbia soon," Reacher said. "Nothing like bad news to hog the spotlight."

Christopher Baglin switched off the TV. He said, "I spent most of the night ass deep in crime scene photos and the ME's reports and all the physical evidence I could lay my hands on. What a messed-up situation. I guess we could frame it as one story of redemption. One of disgrace. And another of, well, I don't know. Someone else can be the judge of that."

Smith said, "Charles Stamoran *was* a disgrace. The secret program he ran in India, and all those other places. The money he and Pritchard stole. The leak it caused, and the thousand lost souls that resulted. May he rot in hell."

Reacher said, "And what value can we put on Morgan Sanson's redemption?"

Baglin said, "His personnel file showed he was a good person. He was worried about safety, not pay or promotions. He was about to expose the corruption and was killed for it. He wasn't a saboteur. He wasn't a suicide. I for one am glad the world now knows."

"And his daughters?" Reacher said. "What have they got to show for it?"

Smith said, "Some of the blame has to go to the scientists. If Owen Buck, for example, had acted at the time, instead of dithering for decades and then giving Roberta and Veronica partial information and provoking this crazy quest of theirs, how different would things have been?"

"Owen Buck," Baglin said. "He wrote the original list of names, I guess. It was in Roberta's pocket when she died. One strange detail about it. Six names were written in one person's handwriting. And the other two in two different hands. Anyone have ideas why that should be?"

Walsh said, "Sorry."

Smith shook her head.

Reacher said nothing.

"Never mind," Baglin said. "It's probably not important."

Smith suggested a drink when the meeting wrapped up but Reacher didn't see the point. The only unfinished business was Neilsen's wake in a day or two and he wasn't thrilled about attending. He figured how you treat people when they're alive is what matters. No amount of drinking and storytelling is going to make a difference after they're gone. So he went back to his hotel. He figured he would grab his things, drop his car keys at reception, and slip out of town without making a big fuss.

It took twice as long as usual for Reacher to pack because he had his Class A's to square away. The pants were going to need some attention from a tailor after getting worn at the pumping station the day before. And the whole thing would need a thorough clean after getting doused with gasoline. He zipped up its garment bag and dropped it on the counter, ready to sweep his other clothes into his duffel, but he noticed something on the side next to the minibar. An envelope. The report Walsh had brought for him the other night. About Susan Kasluga's career. He hadn't read it. Events had overtaken him. And it would be moot now, anyway. The case was closed. Reacher picked up the envelope and started toward the trash can.

He stopped. He slid the contents out of the envelope and began to flick through them. He had time. He figured it would be good to get a sense of the woman whose life he'd saved. He wound up reading every word, and studying every picture. And when he was done, his travel plans were back on hold.

Reacher stepped into Susan Kasluga's outer office at a minute to nine in the morning, two days later.

Kasluga's gray-haired assistant looked up from behind her giant computer and said, "Captain Reacher?" She gestured toward the door to the inner office. "Go ahead. She's ready for you." Then she lowered her voice. "You know, Ms. Kasluga is the backbone of AmeriChem. She's the life and soul of the company. Everyone here is so grateful for what you did to save her."

Reacher said, "Don't thank me yet." Then he gave the inner door a cursory knock and went through.

Susan Kasluga came out from behind her desk to greet him. She was wearing all black. She looked tired and there were dark circles under her eyes. She gave him a gentle hug and said, "I'm glad you're here. Welcome to my sanctuary."

Most of the furniture in the place was a blend of chrome and leather and pale Scandinavian wood. Exactly the kind of tone Reacher expected to find in a chief executive's office. But along one wall there was a surprisingly personal collection of things. Almost sentimental. There was an old lab bench with a jumble of test tubes in wooden racks spread out all over it. There were tongs and Bunsen burners and round glass flasks in various sizes. And on the wall above it there were clusters of framed pictures of experiments in progress and people wearing white coats and safety goggles. There was also a group of five canvas facsimiles of handwritten chemical formulae, complete with crossings-out and scribbled annotations. Reacher guessed they were copies of Kasluga's own work. Presumably milestones that were significant to her in some way.

Reacher shifted his focus back to Kasluga and said, "I'm sorry for your loss."

Kasluga shrugged. "Thank you. It's a complicated situation. I loved Charles. I still do. I always will, I guess. But I have to face facts. He was a murderer. Have you seen what they're saying in the press? It's like they're trying to take away my right to mourn. To shame me. They don't get that I'm a victim, too. Anyway, enough of them and their vindictiveness. Can I offer you some tea? I have orange hibiscus, peppermint leaf, lemon lavender, or huang ju hua. That's yellow chrysanthemum flower. It's delicious." She moved across to a shelf that held a slim electric kettle, a set of mugs in contrasting pastel colors, and half a dozen cylindrical silver caddies.

Reacher said, "Thanks, but no. This won't take long. I just have a couple of loose ends to tie up. Some of our paperwork got lost, unfortunately. A screwup by the admin guys."

"After what you did for me, nothing is too much trouble," she said. "Tell me what you need."

She moved across and sat in a chair by a low coffee table in the center of the office. Reacher took the one opposite.

Reacher said, "The first thing is new, actually. My CO is a bit of an innovator. He's started a study to see if graphology could be applied to our work in any way. The study of handwriting."

"OK?"

"He's looking for samples for his expert to analyze. It's totally anonymous and unofficial, but if I could take him a real-life example it would earn me a load of kudos."

"You want me to write something down?"

Reacher took a notebook and a pen out of a briefcase he'd borrowed and passed them to her. "If you wouldn't mind. A couple of words. *Clears marathons.* Sounds weird, but apparently it's important for every sample to say the same thing and that's what our guy came up with."

Kasluga scribbled on the first page. "Done."

"Thank you. And while you've got the pen, could you give me your phone number? Not your office. I have that one. A home number. In case I have any follow-up. When I have paperwork backed up I tend to work late."

"No problem." She added a string of digits to the second page and handed back the pad.

Reacher hesitated, then said, "I'm sorry if this is an insensitive time to ask, but how much did your husband tell you about his involvement in Project 192?"

"It's OK." Kasluga took a moment to bring her emotions under control. "He didn't tell me much. Just that he suspected someone was killing the scientists from the sixties in order to force one of them to give up the identity of the eighth man on their team, and that he was the eighth man. He didn't want to breach state secrets or anything, but he was worried the killers would come after me to get to him. Which is exactly what did happen, of course."

"What did he tell you about Project Typhon?"

"Nothing. I don't know what that is."

"OK, well I think that pretty much wraps everything up." Reacher started to heave himself out of the chair, then sank back down. "Actually, let me ask you one more thing. I'm curious. I came across an early draft of a press article about your role following that accident in '69. Made you sound a lot more heroic than the one that got published. Heroic is closer to the truth, right? From what I've seen I can't picture you as a passive, talking-head type of person."

Kasluga looked down and smiled. She said, "I didn't realize that original version is still making the rounds. But you're right. It was pretty much spot-on. When the gas leaked, and what a nightmare that was, by the way, there were no senior managers to be found. They all buried their heads in the sand. Someone had to take action, so I did. I organized the work to neutralize the gas that had leaked. And to treat people who had been exposed. Then to clean any contaminated water and repair the damage to the soil."

"And when you'd done all the heavy lifting the bosses resurfaced, took the credit for themselves, and downplayed your role."

"I was seriously pissed at the time. I won't lie. It's one of the reasons I quit that job and founded AmeriChem. But you know what they say. The best revenge is massive success. And look at me now."

"They also say that pride goes before a fall."

Kasluga tipped her head to the side. "What do you mean by that?"

"The gas that leaked in '69 was a product of Project Typhon. So you did know about it."

"It wasn't. It was a new kind of disinfectant from the Mason Chemical plant, where I worked. And look, seven people died which makes it—"

"One thousand and seven." Reacher took a photograph out of his briefcase and laid it on the table. Flemming had given it to him the previous afternoon. It was the wide shot of the bodies strewn out across the desolate field. "You knew which chemicals to use to neutralize the gas. So you knew what kind of gas it was. That's the truth."

Kasluga didn't reply.

Reacher said, "In fact, it's only part of the truth. You didn't just know about the Typhon gas. You stole the formula. And when you set up AmeriChem, it became the basis for your first blockbuster product. In a watered-down form. Your big-deal disinfectant. I bet it's one of the ones you have hanging on the wall."

Reacher saw Kasluga glance at the left-hand canvas.

She said, "That's a lie. I devised the formulas for AmeriChem's first five products myself, on my own, and only after I had established the company."

Reacher set a second photograph on the table. Another from the leak in '69. A close-up of a victim's face. He set a third photo next to it. Also a close-up of a face. With skin stained with the exact same kind of weird purple blotches. Walsh had dug it up when he threw a searchlight on Kasluga's professional life. It was in the envelope he had left at Reacher's hotel.

Reacher said, "That picture was evidence when you were sued after AmeriChem had a gas leak."

Kasluga glanced at the canvas again but didn't say a word.

Reacher said, "Same symptoms. Same gas. No question."

Kasluga picked up the first picture from '69. "Where did you get this?"

Reacher shrugged. "I'm an investigator. I find things."

Kasluga turned the photograph over. There was a stamp on the back, in blue ink, pale to begin with and faded by time. Kasluga brought it closer to her face and peered at the letters. "Copyright Spencer Flemming. And a post office box number. Interesting."

"Don't try to find him. You'd be wasting your time. He's somewhere you'd never expect."

Kasluga got up, crossed to one of her bookcases, and opened a cupboard that took the place of the lower three shelves. There was a machine inside. A document shredder. She fed the picture into it then slammed the door. "Oops."

"That won't help you. Flemming has copies."

"So what are you going to do? Arrest me? Drag the grieving widow out in handcuffs? Good luck with the optics on that one."

Reacher stood. "Not me. Not my jurisdiction. If you were in the military you'd already be in a cell. My next meeting's with the FBI. I'm going to give them everything I have. I'm sure you'll be hearing from them soon. I just wanted to see the look on your face, first."

Chapter 28

Spencer Flemming was sitting on the floor, surrounded by his books and papers and files. He had taken a shower so his hair was hanging down even lower on his back than usual. His clothes had been washed so his shirt was brighter and there were fewer stains on his jeans. A plate was on the desk. A sandwich was spilling over the sides, loaded with tomatoes and peppers and red onions and spinach. His favorite combination. Usually. It was out of his reach, but that was OK. He didn't have the stomach for it just then. He was too busy second-guessing himself. Change was coming. Good things were going to happen, he hoped. But before the sunshine, the storm. Reacher hadn't hidden that from him when he'd asked for his help. It was just a lot easier to be brave when he wasn't on his own.

The guy at the postal store was stubborn. He waved off Susan Kasluga's threats against him and his business. He wasn't interested in her bribes. He wouldn't budge an inch until she spotted the photograph he kept in a frame behind the counter. It showed a woman and two little boys, all hugs and smiles and happiness. Kasluga suggested that two of the men who were with her could track the trio down. She suggested a few things they could do when they caught up with them. Then the guy changed his tune. He gave up Spencer Flemming's address in a heartbeat. He even warned Kasluga that the premises it corresponded to were extremely unorthodox. He didn't want her to think he'd tried to stiff her. He didn't want her coming back. He was extremely clear about that.

Kasluga's driver stopped the Town Car at the end of the asylum's driveway, in the same spot Smith had used six days before. He killed the engine and climbed out. He drew his gun. The other three guards followed and reached for their weapons. Kasluga got out last. The four guys formed up around her and they stood for a moment and stared through the fence at the building. A dark cloud hung low in the sky over the whole site. It felt like some kind of warning. The crumbling brickwork and the rusting screens over the windows seemed to scream, *Run*. Kasluga nudged the guard in front of her. She said, "Come on. What are you waiting for?"

The guard made a gap in the fence and led the way toward the portico and the huge wooden door. He was carrying a set of bolt cutters and he used them to slice through the padlock and knock its rusty remains loose. Then it took two of them to heave the doors apart far enough to squeeze through. Daylight filtered in. They could see the filthy space on the other side. Kasluga pointed at the footprints in the dust that covered the black and white floor tiles. She said, "That way. Let's go."

They stayed close and followed the track past the ruined desk and under the crusted chandelier and all the way out to the court-yard. Kasluga pointed to the line of travel trailers on the far side. "He must be in one of them."

The drapes in the left-hand trailer were drawn but its door was latched open. Kasluga nudged the guard and said, "Try that one."

The guard set his foot on the bottom step. He took the next one slowly, and stepped inside. He paused in the doorway, then crept forward. He disappeared from view. He was gone for a minute. Two. Three. There was no sign of him bringing Flemming out. No sign of him returning alone.

Kasluga called out, "Hey. What's going on in there? What's tak-ing so long?"

There was no reply.

She nudged the next guard. "Go see what's happening."

The guy took the steps at a snail's pace then rushed forward, gun raised. He vanished inside. And did not reappear.

A voice called out from behind them. A man's. Firm. Authorita-tive. It said, "FBI. Drop your weapons. Lie facedown on the ground. Do it now."

The two remaining guards did as they were told. The pair who had gone into the trailer stumbled back out, disarmed, their hands cuffed behind their backs, followed by two agents. Four more agents swarmed around the guys on the floor. They cuffed them. Hauled them onto their feet, and dragged them away.

Susan Kasluga was alone. She remained on her feet. Reacher and Amber Smith approached from the glass doorway. Smith said, "You heard. Get on the ground."

Kasluga folded her arms. She stayed standing.

Reacher stepped in close. He leaned down and loomed over her.

His voice was barely more than a whisper. He said, "I killed a woman because of you. A woman I shouldn't have. So if you think I won't take any chance to rip you to pieces . . ."

Kasluga brushed the ground in front of her with one foot. She lowered herself to her knees. Pushed away a couple of rocks and eased down until she was lying on her front. Smith cuffed her then pulled her back upright and began a search. She was thorough. She checked under Kasluga's arms. Around her chest. Her waist. Her thighs. In the seams of her clothes. Even in her hair.

Kasluga poked at the ground with her toe and sneered. "So what was this about, this wild-goose chase?"

Reacher said, "It's about actions speaking louder than words. Any competent lawyer could have gotten that photo I showed you excluded from a trial. The one with all the bodies from '69. There's no way to prove when it was taken. Where. Whether the people were really dead, or just posing. Whether you even knew about them. But you going to such trouble to find the photographer? That's as good as a guilty plea, all day long."

"Not in a court of law."

"We're not talking about a court. Or the law. Not any longer. I'm not sure society will be best served by you going to jail. Maybe there's another way for you to make amends."

"I'm listening. And I'm betting this has to do with money. How much do you want?"

"AmeriChem made you a very rich woman. You could use that money to provide for the families of the victims you left behind in India. For Morgan Sanson's wife and surviving son. For Kent Neilsen's daughters. A guy from the Treasury Department has drawn up a document. It'll make everything legal. You should sign it."

"Are you insane? I'm not responsible for any of those deaths. I'm not helping those people."

"How much time did you spend in chemistry labs, Susan? Because something's clearly rotted your brain. Start with India. A thousand people died because that gas leaked? Why did it leak?"

"Poor maintenance." She scuffed the dirt with her foot. "Nothing to do with me."

"Everything to do with you. The maintenance was bad because you stole the money that was supposed to pay for it."

"That's a lie."

"You stole the formula to give your new company a head start. You stole the money, too."

"I never—"

"The Cayman Islands, Susan. The property development company. The failed bid. The bogus lawsuit. We know about it all."

Kasluga didn't respond.

Reacher said, "Your stealing caused the leak, and the leak is why you had to silence Morgan Sanson."

"Sanson was a sad loser who messed with the cooling equipment in a fit of temper because he wasn't good enough to get a raise. People died and he couldn't live with it so he killed himself."

"We've read his personnel file, Susan. Safety was his concern. Not pay."

"Speculate all you want. I can listen to this garbage all day long and when you're done I can tell you one thing: I'm not going to jail because some poor people died in a gas leak and I'm not going to jail for killing Morgan Sanson."

"Maybe not," Reacher said. "But you will go to jail for killing your husband. That's for damn sure."

Spencer Flemming struggled to his feet. He was stooped at first, as usual, then he forced himself to stand up straight. He couldn't remember the last time he'd cared about his posture. Or that his skin hadn't been dirty. Or that he'd felt carpet under his toes. He moved until he could catch his reflection in the mirror. He didn't like what he saw. He looked so different, next to the people who had helped him since Reacher and Amber Smith had brought him to the hotel. His hair. His clothes. He was stuck in time, he realized. Not his fault, given that he'd been forced to live in the shadows. And not his choice. But now he could choose to change. He would have to, if he was going to take advantage of this second chance he was being offered. If it actually happened. Reacher had told him the woman most responsible for his plight would be going to jail for the rest of her life. He prayed that was true. But deep down in his gut he didn't believe it. He couldn't. He had a premonition. She was going to skate, and he would wind up back in the asylum.

"You're framing me." Kasluga's voice was practically a shriek. "You're actually trying to frame me. It's unbelievable. You know I didn't kill Charles. You were there. You know Veronica Sanson killed him. She would have killed me, too, if you'd showed up a moment later."

Reacher shrugged and said, "And I used to think punctuality was a virtue."

Kasluga turned to Smith. "Try to arrest me for this and I'll have my lawyer put Reacher on the stand. Make him perjure himself. He'll be the one who winds up in jail. Not me."

Smith said, "Oh, you're getting arrested."

Reacher said, "Try to keep me off the stand."

"This is insane." Kasluga raised her eyes to the sky. "You saw what those women did."

Smith grabbed her by the right arm. "Enough of the histrionics. Come on. Time to go."

Kasluga instantly pulled away. Her right arm appeared from behind her back. Maybe Smith hadn't secured the cuffs properly. Maybe Kasluga's wrists were particularly narrow. But either way, she had somehow wriggled free. Her left arm appeared. She ducked down. Scrabbled in the dirt. Then straightened up with an object in her hand. A four-inch nail, all bent and rusty. Kasluga twisted around behind Smith. She wrapped her right arm around Smith's head, covering her eyes. She used her left to jam the tip of the nail into Smith's neck. She hit a spot right above Smith's carotid. A drop of blood ran down her neck and soaked into her shirt. The nail was still sharp despite the rust. That was clear. A few more ounces of pressure and Smith would be dead.

Kasluga stepped back. She dragged Smith with her and simultaneously pulled her head, stretching her neck and arching her back. She said, "Drop the gun."

Smith did as she was told.

Kasluga shifted her focus to Reacher. "You too."

Reacher raised his hands to shoulder height but he kept hold of his gun. It was side on to Kasluga with its muzzle pointing harmlessly at the sky. He said, "I didn't see those women do anything to your husband. He was already dead when I got there."

"Because they shot him. The younger one did."

"Did she?"

Kasluga pulled back farther. "I said, drop the gun."

Reacher moved the hand holding his gun a little to the side and a little lower, but he didn't let go. "I found the two agents, dead. Then I heard three shots. They were close together. In time, and origin."

Smith started to struggle. She tried to twist her head away from the nail but she couldn't wriggle free. The nail just bit deeper into her skin.

Kasluga said, "Veronica had already shot the agents. Charles fired twice. He hit Roberta and killed her. He hit Veronica and knocked her down but she survived because of her vest. She shot back at the same moment and killed Charles."

Reacher shook his head. "I heard three shots, then a gun hitting the ground. You shot all three of them. Your husband, then the women. Then you tossed your gun at your husband's feet. But you made a mistake. You didn't kill Veronica. And that almost cost you your life."

"Check the police report. See how many shells were missing from each gun."

"I did. Two from your gun. One from Roberta's. Three from Veronica's."

"Two from Charles's gun. Which proves what I said."

"From the gun found by Charles's body. Which proves you're good. For an improvised plan it was adequate in several respects. You asked for time alone with your husband. And you used it to switch one bullet from Veronica's gun into your own. You even noticed it was a different brand. You use Browning. She used Federal. So you unloaded your gun and reloaded it so that her bullet was at the bottom of the magazine."

"I did nothing while I was alone with Charles. With his body. I was too upset."

Smith started to scuffle her feet, trying to pull away. Kasluga elbowed her in the ribs and she stopped moving.

Reacher said, "You switched one bullet. You moved the spent cartridges. The police report noted they were in an odd position. And you wrote your husband's name on Roberta Sanson's list."

"I did not. Now drop the gun. I won't tell you again."

Reacher moved the gun a little lower. A little farther forward. "Remember those words you wrote for me? *Clears marathons*? That's an anagram of *Charles Stamoran*. Same letters, different order. And guess what? The handwriting is a perfect match."

"Drop the damn—"

"The bigger question is why did you write his name at all? Why not leave the list at seven names? Why make him the eighth?"

"He was the eighth. I didn't make him anything."

"Right. He was some kind of a supervisor, 7,500 miles away. He made no difference to the project, day to day. Unlike the ninth person, who was there, on the ground, getting their hands dirty. Cleaning up after the leak. Paying off the relatives and the witnesses."

"There was no ninth person."

"There was. It was you."

Reacher saw Kasluga's knuckles turn white around the nail. He saw her eyes narrow. The tendons in her neck tense up. So he brought his gun the rest of the way around to the front. He was an expert marksman, with a pistol or a rifle. At that moment the range was negligible. There was no wind. No glare. His target wasn't moving. He wasn't out of breath. There were multiple spots he could have picked with minimal risk to Smith. Kasluga's head. Her shoulder. Either knee. Either shin. Either foot. Reacher pulled the trigger. He hit Kasluga dead in the center of her right instep. She screamed, dropped the nail, and fell hard to the side.

Smith stepped back and clamped her hand over her neck.

Kasluga howled and curled up and clenched her teeth. She managed a strangled, "Help me."

Reacher said, "Help you? The way you agreed to help those kids after you killed their parents? To help those bereaved families in India?"

"I was wrong." She was gasping, barely able to breathe through the pain. "Please. I'm begging you."

"I want information. Two questions."

"Anything. Just get me to a damn hospital."

"Who did you call to set up Neilsen's murder?"

"That wasn't—"

"Do you want to lose your whole leg?"

Kasluga shook her head.

"Then stop lying for ten seconds. We know who Neilsen called, asking questions. That person called you. They used the number you wrote in my notebook."

"That's because . . ." Kasluga was panting. ". . . he was calling Charles. We lived together. Same house. Same phone."

"He wasn't. Charles had a whole bunch of Defense Department phone lines in that house. Those lines don't generate records. Why would he take incriminating calls on a line that did?"

Kasluga hissed, "Fine. David Sullivan. Vice president, client satisfaction, Total Security Solutions. They have the AmeriChem account. I have a problem, a lawsuit, someone making trouble, anywhere in the world, he makes it go away."

"Good. I'll give him a call. See if he can make himself go away. Now, Neville Pritchard. What was the deal with him?"

Kasluga let out a long, deep groan. "Hospital. You promised."

"You answer first. Pritchard reported to Stamoran. We pieced that much together. So did he recruit you in-country?"

"Don't make me laugh." Kasluga whimpered for a second from the effort. "Pritchard was an idiot. A pencil pusher. I figured out what he was doing inside a day. Forced him to let me in."

"You stole the money together. Split it later."

"No. I—"

"That's why you gave him the bogus currency loans right after your property development scam. To funnel his share of the laundered cash to him."

Kasluga nodded. Her face was pale and gleaming with sweat.

"When you figured that Buck had spilled his guts to the Sanson sisters you made a call to your buddy Sullivan. Had Pritchard taken out because he was the only one who could identify you."

Kasluga managed a thin smile. "The funny thing? It was Charles who told me about the scientists getting killed. That was why I called Sullivan. Charles thought he was protecting me. He was an idiot, too."

Reacher turned and started toward the glass door. Smith hurried after him and grabbed his sleeve.

She said, "Hold up. You promised we'd get her to the hospital."

"I didn't say how. She can crawl to the car. Or she can bleed out here. Either way is good with me."

"Reacher, that's cold."

He shrugged. "She really should have agreed to help those kids."

Chapter 29

Reacher didn't believe in fate but he had heard it said that the harder a person works, the luckier they become. He thought it would be fair to say he'd worked hard that day. So when he was halfway through putting on his freshly cleaned Class A uniform in preparation for Kent Neilsen's wake and the phone in his hotel room rang, the orders he received seemed fitting. He was being sent back to Illinois with immediate effect. Irregularities had been uncovered with the inventory at the Joliet Army Ammunition Plant. His recent experience at the Rock Island Arsenal was expected to be valuable. And given Joliet's proximity to Chicago, he figured if he worked really hard the case might just expand to include Agent Ottoway . . .

The final flight to Midway airport left in four hours so Reacher decided it would be safe to show his face at the wake. There would be time to pay his last respects to Neilsen and his new posting would be a perfect reason to leave if the whole occasion turned out to be too dire. The venue was easy enough to find. It was an old movie theater, all neon and art deco curves and flourishes, and it had recently been converted into a concert hall. It turned out that Neilsen had been a bit of a musician in his younger days. His thing was the flugelhorn. He was bigger on enthusiasm than technique, according to a woman who'd known him when he played. She was part of a makeshift band that had been rounded up for the evening. It included a couple of his old buddies. They had set an extra place in their semicircle on the stage and propped up a thing that looked to Reacher like a trumpet on the empty chair.

Reacher gravitated to the back of the room and the first person he recognized was Spencer Flemming. Although it took a moment for Reacher to place him. His hair was still gray but it no longer hung down on either side of his face. It was short now. It had been cut into an actual style. And he was wearing jeans and a shirt that didn't look like they were decades out of date. Reacher shook the guy's hand and their conversation quickly turned to the future. Flemming knew Joliet, or had in the sixties. He'd covered a story about a string of accidents at a motor racing track near there. He was hoping to be covering more stories very soon. He just needed to sort out his accommodations. The hotel hadn't worked for him so he was back in his trailer. The FBI had arranged for it to be towed to an RV park. The same one Pritchard had been murdered in, but Flemming didn't know that.

Flemming wandered away after a few minutes, and moments later Reacher bumped into Amber Smith. She had a Band-Aid on her neck as a result of Susan Kasluga's efforts with the rusty nail, and she was wearing a black dress with heels. Reacher had only ever seen her in jeans and boots before. Another person whose appearance had changed. All part of spinning out of one orbit and moving into another, Reacher thought. A natural transition at the end of an intense case.

"Heard anything about Kasluga?" Smith said.

Reacher shook his head. "Done anything about Sullivan? Her wet-work guy?"

"I briefed my supervisor. He said I can run with it. I have a good feeling about it. A chance to do something right again. Get my career back on track."

"And outside of work?"

Smith shrugged. "OK, I think. This is the first funeral I've been to since Philip's. I didn't know how it would be, but I'm handling it. Maybe time really is all I need."

Pretty soon after that Reacher figured he'd had his fill so he started to drift toward the exit. He bumped into Christopher Baglin and Gary Walsh. He heard the band start up for a second session. He saw a man and a woman making for the valet station with an urgent look in their eyes. And when he made it to the foyer he nearly ran into a pair of men in dark suits who were clearly escorting some kind of a bigwig. The guy glanced at Reacher then stopped and backtracked. He said, "Captain Reacher? I thought I might find you here. My name's Jon Essley. Acting Secretary of Defense. I want to thank you for what you did for my predecessor. The fact that we can mourn him as a man who did his duty, albeit in tune with the sensibilities of a bygone time, rather than condemning him as a cold-blooded murderer, is a huge comfort to me personally, and to the nation. If this position becomes mine permanently it's safe to say it won't be long until your silver bars will be gone and your oak leaves will be back."

Reacher said nothing. In his experience, a verbal promise from a politician wasn't worth the paper it was written on.

Lee Child is the author of the #1 *New York Times* bestselling Jack Reacher series and the complete Jack Reacher story collection, *No Middle Name*. Foreign rights in the Reacher series have sold in one hundred territories. A native of England and a former television director, Lee Child lives in New York City and Wyoming.

jackreacher.com
Facebook.com/LeeChildOfficial
Twitter: @LeeChildReacher

To inquire about booking Lee Child for a speaking engagement, please contact the Penguin Random House Speakers Bureau at speakers@penguinrandomhouse.com.

Andrew Child, who also writes as Andrew Grant, is the author of *RUN, False Positive, False Friend, False Witness, Invisible,* and *Too Close to Home.* He is the #1 bestselling co-author of the Jack Reacher novels *The Sentinel, Better Off Dead,* and *No Plan B.* Child and his wife, the novelist Tasha Alexander, live on a wildlife preserve in Wyoming.

andrewgrantbooks.com
Facebook.com/AndrewGrantAuthor
Twitter: @Andrew_Grant

If you enjoyed Lee and Andrew Child's *The Secret*,

read on for a thrilling preview of

In Too Deep

A JACK REACHER NOVEL

Coming in hardcover and ebook from

Delacorte Press

October 2024

Chapter 1

The pain hit first, then the sound followed, the way lightning beats thunder in a storm.

The pain was in Jack Reacher's right wrist. It was sharp and sudden and hot, and it was strong enough to wrestle his attention away from the dull throbbing ache that filled his head. The sound was a single, round, lingering note. Metal on metal. Inconsequential next to the ringing in his ears.

The pain and the sound came after he tried to move his arm. That was all Reacher knew. He had been asleep—no, somewhere deeper and darker than sleep—and when he floated to the surface he was rocked by waves of dizziness. He was lying on his back. Not in a bed. Not on the ground. On something smooth and artificial. And cold. The chill was seeping through his shirt and into his shoulder blades and down his spine. A sharp ridge was cutting into his calves. His head felt like it was being crushed against the hard surface. So he had drawn his right elbow back, ready to lever himself up. Or he had tried to. And it wasn't just the discomfort that had stopped him. Something was fastened around his wrist, preventing it from moving more than a couple of inches. Something cinched in tight. It bit into his skin, but that wasn't what hurt the most. It was one of the bones in his forearm. Maybe more than one. Some kind of major damage had been done beneath the surface. That was clear.

Reacher tried to move his left arm. There was no pain, but that wrist was also restrained by something sharp. So was his left ankle. So was his right. He couldn't see what he was attached to, or what he was bound with, because there was no light. Not the slightest glimmer. The space he was in was completely dark. There was no noise, now that the metallic clink had died away. And no movement of the air. Reacher had no idea where he was. No idea how he had gotten there. But someone must have brought him. And shackled him. And whoever had done those things was going to rue the day. That was for damn sure.

The same time Reacher was slipping back into oblivion a man was standing at the side of the road, five miles away to the north, watching for smoke or flames. His name was Ivan Vidic. He was heavyset and a little stooped which made him look shorter than the six foot two he claimed on his driver's license, and his bald head was all sharp angles and ridges like it had been carved from stone by someone without much skill. His car was parked by the second of a set of three switchbacks. It was a notorious spot for accidents. The turns were sharp and close together and poorly lit. The road was separated from a steep drop by a wide shoulder and a rusty safety rail and the camber coming off the apex of the first bend was way out of whack. Something to do with ancient geological deposits deteriorating and undermining the layers of bedrock way below. Nothing that couldn't be fixed, given the right amount of money. But money was scarce in those parts so the local Department of Roads and Bridges had thrown up a couple of warning signs instead. They didn't help to keep vehicles from crashing, but the department's lawyers said they helped reduce the risk of getting sued.

An SUV had crashed there, earlier that night. A Lincoln Navigator. It had left the road, clipped a tree, rolled three times, and come to rest back on its wheels. Its roof was caved in. Its hood was dented. Its doors were bent and twisted and all its windows were starred and opaque. Vidic had watched the accident unfold. He had been following, close behind. He had pulled over while the Lincoln was still moving, jumped out, and rushed over to investigate. The vehicle had wound up in bad shape, but its driver had fared even worse. He was dead. His neck was broken. At first Vidic thought the passenger was bound for the morgue, too, but when he checked he felt a pulse. He adjusted his diagnosis: just a concussion, and maybe a broken wrist.

Vidic had called a couple of his buddies for help and while he waited for them to arrive he had hauled the driver and the passenger out of the wreckage. That wasn't easy. The driver's head was flopping around all over the place and his body was slack and soft and difficult to grip. The passenger was worse because of his size and weight. Six foot five. Two hundred and fifty pounds. Arms bigger than the driver's legs. Wrists too broad for Vidic to wrap his fingers around. Vidic was out of breath and sweating despite the cool night air when he heard wheels on the asphalt behind him, and he only just had time to finish rifling the passenger's pockets and transferring the few possessions he found there to his own.

The new guys had shown up in a Ford pickup truck, which turned out to be a practical choice. There was no way they'd have been able to manhandle the passenger's unconscious body onto the back-seat of a regular car. He was too big. Too heavy. So they heaved him up onto the load bed and tossed the driver's corpse in next to him.

The guy who had been driving the pickup was called Darren Fletcher. He was a couple of inches taller than Vidic but slimmer and maybe twenty pounds lighter. He slammed the tailgate into place then turned to Vidic and said, "You saw it happen?"

Vidic nodded.

"When you called and said it was Gibson's Lincoln I was hoping you were wrong."

Vidic shrugged.

"How did it go down?"

"Gibson was driving pretty slow. Pretty careful. I caught up to him, heading the same direction, just by chance. He kept going the same steady speed for maybe a mile, then he must have recognized my car. Must have tried to lose me. He hit the gas, but at exactly the wrong time." Vidic nodded at the wrecked vehicle. "Exhibit A."

"Did you flash your lights? Honk your horn? Tailgate him?"

"No. Why would I?"

"So why did he try to lose you?"

Vidic shrugged again.

Fletcher said, "The big guy who's with him. Who is he?"

"No idea."

"No ID?"

"No."

"Luggage? Backpack?"

"Just this." Vidic took a pistol from his waistband and handed it to Fletcher. "A Glock 17. The FBI's weapon of choice. Make of that what you will."

* * *

Fletcher and the other guy had taken off in the Ford and left Vidic to deal with the Lincoln. He had checked the glove box and the trunk for anything containing personal information then turned his attention to the driver's seat. He had been ready to clean up any blood that had been spilled, but there wasn't any. Gibson's skin must not have been pierced in the accident. Or at least not while his heart was still beating. Vidic had smiled. That made his next task easier. He glanced across to the passenger side and noted the position on the doorframe where the bloodstain was. He took a knife from his pocket, made a nick on the pad of his left thumb, and squeezed a few drops of blood onto the frame of the driver's door in a corresponding spot, only around three inches lower. He grabbed the steering wheel. The gear shift. He adjusted the rearview mirror. Then he put his foot on the brake and turned the key. Nothing happened. Some kind of safety system must have shut off the ignition when the vehicle hit the tree. And isolated the fuel supply, with any luck, Vidic thought. He used his knife to pry off the cover from the gearshift release, selected Neutral, then opened the door and jumped down. He climbed into his own car, fired it up, pulled in behind the Lincoln, and gave it a gentle nudge. It rolled a couple of yards and ground to a halt. Vidic leaned a little harder on the gas. The Lincoln rolled faster. It kept going this time and picked up more speed. Enough to help it bust through the safety rail and disappear into the darkness on the other side.

Vidic had hit the brake, shifted into Park, grabbed a flashlight from the glove box, climbed out, and hurried to the gap the Lincoln had made in the rail. He could see the vehicle fifty feet below, on its roof, three wheels still turning. He had stood and watched. There was no explosion. No sign of fire. He waited twenty minutes, to be sure. Then he walked back to his car, got back in behind the wheel and sped away, heading south.

* * *

Reacher was again woken by a sound. A door opening, this time. His eyes were closed but he could sense light. Fairly dim. Then much brighter. He heard footsteps approaching. One set. They came close, then stopped. Reacher opened his eyes, slowly, against the glare. The dizziness had receded a little but everything looked pale and washed out, like a watercolor without enough paint in the mix. A man was standing by his side. He was wearing jeans and a gray T-shirt. He was slim, like a runner, and maybe six foot four. His fists were clenched and Reacher thought he looked angry, maybe even scared, but was trying to hide it.

The man said, "I'm Darren Fletcher. Who are you?"

Reacher ignored him. If they'd searched him, Fletcher would already know his name. And if Fletcher hadn't searched him, he wasn't worth wasting breath on. Reacher concentrated on his surroundings instead. He saw that the restraints on his wrists and ankles were handcuffs, and that he was secured to a rectangular steel table. The floor was covered with white tiles and the walls were lined with steel shelves. The place was some kind of food storage or preparation area, Reacher figured. Then he turned back to Fletcher because the thought of food was making him feel sick.

"This silent act? It isn't helping you," Fletcher said. "You need to understand how serious this situation is. A man is dead. He was my friend. So you need to tell me who you are. You need to explain why you were in his car."

Reacher couldn't remember anything about a car or a dead man but he figured that wouldn't make for a strong negotiating position, so he said, "Release these cuffs. Then I'll tell you."

Fletcher shook his head. "Convince me you had nothing to do with my friend's death. Then I'll unlock the cuffs."

Reacher said nothing.

"Not smart. I can make you tell me, if you don't start talking."

Reacher said, "Can you? Because I can only see one of you."

"You don't want to test me. Believe me. So be sensible. Convince me."

"If I do, you'll release me?"

Fletcher nodded.

"You have the key?"

"Of course."

"Show me."

"No." Fletcher paused for a moment. "Why?"

"To demonstrate good faith. I need to know if you can keep your word."

Fletcher sighed and pulled a small silver key out of his pocket. "Satisfied?"

"One more thing. Release my left hand."

"Talk first."

"Here's the problem. My left wrist is broken. I can feel it swelling. It's getting constricted by the cuff. That can be serious. The damage could be done by the time we've talked. I could lose my hand."

Fletcher didn't respond, but he didn't put the key away.

"Come on. Release one broken limb. What am I going to do with it? My three good ones will still be secure and you have the only key. Release it, and I'll talk. Unless you don't want to know what happened to your friend."

Fletcher hesitated for another moment. A broken wrist had been mentioned at the scene of the accident. He remembered that. But he was a cautious man. He switched the key to his left hand, took the Glock from his waistband and stepped forward, gun raised, finger on the trigger.

Fletcher said, "Try anything and I'll shoot you with your own gun."

Reacher had no idea why Fletcher thought the gun was his but he had no time to waste on questions. He said, "Sure. I get the picture."

Fletcher kept the gun lined up on Reacher's face. He leaned down. Inserted the key into the cuff around Reacher's left wrist. Worked the lock. The cuff sprang open. It swung down, empty, and clanged against the table leg. Fletcher straightened up. The gun was still in his right hand. The key was still in his left. Reacher struggled to focus on either. The dizziness was building again and the images were threatening to split into two. Reacher willed his vision to stay clear then whipped up his hand and caught the Glock by its barrel. He forced it up and to the side. Then he jammed it back. The move was sharp and vicious and Reacher kept it going until the gun was horizontal and the muzzle was pointing at Fletcher's chest. Fletcher's finger was trapped by the trigger guard. It was bent backward, all the way to its limit. Reacher pushed harder. Fletcher's knuckle joint gave way. Cartilage tore. Tendons ripped. Fletcher screamed and let go of the grip. Reacher let the gun fall and dragged his hand across Fletcher's body. He caught Fletcher's left wrist. Pulled until Fletcher's hand was above his chest, then started to squeeze. Hard. Fletcher screamed again. Reacher increased the pressure. He could feel bones and ligaments begin to twist and crack. Fletcher screamed louder. And dropped the key.

The key hit Reacher's chest and bounced straight back up. It was spinning and sparkling and arcing away to the side. Reacher couldn't follow its flight. His vision was too blurred. He pictured it skittling off the shiny surface of the table and rattling down onto the floor tiles. In which case it might as well land in Australia for all the good it would do him. But then he felt something. It was like a butterfly landing on his right bicep. He still couldn't see what it was but Fletcher stretched for it with his damaged hand. Reacher twitched his arm and felt something hard and cold slide down against his side. Fletcher tried to pull away. He scrabbled at the back of his waistband. A second gun was tucked in there. A Sig Sauer. He got it free, but he couldn't hold on to it. His broken finger wouldn't bend. Reacher heard the gun rattle onto the floor. He let go of Fletcher's hand and grabbed his neck instead. He found his Adam's apple. Shifted his thumb down and to the side. Did the same with his middle finger. Then jammed both into the flesh of Fletcher's neck and pinched them together, crushing his carotid arteries. Fletcher howled and grabbed Reacher's wrist with his good hand. He pulled and heaved and scratched and gouged with his nails but Reacher just increased the pressure. He held it for five seconds. Six. Fletcher kept on struggling. Seven seconds passed and Fletcher's energy started to fade. Eight seconds, and that was all Fletcher could take. His brain was out of oxygen. He slumped forward. Reacher pulled his arm aside and Fletcher collapsed face-first onto Reacher's chest.

Reacher gave himself a moment for his heart rate to subside, hoping the hammering in his head would die down with it, then he slammed his fist into Fletcher's temple and let his unconscious body slide onto the floor. He retrieved the key from where it was wedged against his side. Eased himself into a sitting position. Paused to fight a sudden wave of nausea and dizziness, then got to work on the cuff on his right wrist. He moved slowly to avoid jarring the damaged bones. Released his right ankle. His left. Swung his legs around to the side and stood uncertainly on the floor.

Reacher was wearing his only pair of shoes. He had bought them years earlier, in England. They were quality items. Expensive. Solid and sturdy right out of the box, and the leather had only gotten harder with time and weather and hard use. Now the toe caps were like steel. Reacher turned and kicked Fletcher in the head. Hard.

Partly for a practical reason, to make sure Fletcher wouldn't regain consciousness anytime soon. And partly because he was pissed about his wrist and being dragged to this place against his will and the whole business with the handcuffs.

Reacher searched Fletcher's pockets using just his left hand. He found a wallet, which he took. He figured he would check for ID or credit cards later, when he could see better. He retrieved the two fallen guns, crept to the doorway, and peered out. It led to a kitchen. It was large and was kitted out with all kinds of appliances and machines Reacher didn't recognize. He was no expert but he figured it was the kind of place that would belong to a big private house rather than a restaurant or a hotel. Either way, there were no people around, which was what mattered. Reacher could see another door in the corner, diagonally opposite. He started toward it. Made it halfway across the space then the door opened. Reacher had the Glock in his left hand. He raised it. A man stepped into the room. He was heavy and stooped and he had a strange, angular head.

The man said, "Reacher? No need for the gun. I'm here to help."

Reacher didn't lower the gun. He said, "Who are you?"

The man said, "A friend. I saved you from the car wreck."

"How do you know my name?"

"I found your things. Took them. Kept them safe. So the others wouldn't get them."

"Kept them safe? Or tried to steal them?"

"No need for accusations. I'm your friend. Your only friend right now. I have your things here." The guy gestured to his pocket. "Want them back?"

Reacher nodded. "Do nothing stupid."

The guy pulled out Reacher's expired passport, his ATM card, some banknotes, and a folding toothbrush. "I guess you're a light traveler, huh?"

Reacher said, "Put them on the floor. Then step back."

"No time," the guy said. "We've got to hurry. The man in the car with you? Who died? You remember him?"

"No," Reacher said.

"Well, that's a problem. Because he was an FBI agent."

HAVE YOU READ THEM ALL?
The Jack Reacher thrillers in the order in which they were written:

KILLING FLOOR
Reacher gets off a bus in a small town in Georgia.
And is thrown in the county jail for a murder
he didn't commit.

DIE TRYING
Reacher is locked in a van with a
woman claiming to be FBI.

TRIPWIRE
Reacher is digging swimming pools in Key West
when a detective comes around asking questions.
Then the detective turns up dead.

RUNNING BLIND
Two naked women found dead in a bath filled with paint.
Both victims of a man just like Reacher.

ECHO BURNING
In the heat of Texas, Reacher meets a young woman whose
husband is in jail. When he is released, he will kill her.

WITHOUT FAIL
A Washington, D.C., woman asks Reacher for help.
Her job? Protecting the vice president.

PERSUADER
A kidnapping in Boston. A cop dies.
Has Reacher lost his sense of right and wrong?

THE ENEMY
Back in Reacher's army days,
a general is found dead on his watch.

ONE SHOT
A lone sniper shoots five people dead in a heartland city.
But the accused guy says, "Get Reacher."

THE HARD WAY
A coffee on a busy New York street leads to a shoot-out
three thousand miles away.

BAD LUCK AND TROUBLE
One of Reacher's buddies has shown up dead in the
California desert, and Reacher must put his old army unit
back together.

NOTHING TO LOSE
Reacher crosses the line between a town called
Hope and one called Despair.

GONE TOMORROW
On the New York subway, Reacher counts down the twelve
telltale signs of a suicide bomber.

61 HOURS
In freezing South Dakota, Reacher hitches a lift on
a bus heading for trouble.

WORTH DYING FOR
There's deadly trouble in the corn country of
Nebraska . . . and Reacher walks right into it.

THE AFFAIR
An intriguing case, a breaking point, and a twist in Reacher's
own life that he never saw coming.

A WANTED MAN
Reacher sticks out his thumb for a ride to Virginia. He soon
discovers he's hitched a lot more than a ride.

NEVER GO BACK
Never Go Back . . . but Jack Reacher does—
and the past catches up with him.

PERSONAL
Someone has taken a shot at the president of France
in the City of Light. The bullet was American, and
Reacher is making it personal.

MAKE ME
Reacher steps off a midnight train in the remote farming
town of Mother's Rest . . . only to find something dark lurks
beneath the town's idyllic surface.

NIGHT SCHOOL
Reacher is still in the army. In the morning they give him a
medal, and in the afternoon they send him back to school.

THE MIDNIGHT LINE
Some lines should never be crossed.
But then, neither should Reacher.

PAST TENSE
Reacher makes a shocking discovery: The present can be
tough, but the past can be tense . . . and deadly.

BLUE MOON
In a nameless city, two rival gangs compete
for control. But they hadn't counted
on Reacher arriving on their turf.

THE SENTINEL
Reacher spots a hapless soul walking into an
ambush—four against one. So he intervenes, with his own
trademark brand of conflict resolution.

BETTER OFF DEAD
Failure is not an option for Reacher, because in this game,
the loser is always better off dead.

NO PLAN B
Two witnesses to the same tragedy give two
different accounts. One sees a woman die by suicide.
The other witness is Jack Reacher.

THE SECRET
Eight people have been found dead across the US. The
deaths look like unconnected accidents. Reacher is tasked
with uncovering the truth.

IN TOO DEEP
Reacher wakes up, alone, in the dark, handcuffed to a bed
in a makeshift hospital room. He has no memory of getting
there. But whoever did this is about to regret it.